English G 21

B4

für Realschulen

Cornelsen

English G 21 • Band B 4

Im Auftrag des Verlages herausgegeben von
Prof. Hellmut Schwarz, Mannheim

Erarbeitet von
Barbara Derkow Disselbeck, Köln
Allen J. Woppert, Berlin
sowie Susan Abbey, Nenagh, Irland
Laurence Harger, Wellington, Neuseeland

unter Mitarbeit von
Wolfgang Biederstädt, Köln
Joachim Blombach, Herford
David Christie, Banbury, England
Helmut Dengler, Limbach
Jennifer Seidl, München
Andrea Ulrich, Berlin
sowie Ulrike Flach, Köln; Silke Lehmacher, Monheim

in Zusammenarbeit mit der Englischredaktion
Dr. Christiane Kallenbach (Projektleitung);
Klaus G. Unger (verantwortlicher Redakteur);
Susanne Bennetreu (Bildredaktion); Britta Bensmann;
Dr. Philip Devlin; Bonnie S. Glänzer; Uwe Tröger

Beratende Mitwirkung
Anja Bersch, Waldstetten; Peer Brändel, Gütersloh;
Uwe Chormann, Einselthum; Matthew George,
Frankfurt (Main); Prof. Dr. Liesel Hermes, Karlsruhe;
Bernhard Hunger, Dettingen; Gabriele Künstler,
Altlußheim; Michael Semmler, Lünen; Karl Starkebaum,
Diekholzen; Elke Storz, Freiburg i. Br.

Illustrationen
Silke Bachmann, Hamburg; Roland Beier, Berlin;
Stéphane Gamain/NB Illustration, London;
Jörn Hennig, Berlin

Layoutkonzept
Aksinia Raphael; Korinna Wilkes

Technische Umsetzung
Aksinia Raphael; Korinna Wilkes;
Stephan Hilleckenbach; Rainer Bachmaier

Umschlaggestaltung
Klein & Halm Grafikdesign, Berlin

www.cornelsen.de
www.EnglishG.de

Die Internetadressen und -dateien, die in diesem Lehrwerk angegeben sind, wurden vor Drucklegung geprüft. Der Verlag übernimmt keine Gewähr für die Aktualität und den Inhalt dieser Adressen und Dateien oder solcher, die mit ihnen verlinkt sind.

Dieses Werk berücksichtigt die Regeln der reformierten Rechtschreibung und Zeichensetzung.

1. Auflage, 1. Druck 2008

Alle Drucke dieser Auflage sind inhaltlich unverändert und können im Unterricht nebeneinander verwendet werden.

Druck: CS-Druck CornelsenStürtz, Berlin

ISBN 978-3-06-031313-6 – broschiert
ISBN 978-3-06-031363-1 – gebunden

Inhalt gedruckt auf säurefreiem Papier aus nachhaltiger Forstwirtschaft.

Dein Englischbuch enthält folgende Teile:

Introduction	Hier lernst du die jungen Leute von Band 4 kennen.
Units	die fünf Kapitel des Buches
Getting ready for a test	Hier kannst du dich gezielt auf einen Test vorbereiten.
EXTRA: Text File	viele interessante Texte zum Lesen (passend zu den Units)
Skills File (SF)	Beschreibung wichtiger Lern- und Arbeitstechniken
Grammar File (GF)	Zusammenfassung der Grammatik jeder Unit
Vocabulary	Wörterverzeichnis zum Lernen der neuen Wörter jeder Unit
Dictionary	alphabetische Wörterverzeichnisse zum Nachschlagen

Die Units bestehen aus diesen Teilen:

Lead-in	Einstieg in das neue Thema
A-Section	neuer Lernstoff mit vielen Aktivitäten und **Background File**
Practice	Übungen
Text	eine spannende oder lustige Geschichte
How am I doing?	Hier kannst du dein Wissen und Können überprüfen.

In den Units findest du diese Überschriften und Symbole:

Looking at language	Hier sammelst du Beispiele und entdeckst Regeln.
STUDY SKILLS	Einführung in Lern- und Arbeitstechniken
Dossier	Schöne und wichtige Arbeiten kannst du in einer Mappe sammeln.
All about ...	Hier übst du Wortschatz zum Thema der Unit.
READING COURSE	Lesekurs in vier Kapiteln mit Hilfen zum Lesen von Texten
EVERYDAY ENGLISH	Übungen zum Bewältigen wichtiger Alltagssituationen
MEDIATION	Hier vermittelst du zwischen zwei Sprachen.
LISTENING	Aufgaben zu Hörtexten auf der CD
Now you	Hier sprichst und schreibst du über dich selbst.
REVISION	Übungen zur Wiederholung
WORDS	Übungen zu Wortfamilien, Wortfeldern und Wortverbindungen
Extra	Zusätzliche Aktivitäten und Übungen
	Partnerarbeit/Gruppenarbeit
	nur auf CD / auf CD und im Schülerbuch
	Textaufgaben

Inhalt

Welcome to the United States of America

1 What do you know about the US?

Do you know the place in the photo? What other places in the US do you know – cities, National Parks or Monuments, buildings, ...?
What can you say about them?
Can you find the places you have talked about on the US map on the back inside cover?

2 The girl in the photo

What do you suppose the girl in the photo is thinking?

▸ *SF Describing pictures (Revision) (p. 142) • WB 1 (p. 1)*

1 A blog

Caitlin's blog

About me

Name	Caitlin
Age	13
Birthday	July 9
Hometown	New York, New York

August 26

Hi guys – I'm back from my summer vacation, so you can look forward to more of my daily blogs from New York. Where did we go? Like every year, my mom and dad packed me, my little brother and lots of camping gear into our car and drove … and drove and drove. We always go to a National Park, and this year it was the Grand Canyon. The drive there is long, almost 2,500 miles. We crossed three time zones! It took us three and a half days.
I'll never forget this trip. The Grand Canyon is awesome! If you haven't been there, go! We camped at two different places on the rim and took trips in the car or hiked from there. My dad and I went on a two-day hike into the Canyon. It was hard work, and my whole body hurt for three days!

Comments

On 8/27 Ruth wrote
Hi Caitlin, sounds like an awesome trip! Good to have you back. CU Ruth

How far is the Grand Canyon from Caitlin's home in kilometres?
Go to the map on the back inside cover. What time is it in the Canyon when it's 12 o'clock noon in New York?

2 Caitlin at the Grand Canyon

a) *What do you think of Caitlin's summer holidays? Add a comment to her blog.*

b) **Extra** *Where could you go if you travelled as far as Caitlin travelled to the Grand Canyon?*

▸ *SF Learning words (Revision) (p. 138)* • **Text File 1** *(pp. 114–115)*

3 A school essay

Shorecliffs Middle School
San Clemente, California

Student's name: *Luis Morales*

Grade: *8*

Date: *September 3*

My summer vacation

This summer I was very lucky. I was able to go to Grand Canyon National Park with the youth group at my church. For months we were busy with fund-raising: We washed cars, cut grass, cleaned pools and had a bake sale to raise money. (My mother's empanadas were sold out in two hours!)

We were all very excited when the bus came to pick us up. I'm 14 years old, and I'd never been so far from home. The ride took about nine hours with a one-hour lunch break. We sang songs in Spanish and English the whole time – till the driver said we had to stop.

We stayed at the Canyon for three days. We went on long hikes around and into the Canyon. The colors were so beautiful. At night we slept in tents – that was new for me – and cooked our own meals. That was cool.

The Park Rangers were very nice and told us a lot about the Canyon. They showed us how to use binoculars and other ranger tools in a discovery pack and then we were allowed to use them on our own for the rest of the day. One of the Rangers was a Native American. Indian She told us about the Indians who once lived in the Canyon. We all got a patch at the end. My mother is going to sew mine onto my jacket when she has time.

- *How was Luis able to pay for the trip?*
- *Why do you think the group sang songs in English and Spanish?*
- *Go to the map on the back inside cover. Which states did Luis' group drive through?*
- *What does Luis' essay tell you about the job of a Park Ranger? (See also the Americana box.)*

4 Extra Now you

a) *What do kids do at your school or club to raise money for activities?*

b) *If your class had €500, what could you do?*

Americana ★ ★ ★

Park Rangers
US Park Rangers work in National Parks, Forests and Monuments. It's their job to protect the parks from the people and the people from dangers in the park. They also tell visitors about the natural and human history of the area.

5 A summer vacation diary

August 7 – Mom stayed behind to look after the farm and we began our trip from Missouri along the famous highway – Route 66 – to the Grand Canyon.
We traveled west – into Kansas and then Oklahoma. Dad has always dreamed about this journey. He told me about the old TV series "Route 66" and sang the song "Route 66": "Well it winds from Chicago to L.A. More than 2,000 miles all the way." We stopped at every gas station and café and bought Route 66 stuff for him. It's Day 1 and already we have a license plate for the car and a key ring! Tonight we're at a motel outside Tulsa.

August 8 – Early start and another day in the car: boring! We drove through Oklahoma and Texas and into New Mexico. We're spending the night here in Tucumcari. Dad has added a poster and a cap to his Route 66 stuff.

August 9 – On to Santa Rosa and – guess what – the Route 66 Auto Museum! Dad got a Route 66 bag for Mom. It was already dark when we drove into Arizona, so we stopped at a motel in Holbrook.

August 10 – At last! Today we arrived at the Grand Canyon – and wow, IT IS GRAND! We left the car at our motel in the woods and went to the rim of the canyon to look across it. All you can see for miles and miles are walls of multi-colored rock – really awesome. Later, when it got cooler, we walked down part of the Kaibab Trail into the Canyon. We saw a condor! What a bird – 9 feet from wing tip to wing tip. Now I forgive Dad for all the hours in the car and all the "Route 66" songs and stories: today was a day I will never forget.

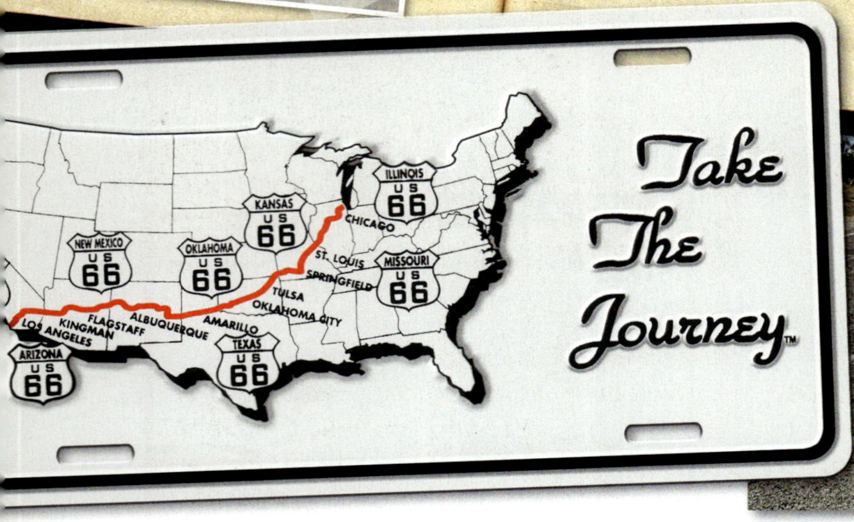

> *What did Mr Kruger and Jake see and do on their trip? Look at the map on the back inside cover:*
> *– What states did they drive through?*
> *– How many kilometres do you think they travelled?*

6 A computer presentation

> *Look at the photos. What do you think Madison did in her summer holidays?*

7 Madison's trip

Read the questions below. Listen to the CD, take notes and answer the questions:

- How much vacation did Madison's parents take this summer? one week
- Did Madison think Las Vegas or the Grand Canyon was more exciting? GC
- What was 'the big adventure'?

ride with a mule train

8 Extra Now you

Write about a summer holiday. You can use one of the text forms from pages 8–10. Brainstorm your ideas. Then look for useful phrases and write the text. Add pictures or maps and put it in your DOSSIER.

► *SF Brainstorming (Revision) (p. 144) • WB 2–8 (pp. 1–4)*

New York, New York

1 You and New York

What do you know about New York? Have you ever been there? Do you know any of the famous sights in these photos or from magazines or films?

2 Places in New York

a) *Copy this list of places. Then listen to Caitlin and Ruth. Who is coming to visit New York? In what order do the girls talk about the places?*

- the Brooklyn Bridge 7 C-
- Central Park 3 R-
- Chinatown 8 C-
- Daniel's Deli 9 C+ R+
- Ellis Island 1 C+ R+
- the Empire State Building 6 C+ R+
- Fifth Avenue 4 C- R+
- the Planetarium 5 C- R+
- the Statue of Liberty 2 (C+ R+
- Times Square 10 C+ R+

b) *Use your list to make a chart. Add Caitlin and Ruth's names.*

Place	Caitlin	Ruth
the Brooklyn Bridge 7	✗	✓
...		

Caitlin and Ruth don't always agree about the places. Listen again. Put a tick if the person is for a place, a cross if she is against it.

d) *Which places does Caitlin have on her final list?*

▸ P 1 (p. 20) • SF Listening for detail (Revision) (p. 148) • WB 1–2 (p. 5)

All about ... getting around an American city

1 Understanding directions

Look at what the woman tells the tourist. Would you know which way you had to go? Match the words to their definitions.

– block	– a bus towards the city centre (in Manhattan: a bus going south)
– a downtown bus	– a group of buildings between two streets
– 34th and Broadway	– the corner of 34th Street and Broadway

2 Understanding American signs

must / mustn't

a) *Where might you find these signs?*

1

outside an underground station

2

in the streets / walk on the other side

3

at a restaurant / must wait for the hostess

museum / bank

4

must wait in the line

in the street

5

mustn't walk

b) *Write down what you think each sign means. Then compare with a partner.*

3 American and British English

Copy and complete the chart below. You can use a German-English dictionary.

American English (AE)	German	British English (BE)
subway	U-Bahn	...
...	(Stadt)Zentrum	...
...	Bürgersteig	...
...	Schlange	
...	Handy	

► SF Using a bilingual dictionary (Revision) (p. 140) • P 2–3 (pp. 20–21) • WB 3–6 (pp. 6–7)

4 Travelling is hard work!

'You look tired,' Caitlin said as Ryan, her cousin from Ireland, sat down at the kitchen table.

'Well,' said Ryan, 'Getting to Dublin airport was awful. I had to leave home at 6 o'clock this morning. Waiting in the security queues meant another two hours. And then flying for six hours ...'

'And then there's the five hour time difference between Ireland and New York' added Caitlin. 'Poor you! But, don't go to bed now. If you sleep now, you'll wake up in the middle of the night and think it's morning. – I know: let's walk over to the fire station and say hi to Dad.'

'Good idea!' said Ryan. He wanted to know all about his uncle's life as a New York firefighter.

What was awful? What took two hours? What took six? When it's 5 p.m. in New York, what time is it in Ireland?

5 I love being a firefighter

My dad and my grandpa were both firefighters. And I can't imagine doing anything else.

I love being a firefighter. Yes, it's hard work. And nobody likes getting up in the middle of the night to fight a fire. But it feels good when you put out a fire and maybe save somebody's life.

We work 15 hour shifts, but we spend a lot of that time at the station. The men and women on my shift are like a family. Some of the guys are great cooks. There was this one guy, Ricardo. He made the best chili con carne, and he sang when he cooked. I always enjoyed listening to him. Good old Ricardo. He's not with us any more – he died on 9/11.

Americana ★ ★ ★

9/11 and Ground Zero

On September 11th (9/11), 2001, 19 hijackers took over four US planes. They flew two of them into the Twin Towers of the World Trade Center in downtown Manhattan. Both Towers burned and collapsed. Almost 3000 people died.

The place where the Towers stood is now called 'Ground Zero'. Every year on 9/11 the 'Tribute in Light' takes place there and people remember the men and women who died that day in 2001.

Looking at language

a) *Write down all the sentences in* **4** *and* **5** *with* **-ing** *forms.*
Travelling is ...

b) *These* **-ing** *forms are like nouns. They're called* **gerunds**. *Translate them into German and compare.*

▸ GF 1 a–b: Gerund (p. 155) • P 4–5 (p. 21) • WB 7–8 (p. 8)

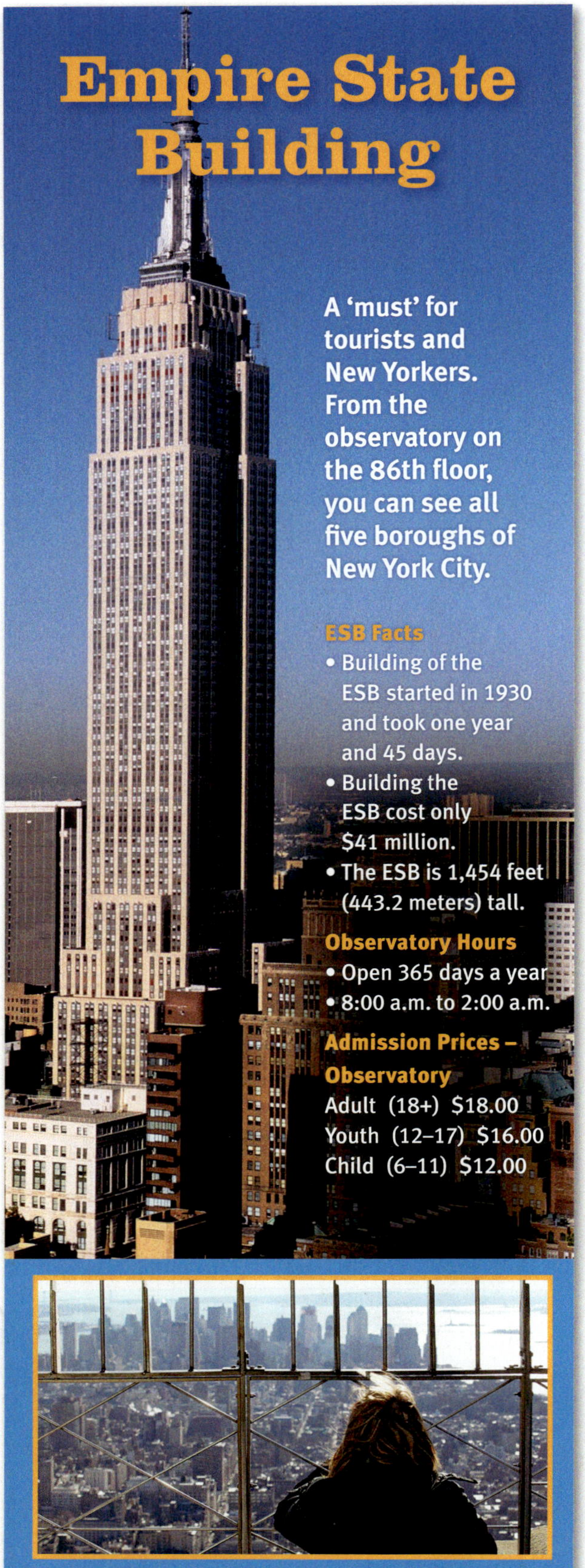

6 On top of the world

'Well, it's a perfect day for going up the Empire State Building!' Caitlin said. She pointed at the sign in the lobby: 'Visibility 45 miles.'

'This way,' she said. 'The ticket office is one floor up.'

'But the sign says it's on the second floor,' said Ryan.

'That's right,' said Caitlin. 'This is the first floor, the next one up is two.'

After buying the tickets, the two cousins went to the elevators. 'I have to warn you,' Ryan said. 'I'm a bit scared of going in lifts. 86 floors – we'll be in that little box forever!'

But in only a minute they were on the 86th floor. Ryan loved looking at New York from above. When they were tired of looking at the sights, they decided to get some lunch.

'I know the perfect place,' Caitlin said. 'We can meet my friend Ruth there. You'll like her!'

Why was it a good day to visit the ESB? Why was Ryan confused about where the 'second floor' is? How much did it cost Katie (13) and Ryan (18) to go up the Empire State Building?

▸ GF 1c: Gerunds after prepositions (p. 156) • P 6–9 (pp. 22–23) • WB 9–12 (pp. 9–10)

7 Group puzzle

a) *Make six groups (A, B, ... F). Each person in the group has a number. Each group finds out more about one of the sights from the unit.*

b) *Join members of other groups (A1, B1, C1, .../A2, B2, C2, ...). Tell the others about your sight.*

c) *Return to your first group and use everything you have learned to plan a day in New York.*

8 At the deli

'Two bagels and cream cheese, one bagel and lox – hi there, Ruthie! – and two coffees to go,' shouted Aaron from behind the counter.

'They know you here, Ruth?' asked Ryan.

'Oh sure, I come here all the time. Look, there's a table. If we get the table, will you get the food, Caitlin?'

'Sure,' said Caitlin. 'What do you want?'

'Ryan has to have a bagel,' said Ruth.

'You're right. When you're in New York, you have to eat bagels. Bagel and lox, Ryan?'

'Er, I don't even know what lox is.'

'Salmon – in Yiddish!' explained Ruth.

'I don't like salmon. Maybe we could ...'

'That's OK. I'll get you a bagel and cream cheese,' smiled Caitlin.

'For me too – and a cola, please!' said Ruth. 'So, Ryan, do you like New York?' she asked as they sat down.

'Yeah, it's great!' He smiled at Ruth. Then he asked: 'Er, Ruth, if we go to Times Square tonight, will you join us?'

'*When* we go to Times Square tonight, Ruth would love to join us, wouldn't you, Ruth!' laughed Caitlin as she brought the food.

Ryan tried his bagel: 'Mmm, you were right, Ruth: This is a great place,' he said. 'If I lived in New York, I'd come here every day!'

> *What would you say if you wanted to take a tea with you from the deli?*
Do you think Ryan likes Ruth? Why?

▸ P 10–13 (pp. 11–13) • WB 13–17 (pp. 24–25)

Americana ★ ★ ★

Delis and Bagels

Bagels are one of the New Yorkers' favourite breakfasts. They run into a deli (the name comes from the German *Delikatessen*) on their way to work and grab a bagel and coffee to go.

Jewish immigrants from Europe brought the bagel – a kind of roll with a hole in it – with them in the 19th century.

9 Extra SONG A heart in New York

New York
To your tall skyline I come
flying in from London
To your door

New York
Looking down on Central Park
Where they say you should not wander
After dark

New York
Like a scene from all those movies
But you're real enough to me
But there's a heart
A heart that lives in New York

by Benny Gallagher and Graham Lyle

a) *Does the singer love or hate New York?*

b) *Which of the photos in the unit go with the song? Why?*

c) *What do the lyrics say about New York?*

▸ **Text File 2–3** (pp. 116–119)

Extra Background File ALL STRANGERS

I had never seen such a big building. Compared to the size of the houses I had left in my town, this was like a whole city in one. I almost felt smaller than I was. It looked beautiful.
Celia Adler
12 when she arrived from Russia, 1914

This is the only country where you're not a stranger, because we are all strangers.
Lazarus Salamon
16 when he arrived from Hungary, 1920

The steamer 'Florida', 14 days out of Naples, with 1600 Italians on board, had come through one of the worst storms the Captain could remember. We were happy, children and adults, to leave the open seas and come at last into the Bay of New York. My family looked with wonder on this land of our dreams.
Edward Corsi
10 when he arrived from Italy, 1907

Our first home in America was a flat near the East River at 112th Street ... our mountain home in Lucania had been full of sunlight and fresh air. Now there were four walls and people over and under and on all sides of us.
Leonard Covello
9 when he arrived from Italy, 1896

Going to America was almost like going to the moon. We were all going to places that we knew nothing about and to a country that was totally strange to us.
Golda Meir
8 when she arrived from Russia, 1906

1 Immigrants

a) *Look at the photos and statements. How did these children feel when they arrived in the US?*

b) *Imagine you're one of the children in the photos. Say what you can see, hear and feel.*
We've just arrived in New York. I can see/hear/feel ...
It is ... My mother and father/family are ...

► *SF Describing pictures (Revision) (p. 142)*

The US is a country of immigrants. In a population of 300 million, only 4 million are Native Americans – all the rest have their roots in other countries around the world. Many immigrants came to America because in their own countries they were not free to practise their religion or take part in politics. But most immigrants came because at home they were poor and hungry.
Until the middle of the 20th century the main gateway to America was the port of New York. In 1892 the city opened the Ellis Island Immigration Station within sight of the Statue of Liberty and Manhattan Island. It was here that – between 1892 and 1921 – more than 12 million immigrants entered the US. Today Ellis Island is a Museum. Through its website you can trace immigrants to the US.

Look at the charts. Which continents did the immigrants come from in 1900? And in 2000? Why do you think the change happened?

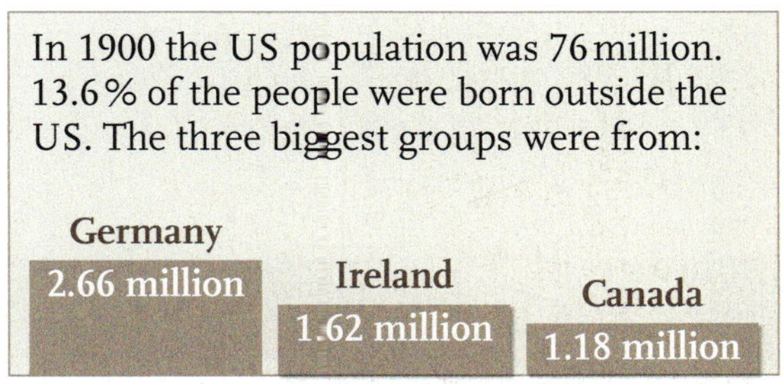

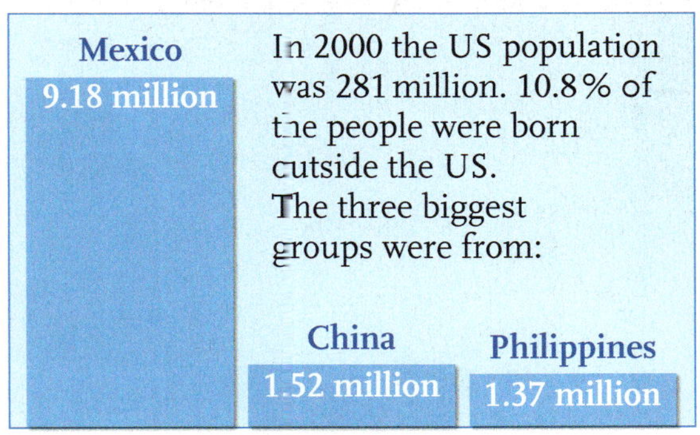

2 Now you

Do either a), b) or c).

a) *Has anybody from your family ever gone to live in the US? Check with your parents or grandparents. If yes, go to* www.ellisisland.org. *Try and trace the person.*

b) *Write a short diary, for an immigrant of your age, about the first day in a new country.*

c) *Have you or anybody in your family or anybody you know come to Germany from another country? Find out as many details as you can.*

► WB 18 (p. 14)

1 The five boroughs of New York

a) *Partner B: Go to p. 108.*
Partner A: Read out the texts below. Your partner must decide which boroughs you're describing.

- This is the biggest of New York's five boroughs. If you fly to Kennedy Airport, this is where you'll land. On the map it's east of Brooklyn.[1]
- A famous bridge over the East River links this borough to the island of Manhattan. New York marathon runners have to run across it.[2]

b) *Now listen to your partner. Which boroughs is he/she describing?*

[1] *The correct answer is 'Queens'.* [2] *The correct answer is 'Brooklyn'.*

2 LISTENING Different words

a) *Look at the photos. Write down the British English (BE) words for the numbered things.*
1 timetable
2 …

b) *You will hear two dialogues. Listen for the American English (AE) words in the box.*

c) *Listen again and write down the correct AE word next to the BE words in your list from a).*

cellphone • +cookie • +eraser • +French fries • +garbage • +pants • +potato chips • +schedule • sidewalk • subway

3 WORDS Verbs and nouns that go together

a) *You can use one verb with all the words in these groups. Find the verbs.*

1 ... a bus, a photo, the subway *take*
2 ... a train, a mouse, a thief catch
3 ... a museum, a city, an aunt visit
4 ... a bike, a horse, a mule ride

b) *Find three words that go with these verbs.*

5 ask for *help* ... directions a book, the way
6 get on *a train,* a bus, a subway
7 look up *train times, ...* a phone number, an address, a word
8 look at *the sights, ...* the view, a picture, a photo, a poster

c) *Compare with a partner.*

4 Getting around New York (Gerund)

a) *Complete the sentences with the gerund of these verbs.*

buy • cross • cycle • drive • spot • take • travel • walk

1 ... is a great way to get around New York – but wear good shoes.
1 Walking is a great way ...
2 ... the street in Manhattan's busy traffic is dangerous, so be careful. Crossing
3 ... can be dangerous too, so wear a helmet. Cycling / Riding
4 ... by bus is a good way to see the city from above ground. Going
5 ... a car can be expensive if you have to pay for parking. Driving
6 ... the subway is fast and cheap, but you don't see much of the city. Taking
7 ... a subway ticket is easy if you've got the correct change. Buying
8 ... a taxi is easy because they're all bright yellow. Finding

b) *Compare your sentences with a partner.*

c) **Extra** *Write down three tips for getting around the place where you live. Use gerunds.*

Going shopping in a big city can be dangerous, so always watch your wallet.

5 I love chatting ... (Gerund)

a) *Finish these sentences. Use a gerund.*

1 (+ + +) I love ...
2 (+ +) I really enjoy ...
3 (+) I like ...
4 (–) I don't like ...
5 (– –) I really don't enjoy ...
6 (– – –) I hate ...

I love chatting with my friends/...
I really enjoy going to .../...

b) *Meet people in your class and listen to their ideas. Take notes on what they like and don't like. Use the symbols.*

Finn *+ watch football on TV*
– – learn English vocabulary

c) *Tell the class.*

Finn likes watching football on TV.
He really doesn't enjoy learning English vocabulary.
He hates ...

d) **Extra** *Write about one of the students you talked to.*

6 Ela is good at … (Gerunds after prepositions)

a) *Complete these sentences with the gerund of the verb in brackets.*

1 Ela is good at (speak) English.
Ela is good at speaking English.
2 So she dreams of (work) in New York.
3 She likes the idea of (go) to concerts in Central Park.
4 And she's very interested in (learn) hip hop.
5 So she'll ask about (join) a dance class when she gets there.
6 And she's thinking of (become) a rapper!

b) *Complete the following sentences with a gerund. Write them on a piece of paper.*

1 I'm tired of …
2 My best friend isn't interested in …
3 I dream of …
4 I'm fed up with …
5 I'm good at …
6 I'm not so good at …

c) *Put the pieces of paper in a box. Take turns to pull out a paper and read what's on it. Can the class guess who wrote it?*

7 REVISION WRITING Taking a break in Central Park

Look at the photo of Central Park. Imagine you are there. Write 80–100 words about your visit. You can use the phrases at the bottom if you need help.

Remember

- First brainstorm your ideas: mind map, list, 5 Ws.
- Think of a good beginning and ending.
- Start a new paragraph for each new topic.
- Use some adjectives, adverbs and linking words.
- Read and correct your text.

… and I went to Central Park to take a break from …

One day in June … asked me to meet …

… next to / in the middle of / under …

All around me I could see …

It was getting dark, so …

We took out our … and started to …

When we got hungry, we …

A few minutes later …

Suddenly …

We sat down/met/saw …

In the background I could hear …

► *SF Writing Course (Revision) (pp. 146–147)* • *SF Brainstorming (Revision) (p. 144)*

8 EVERYDAY ENGLISH MEDIATION At the ticket office 1-11

a) *You are at the ticket office of a tour company in New York. You meet another German who is having trouble with English. Try to help him.*

German man — Entschuldigung, kannst du mir vielleicht helfen? Mein Englisch ist nicht so gut. Ich habe gelesen, dass die Touren auf Deutsch sind. Kannst du bitte mal fragen, ob das stimmt?

You — Excuse me, he'd like to know: Are ...?

Ticket agent — Yes, of course. We have live guides who give their commentary in English. But for those who don't speak English, there's a recorded version in German, French, Spanish and lots of other languages.

You — ...

b) *Listen and go on.*

▸ *SF Mediation (Revision) (p. 143)*

9 EVERYDAY ENGLISH SPEAKING Making plans together

Partner B: Look at p. 108.

Partner A: You and your partner are on holiday in New York. It's your last day. You want to spend the day together, but you have different ideas about what to do.

a) *You want to go to the places below.*
Tell your partner:
- where you want to go
- where the places are, what they cost, when you can go there
- one reason why you would like to go there

b) *Listen to your partner's plans and take notes.*

c) *Now talk to him/her and decide where you'd like to go together – one place in the morning, one place in the afternoon. You each have $20. Check the prices and opening hours.*

▸ *SF Taking notes (Revision) (p. 149)*

The Bronx Zoo

The Bronx Zoo is one of the largest zoos in the United States with over 4000 animals.

The zoo is open 365 days a year!
10:00 a.m. – 5:00 p.m.
Admission:
Adult $14.00
Child (Ages 3–12) $10.00

Skyscraper Museum

The Skyscraper Museum – the only museum of its kind – explores the history of tall buildings. It's at 39 Battery Place in Manhattan. Museum hours are 12–6 p.m., Wednesday–Sunday.
Admission is $5, $2.50 for students.

10 WORDS Jobs in the city

a) *Write down the words for the people who do these jobs.*

1 a person who puts fires out
2 a person who catches thieves
3 a person who helps you in a shop
4 a person who puts on the music at the disco
5 a person who works in an ambulance
6 a person who helps people in hospitals who are ill
7 a person who cuts your hair
8 a person at a National Monument who gives information

b) *Describe two more jobs. Can your partner guess them?*

11 REVISION I might visit New York (*if* and *when*)

Tip

when = sobald, dann wenn (Zeit) *When I take you to Times Square tonight ... (= es steht fest)*

if = wenn, falls (Bedingung) *If I take you to Times Square tonight ... (= es steht nicht fest)*

a) *Complete the short dialogues with **if** or **when**.*

1 *A:* I might visit New York this summer.
B: ... you come to New York, you can stay with me.

2 *A:* My friend Jo will be in New York in July.
B: I'd love to meet him. Ask him to call me ... he's here.

3 *A:* I hope the weather will be OK tomorrow.
B: Don't worry. ... it rains we can go to the Museum of Natural History.

4 *A:* Will we have time to go to Macy's?
B: Well, ... we don't have time today, we can go tomorrow.

5 *A:* We're going to visit Bronx Zoo today.
B: You must see the snakes ... you're there.

6 *A:* There's a film about New York on TV this evening.
B: Great. Can you call me ... it starts?

b) **Extra** *Is the meaning of these two sentences the same? Why (not)?*

1 Call me when you come to New York.
2 Call me if you come to New York.

12 REVISION If I go to New York ... (Conditional sentences 1 and 2)

a) *Complete these conditional sentences.*

1 If I go to New York one day, I'll/I won't ...
2 If it's hot in New York, I'll/I won't be able to ...
3 If I have enough time while I'm there, ...
4 If I see any famous people, ...
5 If I had friends in New York, I'd/I wouldn't ...
6 If I lived in New York, I'd/I wouldn't ...
7 If I was a New York firefighter, ...
8 If I was in a building that was burning, ...

b) *Make an if-chain. You can start like this:*

A: If I had ten million dollars, I'd buy an apartment on Fifth Avenue.
B: If I bought an apartment on Fifth Avenue, ...

13 READING Fire safety (Working out the meanings of words)

a) *Read these fire safety instructions (page* ***1****) from inside a hotel room. Explain (in German) what you have to do if there's a fire.*

Remember

These things help you to understand words you don't know.

1 **pictures**:
What could a high-rise building be?

2 Some words look like **German** words:
What could 'second' mean?

3 the **context** (the words around the word you don't know): What could 'alert' mean?

4 Sometimes you already know **parts of the word** or phrase:
You know 'stairs', you know 'way'.
What could 'stairway' mean? You know 'direction'. What could 'directed' mean?

b) **Extra** *Try these tips with these other words from the instructions:* stay low, report a fire, dial, exit.

c) *Use the tips above to explain the highlighted words and phrases in the safety instructions (page* ***2****) on the right.*

► *SF Reading Course (pp. 150–151)*

1

Fire safety in high-rise buildings

If the fire is IN your room

- If there is a fire, stay calm and think about what to do. Act quickly because every second counts.
- Get everybody out. Stay low, where air is fresher – smoke rises.
- Use your safest and nearest exit.

- CLOSE ALL DOORS as you leave.
- Knock on other guests' doors on your way out and alert them to the danger.
- DO NOT USE THE ELEVATOR.
- Go down the nearest STAIRWAY
- To report a fire, dial 911. Firefighters will be directed to your location.

2

Fire safety in high-rise buildings

If the fire is NOT in your room

- If the hallways are full of smoke, stay in your room.
- Place a wet cloth over your mouth and nose to facilitate breathing.
- Turn off air conditioners.
- Fill your bathtub with water. If your door gets hot, wet it down.

- If you are in great danger, hang a bedsheet out the window so that firefighters can spot you.

You can tell me From *Kelly 'n' Me* by Myron Levoy (adapted)

Anthony (15) plays the guitar and sings in New York's Central Park. That way he makes money to help his mother. One day he meets Kelly Callahan there. She's a singer, and the two decide to work together. Now Anthony is waiting for Kelly and playing the guitar for three young kids.

"Hey, Anthony!" Kelly called as she hurried toward me.

"Hey, Kelly!" I called back.

"Anthoneee!" one of the kids sang out. "Lover boy!"

"Lover boy!" all three kids called out.

Then Kelly gave me a kiss on my cheek.

"Kiss her back, Anthoneee!"

"Let's go for a walk," said Kelly.

We walked up Fifth Avenue on the park side, the Terrible Three right behind us.

One of the kids called to us, "Give us a hundred dollars, and we'll leave you alone!"

"Anthony," Kelly said. "I've got an idea. My mother works in this building on Fifth Avenue. She's a nanny. Let's go there. They can't follow us up."

Kelly opened the back door of the apartment. There was a small hall and some rooms. Nothing special. But these were only the servants' rooms.

We walked down the hall and turned right. I gasped. The room we'd entered was huge, with super-modern furniture. As I walked round, I saw paintings and little statues everywhere. It was like the Museum of Modern Art. This had to be a multi-millionaire's apartment.

Kelly put her guitar down on the long glass table. I wasn't sure that was a good idea.

"Put your guitar down, Anthony!" she said. "This isn't a cathedral."

"Well, you know this place. I don't. I've never seen stuff like this except in a museum. Some of it's pretty strange. Like that painting over there? It looks like a comic book."

"That's by Lichtenstein. Awful, right?"

"Why? What's wrong with it?"

"It's that the Lawrences don't appreciate what they have. Like my mother. They pay my mother almost nothing. That's the Lawrences. Andrew got a suit. He's still growing, but they paid $350 for it. How many poor people could have dinner for that?"

* * *

A few days later, Anthony and Kelly are in the subway.

There were lots and lots of people. We did some of our loudest and wildest stuff. The money was good.

Some people stopped. One of them seemed to be on drugs. He had an eye on our money. I whispered to Kelly between songs and suggested that we move.

"Don't worry," she said. "If he takes any money, it means he needs it more than we do."

"Aren't you afraid of anybody?"

"Oh, sure. I'm afraid of you."

"I don't understand."

"I'll explain later. Let's sing!"

We sang for over an hour. But then all the people and the noise and smells were too much for me.

"Please Kelly! I feel sick. Let's get out of here, please!"

I felt better when we got up to the street. As we walked, I started to feel hungry. "Say, Kelly," I said. "How about feeding the body?"

"You want to have a picnic?"

"You mean here on the street?"

"Come on, Anthony. Don't be silly. We buy some rolls and Swiss cheese and sausage and let's see, chocolate milk, and then we go to the park – I know a nice place there."

Our picnic was in a wild part of the park called the Ramble. There's bridges and hills and small paths. I wouldn't go there when it's dark, but it was safe in the evening. I thought.

As Kelly drank the last of the chocolate milk, I put my arm around her.

"Give me a chocolate mustache," I said.

Kelly leaned over and gave me a very good kiss. And I moved closer.

"Anthony, we really should talk," she said.

"You always want to talk."

"Don't you want to know why I'm afraid of you?"

"OK, why?"

"It's because you're making it hard for me to do what I want to do."

"Huh?"

"To be the new me. To leave everything and take off. I'm nervous enough, and now you've come along."

"You don't look nervous to me."

"Well, I am. I'm scared of everything. Of my parents. And of being alone. And ..."

Suddenly there were tears in her eyes.

"Kelly? Why are you crying? What is it? You can tell me."

"I can and I can't. Why did I have to meet you just now?" She seemed angry.

"Hey, come on. It's not my fault."

"I know. It's – I think I need some time to think about what I'm doing, and about you and me. It's ... that's why I'm afraid of you. Maybe afraid is the wrong word. But you know what I mean. I ..." She was looking past me, toward the path. "Uh-oh-..."

I followed her eyes. On the path, two guys, one with a red beard and one blond, were watching us. One of them, Redbeard, had tattoos all over his arms.

This didn't look good to me. So I said quietly to Kelly, "Let's, maybe, get up slowly and –"

"Yo, blondie!" said Redbeard to Kelly. "You've got a nice body."

"L-leave us alone," I said. It had been stupid to go in this part of the park so late!

"I like your guitar, blondie," said Redbeard. "It's nice – like you." He walked slowly toward her.

What Redbeard didn't know is that when I get angry, I don't think. I just go for it. I jumped up and hit him as hard as I could. He wasn't expecting it, and he fell. My hand hurt.

Kelly screamed. And she really knows how to scream! She tried to hit Blondbeard with her guitar, but he jumped away.

Redbeard was getting up, so I kicked him in the head. It wasn't fair, but I didn't care. I just hoped that they didn't have knives. Or guns.

I turned toward Blondbeard, but it was too late. He hit Kelly – just below her right eye. She fell against a tree and hit her head. She was hurt, but I couldn't help her. Blondbeard was coming toward me. And then I heard shouting down the path.

"Let's get out of here," Blondbeard shouted.

As the people got closer, Blondbeard and Redbeard took off – with Kelly's guitar. They ran down a hill, then out toward the street on the west of the park.

I sat down next to Kelly. There was blood on her face. I tore off a piece of my T-shirt and pressed it against her cheek. Three or four people were around us now.

"Call the police!" said a woman.

"Don't call the – the police," said Kelly. "They'll n-never catch them. And I'm f-fine."

We started to walk slowly toward the street.

"Take me to – to Fifth Avenue and I'll get a cab," Kelly said. She still held the piece of my T-shirt against her cheek.

"No, I'm going all the way home with you. I don't care how your house looks."

"Please. Please, Anthony."

"No! Enough's enough, Kelly. If you don't let me go with you, I'll never see you again."

"OK, let's get out of the park," she said.

As we left the park, I asked Kelly again and again if she was all right.

"It's nothing, Anthony, only blood."

"Very nice blood. You were really brave."

"Thanks. You too."

"I'm sorry about your guitar," I said.

"I've got another guitar," she said. "No problem."

When we got to Fifth Avenue, she tried to get rid of me again.

"No! I'm going with you!"

"OK ... Anthony, could we sit there for a minute?"

We went over to one of the benches along the park wall on Fifth Avenue and sat. Kelly looked out at the tops of some buildings across the street.

"This is what – what I wanted to tell you," she said. "We won't have to walk far. Because I live right there."

"You mean the place where your mother works? Are you using it while they're away?"

"No. It's ... I'm sorry, Anthony. It's that my name isn't really Kelly Callahan. My name's Kelsey. You know? Kelsey Lawrence. I'm sorry ... I'm sorry ..."

Working with the text

1 The story

Look at the headings below and put them in the right order. Which part of the story do they go with? Then say in two or three sentences what happens in each part.

a The Attack
b The Terrible Three
c Inside the Lawrences' apartment
d Kelly's real name
e After the attack
f Making music in the subway station
g Picnic in the park

1 b The Terrible Three (ll. 1–24) Anthony is playing ...

b-c-f-g-a-e-d

2 What do you think?

1 Did you like the story? Why or why not?
2 Why do you think does Kelly want to 'leave everything and take off'? (p. 27, ll. 103–104)
3 How is Anthony making it hard for her to do what she wants to do?
4 Was Kelly unfair toward Anthony?

3 Extra What might happen next?

What do you think will happen next? Will Anthony be angry with Kelsey? Or will he forgive her? Go to page 109 and find out how the story goes on.

▸ WB 19 (p. 15) • **Checkpoint 1** WB (p. 16)

How am I doing?

▸ *SF Check yourself (p. 139)*

STUDY SKILLS Check yourself

Remember: Stop – Check – Go!
Check yourself after every unit. Find out what's giving you problems and make plans to improve your English in these areas. 'How am I doing?' will help you to do that.

a) *Choose the correct answers.*

New York

1 The city of New York has five ...
A areas. B parts.
C boroughs. D sections.

2 Most of the sights and important places in New York are in ...
A Staten Island. B Queens.
C Brooklyn. D the Bronx.
E Manhattan.

3 Downtown Manhattan is ...
A under ground. B a poor area.
C in the south of the island.
D where the airport is.

4 When Americans speak of 9/11, they mean the date when planes flew into ...
A the World Trade Center.
B the Empire State Building.
C Ground Zero. D Times Square.

5 What can't you get at a deli?
A a bagel with cream cheese
B a sandwich C a bagel with lox
D a cellphone

6 A place that's famous for expensive shops and huge apartments is ...
A Staten Island. B Fifth Avenue.
C Macy's. D Broadway.

Words

7 Which word does not mean 'very good'?
A awesome B awful
C great D fantastic

8 The job of a firefighter is to ... fires.
A put on B put off
C put out D put up

9 The library is three ... west of here.
A roads B blocks
C corners D sidewalks

10 Where can you not sleep?
A motel B tent C lodge D deli

British English (BE) and American English (AE)

11 What are these BE words in AE?
pavement • mobile phone • trousers • chips

12 What are these AE words in BE?
elevator • line • subway • vacation

Grammar

13 ... in the Grand Canyon is very exciting.
A Hike B Hiked
C Hiking D Hikes

14 Janet's hobby is ... the guitar.
A playing B a play
C the play of D play

15 Put in *if* or *when*:
A ... I had lots of money, I would fly to New York first class.
B ... I ever go to New York, I want to go up the Empire State Building.
C I'm just going to the tourist information. I'll ask about the Museum of Natural History ... I'm there.

b) *Check your answers on p. 252 and add up your points.*

c) *If you had 19 or more points, well done! Maybe you can help students who had fewer points. If you had 18 points or fewer, it's a good idea to do some more work before you go on to the next unit. Where did you make mistakes? The chart below will tell you what you can do to improve your English.*

No.	Area	Find out more	Exercise(s)
1– 6	New York	pp. 12–19	P1 (p. 20), WB 1–2 (p. 5), 13 (p. 11)
7–10	Words	Unit vocabulary (pp. 169–174)	WB 6 (p. 7), 14 (p. 11)
11–12	American English	All about ... (p. 14)	P 2 (p. 20), WB 3–5 (pp. 6–7)
13–14	The gerund	GF 1, pp. 155–156	P4–6 (pp. 21–22), WB 7–10 (pp. 8–9)
15	if/when	p. 24	P 11–12 (p. 24), WB 15 (p. 12)

1 WORDS In a town

Look at this photo of an American city. Write down words for as many things or people as you can.

2 WORDS Describing towns

a) *Complete the sentences with words that mean the opposite.*

1 A town can be large or *small*.
2 It can be in the east or the ... of a country. west
3 It can be exciting or ... boring
4 It can be noisy or . quiet
5 The buildings can be old or ... new
6 The streets can be clean or ... dirty
7 It can be a safe or a .✓. town. dangerous
8 Life there can be calm or ... busy

b) *Write a text about the photo in 1.*
– Is the city old, clean, ...?
– What things could you do in the city?
– Would you like to live there? Give a reason for your answer.

– shops, life (?), museums (?)

3 You aren't allowed to park here! (Modal verbs)

Complete each sentence with an expression from the box.

4 you don't have to • 2 you have to • 3 you're allowed to • you aren't allowed to 1

1 Look at that NO PARKING sign! .1. park here!
2 2.. drive on the right in the US.
3 But 1 drive on the right in England!
4 Can you play football in the park? – Sure, and 3.. skateboard there too.
5 4.. to take the subway to get to Central Park. It's only two block away.
6 If you visit the sports museum on Saturday, 2.. buy a ticket. It's free on weekends.
7 In many restaurants in the US 2 wait until the hostess seats you.
8 Sorry, no cameras, please. .1. take photos here.

to be allowed to → darf
have to – muss / don't have to – muss nicht
4 = muss nicht,

4 What did you do last weekend? (Simple past and past perfect)

*Rachel is telling her friend what she did last Saturday morning. Finish the sentences for her with the correct forms of the verbs – **simple past** or **past perfect**.*

1 On Saturday morning I ... (get up) at 7 o'clock.
On Saturday morning I got up at 7 o'clock.
2 I had (sleep) well, so I ... (feel) fresh.
3 After breakfast I ... (take) the bus into town.
4 First, I ... (go) to Jeans World.
5 I ... (want) to buy some jeans but I had left my money at home! Arrrgh!
6 Outside in the street, I ... (meet) Karen and Amy from our class.
7 They had (buy) some magazines, so we ... (look at) those and ... (chat).
8 Suddenly I ... (notice) the time! It was 1.30 p.m. I ... (be) in town for three hours. had been
9 I ... (run) to the bus stop.
10 When I ... (get) home, my parents ... (eat) lunch already. My mum ... (not/be) happy! had eaten wasn't

5 STUDY SKILLS Writing better sentences (Linking words)

In a test, you might have to write an e-mail or letter. Remember that linking words can make them more interesting. Join the pairs of sentences with these words.

although • and • because • but • or • so that • that • who

1 I like my town. It's big and exciting.
I like my town because it's big and exciting.
2 I often look at expensive clothes. I never buy them! but
3 I often eat fries. I know they're bad for me! although
4 We could go to the cinema. or (We could) watch a DVD at home.
5 Yesterday we saw a guy. He sells fun T-shirts. who
6 Aaron's is a deli. It sells great bagels. that
7 My mum often gives me money. I can go out with my friends. so
8 My favourite place in town is the park. It's quiet and really pretty. because
9 The film was long. It was boring too. and

► SF Writing Course (Revision) (pp. 146–147)

6 What do you like doing? (Gerunds)

a) *Work with a partner. Brainstorm ideas about things you like doing. Make a mind map.*

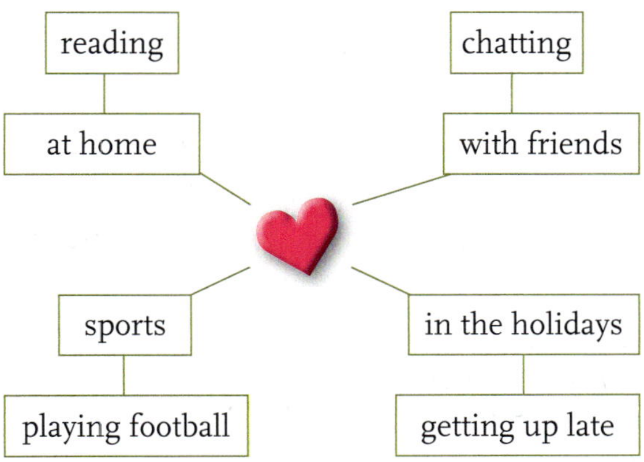

b) *Make sentences that are true for you with words and phrases from your mind map.*
When I'm at home / with friends ...
I (really) like / (absolutely) love ...
I'm (very) interested in ...
My hobby / My favourite thing is ...

STUDY SKILLS How to do well in a test

If you do a test, you should
– know how to prepare yourself
– make sure you understand the instruction
– know what to do with multiple-choice questions.
Go to p. 152 to learn about these things.

► SF How to do well in a test (pp. 152–153)

1 Reading

Greg Zimmermann is a young New Yorker. Read his blog this week and do the tasks below.

Page

New York's yellow taxis are going green!

Hi! What do you think of when you hear the words New York? Skyscrapers? Delis? Central Park? The Statue of Liberty? I love all those things too, but for me, there's another thing that is so typical of the city. Taxis. The famous yellow New York taxicabs.

Taxicabs are everywhere in New York. In fact, there are 13,000 of them. Over half of all the cars you see in Manhattan are taxis. Great if you need a cab, but the problem is they use a lot of gas – around a gallon every hour (that's 3.8 liters for you guys in Europe!). And all that gas makes New York's air pretty dirty.

But now something interesting is happening. The cabs are going green. No, I don't mean that people are painting them a different color. The cabs will still be yellow like always. But they'll be 'environmentally friendly'[1]. The old cabs will slowly go, and there'll be new ones.

The new cabs (there are nearly 400 of them already), will be 'hybrid cabs'.The old cabs use gas all the time, but a hybrid cab uses gas and electricity. It has a normal gas motor, and then it also has a battery[2] and an electric motor. It uses the electric motor in slow traffic and at traffic lights. And it uses the gas motor when it travels more quickly. Result: cleaner air! Cool.

Everybody is excited about the new cabs. The mayor[3] was on TV yesterday. His idea is that New York's image is really important. When tourists come here, they don't want to visit a dirty city. They want to find a place that's modern and that cares about the environment.

And what do the cab drivers think? Our neighbor, Mr Janjma, drives one of the new cabs, so I asked him. "Cab drivers have to buy their cabs," he said, "and the new ones cost more than the old ones. But they don't use so much gas. I save about 30 dollars a day now. I'm really happy!"

Until next week! Stay safe! Greg

a) *Choose the right answers:*

1 New York taxicabs ...
A aren't typical of the city. B don't use much gas. C make the city's air dirty. D aren't a problem.

2 In future, New York's taxicabs will ...
A change colour. B be environmentally friendly. C travel slowly. D all be old.

3 A hybrid taxi ...
A has two motors. B doesn't stop at traffic lights. C uses only gas. D uses only electricity.

4 The mayor of New York says that the city should be ... for tourists.
A dirty B famous C on TV D clean

5 Mr Janjma ... green taxi.
A pays $ 30 a day for his B likes his C never drives his D wants to buy a

b) *Finish the sentences with information from the text.*

1 There are ... taxis in New York and they use about ... litres of gas every hour. 13.000 3,8
2 There are already nearly ... hybrid cabs. 400
3 A hybrid cab only uses gas when it ... travels more quick
4 Millions of people visit new York every year so it's important that ... they find a place [1]
5 Mr Janjma saves money now because... he doesn't use too much gas

► *SF Marking up a text (Revision) (p. 149)*

[1] environmentally friendly *umweltfreundlich* [2] battery *Akku* [3] mayor *Bürgermeister*

1) that is modern and that cares about the environment.

2 Reading

Here are some signs that you might see in town. Write a sentence for six of the signs. You can use the phrases from the box.

Sign 1: This sign …

You aren't allowed to … where you see this sign.
You're allowed to … here.
You don't have to … when you see this sign.
You have to … when you see this sign.

Signs

3 Writing

Choose one of the tasks below. Write an e-mail of 100–120 words. Begin and end your e-mail with suitable phrases. Count your words at the end.

a) *Chloe is your new American penfriend. Tell her about the village/area of town where you live. Include the following things.*

- Where in Germany?
- What's there to do?
- shops and buildings
- Old? Famous?
- Do you like it? Why (not)?

b) *Your British penfriend Robert wants to know what you did last weekend. Tell him:*
– what you did on Saturday/on Sunday
– who you did it with
– if it was fun/boring/…

4 Speaking

You're starting an internet project with a school in Boston in the US. Your class are making audio files about yourselves. Talk for about one minute about what you like doing.

California, the 'Golden State'?

1 California – people and places

a) *Look at the photos. Then read the captions below and match them to the photos.*

1. Endless beaches all along the coast where the 'beautiful people' can surf and party
2. Stars on Hollywood Boulevard
3. Silicon Valley, home of computer and software companies like Apple, Google and EA
4. The Terminator (from the film) + the governor (of the state) = 'the Governator'
5. A Mexican maid
6. Yosemite, one of California's eight National Parks – a great place for a weekend hike
7. A Mexican fruit picker
8. California, home of the movie stars

b) *Which two photos do you find most interesting? Why? Write a few sentences about them. (You can use words from the box.)*

beautiful scenery • expensive houses • film stars • Hollywood • immigrants • minorities • poor • rich • sunny all year • surfers • weekend activities

2 Extra SONG California

Listen to the theme song from the TV series 'The OC', which played in California. What do you feel when you hear it (excited, relaxed, ...)? Are there any photos that match the feeling? Why?

3 Extra PROJECT More on California (I)

Step 1 *: In groups of four, fill in a placemat with interesting topics about California – jobs, free-time activities, minorities, sights, ...*

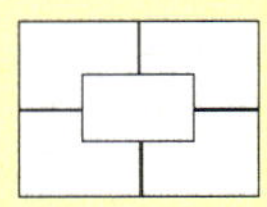

Agree on four topics. Each member of the group takes one.

Step 2*: Start collecting information and words and phrases that have to do with your topic. As you go through the unit, add more information.*

► P 1–4 (pp. 42–43) • WB 00 (p. 00) • **Text File 4** (pp. 120–121)

B
C
D
E
F
G
H
JOHNNY

All about ... growing up in two cultures

1 An e-zine

A youth e-zine asked its readers about their attitudes to immigrants and minorities. Three of the e-mails they published were from California.

"I don't fit in"

I'm Korean, and I hate being different. When I started school, it was a terrible experience. I didn't look like the other kids and I spoke almost no English.

I can't take anyone home with me. My mom doesn't speak much English and she only cooks Korean dishes. So people don't invite me to their houses. I just don't fit in because I belong to the wrong ethnic group.

– Kim L., Eureka, CA

"Learn the language"

I'm not prejudiced against immigrants, and I would never discriminate against them.

But I believe people who want to live in this country should try and fit in. They should learn the language and act like real Americans!

– Ashley S., Los Angeles, CA

"Lucky to live in America"

I'm proud to be a Latino. I've never thought of it as a disadvantage.

I'm growing up in two cultures, so I speak English and Spanish. In my opinion, being bilingual is an advantage. It will be useful when I look for a job and will help me to be successful at what I do.

Where I live, relations between Latinos and "Anglos" are very good – I've never experienced any discrimination. I know that isn't true everywhere – there's a lot of prejudice in our country.

I feel very lucky to live in America, where you can succeed if you have the right attitude.

– Luis M., San Clemente, CA

> *Would any of the three e-mail writers disagree with the statement below?*
'It's important that immigrants learn the language of their new country.'

2 Words and phrases

a) *Complete a copy of the chart with words from 1. You can use these words to talk about growing up in two cultures.*

Noun	Verb	Adjective
experience	...	–––
...	–––	prejudiced
...	discriminate	–––
success	...	successful

b) *Find the English for:*

– Ich würde Immigranten niemals diskriminieren.
– Ich finde, ...
– Ich habe es nie als Nachteil empfunden.
– Meiner Meinung nach ...
– Ich wurde nie diskriminiert.

► *P 5–7 (p. 44)*

3 Where strawberries come from

Luis Morales was trying to do his homework, but his little sister Maria was bored.

'Luis, when is Mama coming home?' Maria shook Luis's arm so hard that he almost dropped the Geography book he was reading.

'Soon,' Luis answered.

His younger brother Diego was next.

'Luis, can you help me with my homework?' he asked.

'Please don't interrupt me,' Luis said. 'I have to finish this by tomorrow. – Now, where was I? Ah, "What percentage of US strawberries come from California?"'

Scan the page from Luis' Geography book and find the answer.

64 Geography Today

1 Machines prepare the ground for planting.

2 Workers from Mexico pick the strawberries.

Food (5): The strawberry industry

Strawberries – like most food – are grown on large industrial farms. There are many steps in the production process:

1 The ground is prepared. (Photo 1)
2 The strawberries are planted.
3 To kill insects, the strawberry plants are sprayed with insecticides.
4 The strawberries are picked by workers from Mexico. (Photo 2)

Fact file

- The United States produces more strawberries than any other country.
- California farmers grow 85% of US strawberries.
- Strawberries are the favorite fruit of over 50% of American children.

Looking at language

1 California farmers **grow** strawberries.
2 Strawberries **are grown** on large farms.

a) *Are the sentences above in the same tense?*

b) *Which of the two sentences tells you who grows the strawberries and which doesn't?*

c) *are grown is a passive verb form. To make this form you need a form of the verb be and the past participle. Find more passive forms in Luis' Geography book.*

d) *Make sentences in the passive.*

Most American strawberries ... (produce) in California.
The strawberries ... (pack) into boxes.
Then the fruit ... (take) to supermarkets.

▸ GF 2a–d: The passive (pp. 157–158) • P 8–9 (p. 45) • WB 00 (p.00)

4 How was your day?

After cleaning and cooking in two houses, Mrs Morales took the bus back to Avenida Pico. It was six o'clock. She had to hurry. Today was one of the days when she had a third job in the evening – as a waitress.

'Hi!' she called out as she opened the front door. Maria ran to her.

Luis looked up from his book: 'Hey, Mom! You look tired. How was your day?'

'Ah, hijo mio! Lots of trouble. At the first job the gardener – old Señor Fuentes – was attacked by the dog. At the second job, the twins were sent home from school ...'

'There was lots of trouble at our school too, Mama,' said Diego. 'Manuel's bike was stolen! And José was bullied by Sam again ... he was taken to the hospital, and ...'

'Oh, no, look at the time!' Mrs Morales saw the clock on the wall. 'I have to leave again in half an hour. I must make your supper.'

'First a story, Mama,' cried Maria. 'About you and Papa when you came across the border.'

'After supper, if there's time, a story, bebita mia.'

> *How was Mrs Morales' day? And Diego's?*

► *P 10–12 (pp. 45–46)*

Americana ★ ★ ★

Many illegal immigrants are killed in car accidents as they run away from the border patrols.

The border

The border between the US and Mexico (1,954 miles) runs from San Diego, California, in the west to Brownsville, Texas, in the east. Thousands of Mexican immigrants reach the border every year with hopes of a better life. But a lot of them are caught by the US Border Patrol when they try to cross illegally. Along parts of the border the Americans have built a high fence to stop illegal immigrants.

Almost half (48.2 %, or 3.8 million) of all Mexican immigrants live in California. Most legal and illegal Mexican immigrants work on farms and in factories.

5 A family story

a) *Read the questions on the right. Then listen to Mrs Morales' story and take notes.*

b) *Answer the questions. Then listen again to check your answers.*

1 Why did Mr and Mrs Morales leave Mexico?
2 Were they legal or illegal immigrants?
3 Did they find work quickly?
4 Where was their first job?
5 After they arrived in California there was an amnesty. What did that mean for them?

► *P 13–15 (pp. 47–48)* • **Text File 5** *(pp. 122–123)*

6 Extra San Clemente – a brochure

San Clemente has
"The World's Finest Weather"
with over 342 sunny days and only 10 inches of rain per year.

Discover San Clemente.

San Clemente has five miles of world-class, white sand beaches, where top American and international surfers can be seen in action all year.

San Clemente is in the south of California's Orange County, close to San Diego and Los Angeles. Sea World and Disneyland can both be reached in about an hour. And if you're a student, take your ID with you. IDs must be shown to enjoy special student admission prices at most attractions.

We're building a new coastal path. From it you'll get wonderful views across the town and the sea. The path will be completed soon!

▸ Extra GF 1e: The passive: will-future + modals (p. 158) • P 16 (p. 48) • WB 00 (p. 00)

7 Extra A postcard puzzle

a) *Look at these details from California postcards. Can you guess what the postcards show?*

b) SONG Picture postcards from L.A.
Look at the beginning of the song. Is there a card that matches it? Listen. Does Rachel go to L.A.?

I'm the piano player, down at Eddie's bar,
and Rachel she's the waitress who wants to be a star.
She swears she's gonna make it, make it big someday,
and she'll send me picture postcards from L.A.

by Joshua Kadison

8 Extra PROJECT
More on California (II)

Step 3 *: In your group decide how you will present your project – posters/OHP/...*
Step 4*: Prepare your presentation.*
Step 5*: Check what you have written.*
Step 6*: Practise and present your information.*

▸ *SF Giving a presentation (Revision) (p. 142)*

Extra Background File **WELCOME TO CALIFORNIA!**

California, the Golden State,

is the third biggest of the fifty united states, but it is the state with the largest population – around 36 million people live there.

In 1848, gold was discovered in California. People from the East heard the news and crossed America to join the Gold Rush. This made California more attractive to the US and in 1850 it became the thirty-first state of the United States of America.

Today California is very rich. Its money comes from:

- farming: fruit, vegetables and wine – you'll find them all in your supermarket
- the computer industry in 'Silicon Valley'
- natural resources – oil, gas and gold etc.
- the entertainment industry – films and TV
- tourism – the National Parks, San Francisco, Hollywood and much more.

Let's go to San Francisco ...

... where you can see the Golden Gate Bridge, gateway to the Pacific Ocean. While New York, on America's East Coast, still has strong links across the Atlantic with Europe, the West Coast's links are with Asia and Australia.

When you're in San Francisco, don't forget to take a ride on a cable car – it's the best way to see the city.

... where the earth moves ...

One problem for the people in San Francisco – and large parts of California – is earthquakes. In 1906 around 3,000 people were killed by a great earthquake and the fire that followed it. More than half of San Francisco's population became homeless. In the 1989 earthquake 57 people died and again there was a lot of damage.

Remember if there's an earthquake:
'Drop, cover and hold on!'

- drop down under a strong table
- cover your eyes
- hold on to something

... or to the world-famous Sequoia National Park ...

... where the giant sequoia trees grow ... and grow ... and grow. There are eight beautiful National Parks in California and this one proves that things in America are bigger than anywhere else!

... and maybe end up in Los Angeles.

It's the largest city in California (second largest in the US) and it has a very famous suburb: Hollywood, or "The Dream Factory". The first Hollywood movie was made in 1910. The great weather and locations (sea, mountains, desert) brought the movie makers and the stars to L.A., and to this day Hollywood dominates the world of film and TV.

1 Gallery walk

a) *Make six groups, one for each statement. In your group, write your statement on a piece of paper. Hang your paper on the classroom wall.*

b) *Discuss your statement for 3 minutes and complete it. Give a reason. Move on to the next group's statement, discuss and complete it, etc.*

c) *When you have added to all papers, return to your own. Discuss what the other groups have added to your statement. Then write a final statement of your own and read it out.*

Statements:

1 The place we'd like to visit in California is ...
2 The things we like best that come from California are ...
3 The Hollywood star we'd like to meet is ...
4 The Hollywood star we wouldn't like to meet is ..
5 For us, California is the Golden State because ..
6 For us, California isn't the Golden State because ...

1 WORDS Who uses these? (Jobs)

a) *Look at the pictures and say who uses these things.*

1

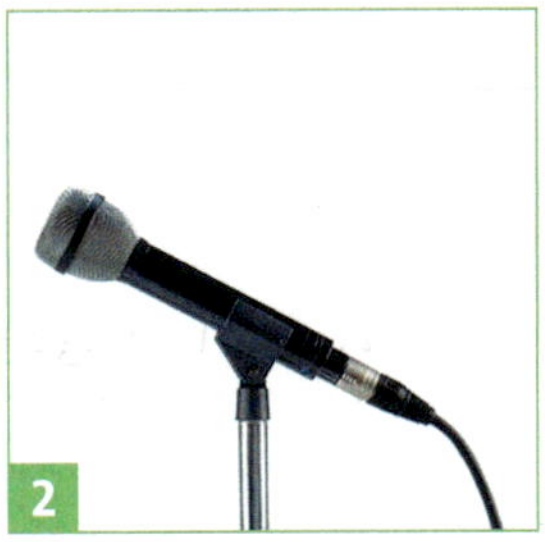
2

3

4

5

6

7

8

1 a waiter/waitress *2 ...*

b) **Extra** *Write one or two sentences about where these people work and what they do.*

2 WORDS Synonyms = words that have the same meaning

a) *Find a word or phrase in the second box that means the same as a word in the first box.*

afraid • also • awful • close • correct • difficult • film • great • kid • leave • loud • now • sad • start

at the moment • begin • child • fantastic • go away • hard • movie • near • noisy • right • scared • terrible • too • unhappy

b) *Choose 6 words from the boxes and make sentences with them.*

We had a great time in California.

c) *Read your sentences to your partner. He/she says the sentence again but uses a synonym.*

A: We had a great time in California.
B: We had a fantastic time in California.

d) **Extra** *Choose three words from each box and try to write a story that uses all of them.*

3 WORDS Word building (-less)

Add -less to the nouns in the box on the right to make adjectives. Then complete the sentences below with them.

cloud • end • head • help • home • job • sleep • tooth

1 I'm so tired – I've had a ... night again.
2 Ben never stops talking. I hate his ... stories.
3 The sun shone from a ... sky.
4 He didn't know what to do – he just ran around like a ... chicken.
5 The number of ... people in the town went up after the factory closed.
6 Little babies always look so ...
7 The old man gave us a ... smile.
8 Thousands of ... people sleep on the streets of L.A.

4 READING COURSE Endless Summer Surf Camp (Skimming and scanning)

Remember

Skimming helps you to find the main ideas of a text quickly.
- Look at the title, words in bold print, pictures and their captions.
- Read the first and last paragraphs quickly.
- Don't read the whole text word for word.

Remember

Scanning helps you to find specific information in a long text.
- Picture specific words in your mind.
- Don't read. Move your eyes over the page:
  – across the page in an 'S' or
  – up and down the page in a 'U'

a) *You want to learn to surf. You'd like to find a surf camp where you can have fun, stay overnight and have all your meals. Skim the Endless Summer Surf Camp website. Has the camp got what you're looking for?*

b) **Extra** *Skim the website again. In a few sentences say what a day at the camp is like.*

c) *You think the Endless Summer Surf Camp might be right for you, but you have some specific questions (see **1–5** on the right). To find the answers, you will have to scan the website.*

Before you scan the website, decide what key words in each of these questions might help you to find the information you need.

1 How many days can I spend at this surf camp?
2 How big are the surf groups?
3 I don't eat meat. Do they have vegetarian meals?
4 Do they do video analysis of students' surfing?
5 Will I be able to watch TV or play games?

▸ *SF Reading Course (pp. 150–151)*

SURF TRAINING

You've never surfed before? You want to learn new tricks and become a better surfer? Then we've got what you're looking for! Our coaches work with you in small groups of 3, so every student gets individual help.

RELAXING AND SLEEPING

You sleep in large and comfortable tents. And at the campsite you'll find a game area with table tennis and beach volleyball. There's also a lounge with sofas where you can watch a movie on TV, read a book or just listen to music and hang out.

MEALS

Three meals a day, plus snacks and drinks! Start the day with a hearty breakfast at the camp. Enjoy a relaxed lunch of sandwiches, summer fruits and other snacks on the beach. And round it all off with a great dinner back at camp every evening. There's a vegetarian alternative at every meal.

5 WORDS Minorities and ethnic groups

a) *Look back at A1 on p. 36 and find the English phrases for:* I'm not prejudiced against

1 Ich gehöre zur falschen ethnischen Gruppe.
2 Ich bin stolz, ein Latino zu sein.
3 Ich wachse in zwei Kulturen auf.
4 Zweisprachig zu sein ist ein Vorteil.
5 Sie sollten versuchen sich anzupassen.
They should try and fit in
6 Ich habe keine Vorurteile gegen Immigranten.
7 Das Verhältnis zwischen ... und ... ist sehr gut.
Relations between

b) *Complete the text below. The phrases from a) will help you.*

I'm white, and I'm ... to be an American. My great-grandfather came from Italy, and he spoke no English when he arrived. Although nobody in my family speaks Italian, I still feel I'm growing ... in two ... We eat Italian food and do lots of traditional Italian things. Where I live, ... between the different ... groups are good! I'm sorry I can't speak Italian – speaking two languages is an ... I think. In the US, of course, you have to speak English if you want to ... Even people who aren't ... against immigrants say that people who come to live in America must learn English.

6 WRITING More on 'Growing up in two cultures' (Writing an e-mail)

a) *Write an e-mail (60–80 words) to the e-zine about one of the e-mails on p. 36 – Kim's, Ashley's or Luis'. Say why you agree or disagree with it. Here are two ideas for how you can start. You can add your e-mail to your DOSSIER.*

b) **Extra** ***Role play*** *Partner A: You're a reporter. Interview Partner B about his/her e-mail. Then swap roles.*

ndl.

> Re: E-mail from Kim L.
> I don't live in the United States, but I belong to an ethnic minority too.
> I agree with everything Kim writes. She says that ...

> Re: E-mail from Ashley S.
> Ashley writes that people who live in America should 'act like real Americans !' I don't belong to a 'minority', but I don't think ...

7 REVISION Being a student is ... (Gerunds)

a) *Complete the sentences. Use gerunds and an adjective. Give reasons.*

1 (be) a student is ...
2 *Being a student is great. You learn lots of interesting things.*
3 (watch) a DVD is ...
4 (get up) early is ...
5 (write) e-mails is ...
6 (go) to school by bike is ...
7 (text) somebody is ...

b) *Make appointments with three partners. Compare your ideas.*

A: I think being a student is great. You learn lots of interesting things.
B: I don't agree. I think being a student is horrible. You have to do lots of homework.

8 The big quiz (Passive – simple present)

Choose the correct answer and write the sentences in your exercise book. The letters behind the correct answers will form a word.

1 Spanish... (speak) in Portugal (B) / Mexico (C) / Italy (D). *Spanish is spoken in ...*
2 Oscars ... (give) to film stars (A) / good sportsmen and sportswomen (B) / famous governors (C).
3 Lots of computer software ... (make) in Death Valley (K) /Silicon Valley (L) / Las Vegas (M).
4 Ferraris ... (produce) in Germany (G) / France (H) / Italy (I).
5 The most bagels ... (eat) in Paris (E) / New York (F) / London (G).
6 Most US strawberries ... (grow) in Alaska (M) / New York (N) / California (O).
7 The fruit on the strawberry farms ... (pick) by young kids (P) / Park Rangers (Q) / Mexicans (R).
8 California ... (call) the Yellow State (M) / Golden State (N) / Orange State (O).
9 Park Rangers ... (find) at all American beaches (H) / National Parks (I) / stations (J).
10 Most of the big films ... (make) in Los Angeles (A) / San Francisco (E) / New York (C).

9 What do you know about California? (Passive – simple present)

Make passive sentences.

1 Some of the best beaches in the US (find)	in Germany, but in German.
2 Software from California (use)	as one of the hottest places on earth.
3 Every year lots of animals (kill)	along California's coast.
4 California's Death Valley (visit)	on California farms.
5 Death Valley is (know)	in large forest fires.
6 California strawberries (sell)	by thousands of tourists every year.
7 Lots of fruit pickers (need)	in computers all over the world.
8 Lots of Hollywood movies (show)	all over the US.

1 Some of the best beaches in the US are found along ...

10 California was discovered by ... (Passive – simple past)

Look at the pictures. Write down what happened when. Use **by** *if you need it*

1
California – discover – Spanish explorers – 1769

2
Golden Gate Bridge – build – Joseph Strauss – 1933–37

3
first film – make – in Hollywood – 1910

4
Disneyland – open – Walt Disney – in Anaheim – 1955

5
gold – find – near Sacramento – 1848

6
forest fires – put out – brave firefighters – last summer

11 Which came first? (Passive – simple past)

a) *Partner B: Go to p. 109. Partner A: Look at each pair of pictures. Guess which of the two came first. Tell your partner what you think.*

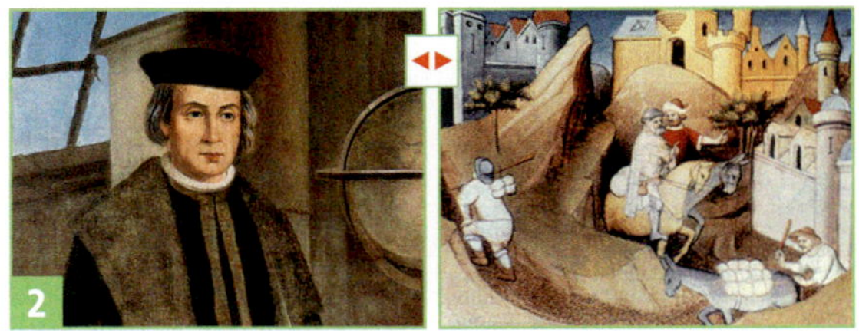

1 Eiffel Tower (build) ◂▸ first car (make)

A: I think the Eiffel Tower was built before the first car was made.
B: That's right. / No, that's wrong. The first car was made in ..., and the Eiffel Tower was ...

2 North America (discover) by Columbus ◂▸ China (visit) by Marco Polo
3 first plane (fly) ◂▸ first underground railway (open)
4 Mona Lisa (paint) ◂▸ St. Paul's Cathedral (finish)

b) *Now your partner is going to say what he/she thinks came first. Listen and correct his/her statements if they're wrong. Use these dates.*
1 planet Uranus (discover): 1781 ◂▸ first slaves (bring) to America: 1502
2 Golden Gate Bridge (finish): 1937 ◂▸ Empire State Building (build): 1930–1931
3 first tea bags (sell): 1904 ◂▸ first helicopter (fly): 1907
4 John F. Kennedy (kill): 1963 ◂▸ Berlin Wall (build): 1961

12 Accident! (Active and Passive)

Read these notes by a reporter and write his report about an accident. Be careful: some sentences have to be in the passive.

- young man on bike ran into old woman
- corner Main Street / Park Road 9.30 am
- man cycling too fast, couldn't stop
- woman fell, lots of blood on her head
- man cycled away, didn't get help
- ambulance called by young woman
- old woman taken to hospital
- police now looking for man
- descriptions sent to all police stations
- same man seen at station minutes after accident
- left bike there
- got on train to airport

A young man on a bike ran into an old woman yesterday. The accident happened at the corner of Main Street and Park Road at 9.30 am. The man was cycling too fast and ...

13 EVERYDAY ENGLISH MEDIATION Sale! (Explaining announcements)

The Walthers from Germany are shopping at a department store in Los Angeles. They're listening to some announcements, but Mr Walther can't understand them. Listen and explain to Mr Walther in German the important points in each announcement.

14 EVERYDAY ENGLISH SPEAKING At a theme park (Asking for information)

a) *Partner B: Go to p. 110.*
Partner A: Read the information on this poster for 'Adventure Park' near San Clemente. Use the information to answer your partner's questions.

b) *Your partner has information on 'Movie Park Hollywood'. Ask him/her about the following:*
1. exciting attractions for teenagers
2. opening hours
3. ticket prices
4. special tickets

15 LISTENING Welcome to San Clemente Cinemas

STUDY SKILLS Interactive listening

If you call somewhere for information, you will often get a recorded message. Then you usually have to press buttons on your phone. Don't panic. You can always listen to the information again.

▸ SF Interactive listening (p. 148)

a) *Imagine you want to take your ten-year-old cousin to the cinema on Saturday afternoon. Listen to the CD (part 1) and fill in a copy of the chart.*

What numbers do you have to press	
– to hear which movies you can see? 1	...
– to hear the information again? 5	
– to get tickets? 3	
– to listen to the child information line? 4	
– to find out when the movies start? 2	

b) *Look at the poster on the right. Then listen to the CD (part 2) and find out which of these three movies you may see with your cousin. Take notes.*

c) *Listen to the CD (part 3). What time do you have to be at the cinema if you need ten minutes to get your tickets and buy drinks and popcorn? Take notes.*

3.55 pm – 3.45 / 7.15 – 7.05

d) *Swap your notes with a partner and check.*

16 Extra The Golden Gate Bridge (Passive – modals and will-future)

Match the sentence halves.

1 *For years, San Francisco Bay*
2 Several engineers wanted to build a bridge,
3 When Joseph Strauss started to build it in 1933, people were still sure:
4 When the bridge was completed in 1937,
5 Over the years, the bridge has had to be closed
6 Today the bridge can be used
7 The Golden Gate Bridge will always be known

6 by more than 100,000 cars and trucks a day.
5 several times because of high winds.
3 'That bridge will never be built!'
7 as the most famous sight in San Francisco.
2 but most people believed it couldn't be done.
had to be crossed by ferry.
4 the bay could be crossed on foot at last.

Santa Monica – Episode 1 of a TV series

Teen TV, a new TV station for teenagers, wants to start with a new teen soap. It has asked a group of teenagers to read the following script and help them to decide if they should film it.

Read the start of the film script for the series 'Santa Monica' and then help to decide if it should become a TV series. Some of the new words in the text aren't in the Dictionary in this book. Try to guess unknown words from the context. Only use your English–German dictionary if you have to.

▸ *SF: Reading Course (pp. 150–151), SF Using a bilingual dictionary (Revision) (p. 140)*

Opening titles

From a helicopter we see the skyscrapers of L.A. We fly out towards the Pacific Ocean and turn down towards Malibu. The series song plays, and as we get near Santa Monica the opening titles appear.

Scene 1 At the beach

A group of five cool, beautiful rich kids – Brad and Josh, Cindy, Jane and Lara – are walking along the beach in Santa Monica, laughing.

Lara ... so I'm going to Alaska with my parents in the summer.

Brad You poor thing – I hate the cold.

Lara It's not cold in Alaska in the summer ... is it?

Brad and Josh look at each other.

Jane Hey, there's Luke!

Luke is waving to them from the road.

Josh He wants us to go surfing with him.

Lara Well, aaaall right! Let's go.

We see the group walk off the beach.

Scene 2 At Luke's car

Luke, beautiful like the others, stands by an expensive SUV. On top of it are surfboards. He holds a door open.

Luke Hey, guys. The surf's good over at Malibu. Make yourselves comfortable and let's go.

Josh Is this the new car?

Luke Sure is.

Cindy Wow! It's real nice, Lukey.

It's clear Cindy likes Luke a lot.

Luke *He doesn't care.* Thanks, Cindy.

Scene 3 On the road

We're inside the car as it drives along by the sea. Lots of laughter. Josh is in the front with Luke. Brad, Lara, Jane and Cindy are in the back, Jane on Brad's knee, Cindy behind the driver.

Brad *Pulls out bottle of water from under him, then an orange.* Hey man, you have a lot of stuff in this new car!

Cindy Right!

She's looking through some clothes she's found on the floor. She holds a T-shirt against herself and shows it to Lara, who is sitting next to her. She throws it into the back. Next a pair of shorts. Both girls laugh. Then she finds a black tie.

Cindy Even a tie! *From behind she puts the tie round Luke.* Hey, Lukey, I didn't even know you could tie one of these.

Luke *He pushes her away.* Hey Cindy, careful! Sure I can tie a tie!

Josh Look, that girl needs help. *He points to a car at the side of the road.* A girl is looking at the engine. Let's make sure she's OK.

Luke *Stops the car.* OK, but make sure you're quick!

Josh gets out and goes over to the girl.

Lara ___ Josh is a real nice guy.

Luke ___ Too nice! Look at the car: it's all old and dirty. It's a real white trash car!

All laugh, except Lara.

Scene 4 By the road

Jenna is looking at the engine. She's puzzled. She's wearing the uniform of a coffee shop waitress – a short skirt and blouse. She's very pretty. Josh walks over.

Josh ___ Hi, can I help you?

She looks up, sees the SUV, sees Josh.

Jenna ___ *Coldly* Normally I'd say no. But if I don't get to Santa Monica in five minutes, I'll lose my job. So, if you know anything about cars ... yes, you can help me.

Josh quickly begins to check the engine.

Luke ___ *Calls from SUV.* Hey, Josh, hurry up!

Josh looks up.

Josh ___ Go on, I'll meet you there.

He turns back to the car and doesn't look up through the rest of the dialogue.

Josh ___ By the way, my name's Josh.

Jenna ___ I'm Jenna.

Josh ___ Nice to meet you Jenna.

Jenna looks at her watch. Josh stands up straight.

Josh ___ There you go!

Scene 5 A street in Santa Monica

A café with tables on the street. The old car arrives. Jenna and Josh get out.

Josh ___ Go! Go! I'll wait.

Boss ___ Well, you won't have to wait long! Jenna, this is the third time you've been late. I warned you: you're fired!

Jenna ___ Larry, please ...

The boss goes into the café. Sadly, Jenna turns away and gets back in the car. Josh gets in too.

Scene 6 In Jenna's car

Josh ___ It was only a café job, Jenna.

Jenna ___ That's what you think!

Jenna is depressed. Josh looks at her and smiles.

Josh ___ Hey Jenna, it's not the end of the world.

Jenna ___ *Angrily* Not for you! You and your friends don't have to work for your money – you just ask your parents.

Josh ___ *Feeling guilty* I'm sorry.

Jenna ___ *Still angry* Yeah. You know... *bitterly* ... I live with my mom in Inglewood – but I guess you never go to that part of town. My dad – at least I think he's my dad – he's in jail. He stole a car, crashed it and then got into a fight. And my mom drinks, so she doesn't have a job. She says that things will change ... But right now I'm the one who has to pay for everything ...

Josh ___ I'm sorry ...

Jenna ___ It's not your fault.

Josh ___ Don't give up, Jenna. I'm sure things will get better. Maybe I can help ...

Jenna turns off the road. We see Luke's SUV and Josh's friends with their surfboards on the beach.

Jenna ___ There are your friends. They're waiting for you.

Josh opens his door.

Josh ___ Do you have a boyfriend, Jenna?

Jenna ___ *Coldly* Why?

Josh ___ *Smiles* What are you doing tonight?

Jenna ___ I'm babysitting for our neighbor.

Josh ___ Give me the address. I might come too.

Jenna looks at him. She's clearly nervous.

Jenna ___ Why?

Josh ___ Because I want to get to know you.

Jenna ___ Seriously?

Josh ___ Seriously.

Jenna ___ But Mrs Alvarez doesn't want me to bring anyone.

Josh: Just this one time.

Jenna: *Pause* 41 Hayden Street.

Josh: 41 Hayden Street. *He jumps out.* Thanks for the ride.

He closes the door and Jenna drives off.

Scene 7 The kitchen at Jenna's house

Jenna is cleaning the small, cheap kitchen. We hear the front door open.

Mom: *Calling* Hi, baby! I'm home.

Jenna: Hi, Mom.

She goes through to the living room, which is small and shabby.

Scene 8 The living room at Jenna's house

Jenna's mom has just dropped her keys on a table by the phone and is falling onto the sofa.

Mom: I met this real nice guy ...

Jenna: *She's heard this often before.* Who is it this time, Mom?

Mom: Whoever you'd like! *She laughs.* Superman, Batman, Rambo ...

Jenna: Oh, Mom. You're drunk again. You promised ...

Mom: Oh, Jenna baby, don't get angry. *She tries to get up.* Where are my cigarettes? *She sees them on the table next to her, takes one and lights it.*

Jenna: And you promised ...

Mom closes her eyes as she smokes. Jenna gives up.

Jenna: I lost my job today.

Mom: *Opens eyes.* My poor baby. Things will change, I'm sure. You'll get another job, I'll get another job – things will work out, baby. Hey, let's go out for a drink tonight, just you and me ...

Jenna: *Sadly* I'm babysitting for Mrs Alvarez tonight, Mom. *Gets ready to go.*

Mom: Aw, don't go, baby. It's so depressing, here, all alone.

Jenna kisses her mom.

Jenna: I'm sorry, Mom. I know. But Mrs Alvarez has to work. And since her niece doesn't have time tonight, I promised to help. And it's ten dollars. See you.

Scene 9 Malibu Beach

Brad and Jane are in the water. The others are sitting on the beach and talking.

Cindy: Hey, look at that girl – she's real fat.

Lara: No, she isn't, Cindy. Just because she isn't a size 6 like you doesn't make her fat.

Luke: I'm not so sure.

He and Cindy laugh. Lara looks at Josh. He's looking out to sea.

Luke: So, what are we doing tonight, guys?

Cindy: There's a party over at Melissa's house. We could ...

Josh: *Angry* Hey Cindy, can't you think of anything except parties and surfing?

Cindy: Shopping!

Cindy and Luke laugh. Josh gets up angrily.

Lara: I think about lots of stuff, Josh – not just parties and surfing.

He looks down at her.

Josh: I know.

Lara: So, what do you want to do tonight?

Josh: I'm busy. I'll call you tomorrow, OK?

He walks off. Cindy leans over to Lara.

Cindy: Don't worry, Lara. He'll be back.

Lara: I'm not so sure ...

Scene 10 The Alvarez house – the living room

The front door opens onto the living room. It's very clean and tidy. Jenna stands at a bedroom door, looking in. She turns off the light and very quietly closes the door – clearly the kids are asleep. Outside somebody knocks. She goes over, checks who it is and opens the door. It's Josh with boxes of Chinese food.

Josh Hi.

Jenna Oh, it's you! You shouldn't be here.

Josh Hungry?

Jenna *Smells the food.* Well, just this one time.

She lets him come in. They sit down.

Scene 11 Party at a rich house

One of the guests, standing alone, is Lara. We see a young waiter offer her some food.

Lara No, thanks.

Waiter *Whispers.* You OK?

Lara Yeah, sure. *She smiles weakly.* Thanks.

Scene 12 The Alvarez house – the living room

The meal is finished. Jenna and Josh are on the white sofa. She's drinking a coffee. Josh suddenly turns to her, the coffee spills on the sofa.

Jenna *Jumps up.* Oh, no!

Josh It's only coffee!

Jenna Only coffee! Look at the sofa – and it's new.

Josh *Gets up.* I'll clean it up. Where's the kitchen?

Jenna No, I'll try to clean it up.

Josh No, let me ...

Jenna goes to the kitchen and gets a towel.

Jenna *Angry* I'll do it! You shouldn't even be here.

Josh Hey, let's not get into an argument over a little coffee.

Jenna I'll take it from here, Josh. I think you should leave.

Josh Hey, Jenna. I thought we were having a good time?

Jenna This whole thing was a bad idea. Just go, Josh!

Josh goes to the door, his feelings hurt.

Josh Bye Jenna.

Jenna Bye.

Working with the text

1 The scenes

Say in one or two sentences what each scene is about.

Scene 1: Brad, Josh, Cindy, Jane and Lara meet at the beach.

Scene 2: Luke invites ...

2 The characters

a) *Write a sentence about how each person feels about the other. Why do you think that? Find examples from the script.*

1 Josh and Lara
2 Brad and Jane
3 Luke and Cindy
4 Josh and Jenna

b) *Think of at least two reasons why the characters say these lines.*

1 Cindy (l.25): 'Wow! It's real nice, Lukey.'
2 Luke (ll.55–56): 'Too nice! ... white trash car!'
3 Josh (l.113): 'I'm sorry.'
4 Lara (l.204): 'I'm not so sure ...'
5 Jenna (l.248): 'This whole thing was a bad idea.'

3 Teen TV series

a) *What do you think makes a good TV series for teens? Think of American and German series you know and like. Do they show romance, comedy, everyday life, social problems, money problems, ...?*

b) *Do you think Teen TV should produce the series Santa Monica or not? Write a short report and give reasons for your opinion.*

I think Teen TV should / shouldn't produce ...
The episode is awesome / boring / ...
I like / don't like ...
The way it shows ... is ...

4 Extra And next week ...

a) *Write one or two scenes for the start of the next episode of Santa Monica.*

b) *Read your scripts. Vote for the favourite. Practise it in your group.*

c) *Each group reads its favourite script to the class. Vote for the best.*

► **Text File 6** *(pp. 124–125)*

How am I doing?

a) *Fill in or choose the correct answers.*

California

1 California is sometimes called ...
A the Golden State. B the Orange State.
C the Sunny State. D the Surfing State.

2 There are lots of computer companies in ...
A San Clemente. B Yosemite.
C Silicon Valley. D San Diego.

3 Because many of the people in California come from Mexico, they speak ...
A Mexican. B English.
C French. D Spanish.

4 People who cross the border to the US without papers are called ... immigrants.
A bad B illegal
C bilingual D border

5 The famous bridge on the west coast of the US is ...
A the Brooklyn Bridge. B Tower Bridge.
C the Golden Gate Bridge.
D Harbour Bridge.

Skills

6 If you skim a text, you don't ...
A look at captions. B look at pictures.
C look at the title. D read every word.

7 Scanning helps you to find ...
A the main ideas of a text.
B good pictures. C specific information.
D a translation.

8 If you call somewhere and get a recorded message ...
A press number 1. B call another number. C don't panic: you can listen again. D wait till somebody talks to you.

Words

9 Mexicans are an important ... in California.
A ethnic group B majority
C attitude D advantage

10 It is illegal to ... people because they belong to a different ethnic group.
A prejudice B prejudice against
C discriminate D discriminate against

11 I've got lots of Latino friends, but my parents don't like it because they're ...
A prejudice. B prejudiced.
C discriminate D discriminated against.

12 Which word does *not* fit in the sentence, 'Most US strawberries are ... in California'?
A planted B produced
C done D grown

13 Large farms are usually called ... farms.
A industry B industrial
C family D process

Grammar

14 Most American films ... in Hollywood.
A become made B will made
C have made D are made

15 Gold ... in California in 1848.
A was discovered B has discovered
C discovered itself D is discovered

16 That film was made ... Steven Spielberg.
A from B by C through D after

17 Which means the same as 'My camera was stolen'?
A I stole a camera.
B A camera stole me.
C Somebody stole my camera.

b) *Check your answers on p. 253 and add up your points.*

c) *If you had 14 or more points, well done! Maybe you can help students who had fewer points. If you had 13 points or fewer, it's a good idea to do some more work before you go on to the next unit. Where did you make mistakes? The chart below will tell you what you can do to improve your English.*

No.	Area	Find out more	Exercise(s)
1– 5	California	Lead-in, Background file	WB 00, p. 00
6– 8	Skills	P 4, p. 43, P 15, p. 48; SF, p. 148	P 4, P 15, WB 00, p. 00
9–11	Words: Minorities	All about, p. 36	P 5–6, p. 44, WB 00, p. 00
12–13	Words: farming	A 4, p. 37	WB 00, p. 00
14–17	The passive	LAL, p. 37; GF 2, pp. 157–158	P 8–12, pp. 45–46, WB 00, p. 00

Hermann says 'Willkommen'

1 What's Hermann like?

a) *Look at the photos of Hermann, Missouri. Would you like to live there? Why (not)? What might you miss? Make notes.*

Living in Hermann:

advantages	disadvantages
lots of festivals	miss old friends
…	…

b) *Make appointments with three classmates. Exchange your ideas about living in Hermann.*

c) **Extra** *Imagine you are on Market Street. Look at the photo. Then close your eyes. What can you see, hear and smell?*

2 Starting a new life

a) *Listen to the CD and find out:*

1 Where does Mr Kruger pick up the German family?
2 Why is the German family going to Hermann?

b) *Listen to the CD again and answer these questions:*

1 Who is going to start at Hermann High School soon?
2 What events take place in the Festhalle?
3 Why does Hermann have more restaurants than most towns its size?
4 Why do tourists go to Hermann?
5 Where will the German family stay at first?

► P 1–2 (p. 62) • SF Listening for detail (Revision) (p. 148) • WB 00 (p. 00)

A Grape harvest at one of Hermann's many wineries.

B Market Street is the main street of Hermann, Missouri.

C Hermann's Festhalle – keeping German traditions alive ...

D ... with festivals ike Maifest and Octoberfest.

E Lots of people live on farms outside town.

F Hermann High School is a modern school with about 400 students.

All about ... American schools

1 The school system

High School	Grades 9–12	Ages 14–18
Middle School	Grades 6–8	Ages 11–14
Elementary School	Grades 1–5	Ages 6–11
Kindergarten		Ages 5–6

In the US, are there different kinds of school for kids of the same age?
Which school and grade would you be in?

2 A class schedule

Hermann High School **Jake Kruger** **Grade: 9**

Period	Time	Subject	Rm.
1	08:20–09:10	English 1	31
2	09:15–10:05	Science	36
3	10:10–11:00	Math	16
4	11:05–11:55	Semester 1: Boys' PE Semester 2: Health	Gym 28
5	Lunch/study hall		
6	01:15–02:05	Sem. 1: Geography Sem. 2: American Government	21 21
7	02:10–03:00	Agricultural Science 1	54

Staatskunde

How is Jake's school day different from yours? (days, rooms, subjects)?

3 From the school bulletin board

Students who want to take part in extracurricular activities: please remember that you can't have any grades below a C.
Mrs. Kay

Arbeitsgemeinschaften

Student Dress Code

1 No hats or caps may be worn inside the school.

2 No clothes with holes should be worn.

3 See-through clothes are not allowed.

STUDENTS WHO BREAK THESE RULES WILL BE SENT HOME TO CHANGE.

US school grades
A excellent **B** good **C** average
D below average **F** failure

What do you think is the reason for the rule about extracurricular activities? Is it fair?
Do you agree with the dress code?

4 School words

Copy and complete the chart. All the AE words you need are in 1, 2 or 3.

German	AE	BE
Jahrgangsstufe	grade	...
...	...	... timetable
(Schul-)Stunde	...	...
schwarzes Brett		... notice board

5 A talk about school

a) *Listen to Jake and Timo as they talk about school. Take notes: school year, school day, lunchtime, school bus*

b) *Divide the four topics above between the people in your group. Listen again for more information on your topic and take notes. Then explain to your group what's the same and what's different in the US and Germany.*

► P 3–5 (p. 63) • WB 00 (p. 00)

6 FFA

'Hey Jake,' Timo said when he saw his friend in the hall. 'Why are you going that way? We've got American Government next – Room 21.'

'Today's Wednesday, Timo,' Jake answered. 'We have extracurriculars in the afternoon.'

'Hey Jake, Timo!' It was Cindy, Jake's girlfriend. 'Are you going to the FFA meeting with us, Timo?'

'FFA? What's that?' Timo asked.

'Future Farmers of America,' she told him. 'This is an important meeting. There'll be lots of information on the County Fair on Saturday. Jake and I are both going to show hogs there.'

Timo found the whole thing very strange. 'I think I'll do my homework then, if that's OK.'

Jake looked hurt. 'Well,' he said, 'homework is important, Timo. But FFA is important too. You'll see.'

So Timo joined them in the auditorium. There was some news about the County Fair, and some of the students talked about their hogs: how much money they had paid for them, how many hours a week they spent on them, and so on. At the end there was a presentation with some information on the Missouri wine industry.

After the meeting Timo asked Jake, 'Are you going to be a farmer like your dad?'

'No,' answered Jake, 'I want to be a teacher. I'm in FFA because it gives you a lot of experience. And it'll look good when I apply for college or my first job.'

Why is today's FFA meeting important for Jake and Cindy? Do you think Timo found it interesting?

Americana ★ ★ ★

Extracurricular activities

'Get involved!' That's what they say at American high schools, where sports and other extracurricular activities are just as important as lessons. Students should be good at their school subjects, but also good at sports and interested in other things. FFA is only one of these activities – there are usually foreign language clubs, debate teams, dance groups, a school band, a drama group, cheerleaders and teams for every kind of sport from golf to football.

7 Now you

a) *Read these statements and decide if you agree or disagree. Think of reasons.*

1 Having extracurricular activities at school would be better than going to private clubs.

2 Having a dress code like the one in Hermann would be good at our school too.

b) *Find somebody who disagrees with you on question **1** and find out his or her reasons. Take notes. Do the same for question **2**. Collect arguments on the board and discuss.*

► GF 3: Countable/uncountable nouns (pp. 159–160) • P 6–8 (p. 64) • WB 00 (p. 000)

8 In Jake's Health class

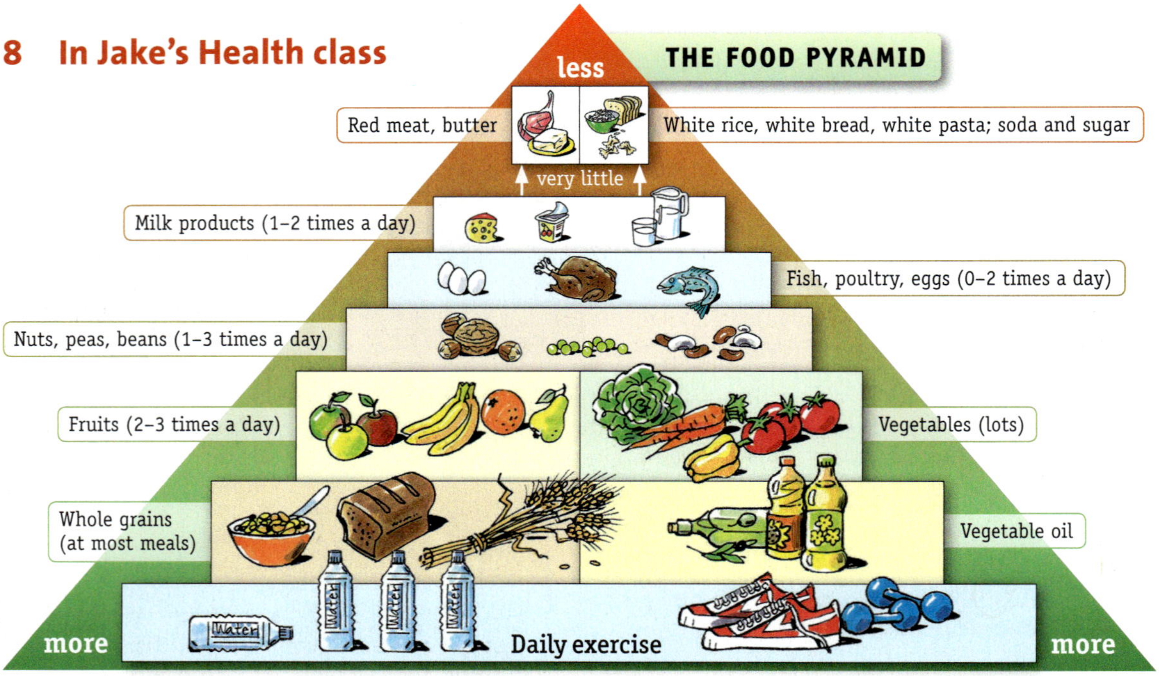

9 Now you

a) *Make a list of everything you ate yesterday.* Morning: muesli, 2 glasses of milk, banana, chocolate, ...

b) *Where would the things you ate yesterday belong in the food pyramid? Did you eat more healthy or more unhealthy things?* I had muesli = whole grains, fruit, nuts and milk

► *P 9 (p. 65)*

10 A discussion in Health class

'Are there any questions about the food pyramid?' Ms. Meerbusch, the Health teacher, asked. 'No? OK. – We've talked about food all week. Now let's talk about the food you eat. Is it healthy? – Yes, Sandy?'

'Yes, I think it is. Everybody says quality is important, and the quality of the food we eat is very good. I mean, most of it comes from farms right here in Missouri. So it's really fresh.'

'I'm not so sure,' Jake said. 'Not everybody cares if their food is fresh, as long as it's cheap. It's a question of money.'

'Yes,' said Tom Bauer, 'but if you're interested in your health, then you'll spend the money you need to buy fresh food.'

Timo was really surprised. 'I always thought that Americans only eat fast food. But you all care about healthy food – just like my family!'

Looking at language

a) *Look at the word 'food' in the two sentences below. In one sentence, it's used in a general way; in the other, it's used to talk about specific food.*
We've talked about food all week.
Let's talk about the food you eat.
Which sentence is general? Which sentence is specific and answers the question 'which food?'?

b) *Now write out the sentences with 'quality' and 'money'. Which sentences are general, which are specific?*

► *GF 4: The definite article (p. 160)* • *P 10–11 (p. 66)* • *WB 00 (p. 00)* • **Text File 7** *(pp. 126–127)*

11 From the local paper

Scrapbook — Hermann Advertiser-Courier — Wedn

New start at local winery is new start for German family

When Andreas Schmidt visited Hermann 20 years ago, he never dreamed that he would return to live here. And his family had never planned to leave their home in Germany. But now they're here in Hermann to start a new life and to restart the old Hermannthal Winery.

Andreas Schmidt was a member of the first group of high school students that visited Hermann from our sister city of Bad Arolsen over 20 years ago. Andreas stayed with the Kruger family, and he has kept in touch with the Krugers all these years.

It was Chuck Kruger who brought him back to Hermann again – this time to stay. Without Chuck, Andreas would not have heard that Hermannthal Winery needed a winemaker to start production again after three years.

"It's a big step to leave your country," Schmidt says. "But we all spoke the language, at least a little, and I already had work."

Karla, Andreas' wife, says it was "an adventure" to move to the US. "But I'm happy that we did it," she adds. Karla has found lots of new friends in Hermann. "I'm even working at Maifest next month," she says.

Son Timo likes his new school. "A lot of things seemed strange at first, but after I understood them better, I really started to like it here." Timo is active in FFA, and he has found a teacher who shares his interest in soccer. "We're starting a soccer team at Hermann High in September," he says. His younger sister Anna already speaks English with a Missouri accent.

To Andreas, Karla, Timo and Anna: Hermann says "Willkommen."

How was the friendship between Andreas and Chuck important? How are the different family members doing in their new home?

► *GF 5: Talking about the future (p. 161) • P 12 (p. 66) • WB 0 (p. 00)*

12 MEDIATION Calling grandmother

Timo wants to call his grandmother to tell her about the newspaper article. Imagine you're Timo. Tell her in three or four German sentences what it says in the article.

► *P 13 (p. 67) • WB 00 (p. 00)*

Extra | Background File | GOING WEST

1 READING Group puzzle I

Divide the class into four groups (A, B, C, D). Each person in the group has a number (1, 2, 3, ...). Group A reads text A, Group B reads text B, etc. Take notes. Then go to 2 on p. 61.

A HERMANN

In the 18th and early 19th centuries, many Germans who had come to the New World were unhappy: English traditions and the English language dominated everyday life. The Germans were afraid that their children wouldn't learn their language and traditions. So they formed the *Deutsche Ansiedlungsgesellschaft zu Philadelphia* in 1836. The following year this group bought land in Missouri and started a German colony there. And so the town of Hermann was born.

The first settlers in Hermann thought it looked like the Rhine Valley.

Hermann stayed very German until World War I (1914–1918). The US was fighting the Germans in Europe, so many Americans worried about Germans in the middle of their country. The school in Hermann was no longer allowed to teach in German. The proud Germans of Hermann stopped speaking their language and gave up their traditions for many years. ■

B THE ROLE OF MISSOURI

The first states in the United States of America were along the east coast. As more and more Europeans came to the US, the country grew towards the West. Missouri became a state in 1821, and by 1840 more than 380,000 people lived there. When gold was discovered in California in 1848, Missouri became the 'Gateway to the West', and the wagon trains to the West started there. But not everybody went west to look for gold. Thousands went to get free or cheap land where they could start a farm and a new life.

People who wanted to go to California, Oregon or other places in the West travelled to St. Louis, where they bought everything they needed for the journey. Most then took a boat up the Missouri River to Independence, where they joined a wagon train. These 'trains' were the safest way to travel until a railway across the continent was finished in 1869. ■

Settlers got off the Missouri river boats and formed wagon trains for the journey to the West.

C THE TRAILS TO THE WEST

The wagon trains followed one of many trails to the West. The Oregon Trail is the most famous. It was more than 2,000 miles long, and the journey often took five months or more.

Many of the pioneers walked the whole way – their wagons were full of the things they needed for their new lives in the West. About ten per cent of the people died from accidents or illnesses. A few were killed in animal or Indian attacks.

Over the years more than half a million people went west this way. The journey was hard, so only those who were very strong were able to do it. There are many stories about the brave men and women who made the journey, and Americans are still very proud of this 'pioneer spirit'. ■

D THE NATIVE AMERICANS

When the first Europeans came to North America, the continent wasn't empty. There were already millions of people there, although nobody can say exactly how many.

In the beginning most of the meetings between the Europeans and the Native Americans (or 'Indians') were peaceful, and the two groups often helped each other. But even then, huge numbers of Native Americans died from diseases that the Europeans had brought with them.

As more and more Europeans arrived and the United States grew bigger, the white settlers pushed the Indians out of their traditional land. The whites promised to leave the Indians alone if they agreed to move, and at first the Indians believed them. But most of these promises were broken, and relations between the groups often became violent.

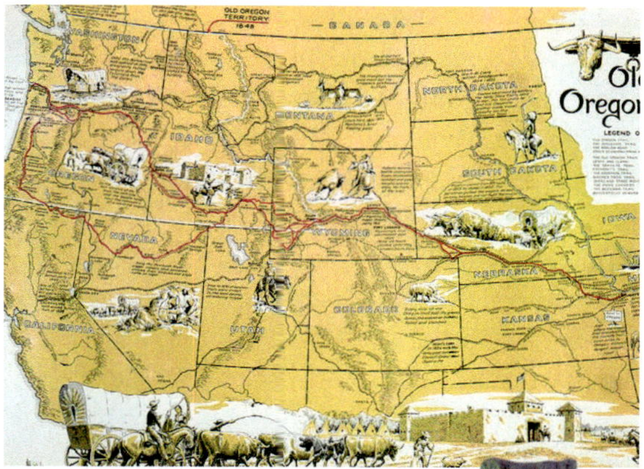

At the beginning of the 21st century, there are about 4,000,000 Native Americans in the US (that's 1.5% of the population). Even today Indians are more often poor or ill than white Americans. ■

2 Group puzzle II

a) In your group (A, B, C or D), compare your notes. Agree on the most important points.

b) Make new groups of four (A1, B1, C1, D1; A2, B2, ...). Tell the others the important information from your text. Take notes on the other texts.

c) Go back to your first group (A, B, C, D) and compare your information. Did you all understand the same things? If not, read the texts to check your information.

► **Text File 8** *(pp. 128–129)*

1 EVERYDAY ENGLISH MEDIATION From Bad Arolsen to Frankfurt

a) *On their way to Frankfurt Airport, the Schmidts met an American woman at the train station. The woman needed their help. Look at the announcement and take Frau Schmidt's role.*

Announcement 1:

Wegen eines technischen Problems verspätet sich die Abfahrt des Regionalexpress von Bad Arolsen nach Kassel-Wilhelmshöhe um voraussichtlich zehn Minuten. Wir bitten um Ihr Verständnis.

Woman ______ Excuse me. What was that about?

Frau Schmidt __ The train to ...

b) *Now listen to more announcements on the CD. How would you help the tourists in these situations?*

▸ *SF Paraphrasing (Revision) (p. 144)*

2 EVERYDAY ENGLISH WRITING A letter (Writing a letter to ask for information)

a) *Before Timo Schmidt and his family moved to Hermann, he wrote a letter to Jake Kruger. Look at the letter on the right. How does Timo start and end it?*

b) *Imagine you are going to go to a new school in the US. You have the name of a student there. Look at the notes below. Then write a letter like Timo's to the student (80–120 words).*

In your letter you can write things like:
- who you are and why you are writing
- what you are interested in

In your letter you can ask things like:
- what the student is interested in
- what you can do in his/her town
- what the school hours are
- if there are special activities for students who are new to the US

Remember

Check the spelling and grammar of your letter and correct it if necessary.

Willy- Brandt-Str. 14
34454 Bad Arolsen
May 27

Dear Jake,

I'm the son of your dad's friend Andreas Schmidt. I'm writing to you because I'd like to know a bit about you and about Hermann before I arrive.
For example what can you do in Hermann after school? What are you interested in? Do you play football? I'm a great fan!
And school: what are the hours? Are there any special activities for students from abroad?
Sorry about all the questions. Please write soon. I'm looking forward to meeting you.

Best wishes,

Timo

▸ *SF Writing Course (Revision) (pp. 146–147)*

3 WORDS American and British schools

a) *Match the definitions to the words in the box.*

break • bulletin board • exam • extracurriculars • grade • member • period • rules • schedule • summer vacation

1 part of a school day when you study a subject period
2 This tells you when lessons begin and end.
3 You see it on a wall. Teachers or students put information on it.
4 the time in the middle of the year when there is no school
5 one of the years that children are at school
6 extra activities at school, usually at the end of the school day
7 a short time to stop work and relax break
8 person who belongs to a club or group
9 These say what you must or mustn't do. rules
10 an important test, usually at the end of the school year exam

b) *In British English there are different words for 1–5 in a). What are they?*
lesson – timetable – notice board – summer holiday – form

4 WORDS School phrases

Read the sentences. Then use the phrases in brackets to write the sentences in a different way.

1 Mike did well in his exam. (get a good grade)
Mike got a good grade in his exam.
2 Do you have to be a member of the drama club to act in the school play? (join a club)
Do you have to ...
3 At US schools, students go from classroom to classroom for each lesson. (change classrooms)
At US schools, students ...
4 Do we have to prepare for the vocabulary test? (revise for a test)
Do we have to ...
5 Two students from our year will be in tonight's discussion. (take part in)
Two students ...
6 Your parents will be upset if you don't pass your exam. (fail an exam)
Your parents will be upset ...
7 You must do what the school rules say. (break the rules)
You mustn't ...

5 LISTENING School announcements and 'Thought for the day'

a) *Read the statements below. Write down the numbers 1–9. Then listen to the morning announcements at Hermann High School. Are the statements right (✓) or wrong (**x**)?*

1 The win against Washington was a surprise.
2 The Hermann High School team is called the Bearcats.
3 Washington usually has a bad baseball team.
4 The school band will meet in the music room this Saturday.
5 The band is going to play at Maifest.
6 The school play is called 'TV Hour'.
7 The play will be on Friday, Saturday and Sunday evenings.
8 Khalil Gibran wrote 'The thought for the day'.
9 It says that not everybody can give something.

b) *Listen to the announcements again. Take notes, then correct the wrong statements.*

c) **Extra** *Write or choose a 'Thought for the day' for your class.*

6 A sandwich – some bread (Countable/uncountable nouns)

Tip

Countable nouns have a singular and a plural (a sandwich, two sandwiches ...). Uncountable nouns have no plural. They describe things you can't count (some bread, lots of bread ... – but not: a ~~bread~~, two ~~breads~~).

a) *Put the nouns from the box in a copy of the chart.*

bread • car • chair • dollar • earring • essay • fact • furniture • homework • information • jewellery • music • money • news • sandwich • song • story • traffic

Countable	Uncountable
sandwich/sandwiches	bread
story/stories	news
essay/...	...

b) *Complete the sentences. Use* ***a/an*** *with countable nouns,* ***some*** *with uncountable nouns.*

1 Can I make ... sandwich?
– Sure. There's ... bread in the kitchen.
What do you need for the salad?
– ... lettuce, ... cheese and ... big tomato.

2 I have to write ... essay for English. And I've got ... French homework for next week.

3 I need ... more information about hogs.
– Well, Tim's got ... book on hogs. Ask him.

4 You can go skiing with us if you want, but you'll have to buy ... equipment.

7 There isn't much furniture ... (Countable/uncountable nouns)

a) *Complete the sentences with the words in brackets. Use plurals where they're needed.*

1 There isn't much ... in the room, only a bed and three or four ... (chair, furniture)

2 Hundreds of ... use this road every day.
– There's a lot of ... on our road too.
(car, traffic)

3 I didn't find much ... about St. Louis, but all the ... are correct. (fact, information)

4 I've done some ..., but I still have to write an ... (essay, homework)

b) **Extra** *Which words from the box can you use to complete sentences **1** to **7**?*

apples • bread • milk • potatoes

1 How much ... do we need?
~~apples~~, bread, milk, ~~potatoes~~

2 How many ... do we need?

3 We need ten ...

4 We need some ...

5 We need lots of ...

6 We need a kilo of ...

7 We need a bottle of ...

8 WORDS Word building (Nouns from verbs and adjectives)

a) *Look at the nouns below. Which verb or adjective do they come from? Can you guess their meanings? Check in a dictionary.*

cleverness • collection • friendliness • illness • happiness • imagination • reality • possibility • sadness • suggestion

A: I think 'cleverness' comes from 'clever', *klug* or *schlau*. It means Klugheit.

B: I think that's right. My turn. 'Collection' ...

Tip

Nouns with: *-ation*, *-ion*, *-ity*, *-ness*

You can often understand nouns with these endings if you know the verb or adjective they come from.

b) *Write sentences with five of the nouns in a). Swap with a partner and check.*

9 READING Soft drinks, hard facts (Finding the main ideas of a text)

You want to find out how healthy soft drinks (soda) are. You have found this article on the internet. If you want to find the main ideas of a text, it's often helpful to look at its structure.

1 Topic:
Every text has a topic. You'll often find it in the first paragraph.

2 Main ideas:
Usually other paragraphs contain main ideas with a link to the topic. You can often find them in the topic sentence.

3 Reasons and examples:
There are examples and reasons for each main idea. They describe the ideas.

Soft drinks, hard facts

(1) Drinking soda is one of the worst things you can do to your health. But some schools are now beginning to do something about it.

(2) Experts agree that sugary soft drinks and fast food are the main reasons why so many American teenagers are fat. About 7% of the calories that they take in come from soft drinks alone. And even if this doesn't cause health problems now, there could be serious trouble later in life.

(3) The problem with soft drinks is that they do not still your hunger, said Wayne Campbell, a professor in the Department of Food and Nutrition at Purdue University. That's because you don't feel satisfied after having a soft drink – although they contain a lot of calories. So if you drink a cola, for example, you take in 400 calories, but you still want a burger.

(4) American kids and teenagers are drinking more soft drinks than ever before, according to the U.S. Department of Agriculture. Soda has taken the place of other, healthier drinks. Thirty years ago, for example, boys drank more than twice as much milk as soft drinks. So what can be done to change the way today's kids drink?

(5) In California, at least, children are no longer able to buy soda at schools: the schools aren't allowed to sell it. That's because experts have found out that having or not having soda machines in schools changes how much soda teenagers drink. If it's easy to buy soda, kids will drink more. If it's difficult, they won't. Experts hope that the new rules will help all children, not just those who are already fat.

a) *Look at the highlighted sentences of the third and fourth paragraphs. Decide which sentence contains the main idea and which a reason or example.*

b) *Read the last paragraph. Find the main idea. What examples and reasons support it?*

c) *Collect and structure the main ideas and examples you've found in the text in a mind map.*

d) **Extra** *What do you think? Should soft drinks be sold at German schools? Why (not)? Write a short text.*

10 Money isn't a problem (The definite article)

Add the where you need it.

1 ... money just isn't a problem for them. They're really rich.
2 I can't find ... money you gave me yesterday.
3 Timo would like to find out more about ... history of Missouri.
4 What can we learn from ... history?
5 We all need ... air to live.
6 Tourists visit Hermann because they enjoy ... fresh air there.
7 ... life of a farmer must be very hard.
8 Is ... life easier if you're rich?
9 Admission to the museum is free for ... students.
10 ... students we met at the museum were from Germany.
11 All ... people I met at the party were very friendly.
12 ... people will usually help you if you ask them nicely.

11 WORDS Using numbers

Partner B: Go to p. 111. Partner C: Go to p. 112.

a) *Partner A: Tell your partners about St. Louis, the second largest city in Missouri. Then listen to them and fill in a copy of the chart.*

	St. Louis	Los Angeles	New York
founded in	1764		
population	348,000		
area	171.3 sq km		
average temperature	– 6° C (winter) 32° C (summer)		
largest ethnic group	black (52%)		

A: St. Louis was founded in 1764. The population ...

St. Louis, Missouri, with the Gateway Arch

b) *Which city is the oldest city? Which has got the most Hispanic people? Which is coldest in winter?*

12 Timo's diary (Present progressive, future meaning)

a) *Look at Timo's diary. What is he doing next week? Use the present progressive.*

MON	afternoon: debate
TUE	after school: cards with Jake evening: St. Louis Blues game
WED	after lunch: FFA meeting
THU	7 pm: meet Emma cinema
FRI	evening: My party! ☺

1 Timo is taking part (take part) in a debate on Monday afternoon.
2 After school on Tuesday he ... (play) cards with Jake.
3 In the evening they ... (go) to St. Louis to see an ice hockey game.
4 On Wednesday after lunch he ... (go) to an FFA meeting.
5 On Thursday at 7 pm Timo ... (meet) Emma at the cinema.
6 On Friday evening he ... (have) a party.

b) *What are you doing next week? Make a diary. Swap diaries with your partner. Write sentences about what your partner is doing.*

13 SKILLS Summary writing

***a)** Read this story about a rafting tour some 11th-graders from Hermann High School took. Watch for the main events.*

A perfect day, by Carrie Langer

I was a bit nervous. It was the first day of the summer vacation and I was going on my first rafting tour. Cindy had tried to talk me out of it.

"Are you crazy, Carrie? You don't even like the water. And the Castor River is pretty wild."

"I know," I said.

"So why are you doing this?"

I mumbled something about looking for adventure. Well, I couldn't tell her the real reason: Jim Nielson. Jim was a really sweet guy who did a lot of rafting. So when I heard he was going to be a guide on the school rafting tour, I put my name down on the list.

Sue sat next to me on the bus to the river and talked endlessly about Maifest. Jim was at the front talking to Nate, the other tour guide. At one point Jim walked down through the bus, so I got up and went toward the bathroom.

"Hi," he said as we met. "Carrie, right?"

"Right," I said. "And you're – er, Jim?"

"Right. – Well, enjoy the tour."

"Thanks," I said. "I'm sure I will."

At first the water was slow, so we talked and laughed as we paddled along. But after an hour it got faster. Suddenly Jim turned and shouted "Left, go left!" but it was too late – the raft hit a rock and I fell into the water. "This is the end," I thought. But then I felt a hand on my arm. It pulled me back onto the raft. When I looked up, I saw Jim.

I was pretty cold, so our group took a short break on shore, and Jim gave me some hot tea from his thermos. We drank out of the same cup!

For the rest of the trip I sat next to Jim, and he asked me every few minutes if I was all right. "Everything's perfect," I told him.

We're going out on Friday night!

***b)** In groups of four, do a placemat activity. Each student writes which four of the ideas below he/she thinks are most important. Then agree on the most important four.*

1 Cindy tries to talk Carrie out of going rafting.

2 Carrie thinks the tour guide, Jim, is sweet.

3 The group takes a bus to the river.

4 On the bus Sue talks about Maifest.

5 On the bus Jim and Carrie say hi.

6 When the raft hits a rock, Carrie falls into the water.

7 Carrie is afraid she'll die.

9 Jim is worried about Carrie.

10 Jim and Carrie plan to go out together.

STUDY SKILLS Summary writing

A summary is a shorter form of a text. It has all the important information from the original.
- In the first one or two sentences tell the reader what the story or text is about.
- In the main part describe the main events.
- Use the simple present.
- Explain **who** does **what** in the story, **when** and **why**.
- Use your own words.
- Leave out examples and direct speech.

***c)** Now write a summary of the story.*

The story is about Carrie, a teenage girl from Hermann who goes on a rafting tour because she wants to meet Jim, the tour guide. ...

► SF Summary writing (p. 145) • WB 00 (p. 00)

Angus Bethune's moment by Chris Crutcher (adapted)

In an American high school, being popular is everything. The coolest boys and the prettiest girls seem to have the most fun. And when there's an important dance and the king and queen of the ball are elected, life becomes even more difficult for the kids who aren't popular – kids like Angus Bethune.

I'm a big kid.

And my parents named me Angus.

"Angus is a cow," I said to my mother. "You named me after a cow."

"Your father's uncle was named Angus," she said.

"So my father's uncle was named after a cow too," I said. "What did he think of that?"

"Actually," Mom said, "I think he was kind of proud. Angus was a farmer, you know."

"Jesus help me," I said, and went to my room.

As Angus, the fat kid, I have my problems, although it isn't as bad as it sounds. I am very, very quick for a fat kid, and I have great reflexes. When I play defense in football, nobody can get away from me. And I'm smart and get good grades. But I'd love to swap reflexes and being smart for a little beauty.

And that brings me to tonight. Tonight is a big night. See, I was elected Winter Ball King. That means I will be out on the dance floor of Lake Michigan High School with Melissa Lefevre, the girl of my dreams – and only my dreams. She was elected Winter Ball Queen. For a minute we'll be out there alone.

Alone with Melissa Lefevre.

Now I don't know how I was elected. I can't even imagine. I mean, it's a joke, I know that. And a good one. I don't know why, but the kids at my school voted for me and not for one of the many cool boys.

The problem is that when Melissa and I are out there on the dance floor, everybody will see me dance. I can't dance.

I fell in love with Melissa in kindergarten. She was a blond girl with long legs and brown eyes that made you ache. You ache a lot more when you're a fat kid, because you know you can never have her.

I've never even talked to her. Until tonight. Tonight I'll *have* to talk to her.

All I want is my moment.

So here I sit. What can Melissa be thinking? She's probably telling herself that it's like a trip to the dentist. He's going to hurt you, but in an hour, you'll walk out of there. And you'll still be alive.

Of course, Melissa hasn't seen me dance.

So now I stand at the door to the gym. Melissa is inside.

Heads turn as I move through the door. I try to look cool and sit down at the nearest empty table. I see Melissa on the dance floor with her boyfriend – a real jerk, Rick Sanford – and

I hear the announcement: the King and Queen have to be behind the stage in five minutes.

I'm sweating. I want my moment.

I get up and start walking to the stage when I see Melissa on her boyfriend's arm. They're walking toward me. As they get closer, I want to run. What am I doing here? What was I thinking?

They stand in front of me. "Angus, my man," Rick slurs, "I'm giving you this pretty thing for a few minutes. So she can compare."

Melissa drops his arm and smiles. "Don't listen to him. He's drunk. And rude."

Then she says, "Why don't we go?" and she takes my arm.

"Yeah," Rick says, "why don't you go, snowball king?"

Melissa drops my arm and grabs his. "Shut up," she whispers. "I'm warning you, Rick. Shut up."

"Have fun," Rick says to me. "Your election cost me a lot of money, probably about two dollars a pound." He looks at me from top to bottom. "And don't put your big fat hands on my girl," he says and starts to point at me. I look at his finger and he takes it back.

Melissa takes my arm and says, "Let's go."

At the side door to the stage I say, "By the way, there's something you should know."

She waits.

"I can't dance."

Melissa smiles. "Not everybody can," she says. "We'll survive."

I say, "I didn't say I can't dance well. I said I can't dance. Good people have been badly hurt when they tried to dance with me."

We're almost ready to start. "What did he mean, my election cost him a lot of money?" I whisper.

"Never mind."

I laugh and say, "I can take it."

"He's rich, and he's rude," she says. "I'm sorry I'm with him." She pauses and puts her arm in mine. "I'm not with him."

The curtains open and the trumpets play.

I look into the lights and smile. This would be silly even if they weren't crowning King Angus the Fat. Without moving her mouth, Melissa says, "I chose a slow song. We don't have to move much. Dance close to me. When you feel me move, you move. And don't listen to the music. It won't help. Just follow."

She takes my arm and we go down the stairs to the dance floor. She smiles, then pulls me close. She says, "Be my shadow."

A part of me goes to heaven. In my wildest dreams I never imagined that Melissa Lefevre would be nice to me in my moment. She whispers, "Relax," into my ear, and I follow her through a song I've never heard.

"Angus?"

"Yeah?"

"Do you ever get tired of who you are?"

I pull back a second, then pull close again. "Do you know who you're talking to?"

I feel her smile. "Yeah," she says, "I thought so. I know it's not the same, but it's not always so great to look like I do. I pay too."

She's right. I think it's not the same.

"I'm bulimic. Do you know what that is?"

"Yes, I know what that is. It means when you eat too much, you throw up so you don't look like me."

"Close enough. Don't worry, I'm in therapy for it," she says. "A lot of pretty girls are."

"Actually," I say, "I even tried it once, but when I put my finger down my throat, I was still hungry and I almost ate my arm."

Melissa laughs and holds me tighter. "You're the only person I've ever told. I just wanted you to know that things aren't always as they seem. Would you do something for me?"

"Yes."

"Would you leave with me?"

"You mean leave this dance? Leave this dance with you?" I feel her nod.

The music ends; all dancers stop and clap politely. "I want to dance one more," Melissa says. "A fast one."

"I'll wait over by the table."

"No. I want to dance it with you."

"You don't understand," I say. "When I dance rock and roll, people across the country feel earthquakes."

She takes my hand. "Listen. Do what you do on the football field. Don't listen to the music; just follow me the way you follow the guy from the other team."

I try to protest, but then the band starts to play "Bad Moon Rising," and the dance floor is full. Melissa pushes me back, and I watch her body the way I would watch another player on the football field. I'm like a mirror and move with her, from top to bottom. Soon lots of kids are watching us; I'm in a circle of kids, and they're cheering. I'm Angus Bethune, the Fat Man, and I'm dancing with Melissa Lefevre.

When the band finishes, everybody is clapping, even Melissa. She wipes sweat from my face with her finger. When she puts the finger in her mouth, I'm in heaven.

"You bitch!" Rick shouts. "You practiced with this fatty. You bitch. You wanted to make me look stupid." He turns to me. "I'm gonna kill you, fat boy," he says. He's looking at my fist.

I say, "Don't even think it. After dancing, fighting is what I do best."

Working with the text

1 Understanding the story

1. Why does Angus think it was a joke that he was elected Winter Ball King?
2. What does Angus mean by his 'moment'?
3. Why does the dance go so well for Angus?
4. Why is Rick angry at the end?

2 Extra What do they mean?

Say who made each statement. What does it mean?

1. 'Angus is a cow.' (p. 68, l. 3)
   Angus says this to his mother. He means that ...
2. 'I'm giving you this pretty thing for a few minutes.' (p. 69, ll. 65–66)
3. 'Be my shadow.' (p. 69, l. 110)

3 The story

a) *What is the story about? Write one sentence about each of the following:*

1. the characters (the people in the story)
   The story is about Angus, a fat high school student; Melissa, a ...
2. the scene (where the story takes place)
   The story takes place in ...
3. the time (when the story takes place)
4. the plot (what happens)

b) *Look at the diagram. Now explain in no more than three sentences how each character in the story feels towards each other character. Do their feelings change? How? Why?*

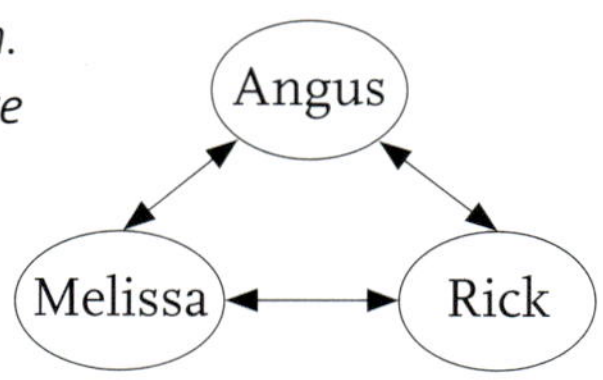

4 Melissa and Angus

a) *Were you surprised by the way Melissa acted towards Angus? Why?/Why not?*

b) *Why do you think Melissa told Angus that she's bulimic?*

5 Extra After the dance

What do you think things will be like between Melissa and Angus the next day? What about between Rick and Angus?

How am I doing?

a) *Fill in or choose the correct answers.*

American schools

1 The school between elementary school and high school is called ...
2 High school starts with the 9th ...
3 Sports and school clubs are known in the US as ...
4 The best grade in school is ...

Hermann and Missouri

5 Missouri is in the ... of the United States.
A north B south C east D west E middle
6 Wineries are an important ... in parts of Missouri.
A drink B industry C food D farm
7 Hermann and other places in Missouri keep German ... alive.
A traditions B sausages C minorities D immigrants

Summary writing

8 Which statement is *not* true of a summary?
A A summary should have all the important information from the original text. B You should write a summary in your own words. C A summary should have lots of details from the original text. D A summary should have complete sentences, not just key words.

Words

9 real – reality • possible – ?
10 invite – invitation • suggest – ?
11 White bread is not as healthy as bread from whole ...
12 To keep fit, eat the right food and get lots of ...
13 Chicken and turkey are a kind of meat we call ...
14 Cheese and cream cheese are ... products.
15 How do you say this number: '7.9'?

Grammar

16 Add 'a/an' or 'some':
A I need ... information.
B Can I have ... glass of milk, please? – Of course, there's ... milk in the fridge.
C Would you like ... fruit with your sandwich? – Yes, ... apple would be nice.
D Dad, can I have ... money for school lunch?
17 Add 'the' where necessary:
A The students talked about ... food in their Health class. They agreed that ... food they eat is healthy. B ... life is boring if you don't have a computer. C My mum says ... quality of ... food we buy at the supermarket is excellent.

b) *Check your answers on p. 253 and add up your points – one point for each correct answer.*

c) *If you had 23 or more points, well done! Maybe you can help students who had fewer points. If you had 22 points or fewer, it's a good idea to do some more work before you go on to the next unit. Where did you make mistakes? The chart below will tell you what you can do to improve your English.*

No.	Area	Find out more	Exercise(s)
1– 4	American schools	All about, p. 56, A 6, p. 57	P 3–4, p. 62; WB 0–0, pp. 0–0
5– 7	Hermann and Missouri	Lead-in, pp. 54–55	WB 0–0, pp. 0–0
8	Summary writing	P 13, p. 67; SF, p. 145	WB 0–0, pp. 0–0
9–10	Word building	P 8, p. 64	WB 0–0, pp. 0–0
11–14	Words: food	A 8, p. 58	WB 0–0, pp. 0–0
15	Words: Numbers	A 8, p. 58	P 11 (p. 66); WB 0–0, pp. 0–0
16	Countable/uncountable	A 6, p. 57; GF 3, pp. 159–160	P 6–7, p. 64; WB 0–0, pp. 0–0
17	The definite article	LAL, p. 58; GF 4, p. 160	P 10 (p. 66); WB 0–0, pp. 0–0

1 WORDS Holidays

a) *Collect ideas about holidays in four lists.*

Getting there	Where to stay	Things to do	Describing things
fly/go by plane go by ...	stay with friends stay at a ...	see the sights relax on the beach visit a ...	the main sights a beautiful/lonely/... beach an interesting ...

b) *Write a short advertisement for an exciting holiday place. Use ideas from your lists.*

Come to ...!
It's easy to get here. ...
Stay at ...
There's lots to do. You can ...
... has something for everyone!

2 WORDS Numbers

Dates, times and prices are important on holidays.
a) *Practise these numbers.*

What's the time?
It's ...

8:04	12:04	20:00
10:47	15:30	22:45
11:15	18:27	22:49

18 April • 12 May • 1 July • 2 October
23/8 • 3/1 • 25/12 • 30/11 • 29/2 • 21/9

$1.50	$8.30	$15	$17.56	$44.99	$71.65

b) *Write down ...*
– the times of three things you're doing next week
– three dates that are important to you
– the prices of three things you bought last week.
Read everything to your partner. He/she writes it down. Then compare.

Tip

	You see	You say
Times	6:00	six o'clock/six am
	9:30	nine thirty/half past nine
	10:47	ten forty-seven
	17:00	five o'clock/five pm
	19:08	nineteen o eight
	22:15	quarter past ten/ten fifteen
Dates	17 March	the seventeenth of March
	22/6	the twenty-second of June
Prices	$1	a/one dollar
	$1.20	a/one dollar twenty
	$5	five dollars
	$8.59	eight dollars fifty-nine

3 My school holidays start ... (prepositions in time phrases)

Complete the sentences with at, in or on.

1. My school holidays start ... Thursday.
2. I want to relax ... the first day of the holidays.
3. Visit Las Vegas ... May – it's too hot ... July.
4. We often go to the beach ... the summer.
5. Hurry! The train leaves ... 8:04.
6. We arrived in London ... Monday morning.
7. We arrived in London ... the morning.
8. When's the concert? – It's ... 10 June.
9. We spent two weeks in the US ... 2006.
10. What do you want to do ... the weekend?

4 SPEAKING Let's go to the park

a) *It's the summer vacation.*
Matt and Jon are talking about things to do today. Read their conversation with a partner.

Matt Let's go to the park. We can skate there.
Jon No, I don't really want to do that again. We went to the park yesterday. We could go to the cinema today.
Matt I'm not sure if I like that idea. I don't have so much money. What about going back to my house? We could play a computer game.
Jon That's a good idea. Let's do that.
Matt Cool. Come on then. Let's go.

Tip

When you talk about things to do, you usually make suggestions, disagree and agree.

Making suggestions
– Let's go/watch/...
– We could/go/watch/...
– What about going/watching/...?

Disagreeing
– I don't really want to do that.
– I'm not sure if I like that idea.

When you disagree, try and give a reason:
– We went there yesterday.
– I haven't got so much money.

Agreeing
– That's a good/great/... idea.
– Yes, let's do that.

b) *Make a conversation like the one on the left. Here are some ideas for things to do.*

go shopping/swimming/... • go on a trip to ... • make a pizza • watch a film • play frisbee/... • visit the natural history museum/...

5 STUDY SKILLS Writing (Linking sentences)

A good text needs linking words and time phrases. Use these words and phrases to complete the text.

and • At about one o'clock • before they went to bed • but (2x) • because • Last year • later in the afternoon • 90 minutes later • One morning in July • On their third day • so • when • where

... (1) there was a competition in UK schools. It was organized by the German Tourist Office and the first prize was four days in Germany. ... (2) the 15 winners left London and just ... (3) landed at Cologne Bonn Airport. From there they went into Cologne to check in at their hotel.

... (4) they had lunch in town and ... (5) they visited the cathedral and a sports museum. For supper they had traditional Rhineland food and ... (6) they went for a walk in the old town. The next day they all went shopping. (They had to speak German ... (7) not all the shop assistants spoke English!) Later they went on a boat trip ... (8) visited a chocolate museum.

... (9) they travelled to Bonn. There they saw the house ... (10) Beethoven was born, ... (11) there wasn't enough time to go to the city's other museums. In the evening they had tickets for a rock festival. It wasn't over until 1 a.m., ... (12) they all went to bed really late. Everyone was very tired ... (13) they arrived back in London the next day, ... (14) they had all had a fantastic time in Germany.

1 Listening

You will hear five travel announcements and mini-dialogues.
For each one choose the correct picture: A, B, or C. At the end you will hear the recordings again.

1 Which gate at the airport must passengers for Denver go to?

A 8 B 18 C 8A

2 Where is the ticket office at this railway station?

A Platform 6 B Platform 9 C Ticket Office next to café →

3 How much does the man pay for his tickets?

A
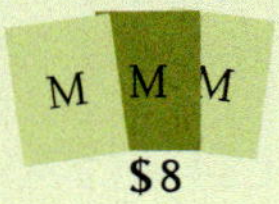

B
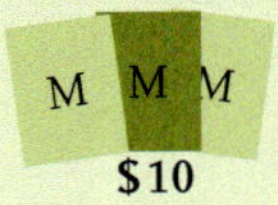

C

4 Which platform must the woman go to?

A S3 Stadtmitte/City Centre 11:07 Gleis 16

B S3 Stadtmitte/City Centre 11:17 Gleis 6

C S3 Stadtmitte/City Centre 11:20 Gleis 2

5 When does the man want a hotel room?

A

B

C

2 Listening

You will hear a radio programme from the US. Read the questions below. Then listen and choose the correct answer: A, B or C. You will hear the programme twice.

1 You can hear the programme once a ...
A day. B week. C month.

2 Later in the show Annie will talk about ...
A school grades. B sport. C fashion.

3 Katie went on an interesting vacation last ...
A summer. B winter. C autumn.

4 She was a ... for a week.
A pop singer B circus clown C cowgirl

5 She went with her ...
A uncle and aunt. B parents. C sisters.

6 On the vacation, Katie ... every day.
A swam B ran 20 miles C rode horses

7 One day she helped Ben and Ted with a ...
A baby cow. B baby horse. C baby lion.

8 Once they had a ... in the mountains.
A camp fire B concert C picnic

9 During the vacation Katie slept in a ...
A hostel. B tent. C cabin.

10 Katie says the vacation would be great for ...
A everyone. B some people. C kids only.

3 Speaking

You're on holiday with your partner. You want to discuss things to do tomorrow.
– Look at the pictures below. Choose three things that you'd like to do.
– Tell your partner about your ideas. How many things can you find that you both want to do?

Give reasons why you want (or don't want) to do something.
Partner A: You begin. Let's ...

1

2

3

4

5

6

7

8

9

4 Writing

'Buddy' is a magazine for teenagers. They want readers' letters about 'The best holiday I've ever had'. Write a short letter to the magazine. Say ...
– when the holiday was
– where you went
– who you went with
– some things you did
– why you liked the holiday so much.

Begin:
Dear Buddy,
You wanted to know about the best holiday I've ever had. It was ...

Atlanta rising

1 An Atlanta timeline

a) *Find Atlanta on the US map on the back inside cover. Which state is it the capital of?*

b) *Look at the pictures and captions. What happened in Atlanta? What is it famous for? Speculate about where the pictures fit on the timeline.*

c) *Listen to the CD. While you listen take notes on a copy of the timeline. What happened when?*

d) *Compare your timelines. Then listen again and check.*

▸ *P1 (p. 85)* • **Text File 9** *(pp. 130–132)*

Atlanta is burned down during the American Civil War 1864

Black slaves on the cotton plantations around Atlanta have a terrible life of hard work and violence

1861

The world's most famous soft drink is born 1886

The 26th Olympic Games 1996

Atlanta timeline — 1847 — *before* 1861 — 1861 — 1864 — 1886

City of Atlanta is founded

Black slaves have ...

Shirley Franklin is elected first African-American woman mayor of Atlanta

2002

Dr Martin Luther King, Jr., leader of the Civil Rights Movement, is born

1929 - 1968

Famous news network CNN is founded in Atlanta

1980

1929 — 1968 — 1980 — 1996 — 2002

All about ... television

1

		7:00 pm	7:30 pm	8:00 pm	8:30 pm	9:00 p
Atlanta, GA ★ cable						
Wednesday, April 15						
3	ABC	World News Tonight	Entertainment Tonight	Grey's Anatomy		Bost
4	FOX	Access Hollywood	The Simpsons (Rerun)	Movie: Dodgeball		
5	NBC	Evening News	Friends (Rerun)	Law & Order		Las
6	CBS	News, Weather, Sports	The Price Is Right	Big Brother		CSI
34	CNN	World News	World News	Business News	World News Europe	Worl Asia
50	MTV	My Super Sweet 16	America's Next Top Model		Pimp My Ride	Nev
61	Animal Planet	Lions of Crocodile River	Animal Cops! Housto	Serenghetti		AP

comedy series
prime time: 8–10pm
drama series
crime series
reality show
news & comment
documentaries
competetion
game show

When can you watch 'Law & Order'? What channel is it on? Can you watch 'America's Next Top Model' if you want to watch 'Dodgeball'? What shows aren't on TV for the first time?

2 TV words

a) *Make a TV network. Use words from **1** and from the box. Check their meaning in the dictionary.*

anchor • comedian • contestant • episode • host • rerun • viewer

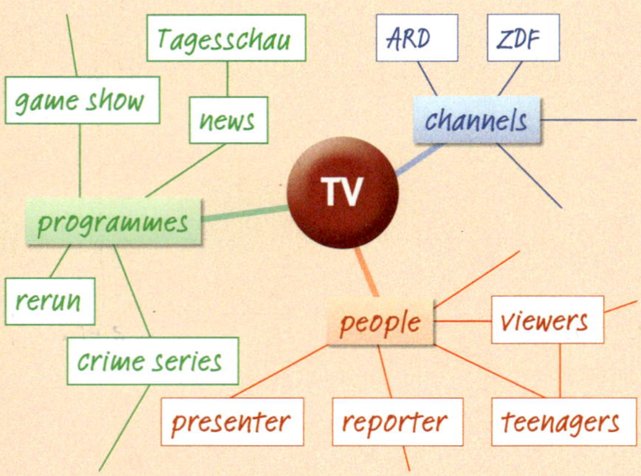

b) *Compare your network with a partner's. Add to yours if you like.*

► P 2 (p. 85) • WB 00 (p. 00)

3 Now you

a) *Write a short text about a TV programme you like, but don't write the name of the programme. You can use these phrases.*

One of my favourite TV programmes is a ...
You can watch it on ZDF/ARD/...
It's on / It isn't on every week/day.
It lasts for ... minutes.
The host/presenter/hero is ...
The contestants have to ...
You can learn a lot about ...

b) *In small groups each student reads out the text they wrote. The others try and guess the name of the programme. When someone has guessed a programme, everyone in the group can give their opinion of it.*

► P 3–5 (pp. 85–86) • WB 00 (p. 00) • **Text File 10** (p. 133)

4 It's 'Take Your Child to Work Day'

'Good morning,' Mrs Young said as she came into the kitchen. Mr Young and Madison were already having breakfast. 'Are you ready to go to work with me, Madison?'

'You bet, Mom!' Madison said. 'I've told everybody at school about it too.'

Mr Young put down his paper. 'You know, Madison, we have 'Take Your Child to Work Day' at the King Center too.'

'I know, Dad. We've already talked about that. But your dusty old archive just can't compete with Mom's international news network. And besides, when I finish school I want to be a reporter, just like Mom.'

What kind of jobs do Mr and Mrs Young do?

► P 6–7 (pp. 87–88) • WB 3–5 (pp. 6–7)

Americana ★ ★ ★

Take Your Child To Work Day

TYCTWD is a day when parents are allowed to take their children to their workplace. The kids can see what their mom or dad does there and get to know the world of work. TYCTWD takes place on the fourth Thursday in April.
Not all companies or schools take part in TYCTWD. But every year more than 25 million children visit their mother's or father's workplace on this special day.

5 Now You

Would you like to have TYCTWD in Germany too? Why? Why not?

6 On the way to the CNN studios

'This is unbelievable, Mom,' said Madison. 'We've been in this traffic jam for 20 minutes. Is it always like this?'

'Well, it's been bad for three months now,' Mrs Young said. 'They're building a new bridge on Paces Ferry Road.'

Just then Mrs Young's cellphone rang. She answered it. It was Dan, her boss at CNN.

'Josephine,' he said, 'I need you at the airport. There's been an explosion, and there've been no flights for over 15 minutes now.'

'Terrorists?' she asked.

'We don't know anything yet, Josephine.'

'Cool,' said Madison after her mom's call. 'My day at CNN is going to be very exciting!'

'No, sorry. Your day at CNN has just ended. I can't take you with me. It might be dangerous. I'll drop you off at Dad's on the way.'

Looking at language

a) *Answer these questions:*
How long have Madison and her mum been in the traffic jam?
They've been in the traffic jam for 20 minutes.

How long has the traffic been bad?
How long have there been no flights?

b) *Translate the sentences you wrote for a) into German. The English sentences use the* ***present perfect****. What tense do you use in German?*

c) **Extra** *Translate these sentences:*
Ich bin seit drei Jahren an dieser Schule.
Meine Eltern leben seit 15 Jahren hier.

► P 8–9 (p. 88) • WB 00 (pp. 00)

The King Center has a library and archives on Martin Luther King.

7 At the King Center

Mr Young was at work in the archives at the King Center when Madison arrived.

'Hey, Madison,' he looked up, surprised. 'What are you doing here? Did you get bored with the TV studios?'

'We never got to the studios,' said Madison angrily. 'There was a big explosion at the airport. So Mom dropped me off here.'

'Well, I have to put away some of Dr King's letters. You could help me with that if you like,' said her dad. 'They've been on display for a few weeks – since April 4th.'

'Since the anniversary of his death,' Madison said.

Her dad was impressed. 'So you know when he died?'

'I've known that for ages, Dad. And we started our school project on Dr King last Monday. Since then I've been even more interested in his life. Are the original letters he wrote really here?'

'They sure are! Just follow me. By the way, when we're through with the letters, I have to work on a video for our website. Maybe you'd like to help ...'

'That sounds great, Dad! Let's go!'

> *Whose job do you find more interesting, Mr or Mrs Young's? What do you think Madison thinks?*

Looking at language

a) *Collect all the phrases with* ***since*** *and* ***for*** *in 7 and add them to a copy of the chart:*

for	*since*
for a few weeks	*since April 4th*
for ...	*since ...*

b) *Which word –* ***since*** *or* ***for*** *– do you use for a period of time, which for a point in time?*

► *GF 6: 'since' and 'for' (pp. 162–163)* • *P 10–11 (p. 89)* • *WB 00 (p. 00))* • **Text File 11** *(pp. 134–135)*

8 Extra Breaking news

Madison worked happily all morning. But when she hadn't heard from her mom by lunchtime, she was worried. Were there terrorists at the airport? Her dad turned on the TV.

9 A timeline on Martin Luther King

a) *Fill in a copy of the timeline for Martin Luther King, Jr. Use information from this page. For three dates you have to do some research on the internet or in an encyclopedia.*

1929 — 1953 — 1955 — 1963 — 1964 — 1968

Martin Luther King, Jr.

Martin Luther King, Jr. (January 15, 1929 – April 4, 1968) became one of the most important leaders of the American Civil Rights Movement. As a young minister in the Baptist church, he saw that blacks were still segregated from whites and that they still didn't have many of the rights that whites had.
King believed in non-violent protest and became world-famous through the March on Washington (1963).

I have a dream that my four little children will one day live in a nation where they will not be judged by the color of their skin but by the content of their character.

It was in Washington, D.C., on August 28, 1963, that he made his most famous speech – 'I have a dream'.

b) *Read the Study Skills box on the right and answer the questions below.*
– What sources could you use to find out more about Martin Luther King?
– What facts do you find if you use the 5 Ws on the website text on Martin Luther King in a)?
– What key words would you use to find out what Martin Luther King did in 1953? And how would you search for more information on the March on Washington?

STUDY SKILLS Research

When you do research
– always use more than one source.
– try to use at least one English source.
– take notes in your own words.
– think of the 5 Ws (**Who, What, When, Where, Why**) to find useful facts in a text.
– If you are using the internet you should choose key words or phrases carefully and put them into your search engine.

▸ *SF Research (p. 141) • P 12 (p. 89) • WB 00 (p. 00)*

10 Extra Now You

a) *Find out about Rosa Parks, another important person in the US Civil Rights Movement. Make a timeline for her.*

b) *Compare timelines. Tell each other what you learned about Rosa Parks. Where did each of you get your information?*

Extra **Background File**

TOWARDS THE AFRICAN-AMERICAN DREAM

A look at black America

Look at the five sections carefully and discuss the questions on the right. You can also use information you already know, or you can do research on the internet, in books etc.

1 Is there still racial discimination in the US?
2 Do you think white Americans and African Americans have equal chances in
A education? B the world of work?
C sports? D politics?

Did you know ...?

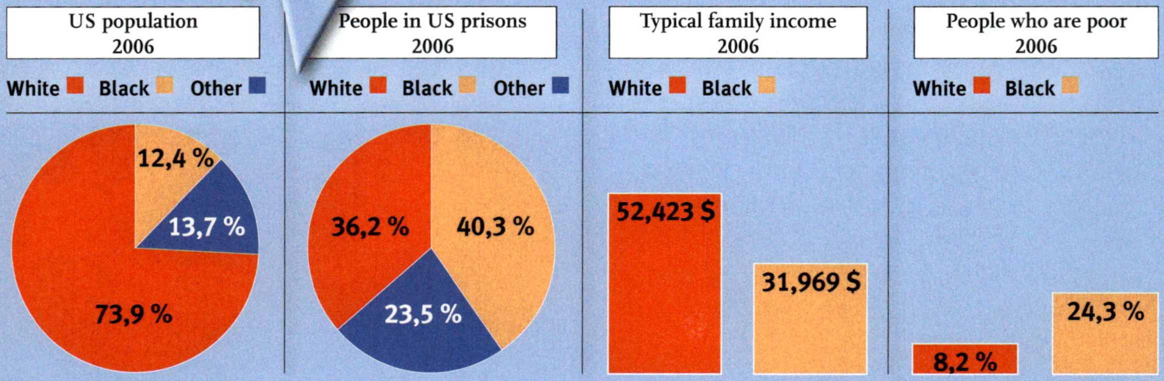

Education

In 2005, 6 % of white students left school without finishing. For blacks the number was 10 %. 69 % of the white students and 57 % of the black students who finished high school in 2005 went on to college.

The Rodney King riots

Rodney King

In 1991, ten Los Angeles policemen – all white – chased and stopped a car that was driven by Rodney King – a black man. Four of the policemen pulled King out of the car and beat him while the others watched.
What they didn't know: someone else was watching too, and he had a video camera. The film was shown on TV, and the four policemen were arrested.
When a mostly white jury decided in 1992 that the policemen had done nothing wrong, there were terrible riots in L. A. The riots lasted six days and more than 50 people were killed.

Politics

Barack Obama

In 2005 Barack Obama became the first African-American presidential candidate. He was only the fifth African-American Senator in US history, and in 2005 he was the only African American in the US Senate.

Sports

LeBron James

Today you can't imagine basketball without players like LeBron James or Stephon Marbury, but it wasn't always like that. The first black players joined the NBA (National Basketball Association) in 1950 after the all-black Harlem Globetrotters beat the all-white national champions in two out of three games.

Music

Beyoncé

Black Eyed Peas

Black artists hold all of Billboard's Top Ten!
October 6: It was on this date in 2003 that – for the first time in the 50-year history of the Billboard music charts – all Top Ten songs in the US were by black artists.

► **Text File 12** *(pp. 136–137)*

12 Extra The day after the airport explosion

13 Extra An hour later ...

Madison Hi, Dad. Mom called while you were out.
Mr Young Oh, what did she want?
Madison She said she had to go back to the airport. And that she wouldn't be home for supper.
Mr Young There's nothing wrong, is there?
Madison That's what I asked her. But she said no, Dan wanted a report on the clean-up. And she wanted me to tell you she would be here around nine.
Mr Young OK. Was there anything else?
Madison Yeah, she said I could go to Marcia's to do homework.
Mr Young Right. Well, I don't want to cook. Why don't we just order a pizza?
Madison I knew you'd say that! Is sausage and mushroom OK with you?

> *When Madison reported what her mother said, what did she leave out?*

Looking at language

a) Extra *What did Madison report to her father? Write the sentences in a chart. Then add the original sentences from the phone call with her mother.*

indirect speech	original (direct speech)
She said she had to go back to the airport. She said she wouldn't be ...	I have to go back to the airport. ...

b) *Underline the verbs in different colours. How do simple present verbs change in indirect speech? And the verbs in the will-future?*

▸ Extra *GF 7: Indirect speech (pp. 163–164) • P 13–15 (p. 90) • WB 00 (p. 00)*

1 REVISION A bit of history (The passive)

Which of the sentences below would be better in the passive? Make changes if necessary.

1 Until 1808, people brought African slaves to the US.
Until 1808, African slaves were brought to the US.
2 Farmers in the South bought the slaves to work on their plantations.
No change.
3 People founded Atlanta in 1847.
4 People discovered gold in California in 1848.
5 Someone built the Hollywood sign in 1923.
6 They built the Empire State Building in only 13 $^1/_2$ months.
7 Millions of European immigrants entered the US through Ellis Island.
8 CNN opened studios in Atlanta in 1980.

Remember

Use the passive when
- it isn't known who did something.
- you're more interested in **what** happened than in who did it.

2 WORDS Adjectives

a) *Fill each gap with an adjective from the box.*

exciting • foreign • local •
old-fashioned • recorded • short

1 three hours – a long programme
twenty minutes – a *short* programme
2 they're playing now – a live match
they played earlier – a ... match
3 Germany – national news
Frankfurt – ... news
4 made in Babelsberg – German films
made abroad – ... films foreign
5 comedy show – funny
adventure film – ... exciting
6 still trendy – modern
not trendy any more – ... old fashioned

b) *Which adjectives from the box can you use for things you like? And which for things you don't like? Make two lists*

exciting • foreign • local •
old-fashioned • recorded • short

awesome *awful*
cool

c) *Compare your lists with your partner's lists. Try and add more adjectives.*

d) *Use adjectives from a) and b) to make sentences about your favourite TV programmes.*
... is a local news programme. You can watch it on ...
... is a fantastic game show. I'm not sure if it's live or recorded.

3 WORDS Media collocations

a) *Choose one verb from the list for each group of nouns.*

▶
– change
– download
– listen to
– read
– record
– send
– surf
– turn on/off
– watch

▶ books • magazines • newspapers • text messages read
computer games • music • ringtones download
CDs • channels • DVDs change
computer • DVD recorder • MP3 player • radio • TV turn on/off

b) *Find a noun for each verb you didn't use in a).*

c) *Write a sentence for each verb in a)*
1 My brother once downloaded a horrible ringtone.

4 EVERYDAY ENGLISH SPEAKING Talking about films

a) *Listen to Madison and Paul's dialogue. Who likes violent movies and who doesn't?*

b) *Look at the dialogue. What might go in the gaps? Listen again and check.*

Paul Have you ... the latest James Bond movie?

Madison James Bond? No way! I don't ... Bond movies. They're so ...

Paul Really? I ... you liked violent movies.

Madison Well, I don't. I ... they're horrible.

Paul Why? Movies aren't real. The violence isn't real. Even the blood ...!

Madison But that's not the ... It's all made to look real.

Paul I think movies are more ... with violence. If there isn't any ... the movie is usually boring.

Madison I disagree. Movies can ... without violence.

Paul Fun, but not realistic. There's violence in real life too.

Madison That's not a good reason ... it in movies!

Paul OK. Maybe you ... see the new Will Smith movie with me then? It's a comedy with a little bit of action in it.

Madison That ... great! I'd ... to see it!

c) *Prepare a dialogue about a film you've seen. Don't write the dialogue out – just make notes. Use them to act out your dialogue.*

d) **Extra** *Write a short essay about what you think about violence in movies.*

5 EVERYDAY ENGLISH WRITING An e-mail about a film

a) *Think about the last film you saw:*

- When was it?
- What kind of film was it?
- What was it about?
- Who was in it?
- How did you like the ending?
- What did you think of the film?
- Do you think your friends should see it? Why?/Why not?

Make notes.

b) *Now write an e-mail to a friend about your film. Use your notes. The phrases in the box might help you.*

c) *Make a correcting circle of four or five students. Rewrite your e-mail with all the corrections. You can put it in your DOSSIER.*

> Dear ...,
> I saw a film yesterday/last week / ... It's called ...
> It's a comedy/drama/ ... about a ... who ...
> Katherine Heigl / ... plays the main character / ...
> I won't tell you how it ends because ...
> I thought it was really ...
> I think you should see it. / Don't go and see it! / Wait till it comes out on DVD.
> Love, / Your friend,
> ...

d) **Extra** *Hang everybody's e-mails on the walls. Walk around and read about the different films. Take notes on one film that interests you. What else would you like to know about it? Write a short e-mail to the person who wrote about the film and ask about it.*

6 READING Students between paid work and schoolwork (Drawing conclusions)

A text doesn't always give you the exact answers you're looking for. But if you look at different parts of the text and try to 'read between the lines', you can often find the answers you want.

It's everywhere you look: Nike, GAP, and J-Lo are trying to sell you something. A lot of students want to wear the latest fashion, so they work after school to be able to buy cars, clothing or iPods without having to ask their parents for money.

We talked to one hundred students from Watsonville High School in California and found that 30% work. What does that mean for their schoolwork?

"A student who wants to be allowed to work has to have certain grades," Ms. Viotti, a counsellor at Watsonville High, said. But that doesn't mean you have to be a good student to be allowed to have a job. Average grades are enough to get the OK.

"Having a job can have advantages for students' school career. Working often makes them more disciplined about doing schoolwork. And they learn how to organize their time," a chemistry teacher at Watsonville High said.

But having a job isn't as great as it sounds. You have to do what others tell you to do and you often aren't paid well. Also, students go to school for seven hours, and then work an average of four hours a day. That's an 11 hour work day.

Having a paid job might be hard but many students have no choice. "Some students have to work to help their families in times of need," Ms. Viotti told us. "A lot of parents in Watsonville are poor or don't have jobs, so their kids have to help out."

Watsonville High has a high rate of students who don't finish their high school education. Their future usually suffers because of that. "When I get home from my job at 10 pm. I'm often too tired to do my schoolwork," Kim, who works at a local supermarket, told us.

In the US millions of teens like Kim work after school. For some it means getting work experience that will help them in their future jobs. But for many it means paying quite a high price: their education.

Information from different parts: You often have to look at different paragraphs of the text to find all the information you need to answer a question.

a) *Why do students work after school? Look at paragraphs 1 and 6. Take notes.*

– *want to buy what they want*

– ...

b) *The text names the advantages of having a job. What are they? In which paragraphs can you find information on this question? Take notes.*

Drawing conclusions: Sometimes the information you need is given indirectly. First find useful facts; then draw conclusions.

c) *The text asks 'What does that mean for their schoolwork?', but doesn't give a direct answer. Find useful facts in the text and draw a conclusion to answer the question.*

Useful facts: – *students go to school*

– ...

Conclusion: ...

d) *Does the author think paid work is good or bad? Find facts in the text and draw a conclusion.*

e) **Extra** *And what do you think? Is paid work good or bad?*

7 REVISION Madison has gone down into the Grand Canyon (Present perfect)

a) *Last year Madison wrote down a list of things she wanted to do. What has she already done? What hasn't she done yet? Write sentences.*

1 *She's already gone down into the Grand Canyon.*
2 *She hasn't …*

b) *In groups of four, brainstorm ten cool things to do and make a list.*

c) *Which of the things from your group's list have you already done? (✓)*
Which haven't you done yet? (✗)

1 go down into the Grand Canyon ✓
2 see the Grand Canyon from a helicopter ✗
3 fly to Washington with my parents ✗
4 visit the CNN studios ✓
5 stay at a hotel in Las Vegas ✓
6 give a computer presentation at school ✗
7 spend a holiday at Disney World, Florida ✗
8 travel to Europe ✗

8 WORDS Word building (-able)

Some adjectives are made by adding -able to a verb, e. g. believe – believable; do – doable

a) *Look at the adjectives in the box and try to say what they mean in German. You can check in the dictionary.*

believable • breakable • doable • downloadable • drinkable • laughable • likeable • understandable

b) *Choose adjectives from the box in a) to complete the sentences.*

1 Do you know a website with … ringtones?
2 Ben is a really … guy. Everyone wants to be his friend.
3 Be careful. Some of the things in the parcel could be …
4 That story can't be true – it just isn't … !
5 The water looks dirty. Are you sure it's … ?

c) **Extra** *Make sentences with the three adjectives you didn't use in b).*

9 I've known him for five years (Present perfect with 'for')

Use the present perfect with for.

1 Sam's my best friend. I / know him / over five years.
I've known him for over five years.
2 Tim isn't at school today. He / have a cold / a few days now.
3 My mum's a waitress. She / work in a café / twelve years.
4 Grandma knows this part of town very well. She / live here / a very long time.
5 Rajif must be very ill. He / be / in hospital / six months.
6 The weather is really awful. It / be very rainy / a week.
7 At last! A holiday in the US! I / want to go there / years.
8 Dad says we need a new car. We / have the old one / ten years.

10 Mr Young at the KIng Center (since/for)

a) *Mr Young is telling Madison about his job. Add* **since** *or* **for** *to complete the sentences.*

1 I've been in my job ... 1999, Madison.
2 I need a new computer. I've had this one ... almost five years.
3 I've known my boss ... about five years.
4 Martin Luther King's wife founded the Center, but she's been dead ... a few years now.
5 Millions of visitors have come to our museum ... 1968.
6 We've also had an online learning programme ... a number of years.
7 Martin Luther King's birthday has been a holiday in the US ... 1986.

b) *Make a chart like the one below and fill it in for yourself.*

How long ...	Me	Partner 1
(be) at this school	4 yrs	
(be) at school today	8.05	
(know) your best friend		
(live) in this town		
(have) your mobile		

c) *Make appointments with three classmates. Ask and answer questions and fill in your chart.*
How long have you been at this school? ...

d) *Write sentences about you and your partners.*
I've been at this school for four years. Today I've been at school since 8.05. ...

11 The US has had 50 states ... (since/for)

a) *Partner B: Look at* *p. 112.*
Partner A: Ask questions with **How long ...** + **present perfect**. *Take notes on your partner's answers.*

1 US/have/50 states?
   A: How long has the US had 50 states?
   B: The US has had 50 states ...
2 Washington/be/the capital of the US?
3 the railway/link/the East Coast with the West Coast?
4 White House/be/the home of US Presidents?

The White House in Washington, D.C.

b) *Answer your partner's questions. Use the present perfect with* **since** *or* **for**.

1 Georgia ... (be) a state ... 1788.
2 Atlanta ... (be) the capital of Georgia ... over 140 years.
3 Atlanta ... (have) black mayors ... 1974.
4 Martin Luther King ... (be) dead ... more than 40 years now.

12 LISTENING 'We shall overcome'

a) *As you listen to the radio programme, write down key words and phrases about*
– what the Civil Rights Movement was trying to change
– who the Freedom Riders were and what they did
– what was happening at the restaurant
– what happened to Ellis Washington's uncle
– what's special about the song 'We shall overcome', and what it meant to black people

b) *Compare notes with a partner. Listen again. Then write a paragraph about one of the topics.*

13 Extra Mrs Young's job (Indirect speech – simple present)

A week after the explosion at the airport, Mrs Young got another call from her boss when she was on her way to work:

1 There's trouble at the downtown police station.
2 There's a man there with a gun.
3 I need a reporter there fast.
4 I can't go – I'm in a terrible traffic jam.
5 I don't have anyone else.
6 OK Dan, but I don't know when I can be there.

later ...
7 Hey, everything's OK! You don't have to go any more.
8 The trouble at the police station is over.

That evening Mrs Young told her family about the phone call. Fill in the missing information.

I was on my way to work when Dan called. He said there 1 *was* trouble at the downtown police station. He told me there 2 a man there with a gun and that he 3 a reporter there fast. I said I 4 go because I was in a terrible traffic jam. But he said he 5 anyone else! So I said OK, but that I 6 when I 6 be there. Anyway, I drove on the wrong side of the street around the traffic jam, and then I drove like a crazy person. The police stopped me – it cost me $ 35! When I was finally outside the police station, Dan called again. He said everything was OK and that I 7 to go any more. The trouble at the police station 8 over. I wanted to kill him.

14 Extra Maybe I'll ... (Indirect speech – will-future)

Later that evening, Madison talked to her mother about her next summer vacation. Write down what she said.

1 *Madison said that maybe she'd ...*

15 Extra He said, she said ... (Indirect speech – mixed bag)

a) *Think of five facts about yourself, e.g.:*

I am/am not ... I can/can't ...
I have/don't have ... I (don't) like/go/...
I have to/don't have to ... I will/won't ...

b) *Make appointments with three partners. At your first two appointments, tell your partners your five things. Write down what they say.*

c) *At your third appointment, tell your partner what the first two told you.*

Melba's story

Background

Before you read 'Melba's story', look at this background information on segregation in the US in the 1950s.

Slavery ended in the US in 1865. But for almost a century after that, blacks in many states, especially in the South, did not have the same rights as whites and were segregated from them.

'Segregation' meant that laws kept African Americans and white Americans apart – on buses and trains, in restaurants and hostels. There were waiting rooms for whites only and drinking fountains for whites and for 'colored' people. There were schools for white children and schools for black children. And the schools for black children were almost always older and smaller.

In 1954, the Supreme Court of the United States ended school segregation: all schools now had to open their doors to black and white children.

In 1957, nine black students were chosen to move from the high school for black children in Little Rock, Arkansas, to the big high school for whites, Central High. But some states didn't want to follow the new law: Arkansas was one of those states. Soon the nine black students would be known as the Little Rock Nine.

Classroom in a black school

Classroom in a white school

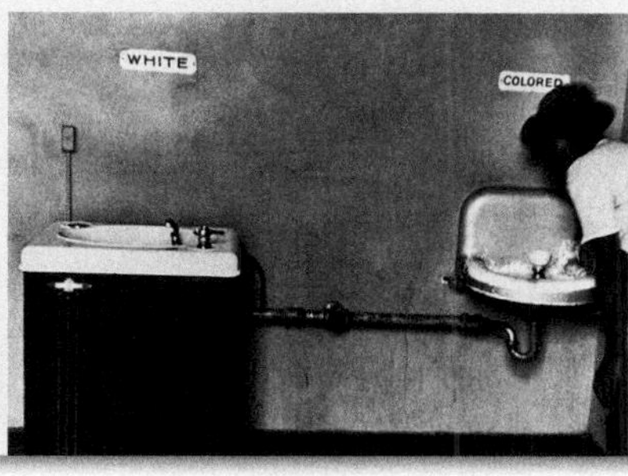

> *What was segregation? Collect as many examples as you can.*

The story

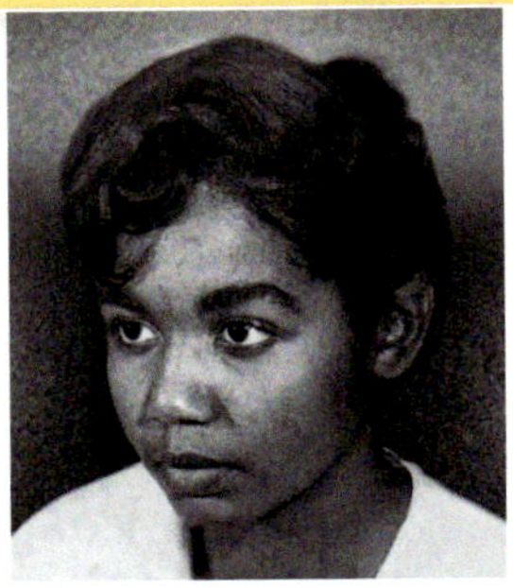

One of the Little Rock Nine was Melba Pattillo, and this is her story.

Melba Pattillo was born in Little Rock, Arkansas, on 7th December 1941. Arkansas was a segregated state, so when Melba was little she spent all her time with black people. Even at the 4th July picnics, the blacks were always in a separate part of the park.

When Melba was five years old, she saved five cents for a ride on the merry-go-round in the park on 4th July. On that day the family packed their holiday picnic and went to the park. Melba, with her five cents in her hand, ran over to the part of the park where the merry-go-round stood. She put the money on the ticket man's counter and asked for a ticket. She wanted to ride the black and white horse and could see that it was empty.

"Could I have one ticket for the merry-go-round please, sir?" she asked.

"There's no place for you here," the ticket man said.

When she pointed to the empty horse, he shouted: "You don't belong here, you little nigger!"

In her book, 'Warriors don't cry', Melba wrote later: "Angry faces looked at me as if I had done something very wrong. As I ran past the people who were waiting I was terrified. I didn't even pick up my money. At the age of five I learned that – even if all the horses on the merry-go-round were empty – there would be no place for me."

In 1955, a year after the Supreme Court had said that segregation in schools was wrong, a teacher at Melba's all-black school asked if any students wanted to go to the white high school. Melba immediately volunteered. She was only 13 years old.

Two years later, in 1957, at the start of the school year on 3rd September, the time had come for nine black students to join the 2000 white students at Little Rock Central High School.

But the Governor of Arkansas supported the white people who didn't want blacks at their children's school. Crowds of angry white people from all over the South came to the school. It was too dangerous for the nine black students: they had to stay home.

The next day, eight of the nine black students met before school and went there together. But the Governor sent the National Guard to the school to stop them. Melba and the others tried to get through the all the angry white crowd to the steps of the school, but they couldn't.

They saw their friend Elizabeth, who hadn't met the others before school. She was trying to get through the National Guard line alone. But whenever she tried to walk past the guards, they moved closer and blocked her way.

The white crowd became angrier and angrier, so Elizabeth tried to get away from the school. She escaped to a bus stop where two white people protected her till the bus came and then took her home.

Melba and her mother ran away from the angry white crowd and escaped in their car. That night Melba wrote in her diary:

> I was sad not to see what is inside Central High School. I don't understand why the governor sent soldiers to keep us out. I don't know if I should go back. But Grandma is right. If I don't go back they will think they have won.

On 23rd September, the black students tried to get into the school again. This time they were able to enter through a side door. All of the white students were cruel to them – they shouted names at them, kicked them and spat at them. And outside the crowd got angrier and angrier. In the end the police decided that they had to get the nine out or they might be killed.

That night Melba wrote in her diary:

> There seems to be no place for me at Central High. I don't want integration to be like the merry-go-round. Please, God, make a place for me.

Two days later the US President sent soldiers to help the black students. The soldiers drove them to the school and protected them as they entered the school through the front door for the first time.

And each of the nine got a soldier as bodyguard for the school day. Melba's was a young soldier called Danny. That night she wrote:

> I feel specially cared about because the guard is there. If he wasn't there I'd hear more of the voices of those people who say I'm a nigger ... that I'm not valuable, that I have no right to be alive. Thank you, Danny.

But even Danny couldn't stop one attack on Melba. This is how she describes it in her book:

"Near the end of the day I was walking down a dark hallway, Danny was following me, when I saw a boy – he was coming straight towards me. I tried to move to one side, but he moved with me. I didn't even have time to call for help.

"The boy threw something in my face. Suddenly I felt a terrible pain in my eyes. I thought I would die. It was like nothing I had ever felt before. I couldn't hear or see or feel anything except the fire in my eyes. I heard myself cry out.

"Someone grabbed my ponytail and pulled me along very fast. Hands pulled my fingers from my eyes. Then cold, cold water was splashed in my eyes. The water felt so good."

The hands were the hands of Danny, Melba's bodyguard. It was his fast action that saved her eyes: what the boy had thrown in them was acid. Melba was one of the eight black students who got through a whole year at Central High. But the following year, the governor of Arkansas closed all high schools in Little Rock to make sure that black kids couldn't go to school with white kids. A family in California offered Melba a new home and the chance to finish her education. They were white.

Melba went on to university and became a journalist. Today she is a successful business woman and lives in San Francisco.

Working with the text

1 Headlines

Which headline fits the events in Little Rock?

Little Rock Nine welcomed at Central High School

☆ LITTLE ROCK NINE ENTER HIGH SCHOOL WITH HELP OF US SOLDIERS

President bans black students from Little Rock Central High

2 Headings for the story

Put these headings for the different parts of the story in the right order. In one or two sentences say what each part is about.

1 Angry whites stop the Nine
2 Schools closed in Little Rock, 1958
3 Attack on Melba
4 Governor sends National Guard
5 Sept. 3, 1957: whites protest on first day
6 Soldiers protect the Little Rock Nine
7 Melba and the merry-go-round
8 Melba volunteers to go to Central High

3 Who are they?

a) *Look at the list of people. Decide who played a good role and who a bad role.*
– the Governor of Arkansas
– the US President
– the soldiers
– the National Guard
– the white people in Little Rock
– Danny

b) *Now explain their roles in the story.*
The governor played a ... role: He didn't want ... to ...

4 Melba's feelings

How do you think Melba felt when ...
... she couldn't go on the merry-go-round
... she volunteered to go to Central High
... she saw the angry white people
... she met her bodyguard, Danny
... a boy threw something in her face
... the governor closed Central High

angry • excited • happy • hopeless • sad • safe • terrified • unhappy • upset • worried

How am I doing?

a) *Fill in or choose the correct answers.*

Atlanta and its history

1 The segregation laws kept ... apart.
A states in the north and states in the south B black and white Americans C CNN and ABC D Native Americans and European immigrants

2 Martin Luther King worked hard to stop ...
A the Civil Rights Movement B the selling of blacks as slaves C Shirley Franklin D discrimination against blacks

3 Which of these is *not* at home in Atlanta?
A Little Rock Central High School B CNN C Coca Cola D the King Center

Words

4 Write down the words that match these definitions:
A a TV show that's on once a week B a show with real people, not actors, who do things naturally C a show with lots of jokes and funny scenes D the best time for TV, in the evening E a film or TV show that tells you about things that really happened

5 Which is not a job in television?
A host B presenter C comedian D viewer

6 A good place to find out what's on TV is ...
A a TV show B a book C the TV listings D CNN

Research

7 When you are doing research, you should always use ...
A Wikipedia B one good source C more than one source D sources in your own language

8 The notes on your research should ...
A use your own words B use the words of your sources as much as possible C never say where you got your information D always use complete sentences

Reading

9 You need special information from a text. When do you have to draw conclusions?
A All answers are directly in the text. B The text is very long and gives lots of facts. C There is nothing about it in the text. D The information is given indirectly.

Grammar

10 Put in the correct form of the verb:
A We ... (live) in the same flat for six years. B My parents ... (be) married for 15 years. C I ... (have) English with Frau Marx since the beginning of last year. D My best friend and I ... (know) each other since the first grade.

11 Decide: 'since' or 'for'?
A ... kindergarten B ... an hour C ... 2007 D ... the accident E ... a long time

b) Check your answers on p. 253 and add up your points.

c) If you had 21 or more points, well done! Maybe you can help students who had fewer points. If you had 20 points or fewer, it's a good idea to do some more work before you go on to the next unit. Where did you make mistakes? The chart below will tell you what you can do to improve your English.

No.	Area	Find out more	Exercise(s)
1– 3	Atlanta and its history	pp. 76–77, A9 (p. 81), p. 91	P1 (p. 85), WB 00, (p. 00)
4– 6	American TV	All about, (p. 78)	P2–3 (p. 85), WB 00, (p. 00)
7– 8	Research	A9, (p. 81), SF, p. 141	WB 00 (p. 00)
9	Reading	P6, (p. 87)	WB 00 (p. 00)
10–11	Grammar: 'since'/'for'	A6, (p. 79), A7, (p. 80)	P9–11 (pp. 88–89), WB 00 (p. 00)

Extra 'There's a boy in the girls' bathroom' abridged from a play by *Louis Sachar*

Before you read

Have you ever been in a situation where everybody knew everybody else but you didn't know anybody? How did it feel?
In the following play Jeff Fishkin has started at a new school in the middle of the semester. How do you think he feels? What problems might he have?

Scene 1 Hallway of Red Hill School, an American public school

Jeff — *(He's in a hurry, but polite.)* Excuse me, Mrs Ebbel. Can you tell me where the counselor's office is please.

Mrs Ebbel — The counselor's office ... Let's see. Go down this hall to the end. Turn right, and it's the third door on your left.

Jeff — Thank you very much. *(He talks to himself as he walks on.)* Right, third door.

Mrs Ebbel — No wait. That's not right. She's in the new office in the other wing. Turn around and go back the way you came, go right, then turn left at the end of the hall and it's the door immediately to your right.

Jeff — Thank you.

Mrs. Ebbel exits. Jeff moves across the stage. He's talking to himself.

Jeff — Turn right. Third door on left. *(Enters girls' bathroom.)* I'm sorry I'm late.

Colleen — *(Buttons her jeans as she leaves the toilet.)* What are you doing in here?

Jeff — *(Puzzled.)* Huh?

Colleen — Get out of here! This is the girls' bathroom!

Jeff stands for a moment, then runs off.

Colleen — *(After Jeff has already left.)* THERE'S A BOY IN THE GIRLS' BATHROOM!

She shouts it one or two more times.

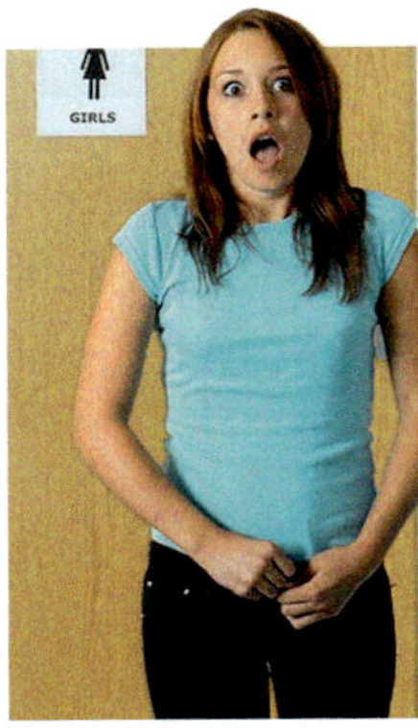

Stage directions

a) *In a play you will find dialogue and stage directions. The stage directions tell you about the scenery and props, or about the actors, e.g.*
- *what they should do*
- *how they should do it*
- *what the characters they are playing feel.*

Find at least one example of each kind of stage direction in Scene 1.

b) *'What are you doing in here?' Take turns to ask this question in different ways:* angrily, coldly, seriously, loudly, quietly, excitedly, ...

Scene 2 The counselor's office

Carla, the school counselor, is putting something up on a bulletin board, but stops when she sees Jeff.

Carla — You must be Jeff. I'm Carla Davis.

She holds out her hand. Jeff numbly shakes it.

Carla — Come in.

They both sit down at the round table.

[1] counselor ['kaʊnsələ] *Berater/in* [2] (to) exit ['eksɪt] *abgehen, von der Bühne gehen* [3] stage direction *Regieanweisung, Bühnenanweisung* [4] scenery ['siːnəri] *Bühnenbild* [5] props *(pl)* [prɒps] *Requisiten* [6] numbly ['nʌmli] *benommen*

Carla You'll have to excuse the mess. I'm still getting moved in.

Jeff stares blankly at her.

Carla So how do you like Red Hill School so far?

Jeff doesn't say anything.

Carla I imagine it must seem a little scary. I think it's scary. It seems so big! Anytime I try to go anywhere, I get lost.

Jeff smiles weakly – if she only knew.

Carla It's hard for me because I'm new here. I don't know anybody. Nobody knows me. The other teachers all look at me strangely. I think some of them don't understand what a counselor does. It's hard for me to make friends with them. They already have their own friends.

Jeff nods.

Carla Maybe you can help me?

Jeff Me? How can I help you? You're supposed to help me.

Carla Maybe we can help each other. What do you think about that?

Jeff smiles and shrugs.

Carla We're the two new kids at school. We can share our experiences and learn from each other.

Jeff Okay, Miss Davis.

Carla Jeff, if we're going to be friends, I want you to call me Carla, not Miss Davis.

Jeff laughs.

Carla Do you think Carla is a funny name?

Jeff Oh, no! I just never called a teacher by her first name, that's all.

Carla But we're friends. Friends don't call each other Miss Davis and Mr. Fishkin, do they?

Jeff *(Laughs again.)* The kids in my class all call me Fishface.

Carla Have you made any friends?

Jeff One. But I don't like him.

Carla How can he be your friend if you don't like him?

Jeff Nobody likes him. At first I felt sorry for him because nobody even wants to sit near him. Even Mrs. Ebbel said so.

Carla It must have hurt his feelings.

Jeff No, he just smiled.

Carla He may have been smiling on the outside, but do you think he really was smiling on the inside?

Jeff I don't know. I guess not. I guess that's why I tried to be friends with him. I told him I didn't mind sitting by him. But then he said, "Give me a dollar or I'll spit on you!"

Carla What'd you do?

Jeff I gave him a dollar. I didn't want to get spit on. But then, today, he said: "I'll give you a dollar if you'll be my friend."

Carla What'd you do?

Jeff I took it. *(Pause.)* So does that mean I have to be his friend, even though I just broke even?

Carla What do you think friendship is?

Jeff I don't know. I mean I know what it is, but I can't explain it.

Carla Is it something you can buy and sell? Can you go to the store and get a quart of milk, a dozen eggs, and a friend?

Jeff *(Laughs.)* No. So does that mean I don't have to be his friend? I don't even know if Bradley wants to be friends.

Carla I think you'll find that if you're nice to Bradley, he'll be nice to you. It's just like with the dollar. You always break even.

Understanding the play

a) *What do the stage directions tell you about how Jeff's feelings change through the scene? Words from the box may help you.*

embarrassed • lonely • puzzled • scared • welcome • worried

b) *What is Jeff thinking of in l. 11 when he 'smiles weakly' and thinks 'if she only knew'?*

---

[1] (to) stare blankly at sb. [ˌsteə 'blæŋkli] *jn. verständnislos anstarren* [2] (to) get lost *sich verirren, sich verlaufen* [3] You're (not) supposed to ... *Du sollst (nicht) ...* [4] (to) shrug [ʃrʌg] *mit den Schultern zucken* [5] I guess (not) *ich denke (nicht), ich glaube (nicht)* [6] even though [ˌi:vn 'ðəʊ] *selbst wenn; obwohl* [7] (to) break even *ausgleichen; gleichziehen* [8] embarrassed [ɪm'bærəst] *verlegen; peinlich berührt*

Friendship

a) *Partner A: Make a list of all the phrases Carla uses with* ***friend*** *or* ***friendship****.*
It's hard for me to make friends (p. 97, ll. 16–18)
Partner B: Make a list of all the phrases Jeff uses.

b) *Compare your lists. What do they tell you about how Carla and Jeff think of friendship?*

c) *What does friendship mean to you?*
'A friend should …'
In groups of four, each fill in 8–10 things on your corner of a placemat e.g. be funny, help me when I'm in trouble, ….
Agree on the three most important qualities for a friend and put them in the middle. Walk round, look at other groups' placemats and discuss them.

Scene 3 The counselor's office

Carla is alone. She's reading a file.

Carla Bradley Chalkers …

She reads something in the file that makes her laugh. Bradley enters.

Bradley I'm here, whadda ya want?

Carla *(Stands and smiles warmly at him.)* Hello Bradley, I'm Carla Davis. It's a pleasure to see you today. *(She holds out her hand.)* I've been looking forward to meeting you.

Bradley just stares at her.

Carla Aren't you going to shake my hand?

Bradley Nah, you're too ugly.

He walks past her and sits down at the table, Carla sits down on the other side.

Carla I appreciate your coming to see me.

Bradley I had to come. Mrs. Ebbel made me.

Carla For whatever reason. I'm glad you came.

Bradley I meant to go to the library. I came here by accident.

Carla Oh, I don't believe in accidents.

Bradley *(Looks at her.)* What about when you spill your milk?

Carla Do you like milk?

Bradley No, I hate it!

Carla So maybe you spill it on purpose. You just think it's an accident.

Bradley stares angrily down at the table. He feels as if she has played a trick on him.

Bradley I don't drink milk. I drink coffee. *(Pause.)* I didn't do anything wrong!

Carla Nobody said you did.

Bradley Then how come I have to be here?

Carla I was hoping you'd like it here. I was hoping we could be friends. Do you think we can?

Bradley No.

Carla Why not?

Bradley Because I don't like you.

Carla I can like you, can't I? You don't have to like me.

Bradley squirms.

Carla I was hoping you'd be able to teach me some things.

Bradley You're the teacher, not me.

Carla That doesn't matter. A teacher can often learn a lot more from a student than a student can learn from a teacher.

Bradley *(Nods.)* I've taught Mrs. Ebbel a lot.

Carla What do you want to teach me?

Bradley What do you want to know?

Carla You tell me. What's the most important thing you can teach me?

Bradley *(Thinks for a moment.)* Nothing. You're not supposed to talk in school.

---

1 pleasure ['pleʒə] *Vergnügen* 2 ugly ['ʌgli] *hässlich* 3 by accident *zufällig* 4 (to) spill [spɪl] *verschütten* 5 on purpose ['pɜːpəs] *absichtlich*
6 (to) squirm [skwɜːm] *sich (verlegen) winden, auf dem Stuhl hin und her rutschen* 7 That doesn't matter. ['mætə] *Das spielt keine Rolle.*

Carla — Why not?

Bradley — It's a rule. Like not sticking gum in the water fountains.

Carla — Well, in this room, there are no rules. In here, everyone thinks for himself. No one tells you what to do.

Bradley — You mean I can stick gum in the water fountain?

Carla — You could, except I don't have a water fountain.

Bradley — Can I break something?

Carla — Certainly.

Bradley gets up and walks round. He's looking for something he can break. Then he looks at Carla.

Bradley — I'm not in the mood.

Carla — Okay. But if you're ever in the mood, there are lots of things you can break – things I like very much and things other children use.

Bradley — I will! *(Sits down again.)* I know karate. *(Raises his hand over the table as if ready to give it a karate chop.)* I can break this table with my bare hand.

Carla — Ooh. Won't that hurt?

Bradley — Nothing ever hurts me. I've broken every table in my house. Call my mother if you don't believe me!

Carla — I believe you.

He looks at her, surprised that she believes him.

Bradley — So now what am I supposed to do?

Carla — Would you like to draw a picture?

She gives Bradley a piece of paper and the box of pencils.

Bradley — *(While he draws.)* My parents only feed me dog food.

Carla — How does it taste?

Bradley — *(Stops drawing and looks up at her, surprised.)* Delicious! Meaty and sweet.

Carla — I've always wanted to try it.

Bradley — *(Draws some more.)* The president called me on the phone last night.

Carla — How exciting! What'd you talk about?

Bradley — *(He's still drawing.)* Hats.

Carla — What about hats?

Bradley — I asked him why he didn't wear a hat like Abraham Lincoln.

Carla — And what did the president say?

Bradley — I'm not allowed to tell you. It's top secret. *(Draws some more.)* Done!

He holds up his picture. It's black.

Carla — That's very nice.

Bradley — It's a picture of night time.

Carla — Oh, I thought it was the floor of a barber shop, after someone with black curly hair got his hair cut. It's very good. May I have it?

Bradley — *(Suspiciously.)* What for?

Carla — I'd like to hang it up on my wall.

Bradley — *(Stares at her, amazed.)* No, it's mine!

Carla — I was hoping you'd let me.

Bradley — It costs a dollar.

Carla — I'm sure it's worth it.

Bradley shakes his head.

Carla — Okay. But, if you ever change your mind...

Bradley — You can make me give it to you.

Carla — No, I can't do that.

Bradley — Sure you can. Teachers make kids do things all the time.

Carla — Not in here. *(She holds out her hand for him to shake. He doesn't take her hand.)* I've enjoyed your visit very much. Thank you for sharing so much with me.

Understanding the play

a) *Is Bradley in Carla's office 'by accident'? Give reasons for your answer.*

b) *How does Bradley try to make Carla angry? How does she react?*

c) *Why doesn't Bradley break anything after Carla says that would be OK?*

d) *Carla says: 'A teacher can often learn a lot more from a student than a student can learn from a teacher.' (p. 98, ll. 48–51) What do you think a teacher can learn from a student? Make a list and report to the class.*

---

[1] (chewing) gum ['tʃu:ɪŋ gʌm] *Kaugummi* [2] water fountain ['faʊntən] *Trinkbrunnen* [3] Certainly. ['sɜ:tnli] *Sicher(lich). / Natürlich.* [4] mood [mu:d] *Stimmung, Laune* [5] (to) taste [teɪst] *schmecken* [6] suspicious(ly) [sə'spɪʃəs(li)] *misstrauisch* [7] (to) change your mind *die Meinung ändern*

Scene 4 The schoolyard

Jeff and Bradley are hanging out in a corner. The three girls enter.

Colleen I was washing my hands and he just walked right in.

Melinda Who was it?

Colleen You know, that new kid.

Lori Jeff Fishnose. He is kind of weird, isn't he?

Colleen I don't know, I think he's kind of cute.

Colleen's two friends look at her, surprised.

Melinda Ooooh!

All three giggle. Then Melinda spots Jeff and hurries to him, with Lori right behind her. Colleen shyly follows.

Melinda Hi, Jeff.

Jeff Hi.

Lori *(In a teasing kind of voice.)* Hello, Jeff.

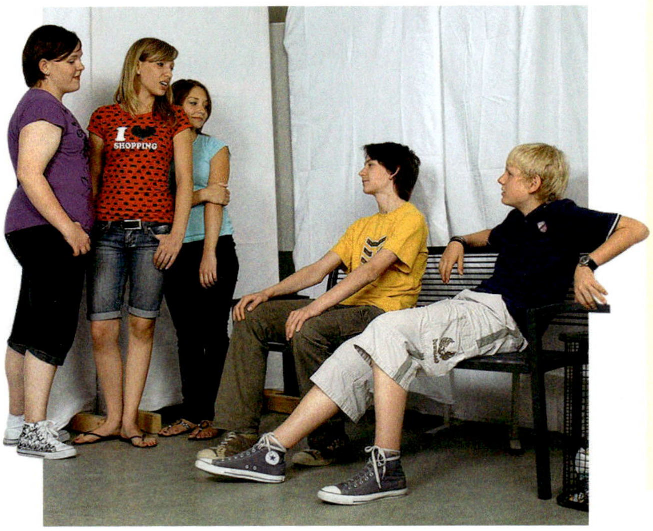

Jeff Hello.

Lori laughs.

Colleen *(Shyly.)* Hi, Jeff.

Jeff Hi.

All three girls giggle.

Bradley Get outta here or I'll punch your faces in.

Lori Euuuu! Bradley Chalkers!

Bradley Lori Loudmouth! The ugliest girl in the school!

Melinda Grow up, Bradley.

Bradley Make me!

He shakes his fist at the girls, and they start to exit, but Lori suddenly stops and turns.

Lori *(Teasingly.)* Hey, Jeff. What were you doing in the girls' bathroom?

The three girls exit – they're laughing – as Jeff covers his face.

Bradley *(Suddenly impressed.)* You went into the girls' bathroom?

Jeff It wasn't – I mean –

Bradley Me too! I go all the time. I like to make them scream.

Bradley now sees Jeff as a friend.

Bradley I know! The next time one of those stupid girls says hello to you – kick her!

Understanding the play

a) *Are these statements right or wrong? Give reasons for your answers.*

- Jeff went into the girls' bathroom by accident.
- Bradley thinks Jeff went into the girls' bathroom by accident.

b) *Why does Bradley think differently about Jeff at the end of the scene? Use the answers from a).*

Reading out loud

a) *Make groups of five. Divide up the roles and read the scene out loud. Practise your reading.*

b) *Now read the scene to the class. Vote for the best group.*

Scene 5 The counselor's office

Bradley enters.

Bradley The reason the president doesn't wear a hat is because the doorways are too low. He used to wear one, but every time he walked through a door, he hit his hat and it would fall off.

Carla *(Almost laughs.)* That makes sense. But, *(looks around, then whispers.)* I thought it was top secret.

Bradley The president says he trusts you.

[1] weird [wɪəd] *seltsam* [2] cute [kjuːt] *süß, niedlich* [3] (to) giggle [ˈɡɪɡl] *kichern* [4] teasing [ˈtiːzɪŋ] *neckend* [5] Jeff covers his face. *Jeff hält die Hände vors Gesicht.* [6] low [ləʊ] *niedrig* [7] sense [sens] *Sinn* [8] (to) trust sb. [trʌst] *jm. (ver)trauen*

Carla Thank you, Bradley, I'm glad you trust me.

Bradley *(Stares at her a moment.)* Jeff trusts you too.

Carla I understand you two have become good friends.

Bradley He's my best friend.

Carla That's very nice. I'm sure Jeff appreciates having you as a friend.

Bradley I'm his only friend.

Carla But even if he had other friends ...

Bradley He won't. I'm his only friend.

Carla But suppose he makes new friends.

Bradley I don't want him to.

Carla But if he made new friends, then his new friends could be your friends too.

Bradley He won't.

Carla Let me ask you something, Bradley. What do you think friendship is? When you say you have a friend, does that mean you own him? I have a book. I have a bicycle. I have a friend. Or is friendship something you share between the two of you?

Bradley stares at her as if she's crazy.

Carla Just because you and Jeff are friends, does that mean he can't be friends with other kids too?

Bradley Yes!

Carla Why?

Bradley *(Proudly.)* Because. So long as Jeff is friends with me, nobody else will like him!

> ***Understanding the play***
>
> ***a)*** *Why is Bradley so sure he will stay Jeff's only friend?*
>
> ***b)*** *Does Bradley like himself or not? Why do you think that?*

Scene 6 Outside after school

Colleen *(Shyly)* Hello, Jeff.

Jeff Hello, Colleen.

Bradley Quit saying hello to him!

Lori It's a free country. We can say hello.

Bradley Not to us!

Lori We didn't say hello to you, just him. Hello, Jeff.

Jeff Hello.

Lori laughs.

Melinda Why don't you just leave us alone, Bradley.

Bradley No. You leave us alone first!

Bradley pushes Melinda. She pushes him back. He stumbles back and falls into a mud puddle. Lori laughs. Bradley climbs out of the mud, angrier than ever.

Bradley You got my clothes dirty!

Lori *(Sings.)* Bradley wet his pants!

Bradley Shut up!

Melinda *(Nervously.)* You started it.

Bradley *(Shakes his fist.)* I'll punch your face in, Melinda!

Bradley comes at her and kicks her. Scared, Melinda hits him hard in the eye. Bradley holds his eye as he stumbles back, but doesn't fall.

Bradley No fair! Four against one!

Bradley runs to the other end of the stage. Jeff is confused. Melinda is shocked. Lori laughs. Colleen looks from one to the other. The three girls exit. Jeff looks after Bradley, then also exits. Mrs. Chalkers, Bradley's mother, enters. Bradley pretends his whole body hurts, not just his eye.

Bradley They beat me up and threw me in the mud. Then they ripped up my homework.

Mrs Ch. Who were they? I want to know their names.

Bradley Uh ... *(Pause.)* I don't know all their names.

Mrs Ch. Don't be afraid. I'll make sure they don't hurt you anymore.

Bradley Jeff Fishkin! He was the leader of the gang.

Mrs Ch. I'll call the school. We won't let Jeff Fishkin get away with this.

Bradley Good! I hope he gets expelled!

> ***Understanding the play***
>
> *Why doesn't Bradley tell his mother the truth at the end of the scene? Explain.*

---

1 (to) own *besitzen* 2 (to) quit doing sth. [kwɪt] *aufhören, etwas zu tun* 3 (to) stumble ['stʌmbl] *stolpern* 4 mud puddle ['mʌd pʌdl] *Schlammpfütze* 5 (to) wet your pants, wet, wet [wet] *sich in die Hose machen* 6 confused [kən'fju:zd] *verwirrt* 7 (to) pretend [prɪ'tend] *so tun, als ob* 8 (to) expel sb. [ɪk'spel] *jn. von der Schule verweisen* 9 truth [tru:θ] *Wahrheit*

Scene 7 The schoolyard

There is a basketball hoop. Jeff walks across stage, confused. Robbie and Brian enter. Brian holds a basketball.

Robbie — Jeff.
Brian — Hey, Jeff.
Jeff — Me?
Robbie — Hi, Jeff.
Jeff — Hi.
Robbie — So, how's it going Jeff?
Jeff — Fine?
Robbie — All right!
Brian — So what did the principal say? Did you get in trouble?
Jeff — No.
Robbie — *(Laughs.)* Probably gave him a medal!
Brian — Man, I've been waiting all year for somebody to teach Chalkers a lesson.

He holds the basketball under his arm, and punches it with his fist as if it's Bradley's head.

Robbie — Yeah. I would have done it myself, but, uh ... you know how it is.
Brian — Yeah. You know how it is. *(Still friendly.)* You're chicken.

Robbie — Well I didn't exactly see you taking on Chalkers either.
Jeff — Uhh...Sure!

They all move toward the basket.

Robbie — All right. Jeff's on my team.
Brian — No, he's on mine.

Brian throws the basketball to Jeff, who dribbles and shoots.

Robbie — All right, Jeff.
Brian — Nice shot, Jeff.

Understanding the play
Why are Robbie and Brian suddenly friendly to Jeff? Explain.

Scene 8 The counselor's office

Jeff — I don't need any help anymore. I have lots of friends now. We play basketball and I'm the best. Everyone says so.
Carla — Good for you Jeff! I'm very proud of you.
Jeff — And I'm not friends with Bradley anymore.
Carla — Oh, I'm sorry to hear that.
Jeff — Why? I'm not. I hate him. In fact ... *(Looks around the room.)* ... I beat him up.
Carla — What happened?
Jeff — Oh, he wouldn't stop bothering me. I never liked him. No one does. So then he tried to hit me *(Jeff pantomimes his fight with Bradley.)* but I ducked and then smashed him right in the face. He came at me again, but I blocked with my left, a right to the gut, and then pow! *(Shrugs.)* I didn't want to have to do it, but I had no choice. *(Pause.)* So, I don't think I need to see a counselor anymore, since I have normal friends.

Scene 9 The schoolyard

Bradley is sitting alone. Lori runs onto the stage. She screams.

Lori — AAAAAAAAAAAHHHHHHHHH! It's a monster!

Bradley looks up at Lori.

Lori — You're not even human! You're a monster from outer space! *(She runs: she wants Bradley to run after her, but he doesn't, so she stops and sings.)* Mon-ster, Mon-ster from outer space!

---

[1] principal ['prɪnsəpl] *(AE) Schulleiter/in* [2] You're chicken. *Du bist feige.* [3] I didn't exactly see you taking on Chalkers either. ['aɪðə, 'iːðə] *(etwa:) Du hast auch nicht gerade gezeigt, dass du es mit Chalkers aufnimmst.* [4] He wouldn't stop bothering me. ['bɒðərɪŋ] *Er hat einfach nicht aufgehört, mich zu belästigen.* [5] choice [tʃɔɪs] *Wahl* [6] outer space [ˌaʊtə 'speɪs] *Weltraum*

Scene 10 The counselor's office

Bradley *(After a long pause.)* Monsters from outer space.

Carla Pardon?

Bradley You said I can pick the topic. I want to talk about monsters from outer space!

Carla What a wonderful topic!

Bradley The only way to kill them is with a ray gun. Regular guns or even hand grenades won't kill them.

He stands up and pretends to shoot a ray gun.

Carla *(Puts up her hands.)* Don't shoot me.

Bradley You're a monster from outer space?

Carla No I'm not. I'm a counselor.

Bradley Do you believe in monsters from outer space?

Carla No. I don't believe in monsters. I believe there are many other types of creatures living in our universe. Some are probably quite primitive, others smarter than you and me. But out of all those creatures, I don't believe there is even one monster.

Bradley I do.

Carla I think everyone has good inside him. Sometimes people think someone's a monster. But that's only because they can't see the "good". And then you know what they do?

Bradley They kill him?

Carla Worse. *(Dramatically.)* They call him a monster! And they all treat him like a monster. And then, after a while, he starts believing it himself! He thinks he's a monster. So he acts like one. But he really isn't a monster. He still has a lot of good, buried deep inside him.

Bradley But what if he's real ugly? What if he has green skin, and three arms, and a big black eye in the middle of his face?

Carla You and I might think that is ugly, but maybe, on that planet, that might be considered beautiful. You may have just described a handsome movie star. *(Bradley laughs.)* On that planet, they would probably think I was ugly because I have two eyes and my skin isn't green.

Bradley No one would ever think you were ugly.

Carla *(Very surprised.)* Why Bradley. That's the nicest thing you ever said to me. Thank you.

Bradley *(Looking down.)* I don't want to talk about monsters anymore.

Carla Okay, I think we had a very good conversation. You picked a great topic.

Bradley *(He begins to draw.)* Carla?

Carla Yes.

Bradley Can you see inside monsters? Can you see the good?

Carla That's all I see.

Bradley Well, how does a monster stop being a monster? I mean, if everyone keeps treating him like a monster?

Carla It isn't easy. I think first he has to realize for himself that he isn't a monster. That I think is the first step. Until he knows he isn't a monster, how is anybody else supposed to know?

Bradley holds up his finished drawing. It's a three-armed green monster with a big black eye. It has a large red heart, to show the "good" inside him.

Bradley He's a movie star on his planet. Everybody loves him.

Carla He's very handsome.

Bradley You want it? I mean, I don't want it anyway, so you can have it.

Carla I'd love it! Thank you.

Bradley I'm going to be good all the time now. Even at school. And then, when everybody sees how good I am, they'll know I'm not a monster.

---

1 ray gun ['reɪ gʌn] *Strahlenpistole, -gewehr* 2 (to) treat [triːt] *behandeln* 3 buried deep inside him ['berid] *tief in ihm vergraben* 4 handsome ['hænsəm] *attraktiv, gut aussehend* 5 conversation [ˌkɒnvə'seɪʃn] *Gespräch, Unterhaltung*

Understanding the play

a) *Why does Bradley choose the topic 'Monsters from outer space' for his talk with Carla? Who does he think 'the monster' is?*

b) *Why doesn't Carla believe in monsters?*

c) *Bradley asks, 'How does a monster stop being a monster'? Take turns to think of how 'monsters' could be friendlier.*

– I think if people smiled when they said hello, that would be good.
– Aggressive people should try to be ...

Scene 11 Outside

Melinda C'mon, Colleen. Ask him.

Colleen looks away.

Lori Colleen has something she wants to ask you.

Colleen Well, see, um, okay, well ...

Jeff Quit bothering me.

Lori We're not bothering you. Colleen just wants to ask you ...

Melinda *(Stops her.)* Let Colleen ask him.

Colleen Well, see ... Okay. *(She takes a breath.)* I'm ...

Jeff I don't want her asking me anything! And quit saying hello to me.

Melinda We can say hello if we want. It's a free country.

Jeff I don't want you saying it to me.

Colleen *(Angry.)* Don't worry! I won't!.

Lori I will. Hello, hello, hello, hello, hello.

Jeff Shut up!

Lori Hello, Jeff, hello, Jeff, Jello, Jeff. *(She laughs.)* Jello, Jeff. Hello Jello. *(She laughs some more.)*

Jeff And quit laughing!

Colleen She can laugh. You can't tell her she can't laugh.

Lori Hello-hello-hello-hello-hello.

Jeff *(Shouts.)* Shut up!

Melinda You shut up.

Jeff I'm not afraid of you, Melinda.

Melinda I'm not afraid of you either.

They both raise their fists. Melinda is much more confident than the last time. Lori is very excited.

Jeff Okay, hit me.

Melinda You hit me first.

Jeff No, you hit me first.

Lori Somebody hit somebody!

Jeff lightly taps Melinda's shoulder with his fist. He doesn't really want to fight. She now hits him over and over again in the face and body. She knocks him down. She climbs on top of him, her knees on his chest. Lori kneels down and hits the ground as she counts.

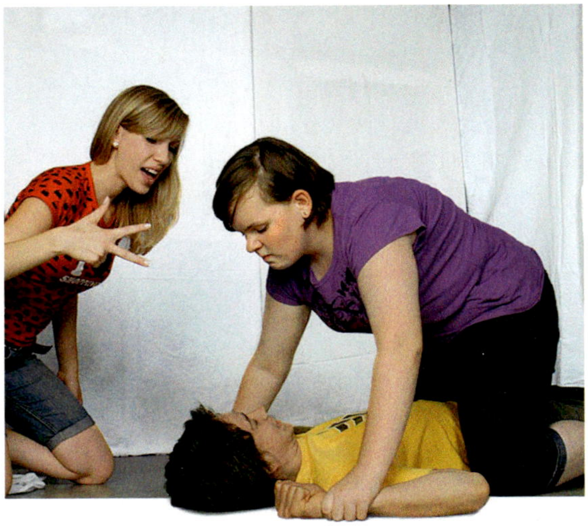

Lori One ... two ... three ... four ... five ... six ... seven ... eight ... nine ... ten!

Melinda gets up. Lori holds Melinda's hand up in the air.

Lori The winner and still champion of the world – Marvelous Melinda!

Colleen claps her hands. The three girls walk away as Jeff is still on the ground.

Understanding the play

Explain why Jeff acts the way he does towards the girls at the beginning of the scene. What does it have to do with him and Bradley?

Scene 12 The schoolyard

Bradley is doing his homework as Colleen walks by.

Bradley Hello Colleen. It's a pleasure to see you today.

Colleen looks at him as if he's the weirdest kid in the world. Enter, Robbie, Brian and Jeff.

---

[1] (to) take a breath [breθ] *Luft holen* [2] not ... either ['aɪðə, 'i:ðə] *auch nicht* [3] confident ['kɒnfɪdənt] *selbstsicher, selbstbewusst* [4] (to) knock sb. down *jn. niederschlagen* [5] chest [tʃest] *Brust(korb)*

Brian holds a basketball.

Robbie Chalkers!

Bradley is backed into a corner.

Brian What's the matter, Bradley. No place to run. *(Threatens Bradley with ball.)*

Robbie Hey, Bradley, what you got there?

Bradley Homework.

Robbie Oh yeah, let me see it.

Bradley holds it to his chest.

Robbie Aw, c'mon Bradley. I just want to see it.

Bradley holds the homework in his left hand. He raises his right fist, ready to defend it.

Robbie Ooh, he wants to fight. *(Robbie backs off.)* Jeff.

Jeff walks toward Bradley, fists raised. Bradley puts his homework in his pocket, then raises both fists.

Robbie C'mon Jeff, teach him a lesson.

Brian Give him another black eye.

Bradley and Jeff stand face to face to each other, then Bradley lowers his hands as he gets an idea.

Bradley Hello, Jeff.

Robbie and Brian giggle.

Jeff Hello.

Robbie and Brian look at Jeff, surprised.

Brian C'mon, Jeff. Let him have it!

Jeff moves closer to Bradley.

Bradley It's a pleasure to see you today.

He holds out his hand. For a moment everyone else stands around unsure what to do.

Jeff So, Bradley. Do you like to play basketball?

Bradley *(After he gets over the shock.)* I'm not very good.

Brian So? *(Throws ball to Bradley.)* None of us are.

Bradley fumbles the pass, then picks up the ball. He dribbles with both hands together, and even then he loses the ball. The ball goes to Colleen. Colleen, unsure, gives the ball back to Bradley.

Bradley Thank you, Colleen.

Bradley dribbles with both hands to the basket, then stops.

Jeff Shoot, Bradley.

Brian Shoot it.

Robbie Go ahead, Bradley. Shoot.

Everyone's quiet as Bradley shoots – he misses.

Understanding the play

a) *How do the other kids react to the 'new' Bradley at first? How does Bradley change that? Find as many examples as you can.*

b) *Why does the fight between Bradley and Jeff not happen?*

Scene 13 The schoolyard

Colleen Hello, Bradley. Would you like to come to my birthday party Saturday? Jeff will be there. He's the only boy.

Bradley tries to speak, but can't.

Colleen Everyone else will be girls.

Bradley Yes!

Colleen Good.

Moves to side of stage where Melinda and Lori enter to meet her.

Bradley You're welcome. I mean thank you.

Melinda *(to Colleen)* Is he coming?

Colleen Yes.

Lori sticks out her tongue and screams.

Melinda Oh, it'll be fun. Bradley's not like he used to be. He's changed.

Colleen Oh, you can't come anymore, Melinda.

Melinda *(Hurt.)* What? Why not?

Colleen *(Looks at Melinda, surprised Melinda has to ask.)* Because, Bradley and Jeff are coming. And you beat them both up.

[1] (to) be backed *(zurück)gedrängt werden* [2] (to) threaten ['θretn] *(be)drohen* [3] (to) defend [dɪ'fend] *verteidigen* [4] (to) back off *zurückweichen* [5] (to) lower ['ləʊə] *sinken lassen* [6] Let him have it! *Gib's ihm!* [7] none of us [nʌn] *keiner von uns* [8] tongue [tʌŋ] *Zunge*

For a moment Melinda is too shocked to speak.

Melinda They started it.

Colleen and Melinda stare at each other.

Melinda I thought I was your best friend.

Colleen You are. But they're boys! *(Sighs.)* Oh, okay. You can come. But you better not cause any more trouble.

Colleen and Melinda exit. Lori follows.

Lori I thought I was your best friend. *(She exits.)*

Scene 14 The counselor's office

Bradley I've never been to a birthday party!

Carla Never?

Bradley A long time ago, in third grade, I went to one. But they made me go home because I sat on the cake.

Carla Well, you're not in third grade anymore.

Bradley But I don't know what to do! Maybe I just shouldn't go.

He waits for Carla to say something, but she just looks at him.

Carla You want to know what I think? I think you're a little overwhelmed by all that has happened to you. *(Pause.)*

Bradley Do I have to bring a present?

Carla You don't have to do anything. But it's a nice thing to do, don't you think?

Bradley What should I get her? Should I get her perfume? Is that what girls like?

Carla *(Shrugs.)* Give her something you like. If you like it, then she probably will too. Give her a gift from the heart.

'A gift from the heart'

Discuss a nice present that Bradley could bring to Colleen's birthday party. Give reasons for your choice and agree on the best present.

Scene 15 The counselor's office

A week later. Bradley enters. He's holding a wrapped present. Carla doesn't notice him.

Bradley It's a pleasure to see you today.

Carla Bradley!

Bradley Well I went to Colleen's birthday party.

Carla How was it?

Bradley The best one I've ever been to.

They both laugh.

Bradley Remember, you told me to give Colleen a gift from the heart. Well you know what I gave her? A real heart. Well not a real one. It was a model of a heart. You can take it apart and put it back together and see what the insides look like. The way the blood goes.

Carla Sounds neat.

Bradley It was my dad's idea. I didn't know what to get a girl. I told him what you said – a gift from the heart. You know what? He once gave my mom a model of a heart for Valentine's Day. That was before they married. I mean, I'm not going to marry Colleen or anything. I just thought it sounded like a neat gift.

Carla *(Points toward the present.)* So, why ...

Bradley *(Embarrassed.)* Oh, that's for you.

Carla For me? Thank –

Bradley Guess what?

Carla What?

Bradley We had a math test. I got a hundred per cent. I'd show it to you, but I can't, know why?

Carla Why?

Bradley Because it's hanging on the wall in Mrs. Ebbel's room.

Carla goes to Bradley as if to hug him, but he holds out his hand. She gives him a firm handshake.

---

1 (to) sigh [saɪ] *seufzen* 2 (to) cause [kɔːz] *verursachen* 3 overwhelmed [ˌəʊvəˈwelmd] *überwältigt* 4 gift [gɪft] *Geschenk, Gabe* 5 neat [niːt] *(AE, infml) super* 6 (to) hug [hʌg] *umarmen, in den Arm nehmen* 7 firm [fɜːm] *fest*

Working with the text

1 Your reactions to the play

a) *Which character do you think is most interesting? Which would you most like to meet? Why?*

I think ... is most interesting because he/she ...
... is the only one who ...
... says what he/she is really thinking.
... tries very hard[1] to be good.
... is very helpful/funny/...

b) *Would you like the character you chose in a) as a friend in real life? Why (not)?*

I'd like ... as a friend because ...
I wouldn't want ... as a friend because ...
... would make me angry / drive me crazy[2] / ...
... would be a great/terrible friend because he/she ...

c) *Which of the following adjectives describes what you think of the play? Explain.*

boring • exciting • funny • heart-warming • realistic • sad • silly • unrealistic

2 The characters

a) *Make a diagram like the one below on a piece of A4 paper. How do the three main characters feel about each other when they first meet? How does each character behave[3] to the others? Make notes on your diagram.*

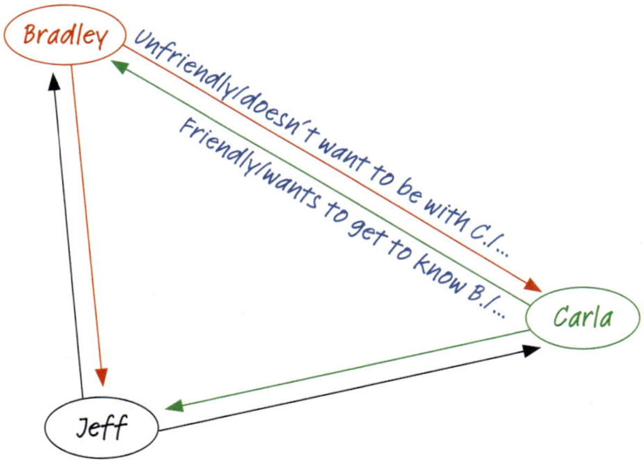

b) *Do the characters' feelings about each other change by the end of the play? How and why? Make notes. Then write a few sentences about each of the characters. Words and phrases from the box may help you.*

+aggressive • at the beginning she thinks ... • at the end he understands that ... • doesn't want to show his/her real feelings • feels very alone • gentle[4] • unfriendly/ ... • isolated[5] • thinks everbody is good • wants to fit in • wants to be friends •

3 Doing the play

a) *Make a list with all the scenes and the characters who appear in each scene. Choose a character you think you could play.*

b) *Form groups, at least one for each scene. Practise your scene: read it out loud three or four times. How does your character speak? How might he/she move etc.?*

c) *If you have time, learn your part and rehearse the play with your group. Put it on for other students in your year/ the school/ your parents/ ...*

Or: Sit in front of the class and do a dramatic reading of the play. Your class could vote for the best group.

---

1 (to) try very hard *sich sehr bemühen, sich anstrengen* 2 (to) drive sb. crazy *jn. wahnsinnig machen* 3 (to) behave [bɪˈheɪv] *sich verhalten*
4 gentle [ˈdʒentl] *sanft(mütig)* 5 isolated [ˈaɪsəleɪtɪd] *isoliert, abgesondert*

Unit 1

1 The five boroughs of New York

a) *Listen to your partner. Which of the five boroughs of New York is she/he describing?*

b) *Now read out the texts below. Your partner must decide which boroughs you're describing.*

- A famous ferry goes between this borough – also an island – and Manhattan. On the way it goes past the Statue of Liberty. It's south west of Manhattan.[1]
- There's a river between this borough and the island of Manhattan. It's north of Manhattan. Lots of famous black singers and bands come from here.[2]

[1] The correct answer is 'Staten Island'.
[2] The correct answer is 'Bronx'.

9 EVERYDAY ENGLISH SPEAKING Making plans together

You and your partner are on holiday in New York. It's your last day. You want to spend the day together, but you have different ideas about what to do.

a) *Listen to your partner's activities and take notes.*

b) *You want to go to the places below. Tell your partner:*

– where you want to go
– where the places are, what they cost, when you can go there
– one reason why you would like to go there

c) *Now talk to her/him and decide where you'd like to go together – one place in the morning, one place in the afternoon. You each have $20. Check the prices and opening hours.*

American Museum of Natural History

Here you'll find the largest and probably one of the most awesome dinosaur collections in the world. You'll find the museum at Central Park West and 79th Street in New York City.
Open daily, 10:00 a.m.–5:45 p.m.
Adults: $14.00, **Children:** (2–12): $8.00

The World's Largest Department Store

Macy's – New York's most famous department store! With 10 floors and half a million things for sale – you'll need lots of time! Open 9 to 9! Herald Square (6th Avenue and 34th Street)

Unit 1

Working with the text

This is the beginning of the next chapter[1].

It was getting dark. I sat in silence. Kelly – Kelsey? – looked at the sidewalk. My world was upside down[2]. That huge Fifth Avenue apartment was hers! But why couldn't she tell me? I bet[3] she was laughing at me all the time! Yes, I was angry. But she looked so sad sitting there, like a kid who had stolen something and didn't know what would happen next.

She was rich, so what[4]! She was just Kelly to me.

"Hey," I said and put my arm around her. "Relax, okay? I'm not going to send you to the principal's[5] office, OK?"

"Oh, Anthony ..." She started crying louder now, I held her close and said again and again,

"It's OK. It's OK." I wished[6] I could hold her forever.

---

[1] chapter ['tʃæptə] *Kapitel* [2] upside down [ˌʌpsaɪd 'daʊn] *auf den Kopf gestellt* [3] (to) bet [bet], bet, bet *wetten*
[4] so what [səʊ 'wɒt] *(infml) na und* [5] principal ['prɪnsəpl] *Schulleiter/in* [6] (to) wish [wɪʃ] *(sich) wünschen*

Unit 2

11 Which came first? (Passive – simple past)

a) *Your partner is going to say what he/she thinks came first. Listen and correct his/her statements if they're wrong. Use these dates.*

1 Eiffel Tower (build): 1887 ◂▸ first car (make): 1885
A: I think the Eiffel Tower was built before the first car was made.
B: No, that's wrong. The first car was made in ..., and the Eiffel Tower was ...

2 America (discover) by Columbus: 1492 ◂▸ China (visit) by Marco Polo: 1266
3 Mona Lisa (paint): 1506–1519 ◂▸ St. Paul's Cathedral (finish): 1708
4 first plane (fly): 1903 ◂▸ first underground railway (open): 1863

b) *Look at each pair of pictures. Guess which of the two came first. Tell your partner what you think.*

5

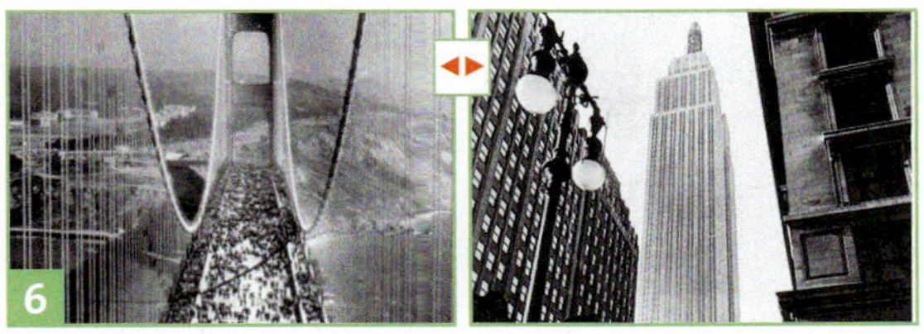
6

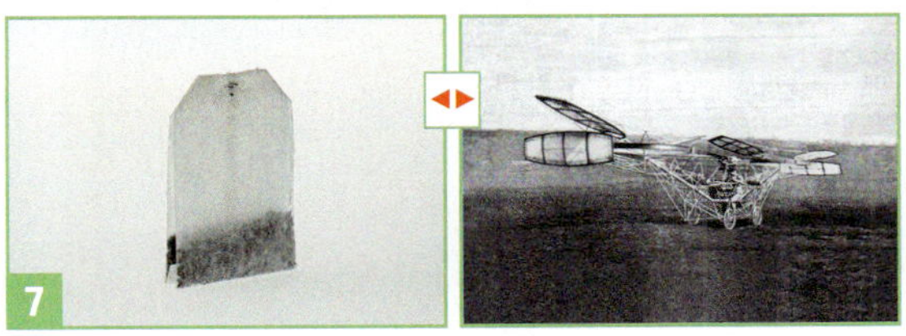
7

8

5 planet Uranus (discover) ◂▸ first slaves (bring) to America
6 Golden Gate Bridge (finish) ◂▸ Empire State Building (build)
7 first tea bags (sell) ◂▸ first helicopter (fly)
8 John F. Kennedy (kill) ◂▸ Berlin Wall (build)

Unit 2

14 EVERYDAY ENGLISH SPEAKING At a theme park (asking for travel information)

a) *Your partner has information on 'Adventure Park' near San Clemente. Ask him/her about the following:*

1 exciting attractions for teens
2 opening hours
3 ticket prices
4 special tickets

b) *Now read the information on this poster for 'Movie Park Hollywood'. Use the information to answer your partner's questions.*

Unit 3

11 WORDS Using numbers

Partner B

a) *Read the following information about Los Angeles, the second largest city in the US. Listen to Partner A and fill in the information about St. Louis in a copy of the chart. Tell your partners about L.A. Then listen to Partner C and fill in the information about New York.*

	St. Louis	Los Angeles	New York
founded in		1781	
population		3,844,00	
area		1290 sq km	
average temperature		12°C (winter) 22°C (summer)	
largest ethnic group		Hispanic (46.5%)	

B: Los Angeles was founded in 1781. The population ...

b) *Which city is the oldest city? Which has got the most Hispanic people? Which is coldest in winter?*

Unit 4

11 The US has had 50 states ... (since/for)

a) *Answer your partner's questions. Use the* ***present perfect*** *with* ***since*** *or* ***for****.*

1 *A:* How long has the US had 50 states?
B: The US has had 50 states ... over 50 years.
2 Washington ... (be) the US capital ... 1800.
3 The railway ... (link) the East Coast with the West Coast ... 1869.
4 The White House ... (be) the home of US presidents ... more than 200 years.

b) *Use the words below to ask questions with* ***How long ... + present perfect****. Note down your partner's answers.*

5 Georgia/be/state?
6 Atlanta/be/the capital of Georgia?
7 Atlanta/have/black mayors?
8 Martin Luther King/be/dead?

Georgia State Capitol, Atlanta

Unit 3

11 WORDS Using numbers

Partner C

c) *Read the following information about New York, the largest city in the US. Listen to your partners and fill in a copy of the chart. Then tell your partners about New York.*

	St. Louis	Los Angeles	New York
founded in			1614
population			8,215,000
area			1214.4 sq km
average temperature			1°C (winter) 25°C (summer)
largest ethnic group			White (44.5%)

C: New York was founded in 1614. The population ...

d) *Which city is the oldest city? Which has got the most Hispanic people? Which is coldest in winter?*

TF 1–12 Inhalt

TF 1 The President and Mr Muir

Read this page about President Roosevelt and John Muir. Find out what both men found interesting.

Theodore Roosevelt
(1858–1919, US President 1901–1909)

Theodore Roosevelt at age 25

As a boy, Theodore Roosevelt was weak and often ill. He had asthma and had to spend lots of time in bed. Because other boys bullied him, his father sent him to boxing lessons. Boxing made Theodore strong and fit. When he was at university, he not only boxed, but rowed[1] for the university team.

Theodore not only loved sports – he loved nature too. When he was only seven, he started his own natural history museum, and at age nine he wrote about insects. Later he published books about birds.

Theodore Roosevelt's other great love was books: he read one or more a day for most of his life. And he could remember everything in those books! He read all the books he could get his hands on[2], and one day he discovered the books of John Muir.

John Muir
(1838–1914)

John Muir at age 23

John Muir was eleven years old when his family left Scotland to live in the US. The Muirs had a farm in the state of Wisconsin, and John later went to university in Madison, Wisconsin. It was there that he had his first botany lesson. After that he decided another university was better for him: the 'university of the wilderness[3]'.

In those days, the eastern US had more nature than cities and towns, and Muir walked from Indiana to Florida to enjoy the wilderness. His plan was to go from Florida to South America, but when he got malaria, he decided that California was a better idea.

When Muir arrived in San Francisco, he found the big city (149,000 people) terrible. He wanted to be outdoors, in nature. He had read about the beautiful Yosemite Valley 300 km east of San Francisco – so he walked there.

---

[1] (to) row [rəʊ] *rudern* [2] all the books he could get his hands on *alle Bücher, die er finden konnte* [3] wilderness ['wɪldənəs] *Wildnis*

Muir loved Yosemite, and over the following years he fought everybody – from the governor of California to big businesses[1] – to protect the place. He wrote books, articles and lots of letters to tell people that they must protect nature everywhere.

A camping trip

When the people of Yosemite Valley heard that the President of the United States was coming, they were very excited. They wanted to welcome him with a bang[2]: they spent $ 400 on fireworks – a lot of money in 1903! They got special lights to light the waterfalls of the Valley. They even got a cook from a French restaurant in San Francisco.

But President Roosevelt had other plans. He had written to Mr Muir and suggested that the two of them go camping. And that's what they did: President Theodore Roosevelt and Mr John Muir spent four days and three nights in Yosemite. Under the stars, without a tent. Muir talked a lot while he was with the President. He talked about nature, and how important it was to protect it. And the President listened. When he got back to Washington, D.C., Roosevelt started the work that saved Yosemite, and later other natural places in the US. By the time he left the White House in 1909, there were 51 national parks. Roosevelt and Muir did more to preserve[3] nature in the US than anyone before or after them. John Muir is often called the 'Father' of the American national parks.

Today the National Park Service (founded[4] in 1916) protects almost 400 different places – 3.6 % of the US! Nearly 300 million people enjoy these places every year – about 3.5 million go to Yosemite alone.

Yosemite Falls

The 'California quarter' remembers Muir.

Roosevelt and Muir in Yosemite

1 What do you think?

Why was the Roosevelt–Muir camping trip important? Could a trip like that happen today?

2 US national parks today

Find out about one of today's US national parks. Where is it? How big is it? What can you see and do there?

---

[1] business ['bɪznəs] *Unternehmen* [2] with a bang [bæŋ] *mit einem Knalleffekt* [3] (to) preserve [prɪ'zɜːv] *bewahren, erhalten*
[4] (to) found [faʊnd] *gründen*

TF 2 New York – poems, an essay and a song

1 Choose a phrase

Read the five texts A–E. Then write down one word or phrase that you like or find interesting in each. Explain why.

I wrote down 'tickle the sun' because it's funny to imagine that a building tickles the sun and …

A The city

If flowers want to grow
right out of the concrete[1] sidewalk cracks[2]
I'm going to bend down[3] to smell them.

by David Ignatow

B Skyscraper

Skyscraper, skyscraper
Scrape[4] me some sky:
Tickle[5] the sun
While the stars go by.
Tickle the stars
While the sun's climbing high,
Then skyscraper, skyscraper
Scrape me some sky.

by Dennis Lee

C Subway rush hour

Mingled[6]
breath[7] and smell
so close
mingled
black and white
so near
no room for fear[8]

by Langston Hughes

[1] concrete ['kɒŋkriːt] *Beton* [2] crack [kræk] *Riss* [3] (to) bend down [bend], bent, bent [bent] *sich hinunterbeugen* [4] (to) scrape *kratzen*
[5] (to) tickle ['tɪkl] *kitzeln* [6] mingled ['mɪŋgld] *vemischt* [7] breath [breθ] *Atem* [8] fear [fɪə] *Angst*

D To the visitor

Visitors force[1] you to think. They arrive with that helpless do-with-me-what-you-will look and when you ask what they'd like to do or see they say, 'Oh, what's good?'

What's good? In New York?

You tell them – gently – that this is New York where everything is good. Everything, baby.

A hot dog at Nathan's in Coney Island is good.

A westward walk on the Brooklyn Bridge when the sun is setting[2] in New Jersey is good.

A ride on the Staten Island Ferry at sunset when the sky is a golden backdrop[3] to the Statue of Liberty and Ellis Island is very good.

Walk down Broadway. Watch people lining up for the ferry to Ellis Island and the Statue of Liberty. Just look at the people. Look. You're looking at the country's history. And listen to them in their various tongues[4]. You're not eavesdropping[5]. You're listening to generations and yourself.

And all that is good.

from an essay by Frank McCourt

E New York, New York

Start spreading[6] the news: I'm leaving today
I want to be a part of it –
New York, New York

These vagabond shoes are longing to stray[7]
Right through the very heart of it –
New York, New York

I want to wake up in a city that doesn't sleep
And find I'm king of the hill, top of the heap[8]

These little town blues are melting away[9]
I'm gonna make a brand new start of it –
in old New York
If I can make it there, I'll make it anywhere[10]
It's up to you – New York, New York

Song by Fred Ebb

2 A word-picture of New York

What picture of New York did the texts give you? Write down phrases that come to your mind.

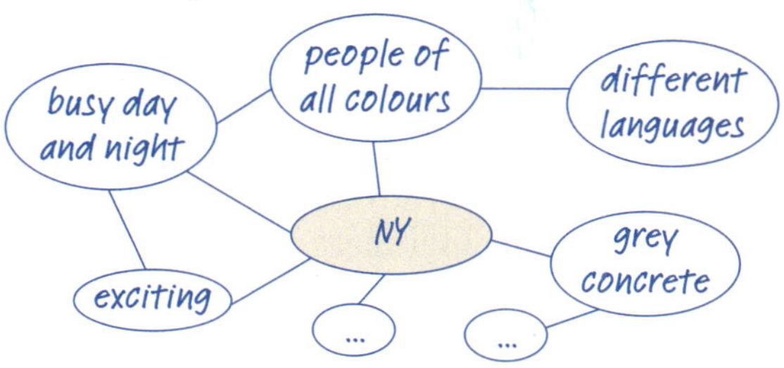

3 Now you

a) *Learn your favourite poem. Say it for your partner. Explain why you like it.*

b) *Would you like to do the things Frank McCourt describes? Why? If not, what would you like to do?*

c) *Why do you think the singer wants to go to New York? Would you like to go there? Why (not)?*

1 (to) force [fɔːs] *zwingen* 2 (to) set [set], set, set *untergehen (Sonne)* 3 backdrop *Hintergrund* 4 tongue [tʌŋ] *Sprache* 5 (to) eavesdrop ['iːvzdrɒp] *lauschen* 6 (to) spread [spred], spread, spread *verbreiten* 7 ... are longing to stray ['lɒŋɪŋ], [streɪ] *etwa: ... wollen in die Welt hinaus* 8 top of the heap [hiːp] *ganz oben* 9 (to) melt away [melt] *dahinschmelzen, sich auflösen* 10 I'll make it anywhere *ich schaffe es überall*

TF 3 'How about them Yankees?' by Louie D'Agostino

Look at the pictures. Do you know what sport this text is about?

"'How about them Yankees?' That's all you need."

"I don't understand," I said to my old English teacher, Signor Bertanelli. I had come to visit him before leaving our little town in Sicily to go to the US – I was emigrating. "Of course you don't understand, Luigi," he said. "You never were very good at English. Just remember this: 'How about them Yankees?'" He repeated it slowly, as he would to any other stupid student. "Then you will be fine when you get to New York."

I had no idea what the old man was talking about, but he had always been nice to me, although I was terrible at English. So I decided that I would remember the question: "How about them Yankees?" It didn't take long before I understood why it was a good sentence to know. And that was before I learned that the Yankees are a baseball team from the Bronx.

I made my way to Rome airport, and soon I was sitting on a plane between two American men from Brooklyn. They asked me lots of easy questions, but after a few minutes, my English was no longer enough. I almost panicked, but then I thought of what Signor Bertanelli had told me.

"How about them Yankees?" I asked. And just as my professore had promised, it was all I needed. The two men talked the rest of the way to New York – I didn't have to say anything. Yes, this one sentence was going to help me a lot.

When I got to New York, I used Signor Bertanelli's question with the Immigration man at JFK airport. I used it to get a room, and it worked when I went to get my first job in America. For three months I washed dishes in a restaurant. (Now I own one.)

I'll never forget the night when I went to my first bar in America. I was talking to a group of guys. When I couldn't think of anything to say, I asked them, "So, how about them Yankees?" I became everybody's best friend! They bought me drinks. And they gave me my American name: Louie. As in "Hey, Joe. Meet Louie. Louie here's a big baseball fan." I had a great time, and I didn't have to pay for my beers: "Joe, Louie's drinks are on me."

Soon after that I learned that the question usually doesn't work with women. (My wife was an exception[1].) And that there are men who don't like baseball. (Not many though.) And that you have to be careful: Queens has its own baseball team, the Mets, and Mets fans aren't very friendly if you ask them the question. (This was especially true in 2000, when the Mets lost the World Series[2] to the Yankees.)

After a few months in the US, I was a big Yankees fan and a regular[3] at their home games at Yankee Stadium in the Bronx. I still am. And now I can talk with the best of them when somebody uses that great conversation opener[4], "How about them Yankees?" Thank you, Signor Bertanelli.

Yankee stadium has room for about 53,000 fans.

---

[1] exception [ɪk'sepʃn] *Ausnahme* [2] World Series *Finale der beiden US-amerikanischen Baseball-Profiligen* [3] regular *Stammgast*
[4] conversation opener [ˌkɒnvə'seɪʃn] *wörtlich: Gesprächseröffner*

Baseball in everyday language

In American English some very common[1] phrases have come from baseball.

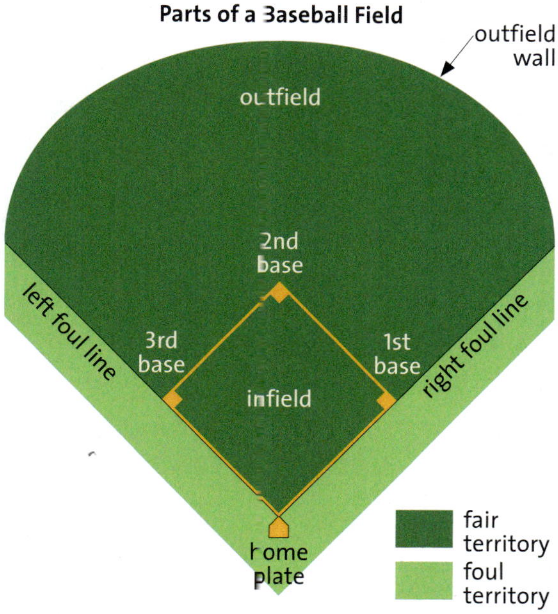

■ out of the ballpark

As in: "The batter hit the ball out of the ballpark."
Common use: "She wants $75 for her old MP3 player. That price is way out of the ballpark."
Means: The price is much too high.

■ get to first base

As in: "It wasn't a very good hit, but he got to first base with it."
Common use: "I tried to do the Math homework, but I couldn't even get to first base."
Means: I couldn't even do a small part of it.

■ throw somebody a curveball

As in: "Wilkins can usually hit the ball well, but not if somebody throws him a curveball."
Common use: "I thought I was ready for the test, but the teacher really threw me a curveball."
Means: The teacher asked questions that I wasn't expecting.

1 Understanding the story

Right or wrong? Correct the wrong statements.

1. Louie has always spoken English well.
2. The question 'How about them Yankees?' works with everybody in New York.
3. Today Louie is a baseball fan.
4. Louie has been successful in the US.

2 Sport phrases in German

What sport expressions do you know in German? Can you explain what they mean in English?

[1] common ['kɒmən] *weit verbreitet, häufig*

TF 4 Earthquakes in California

1 An eyewitness account[1]

Read what a teenager said after the Northridge earthquake in 1994.

- *How did he feel during the earthquake? What happened?*
- *How did he and his father react?*

I was asleep when the earthquake came. I was so scared and I didn't know what to do. The house was shaking so bad that I couldn't even walk. My dad came into my room and got me and we got under the table. We could see the refrigerator[2] sliding back and forth across the kitchen with its door opening and shutting and all of the stuff falling out onto the floor. Our TV went flying across the room and smashed into[3] the wall. All over we could hear things breaking. Then the lights went out. After it stopped we went outside. We could see all of the other people outside too. They were crying and looking around. Part of our apartment building fell down and now those people have to find another place to live. We might have to too.

2 After an earthquake

Explain how an earthquake affects[4] people.

Activate your English

- The photos show different results of an ...
- A lot of roads/buildings are destroyed[5] and ...
- There is a lot of rubble[6] everywhere ...
- Some people are injured ...

[1] eyewitness account ['aɪwɪtnəs‿ə'kaʊnt] *Augenzeugenbericht* [2] refrigerator [rɪ'frɪdʒəreɪtə] *Kühlschrank* [3] (to) smash into sth. [smæʃ] *gegen etwas krachen* [4] (to) affect [ə'fekt] *sich auswirken auf* [5] (to) destroy [dɪ'strɔɪ] *zerstören* [6] rubble ['rʌbl] *Schutt*

3 Southern California earthquakes

a) *Read the text and find the most important facts about earthquakes in Southern California.*

Southern California has thousands of earthquakes every year. A few are damaging[1], but people don't feel most of them. In California there are two continental plates, the Pacific Plate and the North American Plate. An earthquake happens when these plates move and scrape[2] against each other. The boundary[3] between these two plates is the San Andreas fault. It is more than 1,000 km long and up to 15 km deep. The Pacific plate moves northwestward past the North American Plate at a rate of about 50 millimetres per year. That is about how fast your fingernails grow. As a result, Los Angeles City Hall is now 2.7 metres closer to San Francisco than when it was built in 1924.

San Andreas fault

b) *Look at the map and the diagram and answer these questions:*

- Which plates are San Francisco and Los Angeles on?
- What does the diagram show?

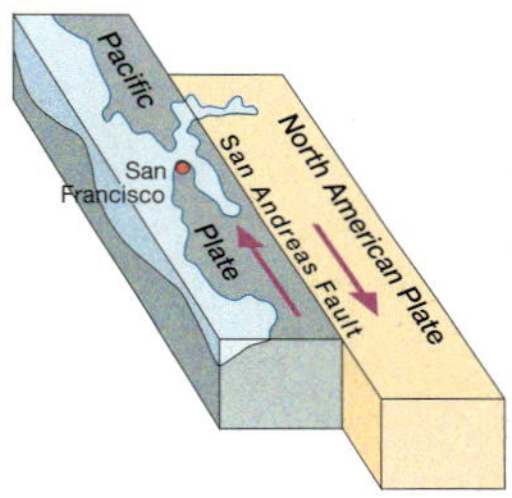

Activate your English

- The diagram shows ... One block moves from ... to ..., the other ... in the opposite direction.
- Part of the Pacific Ocean and Southern California is on ...,

4 Steps to earthquake safety[4]

a) *Look at the poster on the right. Work in groups and find more examples*
- *for things you should secure[5]*
- *for things you should put in a disaster kit*
- *for things you should do after an earthquake.*

b) *Discuss your results in class.*

c) *Design a poster to help people prepare for an earthquake. Add little drawings like this one.*

1 Secure[5] things
as computers, ...

2 Make disaster kits[6]
with food and water, ...

3 Drop, cover, and hold on!
Learn what to do during an earthquake. During earthquakes, drop to the floor, take cover under a desk or table, and hold on to it.

4 Check it out!
One of the first things you should do after an earthquake is to check ...

[1] (to) damage ['dæmɪdʒ] *Schaden anrichten; Schäden verursachen* [2] (to) scrape *reiben* [3] boundary ['baʊndri] *Grenze*
[4] safety ['seɪfti] *Sicherheit* [5] (to) secure [sɪ'kjʊə] *befestigen, sichern* [6] disaster kit [dɪ'zɑːstə kɪt] *Katastrophenausrüstung*

TF 5 Child labour[1] on the US-Mexican border

1 A case study[2]

Many US farmers have large fruit and vegetable farms in northern Mexico because farm workers there get only US$ 11 a day: in California they would earn about US$ 9 an hour. These workers are mainly from southern Mexico. They can't make enough money on their own farms, so they go north and work for the American farmers. Often their children work too. Most of the fruit and vegetables grown on these farms are exported to the US.

> *Why do US farmers have farms in Mexico? Why do workers in Mexico work for so little money?*

■ MEXICO CITY.

by Chris Hawley, The Arizona Republic (adapted)

Adriana Salgado, 10, spends her days in a field in north-western Mexico picking spinach, cabbage and other vegetables that fill American salad bowls.

Adriana attends school for only one hour a day, and still hasn't learned to read. Her 15-year-old sister, who works with her, can't read either. Adriana had an 8-year-old brother too, but he was killed by a tractor while he was working in a tomato field last year.

Even after her brother's death Adriana had to continue to work. This shows how deep the problem is. About 300,000 youngsters like Adriana work illegally in Mexico's fields. Cruz Salgado, Adriana's father, says his family needs the extra $7 a day that Adriana contributes[3]: the $20 a day he and his wife earn as migrant workers just isn't enough to live on. The children are not official employees[4] but because adult workers earn extra money for picking more than their daily quota[5], parents with 'helpers' take more money home.

'I wish they didn't have to work,' Mr Salgado said by telephone from a migrant camp in the state of Sinaloa. 'But we need the money.'

From 6 to 7 pm, Adriana Salgado goes to school. Asked if she enjoyed working, she said, 'Not much. I like school.'

a) *Copy and complete the flow chart below.*

American farmers move their farms to Mexico because ... → Farmers from southern Mexico work on these farms because ... → Their children work there too because ...

↓

Because the children work in the fields, they ... → Because they can't go to school, they ... → Without any education, they ...

b) *Compare the child labour law in Mexico to the information in the article. What do you notice? Compare the laws in Mexico and Germany.*

Child Labour Laws in Mexico

To work full-time, children
- must be at least 14
- must have finished secondary school.

Child Labour Laws in Germany

Children between 13 and 15 are only allowed to
- do a paper round[6]
- do babysitting or look after pets
- go shopping for others

[1] labour ['leɪbə] *Arbeit* [2] case study ['keɪs stʌdi] *Fallstudie* [3] (to) contribute [kən'trɪbjuːt] *beitragen, beisteuern*
[4] employee [ɪm'plɔɪiː] *Arbeitnehmer/in, Angestellte(r)* [5] quota ['kwəʊtə] *Quote, Pensum* [6] (to) do a paper round *Zeitungen austragen*

2 Child labour around the world

a) *Describe what the map below shows. Compare the situation in Mexico, Central Africa and Europe.*

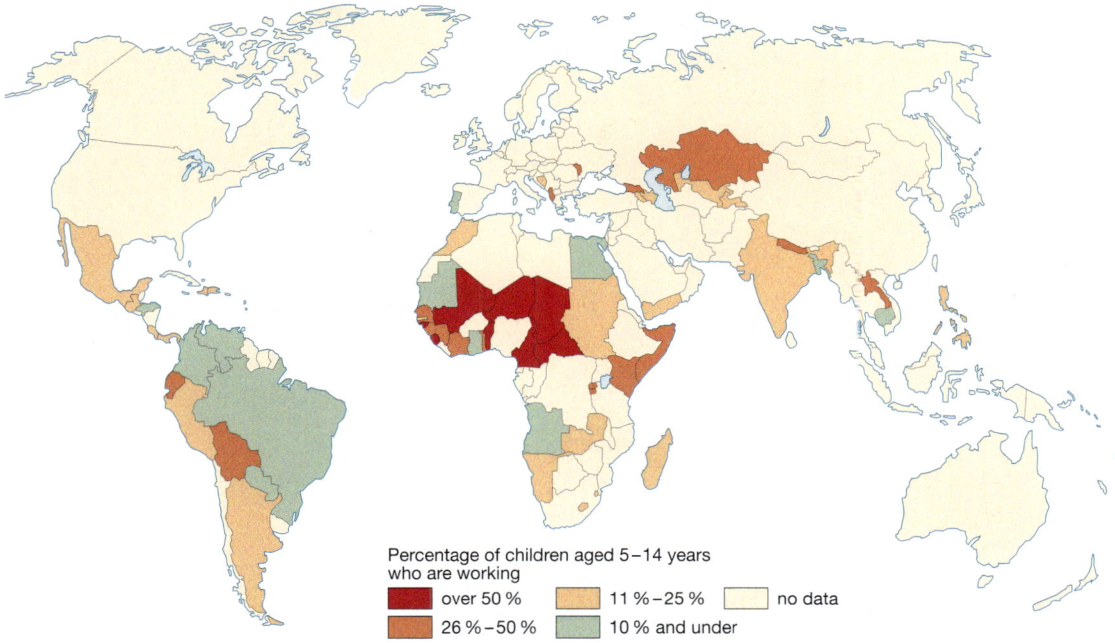

GEOGRAPHY SKILLS **Talking about maps**

When you talk about maps,
- look at the title and the key[1] and make sure you understand what the map is about.
- start with a general statement about the map, then talk about details.

Activate your English
- The map shows/gives information about ...
- This is a map of ...
- It shows the percentage[2] of children ...
- In Mexico between 11 and 25 % of all children aged 5 to 14 ...

b) *Read the Fast facts. If the percentages were the same for Germany, how many working children would there be here? (In Germany there were about 12 million children under 15 in 2006.)*

Fast facts

→ About 17 per cent of the world's children – 246 million in all – have to work.
→ Just over 50 % of the world's working children live in the Asia-Pacific region.
→ Almost a third of all working children (73 million) are under 10.

If 17 per cent of children in Germany worked ...
If the percentage for Germany was the same as for the Asia-Pacific region ...

3 Now you

Write an e-mail to the newspaper that published the article on p. 122. Say
- *what you thought when you read the article.*
- *that you did some more research on child labour and what you found out.*
- *how many working children there would be in Germany if the percentages were as high as in some other countries*
- *what it would mean for you if you didn't have the chance to go to school.*

[1] key *Legende* [2] percentage [pə'sentɪdʒ] *Prozentsatz*

TF 6 Ryan Sheckler, skateboard phenom[1]

When you walk around San Clemente, California, you just might see a TV star. That's not unusual for southern California, and Orange County is as good a place as any to find the rich and the beautiful.

But this star is different: he's only 17, and he's not an actor. In the MTV reality show "Life of Ryan", Ryan Sheckler plays himself, 17-year-old skateboarding phenom Ryan Sheckler. The cameras follow him everywhere.

Ryan first got on a skateboard when he was 18 months old. By the time he was four, he was already doing tricks on the board. His parents built him a skateboard ramp when he was seven, and he soon moved on to skateparks. (He has his own now.)
He became a professional skateboarder at age 13.

Ryan has won lots of competitions[2], but he earns[3] more money from his sponsors. He gets money just for getting dressed in the morning! Lots of companies are happy to pay him money so he'll wear their clothes. Or, of course, use their sports equipment. Ryan's talent takes him all over the world. He has skated in Europe, China, Australia and even Dubai.

What about school? Like lots of young celebrities[4], Ryan goes to Futures High School in Mission Viejo, California. Futures is a private high school where he meets alone with a teacher twice a week for an hour and a half at a time. He goes away "with a pile of homework" after every meeting. But does he do it? You bet[5]! Ryan is "really good" at math, his favorite subject is Science, and he takes English very seriously. He wants to be prepared for having his own business, and good English is important for that.

[1] phenom [fə'nɒm] *(AE, infml) Phänomen* [2] competition [ˌkɒmpə'tɪʃn] *Wettbewerb, Wettkampf* [3] (to) earn [ɜːn] *verdienen*
[4] celebrity [sə'lebrəti] *Prominente(r)* [5] You bet! [bet] *(infml) Und ob! / Aber klar!*

Ryan shows his friends and younger brother the bottom of his board. His friends and family are a big part of "Life of Ryan".

What else does Ryan do? Well, at the top of his list of "likes" are skateboarding and girls. That golf is at number three will be a surprise for lots of fans. But no one will be surprised that "horrible music" and "broken bones" are high on his list of dislikes!

Ryan's advice[1] for young skaters? "Don't ever give up. You've gotta keep trying and never give up."

Skateboard safety

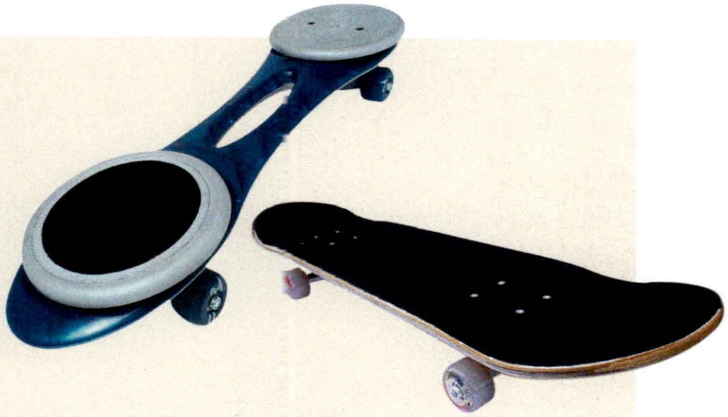

1. **Use the right board.** There are different boards for different kinds of skateboarding.

2. **Wear safety equipment.** Good shoes, helmets and pads are all important. Make sure you wear them correctly, and that they fit well. **Protect your ...**

... head

... knees

... elbows

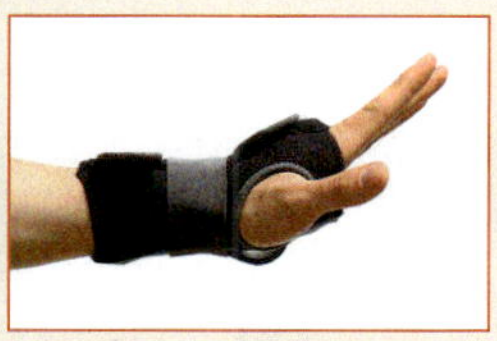

... and wrists.

3. **Learn how to fall.** Even professional skateboarders fall, and you will too. Practise falling on grass or another soft place. Roll when you fall and try to relax your body.

4. **NEVER ride in the street!**

1 What's so special about Ryan Sheckler?

a) *Make a placemat. Write 3–4 things that you find most amazing about Ryan's life in your corner of a placemat. Then agree on the top three points and write them in the middle.*

b) *Present your group's results to the class. Can the class agree on the top three things?*

c) *Write a short text (75–100 words) what's special about Ryan.*

2 Reality TV

a) *Have you ever seen a show like 'Life of Ryan'? What did you like about it? What didn't you like? Make lists.*

b) *Imagine MTV wants to do a show about your life. Would you like that? Why/Why not?*

[1] advice [əd'vaɪs] *Rat*

TF 7 Building the Gateway Arch

Since 1965, the Gateway Arch has been the symbol of St. Louis, Missouri, and a monument to the men and women who settled[1] the western US. The Arch was designed by the architect Eero Saarinen, but a team of engineers was needed to find a way to build it.

Climbing cranes[2]
The first 72 feet of the Arch were made with cranes on the ground. After that, special cranes rode up the sides with their heavy loads[3].

Triangular[4] sections
The sections were made in a factory.

Tracks[5]
Two steel tracks took the cranes up the sides. The tracks were taken away when work was finished.

Elevator
A special elevator carried the workers up to do their jobs.

South Entrance

Observation Room
The view from the windows stretches for miles to the east and west.

Passenger trams
Two trams, one in each leg, take visitors to the top of the Arch. The ride takes 4 minutes.

Jefferson National Expansion Memorial
The Arch is in this park in downtown St. Louis.

Museum of Westward Expansion
Here you can see how the pioneers traveled and how they lived.

---

[1] (to) settle ['setl] *besiedeln* [2] climbing crane [kreɪn] *Kletterkran* [3] heavy load [ˌhevi 'ləʊd] *schwere Last, Ladung*
[4] triangular [traɪ'æŋgjələ] *dreieckig* [5] track [træk] *Gleis*

The skin[1]
The architect wanted it to be timeless, so he chose stainless steel[2].

Construction progress[3]

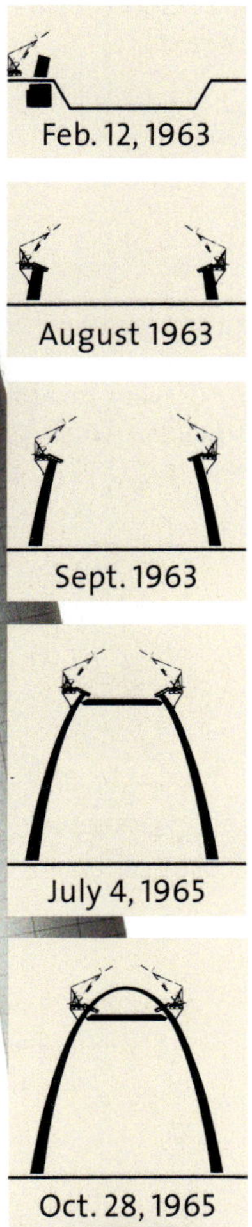

North Entrance

1 Tracks and climbing crane

2 A platform held the two legs during the last few months of construction.

3 A triangular section

4 The last piece of the Arch

1 Understanding the pictures and texts

Look carefully at the drawings, photos and texts and answer the following questions:

1. How tall is the Arch in feet? And in metres?
2. How was the work done up to 72 feet? And above that? What do you think that meant for the construction progress?
3. How long did it take to build the Arch?
4. What is the monument used for today? What can you see and do there?

2 Surprise!

Do you think the Arch is taller than it is wide, or wider than it is tall? Use your ruler to check.

3 Monuments

Find out about a different monument in the US. What is it for? When was it built? How long did it take to build it?

[1] skin [skɪn] *Haut* [2] stainless steel [ˌsteɪnləs 'stiːl] *Edelstahl, rostfreier Stahl* [3] construction progress [kən'strʌkʃn ˌprəʊgres] *Baufortschritt(e)*

TF 8 The Trail of Tears[1]

The darkest time in the history of the Cherokee people was the 'Trail of Tears', when 16,000 of them were removed[2] from the southeastern US.

[1] trail of tears [ˌtreɪl‿əv ˈtɪəz] *Pfad der Tränen* [2] (to) remove [rɪˈmuːv] *entfernen; hier: vertreiben* [3] it ain't [eɪnt] *(infml)* = *it isn't*
[4] territory [ˈterətri] *Gebiet*

5 New Echota, Georgia, November 1838

6 Somewhere in Kentucky, January 1839

7 Somewhere in Missouri, February 1839

8 New Echota Historic Site, Today

1 Getting more out of the story

Study the pictures and text carefully, then answer these questions:

1 Why did the US government want the Indians out of the southeast?
2 Why do you suppose the white settlers called the Cherokee 'civilized'?
3 Why did so many Cherokee die on the 'Trail of Tears'?

2 The Cherokee nation today

Find out about the Cherokee today. Where do they live? What are their lives like? Report to the class.

TF 9 The American Civil War (1861–1865)

1 North and South

Between 1830 and 1860, there was growing conflict between the Northern and Southern states of the US. One problem was the question of slavery. In the South, farming was the main part of the economy and slaves were used as unpaid workers on large plantations. In the Northern states, industry was more important and the economy did not use slaves.

The question of slavery was part of a much bigger problem: the relationship between the federal government[1] in Washington and the state governments. The Southern states were afraid that Washington would force them to end slavery. In their view the federal government did not have that right, and for this reason eleven states left the Union[2] in 1860/1861 and formed the Confederate States of America. They elected Jefferson Davis as their president.

The Northern states were now cut off from the southern seaports[3], which they needed to reach their export markets. They said that the secession of the Confederate States was illegal and sent soldiers to force[4] them back into the Union. A civil war began, in which Americans fought each other.

At the end of the war, the North had won. 620,000 soldiers had died – more than in any other war in US history. Many cities – especially in the South – were destroyed. The slaves were freed and the North and the South were united again under one government.

2 A timeline of the Civil War

1860	1861	1862	1863	1865
Abraham Lincoln (who is against slavery) is elected president	eleven Southern states leave the Union and form the Confederate States of America	**July 17:** blacks are allowed to join the Northern army or navy[5]	**January 1:** President Lincoln declares[6] all slaves in the Confederate States free	**April 9:** the South surrenders[7] **April 14:** President Lincoln is murdered by a supporter of the South **December 18:** slavery is abolished[8] in the US

3 The United States – divided[9] by war

a) *Describe what the map shows.*

Activate your English

- The map shows ...
- Between 1861 and 1865 the states in in the US were divided: ...
- The blue/grey area was part of the Union/...
- The green areas were part of the Union, but ...

b) *Find the following states on the map: California, Missouri, New York, Georgia. Which side were they on in the Civil War? Were they for or against slavery?*

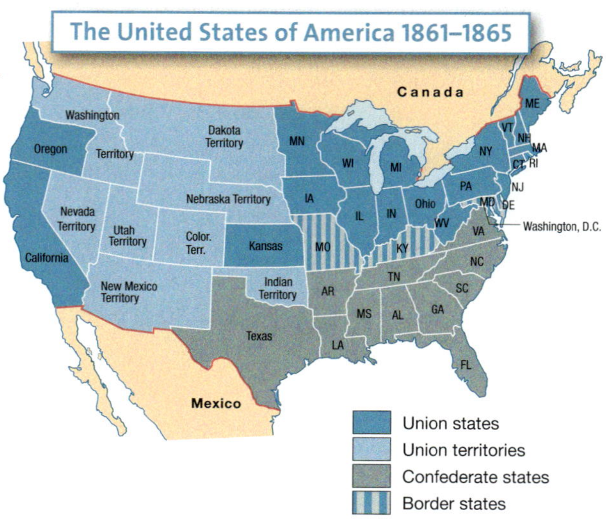

[1] federal government [ˌfedərəl ˈgʌvənmənt] *die amerikanische (Bundes-)Regierung* [2] the Union [ˈjuːniən] *die Vereinigten Staaten* [3] seaport [ˈsiːpɔːt] *Seehafen* [4] (to) force [fɔːs] *zwingen* [5] navy [ˈneɪvi] *Marine* [6] (to) declare [dɪˈkleə] *erklären* [7] (to) surrender [səˈrendə] *kapitulieren, sich ergeben* [8] (to) abolish [əˈbɒlɪʃ] *abschaffen* [9] divided [dɪˈvaɪdɪd] *geteilt* [10] (to) permit [pəˈmɪt] *erlauben*

4 The causes of the Civil War[1]

a) *Complete the notes in the box and put them in the correct column in a copy of the chart.*

didn't want to lose the southern seaports because … • used slaves because … • didn't want to end slavery because … • left the Union because … • sent soldiers south because …

The Southern states …	The Northern states …
used slaves because they needed cheap labour for their plantations. …	didn't …

b) *Write a short text about the causes of the Civil War. Use the notes in your chart.*

5 A face of the Civil War: Sullivan Ballou

a) *Read the text and the letter.*

Sullivan Ballou was a major in the Northern army. He died in the Battle[2] of Bull Run (Virginia) in July 1861. Before the battle he wrote a letter to his wife.

July 14th, 1861
Washington, D.C.

My dear Sarah,

The indications[3] are very strong that we shall move in a few days – perhaps tomorrow. […]
If it is necessary that I should fall on the battlefield for my country, I am ready. […]
And I am willing – perfectly willing – to lay down all my joys[4] in this life, to help maintain[5] this Government […].

b) *Choose the right answers.*

1 Sullivan Ballou … in the battle.
A was afraid to die B was willing to die
C expected to be hurt D lost his friend

2 He went to war because he wanted to save
A his fields. B his life.
C his government. D his family.

c) *Look at the box on the right and try to answer the questions for the letter above:*
The letter was written in … by …

HISTORY SKILLS **Primary sources[6]**

Primary sources are texts or materials that were produced at a certain[7] historical time. To understand a primary source, e.g. a letter, you have to know about its background:
- When and where was it written?
- Why was it written? Who wrote it?
- What can you learn from the text?

Check with what you already know about the background or try to find out more.

[1] causes of the Civil War ['kɔ:zɪz], [ˌsɪvl 'wɔ:] *Ursachen des (US-amerikanischen) Bürgerkriegs* [2] battle ['bætl] *Schlacht* [3] indication [ˌɪndɪ'keɪʃn] *Anzeichen* [4] I am willing to lay down all my joys [dʒɔɪz] *etwa: ich bin bereit, auf alle Freuden zu verzichten* [5] (to) maintain [meɪn'teɪn] *aufrechterhalten* [6] primary sources ['praɪməri ˌsɔ:sɪz] *Primärquellen* [7] certain ['sɜ:tn] *bestimmte(r, s)*

6 The photo and its background

a) Look at the photo and try to answer these questions. Make notes.
- When was the photo taken?
- Who are the men in the photo?
- Which army do they belong to?
- If you saw a photo of soldiers in the US army today, what would be different?
- What does your answer to the last question tell you about the historical background?

b) Read the text on the right to find out about the background of the photo.

c) In groups of three, compare your notes. Agree on answers to all the questions in a).

Activate your English
- I think the photo was taken in/between ...
- These men belonged to ...
- The main thing that would be different today is ...
- This shows that ...

The photo shows soldiers of Company E, 4th Colored Infantry Regiment at Fort Lincoln.

It was taken in 1865, after the end of the Civil War.

About 200,000 black soldiers, many of them former slaves from the South, joined the Northern army. They made up about 10% of the Northern soldiers.

Although they were often discriminated against by their white officers, black soldiers were proud to fight for the North. Many hoped that fighting in the war would help them to become citizens[1].

HISTORY SKILLS Historical photos

Historical photos can tell you a lot about past events. To understand historical photos you have to know about the context in which they were taken. Think about:
- when and where the photo was taken
- who took the photo and for what reason.

Even if you can only answer some of these questions, historical photos will help you to understand history.

TF 10 57 Channels (and Nothin' On) A song by Bruce Springsteen

How many channels can you get on your TV at home? Do you still sometimes feel that there's nothing on that you want to watch? If so, what do you do?

I bought a bourgeois house in the Hollywood hills
With a truckload of hundred thousand dollar bills
Man came by to hook up[1] my cable TV
We settled in[2] for the night my baby and me
We switched[3] 'round and 'round 'til half-past dawn
There was fifty-seven channels and nothin' on

Well now home entertainment was my baby's wish
So I hopped into town for a satellite dish
I tied it to the top of my Japanese car
I came home and I pointed it out into the stars
A message came back from the great beyond[4]
There's fifty-seven channels and nothin' on

Well we might'a[5] made some friends with some billionaires
We might'a got all nice and friendly if we'd made it upstairs
All I got was a note that said "Bye-bye John
Our love is fifty-seven channels and nothin' on"

So I bought a .44 magnum it was solid steel cast
And in the blessed name of Elvis well I just let it blast[6]
'til my TV lay in pieces there at my feet
And they busted[7] me for disturbing the almighty peace[8]
Judge said "what you got in your defense[9] son?"
"Fifty-seven channels and nothin' on"

I can see by your eyes friend you're just about gone
Fifty-seven channels and nothin' on
Fifty-seven channels and nothin' on ...

1 Right or wrong

a) *Correct the wrong statements.*

1 The singer is poor and lives in a house like the one in the photo.
2 The singer's 'baby' left him because their love was as boring as the TV programmes.
3 The TV programmes got better when the singer bought a satellite dish.
4 Elvis shot the singer's TV.

2 The music

Do you find the music exciting or boring? Do you think it fits the story in the song? Why (not)?

---

[1] (to) hook sth. up [hʊk] *etwas anschließen* [2] (to) settle in ['setl] *es sich bequem machen* [3] (to) switch [swɪtʃ] *(um)schalten* [4] the great beyond [bɪ'jɒnd] *das Jenseits* [5] might'a *(infml)* = *might have* [6] (to) blast [blɑːst] *ballern (Pistole)* [7] (to) bust so. [bʌst] *(infml) jn. festnehmen* [8] disturbing the peace [dɪ'stɜːbɪŋ], [piːs] *Hausfriedensbruch* [9] defense [dɪ'fens] *(AE) Verteidigung*

TF 11 Georgia: Portrait of a state

An American magazine has started a series of portraits of the 50 states of the USA for people to collect. This is the one for Georgia.

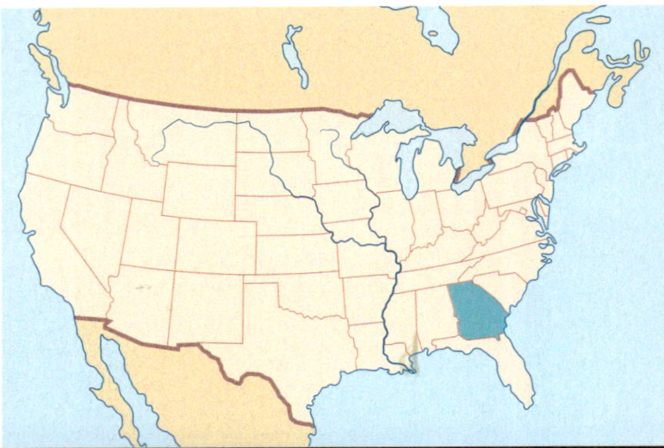

Georgia is 153,909 sq km in size – a little bigger than Greece – with a population of 8.2 million

The state capital is Atlanta (pop. 486,500)

The state bird is the brown thrasher

The state flower is the Cherokee rose

The nickname for Georgia is the Peach[5] State – that's a Georgia peach on this 25 ¢ coin

Things to see

If you go to Atlanta, make sure you see the **Martin Luther King, Jr. National Historic Site.** The museum there will give you an excellent overview of the Civil Rights Movement and Dr. King's role in it. And don't forget to stop at the graves[1] of King and his wife, Coretta Scott King.
CNN Center is always popular, and the **World of Coca-Cola** is a must for fans of the soft drink. And don't miss the **Georgia Aquarium**, one of largest in the world!
If you want to get away from the city, **Stone Mountain Park** offers beautiful nature trails[2], but also a stone carving[3] of southern Civil War generals and a Skyride to see it all from!

For an active vacation, you might want to try the Georgia coast or one of the islands there.

From snorkeling[4] to kite surfing, the Georgia coast has it all.

[1] grave [greɪv] *Grab* [2] nature trail ['neɪtʃə treɪl] *Naturlehrpfad* [3] carving ['kɑːvɪŋ] *Skulptur* [4] snorkeling ['snɔːkəlɪŋ] *Schnorcheln*
[5] peach [piːtʃ] *Pfirsich*

Southern hospitality[1]

Southern hospitality isn't just a legend. The people here really are friendly to guests – even to "Yankees" (anyone from the North). As they say down south: "Y'all are welcome!"
If you want to experience this hospitality and some great southern cooking, go to a B&B in Savannah. They're often in beautiful old homes, some from before the Civil War! You'll get "**grits**[2]" with your breakfast, a traditional iced tea in the afternoon, and if you're really lucky, a slice of home-made **pecan pie**[3] for dessert[4].

Famous Georgians

Margaret Mitchell
(1900–1949) – author of *Gone with the Wind*, a book about Atlanta in the Civil War, which was made into one of the biggest movies of all time

Dr. Martin Luther King, Jr.
(1929–1968) – civil rights leader

Jimmy Carter
(1924–) – President of the US (1977–1981), helps to build houses for poor people.

Ray Charles
(1930–2004) – Rhythm and Blues musician, sang the version of "Georgia on My Mind" that became the official state song.

1 A quiz about Georgia

a) *Write at least five questions about Georgia from the information on these two pages.*

b) *Make a quiz with eight of your best questions. Swap quizzes with another pair.*

2 A state portrait

Use the internet to find out about another US state. Write short texts, print out pictures and make a two-page portrait of your own. You can put it in your DOSSIER.

[1] hospitality [ˌhɒspɪ'tæləti] *Gastfreundschaft* [2] grits *(pl)* [grɪts] *(AE)* *Grütze* [3] pecan pie ['piːkən, *AE:* pɪ'kɑːn] *Kuchen mit Pekannüssen*
[4] dessert [dɪ'zɜːt] *Nachtisch, Dessert*

TF 12 Black music

a) Look at the photos and read the texts. Answer as many quiz questions as you can.

b) Listen to the radio quiz show. Check your answers. Listen again to complete your answers and to correct the wrong ones.

A Black music quiz

1. What were the songs called that the African-American slaves sang in the fields?
2. What were their religious songs called?
3. What's the name of the musical style that has influenced[1] rock musicians to this day?
4. The music style 'Rhythm and Blues' is better known by a shorter name. What is it?
5. What was 'the King's' real name?
6. Name at least three 'Hitsville USA' stars.
7. What are the three elements of hip hop culture?

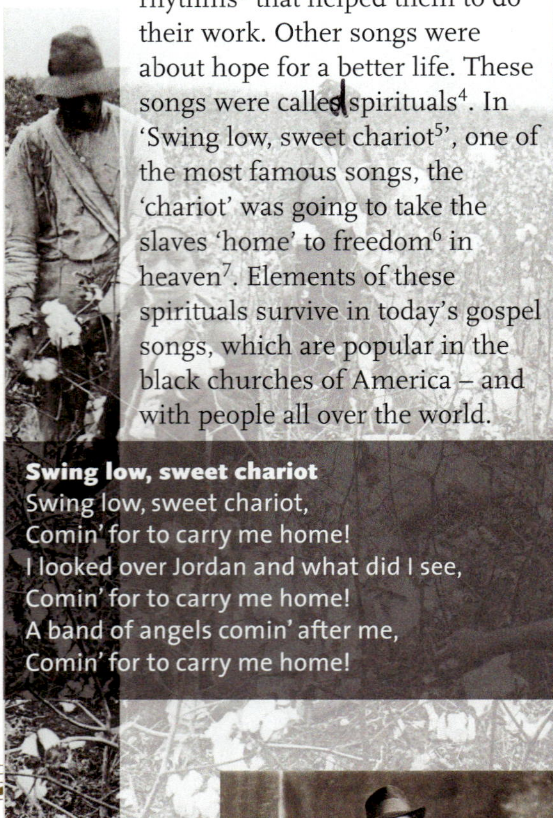

African-American slaves sang songs in the cotton fields, with rhythms[3] that helped them to do their work. Other songs were about hope for a better life. These songs were called spirituals[4]. In 'Swing low, sweet chariot[5]', one of the most famous songs, the 'chariot' was going to take the slaves 'home' to freedom[6] in heaven[7]. Elements of these spirituals survive in today's gospel songs, which are popular in the black churches of America – and with people all over the world.

Swing low, sweet chariot
Swing low, sweet chariot,
Comin' for to carry me home!
I looked over Jordan and what did I see,
Comin' for to carry me home!
A band of angels comin' after me,
Comin' for to carry me home!

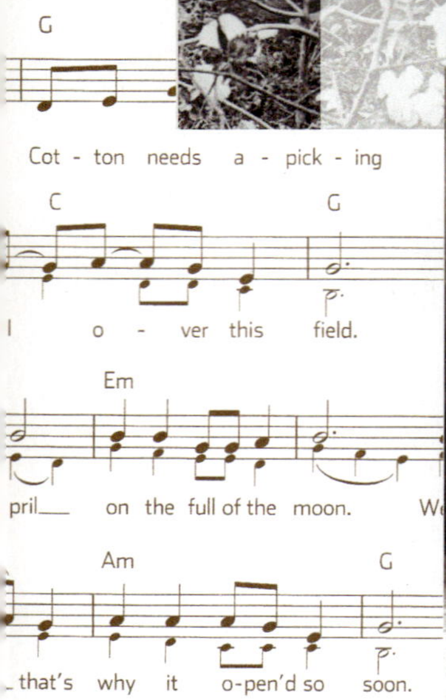

◀ Robert Johnson (1911–1938) was one of the most famous musicians of the Mississippi delta. He sang the Blues, a mix of the early slave work songs and spirituals. His musical style[8] has influenced rock musicians like Eric Clapton.
In the 1940s Blues musicians used elements of Jazz and Gospel: A new music style was created, which was later called rhythm and blues.

[1] (to) influence ['ɪnfluəns] *beeinflussen* [2] cotton ['kɒtn] *Baumwolle* [3] rhythm ['rɪðəm] *Rhythmus* [4] spiritual ['spɪrɪtʃuəl]
[5] Swing low, sweet chariot [ləʊ], ['tʃæriət] *etwa: Schwing dich herab, du himmlischer Wagen* [6] freedom ['fri:dəm] *Freiheit*
[7] heaven ['hevn] *Himmel* [8] style [staɪl] *Stil*

Johnny B. Goode
Deep down Louisiana close to New Orleans Way back up in the woods among the evergreens[1] | There stood a log cabin[2] made of earth and wood | Where lived a country boy named Johnny B. Goode | Who never ever learned to read or write so well. | But he could play the guitar just like ringing a bell. | Go go | Go Johnny go

by Chuck Berry

▲ The songs of the first rock 'n' roller, Chuck Berry (born in 1926) greatly influenced later generations of musicians.
His 'Johnny B. Goode' was a favourite of the Beatles.

▼

'The King of Rock 'n' Roll' was born on January 8, 1935 and died on August 16, 1977. He sang rock 'n' roll songs and sounded like the best African-American singers. But his skin was white. He became one of the most famous American singers and musicians ever – simply 'The King'.

◀ In a studio in this house called 'Hitsville, USA', a new style of black music was born in the 1960s. It was a mixture of rhythm 'n' blues and gospel music – great on the car radio. Its stars were James Brown, Marvin Gaye, ...

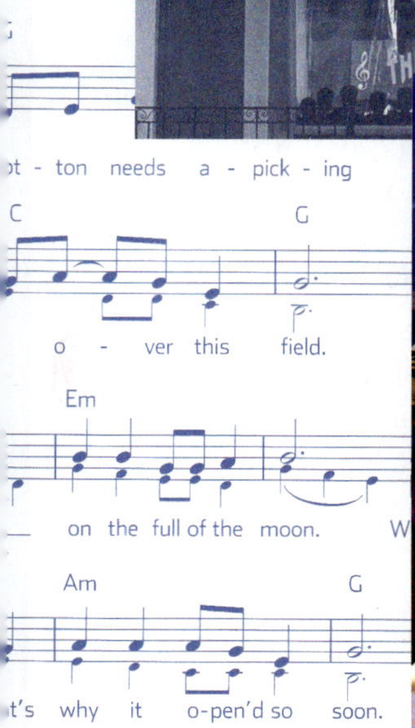

SUGAR HILL GANG

In New York City in the late 1970s DJs began to speak between songs, greeting people, telling jokes and stories, trying to keep the audience excited. A new musical style was born: rap. Although most rappers are male, female artists like Missy Elliot, Lauryn Hill or Lil' Kim have also been very successful.

[1] among the evergreens [ə'mʌŋ] *zwischen den immergrünen Bäumen* [2] log cabin [ˌlɒg 'kæbɪn] *Blockhütte*

Skills File – Inhalt

Im **Skills File** findest du Hinweise zu Arbeits- und Lerntechniken. Was du in den Skills-Kästen der Units gelernt hast, wird hier näher erläutert.

Was du bereits aus Band 3 von English G 21 kennst, ist mit **REVISION** gekennzeichnet,
z. B.
– **REVISION Describing pictures**, Seite 142
– **REVISION Giving a presentation**, Seite 142.

Viele neue Hinweise helfen dir bei der Arbeit mit Hör- und Lesetexten, beim Sprechen, beim Schreiben von eigenen Texten, bei der Sprachmittlung und beim Lernen von Methoden.

Manchmal gibt es auch Aufgaben dazu.

STUDY AND LANGUAGE SKILLS

SF REVISION Learning words

Worauf solltest du beim Lernen und Wiederholen von Vokabeln achten?

- Lerne immer 7–10 Vokabeln auf einmal.
- Lerne neue und wiederhole alte Vokabeln regelmäßig – am besten jeden Tag 5–10 Minuten.
- Lerne mit jemandem zusammen. Fragt euch gegenseitig ab.
- Schreib die neuen Wörter auch auf und überprüfe die Schreibweise mithilfe des *Dictionary* oder *Vocabulary*.

Wie kannst du Wörter besser behalten?

Wörter kannst du besser behalten, wenn du sie in Wortgruppen sammelst und ordnest:

- **Gegensatzpaare** sammeln, z. B. **alive ◄► dead**, **majority ◄► minority**, **forget ◄► remember**
- Wörter mit **gleicher Bedeutung** sammeln, z. B. **(to) train – (to) practise**
- Wörter in **Wortfamilien** sammeln, z. B. **friend**, **boyfriend**, **girlfriend**, **friendly**, **unfriendly**, **make friends, ...**
- Wörter in **Wortnetzen** *(networks)* sammeln und ordnen.

SF Check yourself ▸ *Unit 1, p. 29*

How am I doing?

Damit du weißt, in welchen Bereichen des Englischen du noch Schwächen hast und welche du schon beherrschst, solltest du dich immer wieder selbst überprüfen. Das kannst du auf unterschiedlichen Wegen tun. Eine Reihe von Tipps kennst du schon vom **Stop-Check-Go** aus Band 1–2.
Du kannst dich auch nach jeder Unit mithilfe der *How am I doing*-Seiten selbst überprüfen. Dabei gehst du wie folgt vor:

1. Du machst die einzelnen Aufgaben und überprüfst deine Ergebnisse.
2. Dann schaust du dir die Bereiche, in denen du Fehler gemacht hast, nochmal an. Halte dich dabei an die Hinweise in der Spalte Find out more.
3. Nun übst du gezielt diese Bereiche. Dazu schaust du in der Spalte Exercises nach, wo du im Englischbuch und Workbook Übungen dazu findest.
4. Nach einiger Zeit machst du die Aufgaben in How am I doing? noch einmal und vergleichst die Lösungen mit deinen Ergebnissen vom ersten Mal.

Die Arbeit mit einem persönlichen Fehlerheft

Ein weiterer, sehr hilfreicher Weg ist das Anlegen eines Fehlerheftes.
Dafür legst du dir ein DIN-A4 oder DIN-A5 Heft an. Dieses unterteilst du z. B. nach folgenden Schwerpunkten:

1. Drittel: Words 2. Drittel: Grammar 3. Drittel: Spelling

Dann untersuchst du deine Klassenarbeiten und andere schriftliche Arbeiten auf deine Fehlerquellen hin. Dein/e Englischlehrer/in zeigt durch Abkürzungen am Rand, was für eine Art Fehler du gemacht hast.

WORDS

Wrong	*Correct*	*REMEMBER*
He goes to school ~~with the~~ bus.	*He goes to school by bus.*	*mit dem Bus fahren – go by bus*
We've got a ~~strong~~ teacher.	*We've got a strict teacher.*	*Nicht verwechseln: streng – strict / strong – stark*
I climbed ~~on~~ a tree.	*I climbed a tree.*	*auf einen Baum klettern – climb a tree*

Tipp

- Ergänze das Heft jedes Mal, wenn du eine Klassenarbeit oder einen Text von deinem Lehrer/deiner Lehrerin zurückbekommen oder wenn du eine *„How am I doing"*-Seite bearbeitet hast.
- Überprüfe, ob du bestimmte Fehler immer wieder machst. Wenn ja, such dafür Übungen in deinem Englischbuch, deinem Workbook, deinem *e-Workbook* oder frag deinen Lehrer/deine Lehrerin nach Übungen.
- Schau dir vor jeder Klassenarbeit die Fehler an, die du oft machst.
- Mach dir mithilfe des Grammatikteils die Regeln, die dir besonders schwerfallen, noch einmal bewusst.

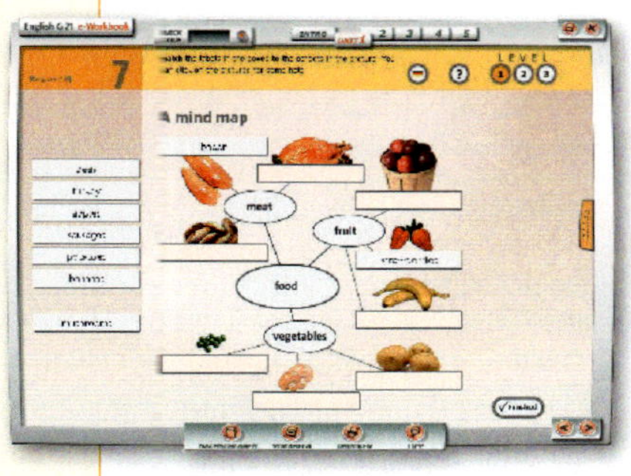

SF REVISION Using a bilingual dictionary

Wann brauche ich ein zweisprachiges Wörterbuch?

Du verstehst einen Text nicht, weil er zu viele Wörter enthält, die dir unbekannt sind, und die Worterschließungstechniken (▸ *SF Working out the meaning of words, p. 150*) helfen dir nicht weiter?
Du sollst einen Text auf Englisch schreiben, und dir fehlt das eine oder andere Wort, um deine Ideen auszudrücken? Du willst z. B. über die Ankunft eines Einwanderers in einem neuen Land schreiben (vgl. S. 19) und kennst das englische Wort für „Grenze" nicht?
In solchen Fällen hilft dir ein zweisprachiges Wörterbuch.

Wie benutze ich ein zweisprachiges Wörterbuch?

- Die **Leitwörter** *(running heads)* oben auf der Seite helfen dir, schneller zu finden, was du suchst. Auf der linken Seite steht das erste Stichwort, auf der rechten Seite das letzte Stichwort der Doppelseite.
- **Grenze** ist das **Stichwort** *(headword)*. Alle Stichwörter sind alphabetisch geordnet: **g** vor **h**, **ga** vor **ge** und **gre** vor **gri** usw.
- Die **kursiv gedruckten** Hinweise helfen dir, die für deinen Text passende Bedeutung zu finden.
- Die **Ziffern 1.**, **2.** usw. zeigen, dass ein Stichwort mehrere ganz verschiedene Bedeutungen hat.
- Dem Stichwort sind **Beispielsätze** und **Redewendungen** zugeordnet. In den Beispielsätzen und Redewendungen ersetzt eine **Tilde** (~) das Stichwort.
- Im englisch-deutschen Teil der meisten Wörterbücher findest du außerdem Hinweise auf **unregelmäßige Verbformen**, auf die **Steigerungsformen der Adjektive** und Ähnliches.
- Die **Lautschrift** gibt Auskunft darüber, wie das Wort ausgesprochen und betont wird.
- Bei kniffligen Wörtern gibt es in vielen Wörterbüchern **Info-Boxes**, in denen dir mehr Hilfen und Hinweise gegeben werden, hier z. B. für das deutsche Wort „schwer".

gottlos

divinely
gottlos godless, wicked
gottverlassen *umg.* godforsaken
Götze, Götzenbild idol ['aɪdl]
Gouverneur governor
Grab grave; *Grabmal* tomb [tu:m]
Graben ditch; MIL trench
graben dig* (**nach** for)

…
Grazie grace
graziös 1 *Adj* graceful (⚠ *nicht* gracious) **2** *Adv* gracefully; **~ tanzen** dance gracefully
greifen 1 *Verb mit Obj* seize, take* hold of **2** *Verb ohne Obj; übertragen: von Maßnahmen* take* effect; **~ nach** reach for; *fest* grab at; ***sie griff in ihre Handtasche*** she reached into her handbag
Greis old man
greisenhaft senile (*auch* MED)
Greisin old woman
grell *Licht* glaring, harsh; *Farbe* garish; *Ton* shrill
Grenze border; *Linie* boundary; *übertragen* limit; ***es hält sich in Grenzen*** it's not too bad
grenzen: ~ an border on (*auch übertragen*)
grenzenlos 1 *Adj* boundless **2** *Adv; sehr* extremely; **~ erstaunt** extremely surprised
Grenzfall borderline case; **Grenzland** borderland; **Grenzübergang** border crossing (point)

schwer krank

schwer

Das deutsche **schwer** hat drei Hauptbedeutungen:
1) *schwer von Gewicht*: **heavy**;
2) *schwerwiegend, ernst*: **serious**, **bad**;
3) *schwierig*: **difficult**, **hard**, **tough**.

Welche englische Entsprechung von **Grenze** brauchst du in diesen Sätzen?
1. Die Grenze zwischen den USA und Mexiko ist 3169 km lang.
2. Beim 15-Kilometer-Lauf gestern kam ich an meine Grenzen.

Tipp

- Nimm nicht einfach die erste Übersetzung, die dir angeboten wird! Lies den Wörterbucheintrag, bis du die richtige Übersetzung gefunden hast.
- Wenn du unsicher bist, bis du die richtige Übersetzung gefunden hast, schau dir den Eintrag zu dieser Übersetzung an. Wenn du z. B. überprüfen willst, ob „limit" im zweiten Satz oben die richtige Übersetzung für „Grenze" ist, lies dir den Eintrag zu „limit" durch.

SF Research ▸ *Unit 4, p. 81*

Wo kann ich Informationen finden?

Find some information about African Americans in the 1960s – so oder so ähnlich lauten Aufgaben, die dir oft als Hausaufgabe gestellt werden.
Wenn du nach Informationen suchst, solltest du immer **mehrere Quellen** verwenden. Du kannst im Internet, in einem Lexikon, Atlas, Wörterbuch oder Schulbuch nachschlagen. Benutze auch möglichst einige englische Quellen, z. B. Websites (s. u.), CDs und DVDs.

- Internet/Lexikon für alle Wissensgebiete, wichtige Personen und Ereignisse
- Atlas: geografische und politische Übersichten, Städte, Flüsse
- Wörterbücher: Rechtschreibung und Bedeutung von Wörtern
- Schulbücher: verschiedene Wissensgebiete

Wie kann ich das Internet zur Recherche nutzen?

Eine wichtige Informationsquelle ist das Internet. Aber manchmal findest du dort so viele Informationen, dass du schnell den Überblick verlierst. Diese Tipps sollen dir dabei helfen, nicht im *world wide web* verloren zu gehen.

- Fertige eine Liste mit Schlüsselwörtern *(keywords)* zu deinem Thema an: *African American , discrimination, history, USA, ...*
- Überlege, welches Schlüsselwort oder welche Kombination von Schlüsselwörtern am besten sein kann. „African Americans"+history oder African+Americans+history
- Wenn du dir zunächst einen Überblick verschaffen willst, kannst du auch ein Nachschlagewerk im Internet anklicken, wie z. B.
  www.infoplease.com
  www.en.wikipedia.org
- Manchmal gibt es dort auch Links, die dir weiterhelfen können.
- Suchmaschinen wie z. B. *Google*, *Altavista* oder *Yahoo* helfen dir, mithilfe deiner Schlüsselwörter Websites zu deinem Thema zu finden. Verwende eine Suchmaschine und gib deine Schlüsselwörter in die Suche ein.
- Wenn die angezeigten Websites dir nicht helfen oder du zu viele Websites angezeigt bekommst, versuch es noch einmal, indem du deine Schlüsselwörter präzisierst.

mit **allen** Wörtern	"African Americans"+history	10 Ergebnisse
mit der **genauen Wortgruppe**	discrimination in the 1960s	
mit **irgendeinem** der Wörter		
ohne die Wörter		

Tipp

- Verwende immer mehrere Quellen, um sicher zu gehen, dass die Informationen stimmen.
- Suche Antworten auf die 5 Ws (**who**, **what**, **when**, **where**, **why**).
- Bei englischen Quellen brauchst du nicht alles verstehen. Konzentrier dich auf das Wesentliche (▸ *Reading Course, p. 150*).
- Schreib die Quellen nicht wortwörtlich ab, sondern mach dir Notizen.

SF REVISION Describing pictures ▸ *Introduction, p. 7*

Wie kann ich Bilder beschreiben?

- Um zu sagen, wo auf einem Bild etwas abgebildet ist, benutze:
  at the top/bottom • **in the foreground/background** • **in the middle** • **on the left/right**
- Diese Präpositionen sind auch hilfreich:
  behind • **between** • **in front of** • **next to** • **under**
- Um zu beschreiben, was die Personen auf dem Bild tun, benutze das **present progressive**.
  The girl is looking down into the Grand Canyon.

Wie kann ich beschreiben, was die Personen fühlen?

Oft sollst du dich in eine Person auf einem Foto hineinversetzen und beschreiben, was sie fühlt oder denkt. Schau dir das Foto genau an und nimm dir Zeit, dir die Situation vorzustellen. Beim Formulieren helfen dir phrases wie:
Maybe the woman/man in the photo is thinking about ... •
I think he/she feels/wants to ...

SF REVISION Giving a presentation

Wie mache ich eine gute Präsentation?

Vorbereitung
- Schreib die wichtigsten Gedanken als Notizen auf, z. B. auf nummerierte Karteikarten – pro Karte einen Gedanke.
- Übe deine Präsentation zu Hause vor einem Spiegel. Sprich laut, deutlich und langsam.

Folien oder Poster
- Overhead-Folien oder Poster sind gut, um
  - zu zeigen, wie dein Vortrag aufgebaut ist
  - Tabellen, Diagramme usw. für alle lesbar zu präsentieren
  - die wichtigsten Punkte zusammenzufassen.
- Schreib groß und für alle gut lesbar.

Durchführung
- Bevor du beginnst, leg deine Folie auf den ausgeschalteten Projektor bzw. häng dein Poster auf..
- Warte, bis es ruhig ist. Schau die Zuhörer an.
- Erkläre zu Anfang, worüber du sprechen wirst. Lies nicht von deinen Karten ab, sondern sprich frei.

My presentation is about ... First, I'd like to talk about ... Second, ...

This picture/photo/ ... shows ...

Schluss
- Sag, dass du fertig bist.
- Frag die Zuhörenden, ob sie Fragen haben. Bedanke dich fürs Zuhören.

That's the end of my presentation. Have you got any questions?

MEDIATION SKILLS

SF REVISION Mediation

REVISION Wann muss ich zwischen zwei Sprachen vermitteln?

Manchmal musst du zwischen zwei Sprachen vermitteln; das nennt man mediation.

1. Du gibst englische Informationen auf Deutsch weiter:
   Du fährst z. B. mit deiner Familie in die USA und deine Eltern oder Geschwister wollen wissen, was jemand in einem Café gesagt hat oder was an einer Informationstafel steht.
2. Du gibst deutsche Informationen auf Englisch weiter:
   Vielleicht ist bei dir zu Hause eine Austauschschülerin aus den USA oder Dänemark zu Gast, die kein Deutsch spricht und Hilfe braucht.
3. In schriftlichen Prüfungen musst du manchmal in einem englischen Text gezielt nach Informationen suchen und diese auf Deutsch wiedergeben.

REVISION Worauf muss ich bei mediation achten?

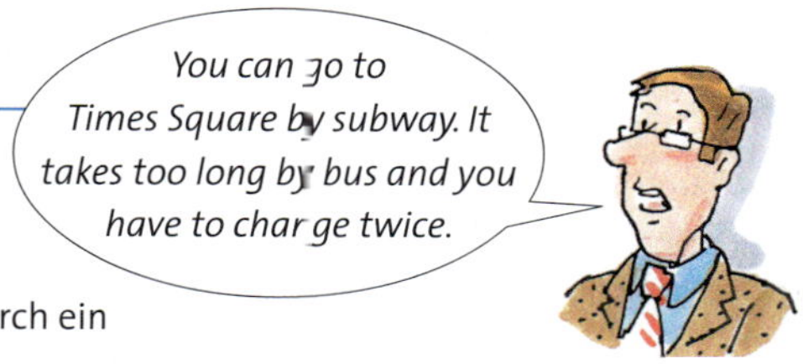

- Übersetze nicht alles wörtlich.
- Gib nur das Wesentliche weiter, lass Unwichtiges weg.
- Verwende kurze und einfache Sätze.
- Wenn du ein Wort nicht kennst, umschreibe es oder ersetze es durch ein anderes Wort.

Was kann ich tun, wenn ich ein wichtiges Wort nicht kenne?

Vielleicht findest du es manchmal schwer, mündliche Aussagen oder schriftliche Textvorlagen in die andere Sprache zu übertragen, z. B. weil:
- dein Wortschatz nicht ausreicht
- dir bekannte Wörter „im Stress" nicht einfallen
- spezielle Fachbegriffe auftauchen.

Manche Wörter kannst du umschreiben, z. B. mithilfe von Relativsätzen wie:
It's somebody/a person who ...
It's something that you use to ...
It's an animal that ...
It's a place where ...

▸ *SF Paraphrasing, p. 144*

SPEAKING AND WRITING SKILLS

SF REVISION Paraphrasing

Worum geht es beim Paraphrasing?

Paraphrasing bedeutet, etwas mit anderen Worten zu erklären. Das ist hilfreich, wenn dir ein bestimmtes Wort nicht einfällt oder wenn dein Gegenüber dich nicht verstanden hat (siehe auch ▸ *SF Mediation, p. 143*).

Wie gehe ich beim Paraphrasing vor?

- Man kann mit einem Wort umschreiben, das dieselbe Bedeutung hat:
  'to wonder' is the same as 'to ask yourself'
  Oder man sagt das Gegenteil.
  'alive' is the opposite of 'dead'
- Manchmal braucht man mehrere Wörter, z. B. wenn man etwas beschreibt oder erklären will, wie man es verwendet. Dabei benutzt man ein allgemeines Wort (**general word**) und nennt weitere Eigenschaften.
  A skyscraper is a very tall building.
- Oder du umschreibst das Wort mit **... is/are like ...**
  A lodge is like a small house or cabin. You find it in the country.
- Du kannst auch einen Relativsatz (**relative clause**) verwenden:
  A nanny is a woman who looks after small children.
  A ticket office is a shop where you can buy tickets for shows and concerts.

SF REVISION Brainstorming

Wofür ist Brainstorming gut?

Bei vielen Aufgaben ist es nützlich, wenn du im ersten Schritt möglichst viele Ideen zum Thema sammelst. Dabei helfen dir die folgenden Techniken.

Drei verschiedene Brainstorming-Techniken

Technik 1: Making a list
Schreib die Ideen so auf, wie sie dir einfallen, und zwar für jede Idee eine neue Zeile. Lies im zweiten Schritt alle deine Ideen durch. Überlege, welche Ideen davon für dein Thema sinnvoll sind und wie du sie zusammenfassen kannst.

Technik 2: Making a mindmap
Leg eine Mind map an.
- Überlege dafür, welche Oberbegriffe zu deinem Thema passen. Verwende unterschiedliche Farben für jeden Oberbegriff.
- Ergänze jede Idee, die zu einem Oberbegriff passt, auf einem Nebenast. Nimm dafür nur wichtige Schlüsselwörter. Du kannst statt Wörtern auch Symbole verwenden und Bilder ergänzen.

Technik 3: The 5 Ws
Schreib die 5 W-Fragen **Who? What? When? Where? Why?** in eine Tabelle. Die Ideen, die dir zu der jeweiligen Frage kommen, werden darunter geschrieben.

SF Summary writing ▸ *Unit 3, p. 67*

Wenn du einen Text (mündlich oder schriftlich) zusammenfasst, gibst du die wichtigen Informationen oder Ereignisse in kürzerer Form wieder.

Wie gehe ich beim *summary writing* vor?

1. Lies den Text einmal ganz durch, damit du verstehst, worum es geht. Mach dir noch keine Notizen.
2. Lies den Text noch einmal gründlich, Satz für Satz, durch und mach dir Notizen zu den 5 Ws:

Who?	Who is the text about?
What?	What happens?/What does somebody do?
When?	When does something happen?
Where?	Where does it happen?
Why?	Why does somebody do something?

Was auf diese Fragen Antwort gibt, ist wichtig. Auslassen kannst du dagegen Beispiele, Vergleiche, Zitate, direkte Rede, ausschmückende Adjektive und andere Textteile, die der Beschreibung dienen.

3. Leg den Text nun beiseite und schreib die *summary* mithilfe deiner Notizen.

– Erklär in den ersten ein oder zwei Sätzen, worum es in dem Text geht.

• Vergleiche diese drei Anfänge einer *summary* von *You can tell me* (S. 26–28). Welcher gibt am besten das Thema der Geschichte wieder?

YOU CAN TELL ME is a story about New York.

YOU CAN TELL ME is a story about Anthony and Kelly, two teenagers from New York.

Anthony and Kelly play music together. A few kids follow them, so they go to Kelly's place.

Du kannst für deine einleitenden Sätze die folgenden phrases verwenden:
The story is about ... • **The text describes ...** • **The article shows ...** • **In the story we get to know ...**

– Im Hauptteil solltest du die wichtigen Ereignisse der Geschichte oder die Hauptpunkte des Artikels wiedergeben.
  • Verwende dafür deine Notizen zu den 5 Ws.
  • Schreib den Text nicht ab, sondern benutze deine eigenen Worte.

Well, I couldn't tell her the real reason: Jim Nielson. Jim was a really sweet guy. → *Carrie thinks Jim is sweet.*

– Schreib die summary im **simple present**, auch wenn die Geschichte oder der Artikel in der Vergangenheit spielt. Nicht vergessen: im **simple present** wird in der 3. Person Singular **-s** angehängt: **Carrie thinks.**

REVISION Writing course – Zusammenfassung

The steps of writing

1. Brainstorming – Ideen sammeln (s. S. ~~135~~). 144
2. Schreiben. Dabei achte darauf,
   - deine Sätze zu verbinden und auszubauen *(Writing better sentences)*
   - deinen Text gut zu strukturieren *(Using paragraphs)*
   - bei einem Bericht die 5 Ws abzudecken *(Writing a report)*
3. Deinen Text inhaltlich und sprachlich überprüfen *(Correcting your text)*

Writing better sentences

Linking words

Eine Geschichte klingt interessanter, wenn man die Sätze mit **linking words** miteinander verbindet. Dabei gibt es mehrere Möglichkeiten:
- **Time phrases** wie at 7 o'clock, every morning, in the afternoons, a few minutes later, suddenly, then, next …
- **Konjunktionen** wie although, because, but, so … that, that, when, while
- **Relativpronomen** wie that und who

Adjektive und Adverbien

- Mit Adjektiven kannst du eine Person, einen Ort, einen Gegenstand oder ein Erlebnis genauer und interessanter beschreiben. Vergleiche:
  The man looked into the room. ▸ The young man looked into the empty room.
- Mit Adverbien kannst du beschreiben, **wie** jemand etwas macht:
  The young man looked nervously into the empty room.

Using paragraphs

Structuring a text

Ein längerer Text ist besser zu verstehen, wenn er mehrere Absätze enthält:
- eine Einleitung **(beginning)** – hier schreibst du, worum es geht
- einen Mittelteil **(middle)** – hier schreibst du mehr über dein Thema
- einen Schluss **(end)** – hier bringst du den Text zu einem interessanten Ende.

Topic sentences

Am Anfang eines Absatzes sind kurze, einleitende Sätze **(topic sentences)** gut, weil sie den Lesern sofort sagen, worum es geht, z. B.
1. Orte: My trip to … was fantastic. / … is famous for … / … is a great place.
2. Personen: … is funny/interesting/clever …
3. Aktivitäten: … is good fun. / Lots of people … every day.

Wie kann ich meine Absätze interessant gestalten?

- Beginne mit einem interessanten Einstiegssatz:
  You'll never guess what happened to me today! / Did I tell you that …?
- Fang für jeden neuen Aspekt einen neuen Absatz an.
- Beende deinen Text mit einer Zusammenfassung oder etwas Persönlichem.

Writing a report – structuring information

Worauf kommt es bei einem Bericht an?

- Gib dem Leser **eine schnelle Orientierung**, was passiert ist.
- Beginne mit **wichtigen Informationen** und gib erst dann Detailinformationen.
- Ein Bericht gibt immer Antworten auf die **5 Ws**:
  Who? What? When? Where? Why? und manchmal auch auf **How?**
- Verwende das *simple past*.

Correcting your text

▸ *Unit 3, p. 62*

Ein Text ist noch nicht „fertig“, wenn du ihn zu Ende geschrieben hast. Du solltest ihn immer mehr als einmal durchlesen:
- einmal, um zu sehen, ob er vollständig und gut verständlich ist
- noch einmal, um ihn auf Fehler zu überprüfen, z. B. **Rechtschreibfehler *(spelling mistakes)*** oder **Grammatikfehler *(grammar mistakes)***.

tomato [tə'mɑːtəʊ], *pl* tomatoes Tomate II

wife [waɪf], *pl* wives [waɪvz] Ehefrau II

drop (-pp-) [drɒp] fallen lassen I

forget (-tt-) [fə'get] vergessen I

Spelling mistakes

Lies deinen Text langsam, Wort für Wort, Buchstabe für Buchstabe. Wenn du unsicher bist, hilft dir ein Wörterbuch. Beachte folgende Regeln:

Tipp
- Manche Wörter haben Buchstaben, die man nicht spricht, aber schreibt, z. B. **autumn**, **climb**.
- Manchmal ändert sich die Schreibweise, wenn ein Wort eine Endung erhält,
  z. B. **take** → **taking**, **terrible** → **terribly**, **lucky** → **luckily**,
  try → **tries** (**aber stay** → **stays**), **run** → **running**, **drop** → **dropped**.
- Beim Plural tritt manchmal noch ein **-e** zum **-s**, z. B. **church** → **churches**.

Grammar mistakes

Diese Tipps helfen dir, typische Fehler zu vermeiden:

Tipp
- Im **simple present** wird in der 3. Person Singular **-s** angehängt: **she knows**
- **Unregelmäßige Verben:** Manche Verben bilden die Formen des *simple past* und des Partizip Perfekt *(past participle)* unregelmäßig. Die unregelmäßigen Formen musst du lernen. Die Liste steht auf S. 250–251.
  go – went – gone; buy – bought – bought
- **Verneinung:** Im *simple present* werden Vollverben mit **don't/doesn't** verneint, im *simple past* mit **didn't**.
- **Satzstellung**: Im Englischen gilt immer (auch im Nebensatz):
  a) subject – verb – object (SVO) ... when **I saw my brother**.
  als **ich meinen Bruder sah**.
  b) Orts- vor Zeitangabe **I bought a nice book in the city yesterday**.

LISTENING AND READING SKILLS

SF REVISION Listening for detail

Was muss ich allgemein beim *Listening* beachten?

Vor dem Hören:
- Lies dir die Fragen durch. So weißt du, worauf du beim Hören achten musst.
- Nutze Überschriften oder Bilder um zu erahnen, um was es geht.
- Bereite dich darauf vor, Notizen zu machen. Leg z. B. eine Tabelle oder Liste an.

Beim Hören:
- Achte auf Geräusche, unterschiedliche Stimmen und wie Leute sprechen.
- Mach nur kurze Notizen, z. B. Symbole oder Stichworte, keine ganzen Sätze.
- Lass dich nicht verunsichern, wenn du mal einen Satz nicht verstehst.

Nach dem Hören:
- Vervollständige deine Notizen sofort.
- Achte beim zweiten Hören auf das, was du zuerst nicht gut verstanden hast.

Wie kann ich Einzelheiten (details) heraushören?

1. Mach dir bewusst, welche Einzelheiten du heraushören sollst bzw. willst. Lass dich von anderen Einzelheiten nicht ablenken.
2. Manche Signalwörter machen es dir leichter, den Hörtext zu verstehen:
   Aufzählung: **and**, **another**, **too**
   Gegensatz: **although**, **but**
   Grund, Folge: **because**, **so**, **so that**
   Vergleich: **larger/older/... than**, **more**, **most**
   Reihenfolge: **before**, **after**, **then**, **next**, **later**, **when**, **at last**, **at the same time**
3. Unterteile Telefonnummern beim Aufschreiben : **0171 572 45 89**.

SF Interactive listening ▸ *Unit 2, p. 48*

Beim Hören von Telefonansagen fehlt dir der Blickkontakt. Aber wenn du dich gut auf die Ansage oder Durchsage vorbereitest, kann dir nichts passieren.

Vor dem Hören:
- Überlege dir vorher, welche Informationen du suchst und auf welche Schlüsselwörter du dafür achten solltest. Schreibe sie auf.
- Geh zum Telefonieren möglichst an einen ruhigen Ort.

Beim Hören:
- Bleib ruhig! Du kannst eine Telefonansage mehrmals hören.
- Achte besonders darauf, ob du für deine Information eine Zahl drücken musst. Zahlen sagen dir, wie du die Ansage fortsetzen kannst. Oft werden sie auch wiederholt.
- Höre besonders genau zu, wenn deine Schlüsselworter genannt werden und mach dir Notizen zu ihnen.

Nach dem Hören:
- Geh das Gehörte noch mal in Gedanken durch. Hast du alles richtig verstanden und hast du alle Informationen? Wenn du nicht sicher bist, ruf einfach noch mal an. Es läuft ein Band und du störst niemanden.

SF REVISION Taking notes

Worum geht es beim Notizen machen?

Wenn du beim Lesen oder Zuhören Notizen machst, kannst du dich später besser an das Gehörte oder Gelesene erinnern, wenn du etwas vortragen, nacherzählen oder einen Bericht schreiben sollst.

Wie mache ich Notizen?

In Texten oder Gesprächen gibt es immer wichtige und unwichtige Wörter. Die wichtigen Wörter werden Schlüsselwörter **(key words)** genannt und nur die solltest du notieren. Meist sind das Substantive und Verben, manchmal auch Adjektive oder Zahlen.

Tipp

- Verwende Ziffern (z.B. „7“ statt „seven“).
- Verwende Symbole und Abkürzungen, z.B. ✔ (für Ja) und + (für und) oder US für United States, C. für Caitlin.
  Du kannst auch eigene Symbole erfinden.
- Verwende **not** oder ✗ statt „doesn't“ oder „don't“.

SF REVISION Marking up a text

Wann sollte ich einen Text markieren?

Du hast einen Text mit vielen Fakten vor dir liegen und sollst später über bestimmte Dinge berichten. Dann wird es dir helfen, die für die Aufgabenstellung wichtigen Informationen im Text zu markieren.

Wie gehe ich am besten vor?

Lies den Text und markiere nur die für dein Thema wichtigen Informationen. Nicht jeder Satz enthält für deine Aufgabe wichtige Wörter, und oft reicht es aus, nur ein oder zwei Wörter in einem Satz zu markieren.

– Du kannst wichtige Wörter einkreisen.
– Du kannst sie unterstreichen.
– Du kannst sie mit einem Textmarker hervorheben.

ABER:
Markiere nur auf Fotokopien von Texten oder in Büchern, die dir gehören.

American Museum of Natural History
In the American Museum of Natural History you'll find the largest and probably one of the most awesome dinosaur collections in the world.

American Museum of Natural History
In the American Museum of Natural History you'll find the largest and probably one of the most awesome dinosaur collections in the world.

American Museum of Natural History
In the American Museum of Natural History you'll find the largest and probably one of the most awesome dinosaur collections in the world.

READING COURSE – Zusammenfassung

REVISION Working out the meaning of words ▸ Unit 1, p. 25

Das Nachschlagen unbekannter Wörter im Wörterbuch kostet Zeit und nimmt auf Dauer den Spaß am Lesen. Oft geht es auch ohne Wörterbuch!

Was hilft mir, unbekannte Wörter zu verstehen?

1. Bilder zeigen oft die Dinge, die du im Text nicht verstehst. Schau sie dir deshalb vor dem Lesen genau an.
2. Oft hilft dir der Textzusammenhang, z. B.
   *When we **reached** the station, Judy went to the ticket machine to buy our tickets.*
3. Zu manchen englischen Wörtern fallen dir vielleicht deutsche, französische oder lateinische Wörter ein, die ähnlich geschrieben oder ausgesprochen werden, z. B.
   excellent, **millionaire**, **nation**, **reality**.
4. Manchmal stecken in unbekannten Wörtern bekannte Teile, z. B.
   friendliness, **helpless**, **understandable**, **gardener**, **tea bag**, **waiting room**.

REVISION Skimming and Scanning ▸ Unit 2, p. 43

Skimming: Lesen, um sich einen Überblick zu verschaffen

Beim **Skimming** überfliegst du einen Text schnell, um dir einen ersten Eindruck zu verschaffen, worum es geht. Das hilft dir herauszufinden, ob ein Text, den du im Internet oder einem Buch gefunden hast, überhaupt die Informationen enthält, nach denen du (z. B. für ein Referat) suchst. Achte dabei auf
- die **Überschrift**
- die **Zwischenüberschriften** und **hervorgehobene** Wörter oder Sätze
- die **Bilder** und **Bildunterschriften**
- den **ersten** und den **letzten Satz** jedes Absatzes
- **Grafiken**, **Statistiken** und die **Quelle** des Textes

Scanning: Lesen, um nach bestimmten Informationen zu suchen

Beim **Scanning** suchst du einen Text nach Schlüsselwörtern *(key words)* ab und liest nur dort genauer, wo du sie findest. Das hilft dir, wenn dich nur bestimmte Aspekte eines Themas interessieren. Geh dabei so vor:

Schritt 1: Denk an das Schlüsselwort, nach dem du suchst, oder schreib es auf.

Schritt 2: Geh mit deinen Augen und dem Finger schnell durch den Text, in breiten Schlingen wie bei einem „S“ oder „Z“ oder von oben nach unten wie bei einem„U“. Dabei hast du das Schriftbild oder das Bild der Wörter, nach denen du suchst, vor Augen. Die gesuchten Wörter werden dir sofort „ins Auge springen“.

Schritt 3: Wenn das Schlüsselwort, nach dem du suchst, im Text nicht vorkommt, überlege dir, welche anderen Wörter mit den benötigten Informationen zu tun haben, und such nach diesen.

Finding the main ideas of a text

▸ *Unit 3, p. 65*

Wenn du Texte wie Zeitungsartikel, Berichte oder Kommentare richtig verstehen willst, ist es gut, wenn du ihre Hauptaussagen erkennst und nachvollziehst, wie sie zusammenhängen. Dabei hilft dir ein Blick auf die Struktur dieser Texte.

Wie finde ich die Hauptaussagen eines Textes?

1. Jeder Text dreht sich um ein Thema oder hat eine Hauptaussage, z. B.
   Drinking soda is one of the worst things you can do to your health.
   Diese Hauptaussage findest du oft im **ersten Absatz**. Lies ihn deshalb besonders gründlich durch.
2. Die Hauptaussage wird in der Regel durch weitere Aussagen bzw. Gedanken unterstützt, z. B.
   Experts agree that sugary soft drinks and fast food are the main reasons why so many American teenagers are fat.
   Du findest sie oft im ersten oder letzten Satz der nachfolgenden Absätze.
3. Diese weiteren Aussagen bzw. Gedanken werden oft durch Beispiele und Begründungen ergänzt, z. B.
   About 7% of the calories that they take in come from soft drinks alone.

Tipp

Die folgenden Wörter oder Ausdrücke werden oft im Zusammenhang mit Begründungen oder Beispielen verwendet:
... % of ... are ... • and so • because • e.g. • etc. • for example • for lots of reasons • this shows that • that's why

Drawing conclusions

▸ *Unit 4, p. 87*

Wenn du bei einer Arbeit Fragen zu einem Text beantworten sollst oder bei einer Recherche Informationen zu einer bestimmten Frage in einem Text suchst, kann es gut sein, dass du an mehreren Stellen schauen musst oder dass die Antwort nicht 1:1 im Text steht.

Wie funktioniert schlussfolgerndes Lesen?

1. Die einfachste Form des schlussfolgernden Lesens besteht darin, die Informationen aus verschiedenen Textstellen zusammenzuführen. Im Text auf S. 87 z. B. musst du mehrere Textstellen anschauen, wenn du alle Gründe finden willst, warum Schüler/innen in den USA arbeiten gehen.
2. Manchmal steht die Antwort auf eine Frage nicht direkt im Text. Dann musst du sie dir erschließen. Im Text auf S. 87 geht es um die Frage, welche Auswirkungen das Arbeiten auf die schulischen Leistungen hat. Dafür musst du Fakten im Text finden, die etwas mit dieser Frage zu tun haben:

FACTS: students have an 11 hour work day; after work they're often too tired to do their homework = negative effects
working makes students more disciplined; they learn to organize their time = positive effects
CONCLUSION: for some students it's good, but for many it means bad grades

EXAM SKILLS

SF How to do well in a test

▸ *Getting ready for a test (p. 31)*

Countdown zum Testerfolg

Ein Test ist angekündigt? Kein Grund zur Panik. Wichtig ist, dass du weißt, worauf du dich vorbereiten musst. Im Zweifelsfall frag deine Lehrerin oder deinen Lehrer. Der Countdown kann beginnen!

Eine Woche vor dem Test

1. Lies noch einmal die **Texte** der zuletzt durchgenommenen Unit (vor allem Lead-in, A-Section und Text, eventuell auch das Background File). Fasse mündlich oder schriftlich zusammen, worum es ging.
2. Wiederhole den **Wortschatz** der Unit mithilfe des Vocabulary, des Wordmaster oder des *English Coach*. Schreibe dir die Wörter und Wortverbindungen, die du immer wieder vergisst, auf ein Blatt Papier. Eine Mindmap oder ein Wortfeld helfen beim Behalten.
3. Geh auch noch mal die neue **Grammatik** durch. Aufgaben zur Selbstüberprüfung und zum Üben findest du im *Practice*-Teil, auf der Seite „How am I doing?", im *Grammar File*, in deinem *Workbook* und im e-*Workbook*. (▸ *SF Check yourself, p. 139*)

Zwei oder drei Tage vor dem Test

1. Wiederhole den **Wortschatz**. Manche Wörter sitzen noch nicht? Schreibe einen kurzen Text, in dem du sie verwendest.
2. Lies die **Schülerbuch-Texte** ein weiteres Mal.
3. Erkläre einem Freund oder einer Freundin die neue **Grammatik**. Klappt nicht richtig? Dann lies nochmal im Grammar File nach.

Am Abend vor dem Test

1. Entspanne dich. Du kannst lesen, dich in die Badewanne legen, Musik hören, fernsehen, ...
2. Geh zur gewohnten Zeit ins Bett.

Am Morgen des Tests

1. Steh rechtzeitig auf, damit du nicht hetzen musst.
2. Lies etwas „zum Aufwärmen", aber schau nicht mehr in dein Schülerbuch.

Während des Tests

1. Denk daran: Du hast dich gut vorbereitet. Es gibt keinen Grund, nervös zu sein.
2. Konzentriere dich auf den Test, lass dich nicht ablenken.
3. Lies dir die Aufgaben genau durch. Dann löse zuerst die Aufgaben, die dir einfach scheinen. Wende dich erst danach den schwereren Aufgaben zu.
4. Aufgaben, die du bearbeitet hast, hakst du ab. So siehst du, wie du voran kommst, und behältst den Überblick.
5. Schau ab und zu auf die Uhr. Du solltest dir für den Schluss noch Zeit einplanen, um deine Antworten nochmal durchzulesen und zu korrigieren.

Good luck!

Aufgabenstellungen verstehen

Bevor du damit anfängst, die Aufgaben zu bearbeiten, stell sicher, dass du genau weißt, was du machen sollst. Lies die Aufgabenstellung Wort für Wort langsam und gründlich und von Anfang bis Ende durch. Sollst du z. B. ganze Sätze schreiben oder dir nur Notizen machen? Du kannst besonders wichtige Dinge der Aufgabenstellung unterstreichen und die Aufgabe, wenn nötig, für dich in einzelne Schritte unterteilen.

Worauf sollte ich bei Multiple-Choice-Aufgaben achten?

- Lies die Frage oder den Satz sehr genau durch.
- Bevor du dir die Lösungsangebote anschaust, deck sie mit Papier ab. Überleg dir, was die richtige Antwort sein könnte. Wenn das dann auch als eine Lösungsmöglichkeit angeboten wird, ist es meistens richtig.
- Lies immer alle vorgegebenen Lösungen, bevor du dich entscheidest.
- Achte darauf, dass du nur **eine** der Antworten ankreuzt – es sei denn, dass in der Aufgabenstellung ausdrücklich gesagt wird, dass mehrere Antworten richtig sein können.
- Mach erst alle Aufgaben so gut du kannst. Lass keine Aufgabe aus, aber geh zum Schluss zu den Fragen zurück, bei denen du unsicher bist.
- Wenn das alles nicht hilft, such nicht mehr nach der richtigen Antwort, sondern nach den falschen Antworten. Weil drei Antwortmöglichkeiten falsch sein müssen, kannst du erschließen, dass die vierte Antwort richtig ist. Hier ist ein Beispiel. Stell dir vor, du hörst folgenden Dialog.

  Boy *Wow, that was great, Dad. Thanks. Can we do it again next weekend?*
  Dad *Sure, Greg – if the weather's nice. But let's find an easier tour then – I'm a bit tired.*

Dazu wird dir die multiple-choice Frage hier rechts gestellt.
Greg und sein Vater müssen etwas im Freien gemacht haben, denn Gregs Dad spricht über das Wetter. Also sind die Antworten **B** und **C** falsch. Man schwimmt keine Touren, also ist **A** auch falsch. Daher muss **D** die richtige Antwort sein.

1. Greg and his dad have just
   - A been swimming.
   - B been to a fitness club.
   - C seen a movie.
   - D been on a bike ride.

Grammar File – Inhalt

Im **Grammar File** (S. 154–166) wird zusammengefasst, was du in diesem Band **über die englische Sprache** lernst.

In der **linken Spalte** findest du **Beispielsätze** und **Übersichten**.

In der **rechten Spalte** stehen **Erklärungen** und nützliche **Hinweise**. Das **rote Ausrufezeichen** (**!**) macht dich auf besondere Fehlerquellen aufmerksam.

Hinweise wie ▸ *Unit 1 (p. 15)* • *P 4–5 (p. 21)* zeigen dir, zu welcher Unit und welcher Seite ein **Grammar-File-**Abschnitt gehört und welche Übungen du dazu im Practice-Teil findest.

Die **grammatischen Fachbegriffe** (*grammatical terms*) kannst du auf den Seiten 165–166 nachschlagen.

Additional information
So gekennzeichnete Abschnitte enthalten Grammatik, die du nicht selbst zu verwenden brauchst. Du solltest aber verstehen, was dort erklärt wird, damit du keine Schwierigkeiten mit Texten hast, in denen diese Grammatik vorkommt.

Am Ende der Abschnitte stehen wieder kleine Aufgaben zur Selbstkontrolle. Schreib die Lösungen in dein Heft. Überprüfe sie dann auf Seite 166.

Unit 1

GF 1 The gerund Das Gerundium

a) Use and form

Flying is exciting.
Fliegen ist aufregend.

Travelling makes me tired.
Reisen macht mich müde.

Taking **a taxi** is quite expensive.
Mit dem Taxi zu fahren / Taxifahren ist ziemlich teuer.

Cycling **in New York** can be dangerous.
In New York Rad zu fahren / Radfahren in New York kann gefährlich sein.

Gebrauch und Form

Wenn die *-ing*-Form eines Verbs im Satz die Funktion eines **Nomens** hat, wird sie **Gerundium** *(gerund)* genannt.
Die *-ing*-Form wird, wie du weißt, durch Anhängen von *-ing* an den Infinitiv gebildet: ***fly*** → ***flying***.

Wie ein Verb kann das Gerundium erweitert werden, z.B. durch ein Objekt *(a taxi)* oder eine Orts- oder Zeitangabe *(in New York)*.

Im Deutschen wird das Gerundium oft durch einen Infinitiv mit „zu" oder durch ein Nomen wiedergegeben.

b) The gerund as subject and object

Das Gerundium als Subjekt und als Objekt

Das Gerundium (und seine Erweiterung) kann wie ein Nomen **Subjekt** oder **Objekt** eines Satzes sein:

Subjekt	
Flying	*is exciting.*
Cycling in a big city	*isn't very healthy.*

	Objekt
My sister likes	***skating.***
I like	***riding my bike in Central Park.***

Ich wohne gern in einer Großstadt. / Ich genieße es, in einer Großstadt zu wohnen. Ich kann mir nicht vorstellen, auf dem Land zu leben.

! Beachte:

◂ **1** Nach einigen Verben – z.B. ***enjoy, finish, imagine, miss, practise*** – muss ein weiteres Verb als Gerundium stehen:

*I **enjoy** living ..., I can't **imagine** living ...*

Anders als im Deutschen darf nach diesen Verben **kein Infinitiv** stehen!
Also nicht: *I ~~enjoy to live~~ ..., I can't ~~imagine to live~~ ...*

When I got to Times Square, it **started** raining. / to rain.

I **like/love** riding / to ride my bike in the rain.

◂ **2** Nach ***begin/start, continue, hate, like, love*** kann – bei gleicher Bedeutung – ein Gerundium oder ein *to*-Infinitiv stehen

I'd like/love to ride in a New York taxi too.
I **would hate** to live in the country.

◂ **3** Nach ***would like, would love, would hate*** kann nur der *to*-Infinitiv stehen.

▸ *Unit 1 (p. 15)* • *P 4–5 (p. 21)*

c) The gerund after prepositions

After so much walking, we were tired.
Nach all der Herumlauferei ... /
Nachdem wir so viel herumgelaufen waren, ...

Never cross a street without looking.
Überquere nie eine Straße, ohne zu schauen.

Ryan is **scared** of going in lifts.
Ryan hat Angst davor, mit dem Lift zu fahren.

Ryan had often **dreamed** of seeing New York from above.
... davon geträumt, New York von oben zu sehen.

Das Gerundium nach Präpositionen

Nach einer Präposition *(after, without, for, of, ...)* muss ein Verb als Gerundium stehen.

Beachte die unterschiedlichen Entsprechungen im Deutschen:

englisch		deutsch
– ***after walking***	→	**Präposition + Nomen** („nach ...“) *oder* **Nebensatz** („nachdem ...“)
– ***without looking***	→	„ohne zu“ + **Infinitiv**
– *scared **of going***	→	„zu“ + **Infinitiv**

Ryan is **interested** in learning about New York firefighters.
Ryan ist daran interessiert, etwas über ... zu erfahren.
He's **excited** about meeting some of them.
Er freut sich sehr darauf, einige von ihnen zu treffen.

Nützliche Wendungen mit Präposition + Gerundium sind:

– *(to) be* ***interested in / excited about / afraid of / good/bad at / tired of*** ***doing** sth.*

Ryan had the **chance** of going to New York.
Ryan hatte die Möglichkeit, nach New York zu fahren.
His **reason** for going there was to visit family.
Sein Grund, dort hinzufahren, war ...

– *the* ***chance of / reason for / idea of / danger of*** ***doing** sth.*

Caitlin **was** against going to Brooklyn Bridge.
Caitlin war dagegen, zur Brooklyn Bridge zu gehen.
Ryan and Caitlin **talked** about meeting Ruth.
Ryan und Caitlin sprachen darüber, Ruth zu treffen.

– *(to)* ***be against / talk about / think of / worry about*** ***doing** sth.*

▸ *Unit 1 (p. 16) • P 6 (p. 22)*

Vervollständige die Sätze in deinem Heft. Wähle ein Verb aus dem Kästchen. Achte auf die richtige Form.

1 ... alone to New York was very exciting for Ryan.
2 He didn't enjoy ... in the security queues at the airport.
3 At first he was a bit afraid of ... up the ESB in a fast lift.
4 He was very interested in ... all the sights.
5 Later he talked about ... down from the ESB for hours.

(to) fly • (to) go • (to) look • (to) see • (to) wait

Unit 2

GF 2 The passive Das Passiv

a) Active and passive

Active: Farmers in California grow strawberries on large farms.
Landwirte in Kalifornien bauen Erdbeeren auf großen Farmen an.

Passive: Strawberries are grown on large farms.
Erdbeeren werden auf großen Farmen angebaut.

Aktiv und Passiv

◂ Mit einem **Aktivsatz** drückst du aus, **wer oder was etwas tut**. Das Subjekt des Aktivsatzes führt die Handlung aus:

Subjekt	**Verb** (aktiv)	**Objekt**
Farmers in California	*grow*	*strawberries ...*

◂ Mit einem **Passivsatz** drückst du aus, **mit wem oder womit etwas geschieht**. Das Objekt des Aktivsatzes *(strawberries)* ist Subjekt des Passivsatzes geworden:

Subjekt	**Verb** (passiv)	
Strawberries	*are grown*	*on large farms.*

b) Form

... wird aufbereitet ...
... werden gepflanzt ...
... wurden angebaut ...

Form

Das Passiv bildest du mit einer **Form von *be*** und der 3. Form des Verbs. Die 3. Form des Verbs heißt **Partizip Perfekt** *(past participle)*.

Simple present: *am/are/is* + ***past participle***
*The ground is **prepared** ...*
*The strawberries are **planted** ...*

Simple past: *was/were* + ***past participle***
*700,000 tons were **grown** ...*

c) Use

At 8.45 yesterday morning a 12-year-old boy was hurt in a car accident on Duke Street. The police were called and the boy was taken to hospital.

Gebrauch

Mit einem Passivsatz kannst du Handlungen beschreiben, ohne zu sagen, wer die Handlung ausführt. Oft ist gar nicht bekannt oder nicht wichtig, wer die Handlung ausführt.
Du findest daher das Passiv oft in Nachrichten und in Zeitungsberichten (z. B. über Unfälle, Verbrechen) oder auf Schildern.

Ein englischer Passivsatz wird im Deutschen oft durch einen Aktivsatz mit „man" wiedergegeben:

*The boy **was taken** to hospital.*
***Man brachte** den Jungen ins Krankenhaus.*

d) Passive sentences with *by* ...

The Golden Gate Bridge **was built** by Joseph Strauss.
... wurde von Joseph Strauss erbaut.

The gardener **was attacked** by a dog.
... wurde von einem Hund angefallen.

My parents' house **was destroyed** by fire.
... wurde durch ein Feuer zerstört.

▸ *Unit 2 (pp. 37–38) • P 8–12 (pp. 45–46)*

Passivsätze mit *by* ...

Wenn du in einem Passivsatz den „Täter" oder „Verursacher" nennen willst, verwendest du die Präposition ***by*** („von", „durch").

Sieh dir die Bilder, die Verben und die Namen an. Schreib die richtigen Passivsätze in dein Heft.

1 

2 

3 

1 The telephone was ... by ...
2 'We will rock you!' was ...
3 Clifton Suspension Bridge ...

build • invent • sing
Alexander Bell • Brunel • Queen

e) Extra The passive: *will*-future and modal auxiliaries

Our new attractions will be opened soon.
... werden bald eröffnet (werden).

Sea World can be visited at any time of the year.
... kann das ganze Jahr über besucht werden.

The fire couldn't be put out.
... konnte nicht gelöscht werden.

▸ *Unit 2 (p. 39) • P 16 (p. 48)*

Das Passiv:
will-future und modale Hilfsverben

Passivsätze mit Hilfsverben (z.B. *will, can, could, must, should, must, may*) bildest du mit *be* + Partizip Perfekt:

will	***be***	***opened***
can	***be***	***visited***
could	***be***	***put out***
must	***be***	***...***
should	***be***	***...***
may	***be***	***...***

Unit 3

GF 3 Countable and uncountable nouns — Zählbare und nicht zählbare Nomen

a) Countable nouns — Zählbare Nomen

a friend – two friends
a CD – lots of CDs
one hour – many hours

◂ Die meisten Nomen sind **zählbar** – sie bezeichnen etwas, das man zählen kann. Zählbare Nomen kommen im Singular und im Plural vor.

b) Uncountable nouns — Nicht zählbare Nomen

bread	Brot	**money**	Geld
butter	Butter	**music**	Musik
furniture	Möbel	**news**	Nachricht(en)
homework	Hausaufgabe(n)	**sugar**	Zucker
information	Information(en)	**traffic**	Verkehr
jewellery	Schmuck	**water**	Wasser
milk	Milch	**work**	Arbeit

◂ **Nicht zählbare** Nomen dagegen bezeichnen etwas, das man nicht zählen kann. Dazu gehören viele Bezeichnungen für Lebensmittel und viele abstrakte Begriffe.

! Auch die Nomen ***furniture, homework, information*** und ***news*** sind nicht zählbar – anders als ihre deutschen Entsprechungen.

! Beachte:

not: ~~a bread; breads~~
~~an information; many informations~~
~~a homework; two homeworks~~

◂ Nicht zählbare Nomen haben **keinen Plural** und stehen **nie mit *a/an* oder mit *one/two/three/...***

That's too much **homework**. I can't do it.
Das sind zu viele **Hausaufgaben**. Ich kann sie nicht machen.

Where did you get this **information**?
Wo hast du diese **Information(en)** her?

◂ Auch die zugehörigen **Begleiter, Verben und Pronomen** stehen immer **im Singular**.

Would you like a glass of **milk**.
Möchtest du **ein Glas Milch**?

That's a useful piece of **information**.
Das ist **eine** nützliche **Information**.

◂ Wenn du **bestimmte Mengen** oder eine **bestimmte Anzahl** nennen willst, musst du passende Wendungen wie ***a glass of ..., a kilo of ..., a piece of ...*** verwenden.

c) Quantifiers: *some, a lot of, many, much* — Mengenangaben: *some, a lot of, many, much*

Countable nouns	Uncountable nouns
some **students** einige/ein paar ...	some **bread/information** etwas Brot/einige Informationen
a lot of **students** viele ...	a lot of **bread/information** viel Brot/viele Informationen
how many **students?** wie viele ...?	
	how much **bread/information?** wie viel Brot? / wie viele Informationen?

Die Mengenangaben *some* und *a lot of* (oder *lots of*) verwendest du sowohl mit dem **Plural von zählbaren Nomen** als auch mit **nicht zählbaren Nomen**.

many („**viele**") steht nur mit dem **Plural von zählbaren Nomen**.

much („**viel**") steht nur mit **nicht zählbaren Nomen**.

▸ Unit 3 (p.57) • P 6–7 (p.64)

Sieh dir die Bilder an und vervollständige die Sätze mit a/an *(2x)*, some *(2x)*, many *(1x)*, much *(3x)*.

1 There's ... milk but there isn't ... bread.

2 Here's ... information about the Grand Canyon. I'm doing ... project on it.

3 We haven't got ... eggs, and we haven't got ... butter.

4 I haven't got ... homework, just ... exercise for French.

GF 4 The definite article *the* Der bestimmte Artikel *the*

1 For Timo and his family, life is exciting at the moment.
... ist **das** Leben im Moment aufregend.

2 Clean air is important to health.
Saubere Luft ist wichtig für **die** Gesundheit.

3 American students do lots of extracurricular activities.

1a At the FFA meeting Timo learned a lot about the life **of Missouri farmers.**
... über das Leben der Farmer in Missouri.

2a The Schmidts are happy that the air **in Hermann** is clean.
... die Luft in Hermann

3a The students **who went to the FFA meeting** were very interested in hogs.

▸ *Unit 3 (p.58) • P 10 (p.66)*

Wenn ein Nomen **ganz allgemein** gebraucht wird, steht es **ohne den bestimmten Artikel** (auch, wenn ein Adjektiv davor steht).

Das gilt insbesondere für

1 **abstrakte Begriffe** wie *life, history, health, quality*

2 **Stoffbezeichnungen** wie *air, oil, gold*

3 **Nomen im Plural** (hier: *students*).

◂ Solche Nomen stehen jedoch **mit bestimmtem Artikel**, wenn sie **näher bestimmt** sind, z.B. durch eine *of*-Fügung (Satz 1a) oder einen Relativsatz (Satz 3a).

Vergleiche die Sätze 1–3 mit den Sätzen 1a–3a.

Mit oder ohne the*? Schreib die Sätze in dein Heft.*

1 We can learn a lot from ... history.
2 What do you know about ... history of England?
3 Is ... food that you like best healthy?
4 In Jake's health class they're talking about ... food.
5 ... tourists like to visit Hermann's Festhalle.
6 ... tourists who asked us the way were from Germany.

GF 5 Talking about the future   Über die Zukunft sprechen

a) REVISION The *will*-future

I think I'll soon find lots of new friends in Hermann. It won't be difficult.

Timo is 14. He'll be 15 next year.
The weather report says that it will be warm and sunny tomorrow.

Tea or coffee? – I think I'll have tea, please.
Those exercises look difficult. I'll help you with them.

Das Futur mit *will*

◂ Mit dem *will-future* kannst du **Vermutungen** und **Vorhersagen** über die Zukunft äußern.
Vermutungen fangen oft mit *I think, I'm sure* oder *maybe* an. Bei Vorhersagen geht es oft um Dinge, die man nicht beeinflussen kann (das Alter; das Wetter).

◂ Das *will-future* verwendest du auch für **spontane Entschlüsse**, die vorher nicht geplant waren (z. B. Hilfsangebote, Versprechen).

b) REVISION The *going to*-future

Timo Are you going to be a farmer like your dad, Jake.

Jake No, I'm not. I'm going to be a teacher.

Timo's books are going to fall.

Das Futur mit *going to*

◂ Mit dem *going to-future* kannst du über **Vorhaben** und **Pläne** für die Zukunft sprechen.

◂ Mit ***going to* + Infinitiv** kannst du auch ausdrücken, dass etwas **wahrscheinlich gleich passieren** wird.
Es gibt dafür schon deutliche **Anzeichen** (hier: die Bücher oben auf dem Stapel, die schon wackeln).

c) The present progressive with future meaning

My mom is working at Maifest **next month**, and we're starting a soccer team at Hermann High **in September**.

▸ *Unit 3 (p. 59)* • *P 12 (p. 66)*

Das *present progressive* mit futurischer Bedeutung

◂ **Feste Pläne** und **Verabredungen** kannst du auch mit dem *present progressive* ausdrücken. Dabei muss klar sein, dass es sich um etwas Zukünftiges handelt, z. B. durch eine Zeitangabe wie *next month, in September, on Friday, at the weekend, tomorrow*.
(Manchmal wird diese Verwendung des *present progressive* auch **diary future**, deutsch „Kalender-Zukunft", genannt, weil es sich oft um Verabredungen handelt, die man schon in seinen Terminkalender eingetragen hat.)

Can you...?

Welche festen Termine und Verabredungen hat Anna nächste Woche?
Schreib die Sätze in dein Heft.

1 On Monday Anna is meeting ...
2 On Tuesday ...
...

Unit 4

GF 6 *since* and *for* (German 'seit') *since* und *for* (Deutsch „seit")

a) The present perfect with *since* and *for*

Das *present perfect* mit *since* und *for*

Du kannst das *present perfect* verwenden, um über einen **Zustand** zu sprechen, der in der Vergangenheit begonnen hat und jetzt noch andauert.

! Wenn du sagen willst, **seit wann** oder **wie lange** der Zustand bereits andauert, musst du aufpassen – es gibt zwei englische Wörter für das deutsche „seit":

◄ **1** Mit *since* gibst du einen **Zeit**punkt an *(since 2001; since May; since 12 o'clock).*
***since* + Zeitpunkt** drückt also aus, **seit wann** ein Zustand andauert.

◄ **2** Mit *for* gibst du einen **Zeit**raum an *(for years; for a month; for a long time).*
***for* + Zeitraum** drückt also aus, **wie lange** ein Zustand bereits andauert.

We've lived in this house since 2004.
Wir wohnen seit 2004 in diesem Haus.

I've had my computer for three years.
Ich habe meinen Computer schon seit drei Jahren.

! Achtung:
Im **Deutschen** benutzt man meist das **Präsens**:
*Wir **wohnen** seit ... / Ich **habe** ... seit ...*

Im **Englischen** muss das ***present perfect*** stehen:
*We**'ve lived** ... since ... / I**'ve had** ... for ...*

***since* + Zeitpunkt** ***for* + Zeitraum**

Madison and her mom are in the car on the way to the CNN studios. **It's 8.20.**

They**'ve been** in the traffic jam since 8 o'clock. ... seit 8 Uhr.

They**'ve been** in the traffic jam for 20 minutes. ... seit 20 Minuten.

How long **have** you **lived** in Atlanta?
– Since 2005. / For a few years.
Wie lange **wohnt** ihr in Atlanta?
– Seit 2005. / Seit ein paar Jahren.

Mit ***How long ...?*** + *present perfect* kannst du fragen, seit wann oder wie lange ein Zustand schon andauert.

► *Unit 4 (pp. 79–80)* • *P 9–11 (pp. 88–89)*

Since *oder* for? *Schreib die vollständigen Sätze in dein Heft.*

1 We've lived here ... four years.
2 Madison has been in the car ... over 20 minutes now.
3 She's been at her school ... 2005.
4 I've known my best friend ... five years.
5 Mr Young has worked at the King Center ... 1999.
6 The weather has been bad ... over a week.

Additional information

b) The present perfect progressive with *since* and *for*

Wir warten in diesem Stau schon seit 20 Minuten – seit 8 Uhr!

Das *present perfect progressive* mit *since* und *for*

Die Verlaufsform des *present perfect* (das *present perfect progressive*) benutzt man für **Vorgänge** und **Handlungen**, die in der Vergangenheit begonnen haben und jetzt noch andauern (oft mit *since* bzw. *for*).

Das *present perfect progressive* besteht aus ***have/has been*** + ***ing*-Form**.

Auch in diesen Fällen benutzt man im **Deutschen** meist das **Präsens**:
*Wir **warten** seit ...*
Im **Englischen** steht das ***present perfect progressive***:
*We**'ve been waiting** since/for ...*

GF 7 Extra Indirect speech Die indirekte Rede

a) Direct and indirect speech

Direkte und indirekte Rede

Das, was jemand sagt (oder gesagt hat), kannst du direkt oder indirekt wiedergeben.

Direct speech Madison says, 'Dad isn't at home.'
Madison sagt: „Dad ist nicht zu Hause."

◀ In der **direkten Rede** *(direct speech)* gibst du **wörtlich** wieder, was jemand sagt oder schreibt.
Direkte Rede steht in der Regel in Anführungszeichen.

Indirect speech Madison **says** (that) her dad isn't at home.
Madison sagt, dass ihr Vater nicht zu Hause ist.

◀ In der **indirekten Rede** (*indirect speech* oder *reported speech*) berichtest du, was jemand sagt oder schreibt. Die indirekte Rede wird mit Verben wie *say, tell sb., answer, explain, write* eingeleitet.

!
- Im Englischen steht vor der indirekten Rede **kein Komma**.
- Das Wort *that* wird oft weggelassen.

b) Indirect speech: tense changes

Indirect speech
Mrs Young **said** that she had to go back to the airport.
She **told** Madison that her boss wanted a report.

Indirekte Rede: Veränderungen der Zeitform

Wenn das einleitende Verb im ***simple past*** steht (*she **said**, she **told** sb., he **wrote*** usw.), werden in der indirekten Rede meist andere Zeitformen verwendet als in der direkten Rede:

Die Zeitformen der direkten Rede werden um eine Zeitstufe in die Vergangenheit „zurückverschoben" *(backshift of tenses)*.

◄ So wird z.B. das *simple present* der direkten Rede in der indirekten Rede zum *simple past*.

Tense changes

		Direct speech	Indirect speech
present ► past	*Madison*	'Dad isn't at home. I'm waiting for him.'	Madison **said** her dad wasn't at home. She **said** she was waiting for him.
past ► past perfect	*Mom*	'There was an explosion at the airport.'	Her mom **told** her there had been an explosion at the airport.
present perfect ► past perfect	*Madison*	'I haven't called Dad since lunchtime.'	Madison **told** her mom she hadn't called her dad since lunchtime.
***will*-future ► *would* + infinitive**	*Mom*	'I'll be home around nine.'	Her mom **said** she would be home around nine.
***going to*-future ► *was/were going to* + infinitive**	*Sam*	'I'm going to do my homework at Marcia's.'	Madison **told** her mom she was going to do her homework at Marcia's.

– Verben im *past perfect* bleiben unverändert, da man sie nicht weiter „zurückverschieben" kann.
– In der Umgangssprache werden *simple past*-Formen der direkten Rede oft nicht ins *past perfect* verändert.

► *Unit 4 (p. 84) • P 13–15 (p. 90)*

Berichte, was Madison am Telefon zu Marcia gesagt hat. Schreib die Sätze in der indirekten Rede in dein Heft.

1 'My mom is very busy.' — Madison **said** her mom ...
2 'She has to work late.' — She **told** Marcia her mom ...
3 'Mom won't be home till nine.' — She **added** that her mom ...
4 'Dad will probably want a pizza.' — She also **said** her dad ...
5 'I'll call again later.' — She **told** Marcia she ...

Grammatical terms (Grammatische Fachbegriffe)

active ['æktɪv]	Aktiv	*Shakira **sang** that song.*
adjective ['ædʒɪktɪv]	Adjektiv	*good, red, new, boring, ...*
adverb ['ædvɜ:b]	Adverb	*always, badly, here, really, today*
adverb of frequency ['fri:kwənsi]	Häufigkeitsadverb	*always, often, never, ...*
adverb of indefinite time [ɪn,defɪnət 'taɪm]	Adverb der unbestimmten Zeit	*already, ever, just, never, ...*
adverb of manner ['mænə]	Adverb der Art und Weise	*badly, happily, quietly, well, ...*
article ['ɑ:tɪkl]	Artikel	*the, a/an*
auxiliary [ɔ:g'zɪliəri]	Hilfsverb	*be, have, do; will, can, must, ...*
backshift of tenses ['bækʃɪft]	Verschiebung der Zeitformen *(bei der indirekten Rede)*	*'I'm sorry.'* ► *He said he **was** sorry.*
comparison [kəm'pærɪsn]	Steigerung	*old – older – oldest*
conditional sentence [kən,dɪʃənl 'sentəns]	Bedingungssatz	*I'd call him if I knew his number.*
conjunction [kən'dʒʌŋkʃn]	Konjunktion	*and, or, but; because, before, ...*
contact clause ['kɒntækt klɔ:z]	Relativsatz ohne Relativpronomen	*She's the girl **I love**.*
countable noun ['kaʊntəbl]	zählbares Nomen	*girl – girls, pound – pounds, ...*
definite article ['defɪnət]	bestimmter Artikel	*the*
direct speech [,daɪrekt 'spi:tʃ]	direkte Rede, wörtliche Rede	***'I'm sorry**.'*
future ['fju:tʃə]	Zukunft, Futur	
gerund ['dʒerənd]	Gerundium	*I like **dancing**. **Dancing** is fun.*
***going to*-future**	Futur mit *going to*	***I'm going to watch** TV tonight.*
***if*-clause** ['ɪf klɔ:z]	*if*-Satz, Nebensatz mit *if*	***If I see Jack**, I'll tell him.*
imperative [ɪm'perətɪv]	Imperativ (Befehlsform)	*Open your books. Don't talk.*
indirect speech [,ɪndərekt 'spi:tʃ]	indirekte Rede	*He said **(that) he was sorry**.*
infinitive [ɪn'fɪnətɪv]	Infinitiv (Grundform des Verbs)	*(to) open, (to) see, (to) read, ...*
irregular verb [ɪ,regjələ 'vɜ:b]	unregelmäßiges Verb	*(to) go – went – gone*
main clause	Hauptsatz	***I like Scruffy** because I like dogs.*
modal, modal auxiliary [,məʊdl‿ɔ:g'zɪliəri]	modales Hilfsverb, Modalverb	*can, could, may, must, ...*
negative statement [,negətɪv 'steɪtmənt]	verneinter Aussagesatz	*I don't like bananas.*
noun [naʊn]	Nomen, Substantiv	*Sophie, girl, brother, time, ...*
object ['ɒbdʒɪkt]	Objekt	*My sister is writing **a letter**.*
object form ['ɒbdʒɪkt fɔ:m]	Objektform (der Personalpronomen)	*me, you, him, her, it, us, them*
passive ['pæsɪv]	Passiv	*That song **was sung** by Shakira.*
past [pɑ:st]	Vergangenheit	
past participle [,pɑ:st 'pɑ:tɪsɪpl]	Partizip Perfekt	*cleaned, planned, gone, seen, ...*
past perfect [,pɑ:st 'pɜ:fɪkt]	Plusquamperfekt, Vorvergangenheit	*He was late because he **had missed** the bus.*
past progressive [,pɑ:st prə'gresɪv]	Verlaufsform der Vergangenheit	*At 7.30 I **was having** dinner.*
personal pronoun [,pɜ:sənl 'prəʊnaʊn]	Personalpronomen (persönliches Fürwort)	*I, you, he, she, it, we, they; me, you, him, her, it, us, them*
plural ['plʊərəl]	Plural, Mehrzahl	
positive statement [,pɒzətɪv 'steɪtmənt]	bejahter Aussagesatz	*I like oranges.*
possessive determiner [pə,zesɪv dɪ'tɜ:mɪnə]	Possessivbegleiter (besitzanzeigender Begleiter)	*my, your, his, her, its, our, their*
possessive form [pə,zesɪv fɔ:m]	*s*-Genitiv	*Jo's brother; my sister's room*
possessive pronoun [pə,zesɪv 'prəʊnaʊn]	Possessivpronomen	*mine, yours, his, hers, ours, theirs*
preposition [,prepə'zɪʃn]	Präposition	*after, at, in, next to, under, ...*
present ['preznt]	Gegenwart	
present perfect [,preznt 'pɜ:fɪkt]	*present perfect*	*We**'ve made** a cake for you.*
present perfect progressive [,preznt ,pɜ:fɪkt prə'gresɪv]	Verlaufsform des *present perfect*	*We**'ve been waiting** for an hour.*

present progressive [ˌpreznt prəˈgresɪv]	Verlaufsform der Gegenwart	*The Hansons **are having** lunch.*
pronoun [ˈprəʊnaʊn]	Pronomen, Fürwort	
quantifier [ˈkwɒntɪfaɪə]	Mengenangabe	*some, a lot of, many, much, ...*
question tag [ˈkwestʃən tæg]	Frageanhängsel	*This place is great, **isn't it?***
question word [ˈkwestʃən wɜːd]	Fragewort	*what?, when?, where?, how?, ...*
regular verb [ˌregjələ ˈvɜːb]	regelmäßiges Verb	*(to) help – helped – helped*
reflexive pronoun [rɪˌfleksɪv ˈprəʊnaʊn]	Reflexivpronomen	*myself, yourself, themselves, ...*
relative clause [ˌrelətɪv ˈklɔːz]	Relativsatz	*There's the girl **who helped me**.*
relative pronoun [ˌrelətɪv ˈprəʊnaʊn]	Relativpronomen	*who, that, which*
reported speech [rɪˌpɔːtɪd ˈspiːtʃ]	indirekte Rede	*He said **(that) he was sorry**.*
short answer [ˌʃɔːt‿ˈɑːnsə]	Kurzantwort	*Yes, I am. / No, I don't. / ...*
simple past [ˌsɪmpl ˈpɑːst]	einfache Form der Vergangenheit	*Jo **wrote** two letters yesterday.*
simple present [ˌsɪmpl ˈpreznt]	einfache Form der Gegenwart	*I always **go** to school by bike.*
singular [ˈsɪŋgjələ]	Singular, Einzahl	
subject [ˈsʌbdʒɪkt]	Subjekt	***My sister** is writing a letter.*
subject form [ˈsʌbdʒɪkt fɔːm]	Subjektform (der Personalpronomen)	*I, you, he, she, it, we, they*
subordinate clause [səˌbɔːdɪnət ˈklɔːz]	Nebensatz	*I like Scruffy **because I like dogs**.*
uncountable noun [ʌnˈkaʊntəbl]	nicht zählbares Nomen	*bread, milk, money, news, work, ...*
verb [vɜːb]	Verb	*hear, open, help, go, ...*
***will*-future**	Futur mit *will*	*I think it **will be** cold tonight.*
word order [ˈwɜːd‿ɔːdə]	Wortstellung	
yes/no question	Entscheidungsfrage	*Are you 13? Do you like comics?*

Lösungen der Grammar-File-Aufgaben

p.156
1 **Flying** alone to New York was very exciting for Ryan.
2 He didn't enjoy **waiting** in the security queues at the airport.
3 At first he was a bit afraid of **going** up the ESB in a fast lift.
4 He was very interested in **seeing** all the sights.
5 Later he talked about **looking** down from the ESB for hours.

p.158
1 The telephone **was invented by Alexander Bell.**
2 'We will rock you!' **was sung by Queen.**
3 Clifton Suspension Bridge **was built by Brunel.**

p.160/1
1 There's **some** milk but there isn't **much** bread.
2 Here's **some** information about the Grand Canyon. I'm doing **a** project on it.
3 We haven't got **many** eggs, and we haven't got **much** butter.
4 I haven't got **much** homework, just **an** exercise for French.

p.160/2
1 We can learn a lot from history.
2 What do you know about **the** history of England?
3 Is **the** food that you like best healthy?
4 In Jake's health class they're talking about food.
5 Tourists like to visit Hermann's Festhalle.
6 **The** tourists who asked us the way were from Germany.

p.161
1 On Monday Anna **is meeting** Elli.
2 On Tuesday she**'s buying** a present.
3 On Wednesday she**'s making** her dad's birthday cake.
4 On Thursday she**'s phoning** friends back home.

p.163
1 We've lived here **for** four years.
2 Madison has been in the car **for** over 20 minutes now.
3 She's been at her school **since** 2005.
4 I've known my best friend **for** five years.
5 Mr Young has worked at the King Center **since** 1999.
6 The weather has been bad **for** over a week.

p.164
1 Madison **said** her mom **was** very busy.
2 She **told** Marcia her mom **had** to work late.
3 She **added** that her mom **wouldn't be** home till nine.
4 She also **said** her dad **would** probably **want** a pizza.
5 She **told** Marcia she**'d call** again later.

Diese Wörterverzeichnisse findest du in deinem Englischbuch:

- Das **Vocabulary** (Vokabelverzeichnis – S. 167–188) enthält alle Wörter und Wendungen, die du lernen musst. Sie stehen in der Reihenfolge, in der sie in den Units vorkommen.
- Das **Dictionary** besteht aus zwei alphabetischen Wörterlisten zum Nachschlagen:
  Englisch – Deutsch: S. 189–219
  Deutsch – Englisch: S. 220–247.

So ist das Vocabulary aufgebaut:

- Hier siehst du, wo die Wörter vorkommen.
  p. 16/A 6 = Seite 16, Abschnitt 6
  p. 21/P 4 = Seite 21, Übung 4
- Die Lautschrift zeigt dir, wie ein Wort ausgesprochen und betont wird.
- Eingerückte Wörter lernst du am besten zusammen mit dem vorausgehenden Wort, weil die beiden zusammengehören.
- Die blauen Kästen solltest du dir besonders gut ansehen.

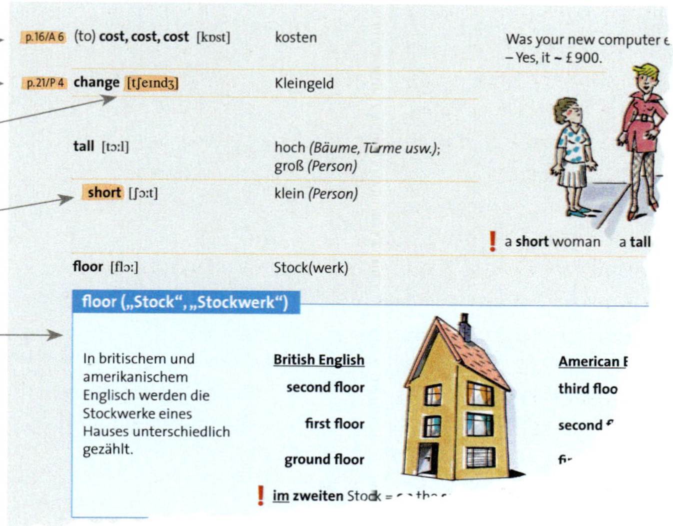
p.16/A 6 (to) **cost, cost, cost** [kɒst] kosten — Was your new computer e… – Yes, it ~ £900.
p.21/P 4 **change** [tʃeɪndʒ] Kleingeld
tall [tɔːl] hoch *(Bäume, Türme usw.)*; groß *(Person)*
short [ʃɔːt] klein *(Person)*
! a **short** woman a **tall**
floor [flɔː] Stock(werk)
floor („Stock", „Stockwerk")
In britischem und amerikanischem Englisch werden die Stockwerke eines Hauses unterschiedlich gezählt.
British English: second floor / first floor / ground floor
American E…: third floo… / second… / fi…
! im zweiten Stock = …

Tipps zum Wörterlernen findest du im Skills File auf Seite 138.

Abkürzungen:

n	= *noun*	*v*	= *verb*
adj	= *adjective*	*adv*	= *adverb*
prep	= *preposition*	*conj*	= *conjunction*
pl	= *plural*	*no pl*	= *no plural*
p.	= page	pp.	= pages
sb.	= somebody	sth.	= something
jn.	= jemanden	jm.	= jemandem
AE	= *American English*	*BE*	= *British English*
infml	= *informal* (umgangssprachlich, informell)		

Symbole:

! Hier stehen Hinweise auf Besonderheiten, bei denen man leicht Fehler machen kann.

◄► ist das „Gegenteil"-Zeichen: **alive** ◄► **dead** (**alive** ist das Gegenteil von **dead**)

~ Die **Tilde** in den Beispielsätzen steht für das neue Wort. Beispiel:
daily – Do your mum and dad get a ~ newspaper?

Introduction – Welcome to the United States of America

p.8	(to) **look forward to** sth. ['fɔːwəd]	sich auf etwas freuen	I'm really **looking ~ to** the weekend. We're going to drive to the Grand Canyon.
	daily ['deɪli]	täglich, Tages-	Do your mum and dad get a ~ newspaper?
	three and a half days/weeks	dreieinhalb Tage/Wochen	! With **'and'**: **three and a half** days
	awesome ['ɔːsəm] *(AE, infml)*	klasse, großartig	very good, great

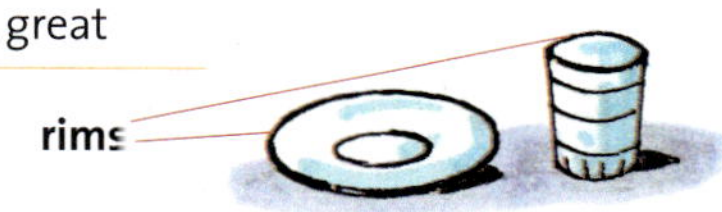

	rim [rɪm]	Rand, Kante	
	(to) **hike** [haɪk]	wandern	(to) go for long walks in the country
	hike	Wanderung, Marsch	a long walk in the country
	comment ['kɒment]	Kommentar, Bemerkung	! stress: **comment** ['kɒment]

p.9	**grade** [greɪd] *(AE)*	Jahrgangsstufe, Klasse	= *BE* year
	middle school	*(USA) Schule für 11- bis 14-Jährige*	
	busy ['bɪzi]	beschäftigt	I'll call you back later. I'm ~ with my homework.
	(to) **raise money (for)** [reɪz]	Geld sammeln (für)	
	(to) **cut the grass** [grɑːs]	Rasen mähen	
	grass	Gras; Rasen	

She's **cutting the grass.**

	sale [seɪl]	Verkauf	
	tent [tent]	Zelt	
	how to do sth.	wie man etwas tut / tun kann / tun soll	

a **tent**

Question words + to-infinitive: how to ... / what to ... / where to ... / ...

Nach **Fragewörtern** kannst du einen **Infinitiv mit *to*** verwenden.
Er entspricht einem Nebensatz mit Modalverb („können", „sollen" usw.).

Can you tell me **how to get** to the station?	Können Sie mir sagen, wie ich zum Bahnhof komme / kommen kann?
I don't know **what to do.**	Ich weiß nicht, was ich machen soll.
He had no idea **where to go** or **who to ask.**	Er hatte keine Ahnung, wohin er gehen sollte oder wen er fragen könnte.

	tool [tuːl]	Werkzeug	
	on my/our/... own [əʊn]	allein, selbstständig *(ohne Hilfe)*	Did you go with Emma? – No, I went **on my ~**. His room looks great. Did he paint it **on his ~**?
	Native American [ˌneɪtɪv‿ə'merɪkən]	amerikanische(r) Ureinwohner/in, Indianer/in	**!** Der Begriff **Native American** wird heute von vielen dem älteren Begriff **Indian** vorgezogen.
	Indian ['ɪndiən]	Indianer/in; indianisch	
	(to) **sew (on)** [səʊ], **sewed** [səʊd], **sewn** [səʊn]	(an)nähen	The doctors were able to ~ his finger back **on**. **!** pronunciation: (to) **sew** [səʊ]
	monument ['mɒnjumənt]	Denkmal, Monument	**!** stress: **<u>mon</u>ument** ['mɒnjumənt] *French:* le monument
	natural ['nætʃrəl]	Natur-, natürlich	*French:* naturel, le
	human ['hjuːmən]	Menschen-, menschlich	When did ~ life on earth begin? Do you know? *French:* humain, e
p.10	**high school** ['haɪ skuːl]	*(USA) Schule für 14- bis 18-Jährige*	
	(to) **stay behind**	zurückbleiben, dableiben	When Mum went away at the weekend, dad **~ed behind** to look after me.
	highway ['haɪweɪ]	*(USA)* Fernstraße *(oft mit vier oder mehr Spuren)*	
	route [ruːt]	Strecke, Route	**!** In den USA werden große Fernstraßen mit <u>**Route** + Nummer</u> bezeichnet.

	gas [gæs] *(AE)*, **petrol** ['petrəl] *(BE)*	Benzin	
	gas station *(AE)*, **petrol station** *(BE)*	Tankstelle	
	license plate ['laɪsns pleɪt] *(AE)*, **number plate** ['nʌmbə pleɪt] *(BE)*	Nummernschild	
	motel [məʊ'tel]	Motel	
	auto ['ɔːtəʊ] *(AE)*	Auto, PKW	
	grand [grænd]	eindrucksvoll, beeindruckend	The hotel looked ~ from outside, but our room was small and dark.
	multi- ['mʌlti]	viel-, mehr-; multi-, Multi-	**multi-**coloured; a **multi-**millionaire
	trail [treɪl]	(Lehr-)Pfad	We learned a lot about trees on the forest ~.
	foot [fʊt], *pl* **feet** [fiːt]	Fuß *(Längenmaß; ca. 30 cm)*	The cabin was quite small, only about 6 **feet** high.
	wing [wɪŋ]	Flügel	
	tip [tɪp]	Spitze	

	(to) **forgive** [fə'gɪv], **forgave** [fə'geɪv], **forgiven** [fə'gɪvn]	vergeben, verzeihen	I know that she has hurt you, but try and ~ her.
p.11	**mule** [mjuːl]	Maultier	
	lodge [lɒdʒ]	Landhaus	
	adventure [əd'ventʃə]	Abenteuer	Our fishing trip in Canada was a great ~. We even saw some bears. *French:* l'aventure *(f)*

Unit 1: New York, New York

p.13	**deli** ['deli]	*Kombination aus Lebensmittelgeschäft und Fastfoodrestaurant*	If you're hungry, we can get some sandwiches at the ~ on the way home.
	avenue ['ævənjuː]	Allee	We moved to a new house in Park **Avenue**. *French:* l'avenue *(f)*
p.14/A 1	**block** [blɒk]	(Häuser-, Wohn-)Block	
	downtown [ˌdaʊn'taʊn] *(AE)*	(im/in das) Stadtzentrum	Dad works in a bank ~.
	the downtown bus *(AE)*	der Bus in Richtung Stadtzentrum	! In New York, the south of Manhattan is called **downtown**.
p.14/A 2	**line** [laɪn] *(AE)*, **queue** [kjuː] *(BE)*	Schlange, Reihe *(wartender Menschen)*	a **queue** *(BE)*, a **line** *(AE)* *French:* la queue
	(to) **form** [fɔːm]	(sich) bilden, formen	*French:* former
	sidewalk ['saɪdwɔːk] *(AE)*, **pavement** ['peɪvmənt] *(BE)*	Gehweg, Bürgersteig	**pavement** *(BE)*, **sidewalk** *(AE)*
	hostess ['həʊstəs]	Gastgeberin *(in USA auch: Frau, die im Restaurant die Gäste empfängt und an ihren Platz führt)*	

American English (I)

p.14/A 3

Different words

American English	British English	
apartment	**flat**	Wohnung
cellphone	**mobile (phone)**	Handy
downtown	**city centre**	Stadtzentrum
elevator	**lift**	Fahrstuhl, Aufzug
gas	**petrol**	Benzin
grade	**year**	Jahrgangsstufe
line	**queue**	Schlange, Reihe
sidewalk	**pavement**	Gehweg, Bürgersteig
subway	**underground**	U-Bahn
vacation	**holiday(s)**	Ferien, Urlaub

Different spelling

American English: *-ter*	British English: *-tre*
cen**ter**	cen**tre**
me**ter**	me**tre**
thea**ter**	thea**tre**

American English: *-or*	British English: *-our*
col**or**	col**our**
fav**or**ite	fav**our**ite
harb**or**	harb**our**
neighb**or**	neighb**our**

American English:	British English:
trave**l**ed, trave**l**ing	trave**ll**ed, trave**ll**ing

p.15/A 4	**security** [sɪ'kjʊərəti]	Sicherheit(svorkehrungen)	At airports, ~ has to be very strict. It's easy to climb in the bottom window, so we have a big ~ problem. *French:* la sécurité
	fire station ['faɪə steɪʃn]	Feuerwache	
	firefighter ['faɪəfaɪtə]	Feuerwehrmann, -frau	another word for 'fireman/-woman'
p.15/A 5	**anything else** [els]	(irgend)etwas anderes	

... else

1. *(anders, unterschiedlich)*

I don't like apple juice. Have you got **anything else**?	... Hast du **irgendetwas anderes**?
I'm tired. **Somebody else** will have to tidy up.	... **Jemand anders** muss aufräumen.
Oh no, not France again! Let's go **somewhere else** this year.	... Lass uns dieses Jahr **woanders** hinfahren.

2. *(außerdem, zusätzlich)*

Do you need **anything else**?	Brauchst du **sonst noch etwas**?
What else do you know about New York?	**Was** weißt du **(sonst) noch** über New York?
I met Susan at the party. – **Who else** did you meet? / Did you meet **anybody else**?	**Wen** hast du **(sonst) noch** getroffen? / Hast du **sonst noch jemanden** getroffen?

(to) **put out a fire**	ein Feuer löschen	
shift [ʃɪft]	Schicht *(bei der Arbeit)*	My dad works 12-hour **~s**. There are eight men and women on his **~**.
guy [gaɪ] *(infml)*	Typ, Kerl	an informal word for 'man' or 'boy'
ground zero [ˌgraʊnd 'zɪərəʊ]	Bodennullpunkt *(Bezeichnung für das zerstörte World Trade Center in New York; ursprünglich die Explosionsstelle einer Bombe oder Rakete über dem Boden)*	
hijacker ['haɪdʒækə]	(Flugzeug-)Entführer/in	

	(to) **take over** a plane	die Kontrolle über ein Flugzeug übernehmen; ein Flugzeug in seine Macht bringen	
	(to) **burn** [bɜːn]	brennen; verbrennen	The light in the bedroom was still **~ing** at 4 am. Don't ~ those newspapers! Recycle them!
	(to) **collapse** [kə'læps]	zusammenbrechen; einstürzen	
	(to) **take place**	stattfinden	Our next school trip will **take** ~ in two months.
p.16/A 6	(to) **cost, cost, cost** [kɒst]	kosten	Was your new computer expensive? – Yes, it ~ £ 900.
	dollar ($) ['dɒlə]	Dollar	How much is £ 900 in **~s**?
	tall [tɔːl]	hoch *(Bäume, Türme usw.)*; groß *(Person)*	
	short [ʃɔːt]	klein *(Person)*	! a **short** woman a **tall** woman
	admission [əd'mɪʃn]	Eintritt, Eintrittspreis	Tickets cost £ 5, but ~ is free for kids under 14.
	perfect ['pɜːfɪkt]	perfekt; ideal	! stress: **perfect** ['pɜːfɪkt] *French:* parfait, e
	lobby ['lɒbi]	Eingangshalle	
	visibility [ˌvɪzə'bɪləti]	Sicht(weite)	The fog was so bad that ~ was only 10 feet. *French:* la visibilité
	ticket office ['tɪkɪt_ˌɒfɪs]	Kasse *(für den Verkauf von Eintrittskarten)*; Fahrkartenschalter	
	floor [flɔː]	Stock(werk)	

floor („Stock", „Stockwerk")

In britischem und amerikanischem Englisch werden die Stockwerke eines Hauses unterschiedlich gezählt.

British English	American English	
second floor	**third floor**	zweiter Stock
first floor	**second floor**	erster Stock
ground floor	**first floor**	Erdgeschoss

! **im zweiten** Stock = **on** the **second** floor *(BE)* / **on** the **third** floor *(AE)*

	forever [fər'evə]	ewig, für immer	always, from now on
	(to) **be tired of** sth.	genug von etwas haben, etwas satt haben	I'm really **~ of** that CD. / I'm really **~ of** listening to that CD. Can't you play something else?
p.16/A 7	**puzzle** ['pʌzl]	Rätsel	
p.17/A 8	**bagel** ['beɪgl]	Bagel *(ringförmiges Brötchen)*	
	cream cheese [ˌkriːm 'tʃiːz]	Frischkäse	
	cream [kriːm]	Sahne; Creme	
	coffee ['kɒfi]	Kaffee	
	counter ['kaʊntə]	Theke, Ladentisch	

	Jewish ['dʒu:ɪʃ]	jüdisch	
	immigrant ['ɪmɪgrənt]	Einwanderer/Einwanderin	! stress: **<u>im</u>migrant** ['ɪmɪgrənt]
p.20/P 1	**borough** ['bʌrə, *AE:* 'bɜ:rəʊ]	(Stadt-)Bezirk	

New York: the five boroughs

the Bronx	[brɒŋks]	der nördlichste Bezirk; liegt als einziger auf dem Festland
Manhattan	[mæn'hætn]	Insel zwischen dem Hudson und dem East River, berühmt für ihre Wolkenkratzer
Queens	[kwi:nz]	der größte Bezirk; im Südwesten der Insel Long Island gelegen; vor allem Wohngebiet
Brooklyn	['brʊklɪn]	wie Queens auf Long Island gelegen; die berühmte Brooklyn Bridge verbindet Brooklyn mit Manhattan
Staten Island !	[ˌstætn‿'aɪlənd]	Insel an der Einfahrt zum Hafen von New York, mit Manhattan durch Fährbetrieb verbunden

(→ Karte auf S. 20)

American English (II)

p.20/P 2

Different words

<u>American English</u>	<u>British English</u>	
cookie ['kʊki]	**biscuit**	Keks
eraser [ɪ'reɪsər; *BE:* ɪ'reɪzə]	**rubber**	Radiergummi
French fries [fraɪz]	**chips**	Pommes frites
garbage ['gɑ:rbɪdʒ]	**rubbish**	Müll, Abfall
pants [pænts]	**trousers**	Hose
potato chips	**crisps**	Kartoffelchips
schedule ['skedʒu:l; *BE:* 'ʃedju:l]	**timetable**	Stundenplan; Fahrplan

Different pronunciation

	AE: [æ]	**BE:** [ɑ:]
ask, last	[æsk], [læst]	[ɑ:sk], [lɑ:st]
	AE: [u:]	**BE:** [ju:]
new, Tuesday	[nu:], ['tu:zdeɪ]	[nju:], ['tju:zdeɪ]
	AE: [ɑ:]	**BE:** [ɒ]
clock, hot	[klɑ:k], [hɑ:t]	[klɒk], [hɒt]

– In American English, you can usually hear the **'r'** in words like **here, more, shirt, farm.**

– A **'t'** between two vowels often sounds more like a **'d'**, for example in **city, better, writer.**

p.21/P 4	**change** [tʃeɪndʒ]	Kleingeld	
p.22/P 7	(to) **take a break**	eine Pause machen	We've worked long enough now. Let's **take a ~**.
p.22/P 8	**ticket agent** ['tɪkɪt‿ˌeɪdʒənt]	*Angestellte(r) in Kartenvorverkaufsstelle*	somebody who sells tickets
p.23/P 9	**zoo** [zu:]	Zoo	*French:* le zoo
	skyscraper ['skaɪskreɪpə]	Wolkenkratzer	
	collection [kə'lekʃn]	Sammlung	verb: (to) **collect** – noun: **collection** *French:* la collection
p.25/P 13	**safety** ['seɪfti]	Sicherheit	

„Sicherheit"

They'll be safe if they stay in the car.

A **security** check at the airport

safety = Sicherheit *(das Sichersein vor Gefahr)*

security = Sicherheit, Sicherheitsvorkehrungen

(to) **work** sth. **out**	etwas herausarbeiten, herausfinden	
context ['kɒntekst]	Kontext, Zusammenhang	*French:* le contexte

You can tell me

p.26 **kiss** [kɪs]	Kuss	
(to) **kiss**	küssen	
cheek [tʃi:k]	Wange	a **kiss** on the **cheek**
(to) **leave** sb. **alone**	jn. in Ruhe lassen	**Leave me ~**. I'm trying to work.
nanny ['næni]	Kindermädchen	a woman who looks after very young children in their home
servant ['sɜ:vənt]	Diener/in, Bedienstete(r)	In the old days, people had lots of **~s** who cleaned the house and cooked for them.
(to) **gasp** [gɑ:sp]	nach Luft schnappen *(auch: vor Überraschung)*	Tim **~ed** as he walked up the hill. 'This is hard work,' he thought.
painting ['peɪntɪŋ]	Gemälde	

except [ɪk'sept]	außer	
(to) **appreciate** [ə'pri:ʃieɪt]	schätzen, zu schätzen wissen	Thank you very much. I really ~ your help.
suit [su:t]	Anzug; (Damen-)Kostüm	
(to) **seem (to be/to do)** [si:m]	(zu sein/zu tun) scheinen	You ~ **(to be)** tired. Did you sleep long enough?
drug [drʌg]	Droge, Rauschgift; Medikament	His eyes look strange. He seems to be on **~s**. Doctors hope the new ~ will help people with heart problems.
(to) **suggest** sth. **(to** sb.**)** [sə'dʒest]	(jm.) etwas vorschlagen	'Let's go for a walk,' Kelly **~ed to** Anthony. **!** My teacher **suggested** that we ask our parents. *(Not:* ... ~~suggested to ask~~ ...)
p.27 **I feel sick.** [sɪk]	Mir ist schlecht.	
(to) **lean over** [ˌli:n_'əʊvə]	sich herüberbeugen, -lehnen	Suddenly Mike **~ed over** and gave me a kiss.
we **should** ... [ʃəd, ʃʊd]	wir sollten ...	I think we ~ ask John before we take his CDs.

	(to) **take off** *(infml)*	sich davonmachen, sich aus dem Staub machen	When they saw the police, the thieves **took ~** in a fast car.
	tear [tɪə]	Träne	 **tears**
	(to) **cry** [kraɪ]	weinen	She's **crying**.
	It's not my fault. [fɔːlt]	Es/Das ist nicht meine Schuld.	Don't blame me! **It wasn't my ~** that we lost the match.
	blond [blɒnd]	blond, hell	*French:* blond, e
	(to) **scream** [skriːm]	schreien, kreischen	The children **~ed** when they saw the mice.
	(to) **kick** [kɪk]	treten	
	I didn't care. [keə]	Es war mir egal.	It wasn't cheap, but **I didn't ~** ... I bought it anyway.
p. 28	(to) **tear** sth. **off** [teə], **tore** [tɔː], **torn** [tɔːn]	etwas abreißen	She **tore ~** a piece of paper and wrote down my phone number.
	(to) **press** sth. [pres]	etwas drücken; auf etwas drücken	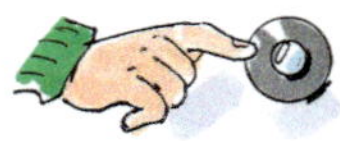
	cab [kæb]	Taxi	another word for 'taxi'
	brave [breɪv]	mutig	! German „brav" = English **good** English **brave** = German „mutig"
	(to) **get rid of** sb./sth. [rɪd]	jn./etwas loswerden	She wasn't very friendly. I think she wanted to **get ~ of** me.
	bench [bentʃ]	(Sitz-)Bank	! **bench** = Bank *(zum Sitzen)* **bank** = Bank *(Geldinstitut)*
	heading ['hedɪŋ]	Überschrift	 a **bench**

Unit 2: California, the 'Golden State'?

p. 34	**endless** ['endləs]	endlos	an **endless** discussion, an **endless** journey
	governor ['gʌvənə]	Gouverneur/in	! stress: **governor** ['gʌvənə]
	maid [meɪd]	Hausangestellte, Zimmermädchen	
	(to) **pick fruit** [pɪk]	Obst pflücken	**Picking fruit** 
	scenery ['siːnəri]	*(schöne)* Landschaft	We just want to relax and enjoy the **~**.
	minority [maɪ'nɒrəti]	Minderheit	There are 16 girls and 11 boys in my class. The boys are in the **~**. *French:* la minorité
	majority [mə'dʒɒrəti]	Mehrheit	The girls are in the **~**. *French:* la majorité **majority ◄► minority**
p. 36/A 1	**culture** ['kʌltʃə]	Kultur	! stress: **culture** ['kʌltʃə] *French:* la culture
	attitude (to, towards) ['ætɪtjuːd]	Haltung (gegenüber), Einstellung (zu)	What's your **~ to/towards** clothes? Do you always buy the latest fashion? *French:* l'attitude *(f)*
	(to) **fit in** (-tt-) [ˌfɪt_'ɪn]	hineinpassen; sich einfügen, sich anpassen	You won't **~ in** if you don't like team work. He didn't like the others, but he tried to **~ in**.

experience [ɪk'spɪəriəns]	Erlebnis, Erfahrung	How was your trip to Canada? – It was a great **~**. He didn't get the job. He hasn't got enough **~**. *French:* l'expérience *(f)*
(to) **experience** [ɪk'spɪəriəns]	erleben, erfahren	Have you ever **~d** bullying at school?

anybody/anyone, everybody/everyone, ...

Neben den Zusammensetzungen **anybody, everybody, somebody, nobody** gibt es auch – bei gleicher Bedeutung – die Zusammensetzungen auf **-one:**

anyone, everyone, someone, ! *(two words:)* **no one**.

anybody / anyone	['eniwʌn]	(irgend)jemand
everybody / everyone	['evriwʌn]	jeder, alle
somebody / someone	['sʌmwʌn]	jemand
nobody / no one	['nəʊ‿wʌn]	niemand

ethnic ['eθnɪk]	ethnisch	There are people from lots of different ~ groups in our city: people from Turkey, Russia, Bosnia, ...
(to) **be prejudiced (against)** ['predʒədɪst]	voreingenommen sein (gegen), Vorurteile haben (gegenüber)	I can't understand why some people **are ~ against** minorities.
prejudice (against) ['predʒudɪs]	Voreingenommenheit (gegen), Vorurteil (gegenüber)	I think Americans speak really awful English. – I'm sorry, but that is just a ~.
(to) **discriminate against** sb. [dɪ'skrɪmɪneɪt]	jn. diskriminieren, jn. benachteiligen	I think it's wrong to ~ **against** minorities. ! **jn.** diskriminieren = (to) discriminate **against sb.**
discrimination (against) [dɪˌskrɪmɪ'neɪʃn]	Diskriminierung (von), Benachteiligung (von)	Men often get more money than women for the same job. That's ~ **against** women.
(to) **act** [ækt]	handeln, sich verhalten	Jane is 15 now, but she still **~s** like a child.
disadvantage [ˌdɪsəd'vɑːntɪdʒ]	Nachteil	Not being able to drive can be a ~ when you're looking for a job. *French:* le désavantage
advantage (over sb./sth.**)** [əd'vɑːntɪdʒ]	Vorteil (gegenüber jm./etwas)	Cats have an ~ **over** dogs: they can climb trees. *French:* l'avantage *(m)*
opinion (of) [ə'pɪnjən]	Meinung (von, zu)	Man U were fantastic. – Do you think so? **In my ~**, Arsenal played better. *French:* l'opinion *(f)* (Meiner Meinung nach ...)
bilingual [ˌbaɪ'lɪŋgwəl]	zweisprachig	~ people = people who speak two languages really well (often because they learned them as children) *French:* bilingue
relations *(pl)* [rɪ'leɪʃnz]	Beziehungen	Germany has good ~ with all its neighbours.
(to) **succeed (in** sth.**)** [sək'siːd]	Erfolg haben, erfolgreich sein (mit etwas, bei etwas)	(to) be successful
p.37/A 3 (to) **be/feel bored** [bɔːd]	gelangweilt sein, sich langweilen	There was no one I knew at the party. I **was ~** and left early.
(to) **shake** [ʃeɪk], **shook** [ʃʊk], **shaken** ['ʃeɪkən]	schütteln; zittern	**Shake** the bottle before you open it. Look, he's nervous: his hands are **shaking**.
hard *(adv)* [hɑːd]	heftig, kräftig	I hit him ~ and he fell to the ground.
(to) **interrupt** [ˌɪntə'rʌpt]	unterbrechen	Please don't ~ me when I'm talking. Wait till I've finished.
(to) **plant** [plɑːnt]	pflanzen, einpflanzen	
plant [plɑːnt]	Pflanze	

(to) **plant**

a **plant**

	industry ['ɪndəstri]	Industrie	! stress: **industry** ['ɪndəstri]
	industrial [ɪn'dʌstriəl]	industriell, Industrie-	noun: **industry** ['ɪndəstri] – adjective: **industrial** [ɪn'dʌstriəl] *French:* l'industrie *(f)* – industriel, le

any („irgendein beliebiger")

Du kennst **any** bereits in verneinten Aussagesätzen und in Fragen:

We haven't got **any** biscuits. Have we got **any** crisps? — Wir haben keine Kekse. Haben wir Chips?

Man verwendet **any** auch, wenn **„irgendein", „jeder beliebige"** gemeint ist.
In dieser Bedeutung kann **any** auch in bejahten Aussagesätzen stehen.

The US produces more strawberries than **any** other country.	... als **jedes** andere Land / ... als **irgendein** anderes Land
You can have **any** bagel with tomato, bacon, ...	... **jeden (beliebigen)** Bagel
It's easy to dance – **anyone** can do it.	... **jeder (Beliebige)**
I was too scared to say **anything.**	... **irgendetwas** zu sagen
You can tell me **anything**.	... **alles (, was es auch sei / egal, was es ist)**

any/anybody wird oft nach **if** verwendet: If **anybody** has **any** questions, I'll try to answer them.

	production [prə'dʌkʃn]	Produktion, Herstellung	! stress: **production** [prə'dʌkʃn] *French:* la production
	process ['prəʊses]	Prozess, Verfahren	! stress: **process** ['prəʊses]
	insect ['ɪnsekt]	Insekt	! stress: **insect** ['ɪnsekt] *French:* l'insecte *(m)*
	(to) **spray** [spreɪ]	sprühen; besprühen	
p.38/A 4	**supper** ['sʌpə]	Abendessen	! **supper**: an evening meal at home, hot or cold **dinner**: a hot meal, at home or at a restaurant
	(to) **cry** [kraɪ]	schreien, rufen	! (to) **cry** = **1.** weinen; **2.** schreien, rufen
	border ['bɔːdə]	Grenze	The US only has a ~ with Canada and Mexico.
	(to) **run**	verlaufen *(Straße; Grenze)*	The cycle path **~s** on both sides of the river.
	(to) **reach** [riːtʃ]	erreichen	When we **~ed** the station, I went to the ticket machine to buy our tickets.
	patrol [pə'trəʊl]	Streife, Patrouille	The thieves saw the police ~ and ran away. *French:* la patrouille
	illegal [ɪ'liːgl]	illegal, ungesetzlich	*French:* illégal, e
	legal ['liːgl]	legal	! stress: **legal** ['liːgl] *French:* légal, e
	fence [fens]	Zaun	a **fence** 
p.38/A 5	**amnesty** ['æmnəsti]	Amnestie, Begnadigung	
p.42/P 2	**synonym** ['sɪnənɪm]	Synonym *(Wort mit gleicher oder sehr ähnlicher Bedeutung)*	Words with the same meaning (or almost the same meaning) are called **~s**. *French:* le synonyme
p.43/P 4	**camp** [kæmp]	Camp, (Ferien-)Lager	
	specific [spə'sɪfɪk]	bestimmte(r, s), spezifische(r, s)	Let's meet between three and six. – No. Let's agree on a ~ time.
	(to) **picture** sth. ['pɪktʃə]	sich etwas (bildlich) vorstellen	I couldn't think of the name of the street, so I tried to ~ the street sign.

	vegetarian [ˌvedʒəˈteəriən]	vegetarisch; Vegetarier/in	We only eat ~ food (= meals without meat). We're **~s**. *French:* végétarien, ne – le végétarien, la végétarienne
	analysis [əˈnæləsɪs], *pl* **analyses** [əˈnæləsiːz]	Analyse, Auswertung	! stress: **analysis** [əˈnæləsɪs]
p.44/P 6	**Re: ...** [riː]	Betreff: ...	
p.45/P 8	**sportsman, sportswoman**	Sportler, Sportlerin	
p.46/P 12	(to) **run into** sth./sb.	gegen etwas fahren / jn. anfahren	He couldn't stop the car and **ran ~** a stone wall. Drive carefully or you'll **run ~** somebody.
p.47/P 14	**theme park** [ˈθiːm pɑːk]	Themenpark *(Freizeitpark mit Attraktionen zu einem bestimmten Thema)*	
	opening hours *(pl)*	Öffnungszeiten	
p.48/P 15	**recorded message**	(automatische) Telefonansage	
	Don't panic. [ˈpænɪk]	Keine Panik. / Bleib ruhig.	
	line [laɪn]	Leitung *(Telefon)*	

Santa Monica – Episode 1 of a TV series

p.49	**episode** [ˈepɪsəʊd]	Folge *(einer Fernsehserie)*	! stress: **episode** [ˈepɪsəʊd] *French:* l'épisode *(f)*
	the Pacific (Ocean) [pəˌsɪfɪk_ˈəʊʃn]	der Pazifische Ozean, der Pazifik	
	the Atlantic (Ocean) [ətˌlæntɪk_ˈəʊʃn]	der Atlantische Ozean, der Atlantik	
	cold [kəʊld]	Kälte	Come in! Don't stand outside in the ~.
	(to) **want** sb. **to do** sth.	wollen, dass jd. etwas tut	! I **want you to help** your sister. = Ich **möchte, dass du** deiner Schwester **hilfst**. *Nie:* ~~I want that you help~~ ...
	comfortable [ˈkʌmftəbl]	bequem	Come in and make yourself ~. (= ... und machen Sie es sich bequem.) ! stress: **comfortable** [ˈkʌmftəbl]
	tie [taɪ]	Krawatte, Schlips	 
	(to) **tie** [taɪ]	binden	He's **tying** his son's tie. She's **tying** her hair back. ! -ing form: **tying**
	engine [ˈendʒɪn]	Motor	
	(to) **make sure** that ...	sich vergewissern, dass ...; dafür sorgen, dass ...	Please **~ sure that** the windows are closed when you leave the house.
p.50	**There you go!** *(infml)*	*etwa:* So, das hätten wir.	**There you go** – your TV's working again.
	depressed [dɪˈprest]	deprimiert, niedergeschlagen	
	depressing [dɪˈpresɪŋ]	deprimierend, trostlos	

guilty ['gɪlti]	schuldbewusst; schuldig	I felt so ~ because I forgot my mum's birthday. He would never steal anything. He can't be ~.
jail [dʒeɪl]	Gefängnis	
(to) **crash** sth. [kræʃ]	einen Unfall mit etwas haben	I **~ed** our car last week, but luckily I wasn't hurt.
fight [faɪt]	Kampf; Schlägerei	verb: (to) **fight** – noun: **fight**
(to) **change** [tʃeɪndʒ]	(sich) ändern; (sich) verändern	We've **~d** our plans. We're having lunch here, not at the café. Water **~s** into ice when it's very cold. *French:* changer
(to) **give up**	aufgeben	
boyfriend ['bɔɪfrend]	(fester) Freund	
girlfriend ['gɜːlfrend]	(feste) Freundin	
(to) **get to know** sb.	jn. kennenlernen	I haven't met Tony's sister, but I'll **get to ~** her at his party on Saturday, I hope.
serious ['sɪəriəs]	ernst, ernsthaft	We've got a ~ problem. I've lost the car keys. *French:* sérieux, sérieuse We could walk home. – **Seriously**? You can't mean that. It's over five miles! („Im Ernst? ...")
p.51 **whoever** [huː'evə]	wer (auch) immer; wen/wem (auch) immer	It's *your* birthday party; you can invite ~ you like.

whoever, whatever, whenever, wherever

Whoever told you that was wrong.	**Wer immer** dir das **(auch)** erzählt hat, hatte Unrecht.
I'll help you **whatever** happens.	Ich werde dir helfen, **was immer auch** geschieht.
Visit us **whenever** you like.	Besuch uns, **wann immer** du magst.
Wherever you go, I'll come with you.	Ich komme mit, **wo auch immer** du hingehst.

drunk [drʌŋk]	betrunken	
cigarette [ˌsɪgə'ret]	Zigarette	*French:* la cigarette
(to) **light** [laɪt], **lit, lit** [lɪt]	anzünden	(to) **light** a firework
(to) **work out** [ˌwɜːk_'aʊt]	gut ausgehen	Don't worry. Things will **work ~** in the end.
since [sɪns]	da (ja), weil	**Since** it was raining, I decided to stay at home.
niece [niːs]	Nichte	a daughter of someone's brother or sister *French:* la nièce
nephew ['nefjuː, 'nevjuː]	Neffe	a son of someone's brother or sister le neveu
fat [fæt]	dick	a **fat** cat
p.52 (to) **offer** ['ɒfə]	anbieten	The language school **~s** French and Spanish courses.
towel ['taʊəl]	Handtuch	
I'll take it from here.	*etwa:* Ich übernehme das jetzt. / Ich komme jetzt allein klar.	Do you need any more help? – No, thanks. **I'll ~ it from here.**
character ['kærəktə]	Person, Figur *(in Roman, Film)*	**!** stress: **<u>cha</u>racter** ['kærəktə]

Unit 3: Hermann says 'Willkommen'

p.54	**grape** [greɪp]	Weintraube	some **grapes** 
	harvest ['hɑ:vɪst]	Ernte	
p.55	**tradition** [trə'dɪʃn]	Tradition	! stress: **tradition** [trə'dɪʃn] *French:* la tradition
	alive [ə'laɪv]	am Leben, lebendig	! pronunciation: **alive** [ə'laɪv] – (to) **live** [lɪv] **alive** ◄► **dead**
	event [ɪ'vent]	Ereignis; Veranstaltung	The first day at school is a big ~ in a child's life.
	at first	zuerst, am Anfang	! • I didn't like him **at first**, but later we became friends. (= **zuerst, am Anfang**) • I'd like to go out, but I have to finish my homework **first**. (= **zuerst, als Erstes**)
p.56/A 1	**system** ['sɪstəm]	System	! stress: **system** ['sɪstəm] *French:* le système
	elementary school [,elɪ'mentri sku:l]	*(USA)* Grundschule *(für 6- bis 11-Jährige)*	
	kindergarten ['kɪndəgɑ:tn]	Kindergarten; *(USA)* Vorschule *(für 5- bis 6-Jährige)*	
p.56/A 2	**period** ['pɪəriəd]	(Unterrichts-/Schul-)Stunde	= *BE* lesson
	semester [sɪ'mestə]	Semester *(Schulhalbjahr in den USA)*	! In Großbritannien ist das Schuljahr in drei **terms** unterteilt, in den USA in zwei **semesters**.
	gym [dʒɪm]	Sporthalle, Turnhalle	! **gym** = Sport-, Turnhalle (*nicht:* ~~Gymnasium~~)
	health [helθ]	Gesundheit; Gesundheitslehre	noun: **health** – adjectives: **healthy, unhealthy**
	study hall ['stʌdi hɔ:l]	*Zeit zum selbstständigen Lernen in der Schule*	At Hermann High students have ~ **hall** every day after lunch.
	(to) **study** ['stʌdi]	studieren; sorgfältig durchlesen; lernen	When I finish school, I'm going to ~ history. My dad **studies** the sports page every morning. There's a test tomorrow, so I have to ~ tonight.
	government ['gʌvənmənt]	Regierung (*als Schulfach etwa:* Staatskunde)	*French:* le gouvernement
p.56/A 3	**bulletin board** ['bʊlətɪn bɔ:d] *(AE)*, **notice board** ['nəʊtɪs bɔ:d] *(BE)*	Anschlagtafel, „schwarzes Brett"	a **bulletin board** *(AE)* / **notice board** *(BE)* 
	(to) **take part (in)**	teilnehmen (an)	(to) join other people in an activity: 12 students **took** ~ **in** the school play.
	extracurricular activities (*or:* **extracurriculars**) [,ekstrəkə'rɪkjələz]	*schulische Angebote außerhalb des regulären Unterrichts, oft als Arbeitsgemeinschaften*	
	grade [greɪd] (*BE auch:* **mark** [mɑ:k])	(Schul-)Note, Zensur	

US school grades

+	A	**excellent** ['eksələnt]	ausgezeichnet, hervorragend
↑	B	**good**	gut
	C	**average** *(n; adj)* ['ævərɪdʒ]	Durchschnitt; durchschnittlich
↓	D	**below average**	unter Durchschnitt; unterdurchschnittlich
–	F	**failure** *(n)* ['feɪljə]	ungenügend

	see-through ['si:θru:]	durchsichtig	
	(to) **be allowed**	erlaubt sein	**!** • See-through clothes **are not allowed** here. = … **sind** hier **nicht erlaubt**. • **I'm not allowed to** wear see-through clothes. = Ich **darf** … **nicht** tragen.
	(to) **break** [breɪk], **broke** [brəʊk], **broken** ['brəʊkən]	(zer)brechen; kaputt gehen	She **broke** the school rules and was sent home. Please be careful with my MP3 player. Don't ~ it. All the plates fell to the floor and **broke**.
	(to) **change** [tʃeɪndʒ]	sich umziehen; wechseln	Your clothes are dirty. Please go home and ~. Do you ~ classrooms after each lesson at your school? *French:* (se) changer

(to) change – change

(sich) ändern, (sich) verändern	We had to **change** our holiday plans. The weather was **changing**, so we hurried home.
wechseln	We **changed** some money at the airport. We were late and didn't have time to **change** clothes.
sich umziehen	I was still wearing my working clothes, so I went upstairs and **changed**.
umsteigen	Can we go directly to Berlin or do we have to **change** at Hanover?
(Ver-)Änderung, Wechsel	It will be a big **change** when you move from London to the country. The **change** from one school to another can be hard for some students.
Wechselgeld; Kleingeld	Always count your **change**! Shop assistants can make mistakes. Have you got enough **change** for the ticket machine?

p.57/A 6	**meeting** ['mi:tɪŋ]	Versammlung, Besprechung; Treffen, Begegnung	The photo club **~s** are on Fridays. verb: (to) **meet** – noun: **meeting**
	and so on (*short:* **etc.** [et'setərə])	und so weiter (usw.)	We need stuff for sandwiches: bread, lettuce, ham, cheese, **and so ~**. (… ham, cheese, **etc.**)
	wine [waɪn]	Wein	*French:* le vin
	(to) **be** a farmer, a teacher, …	Bauer, Lehrer/in, … werden	**!** Wenn es um Berufspläne geht, wird für das deutsche „werden" meist **be** benutzt: What do you want to **be** when you're older? Are you going to **be** a farmer like your dad?
	(to) **apply (for** sth.**)** [ə'plaɪ]	sich bewerben (um/für etwas); etwas beantragen	Did your sister **~ for** the job? – Yes, but she didn't get it.
	college ['kɒlɪdʒ]	Hochschule, Fachhochschule	
	(to) **get involved (in)** [ɪn'vɒlvd]	sich engagieren (für, bei); sich beteiligen (an)	Alex **got ~ in** the drama club soon after he started school.
	foreign ['fɒrən]	ausländisch, fremd	That car must be ~. Look at the number plate. (to) learn ~ languages (Fremdsprachen lernen)
	(to) **debate** [dɪ'beɪt]	debattieren	verb: (to) **debate** – noun: **debate** *French:* débattre – le débat
	cheerleader ['tʃɪəli:də]	Cheerleader *(Stimmungsanheizer/in bei Sportereignissen)*	**cheerleaders** 
p.57/A 7	**private** ['praɪvət]	privat	**!** stress and pronunciation: **private** ['praɪvət] *French:* privé, e

p.58/A 8	**class**	Unterricht; Kurs	What did you learn in French ~ today? I do an evening ~ in painting on Fridays.
	pyramid ['pɪrəmɪd]	Pyramide	**!** stress: **py̲ramid** ['pɪrəmɪd]
	butter ['bʌtə]	Butter	
	rice [raɪs]	Reis	
	pasta *(no pl)* ['pæstə]	Nudeln, Teigwaren	
	little	wenig	**!** These plants need very ~ water. (= nicht viel) These plants need **a̲** ~ water. (= ein bisschen)

little („wenig") – few („wenige")

- **little** + uncountable nouns:
  wenig + nicht zählbare Nomen:
  a little time, money, water, bread, ...
  ein wenig/ein bisschen Zeit, Geld, Wasser Brot, ...
- **few** + plural of countable nouns:
  wenige + Plural von zählbaren Nomen:
  a few hours, dollars, bottles, sandwiches, ...
  wenige/ein paar Stunden, Dollar, Flaschen, Sandwiches, ...

Are you hungry? We've got **a little bacon** and **a few eggs**. ... ein wenig/ein bisschen Schinken und ein paar Eier

Comparison (Steigerung)**:**

little – less – (the) least

I've got so **little** hair.
... so wenig Haare

I've got **less** hair.
... weniger Haare

I've got **the least** hair.
... die wenigsten Haare

	product ['prɒdʌkt]	Produkt, Erzeugnis	**!** verb: (to) **produce** [prə'dju:s] (produzieren) nouns: **production** [prə'dʌkʃn] (Produktion) **product** ['prɒdʌkt] (Produkt)
	poultry ['pəʊltri]	Geflügel	Can you buy a chicken at the ~ shop, please?
	bean [bi:n]	Bohne	
	whole-grain ['həʊlgreɪn]	Vollkorn-	**whole-grain** products: ~-~ bread, ~-~ biscuits
	grain [greɪn]	Korn	
	exercise *(no pl)*	(körperliche) Bewegung, Training	**!** • **exercise(s)** = Übung(en): Which **exercises** have we got for homework? • **exercise** *(no pl, no article)* = Bewegung: The doctors say I need more **exercise**.
p.58/A 9	**muesli** ['mju:zli]	Müsli	
p.58/A 10	**quality** ['kwɒləti]	Qualität	**!** stress: **qu̲a̲lity** ['kwɒləti] *French:* la qualité
	fresh [freʃ]	frisch	
	(to) **care about** sth. [keə]	etwas wichtig nehmen	**!** • I **care about** what I eat. (= What I eat is important to me.) • Many people **don't care** if their food is fresh. (= Fresh food is not important to them.)

everybody ... they

Nach **everybody, someone, nobody** usw. kannst du **they/them/their** verwenden, um die schwer zu lesenden Ausdrücke *he or she / him or her / his or her* zu vermeiden.

Not **everybody** cares if **their** food is fresh. (*statt:* ... if his or her food ...)

Someone left **their** purse on the table. (*statt:* ... his or her purse ...)

Nobody likes it when **they** lose a game. (*statt:* ... he or she loses ...)

a person/friend/student ... they

Auch nach **person, friend, student** usw. kann **they/them/their** stehen, wenn es nicht wichtig oder nicht klar ist, ob ein Mann oder eine Frau gemeint ist.

In this game, you think of a **person** and what clothes **they** might wear. (*statt:* ... he or she ...)

If you have a good **friend** and you ask **them** for help, **they** will help you.

Each **student** reads the sentence **they** wrote to **their** group.

	as long as *(conj)*	solange, sofern	There'll be no trouble **as ~ as** you don't break the rules.
p.59/A 11	**local** ['ləʊkl]	Lokal-, örtlich; am/vom Ort	Find out what's going on in your hometown! Read your ~ paper and listen to your ~ radio station! *French:* local, e
	scrapbook ['skræpbʊk]	Sammelalbum	
	(to) **return** [rɪ'tɜːn]	zurückkehren	I left Britain in May and **~ed** in July. *French:* retourner
	sister city *(AE)*	Partnerstadt	= *BE* twin town
	active ['æktɪv]	aktiv, tätig	! stress: **<u>ac</u>tive** ['æktɪv] *French:* actif, active
	interest (in) ['ɪntrəst]	Interesse (an)	*French:* l'interêt (pour) *(m)*
	soccer ['sɒkə]	Fußball	! In <u>Amerika</u> wird „Fußball" als **soccer** bezeichnet (**football** steht dort für **American football**). In <u>Großbritannien</u> wird meist **football** verwendet; **soccer** klingt dort eher förmlich.
p.62/P 2	**necessary** ['nesəsəri]	nötig, notwendig	You can call me on my mobile if ~.
	Best wishes ['wɪʃɪz]	*etwa:* Alles Gute / Mit besten Grüßen *(als Briefschluss)*	
p.63/P 3	**exam** [ɪg'zæm]	Prüfung, Examen	**exams**: (to) **take/do an exam** – eine Prüfung ablegen; (to) **pass an exam** – eine Prüfung bestehen; (to) **fail an exam** – eine Prüfung nicht bestehen; durchfallen
	member (of) ['membə]	Mitglied (in, von)	! With article: I'm **<u>a</u> member** of the drama club. Ich bin **Mitglied** im Dramaklub. *French:* un membre (de)
p.63/P 5	**thought** [θɔːt]	Gedanke	verb: (to) **think, thought, thought** – noun: **thought**
p.64/P 8	**ending** ['endɪŋ]	Endung	! **ending** = **1.** Ende, Schluss *(eines Films usw.)* **2.** Endung *(eines Wortes)*
p.65/P 9	**soft** [sɒft]	weich	**soft** ◄► **hard**
	soft drink	alkoholfreies Getränk	
	soda ['səʊdə] *(AE)*	Limonade	
	helpful ['helpfl]	hilfreich, nützlich	
	(to) **contain** [kən'teɪn]	enthalten	Soda **~s** a lot of sugar.
	calorie ['kæləri]	Kalorie	*French:* la calorie
p.66/P 11	(to) **found** [faʊnd]	gründen	(to) **found** a new club = (to) start a new club ! Nicht verwechseln: (to) **find, found, found** = finden (to) **found, founded, founded** = gründen

Hispanic *(n; adj)* [hɪ'spænɪk]	*US-amerikanischer Ausdruck für Menschen mit Wurzeln in spanischsprachigen Ländern, besonders in Mittelamerika*	

REVISION: Numbers

You write:	You say:	In German:
10.35	ten **point** three five	10,35 (zehn **Komma** drei fünf)
5.6 %	five **point** six **per cent**	5,6 % (fünf **Komma** sechs **Prozent**)

German 'null':

- phone numbers and dates: **o** [əʊ]
  340926 = three four **o** nine two six
  1907 = nineteen **o** seven
- temperatures: **zero**
  - 3° = three degrees below **zero**
- in most sports: **nil**
  What's the score? – **2–0.** = two **nil**

p. 67/P 13	**summary** ['sʌməri]	Zusammenfassung	What happens in the film? Can you give me a quick ~?
	guide [gaɪd]	(Fremden-)Führer/in, Reiseleiter/in	
	raft [rɑːft]	Schlauchboot *(wildwassertauglich)*	

Going rafting.

	(to) **be worried (about)** ['wʌrid]	beunruhigt sein, besorgt sein (wegen/um)	Hannah **is ~ about** her grandfather. He's very ill. verb: (to) **worry** – adjective: **worried**
	original *(n; adj)* [ə'rɪdʒənl]	Original; Original-	
	(to) **leave** sth. **out** [ˌliːv_'aʊt]	etwas weglassen/auslassen	If an exam question is difficult, **~** it **out** and go back to it later. If you don't like onions, **~** them **out**.
	direct speech [ˌdaɪrekt 'spiːtʃ]	direkte Rede, wörtliche Rede	

Angus Bethune's moment

p. 68	**reflex** ['riːfleks]	Reflex	! stress: **<u>re</u>flex** ['riːfleks] *French:* le réflexe
	smart [smɑːt]	clever, schlau	
	(to) **swap** sth. **(for** sth.**)** **(-pp-)** [swɒp]	etwas (ein)tauschen (für etwas/ gegen etwas)	Jake **~ped** his old bike **for** a new skateboard.
	(to) **elect** sb. sth. [ɪ'lekt]	jn. zu etwas wählen	They **~ed** her leader of the youth club. ! ... **elected her leader** = ... wählten sie **<u>zur</u>** Leiterin
	election [ɪ'lekʃn]	Wahl *(eines Kandidaten bei einer Abstimmung)*	*French:* l'élection *(f)*
	(to) **vote for** sb. [vəʊt]	für jn. stimmen	! Nicht verwechseln: • 14 members **voted for** Fay, but 19 members **voted for** Kate. ... stimmten für Kate • Kate **was elected** leader of the club. Kate wurde zur Leiterin des Klubs gewählt.
	(to) **fall in love (with** sb.**)**	sich verlieben (in jn.)	My best friend **has fallen in ~ with** my sister.
	(to) **ache** [eɪk]	wehtun	! pronunciation: (to) **ache** [eɪk]

dentist ['dentɪst]	Zahnarzt, -ärztin	*French:* le/la dentiste
(to) **sweat** [swet]	schwitzen	! pronunciation: (to) **sweat** [swet], **sweatshirt** ['swetʃɜ:t] verb: (to) **sweat** – noun: **sweat** („Schweiß“)
p.69 (to) **compare** [kəm'peə]	vergleichen	*French:* comparer
Never mind. [ˌnevə 'maɪnd]	*etwa:* Nicht so wichtig. / Ist (doch) egal. / Das willst du gar nicht wissen.	
I can take it.	Ich halt's aus. / Ich kann's aushalten.	

heaven ['hevn]	Himmel *(im religiösen Sinn)*	! • (clouds/planes) in the **sky** = (Wolken/Flugzeuge) am Himmel • (to) be in **heaven** / (to) go to **heaven** = im Himmel sein / in den Himmel kommen
(to) **throw up** [ˌθrəʊ‿'ʌp], **threw up** [θru:], **thrown up** [θrəʊn]	sich übergeben	The man was so drunk that he **threw** ~ all over the taxi.
actually ['æktʃuəli]	nebenbei bemerkt; übrigens	I love Katie Melua. She's a great singer! – And she's a good songwriter too, **~**.
tight [taɪt]	fest	
(to) **clap (-pp-)** [klæp]	(Beifall) klatschen	
polite [pə'laɪt]	höflich	She told me to mind my own business. – That wasn't very **~**. Actually, it was quite rude. *French:* poli, e
p.70 (to) **protest** [prə'test]	protestieren	Hundreds of people came out to **~** against the new road through the forest. *French:* protester
circle ['sɜ:kl]	Kreis	a **circle** 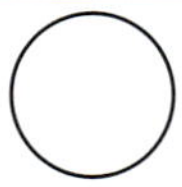 *French:* le cercle
fist [fɪst]	Faust	a **fist** 
plot [plɒt]	Handlung *(eines Romans, Films)*	

Unit 4: Atlanta rising

p.76 (to) **rise** [raɪz], **rose** [rəʊz], **risen** ['rɪzn]	(auf)steigen	The helicopter **rose** and disappeared into the sky. Black smoke was **rising** from the building.
cotton ['kɒtn]	Baumwolle	*French:* le coton
plantation [plɑ:n'teɪʃn]	Plantage	
violence ['vaɪələns]	Gewalt, Gewalttätigkeit	My dad says there's too much sex and **~** on TV.
violent ['vaɪələnt]	gewalttätig; gewaltsam	noun: **violence** – adjective: **violent** *French:* la violence – violent, e
non-violent [nɒn]	gewaltlos, gewaltfrei	**violent** ◄► **non-violent**

	during ['djʊərɪŋ]	während	

German 'während'

- before a noun: **during** *(prep)*
  John phoned **during** the football match. ... **während** des Fußballspiels
- before a clause: **as** *or* **while** *(conj)*
  John phoned **as/while** we were watching the football match. ... **während** wir das Fußballspiel schauten

	civil war [ˌsɪvl 'wɔː]	Bürgerkrieg	
	war [wɔː]	Krieg	
p.77	**network** ['netwɜːk]	*(Radio-, Fernseh-)*Sendernetz	
	African-American [ˌæfrɪkən‿ə'merɪkən]	afro-amerikanisch	If you're in Detroit, try and visit the Museum of **~-American** History.
	mayor [meə]	Bürgermeister/in	❗ pronunciation: **mayor** [meə]
	civil rights *(pl)* [ˌsɪvl 'raɪts]	Bürgerrechte	
	right [raɪt]	Recht	❗ (to) **be right** = Recht haben, im Recht sein
	Olympic Games [əˌlɪmpɪk 'geɪmz]	Olympische Spiele	
p.78/A 1	**TV listings** *(pl)* ['lɪstɪŋz]	das Fernsehprogramm	
	prime time ['praɪm taɪm]	Hauptsendezeit	What kind of programmes can you see at ~ ~?
	cable ['keɪbl]	Kabel *(auch kurz für* Kabelfernsehen)	a piece of **cable** 
	comedy ['kɒmədi]	Komödie; Comedy	*French:* la comédie
	documentary [ˌdɒkju'mentri]	Dokumentarfilm, -beitrag	*French:* le documentaire
	drama ['drɑːmə]	Fernsehspiel; Drama	
	crime series ['kraɪm ˌsɪəriːz]	Krimiserie	
	crime	Kriminalität; Verbrechen	❗ *German* **Krimi** = *English* **crime film, crime story**
	competition [ˌkɒmpə'tɪʃn]	Wettbewerb, Wettkampf	
p.78/A 2	**anchorman/anchorwoman** ['æŋkəmæn, 'æŋkəwʊmən] (*AE auch kurz:* **anchor**)	Moderator/Moderatorin *(von Nachrichtensendungen)*	 the **anchor(woman)**  an **anchor**
	comedian [kə'miːdiən]	Komiker/in	
	contestant [kən'testənt]	Kandidat/in *(in Fernsehshow)*, (Wettkampf-)Teilnehmer/in	
	host [həʊst]	*(Radio-, Fernseh-)*Moderator/in	*French:* le/la hôte
	rerun ['riːrʌn] *(AE)*, **repeat** [rɪ'piːt] *(BE)*	Wiederholung *(einer Fernsehsendung)*	
	viewer ['vjuːə]	Zuschauer/in	
p.78/A 3	(to) **be on**	gezeigt werden, laufen *(im Fernsehen)*	Please be quiet while the news **is ~**.
	(to) **last (for)** [lɑːst]	dauern	The meeting **~ed (for)** over an hour.

p.79/A 4	**You bet!** [bet] *(infml)*	Aber klar! / Und ob!	Did you enjoy your trip to Paris? – **You ~!**
	(to) **bet (-tt-)** [bet], **bet, bet**	wetten	I ~ you can't run faster than me.
	dusty ['dʌsti]	staubig	
	archive ['ɑ:kaɪv]	Archiv	! stress and pronunciation: **archive** ['ɑ:kaɪv] *French:* les archives *(pl)*
	(to) **compete** [kəm'pi:t]	konkurrieren, mithalten	Your pizza just can't ~ with my spaghetti! verb: (to) **compete** – noun: **competition**
	besides [bɪ'saɪdz]	außerdem	It's too late to go to the cinema. And ~, I've already seen the film.
p.79/A 6	**unbelievable** [ˌʌnbɪ'li:vəbl]	unglaublich	This is ~! (= It's hard to believe.)
	traffic jam ['træfɪk dʒæm]	(Verkehrs-)Stau	a **traffic jam** 
	for 20 minutes	seit 20 Minuten; 20 Minuten lang	We've lived here **for** five years now. (Wir wohnen jetzt seit fünf Jahren hier.) ! *Nicht:* We ~~live~~ here **for** five years now.
	explosion [ɪk'spləʊʒn]	Explosion	! stress: **explosion** [ɪk'spləʊʒn] *French:* l'explosion *(f)*
	terrorist ['terərɪst]	Terrorist/in; Terror-, terroristisch	! stress: **terrorist** ['terərɪst]
	(to) **drop** sb. **off (-pp-)** [drɒp]	jn. absetzen *(aussteigen lassen)*	He **~ped** her **off** at the station. 
	How long ...?	Seit wann ...? / Wie lange ...?	**~ ~** have Grandma and Grandpa been married?
p.80/A 7	(to) **be on display** [dɪ'spleɪ]	ausgestellt sein/werden	Her photos **are on ~** at the local museum.
	since April 4th [sɪns]	seit dem 4. April	We've lived here **since** 2003. (Wir wohnen seit 2003 hier.) ! *Nicht:* We ~~live~~ here **since** 2003.

German 'seit'

- **since** mit Zeit**punkt** (wann etwas begonnen hat) — We've been here **since** last Sunday / April / 1998.
  Wir sind **seit** letztem Sonntag / April / 1998 hier.
- **for** mit Zeit**raum** (wie lange etwas bereits der Fall ist) — We've been here **for** three days / a long time / years.
  Wir sind **seit** drei Tagen / langem / Jahren hier.

anniversary [ˌænɪ'vɜ:səri]	Jahrestag	May 8th is the **anniversary** of John's **death**. (Johns **Todestag**) 
death [deθ]	Tod	
impressed [ɪm'prest]	beeindruckt	Jo wrote a great essay. His teacher was really ~. *French:* impressionné, e

	for ages ['eɪdʒɪz]	ewig, eine Ewigkeit	I've known her **for ~**. We went to kindergarten together.
	since then	seitdem	He broke his leg last week and he's been in hospital **~ then**.
p. 81/A 9	**minister** ['mɪnɪstə]	Pastor/in, Pfarrer/in	! stress: **minister** ['mɪnɪstə]
	(to) **segregate** ['segrɪgeɪt]	trennen *(nach Rasse, Religion, Geschlecht)*	Some people say that boys and girls learn better if they're **~d** at school.
	segregation [ˌsegrɪ'geɪʃn]	(Rassen-)Trennung	
	protest ['prəʊtest]	Protest	! noun: **protest** ['prəʊtest] Protest verb: (to) **protest** [prə'test] protestieren
	march [mɑːtʃ]	Marsch, Demonstration	a **protest march** 
	(to) **judge** sb. **(by)** [dʒʌdʒ]	jn. beurteilen, einschätzen (nach)	You shouldn't ~ people **by** their clothes.
	skin [skɪn]	Haut	And you shouldn't judge people by the colour of their ~.
	content ['kɒntent]	Gehalt, Inhalt	*French:* le contenu
	character ['kærəktə]	Charakter, Persönlichkeit	! stress: **character** ['kærəktə]
	(to) **make a speech** [spiːtʃ]	eine Rede halten	
	research *(no pl)* [rɪ'sɜːtʃ, 'riːsɜːtʃ]	Recherche; Nachforschung(en)	I have to do some ~ on Atlanta for homework. ! (to) **do research** = recherchieren
	search engine ['sɜːtʃ‿ˌendʒɪn]	Suchmaschine	
	source [sɔːs]	*(Informations-, Text-)*Quelle	The internet is a good ~ of information if you have to do research. *French:* la source
p. 85/P 3	**collocation** [ˌkɒlə'keɪʃn]	Kollokation *(Wörter, die oft zusammen vorkommen)*	words that go together, for example: – *make the bed* (not: ~~*do*~~ *the bed*), – *do homework* (not: ~~*make*~~ *homework*)
p. 87/P 6	**exact** [ɪg'zækt]	exakt, genau	What's the ~ size of Germany? Do you know?
	(to) **draw conclusions** [ˌdrɔː kən'kluːʒnz], **drew** [druː], **drawn** [drɔːn]	Schlüsse ziehen, schlussfolgern	Don't ~ **conclusions** before you know all the facts.
p. 89/P 10	**holiday** ['hɒlədeɪ]	Feiertag	
p. 89/P 11	**president** ['prezɪdənt]	Präsident/in	! stress: **president** ['prezɪdənt] *French:* le président, la présidente
p. 89/P 12	**freedom** ['friːdəm]	Freiheit	

Melba's story

p. 91	**law** [lɔː]	Gesetz	It's against the ~ to drive a car when you're drunk.
	apart [ə'pɑːt]	auseinander, getrennt	My parents live ~, but they aren't divorced yet.
	court [kɔːt]	Gericht(shof)	Do you have to appear in ~ if you break traffic rules?

p.92	**separate** ['seprət]	getrennt, separat	The library has a ~ room for children's books. ! stress: **separate** ['seprət] *French:* séparé, e
	merry-go-round ['merigəʊraʊnd]	Karussell	a **merry-go-round** 
	sir [sɜː]	*höfliche Anrede für einen Unbekannten (z. B. einen Kunden) oder einen Vorgesetzten*	
	as if [əz‿'ɪf]	als ob	Those flowers look ~ ~ they need water.
	(to) **be terrified (of)** ['terɪfaɪd]	schreckliche Angst haben (vor)	Everyone **was** ~ when the bank robber pulled out a gun.
	immediately [ɪ'miːdiətli]	sofort	My dog usually comes ~ when I call him. *French:* immédiatement
	(to) **volunteer** [ˌvɒlən'tɪə]	sich freiwillig melden, sich bereit erklären	Hundreds of doctors **~ed** to help the earthquake victims.
	volunteer [ˌvɒlən'tɪə]	Freiwillige(r)	*French:* le/la volontaire
	crowd [kraʊd]	(Menschen-)Menge	
p.93	**step** [step]	Stufe	**step** **stairs**
	(to) **block** [blɒk]	blockieren, (ver)sperren	A tree fell down in the storm and **~ed** the road.
	soldier ['səʊldʒə]	Soldat/in	
	cruel [kruːəl]	grausam	Don't you think it's ~ to keep animals in cages? *French:* cruel, le
	(to) **spit (at** sb.**)** **(-tt-)** [spɪt], **spat, spat** [spæt]	(jn. an)spucken	
	God [gɒd]	Gott	
	for the first time	zum ersten Mal	We went on holiday abroad ~ **the first** ~ when I was eight.
	bodyguard ['bɒdigɑːd]	Leibwächter/in, Leibwache	
	valuable ['væljuəbl]	wertvoll; nützlich	She keeps her jewellery in the bank because it's so ~.
	hallway ['hɔːlweɪ] *(AE)*	Korridor, Gang	
p.94	**pain** [peɪn]	Schmerz(en)	
	(to) **splash** [splæʃ]	spritzen	He's **~ing** water on his face.
	acid ['æsɪd]	Säure	*French:* l'acide *(m)*
	education [ˌedʒu'keɪʃn]	(Schul-)Bildung, Ausbildung; Erziehung	You need a good ~ if you want to get a good job.
	university [ˌjuːnɪ'vɜːsəti]	Universität	*French:* l'université *(f)*
	businesswoman/-man ['bɪznəswʊmən, -mæn]	Geschäftsfrau/-mann	
	business ['bɪznəs]	Unternehmen; Geschäft(e)	Mike started his own ~ when he was only 17. We do a lot of ~ with German companies.
	headline ['hedlaɪn]	Schlagzeile	
	(to) **ban** sb. **from** sth. **(-nn-)** [bæn]	jn. von etwas ausschließen	The runner was **~ned from** the Olympic Games because he had taken drugs.

Das Dictionary besteht aus zwei alphabetischen Wörterlisten:

Englisch – Deutsch (S. 189–219)
Deutsch – Englisch (S. 220–247).

Das **English – German Dictionary** enthält den Wortschatz der Bände 1 bis 4 von *English G 21*.
Wenn du wissen möchtest, was ein Wort bedeutet, wie man es ausspricht oder wie es genau geschrieben wird, kannst du hier nachschlagen.

Im **English – German Dictionary** werden folgende **Abkürzungen und Symbole** verwendet:

jm. = jemandem	sb. = somebody	*pl* = *plural*	*AE* = *American English*
jn. = jemanden	sth. = something	*no pl* = *no plural*	*infml* = *informal*

° Mit diesem Kringel sind Wörter markiert, die nicht zum Lernwortschatz gehören.
▶ Der Pfeil verweist auf Kästchen im Vocabulary (S. 167–188), in denen du weitere Informationen zu diesem Wort findest.

Die **Fundstellenangaben** zeigen, wo ein Wort zum ersten Mal vorkommt.
Die Ziffern in Klammern bezeichnen Seitenzahlen:

I = Band 1 • II = Band 2 • III = Band 3 • IV = Band 4
IV Intro (9) = Band 4, Introduction, Seite 9
IV Intro (9/168) = Band 4, Introduction, Seite 168 (im Vocabulary, zu Seite 9)
IV 1 (14) = Band 4, Unit 1, Seite 14
IV 1 (14/170) = Band 4, Unit 1, Seite 170 (im Vocabulary, zu Seite 14)

Tipps zur Arbeit mit einem Wörterbuch findest du im Skills File auf Seite 140.

A

a [ə]
1. ein, eine I
2. once/twice a week einmal/zweimal pro Woche III
a bit ein bisschen, etwas II • **a few** ein paar, einige II • **a little** ein bisschen, ein wenig IV 3 (58)
a lot (of) eine Menge, viel, viele II
He likes her a lot. Er mag sie sehr. I
▶ S.181 little („wenig") – few („wenige")

able ['eɪbl]: **be able to do sth.** etwas tun können; fähig sein / in der Lage sein, etwas zu tun III

about [ə'baʊt]
1. über I
2. ungefähr II
ask about sth. nach etwas fragen I • **This is about Mr Green.** Es geht um Mr Green. I • **How about ...?** Wie wär's mit ...? III • **What about ...? 1.** Was ist mit ...? / Und ...? I; **2.** Wie wär's mit ...? I • **What are you talking about?** Wovon redest du? I • **°What are the pages about?** Wovon handeln die Seiten? • **What was the best thing about ...?** Was war das Beste an ...? II • **°Say what you like about ...** Sag, was du an ... magst

above [ə'bʌv]
1. oben III
2. über, oberhalb (von) III

abroad [ə'brɔːd] im Ausland II
go abroad ins Ausland gehen/fahren II

accent ['æksənt] Akzent II

accident ['æksɪdənt] Unfall II

ache [eɪk] wehtun IV 3 (68)

acid ['æsɪd] Säure IV 4 (94)

across [ə'krɒs]
1. (quer) über III
2. hinüber, herüber III

act [ækt]
1. handeln, sich verhalten IV 2 (36)
2. aufführen, spielen I
°Act out ... Spiele/Spielt ... vor.

°action ['ækʃn]: **in action** in Aktion

active ['æktɪv] aktiv, tätig IV 3 (59)

activity [æk'tɪvəti] Aktivität, Tätigkeit I

actor ['æktə] Schauspieler/in II

actually ['æktʃuəli]
1. eigentlich; in Wirklichkeit III
2. nebenbei bemerkt; übrigens IV 3 (69)

°adapt [ə'dæpt] adaptieren, anpassen; bearbeiten

°adapted [ə'dæptɪd] adaptiert; bearbeitet

add (to) [æd] hinzufügen, ergänzen, addieren (zu) I • **°add up** addieren, zusammenzählen

adjective ['ædʒɪktɪv] Adjektiv I

admission [əd'mɪʃn] Eintritt, Eintrittspreis IV 1 (16)

adult ['ædʌlt] Erwachsene(r) III

advantage (over) [əd'vɑːntɪdʒ] Vorteil (gegenüber) IV 2 (36)

adventure [əd'ventʃə] Abenteuer IV Intro (11)

adverb ['ædvɜːb] Adverb I

afraid [ə'freɪd]
1. be afraid (of) Angst haben (vor) I
2. I'm afraid leider II

African-American [ˌæfrɪkən‿ə'merɪkən] afro-amerikanisch IV 4 (77)

after ['ɑːftə] nach *(zeitlich)* I
after that danach I

after ['ɑːftə] nachdem II

afternoon [ˌɑːftə'nuːn] Nachmittag I • **in the afternoon** nachmittags, am Nachmittag I • **on Friday afternoon** freitagnachmittags, am Freitagnachmittag I

again [ə'gen] wieder; noch einmal I
once again noch einmal III

against [ə'genst] gegen I

age [eɪdʒ] Alter III • **for ages** ewig, eine Ewigkeit IV 4 (80)

ago [ə'gəʊ]: **a minute ago** vor einer Minute I

agree (on) [ə'griː] sich einigen (auf) I • **agree with sb./sth.** jm./etwas zustimmen; mit jm./etwas übereinstimmen II

°**agricultural science** [ˌægrɪˌkʌltʃərəl 'saɪəns] Agrarwissenschaft
air [eə] Luft III
airport ['eəpɔːt] Flughafen III
album ['ælbəm] Album III
alive [ə'laɪv] am Leben, lebendig IV 3 (55)
all [ɔːl] alle; alles I • **2 all** 2 beide (2:2 unentschieden) III • **all around the castle** ganz um die Burg herum II • **all day** den ganzen Tag (lang) I • **all over the world** auf der ganzen Welt III **all right** [ɔːl 'raɪt] gut, in Ordnung II • **all the time** die ganze Zeit I **all we have to do now ...** alles, was wir jetzt (noch) tun müssen, ... II **from all around Wales** aus ganz Wales II • **from all over England/ the UK** aus ganz England/aus dem gesamten Vereinigten Königreich III • **This is all wrong.** Das ist ganz falsch. I
all-day ticket [ˌɔːl deɪ 'tɪkɪt] Tagesfahrkarte III
allowed [ə'laʊd]**: be allowed** erlaubt sein IV 3 (56) • **be allowed to do sth.** etwas tun dürfen III
almost ['ɔːlməʊst] fast, beinahe II
alone [ə'ləʊn] allein I • **leave sb. alone** jn. in Ruhe lassen IV 1 (26)
along the road [ə'lɒŋ] entlang der Straße / die Straße entlang II °**and now you've come along** und jetzt bist du plötzlich aufgetaucht
alphabet ['ælfəbet] Alphabet I
°**alphabetical** [ˌælfə'betɪkl] alphabetisch
already [ɔːl'redi] schon, bereits II
also ['ɔːlsəʊ] auch II
although [ɔːl'ðəʊ] obwohl III
always ['ɔːlweɪz] immer I
am [ˌeɪ‿'em]**: 7 am** 7 Uhr morgens/ vormittags I
amazing [ə'meɪzɪŋ] erstaunlich, unglaublich II
ambulance ['æmbjələns] Krankenwagen III
°**Americana** [əˌmerɪ'kɑːnə] *Sammelbegriff für alles, was als „typisch amerikanisch" empfunden wird*
American football [əˌmerɪkən 'fʊtbɔːl] Football I
amnesty ['æmnəsti] Amnestie, Begnadigung IV 2 (38)
an [ən] ein, eine I • *siehe* **a**
analysis [ə'næləsɪs]**,** *pl* **analyses** [ə'næləsiːz] Analyse, Auswertung IV 2 (43)
anchor ['æŋkə] Anker IV 4 (78/185)
anchorman/anchorwoman ['æŋkəmæn, 'æŋkəwʊmən] (*AE auch kurz:* **anchor)** Moderator/in (*von Nachrichtensendungen)* IV 4 (78)
and [ənd, ænd] und I • **and so on (etc.** [et'setərə]**)** und so weiter (usw.) IV 3 (57)
angel ['eɪndʒl] Engel II
°**Anglo** ['æŋgləʊ] *Person europäischer Abstammung*
angry (about sth./with sb.) ['æŋgri] wütend, böse (über etwas/auf jn.) II
animal ['ænɪml] Tier II
anniversary [ˌænɪ'vɜːsəri] Jahrestag IV 4 (80) • **anniversary of sb.'s death** js. Todestag IV 4 (80/186)
announce [ə'naʊns] ankündigen, bekanntgeben III
announcement [ə'naʊnsmənt] Durchsage, Ansage; Ankündigung, Bekanntgabe III
anorak ['ænəræk] Anorak, Windjacke III
another [ə'nʌðə] ein(e) andere(r, s); noch ein(e) I • **another 45p** weitere 45 Pence, noch 45 Pence II **one another** einander, sich (gegenseitig) III
answer ['ɑːnsə] antworten; beantworten I
answer (to) ['ɑːnsə] Antwort (auf) I
any ['eni] jede(r, s) beliebige; irgendein(e) IV 2 (37/176) • **any ...?** (irgend)welche ...? I • **not (...) any** kein, keine I • **not (...) any more** nicht mehr II
► S.176 any
anybody ['enibɒdi] (irgend)jemand II; jede(r) IV 2 (37/176) • **not (...) anybody** niemand II
► S.176 any
anyone ['eniwʌn] IV 2 (36/175) *siehe* **anybody**
anything ['eniθɪŋ] (irgend)etwas II; alles IV 2 (37/176) • **not (...) anything** nichts II
► S.176 any
anyway ['eniweɪ]
1. sowieso I
2. trotzdem II
anywhere ['eniweə] irgendwo(hin) II • **not (...) anywhere** nirgendwo(hin) II
apart [ə'pɑːt] auseinander, getrennt IV 4 (91)
apartment [ə'pɑːtmənt] *(AE)* Wohnung IV 1 (14/170)
appear [ə'pɪə] erscheinen, auftauchen III
appetite ['æpɪtaɪt] Appetit III
apple ['æpl] Apfel I
apply (for sth.) [ə'plaɪ] sich bewerben (um/für etwas); etwas beantragen IV 3 (57)
appointment [ə'pɔɪntmənt] Termin, Verabredung I
appreciate [ə'priːʃieɪt] schätzen, zu schätzen wissen IV 1 (26)
April ['eɪprəl] April I
archive ['ɑːkaɪv] Archiv IV 4 (79)
are [ɑː] bist; sind; seid I • **How are you?** Wie geht es dir/Ihnen/euch? II • **The pencils are 35p.** Die Bleistifte kosten 35 Pence. I • **You're joking, aren't you?** Du machst Witze, nicht wahr? / Das ist nicht dein Ernst, oder? II
area ['eəriə] Bereich; Gebiet, Gegend III
argue ['ɑːgjuː] sich streiten, sich zanken I
argument ['ɑːgjumənt]
1. Argument, Begründung III
2. Streit III
arm [ɑːm] Arm I
armchair ['ɑːmtʃeə] Sessel I
around [ə'raʊnd] in ... umher, durch; um ... (herum) III • **all around the castle** ganz um die Burg herum II **around six** um sechs Uhr herum, gegen sechs III • **around the lake** um den See (herum) III • **around the town** in der Stadt umher, durch die Stadt III • **from all around Wales** aus ganz Wales II **look around** sich umsehen III **walk/run/jump around** herumgehen/-rennen/-springen, umhergehen/-rennen/-springen III
°**arrest** [ə'rest] verhaften, festnehmen
arrival (arr) [ə'raɪvl] Ankunft III
arrive [ə'raɪv] ankommen, eintreffen II
art [ɑːt] Kunst I
article ['ɑːtɪkl] (Zeitungs-)Artikel I
artificial [ˌɑːtɪ'fɪʃl] künstlich, Kunst- III
artist ['ɑːtɪst] Künstler/in III
as *(conj)* [əz, æz] als, während II **as you can see** wie du sehen kannst II • **as if** als ob IV 4 (92) **as long as** solange, sofern IV 3 (58) **as soon as** sobald, sowie II
► S.185 German 'während'
as *(prep)* [əz, æz] als II • **as a child** als Kind II
as ... as [əz, æz] so ... wie II • **as big/exciting as** so groß/aufregend wie II
ask [ɑːsk] fragen I • **ask about sth.** nach etwas fragen I • **ask questions** Fragen stellen I • **ask**

sb. for sth. jn. um etwas bitten II **ask sb. the way** jn. nach dem Weg fragen II
asleep [ə'sli:p]: **be asleep** schlafen I
Assembly [ə'sembli] Versammlung *(morgendliche Schulversammlung, oft mit Andacht)* III
at [ət, æt]: **at 7 Hamilton Street** in der Hamiltonstraße 7 I • **at 8.45** um 8.45 I • **at 16** mit 16, im Alter von 16 Jahren II • **at break** in der Pause *(zwischen Schulstunden)* II **at first** zuerst, am Anfang IV 3 (55) **at home** daheim, zu Hause I • **at last** endlich, schließlich I • **at least** zumindest, wenigstens I **at night** nachts, in der Nacht I **at school** in der Schule I • **at that table** an dem Tisch (dort) / an den Tisch (dort) I • **at the back (of the room)** hinten, im hinteren Teil (des Zimmers) II • **at the bottom (of)** unten, am unteren Ende (von) II **at the chemist's/hairdresser's** beim Apotheker/Friseur III • **at the end (of)** am Ende (von) I • **at the moment** im Moment, gerade II • **at the Shaws' house** im Haus der Shaws/bei den Shaws zu Hause I • **at the station** am Bahnhof I • **at the top (of)** oben, am oberen Ende, an der Spitze (von) I • **at the weekend** am Wochenende I • **at work** bei der Arbeit / am Arbeitsplatz I
ate [et, eɪt] *siehe* **eat**
athletics [æθ'letɪks] Leichtathletik III
Atlantic: the Atlantic (Ocean) [ət,læntɪk_'əʊʃn] der Atlantische Ozean, der Atlantik IV 2 (49/177)
atmosphere ['ætməsfɪə] Atmosphäre III
attack [ə'tæk] angreifen III
attack [ə'tæk] Angriff III
attitude (to, towards) ['ætɪtju:d] Haltung (gegenüber), Einstellung (zu) IV 2 (36)
attraction [ə'trækʃn] Attraktion, Anziehungspunkt II
°**attractive (to)** [ə'træktɪv] attraktiv (für)
audience ['ɔ:diəns] Publikum; Zuschauer/innen, Zuhörer/innen II
°**auditorium** [,ɔ:dɪ'tɔ:riəm] *(AE)* Hörsaal
August ['ɔ:gəst] August I
aunt [ɑ:nt] Tante I • **auntie** ['ɑ:nti] Tante II
auto ['ɔ:təʊ] *(AE)* Auto, PKW IV Intro (10)
autumn ['ɔ:təm] Herbst I
avenue ['ævənju:] Allee IV 1 (13)
average ['ævərɪdʒ] Durchschnitt; durchschnittlich IV 3 (56/179)
► S.179 US school grades
away [ə'weɪ] weg, fort I
awesome ['ɔ:səm] *(AE, infml)* klasse, großartig IV Intro (8)
awful ['ɔ:fl] furchtbar, schrecklich II

B

baby ['beɪbi] Baby I • **have a baby** ein Baby/Kind bekommen II
back [bæk]
°**1.** Rücken
2. at the back (of) hinten, im hinteren Teil (von) II
back (to) [bæk] zurück (nach) I
back door [,bæk 'dɔ:] Hintertür II
background ['bækgraʊnd] Hintergrund II • **background file** *etwa:* Hintergrundinformation(en) II
°**back inside cover** [,bæk_,ɪnsaɪd 'kʌvə] hintere Umschlaginnenseite
bacon ['beɪkən] Schinkenspeck III
bad [bæd] schlecht, schlimm I **be bad at sth.** schlecht in etwas sein; etwas schlecht können III **bad timing** schlechtes Timing III
badminton ['bædmɪntən] Badminton, Federball I • **badminton racket** ['rækɪt] Badmintonschläger III
bag [bæg] Tasche, Beutel, Tüte I
bagel ['beɪgl] Bagel *(ringförmiges Brötchen)* IV 1 (17)
bagpipes *(pl)* ['bægpaɪps] Dudelsack III
°**bake sale** ['beɪk seɪl] *Verkauf von Selbstgebackenem zum Zwecke der Geldbeschaffung*
ball [bɔ:l]
1. Ball I
2. Ball *(Tanzveranstaltung)* IV 3 (68)
ban sb. from sth. (-nn-) [bæn] jn. von etwas ausschließen IV 4 (94)
banana [bə'nɑ:nə] Banane I
band [bænd] Band, (Musik-)Gruppe I
bank [bæŋk] Bank, Sparkasse I
bank robber ['bæŋk ,rɒbə] Bankräuber/in I
°**Baptist** ['bæptɪst] Baptist/in; Baptisten-
bar [bɑ:] Bar II
baseball ['beɪsbɔ:l] Baseball I
baseball cap ['beɪsbɔ:l kæp] Baseballmütze II
basket ['bɑ:skɪt] Korb I • **a basket of apples** ein Korb Äpfel I
basketball ['bɑ:skɪtbɔ:l] Basketball I
bat [bæt]: **table tennis bat** Tischtennisschläger III
bath [bɑ:θ] Bad, Badewanne II **have a bath** baden, ein Bad nehmen II
bathroom ['bɑ:θru:m] Badezimmer I
bay [beɪ] Bucht III
be [bi:], **was/were, been** sein I **be a farmer, a teacher, ...** Bauer, Lehrer/in, ... werden IV 3 (57)
beach [bi:tʃ] Strand II • **on the beach** am Strand II
bean [bi:n] Bohne IV 3 (58)
bear [beə] Bär II
beard [bɪəd] Bart II
beat [bi:t], **beat, beaten** schlagen; besiegen III
beaten ['bi:tn] *siehe* **beat**
beautiful ['bju:tɪfl] schön I
beauty ['bju:ti] Schönheit III
became [bɪ'keɪm] *siehe* **become**
because [bɪ'kɒz] weil I
°**because of** [bɪ'kɒz_əv] wegen
become [bɪ'kʌm], **became, become** werden II
bed [bed] Bett I • **Bed and Breakfast (B&B)** [,bed_ən 'brekfəst] Frühstückspension I • **go to bed** ins Bett gehen I
bedroom ['bedru:m] Schlafzimmer I
bedspread ['bedspred] Tagesdecke III
beef [bi:f] Rindfleisch III
been [bi:n] *siehe* **be**
before [bɪ'fɔ:] vor *(zeitlich)* I
before [bɪ'fɔ:] bevor II
before [bɪ'fɔ:] (vorher) schon mal II **the night/week/... before** in der Nacht/Woche/... zuvor III
began [bɪ'gæn] *siehe* **begin**
begin (-nn-) [bɪ'gɪn], **began, begun** beginnen, anfangen (mit) III
beginning [bɪ'gɪnɪŋ] Beginn, Anfang; Einleitung II
begun [bɪ'gʌn] *siehe* **begin**
behind [bɪ'haɪnd] hinter II • **stay behind** zurückbleiben, dableiben IV Intro (10)
believable [bɪ'li:vəbl] glaubhaft IV 4 (88)
believe (in) [bɪ'li:v] glauben (an) IV 4 (81)
bell [bel] Klingel, Glocke I
belong (to) [bɪ'lɒŋ] gehören (zu) II
below [bɪ'ləʊ]
1. unten III
2. unter, unterhalb (von) III
bench [bentʃ] (Sitz-)Bank IV 1 (28)

besides [bɪ'saɪdz] außerdem IV 4 (79)
best [best] am besten II • **the best ...** der/die/das beste ...; die besten I • **like sth. best** etwas am liebsten mögen III • **What was the best thing about ...?** Was war das Beste an ...? II • **Best wishes** *etwa:* Alles Gute / Mit besten Grüßen *(als Briefschluss)* IV 3 (62)
bet (-tt-) [bet]**, bet, bet** wetten IV 4 (79) • **You bet!** *(infml)* Aber klar! / Und ob! IV 4 (79)
better ['betə] besser I • **like sth. better** etwas lieber mögen II
between [bɪ'twi:n] zwischen II
big [bɪg] groß I
big wheel [ˌbɪg 'wi:l] Riesenrad III
bike [baɪk] Fahrrad I • **ride a bike** Rad fahren I
bilingual [ˌbaɪ'lɪŋgwəl] zweisprachig IV 2 (36)
°**Billboard** ['bɪlbɔ:d] *amerik. Musikzeitschrift*
bin [bɪn] Mülltonne II
°**binoculars** *(pl)* [bɪ'nɒkjələz] Fernglas
biography [baɪ'ɒgrəfi] Biografie III
biology [baɪ'ɒlədʒi] Biologie I
bird [bɜ:d] Vogel I
birthday ['bɜ:θdeɪ] Geburtstag I **for his birthday** zu seinem Geburtstag III • **Happy birthday.** Herzlichen Glückwunsch zum Geburtstag. I • **My birthday is in May.** Ich habe im Mai Geburtstag. I • **My birthday is on 13th June.** Ich habe am 13. Juni Geburtstag. I **When's your birthday?** Wann hast du Geburtstag? I
biscuit ['bɪskɪt] Keks, Plätzchen I
bit [bɪt]**: a bit** ein bisschen, etwas II
°**bitch** [bɪtʃ] *(infml)* Schlampe, Miststück
black [blæk] schwarz I
black bear ['blæk beə] Schwarzbär III
blame sb. (for) [bleɪm] jm. die Schuld geben (an); jm. Vorwürfe machen (wegen) III
blanket ['blæŋkɪt] Decke *(zum Zudecken)* III
bleep [bli:p] piepsen II
bleep [bli:p] Piepton II
blew [blu:] *siehe* **blow**
block [blɒk] (Häuser-, Wohn-)Block IV 1 (14)
block [blɒk] blockieren, (ver)sperren IV 4 (93)
blog [blɒg] *digitales Tagebuch* IV Intro (8)
blond [blɒnd] blond, hell IV 1 (27)
blood [blʌd] Blut III
blouse [blaʊz] Bluse II
blow [bləʊ]**, blew, blown** wehen, blasen III
blown [bləʊn] *siehe* **blow**
blue [blu:] blau I
board [bɔ:d]
1. (Wand-)Tafel I • **on the board** an der/die Tafel I
°**2. on board** an Bord
boat [bəʊt] Boot, Schiff I
body ['bɒdi] Körper I
bodyguard ['bɒdigɑ:d] Leibwächter/in, Leibwache IV 4 (93)
bold print [ˌbəʊld 'prɪnt] Fettdruck III
book [bʊk] Buch I
booklet ['bʊklət] Broschüre II
boot [bu:t] Stiefel I
border ['bɔ:də] Grenze IV 2 (38)
bored [bɔ:d]**: be/feel bored** gelangweilt sein, sich langweilen IV 2 (37) **get bored** sich langweilen IV 4 (80)
boring ['bɔ:rɪŋ] langweilig I
born [bɔ:n]**: be born** geboren sein/werden II
borough ['bʌrə, *AE:* 'bɜ:rəʊ] (Stadt-)Bezirk IV 1 (20)
► S.172 New York: the five boroughs
boss [bɒs] Chef/in, Boss III
both [bəʊθ] beide I
bottle ['bɒtl] Flasche I • **a bottle of milk** eine Flasche Milch I
bottom ['bɒtəm] unteres Ende II **at the bottom (of)** unten, am unteren Ende (von) II
bought [bɔ:t] *siehe* **buy**
boulevard ['bu:ləvɑ:d] Boulevard IV 2 (34)
bowl [bəʊl] Schüssel I • **a bowl of cornflakes** eine Schale Cornflakes I
box [bɒks] Kasten, Kästchen, Kiste I
boy [bɔɪ] Junge I
boyfriend ['bɔɪfrend] (fester) Freund IV 2 (50)
°**bracket** ['brækɪt] Klammer *(in Texten)*
brainstorm ['breɪnstɔ:m] brainstormen *(so viele Ideen wie möglich sammeln)* III
brave [breɪv] mutig IV 1 (28)
bread *(no pl)* [bred] Brot I
break [breɪk] Pause I • **at break** in der Pause *(zwischen Schulstunden)* II • **take a break** eine Pause machen IV 1 (22)
break [breɪk]**, broke, broken** (zer-)brechen; kaputt gehen IV 3 (56)
breakable ['breɪkəbl] zerbrechlich IV 4 (88)
breakfast ['brekfəst] Frühstück I **have breakfast** frühstücken I
°**breaking news** [ˌbreɪkɪŋ 'nju:z] aktuelle Meldung, aktuelle Nachricht
bridge [brɪdʒ] Brücke I
bridle path ['braɪdl pɑ:θ] Reitweg III
bright [braɪt] hell, leuchtend II
bring [brɪŋ]**, brought, brought** (mit-, her)bringen I
British ['brɪtɪʃ] britisch; Brite, Britin II
°**brochure** ['brəʊʃə] Prospekt, Broschüre
broke [brəʊk] *siehe* **break**
broken ['brəʊkən] gebrochen; zerbrochen, kaputt II • *siehe* **break**
brother ['brʌðə] Bruder I
brought [brɔ:t] *siehe* **bring**
brown [braʊn] braun I
budgie ['bʌdʒi] Wellensittich I
build [bɪld]**, built, built** bauen II
building ['bɪldɪŋ] Gebäude II
built [bɪlt] *siehe* **build**
°**bulimic** [bu'lɪmɪk] bulimisch
bulletin board ['bʊlətɪn bɔ:d] *(AE)* Anschlagtafel, „schwarzes Brett" IV 3 (56)
bully ['bʊli] einschüchtern, tyrannisieren II
bully ['bʊli] (Schul-)Tyrann III
bunk (bed) [bʌŋk] Etagenbett, Koje II
burn [bɜ:n] brennen; verbrennen IV 1 (15) • **burn sth. down** etwas niederbrennen IV 4 (76)
bus [bʌs] Bus I
business ['bɪznəs] Unternehmen; Geschäft(e) IV 4 (94/188) • **Mind your own business.** Das geht dich nichts an! / Kümmere dich um deine eigenen Angelegenheiten! II
businesswoman/-man ['bɪznəswʊmən, -mæn] Geschäftsfrau/Geschäftsmann IV 4 (94)
bus pass ['bʌs pɑ:s] Monatskarte *(für den Bus)* III
bus stop ['bʌs stɒp] Bushaltestelle III
busy ['bɪzi] belebt, verkehrsreich; hektisch III; beschäftigt IV Intro (9)
but [bət, bʌt] aber I
butter ['bʌtə] Butter IV 3 (58)
button ['bʌtn] Knopf III
buy [baɪ]**, bought, bought** kaufen I
°**buzz** [bʌz] *hier:* den Summer/die Glocke betätigen
by [baɪ]
1. von I
2. an; (nahe) bei II

by car/bike/... mit dem Auto/Rad/... II • **by ten o'clock** bis (spätestens) zehn Uhr III • **by the way** [ˌbaɪ ðə ˈweɪ] übrigens; nebenbei (bemerkt) III
Bye. [baɪ] Tschüs! I

C

cab [kæb] Taxi IV 1 (28)
cabin [ˈkæbɪn] Hütte III
cable [ˈkeɪbl] Kabel (*auch kurz für* Kabelfernsehen) IV 4 (78)
°**cable car** [ˈkeɪbl kɑː] *(USA)* Kabelbahn *(von Drahtseilen gezogene Straßenbahn)*
café [ˈkæfeɪ] *(kleines)* Restaurant, Imbissstube, Café I
cage [keɪdʒ] Käfig I
cake [keɪk] Kuchen, Torte I
calendar [ˈkælɪndə] Kalender I
call [kɔːl] rufen; anrufen; nennen I
call sb. names jn. mit Schimpfwörtern hänseln, jm. Schimpfwörter nachrufen III
call [kɔːl] Anruf, Telefongespräch I
make a call ein Telefongespräch führen II
called [kɔːld]: **be called** heißen, genannt werden III
calm down [ˌkɑːm ˈdaʊn] sich beruhigen II
calorie [ˈkæləri] Kalorie IV 3 (65)
came [keɪm] *siehe* **come**
camel [ˈkæml] Kamel II
camera [ˈkæmərə] Kamera, Fotoapparat I
camp [kæmp] Camp, (Ferien-)Lager IV 2 (43)
camp [kæmp] zelten III
camping gear [ˈkæmpɪŋ gɪə] Campingausrüstung, Campingsachen IV Intro (8)
can [kən, kæn]
1. können I
2. dürfen I
Can I help you? Kann ich Ihnen helfen? / Was kann ich für Sie tun? *(im Geschäft)* I
canal [kəˈnæl] Kanal III
canoe [kəˈnuː] paddeln, Kanu fahren III
canoe [kəˈnuː] Kanu, Paddelboot III
canyon [ˈkænjən] Cañon IV Intro (8)
cap [kæp] Mütze, Kappe II
capital [ˈkæpɪtl] Hauptstadt III
capital letter [ˌkæpɪtl ˈletə] Großbuchstabe III
°**captain** [ˈkæptɪn] Kapitän/in
caption [ˈkæpʃn] Bildunterschrift III
car [kɑː] Auto I • **car park** Parkplatz III
caravan [ˈkærəvæn] Wohnwagen II
card [kɑːd] (Spiel-, Post-)Karte I
care about sth. [keə] etwas wichtig nehmen IV 3 (58) • **I don't care.** Es/Das ist mir egal. IV 1 (27/174) • **I didn't care.** Es war mir egal. IV 1 (27) • °**feel cared about** sich behütet/beschützt fühlen
career [kəˈrɪə] Karriere III
careful [ˈkeəfl]
1. vorsichtig II
2. sorgfältig II
caretaker [ˈkeəteɪkə] Hausmeister/Hausmeisterin II
car park [ˈkɑː pɑːk] Parkplatz III
carrot [ˈkærət] Möhre, Karotte I
cartoon [kɑːˈtuːn] Cartoon (Zeichentrickfilm; Bilderwitz) II
case [keɪs] Fall II
castle [ˈkɑːsl] Burg, Schloss II
cat [kæt] Katze I
catch [kætʃ], **caught, caught** fangen; erwischen II
cathedral [kəˈθiːdrəl] Kathedrale, Dom III
caught [kɔːt] *siehe* **catch**
°**cause** [kɔːz] Ursache
°**caution** [ˈkɔːʃn] Vorsicht; Warnung
CD [ˌsiːˈdiː] CD I • **CD player** CD-Spieler I
ceilidh [ˈkeɪli] *Musik- und Tanzveranstaltung, vor allem in Schottland und Irland* III
cellphone [ˈselfəʊn] *(AE)* Handy, Mobiltelefon III
Celsius (C) [ˈselsiəs] Celsius III
cent (c) [sent] Cent I
centimetre (cm) [ˈsentɪmiːtə] Zentimeter III
central [ˈsentrəl] Zentral-, Mittel- III
centre [ˈsentə] Zentrum, Mitte I
century [ˈsentʃəri] Jahrhundert II
°**chain** [tʃeɪn] Kette
chair [tʃeə] Stuhl I
champion [ˈtʃæmpiən] Meister/in, Champion I
championship [ˈtʃæmpiənʃɪp] Meisterschaft III
chance [tʃɑːns] Chance, Möglichkeit, Aussicht II
change [tʃeɪndʒ]
1. (sich) ändern; (sich) verändern IV 2 (50)
2. wechseln IV 3 (56)
3. umsteigen III
4. sich umziehen IV 3 (56)
change channels umschalten *(Fernsehen)* IV 4 (85)
▶ S.180 (to) change – change
change [tʃeɪndʒ]
1. (Ver-)Änderung; Wechsel IV 3 (56/180)
2. Wechselgeld I; Kleingeld IV 1 (21)
▶ S.180 (to) change – change
channel [ˈtʃænl] Kanal, Sender II
character [ˈkærəktə]
1. Charakter, Persönlichkeit IV 4 (81)
2. Person, Figur *(in Roman, Film)* IV 2 (52)
charity [ˈtʃærəti] Wohlfahrtsorganisation II
°**chart** [tʃɑːt] Schaubild, Diagramm, Tabelle • °**charts** *(pl)* Hitliste, Charts
°**chase** [tʃeɪs] jagen, verfolgen
chat (-tt-) [tʃæt] chatten, plaudern II
chat [tʃæt] Chat, Unterhaltung II
chat room [ˈtʃæt ruːm] Chatroom III
cheap [tʃiːp] billig, preiswert II
check [tʃek] (über)prüfen, kontrollieren I
checkpoint [ˈtʃekpɔɪnt] Kontrollpunkt *(hier: zur Selbstüberprüfung)* I
cheek [tʃiːk] Wange IV 1 (26)
cheer [tʃɪə] jubeln, Beifall klatschen II
cheerleader [ˈtʃɪəliːdə] Cheerleader *(Stimmungsanheizer/in bei Sportereignissen)* IV 3 (57)
cheese [tʃiːz] Käse I
chemist [ˈkemɪst] Drogerie, Apotheke II • **at the chemist's** beim Apotheker III
chicken [ˈtʃɪkɪn] Huhn; (Brat-)Hähnchen I
child [tʃaɪld], *pl* **children** [ˈtʃɪldrən] Kind I
°**chili con carne** [ˌtʃɪli kɒn ˈkɑːni] *scharfes Gericht aus Fleisch, Chilischoten und anderen Zutaten*
chips *(pl)* [tʃɪps]
1. *(BE)* Pommes frites I
2. *(AE)* (Kartoffel-)Chips IV 1 (20/172)
chocolate [ˈtʃɒklət] Schokolade I
°**choice** [tʃɔɪs] (Aus-)Wahl, Entscheidung
choir [ˈkwaɪə] Chor I
choose [tʃuːz], **chose, chosen** (sich) aussuchen, (aus)wählen I
chorus [ˈkɔːrəs] Refrain III
chose [tʃəʊz] *siehe* **choose**
chosen [ˈtʃəʊzn] *siehe* **choose**
church [tʃɜːtʃ] Kirche I
cigarette [ˌsɪgəˈret] Zigarette IV 2 (51)
cinema [ˈsɪnəmə] Kino II • **go to the cinema** ins Kino gehen II
circle [ˈsɜːkl] Kreis IV 3 (70)

circus ['sɜːkəs]
1. Zirkus III
2. (runder) Platz *(in der Stadt)* III
city ['sɪti] Stadt, Großstadt I
city centre [ˌsɪti 'sentə] Stadtzentrum, Innenstadt I
civil ['sɪvl]: **civil rights** *(pl)* Bürgerrechte IV 4 (77) • **civil war** Bürgerkrieg IV 4 (76)
clap (-pp-) [klæp] (Beifall) klatschen IV 3 (69)
class [klɑːs]
1. (Schul-)Klasse I
2. Unterricht; Kurs IV 3 (58)
class teacher Klassenlehrer/in I
classical ['klæsɪkl] klassisch III
classmate ['klɑːsmeɪt] Klassenkamerad/in, Mitschüler/in I
classroom ['klɑːsruːm] Klassenzimmer I
°**clause** [klɔːz] (Teil-, Glied-)Satz
clean [kliːn] sauber II
clean [kliːn] sauber machen, putzen I • **I clean my teeth.** Ich putze mir die Zähne. I
cleaner ['kliːnə] Putzfrau, -mann II
°**clean-up** ['kliːn_ʌp] Säuberung(sarbeiten)
clear [klɪə] klar, deutlich I
clever ['klevə] klug, schlau I
cleverness ['klevənəs] Klugheit, Schlauheit IV 3 (64)
click on sth. [klɪk] etwas anklicken II
climb [klaɪm] klettern; hinaufklettern (auf) I • **Climb a tree.** Klettere auf einen Baum. I
clinic ['klɪnɪk] Klinik II
clock [klɒk] (Wand-, Stand-, Turm-)Uhr I
clone [kləʊn] Klon III
close (to) [kləʊs] nahe (bei, an) III
That was close. Das war knapp. II
close [kləʊz] schließen, zumachen I
closed [kləʊzd] geschlossen II
°**closing phrase** ['kləʊzɪŋ freɪz] Schlusswort(e) *(am Briefende)*
clothes *(pl)* [kləʊðz, kləʊz] Kleider, Kleidung(sstücke) II
cloud [klaʊd] Wolke II
cloudless ['klaʊdləs] wolkenlos IV 2 (42)
cloudy ['klaʊdi] bewölkt II
club [klʌb] Klub; Verein I
coach [kəʊtʃ] Trainer/in III
coast [kəʊst] Küste III
°**coastal** ['kəʊstl] Küsten-
coffee ['kɒfi] Kaffee IV 1 (17) • **coffee to go** Kaffee zum Mitnehmen IV 1 (17)
cola ['kəʊlə] Cola I

cold [kəʊld] kalt I • **be cold** frieren I
cold [kəʊld]
1. Kälte IV 2 (49)
2. Erkältung II
have a cold erkältet sein, eine Erkältung haben II
°**collage** ['kɒlɑːʒ] Collage
collapse [kə'læps] zusammenbrechen; einstürzen IV 1 (15)
collect [kə'lekt] sammeln I
collection [kə'lekʃn] Sammlung IV 1 (23)
collector [kə'lektə] Sammler/in II
college ['kɒlɪdʒ] Hochschule, Fachhochschule IV 3 (57)
collocation [ˌkɒlə'keɪʃn] Kollokation *(Wörter, die oft zusammen vorkommen)* IV 4 (85)
°**colony** ['kɒləni] Kolonie
colour ['kʌlə] Farbe I • **What colour is ...?** Welche Farbe hat ...? I
colour ['kʌlə] kolorieren, färben; bunt an-, ausmalen III
column ['kɒləm] Säule III
°**combine** [kəm'baɪn] kombinieren, verbinden
come [kʌm], **came, come** kommen I • **come home** nach Hause kommen I • **come in** hereinkommen I • **Come on. 1.** Na los, komm. II; **2.** Ach komm! / Na hör mal! II • **come out** rauskommen; veröffentlicht werden *(Film, DVD)* IV 4 (86) • °**and now you've come along** und jetzt bist du plötzlich aufgetaucht
comedian [kə'miːdiən] Komiker/in IV 4 (78)
comedy ['kɒmədi] Komödie; Comedy IV 4 (78)
comfortable ['kʌmftəbl] bequem IV 2 (49) • **Make yourself comfortable.** Machen Sie es sich bequem. / Mach es dir bequem. IV 2 (49)
comic ['kɒmɪk] Comic-Heft I
comment ['kɒment] Kommentar, Bemerkung IV Intro (8)
Commonwealth ['kɒmənwelθ]: **the Commonwealth** *Gemeinschaft der Länder des ehemaligen Britischen Weltreichs* III
community [kə'mjuːnəti]: **community centre** Gemeinschaftszentrum, Gemeindezentrum III • **community hall** Gemeinschaftshalle, -saal, Gemeindehalle, -saal III
company ['kʌmpəni] Firma, Gesellschaft III
compare [kəm'peə] vergleichen IV 3 (69)

°**compared to** [kəm'peəd] verglichen mit
comparison [kəm'pærɪsn] Steigerung; Vergleich II • °**make comparisons** Vergleiche anstellen, vergleichen
compete [kəm'piːt] konkurrieren, mithalten IV 4 (79)
competition [ˌkɒmpə'tɪʃn] Wettbewerb, Wettkampf IV 4 (78)
°**complete** [kəm'pliːt] vollständig, komplett
°**complete** [kəm'pliːt] vervollständigen, ergänzen
°**compromise** ['kɒmprəmaɪz] Kompromiss
computer [kəm'pjuːtə] Computer I
concert ['kɒnsət] Konzert III
conclusion [kən'kluːʒn] Schluss(folgerung) IV 4 (87/187) • **draw conclusions** Schlüsse ziehen, schlussfolgern IV 4 (87)
°**condor** ['kɒndɔː] Kondor
°**confused** [kən'fjuːzd] verwirrt
contact sb. ['kɒntækt] sich mit jm. in Verbindung setzen; mit jm. Kontakt aufnehmen III
contain [kən'teɪn] enthalten IV 3 (65)
content ['kɒntent] Gehalt, Inhalt IV 4 (81)
contestant [kən'testənt] Kandidat/Kandidatin *(in Fernsehshow)*, (Wettkampf-)Teilnehmer/in IV 4 (78)
context ['kɒntekst] Kontext, Zusammenhang IV 1 (25)
°**continent** ['kɒntɪnənt] Kontinent, Erdteil
°**continue** [kən'tɪnjuː] fortsetzen; weitermachen (mit)
°**conversation** [ˌkɒnvə'seɪʃn] Unterhaltung, Gespräch
cook [kʊk] kochen, zubereiten II
cook [kʊk] Koch/Köchin III
cooker ['kʊkə] Herd I
cookie ['kʊki] *(AE)* Keks IV 1 (20/172)
cool [kuːl]
1. kühl II
2. cool I
copy ['kɒpi] kopieren II
copy ['kɒpi]
1. Kopie II
2. Exemplar III
corner ['kɔːnə] Ecke I • **on the corner of Sand Street and London Road** Sand Street, Ecke London Road II
cornflakes ['kɔːnfleɪks] Cornflakes I
correct [kə'rekt] berichtigen, korrigieren II • °**correcting circle** *etwa:* Korrekturkreis
correct [kə'rekt] korrekt, richtig III

°**correction** [kə'rekʃn] Korrektur, Berichtigung
cost [kɒst], **cost, cost** kosten IV 1 (16)
cotton ['kɒtn] Baumwolle IV 4 (76)
could [kəd, kʊd]: **he could ...**
1. er konnte ... II
2. er könnte ... III
count [kaʊnt] zählen II
counter ['kaʊntə]
1. Spielstein II
2. Theke, Ladentisch IV 1 (17)
country ['kʌntri] Land *(auch als Gegensatz zur Stadt)* II • **in the country** auf dem Land II
°**county** ['kaʊnti] Landkreis, Bezirk
°**county fair** ['kaʊnti feə] *etwa:* Landwirtschaftsschau, -ausstellung
course [kɔːs] Kurs, Lehrgang III
course: of course [əv 'kɔːs] natürlich, selbstverständlich I
court [kɔːt]
1. Platz, Court *(für Squash, Badminton)* III
2. Gericht(shof) IV 4 (91)
cousin ['kʌzn] Cousin, Cousine I
cover ['kʌvə]
1. (CD-)Hülle I
°2. **inside cover** Umschlaginnenseite
°**cover** ['kʌvə] sich bedecken; sich in Deckung begeben
cow [kaʊ] Kuh II
crash sth. [kræʃ] einen Unfall mit etwas haben IV 2 (50)
crazy ['kreɪzi] verrückt III
cream [kriːm] Sahne; Creme IV 1 (17)
cream cheese [ˌkriːm 'tʃiːz] Frischkäse IV 1 (17)
crime [kraɪm] Kriminalität; Verbrechen IV 4 (78)
crime series ['kraɪm ˌsɪəriːz] Krimiserie IV 4 (78)
crisps *(pl)* [krɪsps] Kartoffelchips I
crocodile ['krɒkədaɪl] Krokodil II
cross [krɒs] überqueren; (sich) kreuzen II
°**cross** [krɒs] Kreuz, Kreuzchen
crowd [kraʊd] (Menschen-)Menge IV 4 (92)
°**crown sb.** [kraʊn] jn. krönen
cruel [kruːəl] grausam IV 4 (93)
crush [krʌʃ]: **have a crush on sb.** in jn. verknallt sein III
cry [kraɪ]
1. weinen IV 1 (27)
2. schreien, rufen IV 2 (38)
cry out aufschreien IV 4 (94)
culture ['kʌltʃə] Kultur IV 2 (36)
cup [kʌp]
1. Tasse III
2. Pokal III
a cup of tea eine Tasse Tee III
cupboard ['kʌbəd] (Küchen-) Schrank I
curtain ['kɜːtn] Vorhang III
customer ['kʌstəmə] Kunde, Kundin II
cut (-tt-) [kʌt], **cut, cut** schneiden III • **cut sth. off** etwas abschneiden, abtrennen III • **cut the grass** Rasen mähen IV Intro (9)
cycle ['saɪkl] (mit dem) Rad fahren II • **cycle path** Radweg II

D

dad [dæd] Papa, Vati; Vater I
daily ['deɪli] täglich, Tages- IV Intro (8)
°**damage** ['dæmɪdʒ] Schaden, Beschädigung
dance [dɑːns] tanzen I
dance [dɑːns] Tanz I
dance floor ['dɑːns flɔː] Tanzfläche, Tanzboden IV 3 (68)
dancer ['dɑːnsə] Tänzer/in II
dancing ['dɑːnsɪŋ] Tanzen I
dancing lessons Tanzstunden, Tanzunterricht I
danger ['deɪndʒə] Gefahr I
dangerous ['deɪndʒərəs] gefährlich II
dark [dɑːk] dunkel I
°**dark** [dɑːk]: **after dark** nach Einbruch der Dunkelheit
date [deɪt]
1. Datum I
2. Date, Verabredung III
date sb. [deɪt] mit jm. (aus)gehen; sich (regelmäßig) mit jm. treffen III
daughter ['dɔːtə] Tochter I
day [deɪ] Tag I • °**a day out** ein Tagesausflug • **one day** eines Tages I • **days of the week** Wochentage I • **that day** an jenem Tag III
dead [ded] tot I
deal [diːl]: **It's a deal!** Abgemacht! III • **make a deal** ein Abkommen/ eine Abmachung treffen III
dear [dɪə] Schatz, Liebling I
Oh dear! Oje! II
dear [dɪə]: **Dear Jay ...** Lieber Jay, ... I
death [deθ] Tod IV 4 (80)
debate [dɪ'beɪt] debattieren IV 3 (57)
debate [dɪ'beɪt] Debatte IV 3 (57/180)
December [dɪ'sembə] Dezember I
decide (on) [dɪ'saɪd] beschließen; sich entscheiden (für) III
deer, *pl* **deer** [dɪə] Reh, Hirsch II
°**defense** [dɪ'fens] *(AE)* Verteidigung
°**definition** [ˌdefɪ'nɪʃn] Definition
degree [dɪ'griː] Grad II
deli ['deli] *Kombination aus Lebensmittelgeschäft und Fastfoodrestaurant* IV 1 (13)
delicious [dɪ'lɪʃəs] köstlich, lecker II
dentist ['dentɪst] Zahnarzt, -ärztin IV 3 (68)
department store [dɪ'pɑːtmənt stɔː] Kaufhaus II
departure (dep) [dɪ'pɑːtʃə] Abfahrt, Abflug; Abreise III
depressed [dɪ'prest] deprimiert, niedergeschlagen IV 2 (50)
depressing [dɪ'presɪŋ] trostlos, deprimierend IV 2 (50/177)
describe sth. (to sb.) [dɪ'skraɪb] (jm.) etwas beschreiben II
description [dɪ'skrɪpʃn] Beschreibung II
°**desert** ['dezət] Wüste
design [dɪ'zaɪn] entwerfen, gestalten II
desk [desk] Schreibtisch I
detail ['diːteɪl] Detail, Einzelheit III
detective [dɪ'tektɪv] Detektiv/in I
°**diagram** ['daɪəgræm] Diagramm, Schaubild
dialogue ['daɪəlɒg] Dialog IV 2 (50)
diary ['daɪəri] Tagebuch; Terminkalender I • °**keep a diary** ein Tagebuch führen
dice, *pl* **dice** [daɪs] Würfel II
°**dictate** [dɪk'teɪt] diktieren
dictionary ['dɪkʃənri] Wörterbuch, *(alphabetisches)* Wörterverzeichnis I
did [dɪd] *siehe* **do** • **Did you know ...?** Wusstest du ...? I • **we didn't go** ['dɪdnt] wir gingen nicht / wir sind nicht gegangen I
die (of) (*-ing form:* **dying**) [daɪ] sterben (an) II
difference ['dɪfrəns] Unterschied III
different (from) ['dɪfrənt] verschieden, unterschiedlich; anders (als) I
difficult ['dɪfɪkəlt] schwierig, schwer I
dining room ['daɪnɪŋ ruːm] Esszimmer I
dinner ['dɪnə] Abendessen, Abendbrot I • **have dinner** Abendbrot essen I
dinosaur ['daɪnəsɔː] Dinosaurier III
direct [də'rekt, daɪ'rekt]: **direct question** direkte Frage II • **direct speech** direkte Rede, wörtliche Rede IV 3 (67)
directions *(pl)* [də'rekʃnz] Wegbeschreibung(en) II
dirty ['dɜːti] schmutzig II
disabled [dɪs'eɪbld] (körper)behindert III

disadvantage [ˌdɪsəd'vɑːntɪdʒ] Nachteil IV 2 (36)
disagree (with) [ˌdɪsə'griː] nicht übereinstimmen (mit); anderer Meinung sein (als) III
disappear [ˌdɪsə'pɪə] verschwinden II
disc jockey (DJ) ['dɪsk dʒɒki, 'diː dʒeɪ] Diskjockey III
disco ['dɪskəʊ] Disko I
discover [dɪ'skʌvə] entdecken; herausfinden II
°**discovery pack** [dɪ'skʌvəri pæk] Entdeckungsset, Kennenlernset
discriminate against sb. [dɪ'skrɪmɪneɪt] jn. diskriminieren, jn. benachteiligen IV 2 (36)
discrimination (against) [dɪˌskrɪmɪ'neɪʃn] Diskriminierung (von), Benachteiligung (von) IV 2 (36)
°**discuss** [dɪ'skʌs] diskutieren, besprechen
discussion [dɪ'skʌʃn] Diskussion II
°**disease** [dɪ'ziːz] Krankheit
dish [dɪʃ] Gericht *(Speise)* III
dishwasher ['dɪʃwɒʃə] Geschirrspülmaschine I
display: be on display [dɪ'spleɪ] ausgestellt sein/werden IV 4 (80)
°**divide (into)** [dɪ'vaɪd] auf-, einteilen (in)
divorced [dɪ'vɔːst] geschieden I
DJ ['diː dʒeɪ] Diskjockey III
DJ ['diː dʒeɪ] (Musik/CDs/Platten) auflegen *(in der Disko)* III
do [duː], **did, done** tun, machen I
Do you like ...? Magst du ...? I
do an exam eine Prüfung ablegen IV 3 (63/182) • **do a gig** einen Auftritt haben, ein Konzert geben III
do a good job gute Arbeit leisten II • **do a project** ein Projekt machen, durchführen II • **do an exercise** eine Übung machen II
do research recherchieren IV 4 (81/187) • **do sport** Sport treiben I
doable ['duːəbl] machbar IV 4 (88)
doctor ['dɒktə] Doktor; Arzt/Ärztin II • **to the doctor's** zum Arzt III
documentary [ˌdɒkju'mentri] Dokumentarfilm, -beitrag IV 4 (78)
dog [dɒg] Hund I
dollar ($) ['dɒlə] Dollar IV 1 (16)
°**dominate** ['dɒmɪneɪt] dominieren, beherrschen
done [dʌn] *siehe* **do**
don't [dəʊnt]: **Don't listen to Dan.** Hör/Hört nicht auf Dan. I • **I don't like ...** Ich mag ... nicht. / Ich mag kein(e) ... I
door [dɔː] Tür I
doorbell ['dɔːbel] Türklingel I
dossier ['dɒsieɪ] Mappe, Dossier *(des Sprachenportfolios)* I
double ['dʌbl] zweimal, doppelt, Doppel- I
double-click ['dʌblklɪk] doppelklicken II
down [daʊn] hinunter, herunter, nach unten I • **down there** dort unten II • **fall down** hinfallen II
download [ˌdaʊn'ləʊd] runterladen, downloaden II
downloadable [ˌdaʊn'ləʊdəbl] herunterladbar IV 4 (88)
downstairs [ˌdaʊn'steəz] unten; nach unten I
downtown [ˌdaʊn'taʊn] *(AE)* (im/in das) Stadtzentrum IV 1 (14) • **the downtown bus** *(AE)* der Bus in Richtung Stadtzentrum IV 1 (14)
drama ['drɑːmə]
1. Schauspiel, darstellende Kunst I
2. Fernsehspiel; Drama IV 4 (78)
drank [dræŋk] *siehe* **drink**
draw [drɔː] Unentschieden III
draw [drɔː], **drew, drawn**
1. zeichnen III
2. draw conclusions Schlüsse ziehen, schlussfolgern IV 4 (87)
drawing ['drɔːɪŋ] Zeichnung III
drawn [drɔːn] *siehe* **draw**
dream [driːm] Traum I
dream (of, about) [driːm] träumen (von) III • **dream on** weiterträumen III
dress [dres] Kleid I
°**dress code** ['dres kəʊd] Kleiderordnung, Bekleidungsregeln
dressed [drest]: **get dressed** sich anziehen I
drew [druː] *siehe* **draw**
drink [drɪŋk] Getränk I
drink [drɪŋk], **drank, drunk** trinken I
drinkable ['drɪŋkəbl] trinkbar, genießbar IV 4 (88)
°**drinking fountain** ['drɪŋkɪŋ faʊntən] Trinkbrunnen
drive [draɪv], **drove, driven** *(ein Auto / mit dem Auto)* fahren II
drive [draɪv] (Auto-)Fahrt III
driven ['drɪvn] *siehe* **drive**
driver ['draɪvə] Fahrer/in II
drop (-pp-) [drɒp]
1. fallen lassen I
2. fallen I
drop sb. off jn. absetzen *(aussteigen lassen)* IV 4 (79)
drove [drəʊv] *siehe* **drive**
drug [drʌg] Droge, Rauschgift; Medikament IV 1 (26)
drum [drʌm] Trommel III • **play the drums** Schlagzeug spielen III
drunk [drʌŋk] betrunken IV 2 (51) *siehe* **drink**
during *(prep)* ['djʊərɪŋ] während IV 4 (76)
► S.185 German 'während'
dustbin ['dʌstbɪn] Mülltonne II
dusty ['dʌsti] staubig IV 4 (79)
DVD [ˌdiː viː' diː] DVD I
DVD recorder DVD-Rekorder IV 4 (85)

E

each [iːtʃ] jeder, jede, jedes (einzelne) I • **each other** einander, sich (gegenseitig) III
ear [ɪə] Ohr I
earache ['ɪəreɪk] Ohrenschmerzen II
early ['ɜːli] früh I
earring ['ɪərɪŋ] Ohrring I
earth [ɜːθ] Erde III • **on earth** auf der Erde III
earthquake ['ɜːθkweɪk] Erdbeben III
east [iːst] Osten; nach Osten; östlich III
eastbound ['iːstbaʊnd] Richtung Osten III
easy ['iːzi] leicht, einfach I
easy-going [ˌiːzi'gəʊɪŋ] gelassen, locker III
eat [iːt], **ate, eaten** essen I
eaten ['iːtn] *siehe* **eat**
editor ['edɪtə] Redakteur/in III
education [ˌedʒu'keɪʃn] (Schul-)Bildung, Ausbildung; Erziehung IV 4 (94)
e-friend ['iːfrend] Brieffreund/in *(im Internet)* I
°**e.g.** [ˌiː 'dʒiː] *(from Latin: exempli gratia)* z.B.
egg [eg] Ei III
°**either ... or ...** ['aɪðə ... ɔː, 'iːðə ... ɔː] entweder ... oder
elect sb. sth. [ɪ'lekt] jn. zu etwas wählen IV 3 (68)
election [ɪ'lekʃn] Wahl *(eines Kandidaten bei einer Abstimmung)* IV 3 (68/183)
electric [ɪ'lektrɪk] elektrisch, Elektro- III
electricity [ɪˌlek'trɪsəti] Strom, Elektrizität III
electronic [ɪˌlek'trɒnɪk] elektronisch III
elementary school [ˌelɪ'mentri skuːl] *(USA)* Grundschule *(für 6- bis 11-Jährige)* IV 3 (56)
elephant ['elɪfənt] Elefant I

elevator ['elɪveɪtə] *(AE)* Fahrstuhl, Aufzug II

else [els]**: anybody else** (sonst) noch jemand / irgendjemand anderes IV 1 (15/170) • **anything else** (sonst) noch etwas / irgendetwas anderes IV 1 (15) • **somebody else** (noch) jemand anderes IV 1 (15/170) **somewhere else** woanders(hin); sonst irgendwo(hin) IV 1 (15/170) **what else?** was (sonst) noch? IV 1 (15/170) • **What else do you know?** Was weißt du sonst noch? II • **who else?** wer/wen/wem (sonst) noch? IV 1 (15/170)
► S.170 ... else

e-mail ['i:meɪl] E-Mail I

°**empanadas** *(pl)* [ˌempə'nɑ:dəz] gefüllte Teigtaschen

empty ['empti] leer I

°**encyclopedia** [ɪnˌsaɪklə'pi:diə] Enzyklopädie, Lexikon

end [end] Ende, Schluss I • **at the end (of)** am Ende (von) I • **in the end** schließlich, zum Schluss III

end [end] enden; beenden III
°**end up (in)** *(infml)* landen (in)

ending ['endɪŋ]
1. Ende, (Ab-)Schluss *(einer Geschichte, eines Films usw.)* III
2. Endung IV 3 (64)

endless ['endləs] endlos IV 2 (34)

enemy ['enəmi] Feind/in II

energy ['enədʒi] Energie; Kraft II

engine ['endʒɪn] Motor IV 2 (49)

engineer [ˌendʒɪ'nɪə] Ingenieur/in II

English ['ɪŋglɪʃ] Englisch; englisch I

enjoy [ɪn'dʒɔɪ] genießen II

enough [ɪ'nʌf] genug I

enter ['entə]
1. betreten; eintreten (in) III
2. **enter sth.** etwas eingeben, eintragen II
enter a country in ein Land einreisen IV 4 (85)

°**entertainment** [ˌentə'teɪnmənt] Unterhaltung, Entertainment

entry ['entri] Eintrag, Eintragung *(in Wörterbuch/Tagebuch)* III

episode ['epɪsəʊd] Folge, Episode *(einer Fernsehserie)* IV 2 (49)

°**equal** ['i:kwəl] gleich

equipment [ɪ'kwɪpmənt] Ausrüstung III

eraser [ɪ'reɪzə, *AE:* ɪ'reɪsər] *(AE)* Radiergummi IV 1 (20/172)

escape (from sb./sth.) [ɪ'skeɪp] fliehen (vor jm./aus etwas); entkommen III

°**especially** [ɪ'speʃəli] besonders, vor allem

essay (about, on) ['eseɪ] Aufsatz (über) I

etc. (et cetera) [et'setərə] usw. (und so weiter) IV 3 (57)

ethnic ['eθnɪk] ethnisch IV 2 (36)

euro (€) ['jʊərəʊ] Euro I

even ['i:vn] sogar II • **even if** selbst wenn; obwohl IV 4 (92) • **not even** (noch) nicht einmal III

evening ['i:vnɪŋ] Abend I • **in the evening** abends, am Abend I **on Friday evening** freitagabends, am Freitagabend I

event [ɪ'vent] Ereignis; Veranstaltung IV 3 (55)

ever? ['evə] je? / jemals? / schon mal? II

every ['evri] jeder, jede, jedes I

everybody ['evribɒdi] jeder, alle II

everyday *(adj)* ['evrideɪ] Alltags-; alltägliche(r, s) III

everyone ['evriwʌn] IV 2 (36/175) *siehe* **everybody**

everything ['evriθɪŋ] alles I

everywhere ['evriweə] überall I

exact [ɪg'zækt] exakt, genau IV 4 (87)

exactly [ɪg'zæktli] genau III

exam [ɪg'zæm] Prüfung, Examen IV 3 (63) • **fail an exam** eine Prüfung nicht bestehen; durchfallen IV 3 (63/182) • **take/do an exam** eine Prüfung ablegen IV 3 (63/182)

example [ɪg'zɑ:mpl] Beispiel I **for example** zum Beispiel I

excellent ['eksələnt] ausgezeichnet, hervorragend IV 3 (56/179)
► S.179 US school grades

except [ɪk'sept] außer IV 1 (26)

exchange [ɪks'tʃeɪndʒ] (Schüler-) Austausch III • **exchange student** Austauschschüler/in III

°**exchange** [ɪks'tʃeɪndʒ] austauschen

excited [ɪk'saɪtɪd] aufgeregt, begeistert III

exciting [ɪk'saɪtɪŋ] aufregend, spannend II

Excuse me, ... [ɪk'skju:z mi:] Entschuldigung, ... / Entschuldigen Sie, ... I

exercise ['eksəsaɪz]
1. Übung, Aufgabe I
2. *(no pl)* (körperliche) Bewegung, Training IV 3 (58)

exercise book ['eksəsaɪz bʊk] Schulheft, Übungsheft I

expect [ɪk'spekt] erwarten III

expensive [ɪk'spensɪv] teuer I

experience [ɪk'spɪəriəns] erleben, erfahren IV 2 (36)

experience [ɪk'spɪəriəns] Erlebnis, Erfahrung IV 2 (36)

explain sth. to sb. [ɪk'spleɪn] jm. etwas erklären, erläutern II

explanation [ˌeksplə'neɪʃn] Erklärung II

explore [ɪk'splɔ:] erkunden, erforschen I

explorer [ɪk'splɔ:rə] Entdecker/in, Forscher/in II

explosion [ɪk'spləʊʒn] Explosion IV 4 (79)

extra ['ekstrə] zusätzlich I

extracurricular activities (*kurz:* **extracurriculars)** [ˌekstrəkə'rɪkjələz] *schulische Angebote außerhalb des regulären Unterrichts, oft als Arbeitsgemeinschaften* IV 3 (56)

eye [aɪ] Auge I

°**e-zine** ['i:zi:n] elektronisches Magazin, elektronische Zeitschrift

F

face [feɪs] Gesicht I

fact [fækt] Tatsache, Fakt III

factory ['fæktri] Fabrik II

fail an exam [feɪl] eine Prüfung nicht bestehen; durchfallen IV 3 (63/182)

failure *(n)* ['feɪljə] ungenügend *(USA, Schulnote)* IV 3 (56/179)
► S 179 US school grades

fair [feə] fair, gerecht II

fall [fɔ:l]**, fell, fallen** fallen, stürzen; hinfallen II • **fall down** hinfallen II • **fall in love (with sb.)** sich verlieben (in jn.) IV 3 (68) • **fall off** herunterfallen (von) II

fallen ['fɔ:lən] *siehe* **fall**

family ['fæməli] Familie I • **family tree** (Familien-)Stammbaum I

famous (for) ['feɪməs] berühmt (für, wegen) II

fan [fæn] Fan I

fantastic [fæn'tæstɪk] fantastisch, toll I

far [fɑ:] weit (entfernt) I • **so far** bis jetzt, bis hierher I

farm [fɑ:m] Bauernhof, Farm II

farmer ['fɑ:mə] Bauer/Bäuerin, Landwirt/in; (Fisch-)Züchter/in III

°**farming** ['fɑ:mɪŋ] Landwirtschaft

fashion ['fæʃn] Mode II

fast [fɑ:st] schnell II • **fast food** Fastfood III

fat [fæt] dick IV 2 (51)

father ['fɑ:ðə] Vater I

°**fatty** ['fæti] *(infml)* Fettsack

fault [fɔ:lt]**: It's not my fault.** Es/Das ist nicht meine Schuld. IV 1 (27)

favourite ['feɪvərɪt] Favorit/in; Liebling III; Lieblings- I

February ['februəri] Februar I
fed [fed] *siehe* **feed** • **be fed up (with sth.)** [ˌfed_ˈʌp] die Nase voll haben (von etwas) II
feed [fi:d], **fed, fed** füttern I
feel [fi:l], **felt, felt** fühlen; sich fühlen; sich anfühlen II • **How do they feel about ...?** Was halten sie von ...? III • **I feel sick.** Mir ist schlecht. IV 1 (27) • °**feel cared about** sich behütet/beschützt fühlen
feeling ['fi:lɪŋ] Gefühl III
feet [fi:t] *pl von „foot"*
fell [fel] *siehe* **fall**
felt [felt] *siehe* **feel**
felt tip ['felt tɪp] Filzstift I
fence [fens] Zaun IV 2 (38)
ferry ['feri] Fähre III
festival ['festɪvl] Fest, Festival III
few: a few [ə 'fju:] ein paar, einige II
► S.181 little („wenig") – few („wenige")
fiddle ['fɪdl] *(infml)* Fiedel, Geige III
play the fiddle Geige spielen III
field [fi:ld] Feld, Acker, Weide II; Sportplatz, Spielfeld III • **in the field** auf dem Feld II
fight (for) [faɪt], **fought, fought** kämpfen (für, um) III • **fight sth.** etwas bekämpfen III
fight [faɪt] Kampf; Schlägerei IV 2 (50)
°**file** [faɪl] (Akten-)Ordner, Hefter
file [faɪl]: **background file** *etwa:* Hintergrundinformation(en) II
grammar file *Grammatikanhang* I
skills file *Anhang mit Lern- und Arbeitstechniken* I • **sound file** Tondatei, Soundfile III
°**fill in** [ˌfɪl_ˈɪn]
1. einsetzen
2. ausfüllen
film [fɪlm] filmen III
film [fɪlm] Film I
film star ['fɪlm stɑ:] Filmstar I
final ['faɪnl] letzte(r, s); End- III
final score Endstand *(beim Sport)* III
final ['faɪnl] Finale, Endspiel III
find [faɪnd], **found, found** finden I
find out (about) herausfinden (über) I
fine [faɪn]
1. gut, schön; in Ordnung II
2. *(gesundheitlich)* gut II
I'm/He's fine. Es geht mir/ihm gut. II
finger ['fɪŋgə] Finger I
finish ['fɪnɪʃ] beenden, zu Ende machen; enden I
fire ['faɪə] Feuer, Brand II
firefighter ['faɪəfaɪtə] Feuerwehrmann, -frau IV 1 (15)
fireman ['faɪəmən] Feuerwehrmann II
fire station ['faɪə steɪʃn] Feuerwache IV 1 (15)
firewoman ['faɪəˌwʊmən] Feuerwehrfrau II
fireworks *(pl)* ['faɪəwɜ:ks] Feuerwerk(skörper) II
first [fɜ:st]
1. erste(r, s) I
2. zuerst, als Erstes I
at first zuerst, am Anfang IV 3 (55)
be first der/die Erste sein I
first floor [ˌfɜ:st flɔ:] erster Stock *(BE)* / Erdgeschoss *(AE)* IV 1 (16/171)
► S.171 floor
fish, *pl* **fish** [fɪʃ] Fisch I
fish [fɪʃ] fischen, angeln III
fist [fɪst] Faust IV 3 (70)
fit (-tt-) [fɪt] passen I • **fit in** hineinpassen; sich einfügen, sich anpassen IV 2 (36)
fit [fɪt] fit III
flash [flæʃ] Lichtblitz III
flat [flæt] Wohnung I
flavour ['fleɪvə] Geschmack, Geschmacksrichtung II
flew [flu:] *siehe* **fly**
flight [flaɪt] Flug II
floor [flɔ:]
1. Fußboden I
2. Stock(werk) IV 1 (16)
first floor erster Stock *(BE)* / Erdgeschoss *(AE)* IV 1 (16/171) • **ground floor** *(BE)* Erdgeschoss IV 1 (16/171)
on the second floor im zweiten Stock *(BE)* / im ersten Stock *(AE)* IV 1 (16/171)
► S.171 floor
flow chart ['fləʊ tʃɑ:t] Flussdiagramm I
flower ['flaʊə] Blume; Blüte III
flown [fləʊn] *siehe* **fly**
flute [flu:t] Querflöte III
fly [flaɪ], **flew, flown** fliegen II
fog [fɒg] Nebel II
foggy ['fɒgi] neblig II
folk (music) [fəʊk] Folk *(englische, schottische, irische oder nordamerikanische Volksmusik des 20. Jahrhunderts)* III
follow ['fɒləʊ] folgen; verfolgen I
the following ... die folgenden ... II
food [fu:d]
1. Essen; Lebensmittel I
2. Futter I
foot [fʊt], *pl* **feet** [fi:t] Fuß I; Fuß *(Längenmaß; ca. 30 cm)* IV Intro (10) • **on foot** zu Fuß III
football ['fʊtbɔ:l] Fußball I
football boots ['fʊtbɔ:l bu:ts] Fußballschuhe, -stiefel I
football pitch ['fʊtbɔ:l pɪtʃ] Fußballplatz, -feld II
football shirt ['fʊtbɔ:l ʃɜ:t] (Fußball-)Trikot III
for [fə, fɔ:] für I • **for ages** ewig, eine Ewigkeit IV 4 (80) • **for breakfast/lunch/dinner** zum Frühstück/Mittagessen/Abendbrot I • **for example** zum Beispiel I • **for his birthday** zu seinem Geburtstag III
for lots of reasons aus vielen Gründen I • **for miles** meilenweit II • **for sale** *(auf Schild)* zu verkaufen IV Intro (9/168) • **for the first time** zum ersten Mal IV 4 (93)
for 20 minutes seit 20 Minuten; 20 Minuten lang IV 4 (79) • **just for fun** nur zum Spaß I • **What for?** Wofür? II • **What's for homework?** Was haben wir als Hausaufgabe auf? I • °**I just go for it.** *etwa:* Ich handle/reagiere einfach nur.
► S.186 German 'seit'
foreground ['fɔ:graʊnd] Vordergrund II
foreign ['fɒrən] ausländisch, fremd IV 3 (57) • **foreign language** Fremdsprache IV 3 (57/180)
forest ['fɒrɪst] Wald II
forever [fər'evə] ewig, für immer IV 1 (16)
forgave [fə'geɪv] *siehe* **forgive**
forget (-tt-) [fə'get], **forgot, forgotten** vergessen III
forgive [fə'gɪv], **forgave, forgiven** vergeben, verzeihen IV Intro (10)
forgiven [fə'gɪvn] *siehe* **forgive**
forgot [fə'gɒt] *siehe* **forget**
forgotten [fə'gɒtn] *siehe* **forget**
fork [fɔ:k] Gabel III
form [fɔ:m]
1. (Schul-)Klasse I
2. Form IV 3 (67)
form teacher Klassenlehrer/in I
form [fɔ:m] (sich) bilden, formen IV 1 (14)
forward ['fɔ:wəd]: **look forward to sth.** sich auf etwas freuen IV Intro (8)
fought [fɔ:t] *siehe* **fight**
found [faʊnd] gründen IV 3 (66)
found [faʊnd] *siehe* **find**
°**fountain** ['faʊntən]: **drinking fountain** Trinkbrunnen
fox [fɒks] Fuchs II
free [fri:]
1. frei I
2. kostenlos I
free time Freizeit, freie Zeit I

freedom ['fri:dəm] Freiheit IV 4 (89)
French [frentʃ] Französisch I
French fries [ˌfrentʃ 'fraɪz] *(AE)* Pommes frites IV 1 (20/172)
fresh [freʃ] frisch IV 3 (58)
Friday ['fraɪdeɪ, 'fraɪdi] Freitag I
fridge [frɪdʒ] Kühlschrank I
friend [frend] Freund/in I
friendliness ['frendlinəs] Freundlichkeit IV 3 (64)
friendly ['frendli] freundlich II
°**friendship** ['frendʃɪp] Freundschaft
frog [frɒg] Frosch II
from [frəm, frɒm]
1. aus I
2. von I
from all around Wales aus ganz Wales II • **from all over England/the UK** aus ganz England/aus dem gesamten Vereinigten Königreich III • **from Monday to Friday** von Montag bis Freitag III • **from my point of view** aus meiner Sicht; von meinem Standpunkt aus gesehen II • **I'm from ...** Ich komme aus ... / Ich bin aus ... I • **Where are you from?** Wo kommst du her? I
front [frʌnt]: **in front of** vor *(räumlich)* I • **to the front** nach vorn I
front door [ˌfrʌnt 'dɔ:] Wohnungstür, Haustür I
°**front inside cover** [ˌfrʌnt‿ˌɪnsaɪd 'kʌvə] vordere Umschlaginnenseite
fruit [fru:t] Obst, Früchte; Frucht I
°**fruit picker** ['fru:t ˌpɪkə] Obstpflücker/in
fruit salad ['fru:t ˌsæləd] Obstsalat I
full [fʊl] voll I
fun [fʌn] Spaß I • **have fun** Spaß haben, sich amüsieren I • **Have fun!** Viel Spaß! I • **just for fun** nur zum Spaß I • **Riding is fun.** Reiten macht Spaß. I
°**fund-raising** ['fʌndreɪzɪŋ] Beschaffung von Geldmitteln
funny ['fʌni] witzig, komisch I
furniture *(no pl)* ['fɜ:nɪtʃə] Möbel III
a piece of furniture ein Möbelstück III
future ['fju:tʃə] Zukunft I

G

°**gallery** ['gæləri] Galerie
game [geɪm] Spiel I • **a game of football** ein Fußballspiel II
°**gap** [gæp] Lücke
garage ['gærɑ:ʒ] Garage II
garbage ['gɑ:bɪdʒ] *(AE)* Müll, Abfall IV 1 (20/172)
garden ['gɑ:dn] Garten I
gardener ['gɑ:dnə] Gärtner/in IV 2 (38)
gas [gæs]
°1. Gas
2. *(AE)* Benzin IV Intro (10)
gasp [gɑ:sp] nach Luft schnappen *(auch: vor Überraschung)* IV 1 (26)
gas station ['gæs steɪʃn] *(AE)* Tankstelle IV Intro (10)
gate [geɪt] Flugsteig III
°**gateway (to)** ['geɪtweɪ] Tor (zu, nach)
gave [geɪv] *siehe* **give**
gear *(no pl)* [gɪə]: **camping gear** Campingausrüstung, Campingsachen IV Intro (8) • **sports gear** Sportausrüstung, Sportsachen II
general ['dʒenrəl] allgemeine(r, s) III
geography [dʒi'ɒgrəfi] Geografie, Erdkunde I
German ['dʒɜ:mən] Deutsch; deutsch; Deutsche(r) I
Germany ['dʒɜ:məni] Deutschland I
get (-tt-) [get], **got, got**
1. bekommen, kriegen II
2. holen, besorgen II
3. gelangen, (hin)kommen I
4. **get angry/hot/...** wütend/heiß/... werden II
5. **get off (the train/bus)** (aus dem Zug/Bus) aussteigen I • **get on (the train/bus)** (in den Zug/Bus) einsteigen I
6. **get up** aufstehen I
get bored sich langweilen IV 4 (80)
get dressed sich anziehen I • **get involved (in)** sich engagieren (für, bei); sich beteiligen (an) IV 3 (57)
get ready (for) sich fertig machen (für), sich vorbereiten (auf) I • **get rid of sb./sth.** jn./etwas loswerden IV 1 (28) • **get sth. off the ground** etwas auf den Weg bringen; etwas auf die Beine stellen III • **get things ready** Dinge fertig machen, vorbereiten I • **get tired of sth.** einer Sache überdrüssig werden, die Lust an etwas verlieren IV 3 (69)
get to know sb. jn. kennenlernen IV 2 (50)
getting by in English [ˌgetɪŋ 'baɪ] *etwa:* auf Englisch zurechtkommen I
°**giant** ['dʒaɪənt] riesig, Riesen-
gig [gɪg] *(infml)* Gig, Auftritt III
do a gig einen Auftritt haben, ein Konzert geben III
giraffe [dʒə'rɑ:f] Giraffe II
girl [gɜ:l] Mädchen I
girlfriend ['gɜ:lfrend] (feste) Freundin IV 2 (50/178)
give [gɪv], **gave, given** geben I
give up aufgeben IV 2 (50)
given ['gɪvn] *siehe* **give**
°**glad** [glæd] froh
glass [glɑ:s] Glas I • **a glass of water** ein Glas Wasser I
glasses *(pl)* ['glɑ:sɪz] (eine) Brille I
glue [glu:] (auf-, ein)kleben II
glue [glu:] Klebstoff I
glue stick ['glu: stɪk] Klebestift I
go [gəʊ], **went, gone** gehen I; fahren II • **coffee to go** Kaffee zum Mitnehmen IV 1 (17) • **go abroad** ins Ausland gehen/fahren II • **go by car/train/bike/...** mit dem Auto/Zug/Rad/... fahren II • °**go crazy** durchdrehen, verrückt werden • **go for a walk** spazieren gehen, einen Spaziergang machen II
go home nach Hause gehen I
go on 1. weitermachen I; weiterreden III; 2. angehen *(Licht)* III
go on a trip einen Ausflug machen II • **go on holiday** in Urlaub fahren II • **go out** weg-, raus-, ausgehen I • **go to bed** ins Bett gehen I • **go to the cinema** ins Kino gehen II • **go together** zusammenpassen IV 1 (21) • **go well** gut (ver)laufen, gutgehen III • **go with** gehören zu, passen zu III
go wrong schiefgehen III • **Let's go.** Auf geht's! I • **There you go!** *(infml) etwa:* So, das hätten wir. IV 2 (50) • °**I just go for it.** *etwa:* Ich handle/reagiere einfach nur.
goal [gəʊl] Tor *(im Sport)* III
goalkeeper ['gəʊlki:pə] Torwart, Torfrau III
God [gɒd] Gott IV 4 (93)
gold [gəʊld] Gold III
golden ['gəʊldən] golden IV 2 (34)
°**gold rush** ['gəʊld rʌʃ] Goldrausch
golf [gɒlf] Golf III
gone [gɒn] *siehe* **go**
good [gʊd]
1. gut I
2. brav II
be good at sth. gut in etwas sein; etwas gut können III • **Good afternoon.** Guten Tag. *(nachmittags)* I • **Good luck (with ...)!** Viel Glück (bei/mit ...)! I • **Good morning.** Guten Morgen. I
► S.179 US school grades
Goodbye. [ˌgʊd'baɪ] Auf Wiedersehen. I • **say goodbye** sich verabschieden I
got [gɒt] *siehe* **get**

got [gɒt]: **I've got ...** Ich habe ... I
I haven't got a chair. Ich habe keinen Stuhl. I
government ['gʌvənmənt] Regierung (*als Schulfach etwa:* Staatskunde) IV 3 (56)
governor ['gʌvənə] Gouverneur/in IV 2 (34)
grab (-bb-) [græb] schnappen, packen III
grade [greɪd]
1. (Schul-)Note, Zensur IV 3 (56)
1. *(AE)* Jahrgangsstufe, Klasse IV Intro (9)
► S.179 US school grades
grain [greɪn] Korn IV 3 (58)
grammar ['græmə] Grammatik I
grammar file *Grammatikanhang* I
grand [grænd] eindrucksvoll, beeindruckend IV Intro (10)
grandchild ['græntʃaɪld], *pl* **grandchildren** ['-tʃɪldrən] Enkel/in I
granddaughter ['grændɔːtə] Enkelin II
grandfather ['grænfɑːðə] Großvater I
grandma ['grænmɑː] Oma I
grandmother ['grænmʌðə] Großmutter I
grandpa ['grænpɑː] Opa I
grandparents ['grænpeərənts] Großeltern I
grandson ['grænsʌn] Enkel II
granny ['græni] Oma II
grape [greɪp] Weintraube IV 3 (54)
grass [grɑːs] Rasen IV Intro (9)
great [greɪt] großartig, toll I
great-grandfather [ˌgreɪt 'grænfɑːðə] Urgroßvater III
great-grandmother [ˌgreɪt 'grænmʌðə] Urgroßmutter III
green [griːn] grün I
°**greeting** ['griːtɪŋ] Gruß, Begrüßung
grew [gruː] *siehe* **grow**
grey [greɪ] grau II
ground [graʊnd] (Erd-)Boden III
get sth. off the ground etwas auf den Weg bringen; etwas auf die Beine stellen III
ground floor [ˌgraʊnd 'flɔː] *(BE)* Erdgeschoss IV 1 (16/171)
► S.171 floor
ground zero [ˌgraʊnd 'zɪərəʊ] Bodennullpunkt (*Bezeichnung für das zerstörte World Trade Center in New York; ursprünglich: Explosionsstelle einer Bombe oder Rakete über dem Boden*) IV 1 (15)
group [gruːp] Gruppe I • **group word** Oberbegriff II
grow [grəʊ], **grew, grown**
1. wachsen II
2. *(Getreide usw.)* anbauen, anpflanzen II
grow up erwachsen werden; aufwachsen III
grown [grəʊn] *siehe* **grow**
grumble ['grʌmbl] murren, nörgeln I
guess [ges] raten, erraten, schätzen II • **Guess what!** Stell dir vor! II
°**guess** [ges] Vermutung, Schätzung
guest [gest] Gast I
°**guard** [gɑːd]: **National Guard** Nationalgarde
guide [gaɪd] (Fremden-)Führer/in, Reiseleiter/in IV 3 (67)
guilty ['gɪlti] schuldbewusst; schuldig IV 2 (50)
guinea pig ['gɪni pɪg] Meerschweinchen I
guitar [gɪ'tɑː] Gitarre I • **play the guitar** Gitarre spielen I
gun [gʌn] (Schuss-)Waffe II
guy [gaɪ] *(infml)* Typ, Kerl IV 1 (15)
guys *(pl) (AE, infml)* Leute III
gym [dʒɪm] Sporthalle, Turnhalle IV 3 (56)

H

had [hæd] *siehe* **have**
hair *(no pl)* [heə] Haar, Haare I
hairdresser ['heədresə] Friseur/in III
at the hairdresser's beim Friseur III
half [hɑːf], *pl* **halves** [hɑːvz]
1. Hälfte III
2. Halbzeit III
the first half die erste Halbzeit III
half [hɑːf]: **half an hour** eine halbe Stunde III • **half past 11** halb zwölf (11.30 / 23.30) I • **three and a half days/weeks** dreieinhalb Tage/Wochen IV Intro (8)
half-pipe ['hɑːfpaɪp] Halfpipe (*halbierte Röhre für Inlineskater*) III
half-time [ˌhɑːf 'taɪm] Halbzeit(pause) III
hall [hɔːl]
1. Flur, Diele I
2. Halle, Saal III
study hall *Zeit zum selbstständigen Lernen in der Schule* IV 3 (56)
hallway ['hɔːlweɪ] *(AE)* Korridor, Gang IV 4 (93)
halves [hɑːvz] *pl von „half"*
hamburger ['hæmbɜːgə] Hamburger I
hamster ['hæmstə] Hamster I
hand [hænd] Hand I
hang [hæŋ], **hung, hung:**
hang out *(infml)* rumhängen, abhängen III • °**hang sth. up** etwas aufhängen
happen (to) ['hæpən] geschehen, passieren (mit) I
happiness ['hæpinəs] Glück IV 3 (64)
happy ['hæpi] glücklich, froh I
Happy birthday. Herzlichen Glückwunsch zum Geburtstag. I
happy ending Happyend II
harbour ['hɑːbə] Hafen II
hard [hɑːd]
1. hart; schwer, schwierig II
2. *(adv)* heftig, kräftig IV 2 (37)
work hard hart arbeiten II
harvest ['hɑːvɪst] Ernte IV 3 (54)
hat [hæt] Hut II
hate [heɪt] hassen, gar nicht mögen I
have [həv, hæv], **had, had** haben, besitzen II • **have a baby** ein Baby/Kind bekommen II • **have a bath** baden, ein Bad nehmen II
have a cold erkältet sein, eine Erkältung haben II • **have a crush on sb.** in jn. verknallt sein III
Have a good time! Viel Spaß! / Viel Vergnügen! III • **have a party** eine Party feiern/veranstalten II
have a sauna in die Sauna gehen II • **have a shower** (sich) duschen I • **have a sore throat** Halsschmerzen haben II • **have a temperature** Fieber haben II • **have breakfast** frühstücken I • **have dinner** Abendbrot essen I • **have ... for breakfast** ... zum Frühstück essen/trinken I • **have fun** Spaß haben, sich amüsieren I • **Have fun!** Viel Spaß! I • **have to do** tun müssen I
have got: I've got ... [aɪv 'gɒt] Ich habe ... I • **I haven't got a chair.** ['hævnt gɒt] Ich habe keinen Stuhl. I
he [hiː] er I
head [hed] Kopf I • °**head of state** Staatsoberhaupt • °**running head** Leitwort (*am Kopf einer Wörterbuchseite*)
headache ['hedeɪk] Kopfschmerzen II
heading ['hedɪŋ] Überschrift IV 1 (28)
headless ['hedləs] kopflos IV 2 (42)
headline ['hedlaɪn] Schlagzeile IV 4 (94)
headphones *(pl)* ['hedfəʊnz] Kopfhörer III
head teacher [ˌhed 'tiːtʃə] Schulleiter/in III
health [helθ] Gesundheit; Gesundheitslehre IV 3 (56)

healthy [ˈhelθi] gesund II
hear [hɪə], **heard, heard** hören I
heard [hɜːd] *siehe* **hear**
heart [hɑːt] Herz II
heaven [ˈhevn] Himmel *(im religiösen Sinn)* IV 3 (69)
hedgehog [ˈhedʒhɒg] Igel II
held [held] *siehe* **hold**
helicopter [ˈhelɪkɒptə] Hubschrauber, Helikopter II
Hello. [həˈləʊ] Hallo. / Guten Tag. I
helmet [ˈhelmɪt] Helm III
help [help] helfen I • **Can I help you?** Kann ich Ihnen helfen? / Was kann ich für Sie tun? *(im Geschäft)* I
help [help] Hilfe I
helpful [ˈhelpfl] hilfreich, nützlich IV 3 (65)
helpless [ˈhelpləs] hilflos IV 2 (42)
her [hə, hɜː]
1. ihr, ihre I
2. sie; ihr I
here [hɪə]
1. hier I
2. hierher I
Here you are. Bitte sehr. / Hier bitte. I
hero [ˈhɪərəʊ], *pl* **heroes** [ˈhɪərəʊz] Held, Heldin II
hers [hɜːz] ihrer, ihre, ihrs II
herself [həˈself, hɜːˈself] sich (selbst) III
Hi! [haɪ] Hallo! I • **Say hi to Dilip for me.** Grüß Dilip von mir. I
hid [hɪd] *siehe* **hide**
hidden [ˈhɪdn] *siehe* **hide**
hide [haɪd], **hid, hidden** sich verstecken; *(etwas)* verstecken I
high [haɪ] hoch III • °**high winds** stürmische Winde
high school [ˈhaɪ skuːl] *(USA) Schule für 14- bis 18-Jährige* IV Intro (10)
°**highlighted** [ˈhaɪlaɪtɪd] hervorgehoben, markiert *(mit Textmarker)*
highway [ˈhaɪweɪ] *(USA)* Fernstraße *(oft mit vier oder mehr Spuren)* IV Intro (10)
hijacker [ˈhaɪdʒækə] (Flugzeug-)Entführer/in IV 1 (15)
hike [haɪk] wandern IV Intro (8)
hike [haɪk] Wanderung, Marsch IV Intro (8)
hill [hɪl] Hügel II
hilly [ˈhɪli] hügelig III
him [hɪm] ihn; ihm I
himself [hɪmˈself] sich (selbst) III
hip hop [ˈhɪp hɒp] Hiphop III
hippo [ˈhɪpəʊ] Flusspferd II
his [hɪz]
1. sein, seine I
2. seiner, seine, seins II

Hispanic *(n; adj)* [hɪˈspænɪk] *US-amerikanischer Ausdruck für Menschen mit Wurzeln in spanischsprachigen Ländern, besonders in Mittelamerika* IV 3 (66)
history [ˈhɪstri] Geschichte I
hit (-tt-) [hɪt], **hit, hit** schlagen I
hit the windscreen gegen/auf die Windschutzscheibe schlagen/prallen III
hit [hɪt] Hit III
hobby [ˈhɒbi] Hobby I
hockey [ˈhɒki] Hockey I
hockey pitch [ˈhɒki pɪtʃ] Hockeyplatz, Hockeyfeld II
hockey shoes [ˈhɒki ʃuːz] Hockeyschuhe I
°**hog** [hɒg] *(bes. AE)* Schwein
hold [həʊld], **held, held** halten II
°**hold sth. up** etwas hochhalten
°**hold on (to sth.)** sich (an etwas) festhalten
hole [həʊl] Loch I
holiday [ˈhɒlədeɪ]
1. Feiertag IV 4 (89)
2. **holiday(s)** Ferien I
be on holiday in Urlaub sein; Ferien haben/machen II • **go on holiday** in Urlaub fahren II
home [həʊm] Heim, Zuhause I
at home daheim, zu Hause I
come home nach Hause kommen I • **get home** nach Hause kommen I • **go home** nach Hause gehen I
homeless [ˈhəʊmləs] obdachlos IV 2 (42)
hometown [ˈhəʊmtaʊn] Heimatstadt IV Intro (8)
homework *(no pl)* [ˈhəʊmwɜːk] Hausaufgabe(n) I • **do homework** die Hausaufgabe(n) machen I
What's for homework? Was haben wir als Hausaufgabe auf? I
Hooray! [huˈreɪ] Hurra! II
hope [həʊp] hoffen II
hope [həʊp] Hoffnung III
hopeless [ˈhəʊpləs] hoffnungslos, verzweifelt IV 4 (94)
horrible [ˈhɒrəbl] scheußlich, grauenhaft II
horse [hɔːs] Pferd I
hospital [ˈhɒspɪtl] Krankenhaus II
host [həʊst] *(Radio-, Fernseh-)* Moderator/in IV 4 (78)
hostel [ˈhɒstl] Herberge, Wohnheim III
hostess [ˈhəʊstəs] Gastgeberin *(in USA auch: Frau, die im Restaurant die Gäste empfängt und an ihren Platz führt)* IV 1 (14)

hot [hɒt] heiß I • **hot-water bottle** Wärmflasche II
hotel [həʊˈtel] Hotel II
hotline [ˈhɒtlaɪn] Hotline II
hour [ˈaʊə] Stunde II • **a 14-hour flight** ein 14-stündiger Flug, ein 14-Stunden-Flug III • **a 24-hour supermarket** ein Supermarkt, der 24 Stunden geöffnet ist III • **half an hour** eine halbe Stunde III
opening hours *(pl)* Öffnungszeiten IV 2 (47)
house [haʊs] Haus I • **at the Shaws' house** im Haus der Shaws/bei den Shaws zu Hause I
how [haʊ] wie I • **How about ...?** Wie wär's mit ...? III • **How am I doing?** Wie komme ich voran? *(Wie sind meine Fortschritte?)* III
How are you? Wie geht es dir/Ihnen/euch? II • **How do you feel about ...?** Was hältst du von ...? III
How do you know ...? Woher weißt/kennst du ...? I • **How long ...?** Seit wann ...? / Wie lange ...? IV 4 (79) • **how many?** wie viele? I
how much? wie viel? I • **How much is ...?** Was kostet ...? / Wie viel kostet ...? I • **how to do sth.** wie man etwas tut / tun kann / tun soll IV Intro (9)
► S. 68 Question words + to-infinitive: how to ... / what to ... / ...
huge [hjuːdʒ] riesig, sehr groß III
human [ˈhjuːmən] Menschen-, menschlich IV Intro (9)
hundred [ˈhʌndrəd] hundert I
hung [hʌŋ] *siehe* **hang**
hungry [ˈhʌŋgri] hungrig I • **be hungry** Hunger haben, hungrig sein I
hunt [hʌnt] jagen III
hunt [hʌnt] Jagd III
hunter [ˈhʌntə] Jäger/in III
hurry [ˈhʌri] eilen; sich beeilen II
hurry up sich beeilen I
hurry [ˈhʌri]: **be in a hurry** in Eile sein, es eilig haben I
hurt [hɜːt], **hurt, hurt** wehtun; verletzen I
hurt [hɜːt] verletzt II
husband [ˈhʌzbənd] Ehemann II
hutch [hʌtʃ] (Kaninchen-)Stall I

I

I [aɪ] ich I • **I'm** [aɪm] ich bin I
I'm from ... Ich komme aus ... / Ich bin aus ... I • **I'm ... years old.** Ich bin ... Jahre alt. I • **I'm sorry.** Entschuldigung. / Tut mir leid. I

ice [aɪs] Eis II
ice cream [ˌaɪs ˈkriːm] (Speise-)Eis I
ice hockey [ˈaɪs hɒki] Eishockey III
ice rink [ˈaɪs rɪŋk] Schlittschuhbahn II
°**ID** [ˌaɪ ˈdiː] (*kurz für:* **identification** [aɪˌdentɪfɪˈkeɪʃn]) Ausweis
idea [aɪˈdɪə] Idee, Einfall I
if [ɪf]
1. falls, wenn II
2. ob II
as if als ob IV 4 (92) • **even if** selbst wenn; obwohl IV 4 (92)
ill [ɪl] krank II
illegal [ɪˈliːgl] illegal, ungesetzlich IV 2 (38)
illness [ˈɪlnəs] Krankheit IV 3 (64)
°**imaginary** [ɪˈmædʒɪnəri] imaginär *(nur in der Vorstellung vorhanden)*
imagination [ɪˌmædʒɪˈneɪʃn] Fantasie, Vorstellung(skraft) IV 3 (64)
imagine sth. [ɪˈmædʒɪn] sich etwas vorstellen III
immediately [ɪˈmiːdiətli] sofort IV 4 (92)
immigrant [ˈɪmɪgrənt] Einwanderer/Einwanderin IV 1 (17)
°**immigration** [ˌɪmɪˈgreɪʃn] Einwanderung
important [ɪmˈpɔːtnt] wichtig II
important to sb. wichtig für jn. III
impossible [ɪmˈpɒsəbl] unmöglich II
impressed [ɪmˈprest] beeindruckt IV 4 (80)
°**improve** [ɪmˈpruːv] verbessern
in [ɪn] in I • **in 1948** im Jahr 1948 II • **in ... Street** in der ...straße I **in English** auf Englisch I • **in front of** vor *(räumlich)* I • **in here** hier drinnen I • **in my opinion** meiner Meinung nach IV 2 (36/175) **in my/your view** meiner/deiner Ansicht nach III • **in other places** an anderen Orten, anderswo III °**in the 1970s** in den 70er-Jahren *(des 20. Jahrhunderts)* • **in the afternoon** nachmittags, am Nachmittag I • **in the country** auf dem Land II • **in the end** schließlich, zum Schluss III • **in the evening** abends, am Abend I • **in the field** auf dem Feld II • **in the morning** am Morgen, morgens I **in the photo** auf dem Foto I • **in the picture** auf dem Bild I • **in the sky** am Himmel II • **in there** dort drinnen I • °**in the world** auf der Welt • **in time** rechtzeitig II
°**inch** [ɪntʃ] Zoll, Inch *(= 2,54 cm)*
°**income** [ˈɪnkʌm] Einkommen
°**incorrect** [ˌɪnkəˈrekt] falsch
Indian [ˈɪndiən] Indianer/in; indianisch IV Intro (9)
indirect question [ˌɪndərekt ˈkwestʃən] indirekte Frage II
industrial [ɪnˈdʌstriəl] industriell, Industrie- IV 2 (37)
industry [ˈɪndəstri] Industrie IV 2 (37)
infinitive [ɪnˈfɪnətɪv] Infinitiv *(Grundform des Verbs)* I
information (about/on) *(no pl)* [ˌɪnfəˈmeɪʃn] Information(en) (über) I
insect [ˈɪnsekt] Insekt IV 2 (37)
°**insecticide** [ɪnˈsektɪsaɪd] Insektizid, Insektenvernichtungsmittel
inside [ˌɪnˈsaɪd]
1. innen (drin), drinnen I
2. nach drinnen II
3. inside the car ins Auto (hinein), ins Innere des Autos II
°**inside cover** [ˌɪnsaɪd ˈkʌvə] Umschlaginnenseite
install [ɪnˈstɔːl] installieren, einrichten II
installation [ˌɪnstəˈleɪʃn] Installation, Einrichtung II
instant messages *(pl)* [ˌɪnstənt ˈmesɪdʒɪz] *Nachrichten, die man im Internet austauscht (in Echtzeit)* III
instructions *(pl)* [ɪnˈstrʌkʃnz] (Gebrauchs-)Anweisung(en), Anleitung(en) II
instrument [ˈɪnstrəmənt] Instrument II
°**integration** [ˌɪntɪˈgreɪʃn] *hier:* Integrationspolitik *(gegen Rassentrennung; USA, 1960er Jahre)*
interactive [ˌɪntərˈæktɪv] interaktiv IV 2 (48)
interest (in) [ˈɪntrəst] Interesse (an) IV 3 (59)
°**interest sb.** [ˈɪntrəst] jn. interessieren
interested [ˈɪntrəstɪd]**: be interested (in)** interessiert sein (an), sich interessieren (für) III
interesting [ˈɪntrəstɪŋ] interessant I
international [ˌɪntəˈnæʃnəl] international III
internet [ˈɪntənet] Internet I
interrupt [ˌɪntəˈrʌpt] unterbrechen IV 2 (37)
interview [ˈɪntəvjuː] interviewen, befragen II
interview [ˈɪntəvjuː] Interview II
into [ˈɪntə, ˈɪntʊ] in ... (hinein) I
run into sth./sb. gegen etwas fahren / jn. anfahren IV 2 (46)
intolerant [ɪnˈtɒlərənt] intolerant III
introduction [ˌɪntrəˈdʌkʃn] Einführung, Einleitung III
invitation (to) [ˌɪnvɪˈteɪʃn] Einladung (zu) I
invite (to) [ɪnˈvaɪt] einladen (zu) I
involved [ɪnˈvɒlvd]**: get involved (in)** sich engagieren (für, bei); sich beteiligen (an) IV 3 (57)
irregular [ɪˈregjələ] unregelmäßig I
is [ɪz] ist I
island [ˈaɪlənd] Insel II
it [ɪt] er/sie/es I • **It's £1.** Er/Sie/Es kostet 1 Pfund. I • **It says here: ...** Hier steht: ... / Es heißt hier: ... II
IT [ˌaɪ ˈtiː]**, information technology** [tekˈnɒlədʒi] IT, Informationstechnologie II
°**italics** [ɪˈtælɪks]**: in italics** kursiv; in Kursivschrift
its [ɪts] sein/seine; ihr/ihre I
itself [ɪtˈself] sich (selbst) III

J

jacket [ˈdʒækɪt] Jacke, Jackett II
jail [dʒeɪl] Gefängnis IV 2 (50)
January [ˈdʒænjuəri] Januar I
jazz [dʒæz] Jazz I
jealous (of) [ˈdʒeləs] neidisch (auf); eifersüchtig (auf) III
jeans *(pl)* [dʒiːnz] Jeans I
°**jerk** [dʒɜːk] *(infml)* Trottel, Blödmann
jewellery *(no pl)* [ˈdʒuːəlri] Schmuck II
Jewish [ˈdʒuːɪʃ] jüdisch IV 1 (17)
job [dʒɒb] Aufgabe, Job I
jobless [ˈdʒɒbləs] arbeitslos IV 2 (42)
join sb. [dʒɔɪn] sich jm. anschließen; bei jm. mitmachen II • °**join up (with)** sich zusammentun (mit)
joke [dʒəʊk] Witz I
joke [dʒəʊk] scherzen, Witze machen II
journalist [ˈdʒɜːnəlɪst] Journalist/in IV 4 (94)
journey [ˈdʒɜːni] Reise, Fahrt II
judge (by) [dʒʌdʒ] beurteilen, einschätzen (nach) IV 4 (81)
judo [ˈdʒuːdəʊ] Judo I • **do judo** Judo machen I
jug [dʒʌg] Krug I • **a jug of milk** ein Krug Milch I
juice [dʒuːs] Saft I
July [dʒuˈlaɪ] Juli I
°**jumble** [ˈdʒʌmbl] gebrauchte Sachen, Trödel
jumble sale [ˈdʒʌmbl seɪl] Wohltätigkeitsbasar I
jump [dʒʌmp] springen II
June [dʒuːn] Juni I

junior ['dʒuːniə] Junioren-, Jugend- I
°**jury** ['dʒʊəri] Jury, Schwurgericht
just [dʒʌst]
1. (einfach) nur, bloß I
2. einfach III • **I just can't find them.** Ich kann sie einfach nicht finden. III
3. gerade (eben), soeben II • **just then** genau in dem Moment; gerade dann II
4. **just like you** genau wie du II

K

kangaroo [ˌkæŋgə'ruː] Känguru II
keep [kiːp], **kept, kept** (be)halten; aufbewahren III • **keep in touch** in Verbindung bleiben, Kontakt halten III • **keep sth. warm/cool/open/...** etwas warm/kühl/offen/... halten II • °**keep a diary** ein Tagebuch führen
kept [kept] *siehe* **keep**
key [kiː] Schlüssel I • **key word** Stichwort, Schlüsselwort I
keyboard ['kiːbɔːd] Keyboard *(elektronisches Tasteninstrument)* III
kick [kɪk] treten IV 1 (27)
kid [kɪd] Kind, Jugendliche(r) I
kill [kɪl] töten I
kilogram (kg) ['kɪləgræm], **kilo** ['kiːləʊ] Kilogramm, Kilo III
a 90-kilogram bear ein 90 Kilogramm schwerer Bär III
kilometre (km) ['kɪləmiːtə] Kilometer III • **a ten-kilometre walk** eine Zehn-Kilometer-Wanderung III
kind (of) [kaɪnd] Art III • **What kind of car ...?** Was für ein Auto ...? III
kind of scary [kaɪnd] *(infml)* irgendwie unheimlich III
kindergarten ['kɪndəgɑːtn] Kindergarten; *(USA)* Vorschule *(für 5- bis 6-Jährige)* IV 3 (56)
king [kɪŋ] König I
kiss [kɪs] küssen IV 1 (26)
kiss [kɪs] Kuss IV 1 (26)
kitchen ['kɪtʃɪn] Küche I
kite [kaɪt] Drachen I
knee [niː] Knie I
knew [njuː] *siehe* **know**
knife [naɪf], *pl* **knives** [naɪvz] Messer III
knock (on) [nɒk] (an)klopfen (an) I
know [nəʊ], **knew, known**
1. wissen I
2. kennen I
know about sth. von etwas wissen; über etwas Bescheid wissen II
get to know sb. jn. kennenlernen IV 2 (50) • **How do you know ...?** Woher weißt du ...? / Woher kennst du ...? I • **I don't know.** Ich weiß es nicht. I • **..., you know.** ..., wissen Sie. / ..., weißt du. I • **You know what, Sophie?** Weißt du was, Sophie? I
known [nəʊn] bekannt IV 4 (85) *siehe* **know**
kph (kilometres per hour) [ˌkeɪ piː ‿ 'eɪtʃ] km/h (Stundenkilometer, Kilometer pro Stunde) III

L

°**label** ['leɪbl] beschriften, etikettieren
°**ladder** ['lædə] *(die)* Leiter
laid [leɪd] *siehe* **lay**
lake [leɪk] (Binnen-)See II
lamb [læm] Lamm III
lamp [læmp] Lampe I
land [lænd] Land, Grund und Boden II • **on land** auf dem Land III
land [lænd] landen II
lane [leɪn] Gasse, Weg III
language ['læŋgwɪdʒ] Sprache I
large [lɑːdʒ] groß II
lasagne [lə'zænjə] Lasagne I
last [lɑːst] letzte(r, s) I • **the last day** der letzte Tag I • **at last** endlich, schließlich I
last (for) [lɑːst] dauern IV 4 (78)
late [leɪt] spät; zu spät I • **be late** zu spät sein/kommen I • **Sorry, I'm late.** Entschuldigung, dass ich zu spät bin/komme. I
later ['leɪtə] später I
latest ['leɪtɪst] neueste(r, s) III
°**Latino** [læ'tiːnəʊ] *US-Einwohner mit lateinamerikanischer Abkunft*
laugh [lɑːf] lachen I • **laugh at sb.** jn. auslachen, über jn. lachen III
laugh out loud laut lachen II
laughable ['lɑːfəbl] lächerlich, lachhaft IV 4 (88)
laughter ['lɑːftə] Gelächter II
law [lɔː] Gesetz IV 4 (91)
lay the table [leɪ], **laid, laid** den Tisch decken I
leader ['liːdə] (An-)Führer/in, Leiter/in III
lean [liːn] sich beugen, sich lehnen IV 1 (27) • **lean over** sich herüberbeugen, -lehnen IV 1 (27)
learn [lɜːn] lernen I • **learn sth. about sth.** etwas über etwas erfahren, etwas über etwas herausfinden II
least [liːst] am wenigsten III
at least zumindest, wenigstens I
leather ['leðə] Leder III
leave [liːv], **left, left**
1. (weg)gehen; abfahren II
2. verlassen II
3. zurücklassen II
leave sb. alone jn. in Ruhe lassen IV 1 (26) • **leave sth. out** etwas weglassen/auslassen IV 3 (67)
left [left] *siehe* **leave**
left [left] linke(r, s) II • **look left** nach links schauen II • **on the left** links, auf der linken Seite I • **turn left** (nach) links abbiegen II
leg [leg] Bein I
legal ['liːgl] legal IV 2 (38/176)
leisure centre ['leʒə sentə] Freizeitzentrum, -park II
lemonade [ˌlemə'neɪd] Limonade I
leotard ['liːətɑːd] Gymnastikanzug; Turnanzug III
less [les] weniger IV 3 (58/181)
lesson ['lesn] (Unterrichts-)Stunde I • **lessons** *(pl)* ['lesnz] Unterricht I
let (-tt-) [let], **let, let** lassen II
Let's ... Lass uns ... / Lasst uns ... I
Let's go. Auf geht's! I • **Let's look at the list.** Sehen wir uns die Liste an. / Lasst uns die Liste ansehen. I
let sb. do sth. jm. erlauben, etwas zu tun; zulassen, dass jd. etwas tut III
letter ['letə]
1. Buchstabe I
2. **letter (to)** Brief (an) II
°**lettering** ['letərɪŋ] Schrift, Schriftbild
lettuce ['letɪs] (Kopf-)Salat II
°**liberty** ['lɪbəti] Freiheit
library ['laɪbrəri] Bibliothek, Bücherei I
license plate ['laɪsns pleɪt] *(AE)* Nummernschild IV Intro (10)
life [laɪf], *pl* **lives** [laɪvz] Leben I
lift [lɪft] Fahrstuhl, Aufzug II
light [laɪt] Licht III
light [laɪt], **lit, lit** anzünden IV 2 (51)
like [laɪk] wie I • **just like you** genau wie du II • **What was the weather like?** Wie war das Wetter? II • **like that / like this** so IV 4 (79)
like [laɪk] mögen, gernhaben I
like sth. better etwas lieber mögen II • **like sth. best** etwas am liebsten mögen III • **I like swimming/dancing/...** Ich schwimme/tanze/... gern. I • **I'd like ... (= I would like ...)** Ich hätte gern ... / Ich möchte gern ... I • **I'd like to go**

(= I would like to go) Ich würde gern gehen / Ich möchte gehen I **I wouldn't like to go** Ich würde nicht gern gehen / Ich möchte nicht gehen I • **Would you like ...?** Möchtest du ...? / Möchten Sie ...? I **°Say what you like about ...** Sag, was du an ... magst

likeable ['laɪkəbl] sympathisch, liebenswert IV 4 (88)

line [laɪn]
1. Zeile II
2. (U-Bahn-)Linie III
3. Leitung *(Telefon)* IV 2 (48)
4. *(AE)* Schlange, Reihe *(wartender Menschen)* IV 1 (14)

link [lɪŋk] verbinden, verknüpfen I

link [lɪŋk] Verbindung, Verknüpfung III

linking word ['lɪŋkɪŋ wɜːd] Bindewort II

lion ['laɪən] Löwe II

list [lɪst] Liste I

list [lɪst] auflisten, aufzählen II

listen (to) ['lɪsn] zuhören; sich *etwas* anhören I • **listen for sth.** auf etwas horchen, achten III

listener ['lɪsnə] Zuhörer/in II

lit [lɪt] *siehe* **light**

little ['lɪtl]
1. klein I
2. wenig IV 3 (58)
► S.181 little („wenig") – few („wenige")

live [lɪv] leben, wohnen I

live music ['laɪv ˌmjuːzɪk] Livemusik II

lives [laɪvz] *pl von „life"*

living room ['lɪvɪŋ ruːm] Wohnzimmer I

lobby ['lɒbi] Eingangshalle IV 1 (16)

local ['ləʊkl] Lokal-, örtlich; am/vom Ort IV 3 (59)

location [ləʊ'keɪʃn]
1. (Einsatz-)Ort, Platz III
°2. Lage, Standort

lock [lɒk] Schleuse III

lock up [ˌlɒk_'ʌp] abschließen II

lodge [lɒdʒ] Landhaus IV Intro (11)

logo ['ləʊgəʊ], *pl* **logos** Logo, Markenzeichen III

lonely ['ləʊnli] einsam III

long [lɒŋ] lang I • **a long time** lange III • **as long as** *(conj)* solange, sofern IV 3 (58) • **How long ...?** Seit wann ...? / Wie lange ...? IV 4 (79)

look [lʊk]
1. schauen, gucken I
2. **look different/great/old** anders/toll/alt aussehen I
look after sth./sb. auf etwas/jn. aufpassen; sich um etwas/jn. kümmern II • **look around** sich umsehen III • **look at** ansehen, anschauen I • **look for** suchen II **look forward to sth.** sich auf etwas freuen IV Intro (8) • **look left/right** nach links/rechts schauen II **look round** sich umsehen I • **look sth. up** etwas nachschlagen III **look up (from)** hochsehen, aufschauen (von) II

°look (at) [lʊk] Blick (auf)

lose [luːz], **lost, lost** verlieren II

lost [lɒst] *siehe* **lose**

lot [lɒt]: **a lot (of)** eine Menge, viel, viele II • **Thanks a lot!** Vielen Dank! I • **He likes her a lot.** Er mag sie sehr. I • **lots more** viel mehr I • **lots of ...** eine Menge ..., viele ..., viel ... I

loud [laʊd] laut I

love [lʌv] lieben, sehr mögen II

love [lʌv]
1. Liebe II
2. Liebes, Liebling III
fall in love (with sb.) sich verlieben (in jn.) IV 3 (68) • **Love ...** Liebe Grüße, ... *(Briefschluss)* I

°lox [lɒks] *(AE)* Räucherlachs

luck [lʌk]: **Good luck (with ...)!** Viel Glück (bei/mit ...)! I

luckily ['lʌkɪli] zum Glück, glücklicherweise II

lucky ['lʌki]: **be lucky (with)** Glück haben (mit) II

lunch [lʌntʃ] Mittagessen I **lunch break** Mittagspause I

lunchtime ['lʌntʃtaɪm] Mittagszeit IV 3 (56)

lyrics *(pl)* ['lɪrɪks] Liedtext(e), Songtext(e) III

M

machine [mə'ʃiːn] Maschine, Gerät III

mad [mæd] verrückt I • **be mad about sth.** verrückt nach/auf etwas sein III

made [meɪd] *siehe* **make**

magazine [ˌmægə'ziːn] Zeitschrift, Magazin I

maid [meɪd] Hausangestellte, Zimmermädchen IV 2 (34)

mail [meɪl] schicken, senden *(per Post oder E-Mail)* I • **mail sb.** jn. anmailen II

main [meɪn] Haupt- III

majority [mə'dʒɒrəti] Mehrheit IV 2 (34/174)

make [meɪk], **made, made** machen; bauen I • **make a call** ein Telefongespräch führen II • **make a deal** ein Abkommen/eine Abmachung treffen III • **make a mess** alles durcheinanderbringen, alles in Unordnung bringen I • **make a point** ein Argument vorbringen III **make a speech** eine Rede halten IV 4 (81) • **°make comparisons** Vergleiche anstellen, vergleichen **°make it** *(infml)* es schaffen, Erfolg haben • **make money** Geld verdienen IV 1 (26) • **°make notes** (sich) Notizen machen • **make sure that ...** sich vergewissern, dass ...; dafür sorgen, dass ... IV 2 (49) • **°make sth. up** sich etwas ausdenken • **°What makes a game a good game?** Was macht ein Spiel zu einem guten Spiel?

make-up ['meɪkʌp] Make-up II

mall [mɔːl], **shopping mall** *(großes)* Einkaufszentrum III

man [mæn], *pl* **men** [men] Mann I

manager ['mænɪdʒə] Manager/in III

many ['meni] viele I • **how many?** wie viele? I

map [mæp] Landkarte, Stadtplan II

marathon ['mærəθən] Marathon IV 1 (20)

march [mɑːtʃ] Marsch, Demonstration IV 4 (81)

March [mɑːtʃ] März I

mark [mɑːk] (Schul-)Note, Zensur IV 3 (56)

mark sth. up [ˌmɑːk_'ʌp] etwas markieren, kennzeichnen II

°marked [mɑːkt] markiert

market ['mɑːkɪt] Markt II

marmalade ['mɑːməleɪd] (Orangen-)Marmelade I

married (to) ['mærɪd] verheiratet (mit) I

match [mætʃ] Spiel, Wettkampf I

°match [mætʃ]
1. passen zu
2. zuordnen
°Match the letters and numbers. Ordne die Buchstaben den Zahlen zu.

mate [meɪt] *(infml)* Freund/in, Kumpel III

math [mæθ] *(AE)* Mathematik IV 3 (56)

maths [mæθs] Mathematik I

matter ['mætə]: **What's the matter?** Was ist los? / Was ist denn? II

may [meɪ] dürfen I

May [meɪ] Mai I

maybe ['meɪbi] vielleicht I

mayor [meə] Bürgermeister/in IV 4 (77)

me [mi:] mir; mich I • **Me too.** Ich auch. I • **more than me** mehr als ich II • **That's me.** Das bin ich. I **Why me?** Warum ich? I

meal [mi:l] Mahlzeit, Essen III
set meal Menü III

mean [mi:n], **meant, meant**
1. bedeuten II
2. meinen *(sagen wollen)* II
What do you mean by ...? Was meinst du mit ...? IV 3 (70)

meaning ['mi:nɪŋ] Bedeutung III

meant [ment] *siehe* **mean**

meat [mi:t] Fleisch I

medal ['medl] Medaille III

media *(pl)* ['mi:diə] Medien III

mediation [ˌmi:di'eɪʃn] Vermittlung, Sprachmittlung, Mediation II

medium ['mi:diəm] mittel(groß) II

meet [mi:t], **met, met**
1. treffen; kennenlernen I
2. sich treffen I
Nice to meet you. Nett, dich kennenzulernen. III

meeting ['mi:tɪŋ] Versammlung, Besprechung; Treffen, Begegnung IV 3 (57)

member (of) ['membə] Mitglied (in, von) IV 3 (63)

men [men] *pl von „man"*

menu ['menju:]
1. Speisekarte III
2. Menü *(Computer)* III

merry-go-round ['merigəʊraʊnd] Karussell IV 4 (92)

mess [mes]**: be a mess** sehr unordentlich sein; fürchterlich aussehen *(Zimmer)* II • **make a mess** alles durcheinanderbringen, alles in Unordnung bringen I

message ['mesɪdʒ] Nachricht III

met [met] *siehe* **meet**

°**method** ['meθəd] Methode, Art und Weise

metre ['mi:tə] Meter II

mice [maɪs] *pl von „mouse"*

microphone ['maɪkrəfəʊn] Mikrofon III

middle (of) ['mɪdl] Mitte I; Mittelteil II

middle school *(USA) Schule für 11- bis 14-Jährige* IV Intro (9)

might [maɪt]**: you might need help** du könntest (vielleicht) Hilfe brauchen III

mild [maɪld] mild III

mile [maɪl] Meile *(= ca. 1,6 km)* II
for miles meilenweit II

milk [mɪlk] Milch I

million ['mɪljən] Million III

millionaire [ˌmɪljə'neə] Millionär/in IV Intro (10/169)

mime [maɪm] pantomimisch darstellen, vorspielen II

°**mime** [maɪm] Pantomime

mind [maɪnd]**: Mind your own business.** Das geht dich nichts an! / Kümmere dich um deine eigenen Angelegenheiten! II • **Never mind.** *etwa:* Nicht so wichtig. / Ist (doch) egal. / Das willst du gar nicht wissen. IV 3 (69)

mind map ['maɪnd mæp] Mindmap („Gedankenkarte", „Wissensnetz") I

mine [maɪn] meiner, meine, meins II

mini- ['mɪni] Mini- II

minister ['mɪnɪstə] Pastor/in, Pfarrer/in IV 4 (81)

minority [maɪ'nɒrəti] Minderheit IV 2 (34)

mints *(pl)* [mɪnts] Pfefferminzbonbons I

minus ['maɪnəs] minus III

minute ['mɪnɪt] Minute I • **Wait a minute.** Warte mal! / Moment mal! II

mirror ['mɪrə] Spiegel II

miss [mɪs]
1. vermissen II
2. verpassen II
3. Miss a turn. Einmal aussetzen. II

Miss White [mɪs] Frau White *(unverheiratet)* I

missing ['mɪsɪŋ]**: be missing** fehlen II • °**the missing information/ words** die fehlenden Informationen/Wörter

mistake [mɪ'steɪk] Fehler I

mix [mɪks] mischen, mixen III
°**mix up** durcheinanderbringen
°**be mixed up** durcheinander/ in der falschen Reihenfolge sein

mix [mɪks] Mix, Mischung III

mixture ['mɪkstʃə] Mischung III

°**mobile** ['məʊbaɪl] Mobile

mobile (phone) ['məʊbaɪl] Mobiltelefon, Handy I

model ['mɒdl] Modell*(-flugzeug, -schiff usw.)* I; (Foto-)Modell II

modern ['mɒdən] modern III

mole [məʊl] Maulwurf II

mom [mɒm, *AE:* mɑ:m] *(AE)* Mama, Mutti; Mutter III

moment ['məʊmənt] Moment, Augenblick II • **at the moment** im Moment, gerade II

Monday ['mʌndeɪ, 'mʌndi] Montag I • **Monday morning** Montagmorgen I

money ['mʌni] Geld I

monitor ['mɒnɪtə] Bildschirm, Monitor III

monkey ['mʌŋki] Affe II

monster ['mɒnstə] Monster, Ungeheuer III

month [mʌnθ] Monat I

monument ['mɒnjumənt] Denkmal, Monument IV Intro (9)

moon [mu:n] Mond II

more [mɔ:] mehr I • **lots more** viel mehr I • **more boring (than)** langweiliger (als) II • **more quickly (than)** schneller (als) II • **more than** mehr als II • **more than me** mehr als ich II • **no more music** keine Musik mehr I • **not (...) any more** nicht mehr II • **once more** noch einmal III • **one more** noch ein(e), ein(e) weitere(r, s) I

morning ['mɔ:nɪŋ] Morgen, Vormittag I • **in the morning** morgens, am Morgen I • **Monday morning** Montagmorgen I • **on Friday morning** freitagmorgens, am Freitagmorgen I

mosque [mɒsk] Moschee III

most [məʊst] (der/die/das) meiste ...; am meisten II • **most people** die meisten Leute I • **(the) most boring** der/die/das langweiligste ...; am langweiligsten II

°**mostly** ['məʊstli] überwiegend, hauptsächlich

motel [məʊ'tel] Motel IV Intro (10)

mother ['mʌðə] Mutter I

mountain ['maʊntən] Berg II

mouse [maʊs], *pl* **mice** [maɪs] Maus I

mouth [maʊθ] Mund I

move [mu:v]
1. bewegen; sich bewegen II
Move back one space. Geh ein Feld zurück. II • **Move on one space.** Geh ein Feld vor. II
2. move (to) umziehen (nach, in) II
move in einziehen II • **move out** ausziehen II

movement ['mu:vmənt] Bewegung II

movie ['mu:vi] Film III

MP3 player [ˌempi:'θri: ˌpleɪə] MP3-Spieler I

Mr ... ['mɪstə] Herr ... I

Mrs ... ['mɪsɪz] Frau ... I

Ms ... [mɪz, məz] Frau ... II

much [mʌtʃ] viel I • **how much?** wie viel? I • **How much is/are ...?** Was kostet/kosten ...? / Wie viel kostet/kosten ...? I • **like/love sth. very much** etwas sehr mögen/ sehr lieben II

muesli ['mju:zli] Müsli IV 3 (58)

mule [mju:l] Maultier IV Intro (11)
multi- ['mʌlti] viel-, mehr-; multi-, Multi- IV Intro (10) • **multi-coloured** vielfarbig, mehrfarbig IV Intro (10) **°multi-cultural** multikulturell **multi-millionaire** Multimillionär/ Multimillionärin IV Intro (10/169)
multiple choice [ˌmʌltɪpl 'tʃɔɪs] Multiple-Choice II
mum [mʌm] Mama, Mutti; Mutter I
murder ['mɜ:də] Mord III
murder ['mɜ:də] (er)morden III
murderer ['mɜ:dərə] Mörder/in III
museum [mju'zi:əm] Museum I
mushroom ['mʌʃrʊm, -ru:m] Pilz III
music ['mju:zɪk] Musik I
musical ['mju:zɪkl] Musical I
musical instrument [ˌmju:zɪkl‿'ɪnstrəmənt] Musikinstrument III
musician [mju:'zɪʃn] Musiker/in III
must [mʌst] müssen I
must *(n)* [mʌst] Muss IV 1 (16)
°mustache ['mʌstæʃ] *(AE)* Schnurrbart
mustn't do ['mʌsnt] nicht tun dürfen II
my [maɪ] mein/e I • **My name is ...** Ich heiße ... / Mein Name ist ... I **It's my turn.** Ich bin dran / an der Reihe. I
myself [maɪ'self] mir/mich (selbst) III
mystery ['mɪstri] Rätsel, Geheimnis II

N

name [neɪm] Name I • **call sb. names** jn. mit Schimpfwörtern hänseln, jm. Schimpfwörter nachrufen III • **My name is ...** Ich heiße ... / Mein Name ist ... I **What's your name?** Wie heißt du? I
name [neɪm] nennen; benennen II
nanny ['næni] Kindermädchen IV 1 (26)
nation ['neɪʃn] Nation IV 4 (81)
national ['næʃnəl] national, National- III • **°National Guard** Nationalgarde • **National Park** Nationalpark IV Intro (8)
Native American [ˌneɪtɪv‿ə'merɪkən] amerikanische(r) Ureinwohner/in, Indianer/in IV Intro (9)
natural ['nætʃrəl] Natur-, natürlich IV Intro (9) • **natural history** Naturkunde III; Naturgeschichte IV Intro (9) • **°natural resources** *(pl)* [rɪ'sɔ:sɪz] natürliche Ressourcen; Rohstoffquellen; Bodenschätze
°NBA [ˌen bi:‿'eɪ] **(National Basketball Association** [əˌsəʊsi'eɪʃn]**)** *nordamerikanische Basketball-Profiliga (wörtlich:* Nationaler Basketball-Verband*)*
near [nɪə] in der Nähe von, nahe (bei) I
neat [ni:t] gepflegt II • **neat and tidy** schön ordentlich II
necessary ['nesəsəri] nötig, notwendig IV 3 (62)
need [ni:d] brauchen, benötigen I **°need to do** tun müssen
needn't do ['ni:dnt] nicht tun müssen, nicht zu tun brauchen II
neighbour ['neɪbə] Nachbar/in I
nephew ['nefju:, 'nevju:] Neffe IV 2 (51/178)
nervous ['nɜ:vəs] nervös, aufgeregt I
network ['netwɜ:k] *(Radio-, Fernseh-)*Sendernetz IV 4 (77); (Wörter-)Netz I
never ['nevə] nie, niemals I **Never mind.** *etwa:* Nicht so wichtig. / Ist (doch) egal. / Das willst du gar nicht wissen. IV 3 (69)
new [nju:] neu I
news *(no pl)* [nju:z] Nachrichten II
newspaper ['nju:speɪpə] Zeitung I
next [nekst]**: be next** der/die Nächste sein I • **the next morning/day** am nächsten Morgen/Tag I • **the next photo** das nächste Foto I • **What have we got next?** Was haben wir als Nächstes? I
next to [nekst] neben I
nice [naɪs] schön, nett I • **Nice to meet you.** Nett, dich kennenzulernen. III
niece [ni:s] Nichte IV 2 (51)
°nigger ['nɪgə] *(abwertend, beleidigend)* Nigger
night [naɪt] Nacht, später Abend I **at night** nachts, in der Nacht I **on Friday night** freitagnachts, Freitagnacht I
nil [nɪl] null III
no [nəʊ] nein I
no [nəʊ] kein, keine I • **no more music** keine Musik mehr I • **no one** niemand IV 2 (36/175) • **No way!** Auf keinen Fall! / Kommt nicht in Frage! II
nobody ['nəʊbədi] niemand II
nod (-dd-) [nɒd] nicken (mit) II
noise [nɔɪz] Geräusch; Lärm I
noisy ['nɔɪzi] laut, lärmend II
non-violent [ˌnɒn'vaɪələnt] gewaltlos, gewaltfrei IV 4 (76/184)
°noon [nu:n] Mittag, 12 Uhr mittags
north [nɔ:θ] Norden; nach Norden; nördlich III
northbound ['nɔ:θbaʊnd] Richtung Norden III
north-east [ˌnɔ:θ'i:st] Nordosten; nach Nordosten; nordöstlich III
°northern ['nɔ:ðən] Nord-, nördlich
north-west [ˌnɔ:θ'west] Nordwesten; nach Nordwesten; nordwestlich III
nose [nəʊz] Nase I
not [nɒt] nicht I • **not (...) any** kein, keine I • **not (...) any more** nicht mehr II • **not (...) anybody** niemand II • **not (...) anything** nichts II • **not (...) anywhere** nirgendwo(hin) II • **not even** (noch) nicht einmal III • **not ... till / not ... until** erst (um); nicht vor III **not (...) yet** noch nicht II
note [nəʊt] Mitteilung, Notiz I **°make notes** sich Notizen machen **take notes** sich Notizen machen I
nothing ['nʌθɪŋ] nichts II
°notice ['nəʊtɪs] Notiz, Mitteilung
notice board ['nəʊtɪs bɔ:d] Anschlagtafel, „schwarzes Brett" IV 3 (56)
November [nəʊ'vembə] November I
now [naʊ] nun, jetzt I
number ['nʌmbə] Zahl, Ziffer, Nummer I
°numbered ['nʌmbəd] nummeriert
number plate ['nʌmbə pleɪt] Nummernschild IV Intro (10)
nut [nʌt] Nuss III

O

o [əʊ] null I
°observatory [əb'zɜ:vətri] Sternwarte
ocean ['əʊʃn] Ozean IV 2 (49/178)
o'clock [ə'klɒk]**: eleven o'clock** elf Uhr I
October [ɒk'təʊbə] Oktober I
°odd [ɒd]**: What word is the odd one out?** Welches Wort passt nicht dazu? / Welches Wort gehört nicht dazu?
of [əv, ɒv] von I • **of the summer holidays** der Sommerferien I
of course [əv 'kɔ:s] natürlich, selbstverständlich I
off [ɒf]**: cut sth. off** etwas abschneiden, abtrennen III • **drop sb. off** jn. absetzen *(aussteigen lassen)* IV 4 (79) • **fall off** herunterfallen (von) II • **get off (the train/bus)**

(aus dem Zug/Bus) aussteigen I
get sth. off the ground etwas auf den Weg bringen; etwas auf die Beine stellen III • **take off** *(infml)* sich davonmachen, sich aus dem Staub machen IV 1 (27) • **take sth. off** etwas ausziehen *(Kleidung)* II; etwas absetzen *(Hut, Helm)* III
take 10c off 10 Cent abziehen I
tear sth. off etwas abreißen IV 1 (28) • **turn sth. off** etwas ausschalten II

offer ['ɒfə] anbieten IV 2 (52)
office ['ɒfɪs] Büro III
often ['ɒfn] oft, häufig I
Oh dear! [əʊ 'dɪə] Oje! II
Oh well ... [əʊ 'wel] Na ja ... / Na gut ... I
°**OHP** [ˌəʊ‿eɪtʃ 'piː] *(kurz für:* **overhead projector** [ˌəʊvəhed prə'dʒektə]) Overheadprojektor
oil [ɔɪl] Öl III
OK [əʊ'keɪ] okay, gut, in Ordnung I
old [əʊld] alt I • **How old are you?** Wie alt bist du? I • **I'm ... years old.** Ich bin ... Jahre alt. I • **thirteen-year-old** Dreizehnjährige(r) III
old-fashioned [ˌəʊld'fæʃnd] altmodisch III
Olympic Games [əˌlɪmpɪk 'geɪmz] Olympische Spiele IV 4 (77)
on [ɒn]
1. auf I
2. weiter III
3. an, eingeschaltet *(Radio, Licht usw.)* II
and so on *(short:* **etc.** [et'setərə]) und so weiter (usw.) IV 3 (57) • **be on** gezeigt werden, laufen *(im Fernsehen)* IV 4 (78) • **be on holiday** in Urlaub sein; Ferien haben/machen II • **go on** angehen *(Licht)* III • **go on holiday** in Urlaub fahren II • **on 13th June** am 13. Juni I
on earth auf der Erde III • **on foot** zu Fuß III • **on Friday** am Freitag I • **on Friday afternoon** freitagnachmittags, am Freitagnachmittag I • **on Friday evening** freitagabends, am Freitagabend I • **on Friday morning** freitagmorgens, am Freitagmorgen I • **on Friday night** freitagnachts, Freitagnacht I • **on my/our/... own** allein, selbstständig *(ohne Hilfe)* IV Intro (9) • **on the beach** am Strand II • **on the board** an die Tafel I • **on the corner of Sand Street and London Road** Sand Street, Ecke London Road II • **on the left** links, auf der linken Seite I
on the phone am Telefon I • **on the plane** im Flugzeug II • **on the radio** im Radio I • **on the right** rechts, auf der rechten Seite I
on the second floor im zweiten Stock *(BE)* / im ersten Stock *(AE)* IV 1 (16/171) • **on the train** im Zug I
on TV im Fernsehen I • **straight on** geradeaus weiter II • **What page are we on?** Auf welcher Seite sind wir? I

once [wʌns]
1. einst, früher einmal III
2. einmal III
once more / once again noch einmal III
one [wʌn] eins, ein, eine I • **a new one** ein neuer / eine neue / ein neues II • **my old ones** meine alten II • **no one** niemand IV 2 (36/175) • **one another** einander, sich (gegenseitig) III • **one day** eines Tages I • **one more** noch ein/e, ein/e weitere(r, s) I
onion ['ʌnjən] Zwiebel III
online [ˌɒn'laɪn] online, Online- III
only ['əʊnli]
1. nur, bloß I; erst III
2. the only guest der einzige Gast I
onto ['ɒntə, 'ɒntʊ] auf (... hinauf) III
open ['əʊpən]
1. öffnen, aufmachen I
2. sich öffnen I
open ['əʊpən] offen, geöffnet II
open-air im Freien; Freilicht- III
open-top bus oben offener (Doppeldecker-)Bus III
opening hours *(pl)* ['əʊpənɪŋ‿aʊəz] Öffnungszeiten IV 2 (47)
°**opening sentence** [ˌəʊpənɪŋ 'sentəns] Einleitungssatz
°**opening titles** [ˌəʊpənɪŋ 'taɪtlz] Vorspann *(Film)*
opera ['ɒprə] Oper III
operation (on) [ˌɒpə'reɪʃn] Operation (an) III
opinion (of) [ə'pɪnjən] Meinung (von, zu) IV 2 (36) • **in my opinion** meiner Meinung nach IV 2 (36/175)
opposite ['ɒpəzɪt] gegenüber (von) II
opposite ['ɒpəzɪt] Gegenteil I
or [ɔː] oder I • °**either ... or ...** ['aɪðə ... ɔː, 'iːðə ... ɔː] entweder ... oder
orange ['ɒrɪndʒ] orange(farben) I
orange ['ɒrɪndʒ] Orange, Apfelsine I
orange juice ['ɒrɪndʒ dʒuːs] Orangensaft I

order ['ɔːdə] Reihenfolge III
°**word order** Wortstellung
°**order** ['ɔːdə] bestellen
organ ['ɔːgən] Orgel II
°**organize** ['ɔːgənaɪz] organisieren
original *(n; adj)* [ə'rɪdʒənl] Original; Original- IV 3 (67)
other ['ʌðə] andere(r, s) I • **the others** die anderen I • **the other way round** anders herum II
Ouch! [aʊtʃ] Autsch! I
our ['aʊə] unser, unsere I
ours ['aʊəz] unserer, unsere, unseres II
ourselves [aʊə'selvz] uns (selbst) III
out [aʊt] heraus, hinaus; draußen II
be out weg sein, nicht da sein I
out of ... aus ... (heraus/hinaus) I
°**a day out** ein Tagesausflug
°**two out of three** zwei von drei
outdoor ['aʊtdɔː] im Freien, Außen- III
outfit ['aʊtfɪt] Outfit *(Kleidung; Ausrüstung)* II
outside [ˌaʊt'saɪd]
1. draußen I
2. nach draußen II
3. outside his room vor seinem Zimmer; außerhalb seines Zimmers I
over ['əʊvə]
1. über, oberhalb von I
2. über, mehr als II
3. be over vorbei/zu Ende sein I
all over the world auf der ganzen Welt III • **from all over England/the UK** aus ganz England/aus dem gesamten Vereinigten Königreich III • **over there** da drüben, dort drüben I • **over to ...** hinüber zu/nach ... II
°**overcome** [ˌəʊvə'kʌm]: **we shall overcome** wir werden siegen *(alle Schwierigkeiten überwinden)*
°**overnight** [ˌəʊvə'naɪt] über Nacht
own [əʊn]: **on my/our/... own** allein, selbstständig *(ohne Hilfe)* IV Intro (9) • **our own pool** unser eigenes Schwimmbad II • °**a statement of your own** eine eigene Aussage
°**owner** ['əʊnə] Besitzer/in

P

Pacific: the Pacific (Ocean) [pəˌsɪfɪk‿'əʊʃn] der Pazifische Ozean, der Pazifik IV 2 (49)
pack [pæk] packen, einpacken II
packet ['pækɪt] Päckchen, Packung, Schachtel I • **a packet of mints**

ein Päckchen/eine Packung Pfefferminzbonbons I
paddle ['pædl] paddeln III
paddle ['pædl] Paddel III
pads *(pl)* [pædz] *(Knie- usw.)* Schützer *(für Inlineskater)*; Schulterpolster *(beim American Football)* III
page [peɪdʒ] (Buch-, Heft-)Seite I **What page are we on?** Auf welcher Seite sind wir? I
paid [peɪd] *siehe* **pay**
pain [peɪn] Schmerz(en) IV 4 (94)
paint [peɪnt] malen, anmalen I
painter ['peɪntə] Maler/in II
painting ['peɪntɪŋ] Gemälde IV 1 (26)
pair [peə]**: a pair (of)** ein Paar II
palace ['pæləs] Palast, Schloss III
panic ['pænɪk]**: Don't panic.** Keine Panik. / Bleib ruhig. IV 2 (48)
pants *(pl)* [pænts] *(AE)* Hose IV 1 (20/172)
paper ['peɪpə]
1. Papier I
2. Zeitung II
paragraph ['pærəgrɑːf] Absatz *(in einem Text)* II
Paralympics *(pl)* [ˌpærə'lɪmpɪks] *olympischer Wettkampf für Behindertensportler/innen* III
paramedic [ˌpærə'medɪk] Sanitäter/in II
paraphrase ['pærəfreɪz] umschreiben, anders ausdrücken III
parcel ['pɑːsl] Paket I
parents ['peərənts] Eltern I
park [pɑːk] Park I
parking ['pɑːkɪŋ] (das) Parken IV 1 (21)
park ranger ['reɪndʒə] *Ranger sind eine Art Aufseher/in in Nationalparks, die auch Führungen machen und als Wald- und Wildhüter/innen arbeiten* IV Intro (9)
parliament ['pɑːləmənt] Parlament III
parrot ['pærət] Papagei I
part [pɑːt] Teil I • **take part (in)** teilnehmen (an) IV 3 (56)
partner ['pɑːtnə] Partner/in I
party ['pɑːti] Party I • **have a party** eine Party feiern/veranstalten II
party ['pɑːti] (Partys) feiern IV 2 (34)
pass [pɑːs]
1. (herüber)reichen, weitergeben I **pass round** herumgeben I • °**pass sth. on** etwas weitergeben
2. pass an exam eine Prüfung bestehen IV 3 (63/182)
past [pɑːst] Vergangenheit II
past [pɑːst] vorbei (an), vorüber (an) II • **half past 11** halb zwölf (11.30 / 23.30) I • **quarter past 11** Viertel nach 11 (11.15 / 23.15) I
pasta *(no pl)* ['pæstə] Nudeln, Teigwaren IV 3 (58)
°**patch** [pætʃ] Aufnäher, Abzeichen *(aus Stoff)*
path [pɑːθ] Pfad, Weg II • **bridle path** ['braɪdl pɑːθ] Reitweg III
patrol [pə'trəʊl] Streife, Patrouille IV 2 (38)
°**pause** [pɔːz] zögern; eine Pause machen
pavement ['peɪvmənt] Gehweg, Bürgersteig IV 1 (14)
pay (for sth.) [peɪ]**, paid, paid** etwas bezahlen II
PE [ˌpiː_'iː]**, Physical Education** [ˌfɪzɪkəl_edʒu'keɪʃn] Sportunterricht, Turnen I
pea [piː] Erbse III
°**peaceful** ['piːsfl] friedlich
pen [pen] Kugelschreiber, Füller I
pence (p) *(pl)* [pens] Pence *(pl von „penny")* I
pencil ['pensl] Bleistift I
pencil case ['pensl keɪs] Federmäppchen I
pencil sharpener ['pensl ʃɑːpnə] Bleistiftanspitzer I
penny ['peni] *kleinste britische Münze* I
people ['piːpl] Menschen, Leute I
pepper ['pepə] Pfeffer III
per [pɜː, pə] pro III
per cent (%) [pə'sent] Prozent III
°**percentage** [pə'sentɪdʒ] Prozentsatz, prozentualer Anteil
perfect ['pɜːfɪkt] perfekt; ideal IV 1 (16)
period ['pɪəriəd]
1. (Unterrichts-/Schul-)Stunde IV 3 (56)
°**2. period of time** Zeitspanne, Zeitraum
person ['pɜːsn] Person II
personal ['pɜːsənl] persönliche(r, s) III
pet [pet] Haustier I
petrol ['petrəl] Benzin IV Intro (10)
petrol station ['petrəl steɪʃn] Tankstelle IV Intro (10)
pet shop ['pet ʃɒp] Tierhandlung I
phone [fəʊn] Telefon I • **on the phone** am Telefon I • **phone call** Anruf, Telefongespräch I • **phone number** Telefonnummer I
phone [fəʊn] anrufen II
photo ['fəʊtəʊ] Foto I • **in the photo** auf dem Foto I • **take photos** Fotos machen, fotografieren I
°**photocopy** ['fəʊtəʊkɒpi] Fotokopie
photographer [fə'tɒgrəfə] Fotograf/in II
phrase [freɪz] Ausdruck, (Rede-)Wendung I
piano [pi'ænəʊ] Klavier, Piano I **play the piano** Klavier spielen I
pick [pɪk]**: pick fruit** Obst pflücken IV 2 (34) • **pick sb. up** jn. abholen III • **pick sth. up** etwas hochheben, aufheben II
picnic ['pɪknɪk] Picknick II
picture ['pɪktʃə] Bild I • **in the picture** auf dem Bild I
picture sth. ['pɪktʃə] sich etwas (bildlich) vorstellen IV 2 (43)
pie [paɪ] Obstkuchen; Pastete II
piece [piːs]**: a piece of** ein Stück I **a piece of paper** ein Stück Papier I
pig [pɪg] Schwein III
pink [pɪŋk] pink(farben), rosa I
°**pioneer** [ˌpaɪə'nɪə] Pionier/in
pipe [paɪp] Pfeife III
pirate ['paɪrət] Pirat, Piratin I
pitch [pɪtʃ]**: football/hockey pitch** Fußball-/Hockeyplatz, -feld II
pizza ['piːtsə] Pizza I
place [pleɪs] Ort, Platz I • **in other places** an anderen Orten, anderswo III • **take place** stattfinden IV 1 (15)
°**placemat** ['pleɪsmæt] Set, Platzdeckchen
plan [plæn] Plan I
plan (-nn-) [plæn] planen II
plane [pleɪn] Flugzeug II • **on the plane** im Flugzeug II
planet ['plænɪt] Planet II
°**planetarium** [ˌplænɪ'teəriəm] Planetarium
plant [plɑːnt] Pflanze IV 2 (37)
plant [plɑːnt] pflanzen, einpflanzen IV 2 (37)
plantation [plɑːn'teɪʃn] Plantage IV 4 (76)
plate [pleɪt] Teller I • **a plate of chips** ein Teller Pommes frites I **license plate** *(AE)* Nummernschild IV Intro (10) • **number plate** Nummernschild IV Intro (10)
platform ['plætfɔːm] Bahnsteig, Gleis III
play [pleɪ] spielen I • **play a trick on sb.** jm. einen Streich spielen II **play the drums** Schlagzeug spielen III • **play the fiddle** Geige spielen III • **play the guitar** Gitarre spielen I • **play the piano** Klavier spielen I
play [pleɪ] Theaterstück I
player ['pleɪə] Spieler/in I
playlist ['pleɪlɪst] Titelliste *(von zu spielenden Songs)* III

please [pliːz] bitte *(in Fragen und Aufforderungen)* I
plot [plɒt] Handlung *(eines Romans, Films)* IV 3 (70)
plug [plʌg] Stecker III
plus [plʌs] plus III
pm [ˌpiː‿ˈem]**: 7 pm** 7 Uhr abends/19 Uhr I
pocket [ˈpɒkɪt] Tasche *(an Kleidungsstück)* II
pocket money [ˈpɒkɪt ˌmʌni] Taschengeld II
poem [ˈpəʊɪm] Gedicht I
point [pɔɪnt] Punkt II • **make a point** ein Argument vorbringen III °**point in time** Zeitpunkt • **point of view** Standpunkt II • **from my point of view** aus meiner Sicht; von meinem Standpunkt aus gesehen II • **10.4 (ten point four)** 10,4 (zehn Komma vier) III
point (at/to sth.) [pɔɪnt] zeigen, deuten (auf etwas) II
police *(pl)* [pəˈliːs] Polizei I
policeman, -woman [pəˈliːsmən, -wʊmən] Polizist, Polizistin II
police station [pəˈliːs steɪʃn] Polizeiwache, Polizeirevier II
polite [pəˈlaɪt] höflich IV 3 (69)
°**politics** [ˈpɒlətɪks] Politik
poltergeist [ˈpəʊltəgaɪst] Poltergeist I
ponytail [ˈpəʊniteɪl] Pferdeschwanz *(Frisur)* III
poor [pɔː, pʊə] arm I • **poor Sophie** (die) arme Sophie I
pop (music) [pɒp] Pop(musik) III
popcorn [ˈpɒpkɔːn] Popcorn II
°**popular** [ˈpɒpjələ] beliebt, populär
population [ˌpɒpjuˈleɪʃn] Bevölkerung, Einwohner(zahl) III
pork [pɔːk] Schweinefleisch III
°**port** [pɔːt] Hafen(stadt)
possibility [ˌpɒsəˈbɪləti] Möglichkeit IV 3 (64)
possible [ˈpɒsəbl] möglich II
post [pəʊst] Post *(Briefe, Päckchen, ...)* III
postcard [ˈpəʊstkɑːd] Postkarte II
poster [ˈpəʊstə] Poster I
post office [ˈpəʊst‿ɒfɪs] Postamt II
potato [pəˈteɪtəʊ], *pl* **potatoes** Kartoffel I
potato chips [pəˈteɪtəʊ tʃɪps] *(AE)* Kartoffelchips IV 1 (20/172)
poultry [ˈpəʊltri] Geflügel IV 3 (58)
pound (£) [paʊnd] Pfund *(britische Währung)* I
practice [ˈpræktɪs] *hier:* Übungsteil I
practice [ˈpræktɪs] *(AE)* üben; trainieren IV 3 (70)
practise [ˈpræktɪs]
1. üben; trainieren I
°2. ausüben *(Religion)*
prejudice (against) [ˈpredʒudɪs] Voreingenommenheit (gegen), Vorurteil (gegenüber) IV 2 (36)
prejudiced [ˈpredʒədɪst]**: be prejudiced (against)** voreingenommen sein (gegen), Vorurteile haben (gegenüber) IV 2 (36)
prepare [prɪˈpeə] vorbereiten; sich vorbereiten II • **prepare for** sich vorbereiten auf II
present [ˈpreznt]
1. Gegenwart I
2. Geschenk I
present sth. (to sb.) [prɪˈzent] (jm.) etwas präsentieren, vorstellen I
presentation [ˌpreznˈteɪʃn] Präsentation, Vorstellung I
presenter [prɪˈzentə] Moderator/in II
president [ˈprezɪdənt] Präsident/in IV 4 (89)
press sth. [pres] etwas drücken; auf etwas drücken IV 1 (28)
pretty [ˈprɪti] hübsch I
pretty cool/good/... [ˈprɪti] ziemlich cool/gut/... II
price [praɪs] (Kauf-)Preis I
prime time [ˈpraɪm taɪm] Hauptsendezeit IV 4 (78)
print: bold print [ˌbəʊld ˈprɪnt] Fettdruck III
print sth. out [ˌprɪnt‿ˈaʊt] etwas ausdrucken II
°**prison** [ˈprɪzn] Gefängnis
private [ˈpraɪvət] privat IV 3 (57)
prize [praɪz] Preis, Gewinn I
probably [ˈprɒbəbli] wahrscheinlich II
problem [ˈprɒbləm] Problem II
process [ˈprəʊses] Prozess, Verfahren IV 2 (37)
produce [prəˈdjuːs] produzieren, herstellen III
product [ˈprɒdʌkt] Produkt, Erzeugnis IV 3 (58)
production [prəˈdʌkʃn] Produktion, Herstellung IV 2 (37)
°**profile** [ˈprəʊfaɪl] Porträt, Beschreibung
programme [ˈprəʊgræm] Programm I
project (about, on) [ˈprɒdʒekt] Projekt (über, zu) I
promise [ˈprɒmɪs] versprechen II
°**promise** [ˈprɒmɪs] Versprechen, Versprechung
°**pronounce** [prəˈnaʊns] aussprechen
pronunciation [prəˌnʌnsiˈeɪʃn] Aussprache I
proof *(no pl)* [pruːf] Beweis(e) II
protect sb. (from) [prəˈtekt] jn. (be)schützen (vor) III
protest [ˈprəʊtest] Protest IV 4 (81)
protest [prəˈtest] protestieren IV 3 (70)
proud (of sb./sth.) [praʊd] stolz (auf jn./etwas) II
°**prove** [pruːv] beweisen
province [ˈprɒvɪns] Provinz III
PS [ˌpiː‿ˈes] **(postscript** [ˈpəʊstskrɪpt]**)** PS *(Nachschrift unter Briefen)* III
pub [pʌb] Kneipe, Lokal II
public [ˈpʌblɪk] öffentliche(r, s) III
public transport *(no pl)* öffentliche Verkehrsmittel, öffentlicher Personennahverkehr III
publish [ˈpʌblɪʃ] veröffentlichen III
pull [pʊl] ziehen I
pullover [ˈpʊləʊvə] Pullover II
punk (rock) [pʌŋk] Punk(rock) III
purple [ˈpɜːpl] violett; lila I
purse [pɜːs] Geldbörse II
push [pʊʃ] drücken, schieben, stoßen I
put (-tt-) [pʊt]**, put, put** legen, stellen, *(etwas wohin)* tun I • **put sth. down** etwas hinlegen IV 4 (79)
put sth. on etwas anziehen *(Kleidung)* II; etwas aufsetzen *(Hut, Helm)* III • **put out a fire** ein Feuer löschen IV 1 (15) • °**Put up your hand.** Heb deine Hand. / Hebt eure Hand.
puzzle [ˈpʌzl] Rätsel IV 1 (16)
puzzled [ˈpʌzld] verwirrt II
pyjamas *(pl)* [pəˈdʒɑːməz] Schlafanzug II
pyramid [ˈpɪrəmɪd] Pyramide IV 3 (58)

Q

quality [ˈkwɒləti] Qualität IV 3 (58)
quarter [ˈkwɔːtə]**: quarter past 11** Viertel nach 11 (11.15 / 23.15) I
quarter to 12 Viertel vor 12 (11.45 / 23.45) I
queen [kwiːn] Königin III
question [ˈkwestʃn] Frage I • **ask questions** Fragen stellen
°**question word** [ˈkwestʃn wɜːd] Fragewort
queue [kjuː] Schlange, Reihe *(wartender Menschen)* IV 1 (14)
quick [kwɪk] schnell I
quiet [ˈkwaɪət] leise, still, ruhig I
quite quickly/well/... [kwaɪt] ziemlich schnell/gut/... II

quiz [kwɪz], *pl* **quizzes** ['kwɪzɪz] Quiz, Ratespiel I
°**quotation marks** [kwəʊ'teɪʃn mɑ:ks] Anführungszeichen, -striche

R

rabbit ['ræbɪt] Kaninchen I
°**racial** ['reɪʃl] Rassen-, rassisch
racket ['rækɪt]: **badminton racket** Badmintonschläger III
radio ['reɪdiəʊ] Radio I • **on the radio** im Radio I
raft [rɑ:ft] Schlauchboot *(wildwassertauglich)* IV 3 (67)
°**rafting** ['rɑ:ftɪŋ] Wildwasserfahrt *(mit großem Schlauchboot)*
railway ['reɪlweɪ] Eisenbahn II
rain [reɪn] Regen II
rain [reɪn] regnen II
rainy ['reɪni] regnerisch II
raise money (for) [reɪz] Geld sammeln (für) IV Intro (9)
ran [ræn] *siehe* **run**
rang [ræŋ] *siehe* **ring**
ranger ['reɪndʒə]: **(park) ranger** *Ranger sind eine Art Aufseher/in in Nationalparks, die auch Führungen machen und als Wald- und Wildhüter/innen arbeiten* IV Intro (9)
rap [ræp] Rap *(rhythmischer Sprechgesang)* I
rap (-pp-) [ræp] rappen III
rapids *(pl)* ['ræpɪdz] Stromschnellen III
rapper ['ræpə] Rapper/in III
RE [,ɑ:r_'i:], **Religious Education** [rɪ,lɪdʒəs_edʒu'keɪʃn] Religion, Religionsunterricht I
Re: ... [ri:] Betreff: ... IV 2 (44)
reach [ri:tʃ] erreichen IV 2 (38)
read [ri:d], **read, read** lesen I **read on** weiterlesen III • °**read out** vorlesen • °**Read out loud.** Lies laut vor. • °**Read the poem to a partner.** Lies das Gedicht einem Partner/einer Partnerin vor.
read [red] *siehe* **read**
reader ['ri:də] Leser/in II
ready ['redi] bereit, fertig I • **get ready (for)** sich fertig machen (für), sich vorbereiten (auf) I • **get things ready** Dinge fertig machen, vorbereiten I
real [rɪəl] echt, wirklich I • **real late** *(AE, infml)* wirklich spät, richtig spät III
realistic [,ri:ə'lɪstɪk] realistisch, wirklichkeitsnah III
reality [ri'æləti] Realität, Wirklichkeit IV 3 (64)
really ['rɪəli] wirklich I
reason ['ri:zn] Grund, Begründung I • **for lots of reasons** aus vielen Gründen I
record ['rekɔ:d] Schallplatte III
record [rɪ'kɔ:d] *(Musik)* aufnehmen, aufzeichnen III
recorded message [rɪ,kɔ:dɪd 'mesɪdʒ] (automatische) Telefonansage IV 2 (48)
recorder [rɪ'kɔ:də] Blockflöte III
recording [rɪ'kɔ:dɪŋ] Aufnahme, Aufzeichnung III
recycled [,ri:'saɪkld] wiederverwertet, wiederverwendet, recycelt II
recycling [,ri:'saɪklɪŋ] Wiederverwertung, Recycling II
red [red] rot I
refer to (-rr-) [rɪ'fɜ:] sich beziehen auf III
reflex ['ri:fleks] Reflex IV 3 (68)
reggae ['regeɪ] Reggae III
rehearsal [rɪ'hɜ:sl] Probe *(am Theater)* I
rehearse [rɪ'hɜ:s] proben *(am Theater)* I
relations *(pl)* [rɪ'leɪʃnz] Beziehungen IV 2 (36)
relax [rɪ'læks] (sich) entspannen, sich ausruhen II
relaxed [rɪ'lækst] locker, entspannt III
release [rɪ'li:s] herausbringen, auf den Markt bringen *(CD, Film usw.)* III
°**religion** [rɪ'lɪdʒən] Religion
remember sth. [rɪ'membə]
1. sich an etwas erinnern I
2. sich etwas merken I
°**Remember ...** Denk dran, ...
repeat [rɪ'pi:t] Wiederholung *(einer Fernsehsendung)* IV 4 (78)
report (on) [rɪ'pɔ:t] Bericht, Reportage (über) I
report (to sb.) [rɪ'pɔ:t] (jm.) berichten II
reporter [rɪ'pɔ:tə] Reporter/in IV 4 (78)
represent [,reprɪ'zent] repräsentieren, vertreten III
rerun ['ri:rʌn] *(AE)* Wiederholung *(einer Fernsehsendung)* IV 4 (78)
research *(no pl)* [rɪ'sɜ:tʃ, 'ri:sɜ:tʃ] Recherche; Nachforschung(en) IV 4 (81) • **do research** recherchieren IV 4 (81/187)
rest [rest] Rest II
°**restart** [,ri:'stɑ:t] wieder in Betrieb nehmen
restaurant ['restrɒnt] Restaurant II
result [rɪ'zʌlt] Ergebnis, Resultat I
return [rɪ'tɜ:n] zurückkehren IV 3 (59)
return ticket [rɪ'tɜ:n ,tɪkɪt] Rückfahrkarte II
revise [rɪ'vaɪz]
1. überarbeiten III
2. wiederholen III
revision [rɪ'vɪʒn] Wiederholung *(des Lernstoffs)* I
°**rewrite** [,ri:'raɪt], **rewrote, rewritten** umschreiben, neu schreiben
°**rewritten** [,ri:'rɪtn] *siehe* **rewrite**
°**rewrote** [,ri:'rəʊt] *siehe* **rewrite**
rhino ['raɪnəʊ] Nashorn II
rice [raɪs] Reis IV 3 (58)
rich [rɪtʃ] reich II
rid [rɪd]: **get rid of sb./sth.** jn./etwas loswerden IV 1 (28)
ridden ['rɪdn] *siehe* **ride**
riddle ['rɪdl] Rätsel III
ride [raɪd], **rode, ridden** reiten I **go riding** ['raɪdɪŋ] reiten gehen I **ride a bike** Rad fahren I
ride [raɪd]: **(bike) ride** (Rad-)Fahrt, (Rad-)Tour II • **take a ride** eine Fahrt machen III
rider ['raɪdə] Reiter/in IV 4 (89)
riding boots *(pl)* ['raɪdɪŋ bu:ts] Reitstiefel III
riding hat ['raɪdɪŋ hæt] Reitkappe, Reiterhelm III
right [raɪt] Recht IV 4 (77)
right [raɪt] richtig I • **all right** [ɔ:l 'raɪt] gut, in Ordnung II • **be right** Recht haben I • **That's right.** Das ist richtig. / Das stimmt. I • **You need a school bag, right?** Du brauchst eine Schultasche, stimmt's? / nicht wahr? I
right [raɪt] rechte(r, s) II • **look right** nach rechts schauen II • **on the right** rechts, auf der rechten Seite I • **turn right** (nach) rechts abbiegen II
right [raɪt]: **right after lunch** direkt/gleich nach dem Mittagessen I **right now** jetzt sofort; jetzt gerade I • **right behind you** direkt/genau hinter dir II
rim [rɪm] Rand, Kante IV Intro (8)
ring [rɪŋ] Ring II
ring [rɪŋ], **rang, rung** klingeln, läuten II
ringtone ['rɪŋtəʊn] Klingelton III
°**riot** ['raɪət] Ausschreitung, Aufruhr
rise [raɪz], **rose, risen** (auf)steigen IV 4 (76)
risen ['rɪzn] *siehe* **rise**
river ['rɪvə] Fluss II
road [rəʊd] Straße I • **Park Road** [,pɑ:k 'rəʊd] Parkstraße I

rock [rɒk] Fels, Felsen III
rock (music) [rɒk] Rock(musik) III
rode [rəʊd] *siehe* **ride**
role [rəʊl] Rolle III
role play ['rəʊl pleɪ] Rollenspiel II
roll [rəʊl] Brötchen I
Roman ['rəʊmən] römisch; Römer, Römerin II
°**romance** [rəʊ'mæns] Romanze
room [ruːm, rʊm] Raum, Zimmer I
°**root** [ruːt] Wurzel
rose [rəʊz] *siehe* **rise**
round [raʊnd] rund II
round [raʊnd] um … (herum); in … umher II • **the other way round** anders herum II
route [ruːt] Strecke, Route IV Intro (10)
royal ['rɔɪəl] königlich III
rubber ['rʌbə] Radiergummi I
rubbish ['rʌbɪʃ] (Haus-)Müll, Abfall II
rucksack ['rʌksæk] Rucksack III
rude [ruːd] unhöflich, unverschämt II
rule [ruːl] Regel, Vorschrift III
ruler ['ruːlə] Lineal I
run [rʌn] (Wett-)Lauf II
run (-nn-) [rʌn], **ran, run**
1. laufen, rennen I
2. verlaufen *(Straße; Grenze)* IV 2 (38)
run into sth./sb. gegen etwas fahren / jn. anfahren IV 2 (46)
rung [rʌŋ] *siehe* **ring**
runner ['rʌnə] Läufer/in II
°**running head** [ˌrʌnɪŋ 'hed] Leitwort *(am Kopf einer Wörterbuchseite)*
running shoes ['rʌnɪŋ ʃuːz] Laufschuhe III
running track ['rʌnɪŋ træk] Laufbahn *(Sport)* III
°**rush** [rʌʃ]: **gold rush** Goldrausch
rush hour ['rʌʃ‿aʊə] Hauptverkehrszeit III

S

sad [sæd] traurig II
saddle ['sædl] Sattel III
sadness ['sædnəs] Traurigkeit IV 3 (64)
safe (from) [seɪf] sicher, in Sicherheit (vor) II
safety ['seɪfti] Sicherheit IV 1 (25) ► S.173 „Sicherheit"
said [sed] *siehe* **say**
sail [seɪl] segeln II
salad ['sæləd] Salat *(als Gericht oder Beilage)* I
sale [seɪl] Verkauf IV Intro (9) • **for sale** *(auf Schild)* zu verkaufen IV Intro (9/168)
salmon ['sæmən], *pl* **salmon** Lachs III
salt [sɔːlt] Salz III
same [seɪm]: **the same …** der-/die-/dasselbe …; dieselben … I • **be/look the same** gleich sein/aussehen I
°**sand** [sænd] Sand
sandal ['sændl] Sandale II
sandwich ['sænwɪtʃ, 'sænwɪdʒ] Sandwich, *(zusammengeklapptes)* belegtes Brot I
sang [sæŋ] *siehe* **sing**
sat [sæt] *siehe* **sit**
Saturday ['sætədeɪ, 'sætədi] Samstag, Sonnabend I
sauna ['sɔːnə] Sauna II • **have a sauna** in die Sauna gehen II
sausage ['sɒsɪdʒ] (Brat-, Bock-) Würstchen, Wurst I
save [seɪv]
1. retten II
2. sparen II
saw [sɔː] *siehe* **see**
saxophone ['sæksəfəʊn] Saxophon III
say [seɪ], **said, said** sagen I • **It says here: …** Hier steht: … / Es heißt hier: … II • **say goodbye** sich verabschieden I • **Say hi to Dilip for me.** Grüß Dilip von mir. I **say sorry** sich entschuldigen II
scan (-nn-) [skæn]
°**1.** (ein)scannen
2. scan a text einen Text schnell nach bestimmten Wörtern/Informationen absuchen II
scared [skeəd] verängstigt II • **be scared (of)** Angst haben (vor) I
scary ['skeəri] unheimlich; gruselig I
scene [siːn] Szene I
scenery ['siːnəri] *(schöne)* Landschaft IV 2 (34)
schedule [*AE:* 'skedʒuːl, *BE:* 'ʃedjuːl] *(AE)*
1. Stundenplan IV 1 (20/172)
2. Fahrplan IV 1 (20/172)
school [skuːl] Schule I • **at school** in der Schule I
school bag ['skuːl bæg] Schultasche I
school subject ['sʌbdʒɪkt] Schulfach I
science ['saɪəns] Naturwissenschaft I
score [skɔː] Spielstand; Punktestand III • **final score** Endstand *(beim Sport)* III • **What's the score?** Wie steht es? *(beim Sport)* III
score (a goal) [skɔː] ein Tor schießen, einen Treffer erzielen III
scrapbook ['skræpbʊk] Sammelalbum IV 3 (59)
scream [skriːm] schreien, kreischen IV 1 (27)
°**script** [skrɪpt] Drehbuch
sea [siː] Meer, *(die)* See I
search (for) [sɜːtʃ] suchen (nach) II
search engine ['sɜːtʃ‿ˌendʒɪn] Suchmaschine IV 4 (81)
°**seat sb.** [siːt] jm. einen (Sitz-)Platz zuweisen, jn. an seinen Platz führen
second ['sekənd] zweite(r, s) I
second-hand [ˌsekənd 'hænd] gebraucht; aus zweiter Hand III
section ['sekʃn] Abschnitt, Teil, (Themen-)Bereich III
security [sɪ'kjʊərəti] Sicherheit(svorkehrungen) IV 1 (15) ► S.173 „Sicherheit"
see [siː], **saw, seen**
1. sehen I
2. see sb. jn. besuchen, jn. aufsuchen II
See? Siehst du? I • **See you.** Tschüs. / Bis bald. I • **Wait and see!** Wart's ab! III
seem (to be/to do) [siːm] (zu sein/zu tun) scheinen IV 1 (26)
seen [siːn] *siehe* **see**
see-through ['siːθruː] durchsichtig IV 3 (56)
segregate ['segrɪgeɪt] trennen *(nach Rasse, Religion, Geschlecht)* IV 4 (81)
segregation [ˌsegrɪ'geɪʃn] (Rassen-)Trennung IV 4 (81/187)
sell [sel], **sold, sold** verkaufen I **be sold out** ausverkauft sein, vergriffen sein III
semester [sɪ'mestə] Semester *(Schulhalbjahr in den USA)* IV 3 (56)
semi-final [ˌsemi'faɪnl] Halbfinale III
°**Senate** ['senət] Senat
°**Senator** ['senətə] Senator/in
send [send], **sent, sent** senden, schicken II
sent [sent] *siehe* **send**
sentence ['sentəns] Satz I
separate ['seprət] getrennt, separat IV 4 (92)
September [sep'tembə] September I
°**sequoia** [sɪ'kwɔɪə] Sequoia, Mammutbaum
series, *pl* **series** ['sɪəriːz] (Sende-)Reihe, Serie II

serious ['sɪəriəs] ernst, ernsthaft IV 2 (50) • **Seriously?** Im Ernst? IV 2 (50/178)
servant ['sɜːvənt] Diener/in, Bedienstete(r) IV 1 (26)
set a trap (for sb.) **(-tt-)** [set], **set, set** (jm.) eine Falle stellen II
set meal [ˌset 'miːl] Menü III
settle down [ˌsetl 'daʊn] sich eingewöhnen III
°**settler** ['setlə] Siedler/in
°**several** ['sevrəl] einige; mehrere
sew (on) [səʊ], **sewed, sewn** (an)nähen IV Intro (9)
sewn [səʊn] *siehe* **sew**
°**shabby** ['ʃæbi] schäbig
shadow ['ʃædəʊ] Schatten III
shake [ʃeɪk], **shook, shaken** schütteln; zittern IV 2 (37)
shaken ['ʃeɪkən] *siehe* **shake**
°**shall** [ʃəl, ʃæl]: **we shall overcome** wir werden siegen *(alle Schwierigkeiten überwinden)*
share sth. (with) [ʃeə] sich etwas teilen (mit) I
she [ʃiː] sie I
sheep, *pl* **sheep** [ʃiːp] Schaf II
shelf [ʃelf], *pl* **shelves** [ʃelvz] Regal(brett) I
shift [ʃɪft] Schicht *(bei der Arbeit)* IV 1 (15) • **on his shift** in seiner Schicht IV 1 (15/170)
shine [ʃaɪn], **shone, shone** scheinen *(Sonne)* II
ship [ʃɪp] Schiff I
shirt [ʃɜːt] Hemd I
shiver ['ʃɪvə] zittern II
shoe [ʃuː] Schuh I
shone [ʃɒn] *siehe* **shine**
shook [ʃʊk] *siehe* **shake**
shop [ʃɒp] Laden, Geschäft I
shop **(-pp-)** [ʃɒp] einkaufen (gehen) I
shop assistant ['ʃɒp‿əˌsɪstənt] Verkäufer/in I
shopping ['ʃɒpɪŋ] (das) Einkaufen I **go shopping** einkaufen gehen I
shopping list ['ʃɒpɪŋ lɪst] Einkaufsliste I
shopping mall ['ʃɒpɪŋ mɔːl] *(großes)* Einkaufszentrum III
shop window [ˌʃɒp 'wɪndəʊ] Schaufenster II
short [ʃɔːt] kurz I; klein *(Person)* IV 1 (16/171)
shorts *(pl)* [ʃɔːts] Shorts, kurze Hose I
shot [ʃɒt]
1. Schuss III
°**2.** Szene *(beim Filmen)*
winning shot Siegtreffer, Siegesschuss III

should [ʃəd, ʃʊd]: **we should ...** wir sollten ... IV 1 (27)
shoulder ['ʃəʊldə] Schulter I
shout [ʃaʊt] schreien, rufen I
shout at sb. jn. anschreien I
show [ʃəʊ] Show, Vorstellung I
show [ʃəʊ], **showed, shown** zeigen I
shower ['ʃaʊə] Dusche I • **have a shower** (sich) duschen I
shown [ʃəʊn] *siehe* **show**
shut up [ˌʃʌt‿'ʌp], **shut, shut** den Mund halten II
shy [ʃaɪ] schüchtern, scheu II
sick [sɪk]: **I feel sick.** Mir ist schlecht. IV 1 (27)
side [saɪd] Seite II
sidewalk ['saɪdwɔːk] *(AE)* Gehweg, Bürgersteig IV 1 (14)
°**sight: within sight** [wɪˌðɪn 'saɪt] in Sichtweite
sights *(pl)* [saɪts] Sehenswürdigkeiten III
sign [saɪn] Schild; Zeichen III
silence ['saɪləns] Stille; Schweigen III
silent letter [ˌsaɪlənt 'letə] „stummer" Buchstabe *(nicht gesprochener Buchstabe)* II
silly ['sɪli] albern, dumm III
since [sɪns]
1. da (ja), weil IV 2 (51)
2. since April 4th seit dem 4. April IV 4 (80) • **since then** seitdem IV 4 (80)
► S.186 German 'seit'
sing [sɪŋ], **sang, sung** singen I
singer ['sɪŋə] Sänger/in II
single ['sɪŋgl] ledig, alleinstehend I
single ['sɪŋgl] Single III
single (ticket) ['sɪŋgl] einfache Fahrkarte *(nur Hinfahrt)* III
sink [sɪŋk] Spüle, Spülbecken I
sir [sɜː] *höfliche Anrede für einen Unbekannten (z. B. einen Kunden) oder einen Vorgesetzten* IV 4 (92)
sister ['sɪstə] Schwester I
sister city ['sɪstə sɪti] *(AE)* Partnerstadt IV 3 (59)
sit **(-tt-)** [sɪt], **sat, sat** sitzen; sich setzen I • **sit down** sich hinsetzen II • **Sit with me.** Setz dich zu mir. / Setzt euch zu mir. I
°**situation** [ˌsɪtʃu'eɪʃn] Situation
size [saɪz] Größe I
skate [skeɪt] Inliner/Skateboard fahren I; Schlittschuh laufen, eislaufen II
skateboard ['skeɪtbɔːd] Skateboard I
skates *(pl)* [skeɪts] Inliner I
sketch [sketʃ] Sketch I

ski [skiː] Ski III
ski [skiː] Ski laufen/fahren III
skills file ['skɪlz faɪl] *Anhang mit Lern- und Arbeitstechniken* I
skim a text **(-mm-)** [skɪm] einen Text überfliegen *(um den Inhalt grob zu erfassen)* III
skin [skɪn] Haut IV 4 (81)
skirt [skɜːt] Rock II
ski slope ['skiː sləʊp] Skipiste III
sky [skaɪ] Himmel II • **in the sky** am Himmel II
°**skyline** ['skaɪlaɪn] Silhouette, Skyline
skyscraper ['skaɪskreɪpə] Wolkenkratzer IV 1 (23)
slave [sleɪv] Sklave, Sklavin II
°**slavery** ['sleɪvəri] Sklaverei
sledge [sledʒ] Schlitten III
sleep [sliːp] Schlaf III
sleep [sliːp], **slept, slept** schlafen I
sleepless ['sliːpləs] schlaflos IV 2 (42)
sleepover ['sliːpəʊvə] Schlafparty III
slept [slept] *siehe* **sleep**
slow [sləʊ] langsam II
°**slur** **(-rr-)** [slɜː] lallen
small [smɔːl] klein II
smart [smɑːt] clever, schlau IV 3 (68)
smell [smel] riechen II
smell [smel] Geruch II
smile [smaɪl] lächeln I • **smile at sb.** jn. anlächeln II
smile [smaɪl] Lächeln II
smoke [sməʊk] rauchen II
smoke [sməʊk] Rauch II
snack [snæk] Snack, Imbiss II
snake [sneɪk] Schlange I
snow [snəʊ] Schnee II
snowball ['snəʊbɔːl] Schneeball IV 3 (69)
snowshoe ['snəʊʃuː] Schneeschuh III
snowshoeing ['snəʊʃuːɪŋ] Schneeschuhwandern III
so [səʊ]
1. also; deshalb, daher I • **So?** Und? / Na und? II
2. so sweet so süß I • **so far** bis jetzt, bis hierher I
3. so that sodass, damit III
4. I think so. Ich glaube (ja). I **I don't think so.** Das finde/glaube ich nicht. I • **Do you really think so?** Meinst du wirklich? / Glaubst du das wirklich? II
soap [səʊp]
1. Seife I
2. *(infml)* Seifenoper IV 2 (49)
soap opera ['səʊp‿ˌɒprə] **(***infml auch:* **soap)** Seifenoper IV 2 (49)
soccer ['sɒkə] Fußball IV 3 (59)

°**social** ['səʊʃl] sozial, gesellschaftlich

sock [sɒk] Socke, Strumpf I

soda ['səʊdə] *(AE)* Limonade IV 3 (65)

sofa ['səʊfə] Sofa I

soft [sɒft] weich IV 3 (65) • **soft drink** alkoholfreies Getränk IV 3 (65)

software ['sɒftweə] Software II

sold [səʊld] *siehe* **sell** • **be sold out** ausverkauft sein, vergriffen sein III

soldier ['səʊldʒə] Soldat/in IV 4 (93)

some [səm, sʌm] einige, ein paar I
some cheese/juice/money etwas Käse/Saft/Geld I

somebody ['sʌmbədi] jemand I
Find/Ask somebody who ... Finde/Frage jemanden, der ... II

someone ['sʌmwʌn] IV 2 (36/175) *siehe* **somebody**

something ['sʌmθɪŋ] etwas I
something to eat etwas zu essen I

sometimes ['sʌmtaɪmz] manchmal I

somewhere ['sʌmweə] irgendwo(hin) II

son [sʌn] Sohn I

song [sɒŋ] Lied, Song I

soon [su:n] bald I • **as soon as** sobald, sowie II

sore [sɔ:]: **be sore** wund sein, wehtun II • **have a sore throat** Halsschmerzen haben II

sorry ['sɒri]: **(I'm) sorry.** Entschuldigung. / Tut mir leid. I • **Sorry, I'm late.** Entschuldigung, dass ich zu spät bin/komme. I • **Sorry?** Wie bitte? I • **say sorry** sich entschuldigen II

sound [saʊnd] klingen, sich *(gut usw.)* anhören I

sound [saʊnd] Laut; Klang I

sound file ['saʊnd faɪl] Tondatei, Soundfile III

soup [su:p] Suppe II

source [sɔ:s] *(Informations-, Text-)* Quelle IV 4 (81)

south [saʊθ] Süden; nach Süden; südlich III

southbound ['saʊθbaʊnd] Richtung Süden III

south-east [ˌsaʊθ'i:st] Südosten; nach Südosten; südöstlich III

south-west [ˌsaʊθ'west] Südwesten; nach Südwesten; südwestlich III

°**souvenir** [ˌsu:və'nɪə] Andenken, Souvenir

space [speɪs]
°**1.** Weltraum
2. Move back one space. Geh ein Feld zurück. II • **Move on one space.** Geh ein Feld vor. II

spaghetti [spə'geti] Spaghetti II

spat [spæt] *siehe* **spit**

speak (to) [spi:k], **spoke, spoken** sprechen (mit), reden (mit) II

special ['speʃl] besondere(r, s) III
What's special about ...? Was ist das Besondere an ...? III

specific [spə'sɪfɪk] bestimmte(r, s), spezifische(r, s) IV 2 (43)

°**speculate (about)** ['spekjuleɪt] Vermutungen anstellen (über), spekulieren (über)

speech [spi:tʃ] Rede IV 4 (81/187)
make a speech eine Rede halten IV 4 (81)

°**speech bubble** ['spi:tʃ bʌbl] Sprechblase

spell [spel] buchstabieren I

spelling ['spelɪŋ] (Recht-)Schreibung, Schreibweise III

spend [spend], **spent, spent: spend money (on)** Geld ausgeben (für) II • **spend time (on)** Zeit verbringen (mit) II

spent [spent] *siehe* **spend**

spicy ['spaɪsi] würzig, scharf gewürzt III

°**spirit** ['spɪrɪt] Geist

spit (at sb.) (-tt-) [spɪt], **spat, spat** (jn. an)spucken IV 4 (93)

splash [splæʃ] spritzen IV 4 (94)

spoke [spəʊk] *siehe* **speak**

spoken ['spəʊkən] *siehe* **speak**

spoon [spu:n] Löffel III

sport [spɔ:t] Sport; Sportart I
do sport Sport treiben I

sports gear *(no pl)* ['spɔ:ts gɪə] Sportausrüstung, Sportsachen II

sports hall ['spɔ:ts hɔ:l] Sporthalle III

sportsman, -woman ['spɔ:tsmən, -ˌwʊmən] Sportler/in IV 2 (45)

spot (-tt-) [spɒt] entdecken III

spray [spreɪ] sprühen; besprühen IV 2 (37)

spring [sprɪŋ] Frühling I

spy [spaɪ] Spion/in I

square [skweə] Platz *(in der Stadt)* II

square km (sq km) [skweə] Quadratkilometer III

squeeze [skwi:z] drücken; (aus-)pressen III

squirrel ['skwɪrəl] Eichhörnchen II

stadium ['steɪdiəm] Stadion III

stage [steɪdʒ] Bühne I

stairs *(pl)* [steəz] Treppe; Treppenstufen I

stamp [stæmp] Briefmarke I

stand [stænd], **stood, stood** stehen; sich (hin)stellen II • **stand up** aufstehen II

star [stɑ:]
1. Stern II
2. (Film-, Pop-)Star I

start [stɑ:t] starten, anfangen, beginnen (mit) I

start [stɑ:t] Start, Anfang, Beginn II

state [steɪt] Staat III

statement ['steɪtmənt] Aussage, Feststellung III

station ['steɪʃn]
1. Bahnhof I • **at the station** am Bahnhof I
2. (radio/pop) station (Radio-/Pop-)Sender III • **fire station** Feuerwache IV 1 (15) • **gas station** *(AE)* Tankstelle IV Intro (10) • **petrol station** Tankstelle IV Intro (10)

statue ['stætʃu:] Statue II

stay [steɪ] bleiben; wohnen, übernachten II • **stay behind** zurückbleiben, dableiben IV Intro (10)
stay out draußen bleiben, wegbleiben III

steak [steɪk] Steak III

steal [sti:l], **stole, stolen** stehlen II

°**steamer** ['sti:mə] Dampfschiff

steel [sti:l] Stahl III

steel drum [ˌsti:l 'drʌm] Steeldrum III

step [step]
1. Stufe IV 4 (93)
2. Schritt I
take steps Schritte machen/unternehmen III

stew [stju:] Eintopf(gericht) III

stick out of sth. [stɪk], **stuck, stuck** aus etwas herausragen, herausstehen III

still [stɪl] (immer) noch I

stole [stəʊl] *siehe* **steal**

stolen ['stəʊlən] *siehe* **steal**

stomach ['stʌmək] Magen II

stomach ache ['stʌmək‿eɪk] Magenschmerzen, Bauchweh II

stone [stəʊn] Stein II

stood [stʊd] *siehe* **stand**

stop (-pp-) [stɒp]
1. aufhören I
2. anhalten I
Stop that! Hör auf damit! / Lass das! I

storm [stɔ:m] Sturm; Gewitter II

stormy ['stɔ:mi] stürmisch II

story ['stɔ:ri] Geschichte, Erzählung I

straight [streɪt]
°**1.** gerade, aufrecht
2. straight on geradeaus weiter II
straight towards sb. direkt auf jn. zu IV 4 (93)

strange [streɪndʒ] seltsam, sonderbar; fremd III

°**stranger** ['streɪndʒə] Fremde(r)
strawberry ['strɔ:bəri] Erdbeere II
street [stri:t] Straße I • **at 7 Hamilton Street** in der Hamiltonstraße 7 I
stress [stres] Betonung III
°**stressed** [strest] betont
strict [strɪkt] streng III
strike [straɪk] Streik III • **be on strike** streiken, sich im Streik befinden III • **go on strike** streiken, in den Streik treten III
strong [strɒŋ] stark II
structure ['strʌktʃə] Struktur; Gliederung III
structure ['strʌktʃə] strukturieren, aufbauen II
stuck [stʌk] *siehe* **stick**
student ['stju:dənt] Schüler/in; Student/in I
studio ['stju:diəʊ] Studio I
study ['stʌdi] studieren; sorgfältig durchlesen; lernen IV 3 (56/179)
study hall ['stʌdi hɔ:l] *Zeit zum selbstständigen Lernen in der Schule* IV 3 (56)
study skills *(pl)* ['stʌdi skɪlz] Lern- und Arbeitstechniken I
stuff [stʌf] Zeug, Kram II
stupid ['stju:pɪd] blöd, dumm III
subject ['sʌbdʒɪkt] Schulfach I
°**suburb** ['sʌbɜ:b] Vorort
subway ['sʌbweɪ]: **the subway** *(AE)* die U-Bahn II
succeed (in sth.) [sək'si:d] Erfolg haben, erfolgreich sein (mit etwas, bei etwas) IV 2 (36)
success [sək'ses] Erfolg III
successful [sək'sesfl] erfolgreich III
°**such a ...** ['sʌtʃ‿ə] so ein(e) ..., solch ein(e) ...
suddenly ['sʌdnli] plötzlich, auf einmal I
sugar ['ʃʊgə] Zucker II
suggest sth. (to sb.) [sə'dʒest] (jm.) etwas vorschlagen IV 1 (26)
suggestion [sə'dʒestʃən] Vorschlag IV 3 (64)
suit [su:t] Anzug; (Damen-)Kostüm IV 1 (26)
suitcase ['su:tkeɪs] Koffer II
°**summarize** ['sʌməraɪz] zusammenfassen
summary ['sʌməri] Zusammenfassung IV 3 (67)
summer ['sʌmə] Sommer I
sun [sʌn] Sonne II
Sunday ['sʌndeɪ, 'sʌndi] Sonntag I
sung [sʌŋ] *siehe* **sing**
sunglasses *(pl)* ['sʌnglɑ:sɪz] (eine) Sonnenbrille I
°**sunlight** ['sʌnlaɪt] Sonnenlicht

sunny ['sʌni] sonnig II
supermarket ['su:pəmɑ:kɪt] Supermarkt II
supper ['sʌpə] Abendessen IV 2 (38)
support [sə'pɔ:t] unterstützen IV 4 (92) • **support a team** eine Mannschaft unterstützen; Fan einer Mannschaft sein III
supporter [sə'pɔ:tə] Anhänger/in, Fan III
suppose [sə'pəʊz] annehmen, vermuten II
°**Supreme: the Supreme Court** [su:ˌpri:m 'kɔ:t] der Oberste Gerichtshof
sure [ʃʊə, ʃɔ:] sicher I • **make sure that ...** sich vergewissern, dass ...; dafür sorgen, dass ... IV 2 (49)
surf [sɜ:f] surfen IV 2 (34) • **surf the internet** im Internet surfen II
surfboard ['sɜ:fbɔ:d] Surfbrett II
surfer ['sɜ:fə] Surfer/in IV 2 (34)
surfing ['sɜ:fɪŋ]: **go surfing** wellenreiten gehen, surfen gehen II
surprise [sə'praɪz] Überraschung II
surprise sb. [sə'praɪz] jn. überraschen III
surprised (at sth.) [sə'praɪzd] überrascht (über etwas) III
surprising [sə'praɪzɪŋ] überraschend, erstaunlich III
survey (on) ['sɜ:veɪ] Umfrage, Untersuchung (über) II
survival [sə'vaɪvl] Überleben II
survive [sə'vaɪv] überleben II
°**SUV** [ˌes ju: 'vi:] **(sport utility vehicle** [ˌspɔ:t ju:'tɪləti ˌvi:əkl]**)** Geländewagen
swam [swæm] *siehe* **swim**
swap sth. (for sth.) **(-pp-)** [swɒp] etwas (ein)tauschen (für etwas/gegen etwas) IV 3 (68)
°**swear** [sweə]**, swore, sworn** schwören
sweat [swet] schwitzen IV 3 (68)
sweat [swet] Schweiß IV 3 (68/184)
sweatshirt ['swetʃɜ:t] Sweatshirt I
sweet [swi:t] süß I
sweetheart ['swi:thɑ:t] Liebling, Schatz II
sweets *(pl)* [swi:ts] Süßigkeiten I
swim (-mm-) [swɪm]**, swam, swum** schwimmen I • **go swimming** schwimmen gehen I
swimmer ['swɪmə] Schwimmer/in II
swimming pool ['swɪmɪŋ pu:l] Schwimmbad, Schwimmbecken I
swimming trunks *(pl)* ['swɪmɪŋ trʌŋks] Badehose III
swimsuit ['swɪmsu:t] Badeanzug III
°**swore** [swɔ:] *siehe* **swear**

°**sworn** [swɔ:n] *siehe* **swear**
swum [swʌm] *siehe* **swim**
syllable ['sɪləbl] Silbe I
°**symbol** ['sɪmbl] Symbol
synagogue ['sɪnəgɒg] Synagoge III
synonym ['sɪnənɪm] Synonym *(Wort mit gleicher oder sehr ähnlicher Bedeutung)* IV 2 (42)
system ['sɪstəm] System IV 3 (56)

T

table ['teɪbl] Tisch I
table tennis ['teɪbl tenɪs] Tischtennis I • **table tennis bat** Tischtennisschläger III
take [teɪk]**, took, taken**
1. nehmen I
2. (weg-, hin)bringen I
3. dauern, *(Zeit)* brauchen III
I can take it. Ich halt's aus. / Ich kann's aushalten. IV 3 (69) • **I'll take it from here.** *etwa:* Ich übernehme das jetzt. / Ich komme jetzt allein klar. IV 2 (52) • **take a break** eine Pause machen IV 1 (22) • **take an exam** eine Prüfung ablegen IV 3 (63/182) • **take a ride** eine Fahrt machen III • **take notes** sich Notizen machen I • **take off** *(infml)* sich davonmachen, sich aus dem Staub machen IV 1 (27) • **take sth. off** etwas ausziehen *(Kleidung)* II; etwas absetzen *(Hut, Helm)* III
take 10c off 10 Cent abziehen I
take sth. out etwas herausnehmen I • **take over a plane** die Kontrolle über ein Flugzeug übernehmen; ein Flugzeug in seine Macht bringen IV 1 (15) • **take part (in)** teilnehmen (an) IV 3 (56)
take photos Fotos machen, fotografieren I • **take place** stattfinden IV 1 (15) • **take steps** Schritte machen/unternehmen III
°**Take turns.** Wechselt euch ab.
taken ['teɪkən] *siehe* **take**
talent ['tælənt] Talent, Begabung III
talk [tɔ:k] Gespräch IV 3 (56)
talk (to sb. about sth.) [tɔ:k] (mit jm. über etwas) reden, sich (mit jm. über etwas) unterhalten I
tall [tɔ:l] hoch *(Bäume, Türme usw.)*; groß *(Person)* IV 1 (16)
tank [tæŋk] Tank III
°**tattoo** [tə'tu:] Tätowierung
taught [tɔ:t] *siehe* **teach**
taxi ['tæksi] Taxi III
tea [ti:] Tee *(auch: leichte Nachmittags- oder Abendmahlzeit)* I
tea bag ['ti: bæg] Teebeutel IV 2 (46)

teach [tiːtʃ], **taught, taught** unterrichten, lehren I
teacher ['tiːtʃə] Lehrer/in I
team [tiːm] Team, Mannschaft I
tear [tɪə] Träne IV 1 (27)
tear sth. off [teə], **tore, torn** etwas abreißen IV 1 (28)
teaspoon ['tiːspuːn] Teelöffel III
teddy bear ['tedi beə] Teddybär III
teen [tiːn] Teenager-, Jugend- III
teenager ['tiːneɪdʒə] Teenager, Jugendliche(r) II
teeth [tiːθ] *pl von „tooth"*
telephone ['telɪfəʊn] Telefon I
telephone number Telefonnummer I
television (TV) ['telɪvɪʒn] Fernsehen I
tell (about) [tel], **told, told** erzählen (von), berichten (über) I • **Tell me your names.** Sagt mir eure Namen. I • **tell sb. the way** jm. den Weg beschreiben II • **tell sb. to do sth.** jn. auffordern, etwas zu tun; jm. sagen, dass er/sie etwas tun soll II
temperature ['temprətʃə] Temperatur II • **have a temperature** Fieber haben II
tennis ['tenɪs] Tennis I
tense [tens] (grammatische) Zeit, Tempus III
tent [tent] Zelt IV Intro (9)
term [tɜːm] Trimester II
terrible ['terəbl] schrecklich, furchtbar I
terrified ['terɪfaɪd]**: be terrified (of)** schreckliche Angst haben (vor) IV 4 (92)
°**territory** ['terətri] Revier, Gebiet, Territorium
terrorist ['terərɪst] Terrorist/in IV 4 (79)
terrorist ['terərɪst] terroristisch, Terror- IV 4 (79)
test [test] Klassenarbeit, Test, Prüfung II
°**test** [test] prüfen, testen
text [tekst] Text I
text message ['tekst ˌmesɪdʒ] SMS III
text sb. [tekst] jm. eine SMS schicken III
than [ðæn, ðən] als II • **more than** mehr als II • **more than me** mehr als ich II
Thank you. ['θæŋk juː] Danke (schön). I • **Thanks.** [θæŋks] Danke. I • **Thanks a lot!** Vielen Dank! I • **Thanks very much!** Danke sehr! / Vielen Dank! II

that [ðət, ðæt]
1. das (dort) I
2. jene(r, s) I
that day an jenem Tag III • **That's me.** Das bin ich. I • **That's right.** Das ist richtig. / Das stimmt. I
That's up to you. Das liegt bei dir./ Das kannst/musst du (selbst) entscheiden. III • **that's why** deshalb, darum I • **That way ...** So .../ Auf diese Weise ... III
that [ðət, ðæt] der, die, das; die *(Relativpronomen)* III
that [ðət, ðæt] dass I • **so that** sodass, damit III
that far/good/bad/... [ðæt] so weit/ gut/schlecht/... III
the [ðə, ði] der, die, das; die I
theatre ['θɪətə] Theater II
their [ðeə] ihr, ihre *(Plural)* I
theirs [ðeəz] ihrer, ihre, ihrs *(Plural)* II
them [ðəm, ðem] sie; ihnen I
theme park ['θiːm pɑːk] Themenpark *(Freizeitpark mit Attraktionen zu einem bestimmten Thema)* IV 2 (47)
°**theme song** ['θiːm sɒŋ] Titelsong, Erkennungsmelodie
themselves [ðəm'selvz] sich (selbst) III
then [ðen] dann, danach I • **since then** seitdem IV 4 (80)
°**therapy** ['θerəpi] Therapie
there [ðeə]
1. da, dort I
2. dahin, dorthin I
down there dort unten II • **in there** dort drinnen I • **over there** da drüben, dort drüben I
there are es sind (vorhanden); es gibt I • **there's** es ist (vorhanden); es gibt I • **there isn't a ...** es ist kein/e ...; es gibt kein/e ... I • **There you go!** *(infml)* *etwa:* So, das hätten wir. IV 2 (50) • **up there** dort oben III
thermometer [θə'mɒmɪtə] Thermometer II
these [ðiːz] diese, die (hier) I
they [ðeɪ] sie *(Plural)* I
thief [θiːf], *pl* **thieves** [θiːvz] Dieb/in II
thing [θɪŋ] Ding, Sache I • **What was the best thing about ...?** Was war das Beste an ...? II
think [θɪŋk], **thought, thought** glauben, meinen, denken I • **I think so.** Ich glaube (ja). I • **I don't think so.** Das finde/glaube ich nicht. I • **think about 1.** nachdenken über II; **2.** denken über, halten von II • **think of 1.** denken über, halten von II; **2.** denken an; sich ausdenken II
third [θɜːd] dritte(r, s) I
thirsty ['θɜːsti] durstig I • **be thirsty** Durst haben, durstig sein I
this [ðɪs]
1. dies (hier) I
2. diese(r, s) I
like this so IV 4 (79) • **This is Isabel.** Hier spricht Isabel. / Hier ist Isabel. *(am Telefon)* II • **this morning/afternoon/evening** heute Morgen/Nachmittag/Abend I
this way 1. hier entlang, in diese Richtung II; **2.** so; auf diese Weise III
those [ðəʊz] die (da), jene (dort) I
thought [θɔːt] *siehe* **think**
thought [θɔːt] Gedanke IV 3 (63)
thousand ['θaʊznd] tausend I
threw [θruː] *siehe* **throw**
throat [θrəʊt] Hals, Kehle II • **have a sore throat** Halsschmerzen haben II
through [θruː] durch II
throw [θrəʊ], **threw, thrown** werfen I • **throw up** sich übergeben IV 3 (69)
thrown [θrəʊn] *siehe* **throw**
Thursday ['θɜːzdeɪ, 'θɜːzdi] Donnerstag I
°**tick** [tɪk] Häkchen
ticket ['tɪkɪt]
1. Eintrittskarte I
2. Fahrkarte II
all-day ticket Tagesfahrkarte III
return ticket Rückfahrkarte II
single ticket einfache Fahrkarte *(nur Hinfahrt)* III
ticket agent ['tɪkɪt‿eɪdʒənt] *Angestellte(r) in Kartenvorverkaufsstelle* IV 1 (22)
ticket machine ['tɪkɪt məˌʃiːn] Fahrkartenautomat III
ticket office ['tɪkɪt‿ɒfɪs] Kasse *(für den Verkauf von Eintrittskarten)*; Fahrkartenschalter IV 1 (16)
tide [taɪd] Gezeiten, Ebbe und Flut II • **the tide is in** es ist Flut II
the tide is out es ist Ebbe II
tidy ['taɪdi] aufräumen I
tidy ['taɪdi] ordentlich, aufgeräumt II
tie (*-ing form:* **tying**) [taɪ] binden IV 2 (49)
tie [taɪ] Krawatte, Schlips IV 2 (49)
tiger ['taɪgə] Tiger II
tight [taɪt] fest IV 3 (69)
tights *(pl)* [taɪts] Strumpfhose III
till [tɪl] bis *(zeitlich)* I • **not ... till** erst (um); nicht vor III

time [taɪm]
1. Zeit; Uhrzeit I • **a long time** lange III • **in time** rechtzeitig II **What's the time?** Wie spät ist es? I
2. time(s) Mal(e); -mal II • **for the first time** zum ersten Mal IV 4 (93)
timeline ['taɪmlaɪn] Zeitstrahl III
timetable ['taɪmteɪbl]
1. Stundenplan I
2. Fahrplan III
timing ['taɪmɪŋ]: **bad timing** schlechtes Timing III
tip [tɪp]
1. Spitze IV Intro (10)
2. Tipp III
tired ['taɪəd] müde I • **be tired of sth.** genug von etwas haben, etwas satt haben IV 1 (16) • **get tired of sth.** einer Sache überdrüssig werden, die Lust an etwas verlieren IV 3 (69)
title ['taɪtl] Titel, Überschrift I
to [tə, tu]
1. zu, nach I • **an e-mail to** eine E-Mail an I • **to Jenny's** zu Jenny I • **to the doctor's** zum Arzt III **to the front** nach vorn I • **I've never been to Bath.** Ich bin noch nie in Bath gewesen. II • **write to** schreiben an I
2. quarter to 12 Viertel vor 12 (11.45 / 23.45) I • **from Monday to Friday** von Montag bis Freitag III
3. something to eat etwas zu essen I • **try to do** versuchen, zu tun I • **we know what to do** wir wissen, was wir tun müssen; wir wissen, was zu tun ist III
4. um zu I
toast [təʊst] Toast(brot) I
tobacco [tə'bækəʊ] Tabak II
today [tə'deɪ] heute I
toe [təʊ] Zeh I
together [tə'geðə] zusammen I **go together** zusammenpassen IV 1 (21)
toilet ['tɔɪlət] Toilette I
told [təʊld] *siehe* **tell**
tolerant ['tɒlərənt] tolerant III
tomato [tə'mɑːtəʊ], *pl* **tomatoes** Tomate II
tomorrow [tə'mɒrəʊ] morgen I **tomorrow's weather** das Wetter von morgen II
°**tongue-twister** ['tʌŋtwɪstə] Zungenbrecher
tonight [tə'naɪt] heute Nacht, heute Abend I • **tonight's programme** das Programm von heute Abend; das heutige Abendprogramm II
too [tuː]: **from Bristol too** auch aus Bristol I • **Me too.** Ich auch. I
too much/big/... [tuː] zu viel/groß/ ... I
took [tʊk] *siehe* **take**
tool [tuːl] Werkzeug IV Intro (9)
tooth [tuːθ], *pl* **teeth** [tiːθ] Zahn I
toothache ['tuːθeɪk] Zahnschmerzen II
toothless ['tuːθləs] zahnlos IV 2 (42)
top [tɒp]
1. Spitze, oberes Ende I • **at the top (of)** oben, am oberen Ende, an der Spitze (von) I
2. Top, Oberteil I
topic ['tɒpɪk] Thema, Themenbereich I • **topic sentence** *Satz, der in das Thema eines Absatzes einführt* II
tore [tɔː] *siehe* **tear**
torn [tɔːn] *siehe* **tear**
tornado [tɔː'neɪdəʊ] Tornado, Wirbelsturm II
tortoise ['tɔːtəs] Schildkröte I
°**totally** ['təʊtəli] völlig
touch [tʌtʃ] berühren, anfassen II
touch [tʌtʃ]: **keep in touch** in Verbindung bleiben, Kontakt halten III
tour (of the house) [tʊə] Rundgang, Tour (durch das Haus) I
°**tourism** ['tʊərɪzəm] Tourismus, Fremdenverkehr
tourist ['tʊərɪst] Tourist/in II **tourist information** Fremdenverkehrsamt II
towards sb./sth. [tə'wɔːdz] auf jn./etwas zu II • °**feel ... towards sb.** sich ... fühlen gegenüber jm.
towel ['taʊəl] Handtuch IV 2 (52)
tower ['taʊə] Turm I
town [taʊn] Stadt I
°**trace** [treɪs] aufspüren, ausfindig machen
track [træk]
1. Stück, Titel, Track *(auf einer CD)* III
2. running track Laufbahn *(Sport)* III
tradition [trə'dɪʃn] Tradition IV 3 (55)
traditional [trə'dɪʃənl] traditionell III
traffic ['træfɪk] Verkehr II
traffic jam ['træfɪk dʒæm] (Verkehrs-)Stau IV 4 (79)
trail [treɪl]
1. (Lehr-)Pfad IV Intro (10)
°**2.** Route, Weg
train [treɪn] Zug I • **on the train** im Zug I
train [treɪn] trainieren III
trainers *(pl)* ['treɪnəz] Turnschuhe II
training session ['treɪnɪŋ ˌseʃn] Trainingsstunde, -einheit III
train times *(pl)* ['treɪn taɪmz] (Zug-) Abfahrtszeiten IV 1 (21)
tram [træm] Straßenbahn III
translate [træns'leɪt] übersetzen III
translation [træns'leɪʃn] Übersetzung III
transport *(no pl)* ['trænspɔːt] Verkehrsmittel III • **public transport** *(no pl)* öffentliche Verkehrsmittel, öffentlicher Personennahverkehr III
trap [træp] Falle II
°**trash** [træʃ]: **white trash** *(AE, infml) abwertende Bezeichnung für die weiße Unterschicht (wörtlich:* weißer Müll*)*
travel (*BE:* **-ll-**) ['trævl] reisen II
Travelcard ['trævlkɑːd] Tagesfahrkarte *(der Londoner Verkehrsbetriebe)* III
tree [triː] Baum I
trendy ['trendi] modisch, schick III
°**tribute** ['trɪbjuːt] Würdigung, Tribut, Anerkennung
trick [trɪk]
1. (Zauber-)Kunststück, Trick I • **do tricks** (Zauber-)Kunststücke machen I
2. Streich II • **play a trick on sb.** jm. einen Streich spielen II
trip [trɪp] Reise; Ausflug I • **go on a trip** einen Ausflug machen II
trombone [trɒm'bəʊn] Posaune III
trouble ['trʌbl] Schwierigkeiten, Ärger II • **be in trouble** in Schwierigkeiten sein; Ärger kriegen II
trousers *(pl)* ['traʊzəz] Hose II
°**truck** [trʌk] Lastwagen
true [truː] wahr II
trumpet ['trʌmpɪt] Trompete III
try [traɪ]
1. versuchen I
2. probieren, kosten I
try and do sth. / try to do sth. versuchen, etwas zu tun I • **try on** anprobieren *(Kleidung)* I
T-shirt ['tiːʃɜːt] T-Shirt I
tube [tjuːb]: **the Tube** *(no pl)* die Londoner U-Bahn III
Tuesday ['tjuːzdeɪ, 'tjuːzdi] Dienstag I
tune [tjuːn] Melodie III
tunnel ['tʌnl] Tunnel II
turkey ['tɜːki] Truthahn, Pute/Puter III
turn [tɜːn]
1. sich umdrehen II • **turn left/right** (nach) links/rechts abbiegen II • **turn to sb.** sich jm. zuwenden; sich an jn. wenden II

2. turn sth. on etwas einschalten I **turn sth. off** etwas ausschalten II **turn sth. up/down** etwas lauter/leiser stellen III

turn [tɜ:n]: **(It's) my turn.** Ich bin dran / an der Reihe. I • **Miss a turn.** Einmal aussetzen. II • °**Take turns.** Wechselt euch ab. • **Whose turn is it?** Wer ist dran / an der Reihe? II

TV [ti:'vi:] Fernsehen I • **on TV** im Fernsehen I • **watch TV** fernsehen I

TV listings *(pl)* ['lɪstɪŋz] das Fernsehprogramm IV 4 (78)

twice [twaɪs] zweimal III

twin [twɪn]: **twin brother** Zwillingsbruder I • **twins** *(pl)* Zwillinge I **twin towers** Zwillingstürme IV 1 (15) • **twin town** Partnerstadt I

type [taɪp] *(infml)* Typ III

°**typical** ['tɪpɪkl] typisch

U

unbelievable [,ʌnbɪ'li:vəbl] unglaublich IV 4 (79)

uncle ['ʌŋkl] Onkel I

unconscious [ʌn'kɒnʃəs] bewusstlos II

uncool [,ʌn'ku:l] *(infml)* uncool III

under ['ʌndə] unter I

underground ['ʌndəgraʊnd]: **the underground** die U-Bahn II

°**underline** [,ʌndə'laɪn] unterstreichen

°**underlined** [,ʌndə'laɪnd] unterstrichen

understand [,ʌndə'stænd], **understood, understood** verstehen, begreifen I

understandable [,ʌndə'stændəbl] verständlich IV 4 (88)

understood [,ʌndə'stʊd] *siehe* **understand**

unfair [,ʌn'feə] unfair, ungerecht III

unfriendly [ʌn'frendli] unfreundlich III

unhappy [ʌn'hæpi] unglücklich III

unhealthy [ʌn'helθi] ungesund III

uniform ['ju:nɪfɔ:m] Uniform I

unit ['ju:nɪt] Kapitel, Lektion I

united [ju'naɪtɪd]: **the United Kingdom (UK)** [ju,naɪtɪd 'kɪŋdəm] das Vereinigte Königreich *(Großbritannien und Nordirland)* III • **the United States (US)** [ju,naɪtɪd 'steɪts] die Vereinigten Staaten (von Amerika) III

university [,ju:nɪ'vɜ:səti] Universität IV 4 (94)

unsafe [ʌn'seɪf] nicht sicher, gefährlich III

untidy [ʌn'taɪdi] unordentlich III

until [ən'tɪl] bis III • **not ... until** erst (um); nicht vor III

up [ʌp] hinauf, herauf, nach oben I **up (the hill)** (den Hügel) hinauf II **up there** dort oben III • **That's up to you.** Das liegt bei dir. / Das kannst/musst du (selbst) entscheiden. III

°**update** [,ʌp'deɪt] aktualisieren, auf den neuesten Stand bringen

upset (about) [,ʌp'set] aufgebracht, gekränkt, mitgenommen (wegen) III

upset sb. **(-tt-)** [ʌp'set], **upset, upset** jn. ärgern, kränken, aus der Fassung bringen III

upstairs [,ʌp'steəz] oben; nach oben I

us [əs, ʌs] uns I

use [ju:z] benutzen, verwenden I

°**used** [ju:zd] gebraucht

useful ['ju:sfl] nützlich III

usually ['ju:ʒuəli] meistens, gewöhnlich, normalerweise I

V

vacation [və'keɪʃn, *AE:* veɪ'keɪʃn] *(AE)* Urlaub, Ferien III

valley ['væli] Tal II • **valley floor** Talboden II

valuable ['væljuəbl] wertvoll; nützlich IV 4 (93)

vegetable ['vedʒtəbl] *(ein)* Gemüse III • **vegetable oil** Pflanzenöl IV 3 (58)

vegetarian [,vedʒə'teəriən] vegetarisch; Vegetarier/in IV 2 (43)

very ['veri] sehr I • **like/love sth. very much** etwas sehr mögen/sehr lieben II • **Thanks very much!** Danke sehr! / Vielen Dank! II

victim ['vɪktɪm] Opfer III

video ['vɪdiəʊ] Video III

view [vju:] Aussicht, Blick II • **in my/your view** meiner/deiner Ansicht nach III • **point of view** Standpunkt II • **from my point of view** aus meiner Sicht; von meinem Standpunkt aus gesehen II

viewer ['vju:ə] Zuschauer/in IV 4 (78)

village ['vɪlɪdʒ] Dorf I

violence ['vaɪələns] Gewalt, Gewalttätigkeit IV 4 (76)

violent ['vaɪələnt] gewalttätig; gewaltsam IV 4 (76/184)

virus ['vaɪrəs] Virus I

visibility [,vɪzə'bɪləti] Sicht(weite) IV 1 (16)

visit ['vɪzɪt] besuchen, aufsuchen II

visit ['vɪzɪt] Besuch II

visitor ['vɪzɪtə] Besucher/in, Gast I

vocabulary [və'kæbjələri] Vokabelverzeichnis, Wörterverzeichnis I

voice [vɔɪs] Stimme I

volleyball ['vɒlibɔ:l] Volleyball I

volunteer [,vɒlən'tɪə] Freiwillige(r) IV 4 (92/188)

volunteer [,vɒlən'tɪə] sich freiwillig melden, sich bereit erklären IV 4 (92)

vote for sb. [vəʊt] für jn. stimmen IV 3 (68)

vowel sound ['vaʊəl saʊnd] Vokallaut II

W

°**wagon train** ['wægən treɪn] Planwagenkolonne, -zug

wait (for) [weɪt] warten (auf) I **I can't wait to see ...** ich kann es kaum erwarten, ... zu sehen I **Wait a minute.** Warte mal! / Moment mal! II • **Wait and see!** Wart's ab! III

waiter ['weɪtə] Kellner II

waiting room ['weɪtɪŋ ru:m] Wartezimmer IV 4 (91)

waitress ['weɪtrəs] Kellnerin II

wake [weɪk], **woke, woken:** **1. wake sb. (up)** jn. (auf)wecken III **2. wake up** aufwachen III

walk [wɔ:k] (zu Fuß) gehen I **walk on** weitergehen III

walk [wɔ:k] Spaziergang II • **go for a walk** spazieren gehen, einen Spaziergang machen II

wall [wɔ:l] Wand; Mauer II

walrus ['wɔ:lrəs] Walross III

°**wander** ['wɒndə] wandern, schlendern

want [wɒnt] (haben) wollen I **want to do** tun wollen I • **want sb. to do sth.** wollen, dass jd. etwas tut IV 2 (49)

war [wɔ:] Krieg IV 4 (76)

wardrobe ['wɔ:drəʊb] Kleiderschrank I

warm [wɔ:m] warm II

warn sb. (about sth.) [wɔ:n] jn. (vor etwas) warnen III

°**warrior** ['wɒriə] Krieger/in

was [wəz, wɒz]: **I/he/she/it was** *siehe* **be**

wash [wɒʃ] waschen I; (auf-) wischen *(Fußboden)* II • **I wash**

my face. Ich wasche mir das Gesicht. I
waste (on) [weɪst] verschwenden, vergeuden (für) III
watch [wɒtʃ] beobachten, sich *etwas* ansehen; zusehen I
°watch for sth. auf etwas achten, nach etwas Ausschau halten
watch TV fernsehen I
watch [wɒtʃ] Armbanduhr I
water ['wɔ:tə] Wasser I
wave [weɪv] winken II
way [weɪ]
1. Weg II • **ask sb. the way** jn. nach dem Weg fragen II • **on the way (to)** auf dem Weg (zu/nach) II • **tell sb. the way** jm. den Weg beschreiben II
2. Richtung II • **the other way round** anders herum II • **the wrong way** in die falsche Richtung II • **this way** hier entlang, in diese Richtung II • **which way?** in welche Richtung? / wohin? II
3. Art und Weise III • **that way/ this way** so; auf diese Weise III • **the way you ...** so wie du ..., auf dieselbe Weise wie du ... IV 3 (70)
4. by the way übrigens; nebenbei (bemerkt) III • **No way!** Auf keinen Fall! / Kommt nicht in Frage! II
we [wi:] wir I
weak [wi:k] schwach II
wear [weə], **wore, worn** tragen, anhaben *(Kleidung)* I
weather ['weðə] Wetter II
webcam ['webkæm] Webcam, Internetkamera II
website ['websaɪt] Website II
Wednesday ['wenzdeɪ, 'wenzdi] Mittwoch I
week [wi:k] Woche I • **days of the week** Wochentage I • **a two-week holiday** ein zweiwöchiger Urlaub III
weekend [ˌwi:k'end] Wochenende I
at the weekend am Wochenende I
welcome ['welkəm]
1. Welcome (to Bristol). Willkommen (in Bristol). I
2. You're welcome. Gern geschehen. / Nichts zu danken. I
welcome sb. (to) ['welkəm] jn. begrüßen, willkommen heißen (in) I
They welcome you to ... Sie heißen dich in ... willkommen I
well [wel]
1. gut II • **go well** gut (ver)laufen, gutgehen III • **You did well.** Das hast du gut gemacht. II • **Oh well ...** Na ja ... / Na gut ... I • **Well, ...** Nun, ... / Also, ... I
2. *(gesundheitlich)* gut; gesund, wohlauf II
Welsh [welʃ] walisisch; Walisisch II
went [went] *siehe* **go**
were [wə, wɜ:]: **we/you/they were** *siehe* **be**
west [west] Westen; nach Westen; westlich III
westbound ['westbaʊnd] Richtung Westen III
western ['westən] westlich, West- III
what [wɒt]
1. was I
2. welche(r, s) I
we know what to do wir wissen, was wir tun müssen; wir wissen, was zu tun ist III • **What about ...? 1.** Was ist mit ...? / Und ...? I; **2.** Wie wär's mit ...? I • **What an interesting life!** Was für ein interessantes Leben! III • **°What are the pages about?** Wovon handeln die Seiten? • **What are you talking about?** Wovon redest du? I • **What colour is ...?** Welche Farbe hat ...? I • **What else do you know ...?** Was weißt du sonst noch ...? II • **What for?** Wofür? II
What have we got next? Was haben wir als Nächstes? I • **What kind of car ...?** Was für ein Auto ...? III • **What page are we on?** Auf welcher Seite sind wir? I
What's for homework? Was haben wir als Hausaufgabe auf? I
What's for lunch? Was gibt es zum Mittagessen? III • **What's the matter?** Was ist los? / Was ist denn? II • **What's the time?** Wie spät ist es? I • **What's wrong with you?** Was fehlt dir? II • **What's your name?** Wie heißt du? I
What was the weather like? Wie war das Wetter? II
whatever [wɒt'evə] was (auch) immer IV 2 (51/178)
▶ S.178 whoever, whatever, whenever, wherever
wheel [wi:l] Rad III • **big wheel** Riesenrad III
wheelchair ['wi:ltʃeə] Rollstuhl I
when [wen] wann I • **When's your birthday?** Wann hast du Geburtstag? I
when [wen]
1. wenn I
2. als I
whenever [wen'evə] wann (auch) immer IV 2 (51/178)
▶ S.178 whoever, whatever, whenever, wherever
where [weə]
1. wo I
2. wohin I
Where are you from? Wo kommst du her? I
wherever [weər'evə] wo(hin) (auch) immer IV 2 (51/178)
▶ S.178 whoever, whatever, whenever, wherever
which [wɪtʃ] welche(r, s) I • **Which picture ...?** Welches Bild ...? I
which way? in welche Richtung? / wohin? II
which [wɪtʃ] der, die, das; die *(Relativpronomen)* III
while *(conj)* [waɪl] während III
▶ S.185 German 'während'
whisky ['wɪski] Whisky II
whisper ['wɪspə] flüstern I
whistle ['wɪsl] pfeifen II
whistle ['wɪsl] (Triller-)Pfeife; Pfiff III
white [waɪt] weiß I • **°white trash** *(AE, infml) abwertende Bezeichnung für die weiße Unterschicht (wörtlich:* weißer Müll*)*
who [hu:]
1. wer I
2. wen / wem II
who [hu:] der, die, das; die *(Relativpronomen)* III
whoever [hu:'evə] wer (auch) immer; wen/wem (auch) immer IV 2 (51)
▶ S.178 whoever, whatever, whenever, wherever
whole [həʊl] ganze(r, s), gesamte(r, s) III
whole-grain ['həʊlgreɪn] Vollkorn- IV 3 (58)
whose? [hu:z] wessen? II
Whose are these? Wem gehören diese? II • **Whose turn is it?** Wer ist dran? / Wer ist an der Reihe? II
why [waɪ] warum I • **Why me?** Warum ich? I • **that's why** deshalb, darum I
wife [waɪf], *pl* **wives** [waɪvz] Ehefrau II
wild [waɪld] wild II
will [wɪl]: **you'll be cold (= you will be cold)** du wirst / ihr werdet frieren II
win (-nn-) [wɪn], **won, won** gewinnen I
win [wɪn] Sieg III
wind [wɪnd] Wind I
°wind [waɪnd], **wound, wound** sich winden, sich schlängeln
window ['wɪndəʊ] Fenster I

windscreen ['wɪndskriːn] Windschutzscheibe III
windy ['wɪndi] windig I
wine [waɪn] Wein IV 3 (57)
°**winery** ['waɪnəri] Weingut
wing [wɪŋ] Flügel IV Intro (10)
winner ['wɪnə] Gewinner/in, Sieger/in II
winning shot [ˌwɪnɪŋ 'ʃɒt] Siegtreffer, Siegesschuss III
winter ['wɪntə] Winter I
°**wipe** [waɪp] wischen
wish [wɪʃ]: **Best wishes** *etwa:* Alles Gute / Mit besten Grüßen *(als Briefschluss)* IV 3 (62)
with [wɪð]
1. mit I
2. bei I
be with sb. mit jm. zusammen sein IV 3 (69) • **go with** gehören zu, passen zu III • **Sit with me.** Setz dich zu mir. / Setzt euch zu mir. I
°**within sight** [wɪˌðɪn 'saɪt] in Sichtweite
without [wɪ'ðaʊt] ohne I
wives [waɪvz] *pl von „wife“* II
woke [wəʊk] *siehe* **wake**
woken ['wəʊkən] *siehe* **wake**
wolf [wʊlf], *pl* **wolves** [wʊlvz] Wolf II
woman ['wʊmən], *pl* **women** ['wɪmɪn] Frau I
won [wʌn] *siehe* **win**
wonder ['wʌndə] sich fragen, gern wissen wollen II
°**wonder** ['wʌndə] Staunen
°**wonderful** ['wʌndəfl] wunderbar
won't [wəʊnt]: **you won't be cold (= you will not be cold)** du wirst nicht frieren / ihr werdet nicht frieren II
wood [wʊd] Holz II
woodpecker ['wʊdpekə] Specht II
woods *(pl)* [wʊdz] Wald, Wälder II
word [wɜːd] Wort I • **word building** Wortbildung II • **word field** Wortfeld III • °**word order** Wortstellung
wore [wɔː] *siehe* **wear**
work [wɜːk]
1. arbeiten I
2. funktionieren III
work hard hart arbeiten II • **work on sth.** an etwas arbeiten I
work out gut ausgehen IV 2 (51)
work sth. out etwas herausarbeiten, herausfinden IV 1 (25)
work [wɜːk] Arbeit I • **at work** bei der Arbeit / am Arbeitsplatz I
worker ['wɜːkə] Arbeiter/in II
workplace ['wɜːkpleɪs] Arbeitsplatz IV 4 (79)
worksheet ['wɜːkʃiːt] Arbeitsblatt I
workshop ['wɜːkʃɒp] Workshop, Werkstatt III
world [wɜːld] Welt I • **all over the world** auf der ganzen Welt III
°**in the world** auf der Welt
worn [wɔːn] *siehe* **wear**
worried ['wʌrid]: **be worried (about)** beunruhigt sein, besorgt sein (wegen/um) IV 3 (67)
worry ['wʌri] Sorge, Kummer II
worry (about) ['wʌri] sich Sorgen machen (wegen, um) I • **Don't worry.** Mach dir keine Sorgen. I
worse [wɜːs] schlechter, schlimmer II
worst [wɜːst]: **(the) worst** am schlechtesten, schlimmsten; der/die/das schlechteste, schlimmste II
would [wəd, wʊd]: **you would ...** du würdest ... III • **I'd like ... (= I would like ...)** Ich hätte gern ... / Ich möchte gern ... I • **Would you like ...?** Möchtest du ...? / Möchten Sie ...? I • **I'd like to go (= I would like to go)** ich würde gern gehen / ich möchte gehen I • **I wouldn't like to go** ich würde nicht gern gehen / ich möchte nicht gehen I
°**wound** [waʊnd] *siehe* **wind**
write [raɪt], **wrote, written** schreiben I • **write down** aufschreiben I • °**write sth. out** etwas ausschreiben • **write to** schreiben an I • °**write sth. up** etwas (schriftlich) ausarbeiten
writer ['raɪtə] Schreiber/in; Schriftsteller/in II
written ['rɪtn] *siehe* **write**
wrong [rɒŋ] falsch, verkehrt I
be wrong 1. falsch sein I; 2. sich irren, Unrecht haben II • **go wrong** schiefgehen III • **the wrong way** in die falsche Richtung II • **What's wrong with you?** Was fehlt dir? II
wrote [rəʊt] *siehe* **write**

Y

yard [jɑːd] Hof II • **in the yard** auf dem Hof II
yawn [jɔːn] gähnen II
year [jɪə]
1. Jahr I
2. Jahrgangsstufe I
thirteen-year-old Dreizehnjährige(r) III
yellow ['jeləʊ] gelb I
yes [jes] ja I
yesterday ['jestədeɪ, 'jestədi] gestern I • **yesterday morning/afternoon/evening** gestern Morgen/Nachmittag/Abend I • **yesterday's homework** die Hausaufgaben von gestern II
yet [jet]: **not (...) yet** noch nicht II
yet? schon? II
°**Yiddish** ['jɪdɪʃ] Jiddisch; jiddisch
yoga ['jəʊgə] Yoga I
you [juː]
1. du; Sie I
2. man III
3. ihr I • **you two** ihr zwei I
4. dir; dich; euch I
You bet! *(infml)* Aber klar! / Und ob! IV 4 (79) • **There you go!** *(infml) etwa:* So, das hätten wir. IV 2 (50)
young [jʌŋ] jung I
your [jɔː]
1. dein/e I
2. Ihr I
3. euer/eure I
yours [jɔːz]
1. deiner, deine, deins II
2. Ihrer, Ihre, Ihrs II
3. eurer, eure, eures II
yourself [jə'self, jɔː'self] dir/dich (selbst) III • **about yourself** über dich selbst III
yourselves [jə'selvz, jɔː'selvz] euch (selbst) III
youth [juːθ] Jugend III

Z

zebra ['zebrə] Zebra II
zero ['zɪərəʊ] null I
zone [zəʊn] Zone, Bereich III
zoo [zuː] Zoo IV 1 (23)

Das **German – English Dictionary** enthält den **Lernwortschatz** der Bände 1 bis 4 von *English G 21*.
Es kann dir eine erste Hilfe sein, wenn du vergessen hast, wie etwas auf Englisch heißt.

Wenn du wissen möchtest, wo das englische Wort zum ersten Mal in *English G 21* vorkommt, dann kannst du im **English – German Dictionary** (S. 189–219) nachschlagen.

Im **German – English Dictionary** werden folgende **Abkürzungen** und **Symbole** verwendet:

jm. = jemandem	sb. = somebody	*pl* = *plural*	*BE* = *British English*	*infml* = *informal*
jn. = jemanden	sth. = something	*no pl* = *no plural*	*AE* = *American English*	

► Der Pfeil verweist auf Kästchen im Vocabulary (S. 167–188), in denen du weitere Informationen findest.

Tipps zur Arbeit mit einem Wörterbuch findest du im Skills File auf Seite 140.

A

abbiegen: (nach) links/rechts abbiegen turn left/right [tɜːn]
Abend evening [ˈiːvnɪŋ]; *(später Abend)* night [naɪt] • **am Abend, abends** in the evening
Abendbrot, -essen dinner [ˈdɪnə]; supper [ˈsʌpə] • **Abendbrot essen** have dinner/supper • **zum Abendbrot** for dinner/supper
Abenteuer adventure [ədˈventʃə]
aber but [bət, bʌt] • **Aber klar!** You bet! [bet] *(infml)*
abfahren *(wegfahren)* leave [liːv]
Abfahrt *(Abreise)* departure (dep) [dɪˈpɑːtʃə]
Abfahrtszeiten *(Zug)* train times
Abfall rubbish [ˈrʌbɪʃ] *(BE)*; garbage [ˈɡɑːbɪdʒ] *(AE)*
Abflug departure (dep) [dɪˈpɑːtʃə]
Abgemacht! It's a deal! [diːl]
abhängen *(rumhängen)* hang out [ˌhæŋ‿ˈaʊt] *(infml)*
abholen: jn. abholen pick sb. up [ˌpɪk‿ˈʌp]
Abkommen: ein Abkommen treffen make a deal [diːl]
ablegen: eine Prüfung ablegen take/do an exam [ɪɡˈzæm]
Abmachung: eine Abmachung treffen make a deal [diːl]
Abreise departure [dɪˈpɑːtʃə]
abreißen: etwas abreißen tear sth. off [teə]
Absatz *(in einem Text)* paragraph [ˈpærəɡrɑːf]
abschließen *(Raum)* lock up [ˌlɒk‿ˈʌp]
abschneiden: etwas abschneiden cut sth. off [ˌkʌt‿ˈɒf]
Abschnitt section [ˈsekʃn]
abschreiben *(kopieren)* copy [ˈkɒpi]
absetzen: etwas absetzen *(Hut, Helm)* take sth. off [ˌteɪk‿ˈɒf] • **jn. absetzen** *(aussteigen lassen)* drop sb. off [drɒp]
abtrennen: etwas abtrennen cut sth. off [ˌkʌt‿ˈɒf]
abwarten: Wart's ab! Wait and see!
abziehen: 10 Cent abziehen take 10c off [ˌteɪk‿ˈɒf]
achten: auf etwas achten *(horchen)* listen for sth. [ˈlɪsn]
Acker field [fiːld]
addieren (zu) add (to) [æd]
Adjektiv adjective [ˈædʒɪktɪv]
Adverb adverb [ˈædvɜːb]
Affe monkey [ˈmʌŋki]
afro-amerikanisch African-American [ˌæfrɪkən‿əˈmerɪkən]
aktiv active [ˈæktɪv]
Aktivität activity [ækˈtɪvəti]
Akzent accent [ˈæksənt]
albern silly [ˈsɪli]
Album album [ˈælbəm]
alkoholfreies Getränk soft drink
alle *(die ganze Gruppe)* all [ɔːl]
Allee avenue [ˈævənjuː]
allein alone [əˈləʊn]; *(selbstständig, ohne Hilfe)* on my/our/... own [əʊn]
alleinstehend single [ˈsɪŋɡl]
alles everything [ˈevriθɪŋ]; anything [ˈeniθɪŋ]; all [ɔːl] • **Alles Gute** *(als Briefschluss)* Best wishes [ˈwɪʃɪz]
alles, was wir jetzt (noch) tun müssen, ... all we have to do now ...
allgemeine(r, s) general [ˈdʒenrəl]
alltägliche(r, s), Alltags- everyday [ˈevrideɪ]
Alphabet alphabet [ˈælfəbet]
als 1. *(zeitlich)* when [wen]; *(während)* as [əz, æz]
2. als ob as if [əz‿ˈɪf]
3. als Kind as a child
4. größer/teurer als bigger/more expensive than [ðæn, ðən] • **mehr als** more than • **mehr als ich** more than me
also *(daher, deshalb)* so [səʊ]
Also, ... Well, ... [wel]
alt old [əʊld]
Alter age [eɪdʒ]
altmodisch old-fashioned [ˌəʊldˈfæʃnd]
am 1. am Bahnhof at the station
am Himmel in the sky • **am oberen Ende (von)** at the top (of)
am Strand on the beach • **am Telefon** on the phone • **am unteren Ende (von)** at the bottom (of) [ˈbɒtəm]
2. *(nahe bei)* **am Meer** by the sea
3. *(zeitlich)* **am 13. Juni** on 13th June • **am Morgen/Nachmittag/Abend** in the morning/afternoon/evening • **am Ende (von)** at the end (of) • **am Freitag** on Friday
am Freitagmorgen on Friday morning • **am nächsten Morgen/Tag** the next morning/day • **am Wochenende** at the weekend
amerikanische(r) Ureinwohner/in *(Indianer/in)* Native American [ˌneɪtɪv‿əˈmerɪkən]
Amnestie amnesty [ˈæmnəsti]
amüsieren: sich amüsieren have fun [hæv ˈfʌn]
an 1. an anderen Orten *(anderswo)* in other places • **an dem/den Tisch (dort)** at that table • **an der Spitze** at the top (of) • **an der/die Tafel** on the board • **an jenem Tag** that day • **schreiben an** write to
2. *(nahe bei)* **an der See** by the sea
3. Was war das Beste an ...? What was the best thing about ...?
4. an sein *(Radio, Licht usw.)* be on
Analyse analysis [əˈnæləsɪs], *pl* analyses [əˈnæləsiːz]
anbauen *(Getreide usw.)* grow [ɡrəʊ]
anbieten offer [ˈɒfə]
andere(r, s) other [ˈʌðə] • **die anderen** the others • **ein(e) andere(r, s) ...** another ... [əˈnʌðə]
(irgend)etwas anderes anything else [els] • **irgendjemand ande-**

res anybody/anyone else • **(noch) jemand anderes** somebody/someone else
▶ S.170 ... else
ändern; sich ändern change [tʃeɪndʒ]
▶ S.180 (to) change – change
anders (als) different (from) ['dɪfrənt] **anders ausdrücken** *(umschreiben)* paraphrase ['pærəfreɪz] • **anders herum** the other way round
anderswo in other places
Änderung change [tʃeɪndʒ]
▶ S.180 (to) change – change
anfahren: jn. anfahren run into sb.
Anfang beginning [bɪ'gɪnɪŋ]; start [stɑ:t] • **am Anfang** at first [fɜ:st]
anfangen (mit) begin [bɪ'gɪn]; start [stɑ:t]
anfassen touch [tʌtʃ]
anfühlen: sich gut anfühlen feel good [fi:l]
Anführer/in leader ['li:də]
angehen *(Licht)* go on
angeln fish [fɪʃ]
angreifen attack [ə'tæk]
Angriff attack [ə'tæk]
Angst haben (vor) be afraid (of) [ə'freɪd]; be scared (of) [skeəd] **schreckliche Angst haben (vor)** be terrified (of) ['terɪfaɪd]
anhaben *(Kleidung)* wear [weə]
anhalten stop [stɒp]
Anhänger/in *(Fan)* supporter [sə'pɔ:tə]
anhören 1. sich etwas anhören listen to sth. ['lɪsn] **2. sich gut anhören** sound good [saʊnd]
Anker anchor ['æŋkə]
anklicken: etwas anklicken click on sth. [klɪk]
anklopfen (an) knock (on) [nɒk]
ankommen arrive [ə'raɪv]
ankündigen announce [ə'naʊns]
Ankündigung announcement [ə'naʊnsmənt]
Ankunft arrival (arr) [ə'raɪvl]
anlächeln: jn. anlächeln smile at sb. [smaɪl]
Anleitung(en) *(Gebrauchsanweisungen)* instructions *(pl)* [ɪn'strʌkʃnz]
anmailen: jn. anmailen mail sb. [meɪl]
anmalen paint [peɪnt]; *(bunt ausmalen)* colour ['kʌlə]
annähen: etwas annähen sew sth. on [səʊ]
annehmen *(vermuten)* suppose [sə'pəʊz]
Anorak anorak ['ænəræk]
anpassen: sich anpassen fit in [ˌfɪt_'ɪn]
anpflanzen *(Getreide usw.)* grow [grəʊ]
anprobieren *(Kleidung)* try on [ˌtraɪ_'ɒn]
Anruf call [kɔ:l]; phone call ['fəʊn kɔ:l]
anrufen call [kɔ:l]; phone [fəʊn]
Ansage *(Durchsage)* announcement [ə'naʊnsmənt]
anschauen look at [lʊk]
Anschlagtafel notice board ['nəʊtɪs bɔ:d] *(BE)*; bulletin board ['bʊlətɪn bɔ:d] *(AE)*
anschließen: sich jm. anschließen join sb. [dʒɔɪn]
anschreien shout at [ʃaʊt]
ansehen: sich etwas ansehen look at sth. [lʊk]; watch sth. [wɒtʃ]
Ansicht: meiner/deiner Ansicht nach in my/your view [vju:]
anspucken: jn. anspucken spit at sb. [spɪt]
Antwort (auf) answer (to) ['ɑ:nsə]
antworten answer ['ɑ:nsə]
Anweisung(en) *(Gebrauchsanweisungen)* instructions *(pl)* [ɪn'strʌkʃnz]
anziehen: etwas anziehen *(Kleidung)* put sth. on [ˌpʊt_'ɒn] • **sich anziehen** get dressed [get 'drest]
Anzug suit [su:t]
anzünden light [laɪt]
Apfel apple ['æpl]
Apfelsine orange ['ɒrɪndʒ]
Apotheke chemist ['kemɪst]
Apotheker: beim Apotheker at the chemist's ['kemɪsts]
Appetit appetite ['æpɪtaɪt]
April April ['eɪprəl]
Arbeit work [wɜ:k] • **bei der Arbeit/ am Arbeitsplatz** at work
arbeiten (an) work (on) [wɜ:k]
Arbeiter/in worker ['wɜ:kə]
Arbeitsblatt worksheet ['wɜ:kʃi:t]
arbeitslos jobless ['dʒɒbləs]
Arbeitsplatz workplace ['wɜ:kpleɪs]
Arbeits- und Lerntechniken study skills ['stʌdi skɪlz]
Archiv archive ['ɑ:kaɪv]
Ärger *(Schwierigkeiten)* trouble ['trʌbl] • **Ärger kriegen** be in trouble
ärgern: jn. ärgern *(kränken)* upset sb. [ʌp'set]
Argument argument ['ɑ:gjumənt] **ein Argument vorbringen** make a point
arm poor [pɔ:, pʊə]
Arm arm [ɑ:m]
Armbanduhr watch [wɒtʃ]
Art 1. *(Sorte)* kind (of) [kaɪnd] **2. Art und Weise** way [weɪ]
Artikel article ['ɑ:tɪkl]
Arzt/Ärztin doctor ['dɒktə] • **zum Arzt** to the doctor's
Atlantik Atlantic (Ocean) [ət'læntɪk]
Atmosphäre atmosphere ['ætməsfɪə]
Attraktion attraction [ə'trækʃn]
auch: auch aus Bristol from Bristol too [tu:]; also from Bristol ['ɔ:lsəʊ] **Ich auch.** Me too.
auf on [ɒn] • **auf (... hinauf)** onto ['ɒntə, 'ɒntʊ] • **auf dem Bild/Foto** in the picture/photo • **auf dem Feld** in the field • **auf dem Hof** in the yard • **auf dem Land** *(im Gegensatz zur Stadt)* in the country; *(nicht auf dem Wasser)* on land **auf dem Weg (zu/nach)** on the way (to) • **auf der Erde** on earth **auf der ganzen Welt** all over the world • **auf diese Weise** that way; this way • **auf einmal** suddenly ['sʌdnli] • **auf Englisch** in English **Auf geht's!** Let's go. • **auf jn./etwas zu** towards sb./sth. [tə'wɔ:dz] **Auf keinen Fall!** No way! • **Auf welcher Seite sind wir?** What page are we on? • **Auf Wiedersehen.** Goodbye. [ˌgʊd'baɪ]
aufbewahren keep [ki:p]
auffordern: jn. auffordern, etwas zu tun tell sb. to do sth.
aufführen *(Szene, Dialog)* act [ækt]
Aufgabe *(im Schulbuch)* exercise ['eksəsaɪz]; *(Job)* job [dʒɒb]
aufgeben give up
aufgebracht (wegen) upset (about) [ˌʌp'set]
aufgeräumt *(ordentlich)* tidy ['taɪdi]
aufgeregt *(nervös)* nervous ['nɜ:vəs]; *(begeistert)* excited [ɪk'saɪtɪd]
aufheben: etwas aufheben *(hochheben)* pick sth. up [ˌpɪk_'ʌp]
aufhören stop [stɒp]
auflegen *(Musik/CDs/Platten; in der Disko)* DJ ['di: dʒeɪ]
auflisten list [lɪst]
aufmachen open ['əʊpən]
Aufnahme *(Aufzeichnung)* recording [rɪ'kɔ:dɪŋ]
aufnehmen 1. *(aufzeichnen; Musik)* record [rɪ'kɔ:d] **2. mit jm. Kontakt aufnehmen** contact sb. ['kɒntækt]
aufpassen: auf etwas/jn. aufpassen look after sth./sb. [ˌlʊk_'ɑ:ftə]
aufräumen tidy ['taɪdi]
aufregend exciting [ɪk'saɪtɪŋ]
Aufsatz essay ['eseɪ]
aufschauen (von) look up (from)
aufschreiben write down [ˌraɪt 'daʊn]
aufschreien cry out [ˌkraɪ_'aʊt]
aufsetzen: etwas aufsetzen *(Hut, Helm)* put sth. on

aufstehen *(sich erheben)* stand up [ˌstænd_ˈʌp]; get up [ˌget_ˈʌp]; *(aus dem Bett)* get up
aufsteigen *(in die Höhe steigen)* rise [raɪz]
aufsuchen: jn. aufsuchen see sb. [siː]
auftauchen *(erscheinen)* appear [əˈpɪə]
Auftritt *(Konzert)* gig [gɪg] *(infml)* **einen Auftritt haben** *(ein Konzert geben)* do a gig
aufwachen wake up [ˌweɪk_ˈʌp]
aufwachsen grow up [ˌgrəʊ_ˈʌp]
aufwecken: jn. aufwecken wake sb. (up) [ˌweɪk_ˈʌp]
aufwischen *(Fußboden)* wash [wɒʃ]
aufzählen *(auflisten)* list [lɪst]
aufzeichnen *(Musik)* record [rɪˈkɔːd]
Aufzeichnung *(Aufnahme)* recording [rɪˈkɔːdɪŋ]
Aufzug lift [lɪft] *(BE)*; elevator [ˈelɪveɪtə] *(AE)*
Auge eye [aɪ]
Augenblick moment [ˈməʊmənt]
August August [ˈɔːgəst]
aus: Ich komme/bin aus ... I'm from ... • **aus ... (heraus/hinaus)** out of ... • **aus der ganzen Welt** from all over the world • **aus dem Zug/Bus aussteigen** get off the train/bus • **aus ganz Wales** from all around Wales / from all over Wales • **aus meiner Sicht** from my point of view • **aus vielen Gründen** for lots of reasons
aus zweiter Hand *(gebraucht)* second-hand [ˌsekənd ˈhænd]
Ausbildung education [ˌedʒuˈkeɪʃn]
ausdenken: sich etwas ausdenken think of sth. [θɪŋk]
Ausdruck *((Rede-)Wendung)* phrase [freɪz]
ausdrucken: etwas ausdrucken print sth. out [ˌprɪnt_ˈaʊt]
ausdrücken: anders ausdrücken *(umschreiben)* paraphrase [ˈpærəfreɪz]
auseinander apart [əˈpɑːt]
Ausflug trip [trɪp] • **einen Ausflug machen** go on a trip
ausgeben: Geld ausgeben (für) spend money (on) [spend]
ausgehen *(weg-, rausgehen)* go out **mit jm. ausgehen** *(regelmäßig)* date sb. [deɪt] • **gut ausgehen** work out [ˌwɜːk_ˈaʊt]
ausgestellt sein/werden be on display [dɪˈspleɪ]
ausgezeichnet excellent [ˈeksələnt] ► S.179 US school grades
aushalten: Ich halt's aus. / Ich kann's aushalten. I can take it.
auslachen: jn. auslachen laugh at sb. [lɑːf]
Ausland: im Ausland abroad [əˈbrɔːd] **ins Ausland gehen/fahren** go abroad
ausländisch foreign [ˈfɒrən]
auslassen: etwas auslassen leave sth. out [ˌliːv_ˈaʊt]
ausmalen *(bunt anmalen, kolorieren)* colour [ˈkʌlə]
auspressen squeeze [skwiːz]
ausruhen: sich ausruhen relax [rɪˈlæks]
Ausrüstung equipment [ɪˈkwɪpmənt]
Aussage statement [ˈsteɪtmənt]
ausschalten: etwas ausschalten turn sth. off [ˌtɜːn_ˈɒf]
ausschließen: jn. von etwas ausschließen ban sb. from sth. [bæn]
aussehen: anders/toll/alt aussehen look different/great/old [lʊk] **fürchterlich aussehen** be a mess [mes] • **gleich aussehen** look the same
außer except [ɪkˈsept]
außerdem besides [bɪˈsaɪdz]
außerhalb seines Zimmers outside his room [ˌaʊtˈsaɪd]
aussetzen: Einmal aussetzen. Miss a turn. [tɜːn]
Aussicht *(Blick)* view [vjuː]
Aussprache pronunciation [prəˌnʌnsiˈeɪʃn]
aussteigen (aus dem Zug/Bus) get off (the train/bus) [ˌget_ˈɒf]
aussuchen: (sich) etwas aussuchen choose sth. [tʃuːz]
Austausch *(Schüleraustausch)* exchange [ɪksˈtʃeɪndʒ]
Austauschschüler/in exchange student [ɪksˈtʃeɪndʒ ˌstjuːdnt]
ausverkauft sein be sold out [ˌsəʊld_ˈaʊt]
auswählen choose [tʃuːz]
Auswertung analysis [əˈnæləsɪs], *pl* analyses [əˈnæləsiːz]
ausziehen 1. *(aus Wohnung)* move out [ˌmuːv_ˈaʊt] **2. etwas ausziehen** *(Kleidung)* take sth. off [ˌteɪk_ˈɒf]
Auto car [kɑː]; auto [ˈɔːtəʊ] *(AE)*
Autofahrt drive [draɪv]
Autsch! Ouch! [aʊtʃ]

B

Baby baby [ˈbeɪbi] • **ein Baby bekommen** have a baby
Badeanzug swimsuit [ˈswɪmsuːt]
Badehose swimming trunks *(pl)* [trʌŋks]
baden *(ein Bad nehmen)* have a bath [bɑːθ]
Badewanne bath [bɑːθ]
Badezimmer bathroom [ˈbɑːθruːm]
Badminton badminton [ˈbædmɪntən]
Badmintonschläger badminton racket [ˈrækɪt]
Bagel *(ringförmiges Brötchen)* bagel [ˈbeɪgl]
Bahnhof station [ˈsteɪʃn] • **am Bahnhof** at the station
Bahnsteig *(Gleis)* platform [ˈplætfɔːm]
bald soon [suːn]
Ball ball [bɔːl]; *(Tanzveranstaltung)* ball
Banane banana [bəˈnɑːnə]
Band *(Musikgruppe)* band [bænd]
Bank *(Geldinstitut)* bank [bæŋk]; *(zum Sitzen)* bench [bentʃ]
Bankräuber/in bank robber [ˈrɒbə]
Bär bear [beə]
Bar bar [bɑː]
Bart beard [bɪəd]
Baseball baseball [ˈbeɪsbɔːl]
Baseballmütze baseball cap [kæp]
Basketball basketball [ˈbɑːskɪtbɔːl]
Bauchweh stomach ache [ˈstʌmək_eɪk]
bauen build [bɪld]
Bauer/Bäuerin farmer [ˈfɑːmə]
Bauernhof farm [fɑːm]
Baum tree [triː]
Baumwolle cotton [ˈkɒtn]
beantragen: etwas beantragen apply (for sth.) [əˈplaɪ]
beantworten answer [ˈɑːnsə]
bedeuten mean [miːn]
Bedeutung meaning [ˈmiːnɪŋ]
Bedienstete(r) servant [ˈsɜːvənt]
beeilen: sich beeilen hurry [ˈhʌri]; hurry up [ˌhʌri_ˈʌp]
beeindruckend grand [grænd]
beeindruckt impressed [ɪmˈprest]
beenden finish [ˈfɪnɪʃ]; end [end]
Begabung talent [ˈtælənt]
Begegnung meeting [ˈmiːtɪŋ]
begeistert excited [ɪkˈsaɪtɪd]
Beginn beginning; start [stɑːt]
beginnen (mit) begin [bɪˈgɪn]; start [stɑːt]
Begnadigung amnesty [ˈæmnəsti]
begreifen understand [ˌʌndəˈstænd]
Begründung *(Grund)* reason [ˈriːzn]; *(Argument)* argument [ˈɑːgjumənt]
behalten keep [kiːp]
behindert disabled [dɪsˈeɪbld]
bei: bei den Shaws zu Hause at the Shaws' house • **bei der Arbeit** at work • **Englisch bei Mr Kingsley** English with Mr Kingsley • **beim Apotheker** at the chemist's **beim Friseur** at the hairdresser's

beide both [bəʊθ] • **2 beide** *(2:2 unentschieden)* 2 all

Bein leg [leg] • **etwas auf die Beine stellen** get sth. off the ground

beinahe almost ['ɔ:lməʊst]

Beispiel example [ɪg'zɑ:mpl] • **zum Beispiel** for example

bekämpfen fight [faɪt]

bekannt known [nəʊn]

Bekanntgabe announcement [ə'naʊnsmənt]

bekanntgeben announce [ə'naʊns]

bekommen get [get] • **ein Baby bekommen** have a baby

belebt *(Straße; Ort)* busy ['bɪzi]

beliebig: jede(r, s) beliebige ... any ... ► S.176 any

Bemerkung *(Kommentar)* comment ['kɒment]

benachteiligen: jn. benachteiligen discriminate against sb. [dɪ'skrɪmɪneɪt]

Benachteiligung (von) discrimination (against) [dɪˌskrɪmɪ'neɪʃn]

benennen name [neɪm]

benötigen need [ni:d]

benutzen use [ju:z]

Benzin petrol ['petrəl] *(BE)*; gas [gæs] *(AE)*

beobachten watch [wɒtʃ]

bequem comfortable ['kʌmftəbl] **Machen Sie es sich bequem. / Mach es dir bequem.** Make yourself comfortable.

Bereich area ['eəriə]; section ['sekʃn]

bereit ready ['redi] • **sich bereit erklären** *(freiwillig)* volunteer [ˌvɒlən'tɪə]

bereits already [ɔ:l'redi]

Berg mountain ['maʊntən]

Bericht (über) report (on) [rɪ'pɔ:t]

berichten (über) tell (about) [tel] **(jm.) etwas berichten** report sth. (to sb.) [rɪ'pɔ:t]

berichtigen correct [kə'rekt]

beruhigen: sich beruhigen calm down [ˌkɑ:m 'daʊn]

berühmt (für, wegen) famous (for) ['feɪməs]

berühren touch [tʌtʃ]

beschäftigt busy ['bɪzi]

Bescheid: über etwas Bescheid wissen know about sth. [nəʊ]

beschließen decide [dɪ'saɪd]

beschreiben: (jm.) etwas beschreiben describe sth. (to sb.) [dɪ'skraɪb] **jm. den Weg beschreiben** tell sb. the way

Beschreibung description [dɪ'skrɪpʃn]

beschützen: jn. beschützen (vor) protect sb. (from) [prə'tekt]

besiegen beat [bi:t]

besondere(r, s) special ['speʃl] • **Was ist das Besondere an ...?** What's special about ...?

besorgen *(holen)* get [get]

besorgt sein (wegen/um) be worried (about) ['wʌrid]

Besprechung meeting ['mi:tɪŋ]

besprühen spray [spreɪ]

besser better ['betə]

beste: am besten (the) best [best] **der/die/das beste ...; die besten ...** the best ... • **Was war das Beste an ...?** What was the best thing about ...?

bestehen: eine Prüfung bestehen pass an exam [pɑ:s] • **eine Prüfung nicht bestehen** fail an exam [feɪl]

bestimmte(r, s) *(spezifische(r, s))* specific [spə'sɪfɪk]

Besuch visit ['vɪzɪt]

besuchen: jn. besuchen visit sb. ['vɪzɪt]; see sb. [si:]

Besucher/in visitor ['vɪzɪtə]

beteiligen: sich beteiligen (an) get involved (in) [ɪn'vɒlvd]

Betonung stress [stres]

Betreff: ... Re: ... [ri:]

betreten *(eintreten in)* enter ['entə]

betrunken drunk [drʌŋk]

Bett bed [bed]

beugen: sich beugen *(sich lehnen)* lean [li:n]

beunruhigt sein (wegen/um) be worried (about) ['wʌrid]

beurteilen (nach) judge (by) [dʒʌdʒ]

Beutel bag [bæg]

Bevölkerung population [ˌpɒpju'leɪʃn]

bevor before [bɪ'fɔ:]

bewegen: sich bewegen move [mu:v]

Bewegung movement ['mu:vmənt]; *(körperlich, als Training)* exercise *(no pl)*

Beweis(e) proof *(no pl)* [pru:f]

bewerben: sich bewerben (um/für etwas) apply (for sth.) [ə'plaɪ]

bewölkt cloudy ['klaʊdi]

bewusstlos unconscious [ʌn'kɒnʃəs]

bezahlen: etwas bezahlen pay for sth. [peɪ]

beziehen: sich beziehen auf refer to [rɪ'fɜ:]

Beziehungen relations *(pl)* [rɪ'leɪʃnz]

Bezirk *(Stadtbezirk)* borough ['bʌrə, *AE:* 'bɜ:rəʊ] ► S.172 New York: the five boroughs

Bibliothek library ['laɪbrəri]

Bild picture ['pɪktʃə] • **auf dem Bild** in the picture

bilden; sich bilden form [fɔ:m]

Bildschirm monitor ['mɒnɪtə]

Bildung education [ˌedʒu'keɪʃn]

Bildunterschrift caption ['kæpʃn]

billig cheap [tʃi:p]

binden tie [taɪ]

Bindewort linking word ['lɪŋkɪŋ wɜ:d]

Biografie biography [baɪ'ɒgrəfi]

Biologie biology [baɪ'ɒlədʒi]

bis *(zeitlich)* until [ən'tɪl]; till [tɪl] **Bis bald.** See you. ['si: ju:] • **bis jetzt / bis hierher** so far • **bis (spätestens) zehn Uhr** by ten o'clock • **von Montag bis Freitag** from Monday to Friday

bisschen: ein bisschen a bit [bɪt]; a little ['lɪtl]

bitte 1. *(in Fragen und Aufforderungen)* please [pli:z] **2. Bitte sehr. / Hier bitte.** Here you are **3. Bitte, gern geschehen.** You're welcome. ['welkəm] **4. Wie bitte?** Sorry? ['sɒri]

bitten: jn. um etwas bitten ask sb. for sth. [ɑ:sk]

blasen *(wehen)* blow [bləʊ]

blau blue [blu:]

bleiben stay [steɪ] • **in Verbindung bleiben** keep in touch [tʌtʃ] • **Bleib ruhig.** Don't panic. ['pænɪk]

Bleistift pencil ['pensl]

Bleistiftanspitzer pencil sharpener ['pensl ʃɑ:pnə]

Blick *(Aussicht)* view [vju:]

Block *(Häuser-, Wohnblock)* block [blɒk]

Blockflöte recorder [rɪ'kɔ:də]

blockieren block [blɒk]

blöd stupid ['stju:pɪd]

blond blond [blɒnd]

bloß just [dʒʌst]; only ['əʊnli]

Blume flower ['flaʊə]

Bluse blouse [blaʊz]

Blut blood [blʌd]

Blüte flower ['flaʊə]

Boden *(Erdboden)* ground [graʊnd]

Bohne bean [bi:n]

Boot boat [bəʊt]

böse sein (über etwas/auf jn.) be angry (about sth./with sb.) ['æŋgri]

Boss boss [bɒs]

Boulevard boulevard ['bu:ləvɑ:d]

brainstormen *(so viele Ideen wie möglich sammeln)* brainstorm ['breɪnstɔ:m]

Brand fire ['faɪə]

brauchen need [ni:d]; *(Zeit brauchen, dauern)* take [teɪk] • **nicht zu tun brauchen** needn't do ['ni:dnt]

braun brown [braʊn]

brav good [gʊd]

brechen *(kaputt gehen)* break [breɪk]

brennen burn [bɜ:n]

Brief (an) letter (to) ['letə]

Brieffreund/in *(im Internet)* e-friend ['i:frend]
Briefmarke stamp [stæmp]
Brille: (eine) Brille glasses *(pl)* ['glɑ:sɪz]
bringen: (mit-, her)bringen bring [brɪŋ] • **(weg-, hin)bringen** take [teɪk] • **auf den Markt bringen** *(CD usw.)* release [rɪ'li:s] • **etwas auf den Weg bringen** get sth. off the ground • **ein Flugzeug in seine Macht bringen** take over a plane
britisch; Brite, Britin British ['brɪtɪʃ]
Broschüre booklet ['bʊklət]
Brot bread *(no pl)* [bred]
Brötchen roll [rəʊl]
Brücke bridge [brɪdʒ]
Bruder brother ['brʌðə]
Buch book [bʊk]
Bücherei library ['laɪbrəri]
Buchstabe letter ['letə]
buchstabieren spell [spel]
Bucht bay [beɪ]
Bühne stage [steɪdʒ]
bunt an-, ausmalen colour ['kʌlə]
Burg castle ['kɑ:sl]
Bürgerkrieg civil war [,sɪvl 'wɔ:]
Bürgermeister/in mayor [meə]
Bürgerrechte civil rights *(pl)* [,sɪvl 'raɪts]
Bürgersteig pavement ['peɪvmənt] *(BE)*; sidewalk ['saɪdwɔ:k] *(AE)*
Büro office ['ɒfɪs]
Bus bus [bʌs]
Bushaltestelle bus stop ['bʌs stɒp]
Bus-Monatskarte bus pass ['bʌs pɑ:s]
Butter butter ['bʌtə]

C

Café café ['kæfeɪ]
Camp camp [kæmp]
Campingausrüstung, Campingsachen camping gear *(no pl)* ['kæmpɪŋ gɪə]
Cañon canyon ['kænjən]
Cartoon cartoon [kɑ:'tu:n]
CD CD [,si:'di:] • **CD-Spieler** CD player [,si:'di: ,pleɪə]
Celsius Celsius (C) ['selsiəs]
Cent cent (c) [sent]
Champion champion ['tʃæmpiən]
Chance *(Gelegenheit; Aussicht)* chance [tʃɑ:ns]
Charakter character ['kærəktə]
Chat *(Unterhaltung)* chat [tʃæt]
Chatroom chat room ['tʃæt ru:m]
chatten chat [tʃæt]
Cheerleader *(Stimmungsanheizer/in bei Sportereignissen)* cheerleader ['tʃɪəli:də]
Chef/in boss [bɒs]
Chor choir ['kwaɪə]
clever clever ['klevə]; smart [smɑ:t]
Cola cola ['kəʊlə]
Comedy comedy ['kɒmədi]
Comic-Heft comic ['kɒmɪk]
Computer computer [kəm'pju:tə]
cool cool [ku:l]
Cornflakes cornflakes ['kɔ:nfleɪks]
Court *(für Squash, Badminton)* court [kɔ:t]
Cousin, Cousine cousin ['kʌzn]
Creme cream [kri:m]

D

da *(weil)* since [sɪns]
da, dahin *(dort, dorthin)* there [ðeə] **da drüben** over there [,əʊvə 'ðeə]
dableiben *(zurückbleiben)* stay behind [,steɪ bɪ'haɪnd]
daheim at home [ət 'həʊm]
daher so [səʊ]
damit *(sodass)* so that
danach *(zeitlich)* after that [,ɑ:ftə 'ðæt]
Danke. Thank you. ['θæŋk ju:]; Thanks. • **Danke sehr!** Thanks very much! • **Vielen Dank!** Thanks a lot!
dann then [ðen]
darstellende Kunst drama ['drɑ:mə]
darum that's why ['ðæts ,waɪ]
das 1. *(Artikel)* the [ðə, ði] **2.** *(Relativpronomen)* **das Mädchen, das ...** the girl who ... / the girl that ... • **das Auto, das ...** the car that ... / the car which ...
das (dort) *(Singular)* that [ðət, ðæt]; *(Plural)* those [ðəʊz] • **Das bin ich.** That's me. • **Das liegt bei dir. / Das kannst/musst du (selbst) entscheiden.** That's up to you.
dass that [ðət, ðæt]
dasselbe the same [seɪm]
Date *(Verabredung)* date [deɪt]
Datum date [deɪt]
dauern last (for) [lɑ:st]; *(Zeit brauchen)* take [teɪk]
davonmachen: sich davonmachen *(sich aus dem Staub machen)* take off *(infml)* [,teɪk‿'ɒf]
Debatte debate [dɪ'beɪt]
debattieren debate [dɪ'beɪt]
Decke *(zum Zudecken)* blanket ['blæŋkɪt]
decken: den Tisch decken lay the table [,leɪ ðə 'teɪbl]
dein(e) ... your ... [jɔ:]
deiner, deine, deins yours [jɔ:z]
Demonstration march [mɑ:tʃ]
denken think [θɪŋk] • **denken an** think of • **Was denkst du über ...?** What do you think about/of ...?
Denkmal monument ['mɒnjumənt]
deprimierend depressing [dɪ'presɪŋ]
deprimiert depressed [dɪ'prest]
der 1. *(Artikel)* the [ðə, ði] **2.** *(Relativpronomen)* **der Mann, der ...** the man who ... / the man that ... • **der Laden, der ...** the shop that ... / the shop which ...
derselbe the same [seɪm]
deshalb so [səʊ]; that's why ['ðæts ,waɪ]
Detail detail ['di:teɪl]
Detektiv/in detective [dɪ'tektɪv]
deuten (auf etwas) *(zeigen)* point (at/to sth.) [pɔɪnt]
deutlich clear [klɪə]
Deutsch; deutsch; Deutsche(r) German ['dʒɜ:mən]
Deutschland Germany ['dʒɜ:məni]
Dezember December [dɪ'sembə]
Dialog dialogue ['daɪəlɒg]
dich you [ju:] • **dich (selbst)** *(Reflexivpronomen)* yourself [jə'self, jɔ:'self]
dick fat [fæt]
die 1. *(Artikel)* the [ðə, ði] **2.** *(Relativpronomen)* **die Frau, die ...** the woman who ... / the woman that ... • **die Jacke, die ...** the jacket that ... / the jacket which ...
die (dort) *(Singular)* that [ðət, ðæt]; *(Plural)* those [ðəʊz] • **die (hier)** *(Singular)* this [ðɪs]; *(Plural)* these [ði:z]
Dieb/in thief [θi:f], *pl* thieves [θi:vz]
Diele hall [hɔ:l]
Diener/in servant ['sɜ:vənt]
Dienstag Tuesday ['tju:zdeɪ, 'tju:zdi] *(siehe auch unter „Freitag")*
dies (hier); diese(r, s) *(Singular)* this [ðɪs]; *(Plural)* these [ði:z]
dieselbe(n) the same [seɪm]
Ding thing [θɪŋ]
Dinosaurier dinosaur ['daɪnəsɔ:]
dir you [ju:] • **dir (selbst)** *(Reflexivpronomen)* yourself [jə'self, jɔ:'self]
direkt: direkt auf jn. zu straight towards sb. [streɪt] • **direkt hinter dir** right behind you • **direkte Frage** direct question [də'rekt, daɪ'rekt] **direkte Rede** direct speech
Diskjockey disc jockey ['dɪsk dʒɒki]; DJ ['di: dʒeɪ]
Disko disco ['dɪskəʊ]
diskriminieren: jn. diskriminieren discriminate against sb. [dɪ'skrɪmɪneɪt]
Diskriminierung (von) discrimination (against) [dɪ,skrɪmɪ'neɪʃn]

Diskussion discussion [dɪ'skʌʃn]
Doktor doctor ['dɒktə]
Dokumentarfilm, -beitrag documentary [ˌdɒkju'mentri]
Dollar dollar ($) ['dɒlə]
Dom cathedral [kə'θi:drəl]
Donnerstag Thursday ['θɜ:zdeɪ, 'θɜ:zdi] *(siehe auch unter „Freitag")*
doppelklicken double-click ['dʌblklɪk]
doppelt, Doppel- double ['dʌbl]
Dorf village ['vɪlɪdʒ]
dort, dorthin there [ðeə] • **dort drinnen** in there • **dort drüben** over there • **dort oben** up there **dort unten** down there
Dossier dossier ['dɒsieɪ]
downloaden download [ˌdaʊn'ləʊd]
Drachen kite [kaɪt]
Drama drama ['drɑ:mə]
dran: Ich bin dran. It's my turn. [tɜ:n] **Wer ist dran** Whose turn is it? [hu:z]
draußen outside [ˌaʊt'saɪd]; out [aʊt] **nach draußen** outside • **draußen bleiben** stay out
dreieinhalb Tage/Wochen three and a half days/weeks [hɑ:f]
Dreizehnjährige(r) thirteen-year-old
drinnen inside [ˌɪn'saɪd] • **dort drinnen** in there [ˌɪn 'ðeə] • **hier drinnen** in here [ˌɪn 'hɪə] • **nach drinnen** inside
dritte(r, s) third [θɜ:d]
Droge drug [drʌg]
Drogerie chemist ['kemɪst]
drüben: da/dort drüben over there [ˌəʊvə 'ðeə]
drücken push [pʊʃ]; press [pres]; *(pressen)* squeeze [skwi:z] • **auf etwas drücken** press sth.
du you [ju:]
Dudelsack bagpipes *(pl)* ['bægpaɪps]
dumm stupid ['stju:pɪd]; *(albern)* silly ['sɪli]
dunkel dark [dɑ:k]
durch through [θru:]; *(in ... umher)* around [ə'raʊnd] • **durch die Stadt** around the town
durcheinander: alles durcheinanderbringen make a mess [ˌmeɪk_ə 'mes]
durchfallen *(eine Prüfung nicht bestehen)* fail an exam [feɪl]
durchführen: ein Projekt durchführen do a project
durchlesen: etwas sorgfältig durchlesen study sth. ['stʌdi]
Durchsage announcement [ə'naʊnsmənt]
Durchschnitt average ['ævərɪdʒ]
durchschnittlich average ['ævərɪdʒ] ► S.179 US school grades
durchsichtig see-through ['si:θru:]
dürfen can [kən, kæn]; may [meɪ]; be allowed to [ə'laʊd] • **nicht dürfen** mustn't ['mʌsnt]
Durst haben, durstig sein be thirsty ['θɜ:sti]
Dusche shower ['ʃaʊə]
duschen; sich duschen have a shower ['ʃaʊə]
DVD DVD [ˌdi: vi: 'di:]
DVD-Rekorder DVD recorder

E

Ebbe und Flut *(Gezeiten)* tide [taɪd] **es ist Ebbe** the tide is out
echt real [rɪəl]
Ecke corner ['kɔ:nə] • **Sand Street, Ecke London Road** on the corner of Sand Street and London Road
egal: Es/Das ist mir egal. I don't care. [keə] • **Ist (doch) egal.** Never mind. [ˌnevə 'maɪnd]
Ehefrau wife [waɪf], *pl* wives [waɪvz]
Ehemann husband ['hʌzbənd]
Ei egg [eg]
Eichhörnchen squirrel ['skwɪrəl]
eifersüchtig (auf) jealous (of) ['dʒeləs]
eigene(r, s): unser eigenes Schwimmbad our own pool [əʊn]
eigentlich *(in Wirklichkeit)* actually ['æktʃuəli]
Eile: in Eile sein be in a hurry ['hʌri]
eilen *(sich beeilen)* hurry ['hʌri]
eilig: es eilig haben be in a hurry ['hʌri]
ein(e) a, an [ə, ən]; one [wʌn] **ein(e) andere(r, s) ...** another ... [ə'nʌðə] • **eine Menge** a lot (of) [lɒt]; lots (of) [lɒts] • **ein neuer / eine neue / ein neues** a new one [wʌn] • **ein paar** some [səm, sʌm]; *(einige wenige)* a few [fju:] • **eines Tages** one day
einander *(sich gegenseitig)* one another [ˌwʌn_ə'nʌðə]; each other [i:tʃ_'ʌðə]
eindrucksvoll grand [grænd]
einfach *(nicht schwierig)* easy ['i:zi] **einfach (nur)** just [dʒʌst] • **einfache Fahrkarte** *(nur Hinfahrt)* single (ticket) ['sɪŋgl]
Einfall *(Idee)* idea [aɪ'dɪə]
einfügen: sich einfügen *(sich anpassen)* fit in [ˌfɪt_'ɪn]
Eingangshalle lobby ['lɒbi]
eingeben: etwas eingeben *(in den Computer)* enter sth. ['entə]
eingeschaltet sein *(Radio, Licht usw.)* be on
eingewöhnen: sich eingewöhnen settle down [ˌsetl 'daʊn]
einige some [səm, sʌm]; *(einige wenige)* a few [fju:]
einigen: sich einigen (auf) agree (on) [ə'gri:]
einkaufen: einkaufen gehen go shopping [ˌgəʊ 'ʃɒpɪŋ]
Einkaufen shopping ['ʃɒpɪŋ]
Einkaufszentrum (shopping) mall [mɔ:l]
einladen (zu) invite (to) [ɪn'vaɪt]
Einladung (zu) invitation (to) [ˌɪnvɪ'teɪʃn]
einmal once [wʌns] • **auf einmal** suddenly ['sʌdnli] • **Einmal aussetzen.** Miss a turn. [tɜ:n] • **früher einmal** once • **(noch) nicht einmal** not even • **noch einmal** once more/once again
einpacken pack [pæk]
einpflanzen plant [plɑ:nt]
einreisen: in ein Land einreisen enter a country ['entə]
eins, ein, eine one ['wʌn]
einsam lonely ['ləʊnli]
einschalten *(Computer usw.)* turn on [ˌtɜ:n_'ɒn]
einschätzen (nach) judge (by) [dʒʌdʒ]
einschüchtern bully ['bʊli]
einst *(früher einmal)* once [wʌns]
einsteigen (in den Zug/Bus) get on (the train/bus) [ˌget_'ɒn]
Einstellung (zu) attitude (to, towards) ['ætɪtju:d]
einstürzen collapse [kə'læps]
eintauschen: etwas eintauschen (für etwas/gegen etwas) swap sth. (for sth.) [swɒp]
Eintopf(gericht) stew [stju:]
Eintrag *(in Wörterbuch/Tagebuch)* entry ['entri]
eintragen: etwas eintragen *(in Formular)* enter sth. ['entə]
Eintragung *(in Tagebuch)* entry ['entri]
eintreffen *(ankommen)* arrive [ə'raɪv]
eintreten (in) *(Zimmer)* enter ['entə]
Eintritt admission [əd'mɪʃn]
Eintrittskarte ticket ['tɪkɪt]
Eintrittspreis admission [əd'mɪʃn]
Einwanderer/Einwanderin immigrant ['ɪmɪgrənt]
Einwohner(zahl) population [ˌpɒpju'leɪʃn]
Einzelheit detail ['di:teɪl]
einziehen *(in Wohnung)* move in [ˌmu:v_'ɪn]
einzig: der einzige Gast the only guest ['əʊnli]
Eis ice [aɪs]; *(Speiseeis)* ice cream [ˌaɪs 'kri:m]

Eisenbahn railway ['reɪlweɪ]
Eishockey ice hockey ['aɪs hɒki]
eislaufen skate [skeɪt]
Elefant elephant ['elɪfənt]
elektrisch, Elektro- electric [ɪ'lektrɪk]
Elektrizität electricity [ɪˌlek'trɪsəti]
elektronisch electronic [ɪˌlek'trɒnɪk]
Eltern parents ['peərənts]
E-Mail (an) e-mail (to) ['i:meɪl]
End- *(letzte/r/s)* final ['faɪnl]
Ende 1. end [end]; *(einer Geschichte, eines Films usw.)* ending ['endɪŋ] **am Ende (von)** at the end (of) • **zu Ende machen** finish ['fɪnɪʃ] • **zu Ende sein** be over ['əʊvə]
2. oberes Ende *(Spitze)* top [tɒp] **am oberen Ende** at the top
3. unteres Ende bottom ['bɒtəm] **am unteren Ende** at the bottom
enden finish ['fɪnɪʃ]; end [end]
endlich at last [ət 'lɑ:st]
endlos endless ['endləs]
Endspiel final ['faɪnl]
Endstand *(beim Sport)* final score [ˌfaɪnl 'skɔ:]
Endung ending ['endɪŋ]
Energie energy ['enədʒi]
engagieren: sich engagieren (für, bei) get involved (in) [ɪn'vɒlvd]
Engel angel ['eɪndʒl]
Englisch; englisch English ['ɪŋglɪʃ]
Enkel grandson ['grænsʌn]; grandchild ['græntʃaɪld], *pl* grandchildren ['græntʃɪldrən]
Enkelin granddaughter ['grændɔ:tə]; grandchild ['græntʃaɪld], *pl* grandchildren ['græntʃɪldrən]
entdecken discover [dɪ'skʌvə]; spot [spɒt]
Entdecker/in *(Forscher/in)* explorer [ɪk'splɔ:rə]
Entführer/in *(eines Flugzeugs)* hijacker ['haɪdʒækə]
enthalten contain [kən'teɪn]
entkommen escape [ɪ'skeɪp]
entlang der Straße / die Straße entlang along the street [ə'lɒŋ]
entscheiden: sich entscheiden (für) decide (on) [dɪ'saɪd] • **Das kannst/musst du (selbst) entscheiden.** That's up to you.
entschuldigen: sich entschuldigen say sorry ['sɒri]
Entschuldigung 1. *(Tut mir leid)* I'm sorry. ['sɒri] • **Entschuldigung, dass ich zu spät komme.** Sorry, I'm late.
2. Entschuldigung, ... *(Darf ich mal stören?)* Excuse me, ... [ɪk'skju:z mi:]
entspannen; sich entspannen relax [rɪ'læks]
entspannt relaxed [rɪ'lækst]
entwerfen design [dɪ'zaɪn]

er 1. *(männliche Person)* he [hi:]
2. *(Ding, Tier)* it [ɪt]
Erbse pea [pi:]
Erdbeben earthquake ['ɜ:θkweɪk]
Erdbeere strawberry ['strɔ:bəri]
Erde earth [ɜ:θ] • **auf der Erde** on earth
Erdgeschoss ground floor *(BE)*; first floor *(AE)*
► S.171 floor
Erdkunde geography [dʒi'ɒgrəfi]
Ereignis event [ɪ'vent]
erfahren experience [ɪk'spɪəriəns] **etwas über etwas erfahren** learn sth. about sth. [lɜ:n]
Erfahrung experience [ɪk'spɪəriəns]
Erfolg success [sək'ses] • **Erfolg haben (mit etwas, bei etwas)** succeed (in sth.) [sək'si:d]
erfolgreich successful [sək'sesfl] **erfolgreich sein (mit etwas, bei etwas)** succeed (in sth.) [sək'si:d]
erforschen explore [ɪk'splɔ:]
ergänzen add (to) [æd]
Ergebnis result [rɪ'zʌlt]
erinnern: sich erinnern (an) remember [rɪ'membə]
erkältet sein have a cold [kəʊld]
Erkältung cold [kəʊld] • **eine Erkältung haben** have a cold
erklären: jm. etwas erklären explain sth. to sb. [ɪk'spleɪn] • **sich bereit erklären** volunteer [ˌvɒlən'tɪə]
Erklärung explanation [ˌeksplə'neɪʃn]
erkunden explore [ɪk'splɔ:]
erlauben: jm. erlauben, etwas zu tun let sb. do sth. [let]
erlaubt sein be allowed [ə'laʊd]
erläutern: jm. etwas erläutern explain sth. to sb. [ɪk'spleɪn]
erleben experience [ɪk'spɪəriəns]
Erlebnis experience [ɪk'spɪəriəns]
ermorden murder ['mɜ:də]
ernst(haft) serious ['sɪəriəs]
Ernst: Im Ernst? Seriously? ['sɪəriəsli]
Ernte harvest ['hɑ:vɪst]
erraten guess [ges]
erreichen reach [ri:tʃ]
erscheinen *(auftauchen)* appear [ə'pɪə]
erst only ['əʊnli] • **erst Montag** *(nicht vor Montag)* not until/not till Monday • **erst um 3** *(nicht vor 3)* not until/not till 3 o'clock
erstaunlich surprising [sə'praɪzɪŋ]; amazing [ə'meɪzɪŋ]
erste(r, s) first [fɜ:st] • **als Erstes** first • **der erste Tag** the first day **der/die Erste sein** be first • **erster Stock** first floor *(BE)*; second floor *(AE)*
► S.171 floor

erwachsen werden grow up [ˌgrəʊ_'ʌp]
Erwachsene(r) adult ['ædʌlt]
erwarten expect [ɪk'spekt] • **ich kann es kaum erwarten, ... zu sehen** I can't wait to see ... [weɪt]
erwischen *(fangen)* catch [kætʃ]
erzählen (von) tell (about) [tel]
Erzählung story ['stɔ:ri]
Erzeugnis product ['prɒdʌkt]
Erziehung education [ˌedʒu'keɪʃn]
erzielen: einen Treffer erzielen *(Tor schießen)* score (a goal) [skɔ:], [gəʊl]
es it [ɪt] • **es gibt** *(es ist vorhanden)* there's; *(es sind vorhanden)* there are
Essen food [fu:d]; *(Mahlzeit)* meal [mi:l]
essen eat [i:t] • **Abendbrot essen** have dinner • **Toast zum Frühstück essen** have toast for breakfast
Esszimmer dining room ['daɪnɪŋ ru:m]
Etagenbett bunk (bed) [bʌŋk]
ethnisch ethnic ['eθnɪk]
etwas something ['sʌmθɪŋ]; *(irgendetwas)* anything ['eniθɪŋ]; *(ein bisschen)* a bit [bɪt]; a little ['lɪtl] **etwas Käse/Saft** some cheese/juice [səm, sʌm]
euch you [ju:] • **euch (selbst)** yourselves [jə'selvz, jɔ:'selvz]
euer, eure ... your ... [jɔ:]
eurer, eure, eures yours [jɔ:z]
Euro euro ['jʊərəʊ]
ewig *(eine Ewigkeit)* for ages; *(für immer)* forever [fər'evə]
Ewigkeit: eine Ewigkeit for ages ['eɪdʒɪz]
exakt exact [ɪg'zækt]
Examen exam [ɪg'zæm]
Exemplar copy ['kɒpi]
Explosion explosion [ɪk'spləʊʒn]

F

Fabrik factory ['fæktri]
Fachhochschule college ['kɒlɪdʒ]
fähig sein, etwas zu tun be able to do sth. ['eɪbl]
Fähre ferry ['feri]
fahren go [gəʊ]; *(ein Auto / mit dem Auto)* drive [draɪv] • **gegen etwas fahren** run into sth. • **in Urlaub fahren** go on holiday • **mit dem Auto/Zug/Rad/... fahren** go by car/train/bike/... • **Inliner/Skateboard fahren** skate [skeɪt] • **Rad fahren** cycle ['saɪkl]; ride a bike [ˌraɪd_ə 'baɪk]
Fahrer/in driver ['draɪvə]

Fahrkarte ticket ['tɪkɪt] • **einfache Fahrkarte** *(nur Hinfahrt)* single (ticket) ['sɪŋgl]
Fahrkartenautomat ticket machine ['tɪkɪt məˌʃi:n]
Fahrkartenschalter ticket office ['tɪkɪt_ˌɒfɪs]
Fahrplan timetable ['taɪmteɪbl] *(BE)*; schedule [*AE:* 'skedʒu:l, *BE:* 'ʃedju:l] *(AE)*
Fahrrad bike [baɪk]
Fahrstuhl lift [lɪft] *(BE)*; elevator ['elɪveɪtə] *(AE)*
Fahrt: (Auto-)Fahrt drive [draɪv] **(Rad-)Fahrt** (bike) ride [raɪd] **eine Fahrt machen** take a ride
fair fair [feə]
Fakt fact [fækt]
Fall 1. *(Kriminalfall)* case [keɪs] **2. Auf keinen Fall!** No way! [ˌnəʊ 'weɪ]
Falle trap [træp] • **(jm.) eine Falle stellen** set a trap (for sb.) [set]
fallen fall [fɔ:l]; drop [drɒp]
fallen lassen drop [drɒp]
falls if [ɪf]
falsch wrong [rɒŋ] • **in die falsche Richtung** the wrong way
Familie family ['fæməli]
Fan fan [fæn]; *(Unterstützer/in)* supporter [sə'pɔ:tə] • **Fan einer Mannschaft sein** support a team [sə'pɔ:t]
fangen catch [kætʃ]
Fantasie imagination [ɪˌmædʒɪ'neɪʃn]
fantastisch fantastic [fæn'tæstɪk]
Farbe colour ['kʌlə] • **Welche Farbe hat ...?** What colour is ...?
färben *(bunt an-, ausmalen)* colour
Farm farm [fɑ:m]
Fassung: jn. aus der Fassung bringen upset sb. [ʌp'set]
fast almost ['ɔ:lməʊst]
Fastfood fast food [ˌfɑ:st 'fu:d]
Faust fist [fɪst]
Favorit/in favourite ['feɪvərɪt]
Februar February ['februəri]
Federball badminton ['bædmɪntən]
Federmäppchen pencil case ['pensl keɪs]
fehlen *(nicht da sein)* be missing ['mɪsɪŋ] • **Was fehlt dir?** *(bei Krankheit)* What's wrong with you?
Fehler mistake [mɪ'steɪk]
feiern *(Party)* party ['pɑ:ti]; have a party
Feiertag holiday ['hɒlədeɪ]
Feind/in enemy ['enəmi]
Feld 1. field [fi:ld] • **auf dem Feld** in the field **2.** *(bei Brettspielen)* **Geh ein Feld vor.** Move on one space. [speɪs] **Geh ein Feld zurück.** Move back one space.

Fels, Felsen rock [rɒk]
Fenster window ['wɪndəʊ]
Ferien holidays ['hɒlədeɪz] *(BE)*; vacation [*AE:* veɪ'keɪʃn, *BE:* və'keɪʃn] *(AE)* **Ferien haben/machen** be on holiday
Fernsehen television ['telɪvɪʒn]; TV [ti:'vi:] • **im Fernsehen** on TV
fernsehen watch TV [ˌwɒtʃ ti:'vi:]
Fernsehprogramm TV listings *(pl)* ['lɪstɪŋz]
Fernsehspiel drama ['drɑ:mə]
Fernstraße *(in den USA, oft mit vier oder mehr Spuren)* highway ['haɪweɪ]
fertig *(bereit)* ready ['redi] • **sich fertig machen (für)** *(sich vorbereiten)* get ready (for) • **Dinge fertig machen (für)** get things ready (for)
fest tight [taɪt]
Fest, Festival festival ['festɪvl]
Feststellung *(Aussage)* statement ['steɪtmənt]
Fettdruck bold print [ˌbəʊld 'prɪnt]
Feuer fire ['faɪə]
Feuerwache fire station ['faɪə steɪʃn]
Feuerwehrfrau firewoman ['faɪəˌwʊmən]; firefighter ['faɪəfaɪtə]
Feuerwehrmann fireman ['faɪəmən]; firefighter ['faɪəfaɪtə]
Feuerwerk(skörper) fireworks *(pl)* ['faɪəwɜ:ks]
Fieber haben have a temperature ['temprətʃə]
Fiedel fiddle ['fɪdl] *(infml)*
Figur *(in Roman, Film)* character ['kærəktə]
Film film [fɪlm]; movie ['mu:vi]
filmen film [fɪlm]
Filmstar film star ['fɪlm stɑ:]
Filzstift felt tip ['felt tɪp]
Finale final ['faɪnl]
finden *(entdecken)* find [faɪnd]
Finger finger ['fɪŋgə]
Firma company ['kʌmpəni]
Fisch fish, *pl* fish [fɪʃ]
fischen fish [fɪʃ]
fit fit [fɪt]
Flasche bottle ['bɒtl] • **eine Flasche Milch** a bottle of milk
Fleisch meat [mi:t]
fliegen fly [flaɪ]
fliehen (vor jm./aus etwas) escape (from sb./sth.) [ɪ'skeɪp]
Flug flight [flaɪt]
Flügel wing [wɪŋ]
Flughafen airport ['eəpɔ:t]
Flugsteig gate [geɪt]
Flugzeug plane [pleɪn] • **im Flugzeug** on the plane
Flur hall [hɔ:l]

Fluss river ['rɪvə]
Flussdiagramm flow chart ['fləʊ tʃɑ:t]
Flusspferd hippo ['hɪpəʊ]
flüstern whisper ['wɪspə]
Flut: Ebbe und Flut *(Gezeiten)* tide [taɪd] • **es ist Flut** the tide is in
Folge *(einer Fernsehserie)* episode ['epɪsəʊd]
folgen follow ['fɒləʊ] • **die folgenden ...** the following ...
Folk *(englische, schottische, irische oder nordamerikanische Volksmusik des 20. Jahrhunderts)* folk (music) [fəʊk]
Football American football [əˌmerɪkən 'fʊtbɔ:l]
Form form [fɔ:m]
formen; sich formen form [fɔ:m]
Forscher/in *(Entdecker/in)* explorer [ɪk'splɔ:rə]
fort away [ə'weɪ]
Foto photo ['fəʊtəʊ] • **auf dem Foto** in the photo • **Fotos machen** take photos
Fotoapparat camera ['kæmərə]
Fotograf/in photographer [fə'tɒgrəfə]
fotografieren take photos [teɪk 'fəʊtəʊz]
Frage question ['kwestʃn] • **Fragen stellen** ask questions • **Kommt nicht in Frage!** No way!
fragen ask [ɑ:sk] • **nach etwas fragen** ask about sth. • **jn. nach dem Weg fragen** ask sb. the way
sich fragen wonder ['wʌndə]
Französisch French [frentʃ]
Frau woman ['wʊmən], *pl* women ['wɪmɪn] • **Frau Brown** Mrs Brown ['mɪsɪz]; Ms Brown [mɪz, məz] • **Frau White** *(unverheiratet)* Miss White [mɪs]
frei free [fri:] • **freie Zeit** free time **im Freien** *(Außen-)* outdoor ['aʊtdɔ:]; *(Freilicht-)* open-air [ˌəʊpən_'eə]
Freiheit freedom ['fri:dəm]
Freilicht- open-air [ˌəʊpən_'eə]
Freitag Friday ['fraɪdeɪ, 'fraɪdi] **freitagabends, am Freitagabend** on Friday evening • **freitagnachts, Freitagnacht** on Friday night
freiwillig: sich freiwillig melden volunteer [ˌvɒlən'tɪə]
Freiwillige(r) volunteer [ˌvɒlən'tɪə]
Freizeit free time [ˌfri: 'taɪm]
Freizeitzentrum, -park leisure centre ['leʒə sentə]
fremd foreign ['fɒrən]; *(nicht vertraut)* strange [streɪndʒ]
Fremdenführer/in guide [gaɪd]
Fremdenverkehrsamt tourist information ['tʊərɪst_ɪnfəˌmeɪʃn]

Fremdsprache foreign language [ˌfɒrən ˈlæŋgwɪdʒ]

freuen: sich auf etwas freuen look forward to sth. [ˈfɔːwəd]

Freund friend [frend]; *(Kumpel)* mate [meɪt] *(infml)*; *(eines Mädchens, einer Frau)* boyfriend [ˈbɔɪfrend]

Freundin friend [frend]; *(Kumpel)* mate [meɪt] *(infml)*; *(eines Jungen, eines Mannes)* girlfriend [ˈgɜːlfrend]

freundlich friendly [ˈfrendli]

Freundlichkeit friendliness [ˈfrendlinəs]

frieren be cold [kəʊld]

frisch fresh [freʃ]

Frischkäse cream cheese [ˌkriːm ˈtʃiːz]

Friseur/in hairdresser [ˈheədresə]
beim Friseur at the hairdresser's

froh happy [ˈhæpi]

Frosch frog [frɒg]

Frucht, Früchte fruit [fruːt]

früh early [ˈɜːli]

früher *(einst, früher einmal)* once [wʌns]

Frühling spring [sprɪŋ]

Frühstück breakfast [ˈbrekfəst]
zum Frühstück for breakfast

frühstücken have breakfast

Frühstückspension Bed and Breakfast (B&B) [ˌbed‿ən ˈbrekfəst]

Fuchs fox [fɒks]

fühlen; sich fühlen feel [fiːl]

führen: ein Telefongespräch führen make a call [ˈkɔːl]

Führer/in *(Leiter/in, Anführer/in)* leader [ˈliːdə]

Füller pen [pen]

funktionieren work [wɜːk]

für for [fə, fɔː] • **Was für ein Auto ...?** What kind of car ...? • **Was für ein interessantes Leben!** What an interesting life!

furchtbar terrible [ˈterəbl]; awful [ˈɔːfl]

fürchterlich aussehen be a mess [mes]

Fuß foot [fʊt], *pl* feet [fiːt] • **zu Fuß** on foot

Fußball football [ˈfʊtbɔːl]; soccer [ˈsɒkə]

Fußballplatz, -feld football pitch [ˈfʊtbɔːl pɪtʃ]

Fußballschuhe, -stiefel football boots [ˈfʊtbɔːl buːts]

Fußballspiel: ein Fußballspiel a game of football [geɪm]

Fußballtrikot football shirt [ˈfʊtbɔːl ʃɜːt]

Fußboden floor [flɔː]

Futter food [fuːd]

füttern feed [fiːd]

G

Gabel fork [fɔːk]

gähnen yawn [jɔːn]

Gang *(Korridor)* hallway [ˈhɔːlweɪ] *(AE)*

ganze(r, s) whole [həʊl] • **auf der ganzen Welt** all over the world **aus der ganzen Welt** from all over the world • **aus ganz Wales** from all around Wales/from all over Wales • **Das ist ganz falsch.** This is all wrong. • **den ganzen Tag (lang)** all day • **die ganze Zeit** all the time • **ganz um die Burg herum** all around the castle

Garage garage [ˈgærɑːʒ]

Garten garden [ˈgɑːdn]

Gärtner/in gardener [ˈgɑːdnə]

Gasse lane [leɪn]

Gast guest [gest]; *(Besucher/in)* visitor [ˈvɪzɪtə]

Gastgeberin hostess [ˈhəʊstəs]

Gebäude building [ˈbɪldɪŋ]

geben give [gɪv] • **ein Konzert geben** do a gig • **es gibt** *(es ist vorhanden)* there's; *(es sind vorhanden)* there are • **jm. die Schuld geben (an)** blame sb. (for) [bleɪm]
Was gibt es zum Mittagessen? What's for lunch?

Gebiet *(Bereich; Gegend)* area [ˈeəriə]

geboren sein/werden be born [bɔːn]

gebraucht *(aus zweiter Hand)* second-hand [ˌsekənd ˈhænd]

gebrochen *(Arm, Bein)* broken [ˈbrəʊkən]

Geburtstag birthday [ˈbɜːθdeɪ]
Ich habe im Mai / am 13. Juni Geburtstag. My birthday is in May / on 13th June. • **Wann hast du Geburtstag?** When's your birthday?
zu seinem Geburtstag for his birthday

Gedanke thought [θɔːt]

Gedicht poem [ˈpəʊɪm]

Gefahr danger [ˈdeɪndʒə]

gefährlich dangerous [ˈdeɪndʒərəs]; *(nicht sicher)* unsafe [ʌnˈseɪf]

Gefängnis jail [dʒeɪl]

Geflügel poultry [ˈpəʊltri]

Gefühl feeling [ˈfiːlɪŋ]

gegen against [əˈgenst] • **gegen sechs** *(um sechs Uhr herum)* around six

Gegend *(Gebiet)* area [ˈeəriə]

Gegenteil opposite [ˈɒpəzɪt]

gegenüber (von) opposite [ˈɒpəzɪt]

Gegenwart present [ˈpreznt]

Gehalt *(Inhalt)* content [ˈkɒntent]

Geheimnis *(Rätsel)* mystery [ˈmɪstri]

gehen 1. go [gəʊ]; *(zu Fuß gehen)* walk [wɔːk]; *(weggehen)* leave [liːv]
Auf geht's! Let's go. • **einkaufen gehen** go shopping; shop [ʃɒp]
Geh ein Feld vor. Move on one space. [speɪs] • **Geh ein Feld zurück.** Move back one space. • **in die Sauna gehen** have a sauna • **ins Ausland gehen** go abroad • **ins Bett gehen** go to bed • **ins Kino gehen** go to the cinema • **mit jm. (aus)gehen** *(regelmäßig)* date sb. [deɪt] • **nach Hause gehen** go home • **reiten/schwimmen gehen** go riding/swimming • **spazieren gehen** go for a walk [wɔːk]
2. Es geht mir/ihm gut. I'm/He's fine. [faɪn] • **Wie geht es dir/ Ihnen/euch?** How are you?
3. Es geht um Mr Green. This is about Mr Green.
4. Das geht dich nichts an! Mind your own business. [ˌmaɪnd jər‿ˌəʊn ˈbɪznəs]

gehören 1. jm. gehören/zu jm. gehören belong to [bɪˈlɒŋ] • **Wem gehören diese?** Whose are these?
2. gehören zu *(passen zu)* go with

Gehweg pavement [ˈpeɪvmənt] *(BE)*; sidewalk [ˈsaɪdwɔːk] *(AE)*

Geige fiddle [ˈfɪdl] *(infml)* • **Geige spielen** play the fiddle

gekränkt (wegen) upset (about) [ˌʌpˈset]

Gelächter laughter [ˈlɑːftə]

gelangen *(hinkommen)* get [get]

gelangweilt sein be/feel bored [bɔːd]

gelassen *(locker)* easy-going [ˌiːziˈgəʊɪŋ]

gelb yellow [ˈjeləʊ]

Geld money [ˈmʌni] • **Geld ausgeben (für)** spend money (on) [spend]
Geld sammeln (für) raise money (for) [reɪz] • **Geld verdienen** make money

Geldbörse purse [pɜːs]

Gelegenheit *(Chance, Möglichkeit)* chance [tʃɑːns]

Gemälde painting [ˈpeɪntɪŋ]

Gemeindehalle, -saal community hall [kəˈmjuːnəti]

Gemeindezentrum community centre [kəˈmjuːnəti]

Gemeinschaftshalle, -saal community hall [kəˈmjuːnəti]

Gemeinschaftszentrum community centre [kəˈmjuːnəti]

Gemüse: *(ein)* **Gemüse** vegetable [ˈvedʒtəbl]

genannt werden *(heißen)* be called [kɔːld]

genau 1. *(Adjektiv)* exact [ɪɡ'zækt]
2. *(Adverb)* exactly [ɪɡ'zæktli]
genau hinter dir right behind you
genau in dem Moment just then
genau wie du just like you
genießbar *(Wasser)* drinkable ['drɪŋkəbl]
genießen enjoy [ɪn'dʒɔɪ]
genug enough [ɪ'nʌf] • **genug von etwas haben** *(etwas satt haben)* be tired of sth. ['taɪəd]
geöffnet open ['əʊpən]
Geografie geography [dʒi'ɒɡrəfi]
gepflegt neat [niːt]
gerade at the moment; *(soeben)* just [dʒʌst] • **gerade dann** *(genau in dem Moment)* just then • **jetzt gerade** *(in diesem Moment)* right now [raɪt 'naʊ]
geradeaus weiter straight on [streɪt_'ɒn]
Gerät *(Maschine)* machine [mə'ʃiːn]
Geräusch noise [nɔɪz]
gerecht fair [feə]
Gericht *(Speise)* dish [dɪʃ]
Gericht(shof) court [kɔːt]
gern: Ich hätte gern ... / Ich möchte gern ... I'd like ... (= I would like ...) **Ich schwimme/tanze/... gern.** I like swimming/dancing/... • **Ich würde gern gehen** I'd like to go • **Ich würde nicht gern gehen** I wouldn't like to go • **Gern geschehen.** You're welcome. ['welkəm]
gernhaben like [laɪk]
Geruch smell [smel]
gesamte(r, s) whole [həʊl] • **aus dem gesamten Vereinigten Königreich** from all over the UK
Geschäft *(Laden)* shop [ʃɒp]
Geschäft(e) business ['bɪznəs]
Geschäftsfrau/-mann businesswoman/-man ['bɪznəswʊmən, -mæn]
geschehen (mit) happen (to) ['hæpən]
Geschenk present ['preznt]
Geschichte 1. story ['stɔːri]
2. *(vergangene Zeiten)* history ['hɪstri]
geschieden divorced [dɪ'vɔːst]
Geschirrspülmaschine dishwasher ['dɪʃwɒʃə]
geschlossen closed [kləʊzd]
Geschmack(srichtung) flavour ['fleɪvə]
Gesellschaft *(Firma)* company ['kʌmpəni]
Gesetz law [lɔː]
Gesicht face [feɪs]
Gespräch talk [tɔːk]
gestalten design [dɪ'zaɪn]
gestern yesterday ['jestədeɪ, 'jestədi]
gestern Morgen/Nachmittag/Abend yesterday morning/afternoon/evening • **die Hausaufgaben von gestern** yesterday's homework
gesund healthy ['helθi]
Gesundheit health [helθ]
Getränk drink [drɪŋk]
getrennt 1. *(Adjektiv)* separate ['seprət]
2. *(Adverb)* apart [ə'pɑːt]
Gewalt violence ['vaɪələns]
gewaltfrei, gewaltlos non-violent [ˌnɒn'vaɪələnt]
gewaltsam violent ['vaɪələnt]
gewalttätig violent ['vaɪələnt]
Gewalttätigkeit violence ['vaɪələns]
Gewinn *(Preis)* prize [praɪz]
gewinnen win [wɪn]
Gewinner/in winner ['wɪnə]
Gewitter storm [stɔːm]
gewöhnlich usually ['juːʒuəli]
gewürzt *(würzig, scharf gewürzt)* spicy ['spaɪsi]
gezeigt werden *(im Fernsehen)* be on
Gezeiten *(Ebbe und Flut)* tide [taɪd]
Gig *(Auftritt, Konzert)* gig [ɡɪɡ] *(infml)*
Giraffe giraffe [dʒə'rɑːf]
Gitarre guitar [ɡɪ'tɑː] • **Gitarre spielen** play the guitar
Glas glass [ɡlɑːs] • **ein Glas Wasser** a glass of water
glauben think [θɪŋk] • **glauben an** believe in [bɪ'liːv] • **Das glaube ich nicht. / Ich glaube nicht.** I don't think so. • **Ich glaube (ja).** I think so. • **Glaubst du das wirklich?** Do you really think so?
glaubhaft believable [bɪ'liːvəbl]
gleich 1. gleich sein/aussehen be/look the same [seɪm]
2. gleich nach dem Mittagessen right after lunch [raɪt]
Gleis *(Bahnsteig)* platform ['plætfɔːm]
Gliederung *(Struktur)* structure ['strʌktʃə]
Glocke bell [bel]
Glück 1. *(das Glücklichsein)* happiness ['hæpinəs]
2. Glück haben (mit) be lucky (with) ['lʌki] • **Viel Glück (bei/mit ...)!** Good luck (with ...)! [ɡʊd 'lʌk]
zum Glück *(glücklicherweise)* luckily ['lʌkɪli]
glücklich happy ['hæpi]
glücklicherweise luckily ['lʌkɪli]
Gold gold [ɡəʊld]
golden golden ['ɡəʊldən]
Golf golf [ɡɒlf]
Gott God [ɡɒd]
Gouverneur/in governor ['ɡʌvənə]
Grad degree [dɪ'ɡriː]
Grammatik grammar ['ɡræmə]
Gras grass [ɡrɑːs]
grau grey [ɡreɪ]
grauenhaft horrible ['hɒrəbl]
grausam cruel [kruːəl]
Grenze border ['bɔːdə]
groß big [bɪɡ]; large [lɑːdʒ]; *(riesig)* huge [hjuːdʒ]; *(Personen, Körpergröße)* tall [tɔːl]
großartig great [ɡreɪt]; awesome ['ɔːsəm] *(AE, infml)*
Großbuchstabe capital letter [ˌkæpɪtl 'letə]
Größe *(Schuhgröße usw.)* size [saɪz]
Großeltern grandparents ['ɡrænpeərənts]
Großmutter grandmother ['ɡrænmʌðə]
Großstadt city ['sɪti]
Großvater grandfather ['ɡrænfɑːðə]
grün green [ɡriːn]
Grund reason ['riːzn] • **aus vielen Gründen** for lots of reasons
gründen found [faʊnd]
Grundschule *(für 6- bis 11-Jährige in den USA)* elementary school [ˌelɪ'mentri skuːl]
Gruppe group [ɡruːp]; *(Musikgruppe)* band [bænd]
gruselig scary ['skeəri]
Gruß: Liebe Grüße, ... *(Briefschluss)* Love ... [lʌv] • **Mit besten Grüßen** *(Briefschluss)* Best wishes ['wɪʃɪz]
Grüß Dilip von mir. Say hi to Dilip for me.
gucken look [lʊk]
gut good [ɡʊd]; *(okay)* OK [əʊ'keɪ]; *(in Ordnung)* all right [ɔːl 'raɪt]; *(gesundheitlich gut, wohlauf)* well [wel]; fine [faɪn] • **Alles Gute** *(Briefschluss)* Best wishes ['wɪʃɪz] • **Es geht mir/ihm gut.** I'm/He's fine.
gut in etwas sein/etwas gut können be good at sth. • **gute Arbeit leisten** do a good job • **Guten Morgen.** Good morning. • **Guten Tag.** Hello.; *(nachmittags)* Good afternoon. • **gut ausgehen** work out [ˌwɜːk_'aʊt] • **gut (ver)laufen** *(gutgehen, klappen)* go well • **Das hast du gut gemacht.** You did well.
gutgehen *(gut (ver)laufen, klappen)* go well
Gymnastikanzug leotard ['liːətɑːd]

H

Haar, Haare hair *(no pl)* [heə]
haben have got ['hæv gɒt]; have [həv, hæv] • **Ich habe keinen Stuhl.** I haven't got a chair. • **Ich habe am 13. Juni/im Mai Geburtstag.** My birthday is on 13th June/in May. **Wann hast du Geburtstag?** When's your birthday? • **haben wollen** want [wɒnt] • **Was haben wir als Hausaufgabe auf?** What's for homework?
Hafen harbour ['hɑ:bə]
Hähnchen chicken ['tʃɪkɪn]
halb: eine halbe Stunde half an hour [ˌhɑ:f_ən_'aʊə] • **halb zwölf** half past 11 • **dreieinhalb Tage/Wochen** three and a half days/weeks
Halbfinale semi-final [ˌsemi'faɪnl]
Halbzeit half [hɑ:f] • **die erste Halbzeit** the first half • **Halbzeit(pause)** half-time [ˌhɑ:f 'taɪm]
Halfpipe *(halbierte Röhre für Inline-skater)* half-pipe ['hɑ:fpaɪp]
Hälfte half [hɑ:f], *pl* halves [hɑ:vz]
Halle hall [hɔ:l]
Hallo! Hi! [haɪ]; Hello. [hə'ləʊ]
Hals throat [θrəʊt]
Halsschmerzen haben have a sore throat [sɔ: 'θrəʊt]
halten 1. hold [həʊld]
2. *(aufbewahren)* keep [ki:p]
etwas warm/kühl/offen/... halten keep sth. warm/cool/open/...
3. *(behalten)* keep
eine Rede halten make a speech [spi:tʃ] • **Halt den Mund!** Shut up. [ˌʃʌt_'ʌp] • **Kontakt halten** keep in touch [tʌtʃ] • **Was hältst du von ...?** What do you think about/of ...? / How do you feel about ...?
Haltung (gegenüber) *(Einstellung)* attitude (to, towards) ['ætɪtju:d]
Hamburger hamburger ['hæmbɜ:gə]
Hamster hamster ['hæmstə]
Hand hand [hænd] • **aus zweiter Hand** *(gebraucht)* second-hand
handeln *(tätig werden; sich verhalten)* act [ækt]
Handlung *(eines Romans, Films)* plot [plɒt]
Handtuch towel ['taʊəl]
Handy mobile (phone) ['məʊbaɪl] *(BE)*; cellphone ['selfəʊn] *(AE)*
hänseln: jn. mit Schimpfwörtern hänseln call sb. names
Happyend happy ending [ˌhæpi_'endɪŋ]
hart hard [hɑ:d] • **hart arbeiten** work hard
hassen hate [heɪt]
häufig often ['ɒfn]
Haupt- main [meɪn]
Hauptsendezeit prime time ['praɪm taɪm]
Hauptstadt capital ['kæpɪtl]
Hauptverkehrszeit rush hour ['rʌʃ_aʊə]
Haus house [haʊs] • **im Haus der Shaws / bei den Shaws zu Hause** at the Shaws' house • **nach Hause gehen** go home [həʊm] • **nach Hause kommen** come home; get home • **zu Hause** at home
Hausangestellte maid [meɪd]
Hausaufgabe(n) homework *(no pl)* ['həʊmwɜ:k] • **die Hausaufgabe(n) machen** do homework • **Was haben wir als Hausaufgabe auf?** What's for homework?
Hausmeister/in caretaker ['keəteɪkə]
Haustier pet [pet]
Haustür front door [ˌfrʌnt 'dɔ:]
Haut skin [skɪn]
heftig hard [hɑ:d]
Heim home [həʊm]
Heimatstadt hometown ['həʊmtaʊn]
heiß hot [hɒt]
heißen 1. *(genannt werden)* be called [kɔ:ld] • **Ich heiße ...** My name is ... • **Wie heißt du?** What's your name?
2. Sie heißen dich in ... willkommen They welcome you to ... ['welkəm]
Held/in hero ['hɪərəʊ], *pl* heroes ['hɪərəʊz]
helfen help [help]
Helikopter helicopter ['helɪkɒptə]
hell *(leuchtend)* bright [braɪt]; *(Haare)* blond [blɒnd]
Helm helmet ['helmɪt]
Hemd shirt [ʃɜ:t]
herauf up [ʌp]
heraus out [aʊt] • **aus ... heraus** out of ... ['aʊt_əv]
herausarbeiten: etwas herausarbeiten work sth. out
herausbringen *(CD, Film usw. auf den Markt bringen)* release [rɪ'li:s]
herausfinden find out [ˌfaɪnd_'aʊt]; *(entdecken)* discover [dɪ'skʌvə]
etwas über etwas herausfinden learn sth. about sth. [lɜ:n]
herausnehmen take out [ˌteɪk_'aʊt]
herausragen aus etwas stick out of sth. [stɪk]
herausstehen aus etwas *(herausragen)* stick out of sth. [stɪk]
Herberge hostel ['hɒstl]
herbringen bring [brɪŋ]
Herbst autumn ['ɔ:təm]
Herd cooker ['kʊkə]
hereinkommen come in [ˌkʌm_'ɪn]
Herr Brown Mr Brown ['mɪstə]
herstellen produce [prə'dju:s]
Herstellung production [prə'dʌkʃn]
herüber across [ə'krɒs]
herüberbeugen: sich herüberbeugen lean over [ˌli:n_'əʊvə]
herüberlehnen: sich herüberlehnen lean over [ˌli:n_'əʊvə]
herum: anders herum the other way round [raʊnd] • **um ... herum** round, around • **ganz um die Burg herum** all around the castle • **um sechs Uhr herum** *(gegen sechs)* around six
herum-: etwas herumgeben pass sth. round [raʊnd] • **herumgehen** walk around • **herumrennen** run around • **herumspringen** jump around
herunter down [daʊn]
herunterfallen (von) fall off [ˌfɔ:l_'ɒf]
herunterladbar downloadable [ˌdaʊn'ləʊdəbl]
hervorragend excellent ['eksələnt]
► S.179 US school grades
Herz heart [hɑ:t]
Herzlichen Glückwunsch zum Geburtstag. Happy birthday. [ˌhæpi 'bɜ:θdeɪ]
heute today [tə'deɪ] • **heute Morgen/Nachmittag/Abend** this morning/afternoon/evening
heute Nacht tonight [tə'naɪt]
das Programm von heute today's programme
heutig: das heutige Programm today's programme
hier here [hɪə] • **Hier bitte.** *(Bitte sehr.)* Here you are. • **hier drinnen** in here [ˌɪn 'hɪə] • **hier entlang** this way ['ðɪs weɪ] • **Hier spricht Isabel. / Hier ist Isabel.** *(am Telefon)* This is Isabel. • **Hier steht: ... / Es heißt hier: ...** *(im Text)* It says here: ...
hierher here [hɪə]
Hilfe help [help]
hilflos helpless ['helpləs]
hilfreich helpful ['helpfl]
Himmel sky [skaɪ]; *(im religiösen Sinn)* heaven ['hevn] • **am Himmel** in the sky
hinauf up [ʌp] • **den Hügel hinauf** up the hill
hinaufklettern (auf) climb [klaɪm] **Klettere auf einen Baum.** Climb a tree.
hinaus out [aʊt] • **aus ... hinaus** out of ... ['aʊt_əv]
hinein: in ... hinein into ... ['ɪntə, 'ɪntʊ]
hineinpassen fit in [ˌfɪt_'ɪn]

hinfallen fall [fɔːl]; fall down

hinkommen *(gelangen)* get [get]

hinlegen: etwas hinlegen put sth. down [ˌpʊt 'daʊn]

hinsetzen: sich hinsetzen sit down [ˌsɪt 'daʊn]

hinstellen: sich hinstellen stand [stænd]

hinten (im Zimmer) at the back (of the room) [bæk]

hinter behind [bɪ'haɪnd] • **im hinteren Teil (des Zimmers)** at the back (of the room) [bæk]

Hintergrund background ['bækgraʊnd]

Hintertür back door

hinüber across [ə'krɒs] • **hinüber zu/nach …** over to … ['əʊvə]

hinunter down [daʊn]

hinzufügen (zu) add (to) [æd]

Hiphop hip hop ['hɪp hɒp]

Hirsch deer, *pl* deer [dɪə]

Hit hit [hɪt]

Hobby hobby ['hɒbi], *pl* hobbies

hoch high [haɪ]; *(Bäume, Türme usw.)* tall [tɔːl]

hochheben: etwas hochheben pick sth. up [ˌpɪk‿'ʌp]

Hochschule college ['kɒlɪdʒ]

hochsehen (von) look up (from) [ˌlʊk‿'ʌp]

Hockey hockey ['hɒki]

Hockeyplatz, -feld hockey pitch [pɪtʃ]

Hockeyschuhe hockey shoes [ʃuːz]

Hof yard [jɑːd] • **auf dem Hof** in the yard

hoffen hope [həʊp]

Hoffnung hope [həʊp]

hoffnungslos hopeless ['həʊpləs]

höflich polite [pə'laɪt]

holen *(besorgen)* get [get]

Holz wood [wʊd]

horchen: auf etwas horchen listen for sth.

hören hear [hɪə] • **Na hör mal!** Come on. [ˌkʌm‿'ɒn]

Hose trousers *(pl)* ['traʊzəz] *(BE)*; pants *(pl)* [pænts] *(AE)*

Hotel hotel [həʊ'tel]

Hotline hotline ['hɒtlaɪn]

hübsch pretty ['prɪti]

Hubschrauber helicopter ['helɪkɒptə]

Hügel hill [hɪl]

hügelig hilly ['hɪli]

Huhn chicken ['tʃɪkɪn]

Hülle cover ['kʌvə]

Hund dog [dɒg]

hundert hundred ['hʌndrəd]

Hunger haben, hungrig sein be hungry ['hʌŋgri]

Hurra! Hooray! [hu'reɪ]

Hut hat [hæt]

Hütte cabin ['kæbɪn]

I

ich I [aɪ] • **Ich auch.** Me too. [ˌmiː 'tuː] • **Das bin ich.** That's me. **Warum ich?** Why me?

Idee idea [aɪ'dɪə]

Igel hedgehog ['hedʒhɒg]

ihm him; *(bei Dingen, Tieren)* it

ihn him; *(bei Dingen, Tieren)* it

ihnen them [ðəm, ðem]

Ihnen *(höfliche Anrede)* you [juː]

ihr *(Plural von „du")* you [juː]

ihr: Hilf ihr. Help her. [hə, hɜː]

ihr(e) … *(besitzanzeigend)* *(zu „she")* her … [hə, hɜː]; *(zu „they")* their … [ðeə]

Ihr(e) … *(höfliche Anrede)* your … [jɔː]

ihrer, ihre, ihrs *(zu „she")* hers [hɜːz]; *(zu „they")* theirs [ðeəz]

Ihrer, Ihre, Ihrs *(höfliche Anrede)* yours [jɔːz]

illegal illegal [ɪ'liːgl]

im: im Alter von 16 Jahren at 16 **im Ausland** abroad [ə'brɔːd] • **Im Ernst?** Seriously? ['sɪəriəsli] • **im Fernsehen** on TV • **im Flugzeug** on the plane • **im Freien** *(Freilicht-)* open-air • **im Haus der Shaws** at the Shaws' house • **im hinteren Teil (des Zimmers)** at the back (of the room) • **im Internet surfen** surf the internet • **im Jahr 1948** in 1948 • **im Mai** in May **im Moment** at the moment • **im Radio** on the radio • **im Zug** on the train

Imbiss snack [snæk]

immer **1.** always ['ɔːlweɪz] • **für immer** forever [fər'evə] • **immer noch** still [stɪl]
2. wann (auch) immer whenever [wen'evə] • **was (auch) immer** whatever [wɒt'evə] • **wer/wen/wem (auch) immer** whoever [huː'evə] • **wo (auch) immer** wherever [weər'evə] • **wohin (auch) immer** wherever
► S.178 whoever, whatever, whenever, wherever

in in • **in … (hinein)** into … ['ɪntə, 'ɪntʊ] • **in … umher** *(durch)* around **in den Zug/Bus einsteigen** get on the train/bus • **in der Stadt umher** around the town • **in der …straße** in … Street • **in der Hamiltonstraße 7** at 7 Hamilton Street • **in der Nacht** at night • **in der Nähe von** near • **in der Pause** *(zwischen Schulstunden)* at break • **in der Schule** at school • **in die falsche Richtung** the wrong way • **in die Sauna gehen** have a sauna • **in Eile sein** be in a hurry • **ins Bett gehen** go to bed • **ins Kino gehen** go to the cinema • **in Schwierigkeiten sein** be in trouble ['trʌbl] **in Urlaub fahren** go on holiday **in Urlaub sein** be on holiday • **in Verbindung bleiben** keep in touch [tʌtʃ] • **in welche Richtung?** which way? • **in Wirklichkeit** *(eigentlich)* actually ['æktʃuəli] • **Ich bin noch nie in Bath gewesen.** I've never been to Bath.

Indianer/in Indian ['ɪndiən]

indianisch Indian ['ɪndiən]

indirekte Frage indirect question [ˌɪndərekt 'kwestʃən]

Industrie industry ['ɪndəstri]

Industrie- industrial [ɪn'dʌstriəl]

industriell industrial [ɪn'dʌstriəl]

Infinitiv infinitive [ɪn'fɪnətɪv]

Information(en) (über) information (about/on) *(no pl)* [ˌɪnfə'meɪʃn]

Informationstechnologie (IT) information technology (IT) [tek'nɒlədʒi], [ˌaɪ 'tiː]

Ingenieur/in engineer [ˌendʒɪ'nɪə]

Inhalt content ['kɒntent]

Inliner skates [skeɪts] • **Inliner fahren** skate

innen (drin) inside [ˌɪn'saɪd]

Innenstadt city centre [ˌsɪti 'sentə]

Insekt insect ['ɪnsekt]

Insel island ['aɪlənd]

Installation installation [ˌɪnstə'leɪʃn]

installieren install [ɪn'stɔːl]

Instrument instrument ['ɪnstrəmənt]

interaktiv interactive [ˌɪntər'æktɪv]

interessant interesting ['ɪntrəstɪŋ]

Interesse (an) interest (in) ['ɪntrəst]

interessieren: sich interessieren (für) be interested (in) ['ɪntrəstɪd]

interessiert sein (an) be interested (in) ['ɪntrəstɪd]

international international [ˌɪntə'næʃnəl]

Internet internet ['ɪntənet] • **im Internet surfen** surf the internet

Interview interview ['ɪntəvjuː]

interviewen interview ['ɪntəvjuː]

intolerant intolerant [ɪn'tɒlərənt]

irgendein(e) any ['eni]
► S.176 any

irgendetwas anything ['eniθɪŋ] **irgendetwas anderes** anything else [els]
► S.176 any ► S.170 … else

irgendjemand anybody ['enibɒdi]; anyone ['eniwʌn] • **irgendjemand**

anderes anybody/anyone else
► S.176 any ► S.170 ... else
irgendwelche any ['eni]
irgendwie unheimlich kind of scary [kaɪnd] *(infml)*
irgendwo(hin) somewhere ['sʌmweə]; anywhere ['eniweə]
irren: sich irren be wrong [rɒŋ]
IT (Informationstechnologie) IT (information technology) [ˌaɪ 'tiː], [tek'nɒlədʒi]

J

ja yes [jes]
Jacke, Jackett jacket ['dʒækɪt]
Jagd hunt [hʌnt]
jagen hunt [hʌnt]
Jäger/in hunter ['hʌntə]
Jahr year [jɪə]
Jahrestag anniversary [ˌænɪ'vɜːsəri]
Jahrgangsstufe year [jɪə] *(BE)*; grade [greɪd] *(AE)*
Jahrhundert century ['sentʃəri]
Januar January ['dʒænjuəri]
Jazz jazz [dʒæz]
je? *(jemals?)* ever? ['evə]
Jeans jeans *(pl)* [dʒiːnz]
jede(r, s) ... *(Begleiter)* **1.** every ... ['evri] **2.** *(jeder einzelne)* each ... [iːtʃ] **3.** *(jeder beliebige)* any ... ['eni]
► S.176 any
jeder *(Pronomen)* **1.** everybody ['evribɒdi]; everyone ['evriwʌn] **2.** *(jeder Beliebige)* anybody ['enibɒdi]; anyone ['eniwʌn]
► S.176 any
jemals? ever? ['evə]
jemand **1.** somebody ['sʌmbədi]; someone ['sʌmwʌn] **2.** *(irgendjemand)* anybody ['enibɒdi]; anyone ['eniwʌn]
► S.176 any
jene(r, s) *(Singular)* that [ðət, ðæt]; *(Plural)* those [ðəʊz]
jetzt now [naʊ] • **jetzt gerade, jetzt sofort** right now
Job job [dʒɒb]
Journalist/in journalist ['dʒɜːnəlɪst]
jubeln cheer [tʃɪə]
jüdisch Jewish ['dʒuːɪʃ]
Judo judo ['dʒuːdəʊ] • **Judo machen** do judo
Jugend youth [juːθ]
Jugend- junior ['dʒuːniə]; *(Teenager-)* teen [tiːn]
Jugendliche(r) kid [kɪd]; teenager ['tiːneɪdʒə]
Juli July [dʒu'laɪ]
jung young [jʌŋ]
Junge boy [bɔɪ]
Juni June [dʒuːn]
Junioren- junior ['dʒuːniə]

K

Kabel cable ['keɪbl]
Kabelfernsehen cable (TV) ['keɪbl]
Kaffee coffee ['kɒfi] • **Kaffee zum Mitnehmen** coffee to go
Käfig cage [keɪdʒ]
Kalender calendar ['kælɪndə]
Kalorie calorie ['kæləri]
kalt cold [kəʊld]
Kälte cold [kəʊld]
Kamel camel ['kæml]
Kamera camera ['kæmərə]
Kampf fight [faɪt]
kämpfen (für, um) fight (for) [faɪt]
Kanal **1.** canal [kə'næl] **2.** *(Fernsehsender)* channel ['tʃænl]
Kandidat/in *(in Fernsehshow)* contestant [kən'testənt]
Känguru kangaroo [ˌkæŋgə'ruː]
Kaninchen rabbit ['ræbɪt]
Kante *(Rand)* rim [rɪm]
Kanu canoe [kə'nuː] • **Kanu fahren** canoe [kə'nuː]
Kappe cap [kæp]
kaputt broken ['brəʊkən] • **kaputt gehen** break [breɪk]
Karotte carrot ['kærət]
Karriere career [kə'rɪə]
Karte *(Post-, Spielkarte)* card [kɑːd]
Kartoffel potato [pə'teɪtəʊ], *pl* -toes
Kartoffelchips crisps *(pl)* [krɪsps] *(BE)*; potato chips *(pl)* [tʃɪps] *(AE)*
Karussell merry-go-round ['merigəʊraʊnd]
Käse cheese [tʃiːz]
Kasse *(für den Verkauf von Eintrittskarten)* ticket office ['tɪkɪt‿ɒfɪs]
Kästchen, Kasten box [bɒks]
Kathedrale cathedral [kə'θiːdrəl]
Katze cat [kæt]
kaufen buy [baɪ]
Kaufhaus department store [dɪ'pɑːtmənt stɔː]
Kehle throat [θrəʊt]
kein(e) no; not a; not (...) any • **Ich habe keinen Stuhl.** I haven't got a chair. • **Ich mag kein(e) ...** I don't like ... • **keine Musik mehr** no more music
Keks biscuit ['bɪskɪt] *(BE)*; cookie ['kʊki] *(AE)*
Kellner waiter ['weɪtə]
Kellnerin waitress ['weɪtrəs]
kennen know [nəʊ]
kennenlernen: jn. kennenlernen get to know sb.; *(zum ersten Mal treffen)* meet sb. [miːt]
kennzeichnen mark up [ˌmɑːk‿'ʌp]
Kerl guy [gaɪ] *(infml)*
Keyboard *(elektronisches Tasteninstrument)* keyboard ['kiːbɔːd]
Kilogramm, Kilo kilogram (kg) ['kɪləgræm], kilo ['kiːləʊ] • **ein 90 Kilogramm schwerer Bär** a 90-kilogram bear
Kilometer kilometre (km) ['kɪləmiːtə] **eine Zehn-Kilometer-Wanderung** a ten-kilometre walk
Kind child [tʃaɪld], *pl* children ['tʃɪldrən]; kid [kɪd]
Kindergarten kindergarten ['kɪndəgɑːtn]
Kindermädchen nanny ['næni]
Kino cinema ['sɪnəmə] • **ins Kino gehen** go to the cinema
Kirche church [tʃɜːtʃ]
Kiste box [bɒks]
Klang sound [saʊnd]
klar clear [klɪə] • **Aber klar!** You bet! [bet] *(infml)*
Klasse class [klɑːs]; form [fɔːm]; grade [greɪd] *(AE)*
klasse *(großartig)* awesome ['ɔːsəm] *(AE, infml)*
Klassenkamerad/in classmate ['klɑːsmeɪt]
Klassenlehrer/in class teacher; form teacher ['tiːtʃə]
Klassenzimmer classroom ['klɑːsruːm]
Klassik *(Musik)* classical music ['klæsɪkl]
klassisch classical ['klæsɪkl]
klatschen clap [klæp]
Klavier piano [pi'ænəʊ] • **Klavier spielen** play the piano
kleben: (auf-, ein)kleben glue [gluː]
Klebestift glue stick ['gluː stɪk]
Klebstoff glue [gluː]
Kleid dress [dres]
Kleider *(Kleidungsstücke)* clothes *(pl)* [kləʊðz, kləʊz]
Kleiderschrank wardrobe ['wɔːdrəʊb]
Kleidung(sstücke) clothes *(pl)* [kləʊðz, kləʊz]
klein little ['lɪtl]; small [smɔːl]; *(Körpergröße)* short [ʃɔːt]
Kleingeld change [tʃeɪndʒ]
► S.180 (to) change – change
Kleinstadt town [taʊn]
klettern climb [klaɪm] • **Klettere auf einen Baum.** Climb a tree.
Klingel bell [bel]
klingeln ring [rɪŋ]
Klingelton ringtone ['rɪŋtəʊn]
klingen sound [saʊnd]
Klinik clinic ['klɪnɪk]
Klon clone [kləʊn]
klopfen (an) knock (on) [nɒk]

Klub club [klʌb]
klug clever ['klevə]
Klugheit cleverness ['klevənəs]
km/h *(Stundenkilometer, Kilometer pro Stunde)* kph (kilometres per hour)
knapp: Das war knapp. That was close. [kləʊs]
Kneipe pub [pʌb]
Knie knee [ni:]
Knopf button ['bʌtn]
Koch cook [kʊk]
kochen cook [kʊk]
Köchin cook [kʊk]
Koffer suitcase ['su:tkeɪs]
Koje *(Etagenbett)* bunk (bed) [bʌŋk]
Kollokation *(Wörter, die oft zusammen vorkommen)* collocation [ˌkɒlə'keɪʃn]
kolorieren colour ['kʌlə]
Komiker/in comedian [kə'mi:diən]
komisch *(witzig)* funny ['fʌni]
Komma: 10,4 (zehn Komma vier) 10.4 (ten point four)
► S.183 REVISION: Numbers
kommen come [kʌm]; *(hinkommen)* get [get] • **Ich komme aus ...** I'm from ... • **Wo kommst du her?** Where are you from? • **nach Hause kommen** come home; get home • **zu spät kommen** be late **Kommt nicht in Frage!** No way! **Ach komm!** Come on. [ˌkʌm‿'ɒn] **Na los, komm.** Come on.
Kommentar comment ['kɒment]
Komödie comedy ['kɒmədi]
König king [kɪŋ]
Königin queen [kwi:n]
königlich royal ['rɔɪəl]
Königreich: das Vereinigte Königreich *(Großbritannien und Nordirland)* the United Kingdom (UK) [ju,naɪtɪd 'kɪŋdəm], [ˌju: 'keɪ]
konkurrieren compete [kəm'pi:t]
können can [kən, kæn]; be able to ['eɪbl] • **etwas gut/schlecht können** be good/bad at sth.
könnte(n): ich/er könnte ... I/he could ... [kəd, kʊd] • **du könntest (vielleicht) Hilfe brauchen** you might need help [maɪt]
konnte(n): ich/er konnte ... I/he could ... [kəd, kʊd]
Kontakt: Kontakt halten keep in touch [tʌtʃ] • **mit jm. Kontakt aufnehmen** contact sb. ['kɒntækt]
Kontext context ['kɒntekst]
Kontrolle: die Kontrolle über ein Flugzeug übernehmen take over a plane
kontrollieren *(prüfen)* check [tʃek]
Konzert concert ['kɒnsət] • **ein Konzert geben** *(einen Auftritt haben)* do a gig *(infml)*
Kopf head [hed]
Kopfhörer headphones *(pl)* ['hedfəʊnz]
kopflos headless ['hedləs]
Kopfschmerzen headache ['hedeɪk]
kopieren copy ['kɒpi]
Korb basket ['bɑ:skɪt] • **ein Korb Äpfel** a basket of apples
Korn grain [greɪn]
Körper body ['bɒdi]
korrekt correct [kə'rekt]
Korridor hallway ['hɔ:lweɪ] *(AE)*
korrigieren correct [kə'rekt]
kosten **1.** cost [kɒst] • **Er/Sie/Es kostet 1 Pfund.** It's £1. • **Sie kosten 35 Pence.** They are 35 p. • **Wie viel kostet/kosten ...?** How much is/are ...?
2. *(Essen probieren)* try [traɪ]
kostenlos free [fri:]
köstlich delicious [dɪ'lɪʃəs]
Kostüm *(Damenkostüm)* suit [su:t]
Kraft *(Energie)* energy ['enədʒi]
kräftig *(heftig)* hard *(adv)* [hɑ:d]
Kram stuff [stʌf]
krank ill [ɪl]
kränken: jn. kränken *(aus der Fassung bringen)* upset sb. [ʌp'set]
Krankenhaus hospital ['hɒspɪtl]
Krankenwagen ambulance ['æmbjələns]
Krankheit illness ['ɪlnəs]
Krawatte tie [taɪ]
Kreis circle ['sɜ:kl]
kreischen scream [skri:m]
kreuzen; sich kreuzen cross [krɒs]
Krieg war [wɔ:]
kriegen get [get]
Kriminalität crime [kraɪm]
Krimiserie crime series ['kraɪm ˌsɪəri:z]
Krokodil crocodile ['krɒkədaɪl]
Krug jug [dʒʌg] • **ein Krug Orangensaft** a jug of orange juice
Küche kitchen ['kɪtʃɪn]
Kuchen cake [keɪk]
Küchenschrank cupboard ['kʌbəd]
Kugelschreiber pen [pen]
Kuh cow [kaʊ]
kühl cool [ku:l]
Kühlschrank fridge [frɪdʒ]
Kultur culture ['kʌltʃə]
Kummer worry ['wʌri]
kümmern **1. sich um etwas/jn. kümmern** look after sth./sb. [ˌlʊk‿'ɑ:ftə]
2. Kümmere dich um deine eigenen Angelegenheiten! Mind your own business. [ˌmaɪnd jər‿ˌəʊn 'bɪznəs]
Kumpel mate [meɪt] *(infml)*
Kunde, Kundin customer ['kʌstəmə]
Kunst art [ɑ:t]
Künstler/in artist ['ɑ:tɪst]
künstlich artificial [ˌɑ:tɪ'fɪʃl]
Kurs *(Lehrgang)* course [kɔ:s]; *(Unterrichtsstunde)* class
kurz short [ʃɔ:t] • **kurze Hose** shorts *(pl)* [ʃɔ:ts]
Kuss kiss [kɪs]
küssen kiss [kɪs]
Küste coast [kəʊst]

L

lächeln smile [smaɪl]
lachen laugh [lɑ:f] • **laut lachen** laugh out loud • **über jn. lachen** laugh at sb.
lächerlich laughable ['lɑ:fəbl]
lachhaft laughable ['lɑ:fəbl]
Lachs salmon ['sæmən], *pl* salmon
Laden *(Geschäft)* shop [ʃɒp]
Ladentisch counter ['kaʊntə]
Lage: in der Lage sein, etwas zu tun be able to do sth. ['eɪbl]
Lager *(Ferienlager)* camp [kæmp]
Lamm lamb [læm]
Lampe lamp [læmp]
Land *(auch als Gegensatz zur Stadt)* country ['kʌntri]; *(Grund und Boden)* land [lænd] • **auf dem Land** *(im Gegensatz zur Stadt)* in the country; *(nicht auf dem Wasser)* on land
landen land [lænd]
Landhaus lodge [lɒdʒ]
Landkarte map [mæp]
Landschaft *(schöne)* scenery ['si:nəri]
Landwirt/in farmer ['fɑ:mə]
lang long [lɒŋ] • **drei Tage lang** for three days • **20 Minuten lang** for 20 minutes • **lange** a long time
langsam slow [sləʊ]
langweilen: sich langweilen be/feel/get bored [bɔ:d]
langweilig boring ['bɔ:rɪŋ]
Lärm noise [nɔɪz]
lärmend noisy ['nɔɪzi]
Lasagne lasagne [lə'zænjə]
lassen let [let] • **Lass uns ... / Lasst uns ...** Let's ... • **Lass das!** Stop that! • **jn. in Ruhe lassen** leave sb. alone [ˌli:v‿ə'ləʊn]
Lauf run [rʌn]
Laufbahn *(Sport)* running track [træk]
laufen run [rʌn]; *(im Fernsehen gezeigt werden)* be on
Läufer/in runner ['rʌnə]
Laufschuhe running shoes

laut loud [laʊd]; *(lärmend)* noisy ['nɔɪzi] • **laut lachen** laugh out loud • **etwas lauter stellen** turn sth. up [tɜ:n]
Laut sound [saʊnd]
läuten ring [rɪŋ]
leben live [lɪv]
Leben life [laɪf], *pl* lives [laɪvz] • **am Leben** *(lebendig)* alive [ə'laɪv]
lebendig alive [ə'laɪv]
Lebensmittel food [fu:d]
lecker delicious [dɪ'lɪʃəs]
Leder leather ['leðə]
ledig single ['sɪŋgl]
leer empty ['empti]
legal legal ['li:gl]
legen *(hin-, ablegen)* put [pʊt]
lehnen: sich lehnen lean [li:n]
lehren teach [ti:tʃ]
Lehrer/in teacher ['ti:tʃə]
Lehrgang *(Kurs)* course [kɔ:s]
Leibwächter/in, Leibwache bodyguard ['bɒdigɑ:d]
leicht *(nicht schwierig)* easy ['i:zi]
Leichtathletik athletics [æθ'letɪks]
leider I'm afraid [ə'freɪd]
leidtun: Tut mir leid. I'm sorry. ['sɒri]
leise quiet ['kwaɪət] • **etwas leiser stellen** turn sth. down [tɜ:n]
Leiter/in *(Anführer/in)* leader ['li:də]
Leitung *(Telefon)* line [laɪn]
Lektion *(im Schulbuch)* unit ['ju:nɪt]
lernen learn [lɜ:n]; *(für die Schule arbeiten)* study ['stʌdi]
Lern- und Arbeitstechniken study skills ['stʌdi skɪlz]
lesen read [ri:d]
Leser/in reader ['ri:də]
letzte(r, s) last [lɑ:st]; final ['faɪnl]
leuchtend bright [braɪt]
Leute people ['pi:pl]; guys [gaɪz] *(AE, infml)*
Licht light [laɪt]
Lichtblitz flash [flæʃ]
Liebe love [lʌv]
Liebe Grüße, ... *(Briefschluss)* Love ... [lʌv]
lieben love [lʌv]
liebenswert likeable ['laɪkəbl]
Lieber Jay, ... Dear Jay ... [dɪə]
lieber: etwas lieber mögen like sth. better
Liebling dear [dɪə]; love [lʌv]; sweetheart ['swi:thɑ:t]; *(Favorit/in)* favourite ['feɪvərɪt]
Lieblings-: meine Lieblingsfarbe my favourite colour ['feɪvərɪt]
liebsten: etwas am liebsten mögen like sth. best
Lied song [sɒŋ]
Liedtext(e) lyrics *(pl)* ['lɪrɪks]
liegen: Das liegt bei dir. *(Das kannst/musst du (selbst) entscheiden.)* That's up to you.
lila purple ['pɜ:pl]
Limonade lemonade [,lemə'neɪd] *(BE)*; soda ['səʊdə] *(AE)*
Lineal ruler ['ru:lə]
Linie: (U-Bahn-)Linie line [laɪn]
linke(r, s) left [left] • **links, auf der linken Seite** on the left • **(nach) links abbiegen** turn left • **nach links schauen** look left
Liste list [lɪst]
Livemusik live music ['laɪv ,mju:zɪk]
Loch hole [həʊl]
locker *(entspannt)* relaxed [rɪ'lækst]; *(gelassen)* easy-going [,i:zi'gəʊɪŋ]
Löffel spoon [spu:n]
Logo logo ['ləʊgəʊ], *pl* logos
Lokal *(Kneipe)* pub [pʌb]
Lokal- local ['ləʊkl]
löschen: ein Feuer löschen put out a fire
loswerden: jn./etwas loswerden get rid of sb./sth. [rɪd]
Löwe lion ['laɪən]
Luft air [eə] • **nach Luft schnappen** *(auch: vor Überraschung)* gasp [gɑ:sp]
Lust: die Lust an etwas verlieren get tired of sth. ['taɪəd]

M

machbar doable ['du:əbl]
machen do [du:]; make [meɪk] • **die Hausaufgabe(n) machen** do homework • **einen Ausflug machen** go on a trip • **eine Fahrt machen** take a ride • **eine Pause machen** take a break • **einen Spaziergang machen** go for a walk **eine Übung machen** do an exercise • **Ferien machen** be on holiday • **Fotos machen** take photos **jm. Vorwürfe machen (wegen)** blame sb. (for) • **Judo machen** do judo • **Mach es dir bequem.** Make yourself comfortable. • **sich aus dem Staub machen** take off *(infml)* • **sich Notizen machen** take notes • **sich Sorgen machen (wegen, um)** worry (about) ['wʌri] **(Zauber-)Kunststücke machen** do tricks • **Reiten macht Spaß.** Riding is fun.
Macht: ein Flugzeug in seine Macht bringen take over a plane
Mädchen girl [gɜ:l]
Magazin *(Zeitschrift)* magazine [,mægə'zi:n]
Magen stomach ['stʌmək]
Magenschmerzen stomach ache ['stʌmək_eɪk]
Magst du ...? Do you like ...?
mähen: Rasen mähen cut the grass [grɑ:s]
Mahlzeit meal [mi:l]
Mai May [meɪ]
Make-up make-up ['meɪkʌp]
Mal(e); -mal time(s) [taɪm], [taɪmz] **zum ersten Mal** for the first time
malen paint [peɪnt]
Maler/in painter ['peɪntə]
Mama mum [mʌm] *(BE)*; mom [mɒm, *AE:* mɑ:m] *(AE)*
man you
Manager/in manager ['mænɪdʒə]
manchmal sometimes ['sʌmtaɪmz]
Mann man [mæn], *pl* men [men]
Mannschaft team [ti:m]
Mappe *(des Sprachenportfolios)* dossier ['dɒsieɪ]
Marathon marathon ['mærəθən]
Markenzeichen *(Logo)* logo ['ləʊgəʊ], *pl* logos
markieren mark up [,mɑ:k_'ʌp]
Markt market ['mɑ:kɪt] • **auf den Markt bringen** *(CD, Film usw. herausbringen)* release [rɪ'li:s]
Marmelade *(Orangenmarmelade)* marmalade ['mɑ:məleɪd]
Marsch march [mɑ:tʃ]; *(Wanderung)* hike [haɪk]
März March [mɑ:tʃ]
Maschine machine [mə'ʃi:n]
Mathematik maths [mæθs] *(BE)*; math [mæθ] *(AE)*
Mauer wall [wɔ:l]
Maultier mule [mju:l]
Maulwurf mole [məʊl]
Maus mouse [maʊs], *pl* mice [maɪs]
Medaille medal ['medl]
Mediation *(Sprachmittlung)* mediation [,mi:di'eɪʃn]
Medien media *(pl)* ['mi:diə]
Medikament drug [drʌg]
Meer sea [si:]
Meerschweinchen guinea pig ['gɪni pɪg]
mehr more [mɔ:] • **mehr als** more than • **mehr als ich** more than me • **nicht mehr** not (...) any more • **viel mehr** lots more **keine Musik mehr** no more music
mehrfarbig multi-coloured ['mʌlti,kʌləd]
Mehrheit majority [mə'dʒɒrəti]
Meile *(= ca. 1,6 km)* mile [maɪl]
meilenweit for miles [maɪlz]
mein(e) ... my ... [maɪ] • **meine neuen** my new ones [wʌnz]

meinen 1. *(glauben)* think [θɪŋk]
Meinst du wirklich? Do you really think so?
2. *(sagen wollen)* **mean** [mi:n]
Was meinst du mit …? What do you mean by …?
meiner, meine, meins mine [maɪn]
Meinung (von, zu) opinion (of) [ə'pɪnjən] • **meiner Meinung nach** in my opinion • **anderer Meinung sein (als)** disagree (with) [ˌdɪsə'gri:]
meist: (der/die/das) meiste …; am meisten most [məʊst] • **die meisten Leute** most people
meistens usually ['ju:ʒuəli]
Meister/in *(Champion)* champion ['tʃæmpiən]
Meisterschaft championship ['tʃæmpiənʃɪp]
melden: sich freiwillig melden volunteer [ˌvɒlən'tɪə]
Melodie tune [tju:n]
Menge 1. *(Menschenmenge)* crowd [kraʊd]
2. eine Menge *(viel, viele)* a lot (of) [lɒt]; lots (of) [lɒts]
Menschen people ['pi:pl]
Menschen- human ['hju:mən]
Menschenmenge crowd [kraʊd]
menschlich human ['hju:mən]
Menü 1. *(im Restaurant)* set meal [ˌset 'mi:l]
2. *(Computermenü)* menu ['menju:]
merken: sich etwas merken remember sth. [rɪ'membə]
Messer knife [naɪf], *pl* knives [naɪvz]
Meter metre ['mi:tə]
mich me [mi:] • **mich (selbst)** myself [maɪ'self]
Mikrofon microphone ['maɪkrəfəʊn]
Milch milk [mɪlk]
mild mild [maɪld]
Million million ['mɪljən]
Millionär/in millionaire [ˌmɪljə'neə]
Minderheit minority [maɪ'nɒrəti]
Mindmap mind map ['maɪnd mæp]
Mini- mini- ['mɪni]
minus minus ['maɪnəs]
Minute minute ['mɪnɪt]
mir me [mi:] • **mir (selbst)** myself [maɪ'self]
mischen mix [mɪks]
Mischung mix; mixture ['mɪkstʃə]
mit with [wɪð] • **mit 16 (Jahren)** at 16 • **Mit besten Grüßen** *(Briefschluss)* Best wishes ['wɪʃɪz] • **mit dem Auto/Zug/Rad/… fahren** go by car/train/bike/…
mitbringen bring [brɪŋ]
mitgenommen (wegen) *(aufgebracht, gekränkt)* upset (about) [ˌʌp'set]
Mitglied (in, von) member (of) ['membə]
mitmachen: bei etwas/jm. mitmachen join sth./sb. [dʒɔɪn]
Mitnehmen: Kaffee zum Mitnehmen coffee to go
Mitschüler/in classmate ['klɑ:smeɪt]
Mittagessen lunch [lʌntʃ] • **Was gibt es zum Mittagessen?** What's for lunch?
Mittagspause lunch break ['lʌntʃ breɪk]
Mittagszeit lunchtime ['lʌntʃtaɪm]
Mitte centre ['sentə]; middle ['mɪdl]
Mitteilung *(Notiz)* note [nəʊt]
Mittel- *(Zentral-)* central ['sentrəl]
mittel(groß) medium ['mi:diəm]
Mittelteil middle ['mɪdl]
Mittwoch Wednesday ['wenzdeɪ, 'wenzdi] *(siehe auch unter „Freitag")*
Mix mix [mɪks]
mixen mix [mɪks]
Möbel furniture *(no pl)* ['fɜ:nɪtʃə]
Möbelstück piece of furniture [ˌpi:s‿əv 'fɜ:nɪtʃə]
Mobiltelefon mobile (phone) [ˌməʊbaɪl 'fəʊn] *(BE)*; cellphone ['selfəʊn] *(AE)*
möchte: Ich möchte gern … (haben) I'd like … (= I would like …) [laɪk]
Ich möchte gehen I'd like to go
Ich möchte nicht gehen I wouldn't like to go • **Möchtest du / Möchten Sie …?** Would you like …?
Mode fashion ['fæʃn]
Modell*(-auto, -schiff; Fotomodell)* model ['mɒdl]
Moderator/in *(Radio, Fernsehen)* presenter [prɪ'zentə]; host [həʊst]; *(von Nachrichtensendungen)* anchorman/anchorwoman ['æŋkəmæn, -wʊmən] *(AE auch kurz:* anchor)
modern modern ['mɒdən]
modisch *(schick, im Trend)* trendy ['trendi]
mögen like [laɪk]; *(sehr mögen)* love [lʌv] • **etwas lieber mögen** like sth. better • **etwas am liebsten mögen** like sth. best
möglich possible ['pɒsəbl]
Möglichkeit possibility [ˌpɒsə'bɪləti]; *(Gelegenheit, Chance)* chance [tʃɑ:ns]
Möhre carrot ['kærət]
Moment moment ['məʊmənt] • **im Moment** at the moment • **genau in dem Moment** just then • **Moment mal!** Wait a minute. ['mɪnɪt]
Monat month [mʌnθ]
Mond moon [mu:n]
Monitor monitor ['mɒnɪtə]
Monster monster ['mɒnstə]
Montag Monday ['mʌndeɪ, 'mʌndi] *(siehe auch unter „Freitag")*
Monument monument ['mɒnjumənt]
Mord murder ['mɜ:də]
morden murder ['mɜ:də]
Mörder/in murderer ['mɜ:dərə]
morgen tomorrow [tə'mɒrəʊ] • **das Wetter von morgen** tomorrow's weather
Morgen morning ['mɔ:nɪŋ] • **am Morgen, morgens** in the morning
Moschee mosque [mɒsk]
Motel motel [məʊ'tel]
Motor engine ['endʒɪn]
MP3-Spieler MP3 player [ˌempi:'θri: ˌpleɪə]
müde tired ['taɪəd]
Müll rubbish ['rʌbɪʃ] *(BE)*; garbage ['gɑ:bɪdʒ] *(AE)*
Mülltonne bin [bɪn]; dustbin ['dʌstbɪn]
multi-, Multi- multi- ['mʌlti] • **Multimillionär/in** multi-millionaire [ˌmʌltiˌmɪljə'neə]
Multiple-Choice multiple choice [ˌmʌltɪpl 'tʃɔɪs]
Mund mouth [maʊθ] • **Halt den Mund!** Shut up. [ˌʃʌt‿'ʌp]
murren grumble ['grʌmbl]
Museum museum [mju'zi:əm]
Musical musical ['mju:zɪkl]
Musik music ['mju:zɪk]
Musiker/in musician [mju:'zɪʃn]
Musikinstrument musical instrument [ˌmju:zɪkl‿'ɪnstrəmənt]
Müsli muesli ['mju:zli]
Muss must [mʌst]
müssen have to; must [mʌst] • **nicht müssen** needn't ['ni:dnt]
mutig brave [breɪv]
Mutter mother ['mʌðə]
Mutti mum [mʌm] *(BE)*; mom [mɒm, *AE:* mɑ:m] *(AE)*
Mütze cap [kæp]

N

Na ja … / Na gut … Oh well … [əʊ wel]
Na und? So? [səʊ]
nach 1. *(örtlich)* to [tə, tu] • **nach draußen** outside • **nach drinnen** inside • **nach Hause gehen** go home • **nach Hause kommen** come home; get home • **nach oben** up; *(im Haus)* upstairs [ˌʌp'steəz] • **nach unten** down; *(im Haus)* downstairs [ˌdaʊn'steəz]
nach vorn to the front [frʌnt]
2. *(zeitlich)* after • **Viertel nach 11** quarter past 11 [pɑ:st]

nach etwas fragen ask about sth. **jn. nach dem Weg fragen** ask sb. the way • **nach Luft schnappen** *(auch: vor Überraschung)* gasp [gɑːsp]
Nachbar/in neighbour ['neɪbə]
nachdem after ['ɑːftə]
nachdenken über think about [θɪŋk]
Nachforschung(en) research *(no pl)* [rɪ'sɜːtʃ, 'riːsɜːtʃ]
Nachmittag afternoon [ˌɑːftə'nuːn] **am Nachmittag, nachmittags** in the afternoon
Nachricht message ['mesɪdʒ] **Nachrichten** *(im Fernsehen, Radio; Neuigkeiten)* news *(no pl)* [njuːz]
nachrufen: jm. Schimpfwörter nachrufen call sb. names
nachschlagen: etwas nachschlagen look sth. up [ˌlʊk‿'ʌp]
nächste(r, s): am nächsten Tag the next day [nekst] • **der Nächste sein** be next • **Was haben wir als Nächstes?** What have we got next?
Nacht night [naɪt] • **heute Nacht** tonight [tə'naɪt] • **in der Nacht, nachts** at night
Nachteil disadvantage [ˌdɪsəd'vɑːntɪdʒ]
nahe (bei) near [nɪə]; close (to) [kləʊs]
Nähe: in der Nähe von near [nɪə]
nähen sew [səʊ]
Name name [neɪm]
Nase nose [nəʊz] • **die Nase voll haben (von)** be fed up (with) [ˌfed‿'ʌp]
Nashorn rhino ['raɪnəʊ]
Nation nation ['neɪʃn]
national national ['næʃnəl]
Nationalpark National Park [ˌnæʃnəl 'pɑːk]
Natur- natural ['nætʃrəl]
Naturgeschichte natural history [ˌnætʃrəl 'hɪstri]
Naturkunde natural history [ˌnætʃrəl 'hɪstri]
natürlich **1.** *(nicht künstlich)* natural ['nætʃrəl] **2.** *(selbstverständlich)* of course [əv 'kɔːs]
Naturwissenschaft science ['saɪəns]
Nebel fog [fɒg]
neben next to ['nekst tə]
nebenbei (bemerkt) by the way [ˌbaɪ ðə 'weɪ]; actually ['æktʃuəli]
neblig foggy ['fɒgi]
Neffe nephew ['nefjuː, 'nevjuː]
nehmen take [teɪk] • **Ich nehme es.** *(beim Einkaufen)* I'll take it. **etwas wichtig nehmen** care about sth. [keə]
neidisch (auf) jealous (of) ['dʒeləs]

nein no [nəʊ]
nennen *(rufen, bezeichnen)* call [kɔːl]; *(benennen)* name [neɪm]
nervös nervous ['nɜːvəs]
nett nice [naɪs] • **Nett, dich kennenzulernen.** Nice to meet you.
neu new [njuː]
neueste(r, s) latest ['leɪtɪst]
nicht not [nɒt] • **nicht mehr** not (...) any more • **Das glaube ich nicht. / Ich glaube nicht.** I don't think so. **..., nicht wahr?** ..., right? • **Du machst Witze, nicht wahr? / Das ist nicht dein Ernst, oder?** You're joking, aren't you? • **nicht vor** *(erst um)* not ... until / not ... till • **noch nicht** not (...) yet [jet] • **(noch) nicht einmal** not even ['iːvn]
Nichte niece [niːs]
nichts nothing ['nʌθɪŋ]; not (...) anything ['eniθɪŋ] • **Nichts zu danken.** You're welcome. ['welkəm]
nicken (mit) nod [nɒd]
nie never ['nevə]
niederbrennen: etwas niederbrennen burn sth. down [ˌbɜːn 'daʊn]
niedergeschlagen depressed [dɪ'prest]
niemals never ['nevə]
niemand nobody ['nəʊbədi]; no one ['nəʊ‿wʌn]; not (...) anybody/anyone ['enibɒdi, 'eniwʌn]
nirgendwo(hin) not (...) anywhere ['eniweə]
noch: noch ein(e) ... another ... [ə'nʌðə]; one more ... [mɔː] • **noch 45 Pence** another 45 p • **noch einmal** again [ə'gen]; once more/once again • **noch jemand anderes** somebody/someone else [els] **noch nicht** not (...) yet [jet] **(immer) noch** still [stɪl] • **(sonst) noch etwas?** anything else? **(sonst) noch jemand?** anybody/anyone else? • **was (sonst) noch?** what else? • **wer/wen/wem (sonst) noch?** who else?
► S.170 ... else
Norden north [nɔːθ] • **nach Norden** north • **Richtung Norden** *(Fahrtrichtung)* northbound ['nɔːθbaʊnd]
nördlich north [nɔːθ]
Nordosten north-east [ˌnɔːθ'iːst] **nach Nordosten** north-east
nordöstlich north-east [ˌnɔːθ'iːst]
Nordwesten north-west [ˌnɔːθ'west] **nach Nordwesten** north-west
nordwestlich north-west [ˌnɔːθ'west]
nörgeln grumble ['grʌmbl]
normalerweise usually ['juːʒuəli]
Note *(Zensur)* grade [greɪd] *(BE auch:* mark [mɑːk])

nötig necessary ['nesəsəri]
Notiz note [nəʊt] • **sich Notizen machen** take notes
notwendig necessary ['nesəsəri]
November November [nəʊ'vembə]
Nudeln pasta *(no pl)* ['pæstə]
null o [əʊ]; zero ['zɪərəʊ]; *(beim Sport)* nil [nɪl]
► S.183 REVISION: Numbers
Nummer number ['nʌmbə]
Nummernschild number plate ['nʌmbə pleɪt] *(BE)*; license plate ['laɪsns pleɪt] *(AE)*
nun now [naʊ] • **Nun, ...** Well, ... [wel]
nur only ['əʊnli]; just [dʒʌst] • **nur zum Spaß** just for fun
Nuss nut [nʌt]
nützlich useful ['juːsfl]; *(hilfreich)* helpful ['helpfl]; *(wertvoll)* valuable ['væljuəbl]

O

ob if [ɪf]
obdachlos homeless ['həʊmləs]
oben above [ə'bʌv]; *(an der Spitze)* at the top (of) [tɒp]; *(im Haus)* upstairs [ˌʌp'steəz] • **dort oben** up there **nach oben** up; *(im Haus)* upstairs
Oberbegriff group word ['gruːp wɜːd]
oberhalb von over ['əʊvə]; above [ə'bʌv]
Oberteil top [tɒp]
Obst fruit [fruːt]
Obstkuchen pie [paɪ]
Obstsalat fruit salad ['fruːt ˌsæləd]
obwohl although [ɔːl'ðəʊ]; even if
oder or [ɔː] • **Das ist nicht dein Ernst, oder?** You're joking, aren't you?
offen open ['əʊpən] • **oben offener (Doppeldecker-)Bus** open-top bus
öffentliche(r, s) public ['pʌblɪk] **öffentliche Verkehrsmittel, öffentlicher Personennahverkehr** public transport *(no pl)* [ˌpʌblɪk 'trænspɔːt]
öffnen; sich öffnen open ['əʊpən]
Öffnungszeiten opening hours *(pl)*
oft often ['ɒfn]
ohne without [wɪ'ðaʊt]
Ohr ear [ɪə]
Ohrenschmerzen earache ['ɪəreɪk]
Ohrring earring ['ɪərɪŋ]
Oje! Oh dear! [əʊ 'dɪə]
okay OK [əʊ'keɪ]
Oktober October [ɒk'təʊbə]
Öl oil [ɔɪl]
Olympische Spiele Olympic Games [əˌlɪmpɪk 'geɪmz]
Oma grandma ['grænmɑː]; granny

Onkel uncle ['ʌŋkl]
online, Online- online [ˌɒn'laɪn]
Opa grandpa ['grænpɑː]
Oper opera ['ɒprə]
Operation (an) operation (on) [ˌɒpə'reɪʃn]
Opfer victim ['vɪktɪm]
Orange orange ['ɒrɪndʒ]
orange(farben) orange ['ɒrɪndʒ]
Orangenmarmelade marmalade ['mɑːməleɪd]
Orangensaft orange juice [dʒuːs]
ordentlich tidy ['taɪdi]
Ordnung: in Ordnung all right [ɔːl 'raɪt]
Orgel organ ['ɔːgən]
Original; Original- original *(n; adj)* [ə'rɪdʒənl]
Ort place [pleɪs]; *(Einsatzort)* location [ləʊ'keɪʃn] • **am/vom Ort** local ['ləʊkl]
örtlich local ['ləʊkl]
Osten east [iːst] • **nach Osten** east **Richtung Osten** *(Fahrtrichtung)* eastbound ['iːstbaʊnd]
östlich east [iːst]
Outfit *(Kleidung; Ausrüstung)* outfit ['aʊtfɪt]
Ozean ocean ['əʊʃn]

P

paar: ein paar some [səm, sʌm]; *(einige wenige)* a few [fjuː]
Paar: ein Paar a pair (of) [peə]
Päckchen packet ['pækɪt] • **ein Päckchen Pfefferminzbonbons** a packet of mints
packen 1. *(Koffer, Auto)* pack [pæk] **2.** *(greifen, schnappen)* grab [græb]
Packung packet ['pækɪt] • **eine Packung Pfefferminzbonbons** a packet of mints
Paddel paddle ['pædl]
Paddelboot canoe [kə'nuː]
paddeln paddle ['pædl]; *(Kanu fahren)* canoe [kə'nuː]
Paket parcel ['pɑːsl]
Palast palace ['pæləs]
Panik: Keine Panik. Don't panic. ['pænɪk]
pantomimisch darstellen mime [maɪm]
Papa dad [dæd]
Papagei parrot ['pærət]
Papier paper ['peɪpə]
Park park [pɑːk]
Parken: *(das)* **Parken** parking ['pɑːkɪŋ]
Parkplatz *(für viele Autos)* car park ['kɑː pɑːk]
Parlament parliament ['pɑːləmənt]
Partner/in partner ['pɑːtnə]
Partnerstadt twin town [ˌtwɪn 'taʊn]; sister city *(AE)*
Party party ['pɑːti] • **eine Party feiern/veranstalten** have a party
passen fit [fɪt]
passieren (mit) happen (to) ['hæpən]
Pastor/in minister ['mɪnɪstə]
Patrouille patrol [pə'trəʊl]
Pause break [breɪk] • **eine Pause machen** take a break • **in der Pause** *(zwischen Schulstunden)* at break
Pazifik Pacific (Ocean) [pə'sɪfɪk]
Pence pence (p) [pens]
perfekt perfect ['pɜːfɪkt]
Person person ['pɜːsn]; *(in Roman, Film)* character ['kærəktə]
Personennahverkehr: öffentlicher Personennahverkehr public transport *(no pl)* [ˌpʌblɪk 'trænspɔːt]
persönliche(r, s) personal ['pɜːsənl]
Persönlichkeit character ['kærəktə]
Pfad path [pɑːθ]; *(Lehrpfad)* trail [treɪl]
Pfarrer/in minister ['mɪnɪstə]
Pfeffer pepper ['pepə]
Pfefferminzbonbons mints [mɪnts]
Pfeife 1. *(zum Rauchen; Orgelpfeife)* pipe [paɪp]
2. *(Trillerpfeife)* whistle ['wɪsl]
pfeifen whistle ['wɪsl]
Pferd horse [hɔːs]
Pferdeschwanz *(Frisur)* ponytail ['pəʊniteɪl]
Pfiff whistle ['wɪsl]
Pflanze plant [plɑːnt]
pflanzen plant [plɑːnt]
Pflanzenöl vegetable oil ['vedʒtəbl]
pflücken: Obst pflücken pick fruit [pɪk]
Pfund *(britische Währung)* pound (£) [paʊnd] • **Es kostet 1 Pfund.** It's £1.
Piano piano [pi'ænəʊ]
Picknick picnic ['pɪknɪk]
piepsen bleep [bliːp]
Piepton bleep [bliːp]
Pilz mushroom ['mʌʃrʊm, -ruːm]
pink(farben) pink [pɪŋk]
Pirat/in pirate ['paɪrət]
Pizza pizza ['piːtsə]
Plan plan [plæn]
planen plan [plæn]
Planet planet ['plænɪt]
Plantage plantation [plɑːn'teɪʃn]
Platz *(Ort, Stelle)* place [pleɪs]; *(in der Stadt)* square [skweə]; *(runder Platz in der Stadt)* circus ['sɜːkəs]; *(für Squash, Badminton)* court [kɔːt]; *(Einsatzort)* location [ləʊ'keɪʃn]
Plätzchen biscuit ['bɪskɪt]
plaudern chat [tʃæt]
plötzlich suddenly ['sʌdnli]
plus plus [plʌs]
Pokal cup [kʌp]
Polizei police *(pl)* [pə'liːs]
Polizeiwache, Polizeirevier police station [pə'liːs steɪʃn]
Polizist/in policeman [pə'liːsmən]/ policewoman [pə'liːswʊmən]
Poltergeist poltergeist ['pəʊltəgaɪst]
Pommes frites chips *(pl)* [tʃɪps] *(BE)*; French fries *(pl)* [fraɪz] *(AE)*
Popcorn popcorn ['pɒpkɔːn]
Pop(musik) pop (music) [pɒp]
Popsender *(Radio)* pop station ['steɪʃn]
Posaune trombone [trɒm'bəʊn]
Post *(Briefe, Päckchen, ...)* post [pəʊst]; *(Postamt)* post office ['pəʊst_ɒfɪs]
Postamt post office ['pəʊst_ɒfɪs]
Poster poster ['pəʊstə]
Postkarte postcard ['pəʊstkɑːd]
prallen: gegen/auf die Windschutzscheibe prallen hit the windscreen ['wɪndskriːn]
Präsentation presentation [ˌprezn'teɪʃn]
präsentieren: (jm.) etwas präsentieren present sth. (to sb.) [prɪ'zent]
Präsident/in president ['prezɪdənt]
Preis 1. *(Kaufpreis)* price [praɪs]
2. *(Gewinn)* prize [praɪz]
pressen squeeze [skwiːz]
privat private ['praɪvət]
pro per [pɜː, pə] • **einmal pro Woche** once a week / once per week
Probe *(am Theater)* rehearsal [rɪ'hɜːsl]
proben *(am Theater)* rehearse [rɪ'hɜːs]
probieren try [traɪ]
Problem problem ['prɒbləm]
Produkt product ['prɒdʌkt]
Produktion production [prə'dʌkʃn]
produzieren produce [prə'djuːs]
Programm programme ['prəʊgræm]
Projekt (über, zu) project (on, about) ['prɒdʒekt] • **ein Projekt machen, durchführen** do a project
Protest protest ['prəʊtest]
protestieren protest [prə'test]
Provinz province ['prɒvɪns]
Prozent per cent (%) [pə'sent]
Prozess *(Verfahren, Vorgang)* process ['prəʊses]
prüfen *(überprüfen)* check [tʃek]
Prüfung *(Examen)* exam [ɪg'zæm] • **eine Prüfung ablegen** take/do an exam • **eine Prüfung bestehen**

pass an exam [pɑːs] • **eine Prüfung nicht bestehen** fail an exam [feɪl]
PS *(Nachschrift unter Briefen)* PS [ˌpiː‿'es] (postscript ['pəʊstskrɪpt])
Publikum audience ['ɔːdɪəns]
Pullover pullover ['pʊləʊvə]
Punk(rock) punk (rock) [pʌŋk]
Punkt *(bei Test, Quiz)* point [pɔɪnt]
Punktestand *(Spielstand)* score [skɔː]
Pute, Puter turkey ['tɜːki]
putzen clean [kliːn] • **Ich putze mir die Zähne.** I clean my teeth.
Putzfrau, -mann cleaner ['kliːnə]
Pyramide pyramid ['pɪrəmɪd]

Q

Quadratkilometer square km (sq km) [skweə]
Qualität quality ['kwɒləti]
Quelle *(Informations-, Textquelle)* source [sɔːs]
quer über across [ə'krɒs]
Querflöte flute [fluːt]
Quiz quiz [kwɪz], *pl* quizzes ['kwɪzɪz]

R

Rad 1. wheel [wiːl]
2. *(Fahrrad)* bike [baɪk]
Rad fahren cycle ['saɪkl]; ride a bike [ˌraɪd‿ə 'baɪk]
Radfahrt bike ride ['baɪk raɪd]
Radiergummi rubber ['rʌbə] *(BE)*; eraser [ɪ'reɪzə, *AE:* ɪ'reɪsər] *(AE)*
Radio radio ['reɪdiəʊ] • **im Radio** on the radio
Radiosender radio station ['reɪdiəʊ ˌsteɪʃn]
Radweg cycle path ['saɪkl pɑːθ]
Rand *(Kante)* rim [rɪm]
Rap rap [ræp]
rappen rap [ræp]
Rapper/in rapper ['ræpə]
Rasen mähen cut the grass [grɑːs]
Rassentrennung segregation [ˌsegrɪ'geɪʃn]
raten guess [ges]
Ratespiel quiz [kwɪz], *pl* quizzes ['kwɪzɪz]
Rätsel riddle ['rɪdl]; puzzle ['pʌzl]; *(Geheimnis)* mystery ['mɪstri]
Rauch smoke [sməʊk]
rauchen smoke [sməʊk]
Raum room [ruːm]
Rauschgift *(Droge)* drug [drʌg]
rauskommen *(Film, DVD: veröffentlicht werden)* come out
realistisch realistic [ˌriːə'lɪstɪk]
Realität reality [ri'æləti]
Recherche research *(no pl)* [rɪ'sɜːtʃ, 'riːsɜːtʃ]
recherchieren do research
Recht right [raɪt] • **Recht haben** be right
rechte(r, s) right [raɪt] • **rechts, auf der rechten Seite** on the right
(nach) rechts abbiegen turn right
nach rechts schauen look right
Rechtschreibung spelling ['spelɪŋ]
rechtzeitig in time [ɪn 'taɪm]
recycelt recycled [ˌriː'saɪkld]
Recycling recycling [ˌriː'saɪklɪŋ]
Redakteur/in editor ['edɪtə]
Rede speech [spiːtʃ] • **eine Rede halten** make a speech
reden (mit, über) talk (to, about) [tɔːk]; speak (to, about) [spiːk]
Wovon redest du? What are you talking about?
Reflex reflex ['riːfleks]
Refrain chorus ['kɔːrəs]
Regal(brett) shelf [ʃelf], *pl* shelves [ʃelvz]
Regel *(Vorschrift)* rule [ruːl]
Regen rain [reɪn]
Reggae reggae ['regeɪ]
Regierung government ['gʌvənmənt]
regnen rain [reɪn]
regnerisch rainy ['reɪni]
Reh deer, *pl* deer [dɪə]
reich rich [rɪtʃ]
reichen *(weitergeben)* pass [pɑːs]
Reihe 1. *(wartende Menschen)* queue [kjuː] *(BE)*; line [laɪn] *(AE)*
2. *(Sendereihe, Serie)* series, *pl* series ['sɪəriːz]
3. Du bist an der Reihe. It's your turn. [tɜːn] • **Wer ist an der Reihe?** Whose turn is it? [huːz]
Reihenfolge order ['ɔːdə]
Reis rice [raɪs]
Reise trip [trɪp]; *(Fahrt)* journey ['dʒɜːni]
Reiseleiter/in guide [gaɪd]
reisen travel ['trævl]
reiten ride [raɪd] • **reiten gehen** go riding
Reiter/in rider ['raɪdə]
Reiterhelm riding hat ['raɪdɪŋ hæt]
Reitkappe riding hat ['raɪdɪŋ hæt]
Reitstiefel riding boots *(pl)* ['raɪdɪŋ buːts]
Reitweg bridle path ['braɪdl pɑːθ]
Religion *(Religionsunterricht)* RE [ˌɑːr‿'iː], Religious Education [rɪˌlɪdʒəs‿edʒu'keɪʃn]
rennen run [rʌn]
Reportage (über) report (on) [rɪ'pɔːt]
Reporter/in reporter [rɪ'pɔːtə]
repräsentieren represent [ˌreprɪ'zent]
Rest rest [rest]
Restaurant restaurant ['restrɒnt]; *(Imbissstube, Café)* café ['kæfeɪ]
Resultat result [rɪ'zʌlt]
retten save [seɪv]
richtig right [raɪt]; *(korrekt)* correct [kə'rekt]
Richtung way [weɪ] • **in diese Richtung** this way • **in die falsche Richtung** the wrong way • **in welche Richtung?** which way?
Richtung Norden northbound ['nɔːθbaʊnd] • **Richtung Osten** eastbound ['iːstbaʊnd] • **Richtung Süden** southbound ['saʊθbaʊnd]
Richtung Westen westbound ['westbaʊnd]
riechen smell [smel]
Riesenrad big wheel [wiːl]
riesig huge [hjuːdʒ]
Rindfleisch beef [biːf]
Ring ring [rɪŋ]
Rock skirt [skɜːt]
Rock(musik) rock (music) [rɒk]
Rolle role [rəʊl]
Rollenspiel role play ['rəʊl pleɪ]
Rollstuhl wheelchair ['wiːltʃeə]
römisch; Römer, Römerin Roman ['rəʊmən]
rosa pink [pɪŋk]
rot red [red]
Route route [ruːt]
Rückfahrkarte return ticket [rɪ'tɜːn ˌtɪkɪt]
Rucksack rucksack ['rʌksæk]
rufen call [kɔːl]; shout [ʃaʊt] • **die Polizei rufen** call the police
Ruhe: jn. in Ruhe lassen leave sb. alone [ˌliːv‿ə'ləʊn]
ruhig quiet ['kwaɪət] • **Bleib ruhig.** Don't panic. ['pænɪk]
rumhängen *(abhängen)* hang out [ˌhæŋ‿'aʊt] *(infml)*
rund round [raʊnd]
Rundgang (durch das Haus) tour (of the house) [tʊə]
runterladen download [ˌdaʊn'ləʊd]

S

Saal hall [hɔːl]
Sache thing [θɪŋ]
Saft juice [dʒuːs]
sagen say [seɪ] • **Sagt mir eure Namen.** Tell me your names. [tel]
jm. sagen, dass er/sie etwas tun soll tell sb. to do sth.
Sahne cream [kriːm]
Salat 1. *(Kopfsalat)* lettuce ['letɪs]
2. *(Gericht, Beilage)* salad ['sæləd]

Salz salt [sɔ:lt]
Sammelalbum scrapbook ['skræpbʊk]
sammeln collect [kə'lekt] • **Geld sammeln (für)** raise money (for) [reɪz]
Sammler/in collector [kə'lektə]
Sammlung collection [kə'lekʃn]
Samstag Saturday ['sætədeɪ, 'sætədi] *(siehe auch unter „Freitag“)*
Sandale sandal ['sændl]
Sandwich sandwich ['sænwɪtʃ]
Sänger/in singer ['sɪŋə]
Sanitäter/in paramedic [,pærə'medɪk]
satt: etwas satt haben be tired of sth. ['taɪəd]
Sattel saddle ['sædl]
Satz sentence ['sentəns]
sauber clean [kli:n] • **sauber machen** clean
Säule column ['kɒləm]
Sauna sauna ['sɔ:nə] • **in die Sauna gehen** have a sauna
Säure acid ['æsɪd]
Saxophon saxophone ['sæksəfəʊn]
Schachtel packet ['pækɪt]
Schaf sheep, *pl* sheep [ʃi:p]
Schale bowl [bəʊl] • **eine Schale Cornflakes** a bowl of cornflakes
Schallplatte record ['rekɔ:d]
scharf *(würzig)* spicy ['spaɪsi]
Schatten *(einer Person, eines Gegenstands)* shadow ['ʃædəʊ]
Schatz dear [dɪə]; sweetheart ['swi:thɑ:t]
schätzen *(erraten)* guess [ges]; *(zu schätzen wissen)* appreciate [ə'pri:ʃieɪt]
schauen look [lʊk] • **nach links/rechts schauen** look left/right
Schaufenster shop window [,ʃɒp 'wɪndəʊ]
Schauspiel drama ['drɑ:mə]
Schauspieler/in actor ['æktə]
scheinen 1. *(Sonne)* shine [ʃaɪn] **2. zu sein/zu tun scheinen** seem to be/to do [si:m]
scherzen joke [dʒəʊk]
scheu shy [ʃaɪ]
scheußlich horrible ['hɒrəbl]
Schicht *(bei der Arbeit)* shift [ʃɪft] **in seiner Schicht** on his shift
schick *(modisch, im Trend)* trendy ['trendi]
schicken (an) *(Post, E-Mail)* send (to) [send]; mail (to) [meɪl] • **jm. eine SMS schicken** text sb. [tekst]
schieben push [pʊʃ]
schiefgehen go wrong
schießen: ein Tor schießen score (a goal) [skɔ:], [gəʊl]
Schiff boat [bəʊt]; ship [ʃɪp]

Schild *(Zeichen)* sign [saɪn]
Schildkröte tortoise ['tɔ:təs]
Schimpfwort: jn. mit Schimpfwörtern hänseln, jm. Schimpfwörter nachrufen call sb. names
Schinkenspeck bacon ['beɪkən]
Schlaf sleep [sli:p]
Schlafanzug pyjamas *(pl)* [pə'dʒɑ:məz]
schlafen sleep [sli:p]; *(nicht wach sein)* be asleep [ə'sli:p]
schlaflos sleepless ['sli:pləs]
Schlafparty sleepover ['sli:pəʊvə]
Schlafzimmer bedroom ['bedru:m]
schlagen hit [hɪt]; *(besiegen)* beat [bi:t] • **gegen/auf die Windschutzscheibe schlagen** hit the windscreen ['wɪndskri:n]
Schlägerei fight [faɪt]
Schlagzeile headline ['hedlaɪn]
Schlagzeug spielen play the drums [drʌmz]
Schlange snake [sneɪk]; *(wartende Menschen)* queue [kju:] *(BE)*, line [laɪn] *(AE)*
schlau clever ['klevə]; smart [smɑ:t]
Schlauchboot *(wildwassertauglich)* raft [rɑ:ft]
Schlauheit cleverness ['klevənəs]
schlecht bad [bæd] • **schlechter** worse [wɜ:s] • **am schlechtesten; der/die/das schlechteste** (the) worst [wɜ:st] • **schlechtes Timing** bad timing • **schlecht in etwas sein; etwas schlecht können** be bad at sth. • **Mir ist schlecht.** I feel sick. [sɪk]
Schleuse lock [lɒk]
schließen *(zumachen)* close [kləʊz]
schließlich at last [ət 'lɑ:st]; *(zum Schluss)* in the end
schlimm bad [bæd] • **schlimmer** worse [wɜ:s] • **am schlimmsten; der/die/das schlimmste** (the) worst [wɜ:st]
Schlips tie [taɪ]
Schlitten sledge [sledʒ]
Schlittschuh laufen skate [skeɪt]
Schlittschuhbahn ice rink ['aɪs rɪŋk]
Schloss castle ['kɑ:sl]; *(Palast)* palace ['pæləs]
Schluss 1. end • **zum Schluss** in the end
2. *(einer Geschichte, eines Films usw.)* ending ['endɪŋ]
3. *(Schlussfolgerung)* conclusion [kən'klu:ʒn] • **Schlüsse ziehen** draw conclusions [,drɔ: kən'klu:ʒnz]
Schlüssel key [ki:]
Schlüsselwort key word ['ki: wɜ:d]
schlussfolgern draw conclusions [,drɔ: kən'klu:ʒnz]

Schlussfolgerung conclusion [kən'klu:ʒn]
Schmerz(en) pain [peɪn]
Schmuck jewellery *(no pl)* ['dʒu:əlri]
schmutzig dirty ['dɜ:ti]
schnappen *(greifen, packen)* grab [græb] • **nach Luft schnappen** *(auch: vor Überraschung)* gasp [gɑ:sp]
Schnee snow [snəʊ]
Schneeball snowball ['snəʊbɔ:l]
Schneeschuh snowshoe ['snəʊʃu:]
Schneeschuhwandern snowshoeing ['snəʊʃu:ɪŋ]
schneiden cut [kʌt]
schnell quick [kwɪk]; fast [fɑ:st]
Schokolade chocolate ['tʃɒklət]
schon already [ɔ:l'redi] • **schon?** yet? [jet] • **schon mal?** ever? ['evə] **(vorher) schon mal** before [bɪ'fɔ:]
schön beautiful ['bju:tɪfl]; *(nett)* nice [naɪs] • **schön ordentlich** neat and tidy [,ni:t_ən 'taɪdi]
Schönheit beauty ['bju:ti]
Schrank cupboard ['kʌbəd]; *(Kleiderschrank)* wardrobe ['wɔ:drəʊb]
schrecklich terrible ['terəbl]; awful ['ɔ:fl] • **schreckliche Angst haben (vor)** be terrified (of) ['terɪfaɪd]
schreiben (an) write (to) [raɪt]
Schreiber/in writer ['raɪtə]
Schreibtisch desk [desk]
Schreibung *(Rechtschreibung, Schreibweise)* spelling ['spelɪŋ]
schreien shout [ʃaʊt]; cry [kraɪ]; *(kreischen)* scream [skri:m]
Schriftsteller/in writer ['raɪtə]
Schritt step [step] • **Schritte machen/unternehmen** take steps
schüchtern shy [ʃaɪ]
Schuh shoe [ʃu:]
Schulbildung education [,edʒu'keɪʃn]
Schuld: Es/Das ist nicht meine Schuld. It's not my fault. [fɔ:lt] **jm. die Schuld geben (an)** blame sb. (for) [bleɪm]
schuldbewusst guilty ['gɪlti]
schuldig guilty ['gɪlti]
Schule school [sku:l] • **in der Schule** at school
Schüler/in student ['stju:dənt]
Schulfach (school) subject ['sʌbdʒɪkt]
Schulheft exercise book ['eksəsaɪz bʊk]
Schulklasse class [klɑ:s]; form [fɔ:m]
Schulleiter/in head teacher [,hed 'ti:tʃə]
Schulnote grade [greɪd] *(BE auch:* mark [mɑ:k]*)*
Schultasche school bag ['sku:l bæg]
Schulter shoulder ['ʃəʊldə]

Schulterpolster *(beim American Football)* pad [pæd]
Schuss shot [ʃɒt]
Schüssel bowl [bəʊl]
Schusswaffe gun [gʌn]
schütteln shake [ʃeɪk]
schützen: jn. schützen (vor) protect sb. (from) [prə'tekt]
Schützer *(Knieschützer usw. für Inlineskater)* pad [pæd]
schwach weak [wi:k]
schwarz black [blæk] • **schwarzes Brett** *(Anschlagtafel)* notice board ['nəʊtɪs bɔ:d] *(BE)*; bulletin board ['bʊlətɪn bɔ:d] *(AE)*
Schwarzbär black bear ['blæk beə]
Schweigen silence ['saɪləns]
Schwein pig [pɪg]
Schweinefleisch pork [pɔ:k]
Schweiß sweat [swet]
schwer *(schwierig)* difficult ['dɪfɪkəlt]; hard [hɑ:d]
Schwester sister ['sɪstə]
schwierig difficult ['dɪfɪkəlt]; hard [hɑ:d]
Schwierigkeiten trouble ['trʌbl] • **in Schwierigkeiten sein** be in trouble
Schwimmbad, -becken swimming pool ['swɪmɪŋ pu:l]
schwimmen swim [swɪm]
schwimmen gehen go swimming
Schwimmer/in swimmer ['swɪmə]
schwitzen sweat [swet]
See 1. *(Binnensee)* lake [leɪk]
2. *(die See, das Meer)* sea [si:]
segeln sail [seɪl]
sehen see [si:] • **Siehst du?** See?
Sehenswürdigkeiten sights *(pl)* [saɪts]
sehr very ['veri] • **Danke sehr!** Thanks very much! • **Er mag sie sehr.** He likes her a lot. [ə 'lɒt]
etwas sehr mögen/sehr lieben like/love sth. very much
Seife soap [səʊp]
Seifenoper soap opera ['səʊp‿ɒprə] *(infml auch:* soap)
sein *(Verb)* be [bi:]
sein(e) ... *(besitzanzeigend) (zu „he")* his ...; *(zu „it")* its ...
seiner, seine, seins his [hɪz]
seit 1. *(mit Zeitraum)* **seit 20 Minuten** for 20 minutes
2. *(mit Zeitpunkt)* **seit dem 4. April** since April 4th [sɪns]
Seit wann ...? How long ...?
► S.186 German 'seit'
seitdem since then
Seite 1. side [saɪd] • **auf der linken Seite** on the left • **auf der rechten Seite** on the right
2. *(Buch-, Heftseite)* page [peɪdʒ]
Auf welcher Seite sind wir? What page are we on?
selbst 1. über dich selbst about yourself [jə'self, jɔ:'self]
2. selbst wenn even if
selbstständig *(ohne Hilfe)* on my/our/... own [əʊn]
selbstverständlich of course [əv 'kɔ:s]
seltsam strange [streɪndʒ]
Semester *(Schulhalbjahr in den USA)* semester [sɪ'mestə]
senden (an) *(Post, E-Mail)* send (to) [send]; mail (to) [meɪl]
Sender *(Fernseh-, Radiokanal)* channel ['tʃænl]; *(Radio-, Popsender)* station ['steɪʃn]
Sendereihe series, *pl* series ['sɪəri:z]
Sendernetz *(Radio, Fernsehen)* network ['netwɜ:k]
separat separate ['seprət]
September September [sep'tembə]
Serie *(Sendereihe)* series, *pl* series ['sɪəri:z]
Sessel armchair ['ɑ:mtʃeə]
setzen: sich setzen sit [sɪt] • **Setz dich/Setzt euch zu mir.** Sit with me. • **sich mit jm. in Verbindung setzen** contact sb. ['kɒntækt]
Shorts shorts *(pl)* [ʃɔ:ts]
Show show [ʃəʊ]
sich (selbst) 1. *(zu „she")* herself [hə'self, hɜ:'self]
2. *(zu „he")* himself [hɪm'self]
3. *(zu „it")* itself [ɪt'self]
4. *(zu „they")* themselves [ðəm'selvz]
5. sich (gegenseitig) *(einander)* each other [i:tʃ‿'ʌðə]; one another [wʌn‿ə'nʌðə]
sicher 1. *(in Sicherheit)* safe (from) [seɪf] • **nicht sicher** *(gefährlich)* unsafe [ʌn'seɪf]
2. sicher sein *(nicht zweifeln)* be sure [ʃʊə, ʃɔ:]
Sicherheit *(das Sichersein vor Gefahr)* safety ['seɪfti]; *(Sicherheitsvorkehrungen)* security [sɪ'kjʊərəti]
in Sicherheit (vor) safe (from) [seɪf]
► S.173 „Sicherheit"
Sicht: aus meiner Sicht from my point of view [,pɔɪnt‿əv 'vju:]
Sicht(weite) visibility [,vɪzə'bɪləti]
sie 1. *(weibliche Person)* she [ʃi:]
Frag sie. Ask her. [hə, hɜ:]
2. *(Ding, Tier)* it [ɪt]
3. *(Plural)* they [ðeɪ] • **Frag sie.** Ask them. [ðəm, ðem]
4. Sie *(höfliche Anrede)* you [ju:]
Sieg win [wɪn]
Sieger/in winner ['wɪnə]
Siegesschuss winning shot [,wɪnɪŋ 'ʃɒt]
Siegtreffer winning shot [,wɪnɪŋ 'ʃɒt]
Silbe syllable ['sɪləbl]
singen sing [sɪŋ]
Single single ['sɪŋgl]
Sitzbank bench [bentʃ]
sitzen sit [sɪt]
Skateboard skateboard ['skeɪtbɔ:d]
Skateboard fahren skate [skeɪt]
Sketch sketch [sketʃ]
Ski ski [ski:] • **Ski laufen/fahren** ski [ski:]
Skipiste ski slope ['ski: sləʊp]
Sklave, Sklavin slave [sleɪv]
SMS text message ['tekst ,mesɪdʒ]
jm. eine SMS schicken text sb. [tekst]
Snack snack [snæk]
so 1. *(auf diese Weise)* like this; like that; this way; that way
2. so weit/gut/schlecht/... that far/good/bad/... • **So süß!** So sweet!
3. so groß/aufregend wie as big/exciting as
4. So, das hätten wir. There you go! *(infml)*
sobald as soon as [əz 'su:n‿əz]
Socke sock [sɒk]
sodass so that
soeben just [dʒʌst]
Sofa sofa ['səʊfə]
sofern as long as
sofort immediately [ɪ'mi:diətli]
Software software ['sɒftweə]
sogar even ['i:vn]
Sohn son [sʌn]
solange as long as
Soldat/in soldier ['səʊldʒə]
sollten: wir sollten ... we should ... [ʃəd, ʃʊd]
Sommer summer ['sʌmə]
sonderbar strange [streɪndʒ]
Song song [sɒŋ]
Songtext(e) lyrics *(pl)* ['lɪrɪks]
Sonnabend Saturday ['sætədeɪ, 'sætədi] *(siehe auch unter „Freitag")*
Sonne sun [sʌn]
Sonnenbrille: (eine) Sonnenbrille sunglasses *(pl)* ['sʌnglɑ:sɪz]
sonnig sunny ['sʌni]
Sonntag Sunday ['sʌndeɪ, 'sʌndi] *(siehe auch unter „Freitag")*
sonst: sonst irgendwo(hin) somewhere else [els] • **sonst noch etwas?** anything else? • **sonst noch jemand?** anybody/anyone else? • **was sonst noch?** what else? • **Was weißt du sonst noch über ...?** What else do you know about ...? • **wer/wen/wem sonst**

noch? who else?
▶ S.170 ... else

Sorge worry ['wʌri] • **sich Sorgen machen (wegen, um)** worry (about) • **Mach dir keine Sorgen.** Don't worry.

sorgen: dafür sorgen, dass ... make sure that ...

sorgfältig careful ['keəfl]

sowie *(sobald)* as soon as [əz 'suːn_əz]

sowieso anyway ['eniweɪ]

Spaghetti spaghetti [spə'geti]

spannend exciting [ɪk'saɪtɪŋ]

sparen save [seɪv]

Spaß fun [fʌn] • **Spaß haben** have fun • **nur zum Spaß** just for fun **Reiten macht Spaß.** Riding is fun. **Viel Spaß!** Have fun! / Have a good time!

spät late [leɪt] • **Wie spät ist es?** What's the time? • **zu spät sein/kommen** be late

später later ['leɪtə]

spazieren gehen go for a walk [wɔːk]

Spaziergang walk [wɔːk] • **einen Spaziergang machen** go for a walk

Specht woodpecker ['wʊdpekə]

Speisekarte menu ['menjuː]

sperren *(blockieren)* block [blɒk]

spezifische(r, s) specific [spə'sɪfɪk]

Spiegel mirror ['mɪrə]

Spiel game [geɪm]; *(Wettkampf)* match [mætʃ]

spielen play [pleɪ]; *(Szene, Dialog)* act [ækt] • **Fußball spielen** play football • **Gitarre/Klavier/Schlagzeug spielen** play the guitar/the piano/the drums • **jm. einen Streich spielen** play a trick on sb.

Spieler/in player ['pleɪə]

Spielstand *(Punktestand)* score [skɔː]

Spielstein *(für Brettspiele)* counter ['kaʊntə]

Spion/in spy [spaɪ]

Spitze *(oberes Ende)* top [tɒp]; *(Flügel-, Schuhspitze)* tip [tɪp] • **an der Spitze (von)** at the top (of)

Sport; Sportart sport [spɔːt] • **Sport treiben** do sport

Sportausrüstung, Sportsachen sports gear *(no pl)* ['spɔːts gɪə]

Sporthalle gym [dʒɪm]; sports hall ['spɔːts hɔːl]

Sportler, Sportlerin sportsman, sportswoman ['spɔːtsmən, -ˌwʊmən]

Sportplatz *(Spielfeld)* field [fiːld]

Sportsachen sports gear *(no pl)* ['spɔːts gɪə]

Sportunterricht PE [ˌpiː_'iː], Physical Education [ˌfɪzɪkəl_edʒu'keɪʃn]

Sprache language ['læŋgwɪdʒ]

Sprachmittlung *(Mediation)* mediation [ˌmiːdi'eɪʃn]

sprechen (mit) speak (to) [spiːk] **Hier spricht Isabel.** *(am Telefon)* This is Isabel.

springen jump [dʒʌmp]

spritzen splash [splæʃ]

sprühen spray [spreɪ]

spucken spit [spɪt]

Spülbecken, Spüle sink [sɪŋk]

Staat state [steɪt] • **die Vereinigten Staaten (von Amerika)** the United States (US) [juˌnaɪtɪd 'steɪts], [ˌjuː_'es]

Stadion stadium ['steɪdiəm]

Stadt *(Großstadt)* city ['sɪti]; *(Kleinstadt)* town [taʊn]

Stadtbezirk borough ['bʌrə, *AE:* 'bɜːrəʊ]
▶ S.172 New York: the five boroughs

Stadtplan map [mæp]

Stadtzentrum city centre [ˌsɪti 'sentə] *(BE)*; downtown [ˌdaʊn'taʊn] *(AE)* **der Bus in Richtung Stadtzentrum** the downtown bus *(AE)* • **im/in das Stadtzentrum** downtown *(AE)*

Stahl steel [stiːl]

Stall *(für Kaninchen)* hutch [hʌtʃ]

Stammbaum family tree ['fæməli triː]

Standpunkt point of view [ˌpɔɪnt_əv 'vjuː] • **von meinem Standpunkt aus gesehen** from my point of view

Star *(Film-, Popstar)* star [stɑː]

stark strong [strɒŋ]

Start start [stɑːt]

starten start [stɑːt]

stattfinden take place [ˌteɪk 'pleɪs]

Statue statue ['stætʃuː]

Stau traffic jam ['træfɪk dʒæm]

staubig dusty ['dʌsti]

Steak steak [steɪk]

Stecker plug [plʌg]

Steeldrum steel drum [ˌstiːl 'drʌm]

stehen stand [stænd] • **Hier steht: ...** *(im Text)* It says here: ... • **Wie steht es?** *(beim Sport)* What's the score?

stehlen steal [stiːl]

steigen rise [raɪz]

Steigerung comparison [kəm'pærɪsn]

Stein stone [stəʊn]

stellen *(hin-, abstellen)* put [pʊt] **Fragen stellen** ask questions **etwas auf die Beine stellen** get sth. off the ground [graʊnd] **etwas lauter/leiser stellen** turn sth. up/down [tɜːn] • **(jm.) eine Falle stellen** set a trap (for sb.) [ˌset_ə 'træp] • **sich (hin)stellen** stand [stænd] • **Stell dir vor! / Stellt euch vor!** Guess what! [ˌges 'wɒt]

sterben (an) die (of) [daɪ]

Stern star [stɑː]

Stichwort *(Schlüsselwort)* key word ['kiː wɜːd]

Stiefel boot [buːt]

still quiet ['kwaɪət]

Stille silence ['saɪləns]

Stimme voice [vɔɪs]

stimmen 1. Das stimmt. That's right. [raɪt] • **..., stimmt's?** ..., right? **2 für jn. stimmen** vote for sb. [vəʊt]

Stock *(Stockwerk)* floor [flɔː] **erster Stock** first floor *(BE)*; second floor *(AE)* • **im ersten Stock** on the first floor *(BE)*; on the second floor *(AE)*
▶ S.171 floor

Stockwerk floor [flɔː]
▶ S.171 floor

stolz (auf jn./etwas) proud (of sb./sth.) [praʊd]

stoßen push [pʊʃ]

Strand beach [biːtʃ] • **am Strand** on the beach

Straße road [rəʊd]; street [striːt]

Straßenbahn tram [træm]

Strecke *(Route)* route [ruːt]

Streich trick [trɪk] • **jm. einen Streich spielen** play a trick on sb.

Streife *(Patrouille)* patrol [pə'trəʊl]

Streik strike [straɪk]

streiken 1. *(sich im Streik befinden)* be on strike [straɪk] **2.** *(in den Streik treten)* go on strike

Streit argument ['ɑːgjumənt]

streiten: sich streiten argue ['ɑːgjuː]

streng strict [strɪkt]

Stromschnellen rapids *(pl)* ['ræpɪdz]

Struktur structure ['strʌktʃə]

strukturieren structure ['strʌktʃə]

Strumpf sock [sɒk]

Strumpfhose tights *(pl)* [taɪts]

Stück 1. piece [piːs] • **ein Stück Papier** a piece of paper **2.** *(Titel auf CD)* track [træk]

Student/in student ['stjuːdənt]

studieren study ['stʌdi]

Studio studio ['stjuːdiəʊ]

Stufe step [step]

Stuhl chair [tʃeə]

stumm: „stummer" Buchstabe *(nicht gesprochener Buchstabe)* silent letter [ˌsaɪlənt 'letə]

Stunde hour ['aʊə]; *(Schulstunde)* lesson ['lesn]; period ['pɪəriəd] • **eine halbe Stunde** half an hour [ˌhɑːf_ən_'aʊə] • **ein 14-Stunden-Flug** a

14-hour flight • **ein Supermarkt, der 24 Stunden geöffnet ist** a 24-hour supermarket
Stundenplan timetable ['taɪmteɪbl] *(BE)*; schedule [*AE:* 'skedʒu:l, *BE:* 'ʃedju:l] *(AE)*
stündig: ein 14-stündiger Flug a 14-hour flight
Sturm storm [stɔ:m]
stürmisch stormy ['stɔ:mi]
stürzen *(hinfallen)* fall [fɔ:l]
suchen: etwas suchen look for sth. ['lʊk fɔ:]; search for sth. ['sɜ:tʃ fɔ:]
Suchmaschine search engine ['sɜ:tʃ‿,endʒɪn]
Süden south [saʊθ] • **nach Süden** south • **Richtung Süden** *(Fahrtrichtung)* southbound ['saʊθbaʊnd]
südlich south [saʊθ]
Südosten south-east [,saʊθ'i:st] **nach Südosten** south-east
südöstlich south-east [,saʊθ'i:st]
Südwesten south-west [,saʊθ'west] **nach Südwesten** south-west
südwestlich south-west [,saʊθ'west]
Supermarkt supermarket ['su:pəmɑ:kɪt]
Suppe soup [su:p]
Surfbrett surfboard ['sɜ:fbɔ:d]
surfen surf [sɜ:f] • **im Internet surfen** surf the internet • **surfen gehen** go surfing
Surfer/in surfer ['sɜ:fə]
süß sweet [swi:t]
Süßigkeiten sweets *(pl)* [swi:ts]
Sweatshirt sweatshirt ['swetʃɜ:t]
sympathisch likeable ['laɪkəbl]
Synagoge synagogue ['sɪnəgɒg]
Synonym *(Wort mit gleicher o. sehr ähnlicher Bedeutung)* synonym ['sɪnənɪm]
System system ['sɪstəm]
Szene scene [si:n]

T

Tabak tobacco [tə'bækəʊ]
Tafel *(Wandtafel)* board [bɔ:d] • **an der/die Tafel** on the board
Tag day [deɪ] • **an jenem Tag** that day • **drei Tage (lang)** for three days • **eines Tages** one day **Guten Tag.** Hello.; *(nachmittags)* Good afternoon. [gʊd‿,ɑ:ftə'nu:n]
Tagebuch diary ['daɪəri]
Tages- daily ['deɪli]
Tagesdecke bedspread ['bedspred]
Tagesfahrkarte all-day ticket; *(der Londoner Verkehrsbetriebe)* Travelcard ['trævlkɑ:d]
täglich daily ['deɪli]
Tal valley ['væli]
Talboden valley floor [,væli 'flɔ:]
Talent talent ['tælənt]
Tank tank [tæŋk]
Tankstelle petrol station *(BE)*; gas station *(AE)*
Tante aunt [ɑ:nt]; auntie ['ɑ:nti]
Tanz dance [dɑ:ns]
Tanzboden dance floor ['dɑ:ns flɔ:]
tanzen dance [dɑ:ns]
Tanzen dancing ['dɑ:nsɪŋ]
Tänzer/in dancer ['dɑ:nsə]
Tanzfläche dance floor ['dɑ:ns flɔ:]
Tanzstunden, Tanzunterricht dancing lessons ['dɑ:nsɪŋ ,lesnz]
Tasche 1. *(Tragetasche, Beutel)* bag [bæg]
2. *(Hosentasche, Jackentasche)* pocket ['pɒkɪt]
Taschengeld pocket money ['pɒkɪt mʌni]
Tasse cup [kʌp] • **eine Tasse Tee** a cup of tea
tätig *(aktiv)* active ['æktɪv]
Tätigkeit activity [æk'tɪvəti]
Tatsache fact [fækt]
tauschen: etwas tauschen (für etwas/ gegen etwas) swap sth. (for sth.) [swɒp]
tausend thousand ['θaʊznd]
Taxi taxi ['tæksi]; cab [kæb]
Team team [ti:m]
Teddybär teddy bear ['tedi beə]
Tee tea [ti:]
Teebeutel tea bag ['ti: bæg]
Teelöffel teaspoon ['ti:spu:n]
Teenager teenager ['ti:neɪdʒə]
Teenager- *(Jugend-)* teen [ti:n]
Teigwaren pasta *(no pl)* ['pæstə]
Teil part [pɑ:t]; *(Abschnitt)* section ['sekʃn]
teilen: sich etwas teilen (mit jm.) share sth. (with sb.) [ʃeə]
teilnehmen (an) take part (in)
Telefon (tele)phone ['telɪfəʊn] • **am Telefon** on the phone
Telefonansage *(vom Band)* recorded message [rɪ,kɔ:dɪd 'mesɪdʒ]
Telefongespräch: ein Telefongespräch führen make a call ['kɔ:l]
Telefonnummer (tele)phone number ['telɪfəʊn ,nʌmbə]
Teller plate [pleɪt] • **ein Teller Pommes frites** a plate of chips
Temperatur temperature ['temprətʃə]
Tempus *(grammatische Zeit)* tense [tens]
Tennis tennis ['tenɪs]
Termin appointment [ə'pɔɪntmənt]
Terminkalender diary ['daɪəri]
Terror- terrorist ['terərɪst]
Terrorist/in terrorist ['terərɪst]
terroristisch terrorist ['terərɪst]
teuer expensive [ɪk'spensɪv]
Text text [tekst]
Theater theatre ['θɪətə]
Theaterstück play [pleɪ]
Theke counter ['kaʊntə]
Thema, Themenbereich topic ['tɒpɪk]
Themenpark *(Freizeitpark mit Attraktionen zu einem bestimmten Thema)* theme park ['θi:m pɑ:k]
Thermometer thermometer [θə'mɒmɪtə]
Tier animal ['ænɪml]; *(Haustier)* pet [pet]
Tierhandlung pet shop ['pet ʃɒp]
Tiger tiger ['taɪgə]
Timing: schlechtes Timing bad timing ['taɪmɪŋ]
Tipp tip [tɪp]
Tisch table ['teɪbl]
Tischtennis table tennis ['teɪbl tenɪs]
Tischtennisschläger table tennis bat [bæt]
Titel title ['taɪtl]; *(Musikstück auf CD)* track [træk]
Titelliste *(von zu spielenden Songs)* playlist ['pleɪlɪst]
Toast(brot) toast [təʊst]
Tochter daughter ['dɔ:tə]
Tod death [deθ]
Todestag: js. Todestag anniversary of sb.'s death [,ænɪ'vɜ:səri]
Toilette toilet ['tɔɪlət]
tolerant tolerant ['tɒlərənt]
toll fantastic [fæn'tæstɪk]; great [greɪt]
Tomate tomato [tə'mɑ:təʊ], *pl* tomatoes
Tondatei *(Soundfile)* sound file ['saʊnd faɪl]
Top *(Oberteil)* top [tɒp]
Tor *(im Sport)* goal [gəʊl] • **ein Tor schießen** score (a goal) [skɔ:]
Torfrau, Torwart goalkeeper ['gəʊlki:pə]
Tornado tornado [tɔ:'neɪdəʊ]
Torte cake [keɪk]
Torwart goalkeeper ['gəʊlki:pə]
tot dead [ded]
töten kill [kɪl]
Tour (durch das Haus) tour (of the house) [tʊə]
Tourist/in tourist ['tʊərɪst]
Track *(auf einer CD)* track [træk]
Tradition tradition [trə'dɪʃn]
traditionell traditional [trə'dɪʃənl]
tragen *(Kleidung)* wear [weə]
Trainer/in coach [kəʊtʃ]
trainieren practise ['præktɪs] *(BE)*; practice ['præktɪs] *(AE)*; train [treɪn]
Training *(körperliche Bewegung)* exercise *(no pl)* ['eksəsaɪz]

Trainingsstunde, -einheit training session ['seʃn]
Träne tear [tɪə]
Traum dream [driːm]
träumen (von) dream (of, about) [driːm]
Traumhaus dream house ['driːm haʊs]
traurig sad [sæd]
Traurigkeit sadness ['sædnəs]
Treffen meeting ['miːtɪŋ]
treffen; sich treffen meet [miːt] **ein Abkommen/eine Abmachung treffen** make a deal [diːl] • **sich (regelmäßig) mit jm. treffen** *(mit jm. (aus)gehen)* date sb. [deɪt]
trennen *(nach Rasse, Religion, Geschlecht)* segregate ['segrɪgeɪt]
Trennung *(nach Rasse, Religion, Geschlecht)* segregation [ˌsegrɪ'geɪʃn]
Treppe(nstufen) stairs *(pl)* [steəz]
treten kick [kɪk]
Trick *(Zauberkunststück)* trick [trɪk]
Trikot: (Fußball-)Trikot football shirt
Trimester term [tɜːm]
trinkbar drinkable ['drɪŋkəbl]
trinken drink [drɪŋk] • **Milch zum Frühstück trinken** have milk for breakfast
Trommel drum [drʌm]
Trompete trumpet ['trʌmpɪt]
trostlos depressing [dɪ'presɪŋ]
trotzdem anyway ['eniweɪ]
Truthahn turkey ['tɜːki]
Tschüs. Bye. [baɪ]; See you. ['siː juː]
T-Shirt T-shirt ['tiːʃɜːt]
tun do [duː] • **tun müssen** have to do • **tun wollen** want to do [wɒnt] **Tut mir leid.** I'm sorry. ['sɒri]
Tunnel tunnel ['tʌnl]
Tür door [dɔː]
Türklingel doorbell ['dɔːbel]
Turm tower ['taʊə]
Turnanzug leotard ['liːətɑːd]
Turnen *(Sportunterricht)* PE [ˌpiː_'iː], Physical Education [ˌfɪzɪkəl_edʒu'keɪʃn]
Turnhalle gym [dʒɪm]
Turnschuhe trainers *(pl)* ['treɪnəz]
Tut mir leid. I'm sorry. ['sɒri]
Tüte bag [bæg]
Typ type [taɪp] *(infml)*; *(Kerl)* guy [gaɪ] *(infml)*
Tyrann *(Schultyrann)* bully ['bʊli]
tyrannisieren bully ['bʊli]

U

U-Bahn: die U-Bahn the underground ['ʌndəgraʊnd] *(BE)*; the subway ['sʌbweɪ] *(AE)*; *(in London)* the Tube *(no pl)* [tjuːb]
U-Bahn-Linie line [laɪn]
üben practise ['præktɪs] *(BE)*; practice ['præktɪs] *(AE)*
über 1. about [ə'baʊt] • **über dich selbst** about yourself
2. *(räumlich)* over ['əʊvə]; *(quer über)* across [ə'krɒs]; *(oberhalb von)* above [ə'bʌv]
3. *(mehr als)* over
überall everywhere ['evriweə]
überarbeiten: etwas überarbeiten revise sth. [rɪ'vaɪz]
überdrüssig: einer Sache überdrüssig werden get tired of sth. ['taɪəd]
übereinstimmen (mit) agree (with) [ə'griː] • **nicht übereinstimmen (mit)** disagree (with) [ˌdɪsə'griː]
überfliegen: einen Text überfliegen *(um den Inhalt grob zu erfassen)* skim a text [skɪm]
übergeben: sich übergeben throw up [ˌθrəʊ_'ʌp]
überleben survive [sə'vaɪv]
Überleben survival [sə'vaɪvl]
übernachten *(über Nacht bleiben)* stay [steɪ]
übernehmen: die Kontrolle über ein Flugzeug übernehmen take over a plane
überprüfen check [tʃek]
überqueren cross [krɒs]
überraschen: jn. überraschen surprise sb. [sə'praɪz]
überraschend surprising [sə'praɪzɪŋ]
überrascht (über etwas) surprised (at sth.) [sə'praɪzd]
Überraschung surprise [sə'praɪz]
Überschrift title ['taɪtl]; heading ['hedɪŋ]
übersetzen translate [træns'leɪt]
Übersetzung translation [træns'leɪʃn]
übrigens *(nebenbei bemerkt)* by the way [ˌbaɪ ðə 'weɪ]; actually ['æktʃuəli]
Übung *(Schulbuch)* exercise ['eksəsaɪz] • **eine Übung machen** do an exercise
Übungsheft exercise book ['eksəsaɪz bʊk]
Uhr 1. *(Armbanduhr)* watch [wɒtʃ]; *(Wand-, Stand-, Turmuhr)* clock [klɒk]
2. elf Uhr eleven o'clock • **7 Uhr morgens/vormittags** 7 am [ˌeɪ_'em] **7 Uhr nachmittags/abends** 7 pm [ˌpiː_'em] • **um 8 Uhr 45** at 8.45
Uhrzeit time [taɪm]

um 1. *(örtlich)* **um ... (herum)** round [raʊnd]; around [ə'raʊnd] • **um den See (herum)** around the lake **ganz um die Burg herum** all around the castle
2. *(zeitlich)* **um 8.45** at 8.45 • **um sechs Uhr herum** *(gegen sechs)* around six
3. Es geht um Mr Green. This is about Mr Green.
4. um zu to
umdrehen: sich umdrehen turn [tɜːn]
Umfrage (über) survey (on) ['sɜːveɪ]
umher: in ... umher round [raʊnd]; around [ə'raʊnd] • **in der Stadt umher** around the town
umher-: umhergehen walk around **umherrennen** run around **umherspringen** jump around
umschalten *(Fernsehen)* change channels
umschreiben *(anders ausdrücken)* paraphrase ['pærəfreɪz]
umsehen: sich umsehen look round [ˌlʊk 'raʊnd]; look around [ˌlʊk_ə'raʊnd]
umsteigen change [tʃeɪndʒ]
► S.180 (to) change – change
umziehen 1. sich umziehen change [tʃeɪndʒ]
2. umziehen (nach, in) *(die Wohnung wechseln)* move (to) [muːv]
► S.180 (to) change – change
uncool uncool [ˌʌn'kuːl] *(infml)*
und and [ənd, ænd] • **Und? / Na und?** So? [səʊ] • **Und ob!** You bet! [bet] *(infml)* • **und so weiter (usw.)** and so on (etc. [et'setərə])
unentschieden: 2:2 unentschieden 2 all
Unentschieden draw [drɔː]
unfair unfair [ˌʌn'feə]
Unfall accident ['æksɪdənt] • **einen Unfall haben (mit dem Auto)** crash the car [kræʃ]
unfreundlich unfriendly [ʌn'frendli]
ungefähr about [ə'baʊt]
Ungeheuer monster ['mɒnstə]
ungenügend *(USA, Schulnote)* failure *(n)* ['feɪljə]
► S.179 US school grades
ungerecht unfair [ˌʌn'feə]
ungesetzlich illegal [ɪ'liːgl]
ungesund unhealthy [ʌn'helθi]
unglaublich unbelievable [ˌʌnbɪ'liːvəbl]; *(sehr erstaunlich)* amazing [ə'meɪzɪŋ]
unglücklich unhappy [ʌn'hæpi]
unheimlich scary ['skeəri]
unhöflich rude [ruːd]
Uniform uniform ['juːnɪfɔːm]

Universität university [ˌjuːnɪˈvɜːsəti]
unmöglich impossible [ɪmˈpɒsəbl]
unordentlich untidy [ʌnˈtaɪdi] • **sehr unordentlich sein** *(Zimmer)* be a mess [mes]
Unordnung: alles in Unordnung bringen make a mess [ˌmeɪk‿ə ˈmes]
Unrecht haben be wrong [rɒŋ]
uns us [əs, ʌs] • **uns (selbst)** ourselves [aʊəˈselvz]
unser(e) ... our ... [ˈaʊə] • **unser eigenes Schwimmbad** our own pool [əʊn]
unserer, unsere, unseres ours [ˈaʊəz]
unten below [bɪˈləʊ]; *(im Haus)* downstairs [ˌdaʊnˈsteəz] • **am unteren Ende (von)** at the bottom (of) [ˈbɒtəm] • **dort unten** down there • **nach unten** down; *(im Haus)* downstairs
unter under [ˈʌndə]; *(unterhalb von)* below [bɪˈləʊ]
unterbrechen interrupt [ˌɪntəˈrʌpt]
untere(r, s): am unteren Ende (von) at the bottom (of) [ˈbɒtəm]
unterhalb (von) below [bɪˈləʊ]
unterhalten: sich unterhalten (mit, über) talk (to, about) [tɔːk]
Unternehmen business [ˈbɪznəs]
Unterricht lessons *(pl)* [ˈlesnz] • **im Unterricht** in class
unterrichten teach [tiːtʃ]
Unterschied difference [ˈdɪfrəns]
unterschiedlich different [ˈdɪfrənt]
unterstützen support [səˈpɔːt]
Untersuchung (über) *(Umfrage)* survey (on) [ˈsɜːveɪ]
unverschämt rude [ruːd]
Urgroßmutter great-grandmother [ˌgreɪt ˈgrænmʌðə]
Urgroßvater great-grandfather [ˌgreɪt ˈgrænfɑːðə]
Urlaub holiday [ˈhɒlədeɪ] *(BE)*; vacation [vəˈkeɪʃn, *AE:* veɪˈkeɪʃn] *(AE)* • **in Urlaub fahren** go on holiday • **in Urlaub sein** be on holiday
usw. etc. [etˈsetərə]

V

Vater father [ˈfɑːðə]
Vati dad [dæd]
Vegetarier/in vegetarian [ˌvedʒəˈteəriən]
vegetarisch vegetarian [ˌvedʒəˈteəriən]
Verabredung appointment [əˈpɔɪntmənt]; *(Date)* date [deɪt]
verabschieden: sich verabschieden say goodbye [ˌseɪ gʊdˈbaɪ]
verändern; sich verändern change [tʃeɪndʒ]
▶ S.180 (to) change – change
Veränderung change [tʃeɪndʒ]
▶ S.180 (to) change – change
verängstigt scared [skeəd]
Veranstaltung event [ɪˈvent]
verbinden *(einander zuordnen)* link [lɪŋk]
Verbindung *(Verknüpfung)* link [lɪŋk] • **in Verbindung bleiben** *(Kontakt halten)* keep in touch [tʌtʃ] • **sich mit jm. in Verbindung setzen** contact sb. [ˈkɒntækt]
Verbrechen crime [kraɪm]
verbrennen burn [bɜːn]
verbringen: Zeit verbringen (mit etwas) spend time (on sth.) [spend]
verdienen: Geld verdienen make money
Verein club [klʌb]
vereinigt: das Vereinigte Königreich *(Großbritannien und Nordirland)* the United Kingdom (UK) [juˌnaɪtɪd ˈkɪŋdəm], [ˌjuː ˈkeɪ] • **die Vereinigten Staaten (von Amerika)** the United States (US) [juˌnaɪtɪd ˈsteɪts], [ˌjuː‿ˈes]
Verfahren *(Prozess, Vorgang)* process [ˈprəʊses]
verfolgen follow [ˈfɒləʊ]
Vergangenheit past [pɑːst]
vergeben *(verzeihen)* forgive [fəˈgɪv]
vergessen forget [fəˈget]
vergeuden (für) waste (on) [weɪst]
vergewissern: sich vergewissern, dass ... make sure that ...
Vergleich comparison [kəmˈpærɪsn]
vergleichen compare [kəmˈpeə]
Vergnügen: Viel Vergnügen! Have a good time!
vergriffen sein *(ausverkauft sein)* be sold out [ˌsəʊld‿ˈaʊt]
verhalten: sich verhalten act [ækt]
verheiratet (mit) married (to) [ˈmærɪd]
Verkauf sale [seɪl]
verkaufen sell [sel] • **zu verkaufen** for sale [seɪl]
Verkäufer/in shop assistant [ˈʃɒp‿əˌsɪstənt]
Verkehr traffic [ˈtræfɪk]
Verkehrsmittel transport *(no pl)* [ˈtrænspɔːt] • **öffentliche Verkehrsmittel** *(öffentlicher Personennahverkehr)* public transport *(no pl)* [ˌpʌblɪk ˈtrænspɔːt]
verkehrsreich *(Straße)* busy [ˈbɪzi]
Verkehrsstau traffic jam [ˈtræfɪk dʒæm]
verkehrt *(falsch)* wrong [rɒŋ]
verknallt: in jn. verknallt sein have a crush on sb. [krʌʃ]
verknüpfen *(einander zuordnen)* link [lɪŋk]
Verknüpfung *(Verbindung)* link
verlassen leave [liːv]
verlaufen *(Straße; Grenze)* run
verletzen hurt [hɜːt]
verletzt hurt [hɜːt]
verlieben: sich verlieben (in jn.) fall in love (with sb.)
verlieren lose [luːz] • **die Lust an etwas verlieren** get tired of sth.
vermissen miss [mɪs]
Vermittlung *(Sprachmittlung, Mediation)* mediation [ˌmiːdiˈeɪʃn]
vermuten suppose [səˈpəʊz]
veröffentlichen publish [ˈpʌblɪʃ] **veröffentlicht werden** *(Film, DVD)* come out
verpassen miss [mɪs]
verrückt mad [mæd]; crazy [ˈkreɪzi] **verrückt nach/auf etwas sein** be mad about sth.
Versammlung meeting [ˈmiːtɪŋ]; *(morgendliche Schulversammlung, oft mit Andacht)* Assembly [əˈsembli]
verschieden different [ˈdɪfrənt]
verschwenden (für) waste (on) [weɪst]
verschwinden disappear [ˌdɪsəˈpɪə]
versperren block [blɒk]
versprechen promise [ˈprɒmɪs]
verständlich understandable [ˌʌndəˈstændəbl]
verstecken; sich verstecken hide [haɪd]
verstehen understand [ˌʌndəˈstænd]
versuchen try [traɪ]
vertreten *(repräsentieren)* represent [ˌreprɪˈzent]
verwenden use [juːz]
verwirrt puzzled [ˈpʌzld]
verzeihen forgive [fəˈgɪv]
Video video [ˈvɪdiəʊ]
viel a lot (of) [lɒt]; lots (of) [lɒts]; much [mʌtʃ] • **viele** a lot (of); lots (of); many [ˈmeni] • **Viel Glück (bei/mit ...)!** Good luck (with ...)! **viel mehr** lots more • **Viel Spaß!** Have fun! / Have a good time! **wie viel?** how much? • **wie viele?** how many? • **Vielen Dank!** Thanks a lot!
vielfarbig multi-coloured [ˈmʌltiˌkʌləd]
vielleicht maybe [ˈmeɪbi] • **du könntest vielleicht Hilfe brauchen** you might need help [maɪt]
Viertel: Viertel nach 11 quarter past 11 [ˈkwɔːtə] • **Viertel vor 12** quarter to 12
violett purple [ˈpɜːpl]

Virus virus ['vaɪrəs]
Vogel bird [bɜ:d]
Vokabelverzeichnis vocabulary [və'kæbjələri]
Vokallaut vowel sound ['vaʊəl saʊnd]
voll full [fʊl] • **die Nase voll haben (von etwas)** be fed up (with sth.) [ˌfed_'ʌp]
Volleyball volleyball ['vɒlibɔ:l]
Vollkorn- whole-grain ['həʊlgreɪn]
von of [əv, ɒv]; from [frəm, frɒm] **ein Aufsatz von ...** an essay by ... [baɪ] • **von Montag bis Freitag** from Monday to Friday
vor 1. *(räumlich)* in front of [ɪn 'frʌnt_əv]
2. *(zeitlich)* **vor dem Abendessen** before dinner [bɪ'fɔ:] • **vor einer Minute** a minute ago [ə'gəʊ]
Viertel vor 12 quarter to 12
nicht vor *(erst um)* not ... until / not ... till
vorankommen: Wie komme ich voran? *(Wie sind meine Fortschritte?)* How am I doing?
vorbei (an) *(vorüber)* past [pɑ:st]
vorbei sein be over ['əʊvə]
vorbereiten prepare [prɪ'peə] • **sich vorbereiten (auf)** prepare (for); get ready (for) ['redi] • **Dinge vorbereiten** get things ready
vorbringen: ein Argument vorbringen make a point [pɔɪnt]
Vordergrund foreground ['fɔ:graʊnd]
Voreingenommenheit (gegen) prejudice (against) ['predʒudɪs]
voreingenommen sein (gegen) be prejudiced (against) ['predʒədɪst]
Vorhang curtain ['kɜ:tn]
Vormittag morning ['mɔ:nɪŋ]
Vorschlag suggestion [sə'dʒestʃən]
vorschlagen: (jm.) etwas vorschlagen suggest sth. (to sb.) [sə'dʒest]
Vorschrift rule [ru:l]
Vorschule *(für 5- bis 6-Jährige in den USA)* kindergarten ['kɪndəgɑ:tn]
vorsichtig careful ['keəfl]
vorspielen *(pantomimisch darstellen)* mime [maɪm]
vorstellen 1. jm. etwas vorstellen *(präsentieren)* present sth. to sb. [prɪ'zent]
2. sich etwas vorstellen imagine sth. [ɪ'mædʒɪn] • **sich etwas bildlich vorstellen** picture sth. ['pɪktʃə]
Stell dir vor! / Stellt euch vor! Guess what! [ˌges 'wɒt]
Vorstellung *(Präsentation)* presentation [ˌprezn'teɪʃn]; *(Show)* show [ʃəʊ]
Vorstellungskraft *(Fantasie)* imagination [ɪˌmædʒɪ'neɪʃn]
Vorteil (gegenüber jm./etwas) advantage (over sb./sth.) [əd'vɑ:ntɪdʒ]
vorüber (an) *(vorbei)* past [pɑ:st]
Vorurteil (gegenüber) prejudice (against) ['predʒudɪs] • **Vorurteile haben (gegenüber)** be prejudiced (against) ['predʒədɪst]
Vorwurf: jm. Vorwürfe machen (wegen) blame sb. (for) [bleɪm]

W

wachsen grow [grəʊ]
Waffe: (Schuss-)Waffe gun [gʌn]
Wahl *(eines Kandidaten bei einer Abstimmung)* election [ɪ'lekʃn]
wählen 1. *(auswählen)* choose [tʃu:z]
2. jn. zu etwas wählen elect sb. sth. [ɪ'lekt]
wahr true [tru:]
während 1. *(vor Nomen)* during ['djʊərɪŋ] • **während des Spiels** during the match
2. *(vor Nebensatz)* as [əz, æz]; while [waɪl] • **während wir zuschauten** as/while we were watching
► S.185 German 'während'
wahrscheinlich probably ['prɒbəbli]
Wald forest ['fɒrɪst]; woods *(pl)* [wʊdz]
walisisch; Walisisch Welsh [welʃ]
Walross walrus ['wɔ:lrəs]
Wand wall [wɔ:l]
wandern hike [haɪk]
Wanderung hike [haɪk]
Wange cheek [tʃi:k]
wann when [wen] • **wann (auch) immer** whenever [wen'evə] • **Seit wann ...?** How long ...?
► S.178 whoever, whatever, whenever, wherever
warm warm [wɔ:m]
Wärmflasche hot-water bottle [ˌhɒt 'wɔ:tə bɒtl]
warnen: jn. (vor etwas) warnen warn sb. (about sth.) [wɔ:n]
warten (auf) wait (for) [weɪt]
Warte mal! Wait a minute. ['mɪnɪt]
Wart's ab! Wait and see!
Wartezimmer waiting room ['weɪtɪŋ ru:m]
warum why [waɪ]
was what [wɒt] • **was (auch) immer** whatever [wɒt'evə] • **Was fehlt dir?** *(bei Krankheit)* What's wrong with you? • **Was für ein Auto ...?** What kind of car ...? • **Was für ein interessantes Leben!** What an interesting life! • **Was gibt es zum Mittagessen?** What's for lunch? • **Was haben wir als Hausaufgabe auf?** What's for homework? • **Was hältst du von ...?** How do you feel about ...? • **Was ist los? / Was ist denn?** What's the matter? ['mætə] • **Was ist mit ...?** What about ...? • **Was kostet/kosten ...?** How much is/are ...?
Was war das Beste an ...? What was the best thing about ...?
Was weißt du sonst noch über ...? What else do you know about ...? [els] • **alles, was wir jetzt (noch) tun müssen, ...** all we have to do now ... • **wir wissen, was wir tun müssen / was zu tun ist** we know what to do
► S.168 Question words + to-infinitive: how to ... / what to ... / ...
waschen wash [wɒʃ] • **Ich wasche mir das Gesicht.** I wash my face.
Wasser water ['wɔ:tə]
Webcam webcam ['webkæm]
Website website ['websaɪt]
Wechsel *((Ver-)Änderung)* change [tʃeɪndʒ]
Wechselgeld change [tʃeɪndʒ]
wechseln change [tʃeɪndʒ]
► S.180 (to) change – change
wecken: jn. wecken wake sb. (up) [weɪk]
weg away [ə'weɪ] • **weg sein** *(nicht zu Hause sein)* be out [aʊt]
Weg way [weɪ]; *(Pfad)* path [pɑ:θ]; *(Gasse)* lane [leɪn] • **auf dem Weg (zu/nach)** on the way (to) **etwas auf den Weg bringen** get sth. off the ground • **jm. den Weg beschreiben** tell sb. the way • **jn. nach dem Weg fragen** ask sb. the way
Wegbeschreibung(en) directions *(pl)* [də'rekʃnz]
wegbleiben *(draußen bleiben)* stay out [ˌsteɪ_'aʊt]
weggehen leave [li:v]; *(raus-, ausgehen)* go out
weglassen: etwas weglassen leave sth. out [ˌli:v_'aʊt]
wehen blow [bləʊ]
wehtun hurt [hɜ:t]; be sore [sɔ:]; ache [eɪk] • **jm. wehtun** hurt sb.
weich soft [sɒft]
Weide field [fi:ld]
weil because [bɪ'kɒz]; *(da ja)* since [sɪns]
Wein wine [waɪn]
weinen cry [kraɪ]
Weintraube grape [greɪp]
Weise *(Art und Weise)* way [weɪ] **auf diese Weise** this way/that way

weiß white [waɪt]
weit *(entfernt)* far [fɑː]
weiter: geradeaus weiter straight on [streɪt_'ɒn]
weitere(r, s): ein(e) weitere(r, s) one more [mɔː] • **weitere 45 Pence** another 45 p [ə'nʌðə]
weiter-: weitergeben pass [pɑːs] **weitergehen** walk on • **weiterlesen** read on • **weitermachen** go on • **weiterreden** go on **weiterträumen** dream on
welche(r, s) which [wɪtʃ] • **Auf welcher Seite sind wir?** What page are we on? [wɒt] • **Welche Farbe hat ...?** What colour is ...?
wellenreiten gehen go surfing ['sɜːfɪŋ]
Wellensittich budgie ['bʌdʒi]
Welt world [wɜːld] • **auf der ganzen Welt** all over the world
wem? who? [huː] • **wem (auch) immer** whoever [huː'evə] • **Wem gehören diese?** Whose are these? [huːz]
► S.178 whoever, whatever, whenever, wherever
wen? who? [huː] • **wen (auch) immer** whoever [huː'evə]
► S.178 whoever, whatever, whenever, wherever
wenden: sich an jn. wenden turn to sb. [tɜːn]
wenig 1. *(mit nicht zählbaren Nomen)* **wenig Zeit/Wasser** little time/water ['lɪtl] • **ein wenig** *(ein bisschen)* a little • **weniger** less [les] • **am wenigsten** least [liːst]
2. *(mit zählbaren Nomen im Plural)* **wenige Stunden/Flaschen** few hours/bottles [fjuː]; *(ein paar)* a few hours/bottles • **weniger** fewer ['fjuːə] • **am wenigsten** fewest ['fjuːɪst]
► S.181 little („wenig") – few („wenige")
wenigstens at least [ət 'liːst]
wenn 1. *(zeitlich)* when [wen]
2. *(falls)* if [ɪf] • **selbst wenn** even if
wer? who? [huː] • **wer (auch) immer** whoever [huː'evə] • **Wer ist dran / an der Reihe?** Whose turn is it? [huːz]
► S.178 whoever, whatever, whenever, wherever
werden become [bɪ'kʌm] • **Bauer, Lehrer/in, ... werden** be a farmer, a teacher, ... • **wütend/heiß/... werden** get angry/hot/... • **du wirst frieren; ihr werdet frieren** you'll be cold (= you will be cold) [wɪl] • **du wirst nicht frieren; ihr werdet nicht frieren** you won't be cold (= you will not be cold) [wəʊnt]
werfen throw [θrəʊ]
Werkstatt workshop ['wɜːkʃɒp]
Werkzeug tool [tuːl]
wertvoll valuable ['væljuəbl]
wessen? whose? [huːz]
Westen west [west] • **nach Westen** west • **Richtung Westen** *(Fahrtrichtung)* westbound ['westbaʊnd]
westlich west [west]; western ['westən]
Wettbewerb competition [ˌkɒmpə'tɪʃn]
wetten bet [bet]
Wetter weather ['weðə]
Wettkampf competition [ˌkɒmpə'tɪʃn]
Whisky whisky ['wɪski]
wichtig (für jn.) important (to sb.) [ɪm'pɔːtnt] • **etwas wichtig nehmen** care about sth. [keə] • **Nicht so wichtig.** Never mind. [ˌnevə 'maɪnd]
wie 1. *(Fragewort)* how [haʊ] • **Wie bitte?** Sorry? ['sɒri] • **Wie geht es dir/Ihnen/euch?** How are you? [ˌhaʊ_'ɑː jʊ] • **Wie heißt du?** What's your name? • **Wie komme ich voran?** *(Wie sind meine Fortschritte?)* How am I doing? • **Wie spät ist es?** What's the time? **Wie steht es?** *(beim Sport)* What's the score? • **wie viel?** how much? **wie viele?** how many? • **Wie war ...?** How was ...? • **Wie war das Wetter?** What was the weather like? • **Wie wär's mit ...?** What about ...? / How about ...?
2. so groß/aufregend wie as big/exciting as • **wie du sehen kannst** as you can see
3. wie ein Filmstar like a film star [laɪk] • **genau wie du** just like you
wieder again [ə'gen]
wiederholen *(Lernstoff)* revise [rɪ'vaɪz]
Wiederholung *(des Lernstoffs)* revision [rɪ'vɪʒn]; *(einer Fernsehsendung)* repeat [rɪ'piːt] *(BE)*; rerun ['riːrʌn] *(AE)*
Wiedersehen: Auf Wiedersehen. Goodbye. [ˌgʊd'baɪ]
wiederverwendet/-verwertet recycled [ˌriː'saɪkld]
Wiederverwertung recycling [ˌriː'saɪklɪŋ]
wild wild [waɪld]
willkommen: Willkommen (in ...). Welcome (to ...). ['welkəm] • **Sie heißen dich in ... willkommen** They welcome you to ...
Wind wind [wɪnd]
windig windy ['wɪndi]
Windjacke anorak ['ænəræk]
Windschutzscheibe windscreen ['wɪndskriːn]
winken wave [weɪv]
Winter winter ['wɪntə]
wir we [wiː]
Wirbelsturm tornado [tɔː'neɪdəʊ]
wirklich 1. *(tatsächlich)* really ['rɪəli] **Meinst du wirklich?/Glaubst du das wirklich?** Do you really think so?
2. *(echt)* real [rɪəl]
Wirklichkeit reality [ri'æləti] • **in Wirklichkeit** *(eigentlich)* actually ['æktʃuəli]
wirklichkeitsnah realistic [ˌriːə'lɪstɪk]
wischen *(Fußboden)* wash [wɒʃ]
wissen know [nəʊ] • **Ich weiß es nicht.** I don't know. • **von etwas wissen; über etwas Bescheid wissen** know about sth. • **..., wissen Sie. / ..., weißt du.** ..., you know. **Weißt du was, Sophie?** You know what, Sophie? • **Woher weißt du ...?** How do you know ...? • **zu schätzen wissen** appreciate [ə'priːʃieɪt]
wissen wollen wonder ['wʌndə]
Witz joke [dʒəʊk] • **Witze machen** joke
witzig funny ['fʌni]
wo where [weə] • **wo (auch) immer** wherever [weər'evə] • **Wo kommst du her?** Where are you from?
► S.178 whoever, whatever, whenever, wherever
woanders(hin) somewhere else
► S.170 ... else
Woche week [wiːk]
Wochenende weekend [ˌwiːk'end] **am Wochenende** at the weekend
Wochentage days of the week
Wofür? What for? [ˌwɒt 'fɔː]
Woher weißt du ...? How do you know ...? [nəʊ]
wohin where [weə]; *(in welche Richtung)* which way • **wohin (auch) immer** wherever [weər'evə]
► S.178 whoever, whatever, whenever, wherever
Wohlfahrtsorganisation charity ['tʃærəti]
Wohltätigkeitsbasar jumble sale ['dʒʌmbl seɪl]
wohnen live [lɪv]
Wohnheim *(Herberge)* hostel ['hɒstl]
Wohnung flat [flæt] *(BE)*; apartment [ə'pɑːtmənt] *(AE)*
Wohnungstür front door [ˌfrʌnt 'dɔː]
Wohnwagen caravan ['kærəvæn]

Wohnzimmer living room ['lɪvɪŋ ru:m]
Wolf wolf, *pl* wolves [wʊlf, wʊlvz]
Wolke cloud [klaʊd]
Wolkenkratzer skyscraper ['skaɪskreɪpə]
wolkenlos cloudless ['klaʊdləs]
wollen *(haben wollen)* want [wɒnt] **tun wollen** want to do • **wollen, dass jd. etwas tut** want sb. to do sth.
Workshop workshop ['wɜ:kʃɒp]
Wort word [wɜ:d]
Wortbildung word building ['wɜ:d ˌbɪldɪŋ]
Wörterbuch dictionary ['dɪkʃənri]
Wörterverzeichnis vocabulary [və'kæbjələri]; *(alphabetisches)* dictionary ['dɪkʃənri]
Wortfeld word field ['wɜ:d fi:ld]
wörtliche Rede direct speech [ˌdaɪrekt 'spi:tʃ]
Wovon redest du? What are you talking about?
wund sein be sore [sɔ:]
würde: du würdest … you would … [wəd, wʊd]
Würfel dice, *pl* dice [daɪs]
Wurst, Würstchen sausage ['sɒsɪdʒ]
würzig *(scharf gewürzt)* spicy ['spaɪsi]
wütend sein (über etwas/auf jn.) be angry (about sth./with sb.) ['æŋgri]

Y

Yoga yoga ['jəʊgə]

Z

Zahl number ['nʌmbə]
zählen count [kaʊnt]
Zahn tooth [tu:θ], *pl* teeth [ti:θ] • **Ich putze mir die Zähne.** I clean my teeth.
Zahnarzt, -ärztin dentist ['dentɪst]
zahnlos toothless ['tu:θləs]
Zahnschmerzen toothache ['tu:θeɪk]
zanken: sich zanken argue ['ɑ:gju:]
Zauberkunststück trick [trɪk] • **Zauberkunststücke machen** do tricks
Zaun fence [fens]
Zebra zebra ['zebrə]
Zeh toe [təʊ]
Zeichen *(Schild)* sign [saɪn]
zeichnen draw [drɔ:]
Zeichnung drawing ['drɔ:ɪŋ]
zeigen show [ʃəʊ] • **auf etwas zeigen** point at/to sth. [pɔɪnt]
Zeile line [laɪn]
Zeit time [taɪm]; *(grammatische Zeit, Tempus)* tense [tens] • **Zeit verbringen (mit)** spend time (on) [spend]
Zeitschrift magazine [ˌmægə'zi:n]
Zeitstrahl timeline ['taɪmlaɪn]
Zeitung newspaper ['nju:speɪpə]; paper ['peɪpə]
Zelt tent [tent]
zelten camp [kæmp]
Zensur *(Schulnote)* grade [greɪd] (*BE auch:* mark [mɑ:k])
Zentimeter centimetre (cm) ['sentɪmi:tə]
Zentral-, Mittel- central ['sentrəl]
Zentrum centre ['sentə]
zerbrechen break [breɪk]
zerbrechlich breakable ['breɪkəbl]
zerbrochen broken ['brəʊkən]
Zeug *(Kram)* stuff [stʌf]
ziehen pull [pʊl] • **Schlüsse ziehen** draw conclusions [ˌdrɔ: kən'klu:ʒnz]
ziemlich gut pretty good ['prɪti]; quite good [kwaɪt]
Ziffer number ['nʌmbə]
Zigarette cigarette [ˌsɪgə'ret]
Zimmer room [ru:m]
Zimmermädchen maid [meɪd]
Zirkus circus ['sɜ:kəs]
zittern shiver ['ʃɪvə]; shake [ʃeɪk]
Zone zone [zəʊn]
Zoo zoo [zu:]
zu 1. *(örtlich)* to [tə, tu] • **auf jn./etwas zu** towards sb./sth. [tə'wɔ:dz] **direkt auf jn. zu** straight towards sb. • **zu Jenny** to Jenny's • **zu Hause** at home • **zum Arzt** to the doctor's • **Setz dich zu mir.** Sit with me.
2. zu Fuß on foot • **zum Beispiel** for example [ɪg'zɑ:mpl] • **zum ersten Mal** for the first time • **zum Frühstück/Mittagessen/Abendbrot** for breakfast/lunch/dinner **zum Schluss** *(schließlich)* in the end • **zu seinem Geburtstag** for his birthday
3. zu viel too much [tu:] • **zu spät sein/kommen** be late
4. versuchen zu tun try and do / try to do
5. um zu to
zubereiten *(kochen)* cook [kʊk]
Zucker sugar ['ʃʊgə]
zuerst *(als Erstes)* first [fɜ:st]; *(zu Beginn)* at first
Zug train [treɪn] • **im Zug** on the train
Zuhause home [həʊm]
zuhören listen (to) ['lɪsn]
Zuhörer/in listener ['lɪsnə] • **Zuhörer/innen** *(Publikum)* audience ['ɔ:diəns]
Zukunft future ['fju:tʃə]
zulassen, dass jd. etwas tut *(erlauben)* let sb. do sth. [let]
zum *siehe „zu"*
zumachen close [kləʊz]
zumindest at least [ət 'li:st]
zurück (nach) back (to) [bæk]
zurückbleiben stay behind [ˌsteɪ bɪ'haɪnd]
zurückkehren return [rɪ'tɜ:n]
zurücklassen leave [li:v]
zusammen together [tə'geðə] • **mit jm. zusammen sein** be with sb.
zusammenbrechen collapse [kə'læps]
Zusammenfassung summary ['sʌməri]
Zusammenhang *(Kontext, Textzusammenhang)* context ['kɒntekst]
zusammenpassen go together
zusätzlich extra ['ekstrə]
Zuschauer/in viewer ['vju:ə] • **Zuschauer/innen** *(Publikum)* audience ['ɔ:diəns]
zusehen watch [wɒtʃ]
zustimmen: jm./etwas zustimmen agree with sb./sth. [ə'gri:]
zuvor: in der Nacht/Woche/… zuvor the night/week/… before [bɪ'fɔ:]
zuwenden: sich jm. zuwenden turn to sb. [tɜ:n]
zweimal twice [twaɪs]
zweisprachig bilingual [ˌbaɪ'lɪŋgwəl]
zweite(r, s) second ['sekənd]
zweiwöchig: ein zweiwöchiger Urlaub a two-week holiday
Zwiebel onion ['ʌnjən]
Zwillinge twins *(pl)* [twɪnz]
Zwillingsbruder twin brother ['twɪn ˌbrʌðə]
Zwillingstürme twin towers
zwischen between [bɪ'twi:n]

First names
(Vornamen)

Aaron ['eərən]
Abraham ['eɪbrəhæm]
Adriana [ˌeɪdri'ɑ:nə]
Andrew ['ændru:]
Angus ['æŋgəs]
Anthony ['æntəni]
Ashley ['æʃli]
Barack ['bærək, bə'ræk]
Beyoncé [bi'jɒnseɪ]
Brad [bræd]
Bradley ['brædli]
Brian ['braɪən]
Bruce [bru:s]
Caitlin ['keɪtlɪn, 'kætlɪn]
Chris [krɪs]
Chuck [tʃʌk]
Colleen [kɒ'li:n]
Coretta [kə'retə]
Cruz [kru:z]
David ['deɪvɪd]
Diego [di'eɪgəʊ]
Eileen ['aɪli:n]
Elizabeth [ɪ'lɪzəbəθ]
Frank [fræŋk]
Jake [dʒeɪk]
James [dʒeɪmz]
Jane [dʒeɪn]
Janet ['dʒænɪt, 'dʒænət]
Jeff [dʒef]
Jefferson ['dʒefəsən]
Jenna ['dʒenə]
Jesus ['dʒi:zəs]
José [həʊ'zeɪ]
Josephine ['dʒəʊzəfi:n]
Josh [dʒɒʃ]
Katherine ['kæθrɪn]
Katie ['keɪti]
Kelsey ['kelsi]
Khalil [kə'li:l, kɑ:'li:l]
Langston ['læŋstən]
Lara ['lɑ:rə]
Lauryn ['lɒrən]
LeBron [lə'brɒn]
Lori ['lɒri]
Louie ['lu:i]
Louis ['lu:ɪs, 'lu:i]
Luis [lu:'i:s, 'lu:ɪs]
Luke [lu:k]
Madison ['mædɪsn]
Manuel [ˌmæn'wel]
Marcia ['mɑ:siə, 'mɑ:ʃə]
Margaret ['mɑ:grət]
Maria [mə'ri:ə]
Martin ['mɑ:tɪn]
Marvin ['mɑ:vɪn]
Melba ['melbə]
Melinda [mə'lɪndə]
Melissa [mə'lɪsə]
Nate [neɪt]
Nathan ['neɪθn]
Patrick ['pætrɪk]
Paul [pɔ:l]
Rachel ['reɪtʃəl]
Rajif [ræ'dʒi:f]
Ray [reɪ]
Ricardo [rɪ'kɑ:dəʊ]
Robert ['rɒbət]
Rodney ['rɒdni]
Ruth [ru:θ]
Ryan ['raɪən]
Sarah ['seərə]
Shirley ['ʃɜ:li]
Stephon ['sti:vn]
Sue [su:]
Sullivan ['sʌlɪvən]
Theodore ['θi:ədɔ:]
Thomas ['tɒməs]
Wayne [weɪn]

Family names
(Familiennamen)

Alvarez ['ælvərez]
Ballou [bə'lu:]
Bertanelli [ˌbɜ:tə'neli]
Bethune [be'θu:n]
Bond [bɒnd]
Callahan ['kæləhən]
Campbell ['kæmbəl]
Carter ['kɑ:tə]
Chalkers ['tʃɔ:kəz]
Charles [tʃɑ:lz]
Clapton ['klæptən]
Clinton ['klɪntən]
Columbus [kə'lʌmbəs]
D'Agostino [ˌdægə'sti:nəʊ]
Davis ['deɪvɪs]
Ebb [eb]
Ebbel ['ebl]
Elliot ['eliət]
Fishkin ['fɪʃkɪn]
Franklin ['fræŋklɪn]
Fuentes [fu'entez, 'fwentes]
Gallagher ['gæləhə, 'gæləgə]
Gaye [geɪ]
Gibran [dʒɪ'brɑ:n]
Hawley ['hɔ:li]
Heigl ['haɪgl]
Hughes [hju:z]
Johnson ['dʒɒnsn]
Kennedy ['kenədi]
Kruger ['kru:gə]
Lawrence ['lɒrəns]
Lee [li:]
Lefevre [lə'fi:və]
Levoy ['li:vɔɪ]
Lichtenstein ['lɪktənstaɪn]
Lincoln ['lɪŋkən]
Lucas ['lu:kəs]
Luther ['lu:θə]
Lyle [laɪl]
Marbury ['mɑ:bəri]
Marx [mɑ:ks]
McCourt [mə'kɔ:t]
Meir [meɪ'ɪə]
Mitchell ['mɪtʃəl]
Morales [mə'rɑ:lez, mə'ræləs]
Muir [mjʊə]
Nielson ['ni:lsən]
Obama [əʊ'bɑ:mə]
Pattillo [pə'tɪləʊ]
Pemberton ['pembətən]
Polo ['pəʊləʊ]
Roosevelt ['rəʊzəvelt]
Sachar ['sækə]
Salgado [sæl'gɑ:dəʊ]
Sanford ['sænfəd]
Sheckler ['ʃeklə]
Sherman ['ʃɜ:mən]
Smith [smɪθ]
Springsteen ['sprɪŋsti:n]
Strauss [straʊs]
Viotti [vi'ɒti]
Washington ['wɒʃɪŋtən]

Place names
(Ortsnamen)

(siehe auch S. 256: The United States of America*)*

Anaheim ['ænəhaɪm]
Atlanta [ət'læntə]
Avenida Pico [ˌɑ:və'ni:də 'pi:kəʊ, ˌævə'ni:də 'pi:kəʊ]
Bellagio [bə'lɑ:dʒɪəʊ]
Broadway ['brɔ:dweɪ]
Bronx [brɒŋks]
Brooklyn ['brʊklɪn]
Brownsville ['braʊnsvɪl]
Castor River [ˌkɑ:stə 'rɪvə]
Chicago [ʃɪ'kɑ:gəʊ]
Coney Island [ˌkəʊni_'aɪlənd]
Dahlonega [də'lɒnəgə]
Dublin ['dʌblɪn]
Eiffel Tower [ˌaɪfl 'taʊə]
Ellis Island [ˌelɪs_'aɪlənd]
Empire State Building [ˌempaɪə 'steɪt ˌbɪldɪŋ]
Eureka [ju'ri:kə]
Fort Lincoln [ˌfɔ:t 'lɪŋkən]
Frankfurt ['fræŋkfɜ:t]
Gateway Arch [ˌgeɪtweɪ_'ɑ:tʃ]
Grand Canyon [ˌgrænd 'kænjən]
Hayden Street ['heɪdn stri:t]
Herald Square [ˌherəld 'skweə]
Hermann ['hɜ:mən]
Hermannthal Winery [ˌhɜ:məntɑ:l 'waɪnəri]
Holbrook ['həʊlbrʊk]
Hollywood ['hɒliwʊd]
Inglewood ['ɪŋglwʊd]
Jefferson National Expansion Memorial [ˌdʒefəsən ˌnæʃnəl_ɪk'spænʃn məˌmɔ:riəl]
Lambert-St. Louis [ˌlæmbət sənt 'lu:ɪs]
Las Vegas [læs 'veɪgəs]
Los Angeles [lɒs_'ændʒəli:z]
Macy's ['meɪsiz]
Madison ['mædɪsən]
Malibu ['mælɪbu:]
Manhattan [mæn'hætn]
Mission Viejo [ˌmɪʃn vi'eɪhəʊ]
Naples ['neɪplz]
New Echota [ˌnju:_i'kəʊtə]
New York [ˌnju: 'jɔ:k]
Northridge ['nɔ:θrɪdʒ]
Paces Ferry Road [ˌpeɪsɪz ˌferi 'rəʊd]
Paris ['pærɪs]
Purdue University [ˌpɜ:dju: ju:nɪ'vɜ:səti]
Queens [kwi:nz]
The **Ramble** ['ræmbl]
Rome [rəʊm]
Sacramento [ˌsækrə'mentəʊ]
San Andreas [ˌsæn_æn'dreɪəs]
San Clemente [ˌsæn klə'menti]
San Diego [ˌsæn di'eɪgəʊ]
San Francisco [ˌsæn frən'sɪskəʊ]
Santa Monica [ˌsæntə 'mɒnɪkə]
Santa Rosa [ˌsæntə 'rəʊzə]
Savannah [sə'vænə]
Sequoia National Park [sɪˌkwɔɪə ˌnæʃnəl 'pɑ:k]
Shorecliffs Middle School ['ʃɔ:klɪfs]
Sicily ['sɪsəli]
Silicon Valley [ˌsɪlɪkən 'væli]
Staten Island [ˌstætn_'aɪlənd]
St. Louis [sənt 'lu:ɪs]
Tucumcari [ˌtu:kəm'keəri]
Tulsa ['tʌlsə]
Washington ['wɒʃɪŋtən]
Watsonville ['wɒtsnvɪl]
Yankee Stadium [ˌjæŋki 'steɪdiəm]
Yosemite [jəʊ'seməti]

Other names
(Andere Namen)

Bearcats ['beəkæts]
Cherokees ['tʃerəki:z]
Ferrari [fə'rɑ:ri]
Harlem Globetrotters [ˌhɑ:ləm 'gləʊbˌtrɒtəz]
Kaibab Trail ['kaɪbæb treɪl]
Mona Lisa [ˌməʊnə 'li:sə]
Olympiad [ə'lɪmpiæd]
Phoenix ['fi:nɪks]
Terminator ['tɜ:mɪneɪtə]
Uranus ['jʊərənəs]
Yankees ['jæŋkiz]

Country/Continent	Adjective	Person	People
Africa ['æfrɪkə] *Afrika*	African ['æfrɪkən]	an African	the Africans
America [ə'merɪkə] *Amerika*	American [ə'merɪkən]	an American	the Americans
Asia ['eɪʃə, 'eɪʒə] *Asien*	Asian ['eɪʃn, 'eɪʒn]	an Asian	the Asians
Australia [ɒ'streɪliə] *Australien*	Australian [ɒ'streɪliən]	an Australian	the Australians
Austria ['ɒstriə] *Österreich*	Austrian ['ɒstriən]	an Austrian	the Austrians
Belgium ['beldʒəm] *Belgien*	Belgian ['beldʒən]	a Belgian	the Belgians
Canada ['kænədə] *Kanada*	Canadian [kə'neɪdiən]	a Canadian	the Canadians
China ['tʃaɪnə] *China*	Chinese [ˌtʃaɪ'ni:z]	a Chinese	the Chinese
Croatia [krəʊ'eɪʃə] *Kroatien*	Croatian [krəʊ'eɪʃn]	a Croatian	the Croatians
the Czech Republic [ˌtʃek rɪ'pʌblɪk] *Tschechien, die Tschechische Republik*	Czech [tʃek]	a Czech	the Czechs
Denmark ['denmɑ:k] *Dänemark*	Danish ['deɪnɪʃ]	a Dane [deɪn]	the Danes
England ['ɪŋglənd] *England*	English ['ɪŋglɪʃ]	an Englishman/-woman	the English
Europe ['jʊərəp] *Europa*	European [ˌjʊərə'pi:ən]	a European	the Europeans
Finland ['fɪnlənd] *Finnland*	Finnish ['fɪnɪʃ]	a Finn [fɪn]	the Finns
France [frɑ:ns] *Frankreich*	French [frentʃ]	a Frenchman/-woman	the French
Georgia ['dʒɔ:dʒə] *Georgien*	Georgian ['dʒɔ:dʒən]	a Georgian	the Georgians
Germany ['dʒɜ:məni] *Deutschland*	German ['dʒɜ:mən]	a German	the Germans
(Great) Britain ['brɪtn] *Großbritannien*	British ['brɪtɪʃ]	a Briton ['brɪtn]	the British
Greece [gri:s] *Griechenland*	Greek [gri:k]	a Greek	the Greeks
Holland ['hɒlənd] *Holland, die Niederlande*	Dutch [dʌtʃ]	a Dutchman/-woman	the Dutch
Hungary ['hʌŋgəri] *Ungarn*	Hungarian [hʌŋ'geəriən]	a Hungarian	the Hungarians
India ['ɪndiə] *Indien*	Indian ['ɪndiən]	an Indian	the Indians
Ireland ['aɪələnd] *Irland*	Irish ['aɪrɪʃ]	an Irishman/-woman	the Irish
Italy ['ɪtəli] *Italien*	Italian [ɪ'tæliən]	an Italian	the Italians
Japan [dʒə'pæn] *Japan*	Japanese [ˌdʒæpə'ni:z]	a Japanese	the Japanese
the Netherlands ['neðələndz] *die Niederlande, Holland*	Dutch [dʌtʃ]	a Dutchman/-woman	the Dutch
New Zealand [ˌnju: 'zi:lənd] *Neuseeland*	New Zealand [ˌnju: 'zi:lənd]	a New Zealander	the New Zealanders
Norway ['nɔ:weɪ] *Norwegen*	Norwegian [nɔ:'wi:dʒən]	a Norwegian	the Norwegians
Pakistan [ˌpækɪ'stæn, ˌpɑ:kɪ'stɑ:n] *Pakistan*	Pakistani [ˌpækɪ'stæni, ˌpɑ:kɪ'stɑ:ni]	a Pakistani	the Pakistanis
the Philippines ['fɪlɪpi:nz] *die Philippinen*	Philippine ['fɪlɪpi:n]	a Filipino [ˌfɪlɪ'pi:nəʊ]/ Filipina [ˌfɪlɪ'pi:nə]	the Filipinos/ Filipinas
Poland ['pəʊlənd] *Polen*	Polish ['pəʊlɪʃ]	a Pole [pəʊl]	the Poles
Portugal ['pɔ:tʃʊgl] *Portugal*	Portuguese [ˌpɔ:tʃu'gi:z]	a Portuguese	the Portuguese
Russia ['rʌʃə] *Russland*	Russian ['rʌʃn]	a Russian	the Russians
Scotland ['skɒtlənd] *Schottland*	Scottish ['skɒtɪʃ]	a Scotsman/-woman, a Scot [skɒt]	the Scots, the Scottish
Slovakia [sləʊ'vɑ:kiə, sləʊ'vækiə] *die Slowakei*	Slovak ['sləʊvæk]	a Slovak	the Slovaks
Slovenia [sləʊ'vi:niə] *Slowenien*	Slovenian [sləʊ'vi:niən], Slovene ['sləʊvi:n]	a Slovene, a Slovenian	the Slovenes, the Slovenians
Spain [speɪn] *Spanien*	Spanish ['spænɪʃ]	a Spaniard ['spænɪəd]	the Spaniards
Sweden ['swi:dn] *Schweden*	Swedish ['swi:dɪʃ]	a Swede [swi:d]	the Swedes
Switzerland ['swɪtsələnd] *die Schweiz*	Swiss [swɪs]	a Swiss	the Swiss
Turkey ['tɜ:ki] *die Türkei*	Turkish ['tɜ:kɪʃ]	a Turk [tɜ:k]	the Turks
the United Kingdom (the UK) [juˌnaɪtɪd 'kɪŋdəm, ju:'keɪ] *das Vereinigte Königreich (Großbritannien und Nordirland)*	British ['brɪtɪʃ]	a Briton ['brɪtn]	the British
the United States of America (the USA) [juˌnaɪtɪd ˌsteɪts_əv_ə'merɪkə, ˌju:_es_'eɪ] *die Vereinigten Staaten von Amerika*	American [ə'merɪkən]	an American	the Americans
Wales [weɪlz] *Wales*	Welsh [welʃ]	a Welshman/-woman	the Welsh

Infinitive	Simple past form	Past participle	
(to) **be**	**was/were**	**been**	sein
(to) **beat**	**beat**	**beaten**	schlagen; besiegen
(to) **become**	**became**	**become**	werden
(to) **begin**	**began**	**begun**	beginnen, anfangen (mit)
(to) **bet**	**bet**	**bet**	wetten
(to) **blow**	**blew**	**blown**	wehen, blasen
(to) **break** [eɪ]	**broke**	**broken**	(zer)brechen; kaputt gehen
(to) **bring**	**brought**	**brought**	(mit-, her)bringen
(to) **build**	**built**	**built**	bauen
(to) **buy**	**bought**	**bought**	kaufen
(to) **catch**	**caught**	**caught**	fangen; erwischen
(to) **choose** [uː]	**chose** [əʊ]	**chosen** [əʊ]	(aus)wählen; (sich) aussuchen
(to) **come**	**came**	**come**	kommen
(to) **cost**	**cost**	**cost**	kosten
(to) **cut**	**cut**	**cut**	schneiden
(to) **do**	**did**	**done** [ʌ]	tun, machen
(to) **draw**	**drew**	**drawn**	zeichnen; ziehen
(to) **drink**	**drank**	**drunk**	trinken
(to) **drive** [aɪ]	**drove**	**driven** [ɪ]	*(ein Auto)* fahren
(to) **eat**	**ate** [et, eɪt]	**eaten**	essen
(to) **fall**	**fell**	**fallen**	(hin)fallen, stürzen
(to) **feed**	**fed**	**fed**	füttern
(to) **feel**	**felt**	**felt**	(sich) fühlen; sich anfühlen
(to) **fight**	**fought**	**fought**	kämpfen
(to) **find**	**found**	**found**	finden
(to) **fly**	**flew**	**flown**	fliegen
(to) **forget**	**forgot**	**forgotten**	vergessen
(to) **forgive**	**forgave**	**forgiven**	vergeben, verzeihen
(to) **get**	**got**	**got**	bekommen; holen; werden; (hin)kommen
(to) **give**	**gave**	**given**	geben
(to) **go**	**went**	**gone** [ɒ]	gehen, fahren
(to) **grow**	**grew**	**grown**	wachsen; anbauen, anpflanzen
(to) **hang out** *(infml)*	**hung out**	**hung out**	rumhängen, abhängen
(to) **have (have got)**	**had**	**had**	haben, besitzen
(to) **hear** [ɪə]	**heard** [ɜː]	**heard** [ɜː]	hören
(to) **hide** [aɪ]	**hid** [ɪ]	**hidden** [ɪ]	(sich) verstecken
(to) **hit**	**hit**	**hit**	schlagen
(to) **hold**	**held**	**held**	halten
(to) **hurt**	**hurt**	**hurt**	wehtun; verletzen
(to) **keep**	**kept**	**kept**	(be)halten
(to) **know** [nəʊ]	**knew** [njuː]	**known** [nəʊn]	wissen; kennen
(to) **lay** the table	**laid**	**laid**	den Tisch decken
(to) **leave**	**left**	**left**	(weg)gehen; abfahren; verlassen; zurücklassen
(to) **let**	**let**	**let**	lassen

Infinitive	Simple past form	Past participle	
(to) **light**	**lit**	**lit**	anzünden
(to) **lose** [uː]	**lost** [ɒ]	**lost** [ɒ]	verlieren
(to) **make**	**made**	**made**	machen; bauen; bilden
(to) **mean** [iː]	**meant** [e]	**meant** [e]	bedeuten; meinen
(to) **meet**	**met**	**met**	(sich) treffen
(to) **pay**	**paid**	**paid**	bezahlen
(to) **put**	**put**	**put**	legen, stellen, *(wohin)* tun
(to) **read** [iː]	**read** [e]	**read** [e]	lesen
(to) **ride** [aɪ]	**rode**	**ridden** [ɪ]	reiten; *(Rad)* fahren
(to) **ring**	**rang**	**rung**	klingeln, läuten
(to) **rise** [aɪ]	**rose**	**risen** [ɪ]	(auf)steigen
(to) **run**	**ran**	**run**	rennen, laufen; verlaufen *(Straße, Grenze)*
(to) **say** [eɪ]	**said** [e]	**said** [e]	sagen
(to) **see**	**saw**	**seen**	sehen; besuchen, aufsuchen
(to) **sell**	**sold**	**sold**	verkaufen
(to) **send**	**sent**	**sent**	schicken, senden
(to) **set** a trap	**set**	**set**	eine Falle stellen
(to) **sew** [əʊ]	**sewed**	**sewn**	nähen
(to) **shake**	**shook**	**shaken**	schütteln; zittern
(to) **shine**	**shone** [ɒ]	**shone** [ɒ]	scheinen *(Sonne)*
(to) **show**	**showed**	**shown**	zeigen
(to) **shut up**	**shut**	**shut**	den Mund halten
(to) **sing**	**sang**	**sung**	singen
(to) **sit**	**sat**	**sat**	sitzen; sich setzen
(to) **sleep**	**slept**	**slept**	schlafen
(to) **speak**	**spoke**	**spoken**	sprechen
(to) **spend**	**spent**	**spent**	*(Zeit)* verbringen; *(Geld)* ausgeben
(to) **spit**	**spat**	**spat**	spucken
(to) **stand**	**stood**	**stood**	stehen; sich (hin)stellen
(to) **steal**	**stole**	**stolen**	stehlen
(to) **stick**	**stuck**	**stuck**	herausragen, herausstehen
(to) **swim**	**swam**	**swum**	schwimmen
(to) **take**	**took**	**taken**	nehmen; (weg-, hin)bringen; dauern, *(Zeit)* brauchen
(to) **teach**	**taught**	**taught**	unterrichten, lehren
(to) **tear off** [eə]	**tore**	**torn**	abreißen
(to) **tell**	**told**	**told**	erzählen, berichten
(to) **think**	**thought**	**thought**	denken, glauben, meinen
(to) **throw**	**threw**	**thrown**	werfen
(to) **understand**	**understood**	**understood**	verstehen
(to) **upset**	**upset**	**upset**	ärgern, kränken, aus der Fassung bringen
(to) **wake** up	**woke**	**woken**	aufwachen; wecken
(to) **wear** [eə]	**wore** [ɔː]	**worn** [ɔː]	tragen *(Kleidung)*
(to) **win**	**won** [ʌ]	**won** [ʌ]	gewinnen
(to) **write**	**wrote**	**written**	schreiben

Key to 'How am I doing?'

Unit 1 ▸ p. 29

1 C boroughs
2 E Manhattan
3 C in the south of the island
4 A the World Trade Center
5 D a cellphone
6 B Fifth Avenue
7 B awful
8 C put out
9 B blocks
10 D deli
11 sidewalk • cellphone • pants • French fries
12 lift • queue • underground • holiday(s)
13 C Hiking
14 A playing
15 A If I had lots of money, I would fly to New York first class.
B If I ever go to New York, I want to go up the Empire State Building.
C I'm just going to the tourist information. I'll ask about the Museum of Natural History when I'm there.

Unit 2 ▸ p. 53

1 A the Golden State
2 C Silicon Valley
3 D Spanish
4 B illegal
5 C the Golden Gate Bridge
6 D read every word
7 C specific information
8 C don't panic: you can listen again
9 A ethnic group
10 D discriminate against
11 B prejudiced
12 C done
13 B industrial
14 D are made
15 A was discovered
16 B by
17 C Somebody stole my camera.

Unit 3 ▸ p. 71

1 The school between elementary school and high school is called middle school.
2 High school starts with the 9th grade.
3 Sports and school clubs are known in the US as extracurricular activities.
4 The best grade in school is A (excellent).
5 E middle
6 B industry
7 A traditions
8 Not true: C A summary should have lots of details from the original text.
9 possibility
10 suggestion
11 White bread is not as healthy as bread from whole grain(s).
12 To keep fit, eat the right food and get lots of exercise.
13 Chicken and turkey are a kind of meat we call poultry.
14 milk products
15 seven point nine
16 A I need some information.
B Can I have a glass of milk, please?
– Of course, there's some milk in the fridge.
C Would you like some fruit with your sandwich?
– Yes, an apple would be nice.
D Dad, can I have some money for school lunch?
17 A The students talked about food in their Health class. They agreed that the food they eat is healthy.
B Life is boring if you don't have a computer.
C My mum says the quality of the food we buy at the supermarket is excellent.

Key to 'How am I doing?'

Unit 4

▸ p. 95

1 B black and white Americans
2 D discrimination against blacks
3 A Little Rock Central High School
4 A series
B reality show
C comedy
D prime time
E news
5 D viewer
6 C the TV listings
7 C more than one source
8 A use your own words
9 D The information is given indirectly.
10 A We have lived in the same flat for six years.
B My parents have been married for 15 years.
C I've had English with Frau Marx since the beginning of last year.
D My best friend and I have known each other since the first grade.
11 A since kindergarten B for an hour
C since 2007 D since the accident
E for a long time

Illustrationen

Silke Bachmann, Hamburg: 49–51; 68–69; 79–80; 84; 90; **Roland Beier**, Berlin: 25; 40; 44; 48; 56; 58; 64; 85; 88; 119; 121 unten; 133; 138–188; **Carlos Borrell**, Berlin: 20 oben (u. 108); 121 oben; 123; 130; 134; **Stéphane Gamain/NB Illustration**, London: 20 Mitte, unten; 24; 26 unten–28; 38; 46; **Jörn Hennig**, Berlin: 128–129

Bildquellen

Michelle Abesamis, New York: S. 23 zoo; **Agentur Focus**, Hamburg: S. 91 unten: Magnum Photos/Elliott Erwitt; **Alamy**, Abingdon: Inhaltsverz. Caitlin (u. 8 oben li.): Geoff du Feu (RF), Luis (u. 9 u. 36 oben re.) David R. Frazier Photolibrary, Inc., skyline (M): JUPITERIMAGES/ Thinkstock (RF), Inhaltsverz. surfers (u. 34/35): Juice Images Limited (RF), Market Street (u. 55): Danita Delimont/Chuck Haney; S. 9 Mitte school bus: Directphoto.org; S. 10 oben li.: Robert Harding Picture Library Ltd; S. 12 oben re.: Ellen McKnight; S. 14 oben girls (M): Andrew Rubtsov, Bild 2: John Taylor, Bild 5: Dieter Melhorn; S. 15 oben: Picture Partners, Mitte: eStock Photo/Gg; S. 16 oben: Sandra Baker, unten: Arcaid/G Jackson; S. 17 oben: dbimages/Derek Brown; S. 24 oben li.: Janine Wiedel Photolibrary, unten li.: WorldFoto; S. 30: Kevin Browne; S. 35 Bild F: David R. Frazier Photolibrary, Inc.; S. 36 oben li.: Form-court (Form Advertising) (RF); S. 45 Bild 5: Pick and Mix Images; S. 46 Bild 3 li.: History Archive, re.: INTERFOTO Pressebildagentur; S. 47 ride: EuroStyle Graphics, sky: Greg Gilman; S. 87: VStock (RF); S. 109 Bild 5 li. u. 7 re.: Mary Evans Picture Library; S. 110: Picture Contact/ jochem wijnands; S. 113 TF 3 (u. 118): Gail Mooney-Kelly, TF 7 (u. 126): Rich Iwasaki, TF 10 (u. 133): Nordicphotos/Nina Korhonen; S. 116 oben re.: LOOK Die Bildagentur der Fotografen GmbH/Konrad Wothe; S. 125 Mitte li.: Stockbyte (RF); S. 125 helmet: Photodisc (RF), knee pads: Studiomode; S. 126 observation room: Andre Jenny; S. 134 unten Mitte: Graat Heilman Photography/Jim Strawser, unten li.: coinery (RF); **Animal Planet**, München: S. 78 Animal Planet logo; **Arteaga Photos LTD.**, St. Louis: S. 127 Bild 1 u. 3; **Artothek**, Weilheim: S. 26 oben © Christie's/VG Bild-Kunst Bonn; **Associated Press**, Frankfurt/Main: S. 14 Bild 4: Ed Reinke; S. 37 Bild 2: PAUL SAKUMA; S. 91 oben re.; S. 92 oben; S. 113 TF 5 (u. 122): Amy Sancetta; S. 135 Jimmy Carter: Pat Roque; **Britta Bensmann**, Berlin: S. 125 elbow pads; **Dave Briccetti**, Lafayette: S. 43 unten; **Bridgeman**, Berlin: S. 61 oben: Peter Newark American Pictures, unten: Private Collection; **Cable News Network. A Time Warner Company**, Atlanta: S. 78 CNN logo; **CBS Broadcasting Inc.**, Los Angeles: S. 78 CBS logo: Use of logo from CBS Eye Logos - Courtesy of CBS Broadcasting Inc., Los Angeles; **Cinetext**, Frankfurt/Main: S. 45 Bild 3: Cinetext Bildarchiv; S. 47 Bild 1: Cinetext Bildarchiv; S. 48 Mitte: Buena Vista; S. 86: Sony Pictures; S. 135 film poster: Sammlung Richter; **City of Atlanta**: S. 77 unten li.; **The Coca-Cola Company**, Atlanta: S. 76 unten Mitte; **copy-us Verlags GmbH**, Kleve: S. 136 sheet music background: © 2007 by copy-us-Verlags GmbH, Kleve, arrangiert für Männerchor von Manni Bernhard; **Corbis**, Düsseldorf: S. 7 (u. 142): Reuters/Jeff Topping; S. 12/13 background: David Ball; S. 35 Bild D: Catherine Karnow; S. 77 unten re.: Franz-Marc Frei; S. 81 unten: Bettmann; S. 82 oben: Comstock (RF); S. 91 Mitte li.: Bettmann; S. 92 unten: Bettmann; S. 93: Bettmann; S. 109 Bild 5 re.: Adam Woolfitt, Bild 8 li.: Bettmann; S. 113 TF 4 (u. 120 unten re.): Grant Smith, TF 6 Sheckler (u. 124): Bo Bridges, TF 9 (u. 132): Bettmann/William Horace Smith; S. 120 unten li.: Lloyd Cluff; S. 127 Bild 2: Bettmann, Bild 4: Bettmann; S. 135 oben: Kevin Schafer, Margaret Mitchell: Bettmann, Ray Charles: John Van Hasselt/Sygma, Martin Luther King: Flip Schulke; S. 137 unten re.: Laura Levine; **Angel & Wilma Delgadillo's Route 66 Gift Shop & Visitor's Center**, Seligman: S. 10 unten li.; **Denver Public Library**, Denver: S. 60 unten: Colorado Historical Society & Denver Art Museum; **FDNY/NYC & Company**, New York: S. 25 FDNY logos: All New York City logos and marks depicted herein are the property of the City of New York and may not be used without prior written consent; **First National Bank of Atlanta**, Atlanta: Inhaltsverz. (u. 76 (M)): Atlanta burning photo: Taken from "Atlanta Rusurgens". Written and published by the First National Bank of Atlanta. November 1971, Atlanta. Photo: Metro-Goldwyn-Mayer; **FOX Broadcasting Company**: S. 78 FOX logo: FOX is the trademark of FOX Broadcasting Company and is used with permission of FOX Broadcasting Company; **Fricke Studio**, Hermann: Inhaltsverz. Jake (u. 10 oben); S. 54/55 Bild A; S. 55 Bild C, E, F, S. 57 oben; S. 59; **Getty Images**, München: S. 6, S. 11 skywalk: David McNew uS. 11 skywalk: David McNew; S. 15 unten: Aurora/Ian Shive; S. 19 re.: Stone/Archive Holdings Inc.; S. 24 oben re.: Getty Images News/Gilles Mingasson; S. 32: AFP/Stan Honda; S. 35 Bild B: Stone/Gala Narezo; S. 38 li.: Getty Images News/ Chip Somodevilla; S. 41 oben re.: Photographer's Choice/Grant Faint; S. 43 oben: Justin Sullivan; S. 61 Mitte: The Bridgeman Art Library/Charles Marion Russell; S. 65: Justin Sullivan; S. 73: Image Source (RF); S. 77 unten Mitte: Hulton Archive/Agence France Presse; S. 81 oben: München: Popperfoto/Rolls Press; S. 82 unten: CNN/Handout; S. 83 Mitte: NBAE/ David Liam Kyle; S. 91 oben li.: Hulton Archive/William Lovelace; S. 92 Mitte: Hulton Archive/Moore; S. 112: Photographer's Choice/Louis Schwartzberg; S. 113 TF 2 (u. 116): Photographer's Choice/Mitchell Funk, TF 12 (u. 136): FPG; S. 116 unten re.: Mario Tama; S. 120 oben: Cindy Karp; S. 125 oben re.: FilmMagic/Jon Kopaloff; S. 137 oben: Michael Ochs Archives; **www.Gleis4.de**: S. 62; **Grand Canyon National Park**, Grand Canyon: S. 11 lodge: NPS Photo; **Grand Canyon NP Museum Collection**, Grand Canyon: S. 9 Mitte scorpion patch; S. 24 ranger; **Howard Architectural Models, Inc.**, Toldedo: S. 117 unten re.; **iStockphoto**, Calgary: S. 35 Bild E: Paige Falk; S. 37 Bild 1: Arthurpreston; S. 39 oben: stevegeer; S. 47 Bild 3: Greg Nicholas; S. 75 Bild 4: dwphotos, Bild 7: Sergia Kishan, Bild 8: Lisa Fletcher; S. 113 TF 11 (u. 134): Stephen Muskie; S. 117 unten li.: Frank van den Bergh; S. 134 unten re.: catman73; **Chris Junker**, Portland: S. 127 Arch skin; **jupiterimages**, Ottobrunn/München: Inhaltsverz. Madison (u. 11): Polka Dot Images (RF); **Adam Kuban**, New York: S. 117 oben; **Tom Lohdan**, Melbourne: S. 35 Bild H; **Major League Baseball Properties, Inc.**: S. 118 oben: Major League Baseball trademarks and copyrights are used with permission of Major League Baseball Properties, Inc.; **Massachusetts Commandery Military Order of the Loyal Legion and the U.S. Army Military History Institute**: S. 131; **mauritius images**, Mittenwald: S. 11 mule train: Jeff O'Brien; S. 13: age; S. 14 oben street (M): age; **Jeri Mearns**, Mill Valley: S. 94; **Most Wanted Pictures**, Los Angeles: S. 35 Bild G Hintergrund (M); **MTV Music**: S. 125 oben li.: Ewan Burns; **MTV Networks Germany GmbH**, Berlin: S. 78 MTV logo; **National FFA Organization**, Indianapolis: S. 57 unten; **The New York Public Library**, New York: S. 18 unten re., S. 19 oben Mitte: Lewis Wickes Hine; **Barack Obama Office**, Washington D.C.: S. 83 oben; Thomas Parker, Vienna, Missouri, USA: S. 55 Bild D; **Photolibrary**, London: S. 8 oben re.: Nonstock/Joseph De Sciose; S. 41 oben li.: Nordic Photos/Chad Ehlers; S. 42 Bild 1 tray; S. 66: Owaki-Kulla; S. 77 oben: Jon Arnold Travel/ Walter Bibikow; **Picture-Alliance**, Frankfurt/Main: S. 9 unten: dpa/Jörg Schmitt; S. 10 unten re.: MAXPPP/Marianna Day Massey; S. 25 unten li.: dpa-Report/PA Magdalena Mayo; S. 35 Bild C: dpa-Report/Ken James, Bild G Will Smith (M): SCHROEWIG/Graylock; S. 38 re.: dpa/Jerzy Dabrowski; S. 45 Bild 4: dpa-Bildarchiv/Bert Reisfeld, Bild 6 (u. 47): dpa-Fotoreport/epa afp Scott Nelson; S. 76 unten li.: akg-images; S. 80: dpaweb,dpa-Report/Thomas S. England; S. 83 unten li.: Sven Simon, unten re.: dpa-Report/ epa Peter Fowley; S. 108 li. (u. 149) u. re.: HB-Verlag/Martin Sasse; S. 137 Mitte li.: Newscom/Andre Jenny; **Picture Desk**, London: S. 48 li. u. re.: The Kobal Collection/Universal; **Marion Schönenberger**, Berlin: Inhaltsverz. Teenagers (u. 100); S. 96–106; **Redferns**, London: S. 136 unten: Deltahaze Corporation; S. 137 unten li.: Martin Philebey; **Ohad Shahar/Photo-Stock-Israel**: www.photographersdirect.com: S. 126 tram; **Shutterstock**, New York: Inhaltsverz. Statue of Liberty (M) (u. 12): gary718; S. 8 unten: Bruce Grubbs; S. 10 book (M): Martina I. Meyer, Mitte: Condor 36; S. 11 Bellagio: Andy Z.; S. 12 unten re.: Zina Seletskaya; S. 14 Bild 1: emin kuliyev; S. 17 Mitte: Hannamariah, unten: Scott Rothstein; S. 21: Steven Pepple; S. 22: Vladimir Korostyshevskiy; S. 23 unten li.: Bill Kennedy, re.: Ilja Mašík; S. 33 Bild 1: Ali Mazraie Shadi, Bild 2: Jason Kasumovic, Bild 3: cardiae, Bild 4: Jostein Hauge, Bild 5: Christa DeRidder, Bild 6: Miguel Angel Salinas Salinas, Bild 7: Sebastian Kaulitzki, Bild 8: Max Blain, Bild 9: erikdegraaf fotografie; S. 36 unten: Edyta Pawlowska; S. 37 strawberries: Norman Chan; S. 39 unten li. (u. 40/41): Brandon Holmes, unten Mitte (u. 41): Oliver Johannes Uhrig, unten re. (u. 41): Byron W. Moore; S. 40 oben: Albo; S. 41 skyline: David Alexander Liu; S. 42 Bild 1 notepad: luminouslens, pen: EuToch, Bild 2: amfoto, Bild 3 camera: terekhov igor, tripod: design56, Bild 4 costume: Margo Harrison, clipboard: Natalia Siverina, powder: Sean O. S. Barley, Bild 5: Bjorn Heller, Bild 6 teacher: Adam Borkowski, chalk: Kuzma, books: pixelman, Bild 7 duster: Mark Stout Photography, vacuum cleaner: angelo gilardelli, Bild 8 money: Morgan Lane Photography, gun: vadim kozlovsky; S. 45 Bild 1: Feverpitched, Bild 2: Stas Volik; S. 46 Bild 1 li.: Guus van Raaphorst, Bild 4 St. re.: Deborah Reny; S. 47 Bild 2: stocksnapp, Bild 4: Ivan Stevanovic; S. 47 adventure park: Peter Brett Charlton; S. 54/55 vine: Lezh; S. 67: Ron Hilton; 75 Bild 1: Maxim Petrichuk, Bild 2: Palto, Bild 3: Jose Marines; Bild 5: B. Speckart, Bild 6: Olga Chernetskaya, Bild 9: Glenda M. Powers; S. 76/77 (M) flames: David Lee; S. 82/83 US flag background: Goxy; S. 89: Condor 36; S. 111 oben: David Alexander Liu, unten (u. 134 oben li.): iofoto; S. 115 oben: Chee-Onn Leong; S. 125 Mitte re.: Alexander Kalina, wrist guard: triaphoto; S. 134 oben re.: Jeff Kinsey; **Stone Hill Winery**, Hermann: S. 60 oben; **Makoto Takami**, Japan: S. 14 Bild 3; **Topeka Room, Topeka & Shawnee County Public Library**, Topeka: S. 91 Mitte re.; **ullstein bild**, Berlin: S. 18/19 Ellis Island : histopics; S. 40 unten: Peter Arnold Inc.; S. 46 Bild 1 re.: Granger Collection, Bild 2 li.: AISA, re.: Granger Collection, Bild 4 li.: Granger Collection; S. 76 unten re.: dpa; S. 78 NBC logo: Keith (used by permission of NBC Universal, Inc., New York); S. 109 Bild 8 re.: AP, Bild 6 re.; Granger Collection, Bild 7 li.: Imagebroker.net, Bild 6 li.: TopFoto; S. 113 TF 1 (u.115 unten re.): Granger Collection; S. 114 li. u. re.: Granger Collection; S. 121: Still Pictures; S. 137 Mitte re.: Probst; **U.S. Department of the Interior, National Park Service**: S. 126/127 Gateway Arch (Artist: David Leech); S. 126 Gateway Arch triangle detail (Artist David Leech); S. 127 construction progress (Artist: David Leech)

Titelbild

Corbis, Düsseldorf: yellow cab (M): image100 (RF), Times Square (M): Jose Fuste Raga; **Corel Library**: US Flag Hintergrund (M)

Textquellen

S. 18: Statements by Celia Adler, Lazarus Salamon, Edward Corsi, Golda Meir taken from "I was dreaming to come to America" by Veronica Lawlor, © 1995 by Veronica Lawlor. Used by permission of Viking Penguin, A Division of Penguin Young Readers Group, A Member of Penguin Group (USA) Inc., 345 Hudson Street, New York, NY 10014. All rights reserved, Statement by Leonard Covello taken from "Immigrant Kids" by Russel Freedman. Used by permission of Dutton Children's Books, A Division of Penguin Young Readers Group, A Member of Penguin Group (USA), Inc., 345 Hudson Street, New York, NY 10014. All rights reserved. S. 26–28: *You can tell me.* Adapted from "Kelly 'n' Me" by Myron Levoy. Published by iUniverse.com, Inc. Lincoln. All Rights Reserved © 1992, 2000 by Myron Levoy. Reprinted by arrangement with the author and Writers House LLC, acting as agent for the author; S. 68–70: *Angus Bethune's moment.* Adapted from „Telephone Man" from "Athletic Shorts" © 1989, 1991 by Chris Crutcher. Printed with permission from Greenwillow Books, an imprint of HarperCollins Publishers; S. 92–94: *Melba's story.* Excerpts taken from „Warriors don't Cry. The Searing Memoir of the Battle to Integrate Little Rock's Central High" by Melba Pattillo Beals. Abridged edition. Simon Pulse, 1995; S. 96–106: *There is a boy in the girls' bathroom* by Louis Sachar. Abridged and adapted. All Rights reserved. Professionals and amateurs are hereby warned that this play is subject to a royalty. It is fully under the copyright laws of the United States of America, the British Commonwealth, including Canada, and all other countries of the Copyright Union. All rights, including professional, amateur, motion picture, recitation, lecturing, public reading, radio and television broadcasting, internet and electronic rights, and the rights of translation into foreign lanugages are strictly reserved. These rights are controlled exclusively by Susan Schulman, A Literary Agency, 545 West 44th St., New York, NY, 10036 E: Schulman@aol.com and royalty arrangements and licenses must be secured in advance or presentation and/or use; S. 106: *The City* by David Ignatow. Reprinted with permission from the March 17, 1969 issue of "The Nation". For subscription information, call 1-800-333-8563. Portions of each week's Nation magazine can be accessed at http://www.thenation.com; S. 116: *Skyscraper* by Dennis Lee. From "Alligator Pie" (Macmillan of Canada, 1974; Key Porter Books, 2001). Copyright © 1974 Dennis Lee. With permission of the author; S. 116: *Subway rush hour* © 1994 by the Estate of Langston Hughes; S. 117: To the visitor. © 2003 Frank McCourt; S. 122: *Child labour on the US-Mexican border.* Abridged and adapted from "Illegal child labor in Mexico puts food on tables of Americans" by Chris Hawley. The Arizona Republic, May 9, 2008; S. 140: Auszug von S. 582 aus „English G 2000 Wörterbuch - Das Wörterbuch zum Lehrwerk". Herausgegeben von der Langenscheidt-Redaktion Wörterbücher und der Cornelsen-Redaktion Englisch. © 2002 Cornelsen Verlag GmbH & Co. OHG, Berlin und Langenscheidt KG, Berlin und München.

Liedquellen

S. 17: *A heart in New York*: K+T: Gallagher, Benny/Lyle, Graham. © Good Single Ltd./Imagem Songs Ltd. Tj musicservice GmbH, Hamburg. Imagem Music GmbH, Hamburg; S. 39: *Picture postcards from L.A.*: T: Kadison, Joshua. © Joshuasongs/Seymour Glass Songs/EMI Blackwood Music Inc. EMI Music Publishing GmbH, Hamburg; S. 117: *New York, New York*: K+T: Ebb, Fred. © by EMI Unart Catalog Inc. D/A/CH/Osteuropäische Länder: EMI Partnership Musikverlag GmbH, Hamburg; S. 133: *57 Channels*: T: Springsteen, Bruce. © Bruce Springsteen Music. D/A/CH: Rondor Musikverlag GmbH, Hamburg; S. 137: *Johnny B. Goode*: T: Berry, Chuck. © ARC Music Corp. Good Tunes Music AG, Geneva.

Classroom English

Was *du* im Klassenzimmer sagen kannst	What *you* can say in the classroom
Du brauchst Hilfe	**You need help**
Können Sie mir bitte helfen?	**Can you help me, please?**
Auf welcher Seite sind wir, bitte?	**What page are we on, please?**
Was heißt ... auf Englisch/Deutsch?	**What's ... in English/German?**
Wie spricht man das erste Wort in Zeile 2 aus?	**How do you say the first word in line 2?**
Können Sie bitte ... buchstabieren?	**Can you spell ..., please?**
Können Sie es bitte an die Tafel schreiben?	**Can you write it on the board, please?**
Kann ich es auf Deutsch sagen?	**Can I say it in German?**
Können Sie/Kannst du bitte lauter sprechen?	**Can you speak louder, please?**
Können Sie/Kannst du das bitte noch mal sagen?	**Can you say that again, please?**
Über Texte und Themen sprechen	**Talking about texts and topics**
Ich finde die Geschichte ...	**I think the story is ...**
schön/interessant/langweilig/schrecklich/....	**nice/interesting/boring/terrible/...**
Es war lustig/gruselig/langweilig/..., als ...	**It was funny/scary/boring/... when ...**
Ich fand es gut/nicht gut, als ...	**I liked it/didn't like it when ...**
Ich finde Tom hat recht/nicht recht, weil ...	**I think Tom is right/wrong because ...**
Ich bin mir nicht sicher. Vielleicht ...	**I'm not sure. Maybe ...**
Was meinst du?	**What do you think?**
Ich stimme ... zu/nicht zu, weil ...	**I agree/disagree (with ...) because ...**
Hausaufgaben und Übungen	**Homework and exercises**
Tut mir leid, ich habe mein Schulheft nicht dabei, Herr ...	**Sorry, I haven't got my exercise book, Mr ...**
Ich habe meine Hausaufgaben vergessen, Frau ...	**I've forgotten my homework, Mrs/Ms/Miss ...**
Ich kann Nummer 3 nicht lösen.	**I can't do number 3.**
Entschuldigung, ich bin noch nicht fertig.	**Sorry, I haven't finished yet.**
Ich habe ... Ist das auch richtig?	**I've got ... Is that right too?**
Tut mir leid, das weiß ich nicht.	**Sorry, I don't know.**
Was haben wir (als Hausaufgabe) auf?	**What's for homework?**
Bei der Partnerarbeit	**Work with a partner**
Kann ich mit Julian arbeiten?	**Can I work with Julian?**
Wer ist dran? - Du bist dran.	**Whose turn is it? - It's your turn.**
Ich finde, wir sollten/könnten ...	**I think we should/could ...**
Was machen wir zuerst?	**What are we going to do first?**
What your teacher says	**Was dein/e Lehrer/in sagt**
Open your books at page 24, please.	Schlagt bitte Seite 24 auf.
Look at the picture/line 8/... on page 24.	Seht euch das Bild/Zeile 8/... auf Seite 24 an.
Copy/Complete the chart/network/...	Übertragt/Vervollständigt die Tabelle/das Wörternetz/...
Correct the mistakes.	Verbessert die Fehler.
Take notes.	Macht euch Notizen.
Do exercise 3 for homework, please.	Macht bitte Übung 3 als Hausaufgabe.
Have you finished?	Seid ihr fertig? / Bist du fertig?
Switch off your mobile phones.	Schaltet eure Handys aus.
Walk around the class and ask other students.	Geht durch die Klasse und fragt andere Schüler/innen.
Discuss ... with ...	Diskutiere/Diskutiert ... mit ...
Give a presentation about ...	Halte/Haltet einen Vortrag über ...
Report to the class.	Berichte/Berichtet der Klasse.

Staat		Abkürzung	Hauptstadt	
Alabama	[ˌæləˈbæmə]	AL	**Montgomery**	[məntˈgʌməri]
Alaska	[əˈlæskə]	AK	**Juneau**	[ˈdʒuːnəʊ]
Arizona	[ˌærɪˈzəʊnə]	AZ	**Phoenix**	[ˈfiːnɪks]
Arkansas	[ˈɑːkənsɔː]	AR	**Little Rock**	[ˌlɪtl ˈrɒk]
California	[ˌkæləˈfɔːniə]	CA	**Sacramento**	[ˌsækrəˈmentəʊ]
Colorado	[ˌkɒləˈrɑːdəʊ]	CO	**Denver**	[ˈdenvə]
Connecticut	[kəˈnetɪkət]	CT	**Hartford**	[ˈhɑːtfəd]
Delaware	[ˈdeləweə]	DE	**Dover**	[ˈdəʊvə]
Florida	[ˈflɒrɪdə]	FL	**Tallahassee**	[ˌtæləˈhæsi]
Georgia	[ˈdʒɔːdʒə]	GA	**Atlanta**	[ətˈlæntə]
Hawaii	[həˈwaɪi]	HI	**Honolulu**	[ˌhɒnəˈluːluː]
Idaho	[ˈaɪdəhəʊ]	ID	**Boise**	[ˈbɔɪzi]
Illinois	[ˌɪləˈnɔɪ]	IL	**Springfield**	[ˈsprɪŋfiːld]
Indiana	[ˌɪndiˈænə]	IN	**Indianapolis**	[ˌɪndiəˈnæpəlɪs]
Iowa	[ˈaɪəwə]	IA	**Des Moines**	[də ˈmɔɪn]
Kansas	[ˈkænzəs]	KS	**Topeka**	[təʊˈpiːkə]
Kentucky	[kenˈtʌki]	KY	**Frankfort**	[ˈfræŋkfət]
Louisiana	[luˌiːziˈænə]	LA	**Baton Rouge**	[ˌbætn ˈruːʒ]
Maine	[meɪn]	ME	**Augusta**	[ɔːˈgʌstə]
Maryland	[ˈmeərilənd]	MD	**Annapolis**	[əˈnæpəlɪs]
Massachusetts	[ˌmæsəˈtʃuːsɪts]	MA	**Boston**	[ˈbɒstən]
Michigan	[ˈmɪʃɪgən]	MI	**Lansing**	[ˈlɑːnsɪŋ]
Minnesota	[ˌmɪnɪˈsəʊtə]	MN	**Saint Paul**	[sənt ˈpɔːl]
Mississippi	[ˌmɪsɪˈsɪpi]	MS	**Jackson**	[ˈdʒæksən]
Missouri	[mɪˈzʊəri]	MO	**Jefferson City**	[ˌdʒefəsən ˈsɪti]
Montana	[mɒnˈtænə]	MT	**Helena**	[ˈhelənə]
Nebraska	[nəˈbræskə]	NE	**Lincoln**	[ˈlɪŋkən]
Nevada	[nəˈvɑːdə]	NV	**Carson City**	[ˌkɑːsn ˈsɪti]
New Hampshire	[ˌnjuː ˈhæmpʃə]	NH	**Concord**	[ˈkɒŋkɔːd, ˈkɒŋkəd]
New Jersey	[ˌnjuː ˈdʒɜːzi]	NJ	**Trenton**	[ˈtrentən]
New Mexico	[ˌnjuː ˈmeksɪkəʊ]	NM	**Santa Fe**	[ˌsæntə ˈfeɪ]
New York	[ˌnjuː ˈjɔːk]	NY	**Albany**	[ˈɔːlbəni]
North Carolina	[ˌnɔːθ kærəˈlaɪnə]	NC	**Raleigh**	[ˈrɔːli]
North Dakota	[ˌnɔːθ dəˈkəʊtə]	ND	**Bismarck**	[ˈbɪzmɑːk]
Ohio	[əʊˈhaɪəʊ]	OH	**Columbus**	[kəˈlʌmbəs]
Oklahoma	[ˌəʊkləˈhəʊmə]	OK	**Oklahoma City**	[ˌəʊkləˌhəʊmə ˈsɪti]
Oregon	[ˈɒrɪgən]	OR	**Salem**	[ˈseɪləm]
Pennsylvania	[ˌpenslˈveɪniə]	PA	**Harrisburg**	[ˈhærɪsbɜːg]
Rhode Island	[ˌrəʊd‿ˈaɪlənd]	RI	**Providence**	[ˈprɒvɪdəns]
South Carolina	[ˌsaʊθ kærəˈlaɪnə]	SC	**Columbia**	[kəˈlʌmbiə]
South Dakota	[ˌsaʊθ dəˈkəʊtə]	SD	**Pierre**	[pɪə]
Tennessee	[ˌtenəˈsiː]	TN	**Nashville**	[ˈnæʃvɪl]
Texas	[ˈteksəs]	TX	**Austin**	[ˈɒstɪn]
Utah	[ˈjuːtɑː]	UT	**Salt Lake City**	[ˌsɔːlt leɪk ˈsɪti]
Vermont	[vəˈmɒnt]	VT	**Montpelier**	[mɒntˈpiːliə]
Virginia	[vəˈdʒɪniə]	VA	**Richmond**	[ˈrɪtʃmənd]
Washington	[ˈwɒʃɪŋtən]	WA	**Olympia**	[əˈlɪmpiə]
West Virginia	[ˌwest vəˈdʒɪniə]	WV	**Charleston**	[ˈtʃɑːlstən]
Wisconsin	[wɪsˈkɒnsɪn]	WI	**Madison**	[ˈmædɪsən]
Wyoming	[waɪˈəʊmɪŋ]	WY	**Cheyenne**	[ˌʃaɪˈæn]